WESTMAR COLLEGE  W9-BVH-174

Cornell International Industrial and Labor Relations Report Number 15

A SECRETARY AND A COOK

Challenging Women's Wages in the Courts of the United States and Great Britain

STEVEN L. WILLBORN

ILR Press
School of Industrial and Labor Relations
Cornell University

Copyright © 1989 by Cornell University
All rights reserved

Library of Congress Cataloging-in-Publication Data
Willborn, Steven L.
A secretary and a cook : challenging women's wages in the courts of
the United States and Great Britain / Steven L. Willborn.
    p.   cm.—(Cornell international industrial and labor
                    relations report ; no. 15)
            Includes bibliographical references.
    ISBN 0-87546-157-3 (alk. paper).—ISBN 0-87546-158-1
                    (pbk. : alk. paper)
1. Pay equity—Law and legislation—United States. 2. Pay equity—
Law and legislation—Great Britain. I. Title. II. Series:
Cornell international industrial and labor relations reports ; 15.
                K1770.W55   1989
                344.73'0121—dc20
[347.304121]   89-39540
                                                                CIP

Copies may be ordered through bookstores or from
ILR Press
School of Industrial and Labor Relations
Cornell University
Ithaca, NY 14851-0952

Printed on acid-free paper in the United States of America

5   4   3   2   1

To Emily

Contents

Preface

THE LAW IS an abstraction machine. It takes the concrete realities of our lives—traffic tickets, job promotions, check writing—and organizes them into abstractions such as criminal law, labor law, and commercial law. Law professors like me are the principal cogs in this machine. One of our main jobs is to look briefly at lots of cases—lots of job promotions or whatever—and articulate an abstract rule that explains the result in all the cases. There is value in that. There must be. Hundreds of pages of these abstractions are published in law reviews every week. But there is danger in doing *only* that. What one learns by looking briefly at many cases may be different from what one learns by looking carefully at one or two cases. This book looks carefully at two. In a sense, the book puts the abstraction machine in reverse. It de-abstracts an issue by examining two cases in detail. Now I must admit that near the end of the book I crank up the abstraction machine once again, but my hope is that by that time the abstractions will have been made richer and clearer by my close examination of the two cases.

It was partly in a flight from abstraction that I found myself examining these two cases in the first place. I lived in London during the 1985–86 academic year. Most of my time there was spent in libraries, in the reading room of the British Library and in the library at the Institute of Advanced Legal Studies. I learned a great deal, but near the end of my time there I was ready, very ready, to get out of those libraries and talk to someone. I began to contact people who were associated in one way or another with an important lawsuit. Julie Hayward, a cook, had sued her employer, Cammell Laird Shipbuilders, claiming that Cammell Laird had violated a British law requiring employers to pay the same wages to men and women who were performing work of equal value.

Eventually, I talked with virtually everyone, other than the judges themselves, who had been significantly involved in the lawsuit. Everyone was very forthcoming and friendly. I continued to learn—and I had escaped the libraries.

When I returned to the United States in May 1986, I traveled to Washington State to talk with people there who were associated with an equally significant American comparable worth case. A number of state employees, including a secretary named Helen Castrilli, had sued the state, claiming that it discriminated against them because they worked in occupations in which most of the workers were female. The people in Washington were also very forthcoming and friendly, and those conversations did not take place in libraries either.

My escape from libraries ended soon after that. I returned to my university and to my office, which is located in a library, and began writing. Except for a brief furlough or two, I have been there ever since. But since my return, the library has not been so bad. I had been invigorated by the people I talked with. I thank them, and others, for making this book possible. I extend special thanks to Nick Carter, Andrew Davies, Terry Dillon, Mary Donnelly, Rhonda Dunaway, Bob Fiddaman, Mitch Fontenot, Erica Fox, Penny Gardner, Richard Heath, Craig Lawson, Pippa Lawson, Timothy Loudon, George Masten, Diane McCombs, J. B. McCombs, Keith Moxon, Ramona Paetzold, Harvey Perlman, Louise Peterson, Josephine Potuto, Helen Remick, Jim Rogers, Terry Sebring, Patricia Sterling, John Swift, Sue Thomas, Richard Townshend-Smith, David Wainwright, Marie Wiechman, Elizabeth Hazen Willborn, and Norman Willis. I am also grateful to the Fulbright Commission and the University of Nebraska Foundation for financial support.

Finally, I am especially grateful to two people who risked a great deal to keep alight the often flickering flame of equal pay, two women with a great deal of courage and energy: Helen Castrilli and Julie Hayward—a secretary and a cook.

Introduction

"IN AN OFFICE I used to have before the lab moved to this hospital, we had windows and I would look outside and I would see a fellow out there mowing a lawn, raking leaves, and he was paid $300 to $500 more a month than I was. His job specifications did not require that he could read nor write. They only required that he could push a lawn mower and rake leaves. . . . There was not any skill required in it. Just some muscles." Helen Castrilli recalls looking out her window and seeing inequality. She is a secretary. She works for the state of Washington at the Western State Hospital near Tacoma.

Julie Hayward had just finished her apprenticeship as a cook and had begun working full time for the Cammell Laird shipbuilding company near Liverpool, England. She talked with friends who had just finished their apprenticeships as painters and light carpenters. While Julie and her friends were apprentices, they were all paid the same. Now that they were no longer apprentices, she was paid less. As Julie tells it, by talking with her friends she discovered that she was "serving meals to men at the yard, including former schoolmates, who had a comparable level of training, easier jobs, and higher salaries." Julie Hayward talked with her friends and heard inequality.

Helen Castrilli and Julie Hayward decided to do something about the inequality they saw and heard. This is the story of their rather remarkable odysseys. It is also the story of an idea and the struggles of two societies to come to grips with that idea. The idea is that jobs such as secretaries and cooks become identified as "women's work" and then pay less *because* women do them. There is no doubt that in both the United States and Great Britain there are "women's" jobs. Most secretaries and cooks (and child-care workers and nurses and teachers of

1

young children and librarians and telephone operators and on and on) are women.[1] And there is no doubt that "women's" jobs often, perhaps even usually, do not pay very much. The five lowest-paying occupations in the 1980 United States Census were all "women's" jobs.[2] But there is a great debate about whether "women's" jobs pay less because women do them or whether they pay less for other reasons.[3] The answer to that question is important. If the jobs pay less because women do them, that is sex discrimination, and there are laws in both the United States and Britain that make sex discrimination illegal.[4] This idea—that "women's work" pays less because women do it—is the basis of the struggle for what is called "comparable worth" in the United States and "equal pay for work of equal value" in Britain. (I will generally use the term "comparable worth" for a very simple reason—it is shorter.)[5]

Comparable worth is a controversial issue. It has been called the women's issue of the 1980s and the feminist road to socialism.[6] Former president Ronald Reagan called it a "cockamamie idea," and the chairman of the U.S. Civil Rights Commission dubbed it "the looniest idea since 'Looney Tunes.' "[7] But this cockamamie, looney idea is the law in the European Economic Community[8] and in the 104 countries that have adopted Convention No. 100 of the International Labour Organization.[9]

Comparable worth is also a very important issue. Women in both the United States and Great Britain are now, and always have been, paid much less than men. In the United States, the ratio of female-to-male wages hovered around 60 percent for decades.[10] There have been steady increases in the ratio in the 1980s, but by 1987 the median annual earnings of full-time working women in the United States were still only 65 percent of the earnings of their male equivalents.[11] In the United Kingdom, except for a significant increase between 1973 and 1977 that has been attributed to the enactment of antidiscrimination legislation,[12] the ratio has also been quite stable over time.[13] In 1987 the mean weekly earnings of full-time working women in the United Kingdom were 66 percent of the earnings of their male equivalents.[14] Comparable worth may be one way to address this troubling and persistent wage gap.

Finally, although comparable worth cases often begin with alluring simplicity—with Helen Castrilli looking out her window or Julie Hayward talking with her friends—the issue is very complex. To understand the economists who work on the issue, for example, one must understand human capital and dual labor market theories, multiple regression, t-statistics, multicollinearity, heteroscedasticity, and dozens of other technical or specialized concepts that are often even more difficult to understand than they are to spell. Consider the economist from Helen Castrilli's case who said that a *"simple* method of calculation is to calculate the natural logarithm of each benchmark salary, $\ln (SAL_i)$, where SAL_i is the mean salary in the ith benchmark. Using a standard linear regression computer program, calculate: $\ln (SAL_i) = b_o + b_1 (EP_i) + b_2 (M_i)$, where EP is the . . . " You get the idea. One wonders what his *complex* method of calculation would have looked like. And economists are only one type of specialist that must be understood to grasp this issue fully. One must also deal with lawyers, job evaluation experts, feminists, anthropologists, and a host of other people with knowledge as technical and specialized as that of economists. The comparable worth issue is complex because the world in which it arises is complex and because those interested in exploring the issue have relied on all the weapons at their disposal to deal with that complexity, including weapons that are very difficult for nonspecialists to understand.

When Helen Castrilli and Julie Hayward decided to do something about the inequality they saw and heard, they and their cases became lightning rods for this controversial, important, and complex issue. By acting, they hoped to improve their own positions, of course, but also the positions of all people working in "women's" jobs in Britain and America. And by acting, they fostered national debates on comparable worth, an issue of great significance and political impact in the two societies, but an issue that to Helen and Julie seemed as natural as looking out a window or talking with friends.

PART ONE
COMPARABLE ODYSSEYS

1

Secretaries and
Campus Police Officers

HELEN CASTRILLI'S STORY begins on November 20, 1973, when Norm Schut, executive director of the Washington Federation of State Employees, wrote a letter to Daniel J. Evans, who was then governor of the state of Washington (he was subsequently a United States senator from Washington for six years). In the letter Schut for the first time formally raised the issue that was later to form the heart of Helen Castrilli's case; he said that "the major issue" in that year's salary negotiations was whether there was "blatant discrimination in the [state's] salary setting process against women who work."

Governor Evans responded quickly. On November 28 he wrote to Douglas Sayan, director of the state's Higher Education Personnel Board (which has jurisdiction over employees of the state-supported universities, the college, and the community colleges) and Leonard Nord, director of the state's Department of Personnel (which has jurisdiction over most other state employees). Referring to the letter he had just received from Norm Schut, the governor said, "It is the position of this administration that the state take the lead, by enforcement and example, in eliminating all forms of discrimination. . . . If the state's salary schedules reflect a bias in wages paid to women compared to those of men, then we must move to reverse this inequity." The letter directed Sayan and Nord to determine whether there truly was discrimination in the way the state set salaries for its employees.

Sayan and Nord responded by conducting a study, the first (and the simplest) of many comparable worth studies in Washington. The study examined 12 state positions that were occupied primarily by women and 12 that were occupied primarily by men. It compared the pay and the difficulty of the occupations. The difficulty of the occupations was com-

7

pared by assessing each occupation on the basis of five factors: (1) working conditions, (2) complexity of the work, (3) physical effort, (4) responsibility, and (5) education and/or experience required. The study found that when occupations were equal in difficulty, the predominantly male jobs were paid, on average, 15 percent more than the predominantly female jobs.

Governor Evans once again responded quickly. He received the results of the preliminary study in January 1974 and immediately issued a press release calling for a more comprehensive study of the problem. By April, Norman Willis, a well-recognized expert in job evaluation, had been hired. Willis, however, was not hired to produce a report on "comparable worth." In 1974 the term did not exist. When I saw Willis in his Seattle office overlooking Puget Sound, he recalled the cavalier manner in which the term was coined. "We had to call [the report] something, so we said, well, let's call it comparable worth, and it stuck. . . . We never had any idea at all in 1974 that this thing would mushroom the way it has." So in September of that year, Willis produced for the state his "Comparable Worth Study," the study that a decade later would form the crux of Helen Castrilli's lawsuit and provide a name for the most important discrimination issue of the 1980s.[1]

Willis's study was designed to determine whether there were salary differences between male- and female-dominated positions that could not be explained by differences in job duties. To do this, Willis examined 121 state positions, 62 female-dominated and 59 male-dominated positions. (A position was said to be dominated by a sex if 70 percent of the people employed in the position were of that sex.) Before Willis could evaluate all these positions, he had to know what the jobs were. What was someone required to do who was, like Helen Castrilli, employed as a "Secretary I, Shorthand"? The first step of the study, then, was to gather the data required to evaluate the positions. Willis first looked at the job descriptions provided by the state, but they lacked the detail needed for his purposes, so Willis developed a questionnaire that asked employees about their jobs and sent it to 1,600 state employees who were working in the positions he was studying. (The 1,600 employees were selected randomly and constituted about 12 percent of all employees working in the 121 positions at the time of the study.) But Willis was not certain that the results from the questionnaire would be completely accurate. So in addition, Willis and his assistants personally interviewed 800 of the 1,600 employees selected to complete the questionnaires. The questionnaires, some supplemented by interviews, were then screened, and those that were most typical of the position and that were the most complete and factual were selected for use in the evaluation process.

A committee then evaluated all the positions on the basis of four factors: (1) knowledge and skills, (2) mental demands, (3) accountability, and (4) working conditions. Each job was evaluated and assigned a number of evaluation points on each factor. The highest possible number of job evaluation points that could be earned for knowledge and skills was 280; for mental demands, 140; for accountability, 160; and for working conditions, 20. Helen Castrilli's position was one of those evaluated. A Secretary I, Shorthand, received 122 points on the knowledge and skills factor, 30 on mental demands, 35 on accountability, and 0 on working conditions, for a total of 187 evaluation points. The male-dominated position of Campus Police Officer was also evaluated. It received 106 points on knowledge and skills, 30 on mental demands, 35 on accountability, and 11 on working conditions, for a total of 182 evaluation points. Even though their job was slightly less difficult, campus police officers earned about $400 per month more than Helen Castrilli.

The Willis study demonstrated that this type of disparity between job difficulty (as measured by the study) and pay was the rule, rather than the exception, in the state of Washington and, moreover, that the disparity almost always worked to the disadvantage of women's jobs. The study concluded that "the tendency is for women's [positions] to be paid less than men's [positions] for comparable job worth. . . . Overall . . . the disparity is approximately 20 percent."

Although Helen Castrilli had looked out her window and seen discrimination many years before, this was the first time the state of Washington had looked out her window. It also saw discrimination. The state, however, like Helen, did not react quickly to what it saw. Nearly two years passed. In 1976 Willis was hired again. This time he was asked to develop a salary system for the state that would base salaries on job content.[2]

Willis's second assignment marked a significant turningpoint for the state in two respects. First, in contrast to the 1974 study, this study (and the subsequent studies) did not consider whether positions were male or female dominated. It did not consider sex at all. Instead, Willis's sole task was to develop a system to ensure that all jobs, irrespective of their sex composition, were paid in accordance with job duties. Second, the assignment indicated that the state might modify its previous method of setting salaries. Historically, the state had attempted to pay its employees what they would have been paid for the same job outside the state's employ; it had regularly surveyed private sector employers and other units of government (such as city and county government) to determine their pay scales, and then had attempted to pay state employees the same amount.[3] Willis's assignment indicated that the state might reduce its reliance on the "market" to set salaries and increase correspondingly its reliance on job content to determine what state employees should be paid.

Why did the state shift its focus away from sex discrimination? Willis had already surveyed 121 of the state's sex-dominated positions, and it certainly would have been much easier for him to survey the remaining sex-dominated positions than to develop a salary system for the 3,000 positions in the state system overall. We do not know for sure, but it is likely that the state began to appreciate the hazards of its previous focus on sex discrimination. Say that the state had surveyed the remaining sex-dominated positions and had found, as it was likely to, that female-dominated positions were paid 20 percent less than one would expect by looking at job duties. That would further support Helen Castrilli's opinion as she looked out her office window. But if discrimination could be proved, the employment discrimination laws would require the state not only to increase the pay of "women's" occupations in the future (which it was presumably planning to do anyway) but also to provide compensation for the discrimination that had occurred in the past. That back pay would have amounted to millions of dollars.[4] So the state had a very real economic interest in shifting the focus away from sex discrimination. Helen Castrilli, of course, had an interest in keeping the focus on sex discrimination. She would be one of those that would share in the millions of dollars of back pay if sex discrimination could be proved.

Willis's new assignment—to develop a salary system for the state that would base salaries on job content—was formidable. To evaluate the job content of each of the 3,000 positions in the state system would have been an overwhelming task. Clearly, a shortcut had to be found. Willis found one in the system the state had used to set salaries before it contacted him. Under the prior system for setting salaries, Washington State had grouped similar types of jobs together. The jobs in one group, for example, included Office Assistant I and II, Copy Machine Operator I and II, Microfilm Technician, and Telephone Operator. One or two jobs from each group were then selected as "benchmarks." In the example, the Office Assistant II job was selected as the "benchmark." Other employers in the state would be surveyed about each benchmark to determine what they paid for that job. The state would then attempt to pay the benchmark jobs the same as other employers in the state paid for that job. So the pay for the Office Assistant II job, the "benchmark" job, would be based on the results of the survey of other employers. The pay for the other jobs in an occupational grouping would then be determined by a process known as indexing: each nonbenchmark job would be "indexed" to the benchmark, principally on the basis of job duties. In our example, Office Assistant I was indexed four salary ranges below the benchmark Office Assistant II (a salary range represented a pay differential of 2.5 percent); Copy Machine Operator I was indexed at the same level as the benchmark; Microfilm Technician, one salary range above the benchmark; Copy Machine Operator II, four salary ranges above the benchmark, and so on.

Willis decided to use the state's indexing system as his shortcut. Instead of evaluating all 3,000 state positions, he evaluated only the 55 benchmarks. (He also evaluated a few others and reviewed the 121 evaluations made in the 1974 study.) He then relied on the state's indexing system to position the remaining jobs.

Willis's difficulties, however, were not over once he had found this shortcut. His evaluation of the 55 benchmarks yielded only job evaluation points—he knew after the evaluation that Helen Castrilli's job received 187 evaluation points and that it was so many points more or less difficult than the other benchmark jobs—but a job evaluation alone does not determine what a job should be paid. To determine what a job should be paid under a system that paid according to job content, Willis had to take an additional step. Using a statistical technique called regression analysis, he determined the relationship between job content (between job evaluation points) and the salary that the state's market survey indicated for each benchmark.[5] That is, Willis determined the salary that the state would pay if it based its salary decisions on job content.

Willis presented his "comparable worth salary" in an equation and in a graph. In an equation, it looked like this:

$$\text{monthly salary} = \$2.51 \times \text{job evaluation points} + \$518$$

Thus, the monthly salary for Helen Castrilli's job—Secretary I, Short-hand—would have been $987 ($2.51 × 187 + $518) if the state had based its salary decisions on job content. Her actual pay was about $100

FIGURE 1.1. Willis Comparable Worth Line

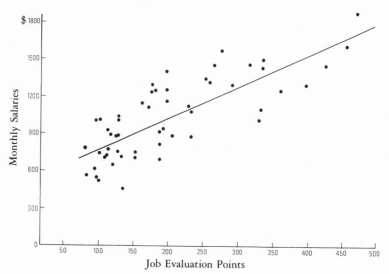

Job Evaluation Points

Source: Norman D. Willis, Washington State Comparable Worth Study 1976, chart A-CW.

less. In graph form, Willis's "comparable worth salary" looked like figure 1.1. The line on this graph—Willis called it the "comparable worth line"—presented the state of Washington with a major problem. The line represented what the state would pay its employees if it based their pay on job content. But the state, like almost every other employer in America, based its employees' pay not on job content but on an undifferentiated amalgam of factors such as the "market" rate for the occupation, whether the occupation was represented by a union, the difficulty of filling vacancies, and (according to some) the sex composition of the occupation. As a result, the actual pay for particular occupations varied considerably from the comparable worth line. The pay for Helen's job (187 evaluation points) was considerably below the comparable worth line; the pay for campus police officers (182 evaluation points) was considerably above the line. Moreover, even though Willis's evaluation did not explicitly take sex into consideration, the results once again indicated that the sex composition of an occupation was related to the pay for that occupation. Almost all the predominantly female occupations were paid below the comparable worth line, and almost all of the predominantly male occupations were paid above the comparable worth line.

So what was the state to do? One option was to begin paying all state employees based on job content. That would have required the state to increase the salaries of people like Helen who were in jobs in which the pay fell below the comparable worth line. But it also would have required the state to reduce the salaries of people in jobs in which the pay fell above the line. The pay of campus police officers, for example, would be reduced. This option would have solved the comparable worth problem on both a theoretical and a practical level. Theoretically, the comparable worth claim is that the pay for occupations is based in part on the sex composition of the occupations. This option would have answered that claim by basing pay solely on job content. Practically, the comparable worth claim is that "women's" occupations are underpaid. Because most of the occupations below the comparable worth line were "women's" occupations, this option would have answered that claim by raising the pay of those occupations. The option also had the advantage of being virtually free to the state, because for every increase in pay for an occupation below the line, there would have been a corresponding decrease in pay for an occupation above the line.[6]

But the option also raised serious problems. The first and most obvious is the resentment it would have caused among those whose pay would have been reduced. Workers strongly resist pay cuts even when their jobs and industries are in dire economic jeopardy. They would likely have resisted these pay cuts even more strongly. Moreover, the group of employees suffering pay cuts would have been predominantly male, and, as indicated above, the group of employees benefited would have been predominantly female. Despite the state's efforts to shift the focus away from sex discrimination, the dispute would undoubtedly have taken on discrimination overtones: why should this group of "innocent" male employees have to suffer to undo the effects of the "guilty" state's discriminatory wage structure? There were also potential economic problems. The actual pay for state occupations reflected the state's attempt to pay the same as other employers in the state paid for that occupation. If the state began to pay male-dominated occupations less than that, one would expect it to have difficulty recruiting and retaining employees in those occupations. Employees would simply accept better offers elsewhere.

Perhaps because of these problems, Willis suggested another option.

(Willis's job, it appears, was political as well as technical. He not only performed the technical job evaluations but he also suggested politically palatable responses.) He proposed that jobs above and below the comparable worth line be treated differently. The pay for jobs below the line, such as Helen's, should be raised to the comparable worth line. The pay for jobs above the line, however, should not be reduced. Instead, the state should continue to pay those jobs as it had in the past, that is, in accordance with the state's survey of other employers.

Willis's suggestion was a compromise. By raising the pay of occupations below the line (most of which were female dominated), it addressed the comparable worth claim that occupations dominated by women were underpaid. But because it failed to reduce the pay of occupations above the line (most of which were male dominated), the gap between the pay of male- and female-dominated occupations would persist. The pay for female-dominated occupations would be increased, but not to the level of the male-dominated occupations above Willis's comparable worth line. Willis's suggestion, then, would reduce but not eliminate the wage gap between male- and female-dominated jobs that ranked equally on the job evaluation study.

Willis's suggestion was also a compromise because, although it permitted the state to avoid the problems that would have been created by reducing the salaries of jobs above the line, it was not free to the state. Under the first option the state would have been able to finance the wage increase for jobs below the line with the money it saved by decreasing the wages of jobs above the line. Willis proposed increasing the wages of jobs below the line but did not propose the corresponding decrease. Willis estimated that the total annual cost to the state to finance the wage increases would be $37.9 million.

So the state had looked out Helen Castrilli's window a second time. Once again, it saw discrimination. Governor Evans decided that enough studies had been done. In his proposed state budget for the 1977–79 biennium, he requested $7 million to begin implementing Willis's suggestion. If Evans had had anything to say about it, Helen Castrilli would soon have received a raise.

Governor Evans, as it turned out, did not have much to say about it. By the time he presented his proposed budget to the legislature in January 1977, he was already a lame duck. (He had not sought reelection.) Governor Dixy Lee Ray, his successor, did not include the $7 million appropriation in her state budget. (This was quite a disappointment to Helen Castrilli and her union because, as a candidate, Governor

Ray had supported comparable worth.) Instead, the legislature required additional comparable worth studies to be done and publicized "for purposes of full disclosure and visibility."[7] As a result, in 1979 and 1981, studies modeled after the 1976 Willis study were done. The studies showed—not unexpectedly—that the state of Washington was not paying occupations on the basis of job content and, tacitly, that occupations with predominantly female incumbents generally fared less well than occupations with predominantly male incumbents. So the state now had five studies, conducted over a period of seven years, all indicating that the state's method of setting salaries worked to the disadvantage of its female employees. But the state still did not change its method of setting salaries; nor did it appropriate any money to raise Helen's pay.

By 1981, Helen Castrilli had moved to an office without any windows, but because of the legislature's policy of full disclosure and visibility, she thought she could see discrimination even without the window. She recalls the phone call from George Masten, executive director of the Washington Federation of State Employees, that allowed her to do something about it. "When George Masten called and said, 'Helen, how would you like to be a plaintiff in a comparable worth lawsuit?' I said, 'Where do I sign?' I thought that was terrific, just great!"

2
A New Recipe for a Cook

ON AUGUST 19, 1975, Julie Hayward began working for the Cammell Laird shipbuilding company near Liverpool, England, as an apprentice cook. She was sixteen years old. For the next four years she learned her trade by spending one day each week at a local technical college and the other four days working in the Cammell Laird canteen. The company paid her for all five days.

Cammell Laird paid Hayward the same amount during her training as it paid all of its apprentices, regardless of their skill. So Hayward was paid the same as Cammell Laird's apprentice painters and light carpenters. But when she ended her apprenticeship and became a fully qualified cook in 1979, she was no longer paid the same as the painters and light carpenters who had also just ended their apprenticeships. She was paid less. Julie Hayward was ready to take action as soon as she discovered that she was being paid less. British law, however, was not yet ready to accommodate her claim.

In 1979 British law required men and women to be paid equally in two circumstances. First, the Equal Pay Act 1970[1] required men and women to be paid equally if they were employed on "like work" in the same establishment. "Like work" was defined as work of "the same or a broadly similar nature" where any differences were "not of practical importance." In common language, this meant that men and women had to be paid equally if they were doing the same job. Thus, if Hayward's claim had been that she was being paid less than a man doing the same work as she (less than a newly qualified male cook), the Equal Pay Act 1970 might have helped. But that was not Hayward's claim. Her claim was that she was being paid less than men doing different but no more difficult work. Her claim was one of comparable worth.

The Equal Pay Act 1970 also required equal pay for men and women who were doing work that had been rated as equivalent by a job evaluation study. This requirement would have been of considerable assistance to Helen Castrilli. In Washington, Norm Willis's job evaluation study had determined that Castrilli's job was equal in difficulty to the campus police officer's job. The British Equal Pay Act 1970, then, would have required Castrilli to be paid the same as campus police officers. The problem for Castrilli was that there is no American equivalent to this part of the British Equal Pay Act. American law simply does not require that jobs rated as equivalent on a job evaluation study be paid equally. The problem for Julie Hayward was that Cammell Laird had never conducted a formal job evaluation study. Nor was Cammell Laird likely to conduct such a study. If it did so, Julie Hayward (and people like her) would have asked for a pay raise under the Equal Pay Act. But couldn't Hayward, with the assistance of her union, conduct her own job evaluation study demonstrating that her job was equivalent to the jobs of painters and light carpenters, and then claim equal pay under the Equal Pay Act? The answer to that question is no, and it points out a substantial shortcoming of the British law. Only job evaluation studies accepted as valid by the parties, *including the employer,* could be used to claim equal pay under the Equal Pay Act 1970. Thus, jobs could be "rated as equivalent" only on the basis of a job evaluation study, but a job evaluation study could be used for that purpose only if the employer accepted it as valid.[2] It is not surprising under these circumstances that few employers in Britain were willing to accept job evaluation studies as valid when women constituted a substantial proportion of their work force.[3] By 1979, when Hayward's claim arose, this section of the Equal Pay Act was virtually a dead letter.[4]

In 1979, then, British law did not provide Julie Hayward with a legal claim that she should be paid the same as Cammell Laird's painters and light carpenters. But things were changing. The United Kingdom had become a member of the European Economic Community in 1973. (The EEC was initially formed by Belgium, France, Italy, Luxembourg, the Netherlands, and West Germany in 1957; it has since been joined by Denmark, Ireland, and the United Kingdom in 1973, Greece in 1981, and Portugal and Spain in 1986.) The main agreements of the countries that make up the EEC are contained in the Treaty of Rome. Article 119 of the Treaty requires each member country to "ensure and subsequently maintain . . . the principle that men and women should receive equal pay for equal work."[5]

At first glance, Article 119 does not seem to require anything more than the British Equal Pay Act. Article 119 requires equal pay for equal work; the British Equal Pay Act requires equal pay for like work. Neither appeared to be of much use to Hayward, because she was claiming not equal pay for the same (or "equal" or "like") work but rather equal pay for different work requiring the same effort. But the Treaty of Rome and Article 119 were originally drafted not in English but in French, Italian, Dutch, and German. The French (*même travail*), Italian (*stesso lavoro*), and Dutch (*gelijke arbeid*) texts, like the English text, seemed to require only equal pay for the same work, but the German text (*gleicher arbeit*) can be interpreted to require equal pay for the same work *and* for similar work. Thus, the German text of Article 119 might have provided Hayward with a legal claim, since she was seeking equal pay for similar work. The EEC does not have a single, official text, so for a long time there was a great deal of uncertainty about the meaning and effect of Article 119.

By the time Hayward's case arose, however, the meaning of Article 119 had been settled within the EEC. In 1975 the Council of Ministers of the European Communities, the principal legislative branch of the EEC, adopted a directive that interpreted Article 119 in a way that included Hayward's claim:

> The principle of equal pay for men and women outlined in Article 119 . . . means for the same work *or for work to which equal value is attributed,* the elimination of all discrimination on grounds of sex with regard to all aspects and conditions of remuneration.[6]

The directive also required member states to enact laws to effectuate fully the principle of Article 119 that men and women be paid equally for work of equal value to the employer.

Despite this directive, by the time Hayward began serving meals to more highly paid men in 1979, the United Kingdom had taken no action to implement Article 119. This troubled not only Hayward (although she, of course, was scarcely aware of it at the time), but also the Commission of the European Communities, the principal executive organ of the EEC. After an investigation, the commission announced that it was going to sue the United Kingdom in the European Court of Justice.[7] The commission's claim was that the United Kingdom was violating Article 119 of the Treaty of Rome, and the 1975 directive interpreting the article, because its laws did not require equal pay for work of equal value. (The commission also sued six other members of the EEC—Belgium, Denmark, France, West Germany, Luxembourg, and the Netherlands—claiming that they too were in violation of Article 119, but that's another six stories.)[8]

The United Kingdom put up a spirited defense. It claimed that the Equal Pay Act 1970 brought it into compliance with the requirements of Article 119. Where the employer had agreed to a job evaluation study, women were entitled to all that Article 119 required—equal pay for jobs that had been rated as equivalent. Where no job evaluation study had been done, Britain adopted "the closest approach to a comparison." British law required equal pay where the work of men and women was the same. The United Kingdom argued that Article 119, for good reason, did not require that employees have the right to insist that a job evaluation be done. Job evaluations were very expensive, and the EEC had not discussed at all the implications of such a requirement (what criteria should be used to compare jobs, how they should be weighed, what exceptions should apply, and so forth).

But the United Kingdom's defense failed. On July 6, 1982, the European Court of Justice held that the United Kingdom was not in compliance with Article 119 of the Treaty of Rome. The court rejected the United Kingdom's claim that employees did not have the right to insist that a job evaluation be done. That, the court said, would amount "to a denial of the very existence of a right to equal pay for work of equal value where no [job evaluation study] has been made."[9] The court said that under Article 119 and the 1975 directive the United Kingdom had to provide a way for employees like Julie Hayward, whose jobs had never been evaluated, to have their claims heard. British law had to require equal pay for work of equal value, and it had to provide Julie Hayward with a forum in which to present her claim that her job was equal in value to that of painters and light carpenters.

In one of the many ironies of this case, then, the British government, headed by Margaret Thatcher and perhaps the most conservative in Europe, was required by its treaty obligations to the EEC to enact a law that was more liberal than the one passed by the Labour government in 1970, the Equal Pay Act 1970. The Thatcher government was required to enact a law that would require comparable worth and provide a procedure for enforcing the requirement. Despite its ideological aversion to the task, the government immediately set out to do its duty. By August, only a month after the decision of the European Court of Justice, the government had already circulated a document that discussed changes that needed to be made in the Equal Pay Act to comply with the decision.

And in July 1983, after publishing and receiving comments on consultative regulations, the government presented to Parliament its proposal for complying with the decision, the "Equal Pay (Amendment) Regulations 1983."[10]

The Equal Pay (Amendment) Regulations required that a woman be paid the same as a man when she was employed on work that was of "equal value" to that of the man. Equal value, the regulations said, was to be determined "in terms of the demands made [on the man and woman], for instance under such headings as effort, skill and decision."[11] The regulations, on their face, seemed tailor-made for Julie Hayward. Her claim was that her work as a cook required the same "effort, skill and decision" as the work of men working as painters and light carpenters. Thus, her claim was that her work was equal in value to their work and, hence, that she was entitled to be paid the same as they. With another set of regulations, the government provided procedures for people like Hayward to follow in making their claims. As if to emphasize the complexity of the procedures (or perhaps simply to warn nonlawyers away), the procedural regulations were entitled "Industrial Tribunals (Rules of Procedure) (Equal Value Amendment) Regulations 1983."[12]

The Thatcher government, however, was still the Thatcher government—a very conservative government that had vigorously defended its compliance with Article 119 in the proceeding before the European Court of Justice. It was clear from the manner in which the regulations were presented that although the government was attempting to comply with the judgment of the court, it was doing so grudgingly. A leading British commentator has described the introduction of the regulations in the House of Commons by Alan Clark, the undersecretary of state for employment:

> He left no doubt about his lack of commitment to the [comparable worth] policy [of the Regulations]. He told the House of Commons that "a certain separation between expressed and implied beliefs is endemic among those who hold office." He warned the House that there were in the draft Regulations "certain legalistic passages which I might have to deal with at 78 rpm instead of 33." He did so. . . . The quality of the speech of the Under-Secretary of State was indicated by the fact that it was warmly applauded by Mr. Tony Marlow, a Conservative back-bencher, whose own contribution to the debate was a criticism of the very idea of entitling women to equal pay for work of equal value. Mr. Marlow was worried that "[a]ny troublemaker . . . is going to pretend that her work is of equal value. It is an open

invitation to any feminist, any harridan, or any rattle-headed female with a chip on her bra-strap to take action against her employer."[13]

The substance of the regulations, in addition to the manner in which they were introduced, clearly indicated that the government was attempting to comply with the decision of the European court in as narrow a fashion as possible. As Clark put it, the government was merely closing "a small gap" in the equal pay laws that had been pointed out by the European Court of Justice.[14] The House of Lords took a different view. It did not think that the gap pointed out by the European Court of Justice, whether small or large, had been closed by the government's proposed regulations. In an unusual move, it attached an amendment to the motion to approve the regulations which said "that this House believes that the regulations do not adequately reflect the 1982 decision of the European Court of Justice."[15] Nevertheless, the House of Lords approved the regulations, perhaps thinking that closing some of the gap was better than not closing the gap at all.

It was also clear from the regulations that the government did not intend to make it easy for people like Julie Hayward to pursue their claims. The proposed procedural regulations were very complicated, so complicated in fact that when they were presented to the House of Commons for approval, the opposition called them "incomprehensible."[16] (An early comment on them was headed "Legislating Nonsense.")[17] Nevertheless, the House of Commons also approved the regulations. So as of January 1, 1984, the effective date of the Equal Pay Regulations, a law was in force in Great Britain that required comparable worth.

But Julie Hayward had been serving meals to more highly paid painters and light carpenters since 1979. Julie Hayward was not one to wait patiently, nor was she one to shy away from difficult odds. In 1980 she had filed a claim under the collective bargaining agreement, but the company had the final word under that procedure, and so the final word was not good. Then, in 1982, like a novice gambler betting on a long shot, Hayward filed an action under the Equal Pay Act as it existed prior to the effective date of the Equal Pay Regulations. Under the Equal Pay Act, Hayward was entitled to equal pay only if she could prove that she was doing the same work ("like work") as a more highly paid man. (The major change made by the Equal Pay Regulations in 1984, then, was that Hayward would be entitled to equal pay if she was doing work of "equal value" to that of a man, work that although it was not the same, required the same effort, skill, and decision.) Since there were no men doing exactly the same work as Hayward, no male cooks, Hayward claimed in her action that her work was the same as the work of her male supervisor, who was paid more. But the claim was not likely to succeed. "Like work" meant work that was virtually identical, and Hayward's work was not virtually identical with that of her supervisor. The major difference, of course, was that Hayward did not supervise any other workers. Such a difference in job duties was usually sufficient to defeat claims under the "like work" provision of the Equal Pay Act. Indeed, such a difference probably would have been sufficient to defeat a claim even under the new Equal Pay Regulations: Hayward's work and that of her supervisor were not of equal value because of this difference in responsibility.

Despite the weakness of her legal claim, Hayward had some success in this preliminary suit, success that eventually was to become bittersweet. In October 1983, when it was quite clear that the Equal Pay Regulations would soon come into force, Hayward and Cammell Laird settled her "like work" claim. Cammell Laird did not admit that Hayward's job was the same as her supervisor's, but to dispose of the action, the company agreed to place Hayward on staff status in return for Hayward's agreement to withdraw her claim under the Equal Pay Act. The elevation to staff status did not increase Hayward's basic pay of about £100 per week, but it did increase some of her benefits. Her sick pay was improved considerably; her lunch break became paid time, and the company provided the lunch; and she received two extra vacation days per year.

In settling her equal pay action, however, Hayward specifically reserved the right to file another action under the new regulations when they became effective. So in January 1984, Julie Hayward became one of the first people in Great Britain to file a claim under the new and untested Equal Pay Regulations that required equal pay for work of equal value. Julie Hayward wanted to be paid the same as those men she served every day.

3
A Secretary Files . . .
a Lawsuit

HELEN CASTRILLI WORKS at the Western State Hospital, which is located a couple of miles east of Steilacoom (pronounced still-a-cum) and about seven miles southwest of Tacoma. Steilacoom is a small wooded town built on a hill that overlooks Puget Sound. The Olympic Mountains are in the distance to the west, across the sound. Steilacoom is the kind of place where the town hall, municipal court, and city library are all located in the same small, bright-white clapboard building; where the shops do not open until 11:00 A.M.; and the bank has the longest hours in town. It is the kind of place that has a soda fountain with overhead fans, a crank telephone, candy in jars, and elderly patrons who sit around drinking coffee, talking about the weather, and asking newcomers questions like "How long are you staying here with your grandpa?" Steilacoom could be the perfect resort town, except for a couple of things. For one, McNeil Island is just off its shores in Puget Sound, and the ferries regularly leave its dock to take prisoners and visitors to the state prison there. For another, the Western State Hospital, where Helen Castrilli works, is the oldest mental hospital in the Pacific Northwest.

Western State Hospital is located on the site of Fort Steilacoom, which was established in 1849 when troops of the United States Army arrived to protect settlers from Indians. When the military abandoned the site in 1868, a bill was introduced in Congress to give the property to Washington Territory for use as an institution for the insane. That bill failed, but when the site was offered for sale by the United States War Department in 1870, the territory bought it for $850. The hospital, then known as Fort Steilacoom, was opened as an asylum for the insane in August 1871 with twenty-one patients. For the first few years it was run by private individuals, but in 1875, after claims that inmates were poorly treated, the territory took over. The hospital has been a public institution ever since.

For its $850 Washington Territory had received some eight hundred acres of prairie land, overlooked to the east by the brooding presence of Mount Rainier and to the west by the Olympic range. There was a lake on the land and a stream fed by numerous springs. The setting was perfect for the best treatment, perhaps, before modern times—"beauty all around is the cure."[1] There were also about twenty-five structures on the land, and some of them still exist as historic sites. But the buildings used as the hospital, of course, have changed.

Helen Castrilli works in a modern, two-story, white concrete building on the east campus of Western State Hospital. The area is wooded and clean. A few people meander between buildings as if it were a college campus. The east campus is connected to the hospital's older brick and red tile buildings by a jogging and exercise trail. But the hospital is for the mentally ill, and as I first approached it, the bucolic setting was disrupted by agitated yelling coming from somewhere inside a building: "Get out of here! Go!" I decided to ignore the advice.

Helen Castrilli is an enthusiastic person. She often uses words of exclamation to end her sentences, words like "You bet!" or "Right!" or "Terrific!" She works in a small windowless office, but it is an office with two doors, a busy office. When I spoke with her, she was doing several things at once, as secretaries often do—talking with me, giving directions to and taking them from people who came in one door or the other, and eating lunch. She spoke with me about her job. Once again like many other secretaries, she was not "just" a secretary.

The state's employment records show that Helen Castrilli began her current job in 1970, after working for the state for ten years in other positions. At that time, she became secretary to the director of the Western State Hospital laboratory. When she started, her duties were what one would expect for a secretary: shorthand, typing, filing. But as Castrilli explains, her duties gradually changed:

> Over the years, we have had a reduction in personnel in the laboratory. The woman who was laboratory supervisor when I was hired retired. For a period of time, a man was filling the position, but he left. I'm not sure of the exact dates. At the time he left, Dr. Wood [then director of the laboratory] requested I take over as many of the duties as I could, short of supervising. So I now do all of the timekeeping, the ordering of all the supplies (which may be $5,000–$6,000 worth of disposable items in any week), writing justifications for new equipment, scheduling some of the lab work, attempt-

ing to be the person who would smooth things over internally in the department. I even lend a hand in the clinical lab whenever I can. I've spun down specimens and separated them and sent them out to our reference laboratory. You bet!

Despite these additional duties, Helen Castrilli never became the laboratory supervisor. To the state, she was still a Secretary I, Shorthand. As a result, she continued to earn Secretary I, Shorthand, wages. So when Norman Willis did his job evaluations and found that the Secretary I, Shorthand, and Campus Police Officer positions were equal in job difficulty but paid quite differently (entry-level salaries of $1,035 versus $1,392 per month), the disparity was even more troubling to Helen Castrilli. She knew that her *real* job was much more difficult than her job title indicated. She knew that for her the disparity in pay was quite understated.

So Castrilli was excited when she was called in 1981 and asked to be a plaintiff in a comparable worth lawsuit. The call, of course, was not totally unexpected. The political negotiations for a solution to the problem had been unsuccessful for years, and a lawsuit seemed the next logical step. The largest union representing state employees—the national American Federation of State, County, and Municipal Employees (AFSCME) and its state affiliate, the Washington Federation of State Employees—would be the primary sponsor and paymaster of the lawsuit. Castrilli was active in the union and thus a likely person to call on as a plaintiff. She had served as a local union officer at Western State Hospital and later as president of the local, and she sat on the state executive board of the Washington Federation of State Employees. Nevertheless, Castrilli was excited to be called.

> I knew then it would take a long time to have to go through all the due process, but we knew it would happen. I just knew, I don't know why, but I guess my gut feeling was that I knew it was the right thing to happen and that there is never an excuse for discrimination, no matter what area you discriminate in. There isn't any excuse for it. Right!

But lawsuits must be based on laws, and despite Castrilli's gut feeling, the laws in the United States prohibiting sex discrimination provided only an uncertain basis for her lawsuit—and almost failed to provide even that. The law her suit was based on was Title VII of the Civil Rights Act of 1964.[2] When the bill that eventually became Title VII was initially introduced in Congress, it prohibited employment discrimination on the basis only of race, color, religion, and national origin.

Sex discrimination in employment was not prohibited. But before the bill was enacted into law, an amendment was passed that added sex to the bill as a type of discrimination that was prohibited.

There were several curious things about that amendment, however. First, it was proposed by Howard Smith, a Virginian who was opposed to Title VII and who eventually voted against it. Second, when Congressman Smith introduced his amendment, he treated it as a joke. He read a letter from a "lady" who pointed out that there were two million more women than men in the United States and then argued that this disparity "shut off the 'right' of every female to have a husband of her own." She asked Congress to do something about this "grave injustice." Third, many of the natural proponents of Title VII—the President's Commission on the Status of Women, the American Association of University Women, and others—were opposed to the amendment adding sex to the bill. And fourth, many of the representatives voting in favor of the amendment were people who, like Smith, opposed Title VII and eventually voted against it.[3]

So why was the prohibition on sex discrimination added to the bill? Two explanations have been forwarded. Perhaps Smith proposed his amendment in an effort to clutter up Title VII and thus create a bill that could be defeated.[4] Or, as was suggested in the *New Republic,* perhaps the amendment was merely "a mischievous joke."[5] Whether it got there as a parliamentary strategy that failed or as a joke or for some other reason long lost in the corridors of Congress,[6] the amendment that added sex to Title VII provided Helen Castrilli with a law upon which to base her lawsuit.

Even with its prohibition against sex discrimination, however, Title VII applied only uncertainly to Castrilli's case. The language of Title VII is broad and vague: "It shall be [illegal] for an employer . . . to discriminate against any individual with respect to his compensation, terms, conditions, or privileges of employment, because of such individual's race, color, religion, sex, or national origin."[7] Castrilli was to claim in her lawsuit that it was discrimination for the state consistently to pay female-dominated jobs like hers less than it paid male-dominated jobs that required the same amount of skill, effort, and responsibility. Her claim was that paying a Secretary I, Shorthand, less than a Campus Police Officer was illegal sex discrimination.

But that result was by no means clear. For one thing, Congress had considered bills in 1961 and 1962 that would have required employers to pay men and women equally "for work of comparable character on jobs the performance of which required comparable skills."[8] That would have been perfect for Castrilli; she was claiming that she was paid less than campus police officers even though the Willis studies demonstrated that the secretarial and campus police positions were "comparable" in job content. But Congress did not pass those bills. Instead, in 1963 it passed the Equal Pay Act, which required equal pay only if men and women were doing exactly the same work.[9] So the state had a legal argument against Castrilli's claim: since Congress had specifically *rejected* comparable worth in 1963 when it enacted the Equal Pay Act, Congress certainly could not have intended to *require* comparable worth when it enacted the vague language of Title VII in 1964.[10]

Castrilli's claim was uncertain for other reasons as well. Was it true that the Secretary I, Shorthand, and Campus Police Officer positions were equal in job content, or were the Willis studies methodologically flawed? Even if the positions were equal in job content, did that necessarily mean that the pay difference was based on the sex of the people doing the jobs, or could there be other explanations for the difference? And even if the pay difference was based in part on the sex of the people in those positions, would it be fair to hold the state of Washington liable for a type of discrimination engaged in by *all* employers?

These uncertainties, for good reason, did not discourage Helen Castrilli. Lawsuits are *always* the result of uncertainties: when a law is clear, the parties need not go to the expense of asking a judge what it means. But there are varying degrees of uncertainty, and like a skater on an ice-covered lake in the spring who, despite the cracking noises, edges ever closer to the perilous center, Helen Castrilli with Title VII as her base was about to skate on thin ice. On September 16, 1981, she took the first step required to begin her lawsuit. She filed a charge with the United States Equal Employment Opportunity Commission (EEOC). Title VII requires people who want to file discrimination claims in federal court to file a charge with the EEOC first. The EEOC doesn't have the power to decide finally whether discrimination has occurred (Title VII gives that power to the federal courts), but it does have authority to investigate charges and, if it believes discrimination has occurred, to bring the parties together to try to settle the issue before a lawsuit is filed.

Helen Castrilli's charge read as follows:

The State of Washington, through the State Personnel Board, discriminates against women on the basis of sex in compensation.

Specifically, the State of Washington, through the State Personnel Board and Western State Hospital, discriminates against me on the basis of sex in compensation by intentionally paying my job, Secretary I, Shorthand, less than predominantly male jobs of equal or lesser value to the employer and equal or lesser levels of skill, effort and responsibility.

Castrilli's charge made it clear that her case was to extend far beyond her narrow complaint that she was paid less than campus police officers. Her charge was not directed only against her immediate employer, Western State Hospital, or even against the state personnel board, which governed most non-higher education state employees. Rather, the employer, the alleged discriminator, was identified broadly as the state of Washington. Moreover, the charge claimed that the state discriminated not only against her and other secretaries but against women generally: "The State of Washington . . . discriminates against women on the basis of sex in compensation."

Castrilli did not act alone in this endeavor. On the same day that she filed her charge of discrimination with the EEOC, charges were also filed by eight other individuals, by the statewide union representing Castrilli and other state employees (the Washington Federation of State Employees), and by the national union with which the statewide union was affiliated (the American Federation of State, County, and Municipal Employees). All the charges made the same basic claim, that the state of Washington discriminated against women by setting lower wages for predominantly female jobs than for predominantly male jobs requiring equal or lesser skill, effort, and responsibility.

In the next six months the EEOC took no action on Castrilli's charge or any of the others. That was not unexpected. The EEOC is a busy agency and does not always get to a charge immediately. In addition, if the EEOC had found reason to believe that discrimination had occurred, its next step would have been to try to settle the case. Castrilli's case, because it was against the state (and hence would require legislative action to settle) and because it was so massive (potentially involving all state employees), would have been very difficult, perhaps impossible, to settle without a lawsuit. So it made some sense for the EEOC not to expend resources investigating a case it could not settle. Finally, although the federal government (in this case the Department of Justice) has the authority to file a lawsuit on behalf of people like Castrilli who file charges, the government (and especially the administration of President Ronald Reagan and the head of his Civil Rights Division, William

Bradford Reynolds) had never filed a lawsuit in a case claiming comparable worth.

The EEOC's failure to act did not prejudice Castrilli's case. Title VII provides that 180 days after a charge has been filed with the EEOC, regardless of whether the EEOC has taken any action or not, the charging party can request a right-to-sue letter. A right-to-sue letter comes from the government and authorizes the charging party to file a lawsuit in federal court.[11] So, on April 23, 1982, following her attorney's request, Helen Castrilli received a right-to-sue letter authorizing her to file a lawsuit in federal court.

Castrilli's lawsuit was filed in the United States District Court in Tacoma on July 20, 1982. Why Tacoma, rather than Seattle or Spokane where the other U.S. district courts in Washington are located? The simple answer, that Castrilli lived closest to Tacoma, is almost certainly not the right one. Castrilli was not the only plaintiff in the lawsuit, and her personal involvement in the trial of the case would be minimal, so proximity to her residence was not important. The principal attorney for the plaintiffs, Winn Newman, came from Washington, D.C., so his location was not a consideration in selecting Tacoma either. Nevertheless, there was an important reason for choosing Tacoma over Seattle or Spokane. When a case is filed in Seattle and Spokane, it is randomly assigned to one of several judges. But in Tacoma at the time the case was filed, there was only one judge, so by filing there the plaintiffs knew who the judge for the case would be: Jack E. Tanner, a black man who had not shied away from controversial decisions.[12] Castrilli's case was filed in Tacoma because the plaintiffs wanted the case to be tried before Judge Tanner.

The document filed to begin the lawsuit, the complaint, was only eleven pages long, with twenty-one pages of attachments, but the lawsuit was by no means small. AFSCME and the Washington Federation of State Employees were also plaintiffs in the suit, and they represented 22,000 state employees. (AFSCME was the first plaintiff named in the complaint, so the case would officially be known as *AFSCME v. State of Washington.*) The eight other individual plaintiffs, like Castrilli, worked for the state in female-dominated occupations. There were two other secretaries, two nurses, a food service worker, a librarian, a counselor, and a job service interviewer. The complaint also named an imposing list of defendants. There was the state of Washington, of course, but also the governor, the director of financial management, the members and director of the Higher Education Personnel Board, the Department of Personnel and its director, the speaker of the Washington House of Representatives and the president of the Washington Senate, and *all* state agencies, boards, and institutions of higher education.

The lawsuit was even larger than the list of plaintiffs and defendants would indicate, because the case was filed as a class action. In the United States, a plaintiff in a lawsuit can, if certain conditions are met to ensure that the plaintiff is a fair and adequate representative, represent people who are not explicitly named in the complaint but who share the same injury or legal claim as the plaintiff. So in this case, Castrilli sought to represent everyone who worked for the state in a position that was female dominated, that had 70 percent or more female incumbents. (Since Title VII protects only claims that arise within three hundred days of the filing of a charge with the EEOC, Castrilli's proposed class included only people who had worked for the state in female-dominated positions since November 20, 1980—three hundred days before Castrilli filed her charge with the EEOC.) Castrilli argued that she should be allowed to represent these people because they all shared the same injury (they were paid less because they worked in female-dominated jobs) and the same legal claim (that Title VII prohibits lower pay because of the "sex" of an occupation). In a decision made before the trial began, Judge Tanner agreed to permit Castrilli and the other named plaintiffs in the lawsuit to represent these other people, so the case expanded to include thousands of state employees (no one knew the exact number) who worked in female-dominated positions. Estimates of the potential liability to the state if it lost the case ranged from hundreds of thousands to billions of dollars.

Making the lawsuit a class action increased not only its size but also its complexity. Consider, for example, the definition of the class. Castrilli now represented all persons who worked or had worked since November 20, 1980, in a state position that was 70 percent or more female. But the sex composition of state positions is not a static ratio. How should someone be treated who was in an occupation that was once 70 percent but is now 50 percent female? What about someone in an occupation that was once 50 percent and is now 80 percent female? In addition, the state had a number of job positions with only one incumbent; each of these positions was either 100 percent male or 100 percent female, depending on the sex of the person who happened to be occupying it. When women held those (usually managerial) positions, they were in the class Castrilli was representing, but did they share the injury and legal claim that Castrilli was asserting?

After a lawsuit is filed, the parties have a right to get information from the opposing side about the lawsuit. This process is called discovery; the parties are trying to discover all the facts relevant to the case. The law provides several ways in which one side can obtain information from the other. It can ask the other side to make admissions (Castrilli, for example, might ask the state to admit that it had conducted a job evaluation study in 1976); to submit to a recorded interview known as a deposition (the state "deposed" Helen Castrilli: that is, she was placed under oath and asked several questions by the state's attorneys, and her answers were transcribed verbatim); to answer written questions known as interrogatories (Castrilli sent an interrogatory to the state asking it to list all the state positions that were 70 percent or more female); and to produce documents. Discovery enables the parties to obtain the information required to prove their case. When the case actually comes to trial and is heard by a judge or jury, each side should be able to present its case in an orderly fashion and should not be unduly surprised by what the other side presents.

From the time Castrilli's case was filed in July 1982 until it came to trial in August 1983, the parties engaged in discovery. This was actually a very short time for discovery. Discovery in large and complex cases like this sometimes takes a decade or more. Hence, this was a very busy time for Castrilli's attorneys and the attorneys for the state—and a time of great tension. Richard Heath, an attorney for the state, talked about the pressure:

> Working day and night and every day for a long period of time just kind of gets to you after a while. And everybody was doing it, both sides were doing it. On the personal side, that takes you away from your family, you never get to see your family at all, and so that's hard on you physically and emotionally and mentally.

The pressure also took its toll professionally. Richard Heath again:

> What they wanted [in discovery] to prove their case was every record the state produced from 1960 on or that had anything whatsoever to do with personnel. I mean that's a big field—personnel. And you're talking 110 or 112 state agencies over a twenty-two-, twenty-three-year period. You're talking a massive amount of documents. And they wouldn't cut down on what they wanted. We resisted, saying there was absolutely no way we could go back twenty-some years with 110 agencies and dig out all those records.

So the state resisted. When Castrilli's attorneys sent a set of forty-nine interrogatories (written questions) to Heath, Heath sent back a response refusing to answer all forty-nine questions. So Castrilli's attorneys asked Judge Tanner to require the state to answer the interrogatories, which he did. Certainly, there was an element of legal strategy in refusing to answer the interrogatories, but principally the refusal was a reaction to the massive amounts of information that were being requested and the short period of time available for response.

The state's attorneys, of course, were not the only ones to feel the pressure. Castrilli's attorneys, without notifying the state's attorneys, approached the former governor, Daniel Evans, and obtained an affidavit from him about his role in the events leading up to the case. Evans at that time was president of Evergreen State College in Washington and thus technically one of the defendants in the suit. (The suit had named as defendants all institutions of higher education in the state. That included Evergreen State College and its chief representative, Daniel Evans.) Consequently, Castrilli's attorneys had engaged in a technical violation of the Code of Professional Responsibility for attorneys. When a lawyer knows that a person has an attorney, Disciplinary Rule 7-104(A)(1) of the code requires the lawyer to obtain the consent of the person's attorney before speaking with that person about a lawsuit.[13] (In this case, Castrilli's attorneys knew that Heath and his colleagues represented everyone named as a defendant in the suit.) Once again, there may have been an element of legal strategy involved in contacting Evans without notifying the state's attorneys, but more likely the technical violation of the code was the result of the complexity of the lawsuit (which, after all, involved thousands of plaintiffs and hundreds of defendants) and the pressures of the discovery process.

The pressure also took its toll on the relationship between the attorneys for the two sides. Before a trial begins the attorneys are expected to agree on a pretrial brief setting out the facts that are agreed upon, the issues in the case, the witnesses the parties expect to call, and so forth. The pretrial brief is of great assistance to the judge in understanding the case and the issues he or she is being asked to decide. But in this case the relationship between the attorneys had so broken down that they were unable to agree on a pretrial brief. Judge Tanner would not be happy about that.

Nevertheless, on August 30, 1983, a year after filing her lawsuit, two years after filing her charge of discrimination with the EEOC, seven years after Governor Evans had proposed raising her salary and the salaries of other workers in female-dominated positions (and then had left office and had his proposal rejected by the new governor); nine years after the first Willis study had said that she was paid too little, and twenty-three years after she began working for the state as a secretary, Helen Castrilli sat in the back of the federal courtroom in Tacoma, Washington, and watched the trial of her case begin.

4

Painters, Joiners, Laggers, and a Cook

AS ONE LOOKS across the River Mersey from Liverpool, the Cammell Laird shipyard, where Julie Hayward works, captures the eye and the imagination. Covering more than two miles of river frontage, the shipyard has a dozen or so permanent yellow cranes stretching 150 feet into the air above a complex of buildings, including at least two that could easily double as enclosed football fields. Squinting, one can almost see *L'Egyptien*, a ship made for Mohammed Ali, the pasha of Egypt, steaming away from the shipyard in 1837 to become the first iron ship to sail from England and then up the Nile; or the *Alabama* sailing for America in 1862 to serve the Confederate cause and capture or sink 67 Union ships; or one of the 106 fighting ships ("a ship every 20 days") that Cammell Laird built during World War II.

The shipyard is located in the borough of Birkenhead on the eastern edge of the Wirral Peninsula, facing the River Mersey. Five miles to the north is Liverpool Bay, leading to the Irish Sea, and seven miles to the west is the River Dee. Rather than saying the shipyard is located in Birkenhead, though, it may be more appropriate to say that Birkenhead grew up around the Cammell Laird shipyard. When William Laird and his son John began building ships on the site in 1828, Birkenhead was a rural area across the river from Liverpool, which was already a major port for trade with the Americas (for a short time it had gained notoriety as Europe's principal slave trade port, and it was a popular point of embarkation for emigrants to the New World). But the shipyard became a major employer, and the employees lived in the area and attracted other businesses. By 1861, Birkenhead was large enough to be recognized as a parliamentary borough, and John Laird was elected its first member of Parliament. By the time he died in 1874, after being returned to Parliament through three general elections, John Laird was recognized as the "Father of Birkenhead," and a statue of him was erected in Hamilton Square, opposite the town hall. So when Julie Hayward tried to increase her pay as a cook, she was not suing just any shipbuilding company. She was suing the company that *was* Birkenhead. She was suing a statue in Hamilton Square.

Julie Hayward lives about two and a half miles from the Cammell Laird shipyard. She lives with her parents and one of her brothers in a small brick house that was originally built as public housing. In January 1984, when her equal value claim was filed, Hayward was twenty-four years old and had been working for Cammell Laird for eight years. Every work morning, she left the house at about 6:45 A.M. She caught a bus and arrived at the shipyard about half an hour later. She changed into her work clothes, including a white apron and chef's hat, and reported to work promptly at 7:30. Until 3:30 P.M., except for tea and lunch breaks, she was a cook in the company canteen. She helped prepare, cook, and serve the midday meal offered by the canteen and then cleaned up afterward. She was paid about £100 per week.

When Hayward filed her equal value claim in early 1984, Paul Brady was reporting for work at Cammell Laird each morning at about the same time as Julie Hayward. Depending on what needed to be done that day, he might report to a quiet and clean room to do spot painting with a brush or he might need to don special protective clothing to do spray painting in an awkward position on a ship under construction. During his lunch break he could go to the canteen and sample the products of Julie Hayward's morning labors or, as I saw many workers do, go to the Brittania Pub across the street and have two pints of bitter for lunch. To Julie Hayward, Paul Brady's job as a painter did not seem any more difficult than her job. Nor did the jobs of Tim Cox and Derek Gilbert seem more difficult than hers. Cox was a joiner, or what we would call a light carpenter. Gilbert was a lagger, or, in the modern terminology, a thermal insulation engineer; he installed insulation. So it disturbed Julie Hayward that at the end of the week, Paul Brady, Tim Cox, and Derek Gilbert received not £100, as she did, but £125.

As a result, Julie Hayward filed a claim as soon as the Equal Pay Regulations became effective in January 1984. The Equal Pay Regulations, once again, required that employers pay men and women equal wages if they were employed on work of equal value as measured by the skill, effort, and responsibility required to do the job. Julie Hayward's claim, then, was that Cammell Laird was violating the Equal Pay Regulations because Paul Brady, Tim Cox, and Derek Gilbert were employed on work of equal value to hers but were paid more.

Julie Hayward was not alone in filing her claim. When she first began to think her pay was unfair, she went to her union (the General, Municipal, Boilermakers and Allied Trades Union) and talked with Andrew Davies, its legal officer. It was Andrew Davies who went to the shipyard before the claim was filed to try to find workers whose jobs might be compared with Hayward's. Using very crude job comparisons that he had devised himself, he decided that the painter's, joiner's, and lagger's jobs were comparable to the cook's job. He then asked Paul Brady, Tim Cox, and Derek Gilbert to help Hayward with her case. And perhaps most important, Andrew Davies found the money needed to bring the suit.

Despite the obvious interest and energy of Andrew Davies, however, Julie Hayward's case placed the union in a somewhat difficult position for several reasons. First, the union represented Hayward *and* Brady, Cox, and Gilbert. Through collective bargaining, the union had agreed to the wages for all of them, including the wages it was now helping Hayward to challenge. Second, the union and its leadership were composed mostly of men, and too strong a push for equal pay for women could create a backlash. As Andrew Davies put it when I spoke with him, "There's a great deal of hostility to equal pay beneath the surface— hostility from male members and from male union officers who think the issue will only cause trouble in the union." Another knowledgeable observer put it less delicately: "Unions have problems with the troops— they don't see women as full human beings." Finally, Hayward's case was a problem for the union because, like virtually all unions in Britain, it was ideologically opposed to the use of the law in labor relations. (This opposition, in the tongue-twisting language of lawyers, is called legal abstentionism.)[1] Hayward's case, of course, required the union to lean on the law to support her claim for higher pay. Nevertheless, despite these difficulties, the union did all it could to help Julie Hayward. It provided an active and effective advocate in Andrew Davies, and, just as important, it guaranteed that Hayward would not have to pay for the lawsuit.

Julie Hayward also received help from another quarter. The Equal Opportunity Commission (EOC), which is roughly equivalent to the Equal Employment Opportunity Commission (EEOC) in the United States, agreed to pay for a barrister and a job evaluation expert. The EOC does not have the resources to support many cases, but it supported

Hayward's because it was the first to be heard under the new Equal Value Regulations and, since the regulations were very complex, the EOC wanted to ensure that the first cases (from which important legal precedents would be set) were handled by able lawyers.

By the time Hayward's case was to be heard for the first time in April 1984, an impressive litigation team had been assembled. Andrew Davies, of course, had already provided valuable service as the union representative and would continue to do so. David Pannick had been retained by the EOC as Hayward's barrister. Pannick was an impressive person; he was a fellow of All Souls College at Oxford University, would soon publish an important book on British sex discrimination law,[2] and was already well known and highly respected as a barrister in discrimination cases. The union supplied a solicitor, Nick Carter, from a large firm based principally in Manchester. (The British, of course, still have a split legal profession. Barristers, in effect, are litigation specialists; they handle matters in court. They are advised by solicitors, who maintain contact with the client and handle legal matters outside the courtroom.) Finally, the EOC paid one of the best-known job evaluators in England, David Wainwright, to advise Hayward. I suppose if one is to attack a statue in the main town square, the modern way to do it (in Britain and America) is with a team of lawyers and experts. Julie Hayward, with a little help from her friends, came prepared.

On April 10, 1984, Julie Hayward and her friends went to the offices of the Liverpool Industrial Tribunal for the first hearing in her case. The offices of the tribunal are located on the corner of Cook Street and Union Court just beyond Mathew Street, where a couple of decades earlier the Beatles had sung about help and friends (and a few other things). Hayward and the others walked through the men's clothing section of the Watson Prickard store and took the elevator to the fourth floor (fifth floor, to Americans) where the tribunal's offices are located.

The industrial tribunal that was to hear Hayward's case consisted of three people: Mr. A. M. Coventry, the chairman and a barrister, and two nonlawyers, Mr. N. Thompson and Mrs. G. Taylor.[3] They sat behind a table on a low platform that enabled them to look down at the parties in the small, crowded room. David Pannick, speaking on behalf of Julie Hayward, was behind a table facing them and to their left. Behind another table to their right was Donald Munro, the solicitor for Cammell Laird. (Wigs and robes à la Rumpole and the American image of British courtrooms, alas, are not used in industrial tribunal hearings.)

The issue before the tribunal on that day was whether it should send the case to an independent job evaluation expert who would examine Hayward's job and those of Brady, Cox, and Gilbert to determine whether they were of equal value. The tribunal could decide *not* to send the case to an expert (and hence decide the case against Hayward) if Cammell Laird could prove one of two things. First, the tribunal could dismiss the case if Cammell Laird proved that there were no "reasonable grounds for determining that the work is of equal value."[4] The tribunal could dismiss on this ground, though, only if Hayward's case appeared hopeless, only if there was virtually no chance that a job evaluation expert would judge her job to be equal in value to those of Brady, Cox, and Gilbert. Second, the tribunal could dismiss the case if Cammell Laird could prove that the difference in pay between Hayward and the others was caused by a material factor other than sex, for example, that the men were paid more than Hayward because they had more seniority or because they worked a more undesirable shift. (Cases can also be dismissed at this stage if the employer can prove that a job evaluation study has already been done, that it ranks the applicant's job lower than the comparator's job, and that there are no reasonable grounds for believing that the study is discriminatory. That ground for dismissal was not at issue in Hayward's case, because no prior job evaluation study had been done.)

Cammell Laird, then, bore the heavier burden in this preliminary proceeding. The case would be sent to an independent job evaluator unless Cammell Laird could prove that Hayward's case was hopeless or that there were factors other than sex to explain the difference in pay. Donald Munro, Cammell Laird's solicitor, called two witnesses at the hearing. John Swift testified first. He was the catering manager at Cammell Laird, and Julie Hayward's boss. He testified about Julie Hayward's job duties as a cook. Then Charles Kelly, production administration manager at Cammell Laird, testified about the job duties of Brady, Cox, and Gilbert, the painter, the joiner, and the lagger. Cammell Laird was trying to prove that Hayward's case was hopeless, that there were no reasonable grounds for believing that her job was equal in value to the jobs of the men.

There was a fundamental problem with Cammell Laird's approach, however, and David Pannick, Hayward's barrister, quickly pointed it out. Swift knew what cooks did, and Kelly knew what painters, joiners, and laggers did, but neither could testify about *both* Hayward's job and the jobs of the men. Neither could *compare* the jobs to determine whether they were equal in value. But that, of course, was what the tribunal had to do if it was not to send the case to a job evaluator. It had to determine that when the jobs were compared, there was virtually no possibility that a job evaluator would find them to be of equal value. This error, although unfortunate, may not have been too damaging to Cammell Laird. Given the heavy burden of proving that there were "no reasonable grounds" for believing the jobs were of equal value, the company probably would have been unable to win on this issue even if it had presented witnesses who could compare the jobs.

But Cammell Laird made another error at this initial hearing, which, like a time bomb, was waiting to explode at a later hearing. Cammell Laird decided not to call any other witnesses; it decided not to present any evidence to support the second reason for not sending the case to a job evaluator: that material factors other than sex might explain the wage difference between Hayward and the men. Cammell Laird's attorneys were calculating that it would be better to present that defense at a later stage of the proceeding. It was this strategy that exploded later in the case: the tribunal later held that the company had waived the defense when it failed to present any evidence on it at this early hearing (the later hearing is discussed below).

Both these errors (failing to call a witness who could compare jobs, and failing to present evidence on material factors other than sex that might explain the wage difference) are understandable. This was the first case under the new Equal Pay Regulations. There were no cases that said the "material factor" defense was waived if not presented at the first hearing—until this tribunal said so. There was little chance of winning on the job comparison defense regardless of the evidence presented, so it made some sense not to spend too much time or energy on it. Nevertheless, I have never examined a case before (and as a law professor and an attorney I have examined many) in which there was greater unanimity that one side made prejudicial legal mistakes. On the applicant's side, Andrew Davies said Cammell Laird "rather mishandled the case at the beginning"; Julie Hayward said the company "made a complete botch of it." Bob Fiddaman, Cammell Laird's industrial relations manager, recognized the mistakes at the initial hearing but, circumspect as always, said that "this case was the first; we didn't know what the new regulations meant." But he also listened without contradicting as a colleague asserted that the company was "poorly represented," that the hearing was a "travesty."

In any event, Julie Hayward won at the first hearing without presenting any witnesses or evidence whatsoever. But winning there did not mean much. It meant only that the case would be sent to a job evaluation expert, who would examine Hayward's job and the jobs of the men to see whether they were of equal value. He or she would submit his or her conclusions to the industrial tribunal, and then there would be another hearing. All Hayward had won was the right to have an independent expert take a closer look at her case.

So the focus of the case shifted to Wales and to Terence Anthony Dillon. Terry Dillon is a lecturer in industrial relations at University College of North Wales in Wrexham. He is youngish middle-aged, wears spectacles, and has a floating eye that creates a moment of uncertainty when one wants to look at him directly. He works in a small, sparsely furnished office with an unvarnished wood floor and half-filled bookshelves. He was soon to be the most important person in Julie Hayward's case: the independent job evaluation expert.

How does one become an independent job evaluation expert? Terry Dillon became one by replying to an advertisement in the Sunday newspaper. The Equal Pay Regulations required that industrial tribunals refer cases like Hayward's to a job evaluation expert, and they assigned the task of compiling a list of experts to the Advisory, Conciliation and Arbitration Service (ACAS). ACAS decided to do that by first advertising for self-described experts. There were hundreds of self-described experts; ACAS received about 1,300 applications in response to its advertisements. ACAS then whittled that number down to about sixty people to interview and finally to fifteen people, including Terry Dillon, who were placed on the list of experts.

The people on this list were not "experts" in a strict sense. Most of them, including Dillon, had never formally studied job evaluation in an academic setting. Most, including Dillon, had never conducted scientific studies on the validity of various job evaluation techniques. Some, not including Dillon, had never even done a job evaluation. (Dillon had done evaluations when he was on the research staff of a union.) ACAS was not looking for people who were experts in this strict sense (although it certainly would have accepted them), but rather for people who had a good knowledge of industrial relations and pay systems, who had sufficient experience to have developed an "industrial relations sensitivity," and who were sufficiently literate to produce a report and sufficiently articulate to defend it before an industrial tribunal. ACAS, then, had compiled a list of "nonexpert experts" to do the job evaluations in equal value cases like Julie Hayward's.

It may not have been only humor and modesty, then, when Terry Dillon said that he was appointed to Hayward's case, the first case, to his "shock and horror." His expertise was limited, and it was not possible to rely on the experience of others—there was no other experience. And when he looked at the Equal Pay Regulations, he found little there to guide him. The regulations told him to compare the jobs and to "act fairly," but they provided virtually no guidance on *how* to compare the jobs. Which aspects of the jobs should he examine? The regulations suggested but did not require that he look at effort, skill, and decision. Should he also look at responsibility? working conditions? How should he quantify the factors he looked at? The regulations did not say. To what extent should he defer to assessments by the employer or collective bargaining agreements? Once again, there was no guidance from the Equal Pay Regulations.[5]

Dillon said that after he was appointed he was left "holding the baby," and he was—a "baby" that included responsibility not only for a job evaluation in one case but for setting the course for all equal value cases in the future. His actions would have a great deal of influence on the future development of comparable worth in Great Britain.

But how could this be—a lecturer from Wales influencing the development of comparable worth, nonexpert experts deciding cases, little or no guidance from the law designed to require comparable worth? The general rules of procedure in Great Britain provide the primary explanation for this state of affairs. British rules of procedure do not recognize class actions. Julie Hayward could not, as Helen Castrilli did in the United States, file an action on behalf of all her co-employees who worked in female-dominated occupations. Instead, Hayward could file only on her own behalf.[6] But comparable worth is a problem that affects a large number of people. Because having a relatively small number of very large comparable worth cases was not possible in Britain, Britain designed a system to hear a great number of small cases very quickly. Instead of a long and detailed job comparison by a professional evaluation expert, which would presumably take some time to prepare, the system sought quasi-experts who could prepare job comparisons quickly. And instead of an inflexible procedure prescribed by the regulations, the system permitted the procedures (and the job evaluation) to be tailored to the individual case. The job evaluations would probably be less than fully accurate and precise, but that was the price to be paid for quickness and efficiency.

Dillon was appointed as the independent job evaluator in Hayward's case early in the summer of 1984. Because no standard procedure had been established, he first met with the parties separately to discuss procedures. Without any major difficulties, a basic procedure was agreed upon. Dillon would go to the Cammell Laird shipyard and observe Julie Hayward doing her job and Brady, Cox, and Gilbert doing their jobs. (By the time Dillon got to the shipyard, Brady was no longer working at Cammell Laird, and Cox was a full-time shop steward. Another painter and two other joiners were added as comparators for Dillon to observe, but to avoid confusion I will continue to refer to Brady, Cox, and Gilbert as the comparators.) While he was observing, Dillon would be accompanied by representatives from the company and the union. He would also accept submissions from Cammell Laird and the union about the jobs. Dillon would then prepare a summary of his conclusions and submit it to the parties, who would be given an opportunity to respond in writing and in person during a meeting with Dillon. After that, Dillon would prepare his final report (which, of course, would indicate whether he thought Hayward's job was of equal value to those of the men) and submit it to the industrial tribunal.

So on three pleasant and sunny days in June 1984, Terry Dillon watched a cook, a painter, a joiner, and a lagger doing their jobs. It quickly became apparent that determining whether the jobs were of "equal value" would be no easy task. For example, Dillon had to go deep into the bowels of the ship then under construction, through tiny holes on shaky ladders down five levels, to see Brady "red-leading." Red-leading was painting with a lead-based paint, and it was not pleasant work—it was cramped down there, and misty, and dirty. But when Dillon made it back to the top of the ship, the union representative who was accompanying him (but who had decided not to accompany him all the way down into the ship) told him that he should not consider red-leading in comparing Brady's work to Hayward's because Brady received extra pay for red-leading. He received pay on top of his usual salary for going so far down into the ship, for working in the fume-filled environment, for putting on the special clothes required to work with lead-based paint. Was that right? Should Dillon not consider work for which Brady was paid extra? Despite the extra pay, it was still work that a painter had to do, work that obviously had value to Cammell Laird. Or did the extra pay take that task outside the normal duties of a painter? Did the extra pay make the performance of that task, in effect, another job?

And what about mistakes? A ship had once been returned to Cammell

Laird because the wrong kind of paint had been used. The company had the ship in drydock for two weeks, scraping off the bad paint and putting on new paint. And on top of that expense, it had to make payments to the ship owner on a penalty clause in the contract. Mistakes by Brady, the painter, could be very costly. What happened when Hayward made a mistake? Replacing burned potatoes is much cheaper than putting ships into drydock. But should Dillon consider the cost of mistakes at all? If equal value is to be determined on the basis of job duties, perhaps not. Job duties are what one does on the job, not what happens if one makes a mistake.

And should Dillon consider the relationship of the jobs to the principal business of the company? Bob Fiddaman argued that Cammell Laird's business is making ships, and the painter, joiner, and lagger are all essential workers in that enterprise. A cook, on the other hand, is not essential to that task; Cammell Laird could make ships without any cooks and in fact did so for well over a century. If Dillon's job was to measure the "value" of the work, Fiddaman argued, attention should be paid to the relationship of the jobs to shipbuilding.

And what about the fact that Dillon made his observations on pleasant, sunny days in June? Hayward's work was all done indoors in the canteen, so the weather did not affect Dillon's impressions of her job. But painters, joiners, and laggers did not always work indoors, and it was not always pleasant and sunny when work needed to be done outdoors. Could Dillon fairly evaluate work that might be done outdoors in February with a cold wind blowing off the Mersey by observing it only on pleasant days in June?

By September, Dillon had prepared his report. When I talked with him about it later, he acknowledged his difficulties; he said everyone involved was "learning as we went along." He recognized that the report was relatively crude and was not an "expert" job evaluation. It was, he said, "a subjective process at the end of the day"; he simply looked at the jobs and applied "common sense." He even argued that an expert job evaluation could not be done in the context of an equal value case like Julie Hayward's. An expert evaluation could be done, he argued, only if larger numbers of employees were being evaluated. (Norm Willis, the job evaluation expert in Seattle, later told me that in his opinion a valid job evaluation could be done with only two employees if the goal is, as it is under the Equal Pay Regulations, simply to determine whether a woman's job is equal in value to a man's job. Attempting to determine the degree of difference between the two jobs, however, would not be possible with only two employees.) Nevertheless, despite the difficulties, despite the crudeness of the report, despite Dillon's doubts about whether job evaluation could even be done in this context, a report was issued. If it determined that Hayward's job was not equal in value to those of the painter, joiner, and lagger, the case would be over. Hayward would lose.[7] If the report determined that Hayward's job was equal in value to one or more of the men's jobs, Hayward would be one step closer to earning the same salary as her male co-workers.

Dillon structured his job evaluation in much the same way as Norm Willis had structured his much larger evaluations in the state of Washington. Dillon first isolated the factors he was going to examine in evaluating the jobs. He was going to examine the jobs for (1) their physical demands (the need for physical effort and stamina); (2) their environmental demands (the general conditions under which the work had to be performed); (3) their planning and decision-making demands (the level of discretion allowed); (4) their skill and knowledge demands (the knowledge and ability required to perform the jobs); and (5) their responsibility demands (their accountability for tools, equipment, and materials). Instead of attempting to assign points on each factor as Willis did, however, Dillon simply determined whether each job should be ranked low, moderate, or high on each factor. For example, in comparing the physical demands of the cook's and joiner's jobs, Dillon said:

> The cook stands when preparing and cooking meals and snacks. She exerts low levels of effort when mixing, cutting and slicing ingredients, with moderate levels of effort needed for lifting, carrying and sliding items of equipment, foodstuffs, semi-prepared and finished dishes. She has routine daily and weekly cleaning duties, which involve moderate levels of effort.
> The joiner works on a vessel, in the joinery shop, or about the yard, as required. Much of his activity in cutting, shaping and fixing involves low levels of effort, although these tasks can require moderate and sometimes high levels of effort when working in awkward postures on board a vessel. The higher level of effort required on occasions by the joiner is, in my judgment, counterbalanced by the extra stamina required by the [cook], each day, during the period of increased working pace and level of activity preceding the mealtime deadline.[8]

With that explanation, Dillon concluded that both jobs ranked as "moderate" on the physical demands factor.

And so Dillon proceeded, comparing the job of cook to each of the other three jobs on each of the factors and making his crude low, moderate, or high determinations. At one point he seemed to forget his

TABLE 4.1. Summary of Dillon Job Evaluation

Factor	Cook	Painter	Joiner	Lagger
Physical demands	moderate	moderate	moderate	moderate
Environmental demands	moderate	moderate	moderate	moderate
Planning and decision-making demands	moderate	low	low	low
Skill and knowledge demands	equal	equal	equal	equal
Responsibility demands	low	moderate	moderate	low

Source: Report of independent expert in *Hayward v. Cammell Laird.*

own process: on the skill and knowledge factor he failed to rank the jobs as low, moderate, or high; he said only that all the jobs were equal (see table 4.1). Dillon simply ignored many of the most contentious issues; he did not even discuss the extra pay for certain tasks, the relative costliness of mistakes, or the relationship of the jobs to the company's principal task of shipbuilding. But whatever the shortcomings of Dillon's technique, his was to be the only job evaluation in Hayward's case and the first one in an equal value case in Great Britain. He concluded that Julie Hayward's job as a cook was equal in value to the job of Paul Brady, the painter; equal in value to the job of Tim Cox, the joiner; *and* equal in value to the job of Derek Gilbert, the lagger.[9] Julie Hayward had made it over a significant hurdle, but there were still others in her path.

On October 4, 1984, the three members of the industrial tribunal in Hayward's case met once again in the tribunal's office above the Watson Prickard clothing store. Dillon had submitted his report. The tribunal's task was to decide whether to accept its conclusion that Hayward's job was equal in value to the jobs of the men. At this hearing, in contrast to the earlier one, Cammell Laird was represented by a barrister, Charles James. (Cammell Laird was not about to repeat the mistakes of the first hearing, but as it was soon to find out, in some respects it was already too late.) David Pannick was there once again to represent Julie Hayward. Terry Dillon was called as the first witness.

Cammell Laird, of course, was not happy with Dillon's conclusion. Throughout the day of October 4 and into the morning of October 5, James questioned Dillon at length and in detail. It was not friendly questioning; Dillon later said that he was "roughed up." James attacked Dillon because of the relatively short time he had spent in the shipyard observing the jobs. The report had taken five months to prepare, but

Dillon had spent only three days in the shipyard. James challenged the method Dillon had used in evaluating the jobs. The crude "low, moderate, and high" evaluation scale, James asserted, was not sufficiently precise and reliable to measure the relative value of jobs. And why, James asked, had Dillon not considered the collective bargaining agreement? The agreement not only approved (and, indeed, required) the pay rates of cooks, painters, joiners, and laggers, it also affected the job evaluation because it classified cooks as "unskilled" workers but classified painters, joiners, and laggers as "skilled tradesmen." How, James asked, could Dillon treat the jobs as equal when Hayward's own union had agreed that they were unequal?

But James was operating against several formidable obstacles. One was the time bomb resulting from Cammell Laird's presentation of its case at the first hearing. The Equal Pay Regulations permit unequal pay for work of equal value if the employer can prove that the difference is based on some factor other than sex. Thus, even assuming that Hayward's job was equal in value to the other jobs (and Cammell Laird certainly disputed that), the difference in pay was legal if Cammell Laird could prove that it was caused by some factor other than sex. The factor James wanted to point to was the collective bargaining agreement. Hayward was paid less not because of her sex but because of an independent factor, the collective bargaining agreement. This was the argument Cammell Laird could have presented at the first hearing when the Tribunal was deciding whether to send the case to an independent expert, but did not. At the second hearing, the tribunal decided that the "factor other than sex" defense could be presented only if it had been raised at the first hearing. Hence, James was not permitted to raise the defense.

The tribunal's decision makes some sense. If there is a reason for a pay disparity other than sex (such as the collective bargaining agreement in this case), the employer should know about it at the time of the first hearing and, arguably, should be required to present the defense at that time, because, if successful, the defense would then save the time and expense of the job evaluation. But because this was the first case under the Equal Pay Regulations, Cammell Laird did not know at the time of the first hearing that if it did not present the "factor other than sex" defense, it would not be permitted to do so later. In this case, what Cammell Laird did not know could and did hurt it.

James faced other obstacles as well. One way in which Cammell Laird had planned to challenge Dillon's report was to present its own job evaluation. The company had hired a job evaluation expert who had

looked at Hayward's job and the other jobs and had determined that
they were not of equal value. James planned to call this expert as a
witness, as was his right under the Equal Pay Regulations. But when
the second hearing, originally scheduled to begin on October 1, was
postponed until October 4, Cammell Laird's expert was unavailable.
Bob Fiddaman, the company's industrial relations manager, recalls pleading with the expert for an hour—"I told him if you don't testify, we
lose"—but the expert told Fiddaman he could not testify on October 4
or 5. Then Fiddaman talked with James, his barrister, and Munro, his
solicitor, about rescheduling the hearing, but they felt that asking for
a postponement would prejudice the case as badly as not having the
expert. So James had to mount his challenge to Dillon's report without
the supporting testimony of Cammell Laird's job evaluation expert.
(Julie Hayward had also hired an expert, David Wainwright, to do an
evaluation, and he, unsurprisingly, had agreed with Dillon that the jobs
were of equal value. Because Dillon's conclusion supported Hayward's
claim, Wainwright did not have to testify.)

James also wanted to challenge Dillon's report by presenting testimony that would undermine the facts Dillon relied on to reach his
conclusion. He wanted, for example, to have a painter testify about
climbing down those shaky ladders to apply lead-based paint in a fume-
filled hold, so that the tribunal could decide for itself whether Dillon
was right when he said the working environments of the cook and the
painter were about the same. But once again, James confronted an
insurmountable obstacle. The Equal Pay Regulations provided that "no
party to a case involving an equal value claim may give evidence upon,
or question any witness upon, any matter of fact upon which a conclusion
in the report of the expert is based."[10] And Dillon, of course, had based
the conclusions in his report on precisely the types of information that
James wanted to present to the tribunal. As a result, James could not
present any evidence to challenge the factual basis of Dillon's report.
He could not have a painter testify about red-leading.

The industrial tribunal did show some concern for James's predicament. It said that

> such a rule does, of course, cut across what is taken for granted in other
> types of cases as being normal procedure, and imposes a severe constraint
> upon the manner in which the content of the report can be tested. That
> that must prove difficult, and indeed irksome, to [James and Cammell Laird]
> is entirely understandable but, nevertheless, it is a part of the scheme of
> things which the legislature has, in its wisdom, thought proper to adopt.[11]

But what could the wisdom of the legislature have been? Why prevent James from presenting facts that might expose errors in Dillon's analysis? The reason is that the legislature had decided to make the equal value procedure quick and efficient, and the cases could not be heard and disposed of quickly if people like Charles James were allowed to present all the evidence they wanted to industrial tribunals. So the legislature included in the Equal Value Regulations the provision that prohibited James from calling a painter as a witness. (As mentioned earlier, there was a need for a quick and efficient procedure because Britain does not recognize class actions. Since it could not have a few very large cases like Helen Castrilli's, it wanted to have a procedure that would permit many small cases to be decided quickly.)

The corollary of this legislative wisdom was the final obstacle James faced. Because the legislature had prohibited the industrial tribunal from hearing evidence challenging the factual basis of Dillon's report, it obviously intended the tribunal to give great weight to Dillon's conclusions. The tribunal in Hayward's case complained about this; it said that the regulations resulted in "the effective removal from the Tribunal of its own primary fact-finding role" and the transfer of that role to job evaluation experts like Terry Dillon. But that was what the legislature had said, and the tribunal conceded that it could make findings at odds with Dillon's only if it found that Dillon "had gone badly wrong."[12] (British tribunals have certainly not gone badly wrong in delightfully phrasing their legal standards.)

James, then, faced a whole series of obstacles in attempting to get around Dillon's conclusion that Hayward's job was equal in value to the jobs of painters, joiners, and laggers. The tribunal would not permit him to attempt to prove that a factor other than sex caused the pay difference between Hayward and the men because Cammell Laird had not raised that issue at the first hearing. He could not call the company's job evaluation expert to testify that, in his opinion, Hayward's job was not equal in value to the other jobs because the expert was unavailable on the days the industrial tribunal met. The Equal Pay Regulations prohibited James from presenting evidence that might have undermined the factual basis of Dillon's conclusion. And the tribunal held that it was going to accept Dillon's conclusion unless James could somehow prove, without being allowed to present much evidence, that Dillon had "gone badly wrong."

The tribunal's decision, then, was no great surprise. The tribunal accepted Dillon's conclusions. In a decision issued on October 29, 1984, the tribunal decided that Julie Hayward's work was equal in value to that of painters, joiners, and laggers. Julie Hayward had won. She was, the tribunal said, entitled to pay equal to that of the men. The tribunal ended its opinion with a statement that seemed innocent at the time: if the parties could not agree on Hayward's new pay level, then Hayward could "request that her application be further considered by the Tribunal on a date to be fixed."[13]

On the day the tribunal issued its decision in her case, Julie Hayward was at work in the canteen at the Cammell Laird shipyard. The canteen was noisy and full; workers were eating and (mostly female) workers were serving food. But Julie and the others knew that a decision was imminent, and when the phone rang, there was a momentary hush in the noontime bustle. The call was for Julie. She spoke for a moment, hung up the phone, and then modestly informed the crowd that she had won. The workers began to applaud and gradually to stand. The applause grew, and suddenly Julie's fellow canteen workers were on the tables performing a short dance in celebration. Julie Hayward, a canteen worker for a third of her lifetime, first enjoyed her victory, the first victory in Britain for a woman seeking equal pay for work of equal value, with her fellow workers in the canteen where she spent much of her life.

5
A Secretary's Case Is Heard

ON AUGUST 30, 1983, Helen Castrilli was in Tacoma, a city surrounded by natural beauty. Mount Rainier looks down on it from the east, a snow-capped peak often resting on a white cushion of low clouds, and the city looks out toward the shimmering blue of Puget Sound to the west. But, perhaps to balance nature, the city has the pungent aroma of paper mills and is marred by religious graffiti. (Actually, there may be an equal number of religious and nonreligious graffitists in Tacoma, because although the message I saw most often on downtown walls read "Trust Jesus," a rival graffitist had added the word "Alou" to most of the messages. Jesus Alou was a baseball player.) Tacoma is built on a hill overlooking Commencement Bay, and Helen Castrilli was in town on that day for a commencement—the commencement of the trial of her lawsuit against the state of Washington, the commencement of the most important comparable worth case in America.

Judge Jack Tanner entered a full courtroom that day. With everyone in the courtroom standing, he climbed the few steps to the bench and sat directly in front of the large gold seal of the United States, just to the right of the American flag. When he looked down, he might have seen Helen Castrilli, who was seated in the section for the public in the back of the courtroom with her fellow plaintiffs and the television and newspaper reporters. In front of Judge Tanner and to his right were the attorneys who represented Castrilli. The team was led by Winn Newman from Washington, D.C., a well-known and highly respected plaintiff's lawyer in discrimination cases. Newman had argued discrimination cases before the United States Supreme Court and—significantly, since there were not many of them—he had litigated comparable worth cases before. To the judge's left were the attorneys for the state of Washington:

Christine Gregoire, deputy attorney general, and Richard Heath and Clark Davis, assistant attorneys general. The team for the state was not as well known in legal circles. None of them had any experience in discrimination cases, and they had only very limited experience in the federal courts in any type of case. Davis had been specially hired for this case because of his federal court experience, yet he had been out of law school for only three years, and his federal court experience was as a law clerk to a federal judge, not as a litigator. Gregoire and Heath had even less experience: a computer search uncovered only one federal court case in which either of them had participated.

The attorneys must have been quite apprehensive as Judge Tanner entered and got settled. The case was not only large in its own right (estimates of the state's potential liability ranged to well over $1 billion); it was also significant for the effect it might have throughout the country. If the state won, litigation on the comparable worth issue might be stopped dead in its tracks. If Helen Castrilli won, suits like this might become commonplace.

The attorneys must have also been apprehensive because Judge Tanner was hearing the case. He is not an easy judge to work before. As one commentator has noted, Judge Tanner is not like "other judges who maintain the traditional stony 'courtroom demeanor': [rather, he] is an aggressive and animated questioner."[1] He can also be abrupt and sarcastic. When Christine Gregoire, for example, was presenting her opening statement, Judge Tanner thought he noticed an inconsistency between what she was saying and a brief she had previously filed with the court.

TANNER: I get the feeling that you're disavowing your [brief].
GREGOIRE: No, we're not, Your Honor.
TANNER: Have you read it lately?
GREGOIRE: I believe so, yes.[2]

Judge Tanner's sarcasm was certainly not reserved solely for the state's attorneys. Consider the time he thought Winn Newman was taking too much time with a witness:

TANNER: I asked you three times . . . to ask him his opinion for
             what you called him for. And you don't want to do that
             for some reason.

NEWMAN: Well, I will attempt to go through that, but I do think
             we have not finished [questioning him yet]. I think,
             Your Honor, that we can finish with him in half an hour
             and I would like the opportunity, your permission to
             do so.

TANNER: You don't hear very well, do you?

NEWMAN: I hear, but I—

TANNER: Bring [the witness] back.[3]

Judge Tanner's courtroom demeanor has made him unpopular with
attorneys. In a study conducted by a national lawyers' magazine and
released shortly before Helen Castrilli's trial began, Tanner was named
the worst federal judge in the West. The study quoted an unnamed
lawyer: "[Judge Tanner] is unpleasant to everyone who appears before
him. I've known Jack for many years, and I like him outside the courtroom. But he puts on the black robe and he just goes berserk."[4] Judge
Tanner could hardly care less about what attorneys think of him. In
fact, he may prefer things the way they are. "I kind of like people to
talk about me," he says. "At least they know I'm there."[5]

It did not take long for Judge Tanner to let the parties in Helen
Castrilli's case know he was there. He quickly displayed his judicial
temperament. Before a case begins, the parties are supposed to agree to
a pretrial order that tells the judge what the issues in the case are, what
facts have been agreed upon, what witnesses will be called, and so on.
The attorneys in this case could not agree on a pretrial order, so each
side submitted one. Judge Tanner began the case by expressing his
displeasure:

> Both parties' pretrial orders are terrible. Apparently it results from—the
> pretrial order is a result of the inability of counsel to get together on the
> case. . . . The Court just can't accept the reasons for two pretrial orders.
> There's just no reason for it. It's just a complete failure of counsel to follow
> the rules.[6]

Nothing was to be done about this failure. The parties were not sanc-
tioned in any way. The case was not delayed until the parties agreed to
a pretrial order. But the episode immediately put the parties on notice
that Judge Tanner was not simply going to sit above them and listen
to the evidence. He and his temperament would play a considerable part
in the trial of Helen Castrilli's case.

After Judge Tanner's outburst, Winn Newman made his opening
statement, presenting the broad outline of Helen Castrilli's case against

the state of Washington. (The parties had agreed that at this stage of the trial the only issue before the court would be whether the state had discriminated. If the court found that the state had discriminated, the issue of how to remedy the discrimination would be presented to the court later.) Helen Castrilli's claim was that the state of Washington had discriminated against her and other people working in female-dominated jobs by paying them less because of the "sex" of their occupations. To prove that, Newman would rely principally on Willis's job evaluation studies. The studies, Newman argued, proved discrimination because among jobs ranked equal by the studies, female-dominated occupations were always paid less than male-dominated occupations. That result, he continued, was not the result of chance or happenstance; instead, it was caused by the state's discrimination against women, discrimination that had been admitted by a former governor of the state, Daniel Evans, and that was evident in the state's attempts in the past to segregate jobs by sex (for example, by advertising job openings in newspaper advertisements as "men's jobs" and "women's jobs").

Then it was the state's turn to make an opening statement, and Christine Gregoire quickly summarized the thrust of the defense:

> The question before this Court, Your Honor, is whether you should ratify an individual's subjective evaluation of the worth of a job with no reference whatsoever to the marketplace and the marketplace determination as to the value of that job insofar as pay is concerned.[7]

The state's defense, then, had two principal components. First, the state would attack the validity of Willis's job evaluations. They were, according to the state, merely "subjective evaluation[s] of the worth of a job" and, therefore, the court should not rely upon them as evidence of discrimination. Second, even if the job evaluations had some minimal validity, the pay difference they showed between male- and female-dominated jobs was caused not by discrimination on the basis of sex but by the state's attempt to pay the market rate—the rate other employers in Washington were paying—for doing a particular job. Paying the market rate, Gregoire argued, is entirely sex-neutral and should therefore be a complete defense against Helen Castrilli's claim.

The arguments of the two sides displayed a confounding symmetry. Newman worshiped the god of job evaluation, that neutral and reliable giver of pay equity between the sexes. Gregoire worshiped the god of market rates whose invisible hand sent the wage rates for secretaries and campus police officers up or down depending on his need for workers in those jobs.

In the trial, Newman and Gregoire were missionaries each singing the praises of his or her own god while crusading against the other's god. This symmetry was confounding because every idea that was used to crusade against one god was later reformulated and directed against the other. Judge Tanner was the potential convert. But this battle was to be fought not in the heavens but in a courtroom in slightly smelly, graffiti-ridden, downtown Tacoma, Washington, where neither Newman's god nor Gregoire's god was a pure, omnipotent giver of truth.

After the opening statements Newman began to present Helen Castrilli's case. The star witness, of course, was Norm Willis, the author of the job evaluation studies. But the reason for having Willis testify is not as clear as one might imagine. The studies themselves had already been admitted into evidence by agreement of the parties, so Willis was not called so that his studies could be presented to the court for its consideration. Newman obviously wanted Judge Tanner to infer from the studies that the state had discriminated against female-dominated occupations, but Willis was not called to guide the judge in making that inference. Another witness would do that. So why was Norm Willis called as a witness? From the questioning, it became clear that Newman wanted Willis to testify so that Judge Tanner could evaluate Willis's competency firsthand and, by doing so, judge *ad hominem* the reliability of his job evaluation studies. Newman asked Willis how long he had been conducting job evaluations (almost two decades), for whom he had done job evaluation studies (an impressive list including the states of Alaska, Connecticut, and Oregon and several large companies, such as Weyerhaeuser and the Northwest Natural Gas Company), and how many job evaluation studies he had done (somewhere in the low three figures, perhaps 200). Newman also emphasized Willis's competency with another line of questioning:

NEWMAN: [The first job evaluation] study that you did [for the state of Washington] was not called a comparable worth study, was it?

WILLIS: In 1973 there was no such term.

NEWMAN: Do you know how the name comparable worth came about?

WILLIS: I guess we have to claim responsibility for it. As in any study, we'll talk out the intent with the client, the purpose of the study. In this case . . . we arrived at comparable worth as being [the] most appropriate [name for the study].[8]

Newman had Norm Willis testify, then, primarily so that Willis could be presented to Judge Tanner as a man who had been doing job evaluations for a long time, who had done a great many of them for many important clients, and, indeed, who had coined the term "comparable worth." Newman presented Norm Willis as the wise and benevolent founding father of comparable worth.

Once he was called as a witness, however, Willis also had to face questioning from the state's attorneys, and their goal was to show that "wise" and "benevolent" were not terms that applied at all to the notion of comparable worth. Their goal was to undermine the validity of Willis's job evaluation studies. They certainly had plenty of cards in their hands to do so, but the cards they played were played poorly, and they simply failed to play other cards.[9]

The state's attorneys attempted to make three points in questioning Willis. First, they asked him how many different state jobs there were in Washington when he did his studies (more than 3,000), and then they asked him how many jobs he had actually evaluated in his studies (about 200).[10] The implication was clear. Judge Tanner should not rely on Willis's studies of about 200 jobs to overturn the state's wage-setting practices for more than 3,000 jobs. Second, the state's attorneys asked Willis about the types of jobs his system was originally designed to evaluate. He acknowledged that the system was originally designed for use in evaluating white-collar office jobs. The implication here was that the system was suspect when it was used for other jobs, especially blue-collar jobs. Third, the state's attorneys asked Willis about the maximum number of points that any job could score on each of the factors. Willis reported that the highest possible number of job evaluation points that could be earned for knowledge and skills was 280, for mental demands 140, for accountability 160, and for working conditions 20. The state's attorneys then had Willis acknowledge the obvious: the highest possible ranking for knowledge and skills was fourteen times the highest possible ranking for working conditions. The implication was that the job evaluation system was suspect because it unfairly (or perhaps arbitrarily) compared knowledge and skills with working conditions; a job performed under the harshest of working conditions but requiring little knowledge or skill could not rank favorably against a job that required even a moderate or low level of knowledge and skill.

All the points made by the state's attorneys in their questioning of Willis were well worth making, but the points were only half-formed so they lost much of their impact, and other points that could have been made were not even touched upon. And these shortcomings in the state's defense went well beyond Willis's questioning. The points I discuss here were not effectively raised by the state at any point in the case.

Consider the first point made by the state: Willis's conclusions were based on evaluations of only 200 of the more than 3,000 different jobs in the state of Washington's personnel system. The state missed an opportunity to make the point even more forcefully. Although Willis had evaluated about 200 jobs, the core of his analysis, his comparable worth line, was based on only 55 jobs. More important, the state failed to present additional evidence that was crucial to its point. Willis's reliance on 200 (or 55) jobs would undermine his conclusions *only* if the 200 jobs he evaluated were not a representative sample of the 3,000 state jobs. If the jobs Willis evaluated *were* a representative sample of all state jobs, his conclusions could have been quite reliable even though he did not look at the vast majority of the jobs. (In the same way, newspaper surveys reporting, for example, that 50 percent of the public supports the president's stand on an issue are quite reliable even though the newspapers actually obtain the opinions of only a very small number of people. The conclusions reached are reliable because the opinions are obtained from a representative sample of the entire population.) By itself, then, the state's bald assertion that only 200 of 3,000 jobs were evaluated did not undermine the reliability of Willis's studies. But if the state had demonstrated in addition that the 200 jobs Willis evaluated were not a representative sample of the 3,000 jobs, its criticism would have had some force—but the state did not even attempt to prove that.

Looked at in one way, this was a lost opportunity, because the state could have presented evidence that Willis did not examine a representative sample. Willis had decided to evaluate particular jobs primarily because the state had selected them as benchmarks. But the state had selected jobs as benchmarks not because they were representative of all state jobs but because they would make it easy to do a salary survey. The state selected the benchmarks, among other reasons, because it was easy to describe the content of the benchmark jobs and because other employers employed people in similar jobs.[11] Looked at in another way, however, the state's failure to present this evidence was entirely understandable. It was a consequence of the confounding symmetry of the case. Later, the state was going to rely on the salary survey as a defense against Helen Castrilli's claim. If it now attacked one part of the salary survey (the selection of the benchmark jobs), Newman would use the evidence later to attack that state defense. Nevertheless, even though there may have been good reasons for its failure to present the evidence, the state's attack on the reliability of Willis's job evaluation studies was weak because it presented only half an argument.

Half an argument, however, was better than the state did on its other two objections to Willis's job evaluations. On those, the state merely presented the seed of an objection; it failed to nurture the objection into full flower. These objections were that Willis's methodology was designed for white-collar office jobs and could not reliably be applied to predominantly male, blue-collar occupations, and that differences in the maximum number of points assigned to the various factors (280 possible points for knowledge and skills and only 20 for working conditions) skewed Willis's results in some undefined way. Both were potentially powerful arguments; both were mishandled. The state's first shortcoming was in failing to relate the two objections to each other. Willis's evaluation system could not be reliably applied to blue-collar workers *because* of the differences in the maximum number of points available under the various factors. Blue-collar workers did poorly on Willis's job evaluation because they ranked high on the working conditions factor, a factor that was given very little weight in Willis's evaluation scheme.

The state could have vividly illustrated the importance of this point. Under Willis's weighting scheme the average male-dominated job in Washington scored 195 points and the average female-dominated job scored 240 points. That result, however, would have changed dramatically if Willis's weighting scheme had been different and everything else had been exactly the same, including the relative ranking of male and female jobs on each factor. If, for example, the weighting scheme had been changed by multiplying the scores on the working conditions factor by 10 and the scores on the other factors by 0.5, male jobs would have averaged 186 points and female jobs 162 points. [12] Suddenly, simply because the relative weighting of the factors had been changed, male jobs would have been worth more than female jobs.

Despite its potential impact, the state decided not to use this type of illustration. But let us imagine what would have happened if the argument had been pursued. Willis was not without his defenses. His principal counterargument would have been that any different weighting scheme would have been "extremely difficult to validate." (Willis began to make this argument even against the state's relatively undeveloped attack.) But that would have opened up a new opportunity for the state.

Willis explained to me what he meant by validation:

[When we talk] of validation of an evaluation system, all we are [doing] is using compensability as the frame of reference. There has got to be some frame of reference; you can't just say it's nice to have more points for this and more points for that. There has to be some frame of reference, and compensability in the marketplace [is the frame of reference we use]. That's how you validate.

Willis validated his studies, then, by comparing the job rankings he received from his job evaluation to the job rankings provided by the marketplace. If the job evaluation ranked jobs quite similarly to the way the market ranked them, Willis considered the job evaluation to be valid. His counterargument to an attack on his weighting scheme, then, was that any weighting scheme other than the one he used would have resulted in job rankings that were more different from the job rankings provided by the marketplace. Any other weighting scheme would have resulted in a job evaluation system that was less valid than his.

If Willis had been forced to articulate this defense of his job evaluation system, the state could have mounted a formidable attack. If, as Willis argued, the market is the "frame of reference," then the most valid job evaluation system is not Willis's system but the market itself. No job evaluation system can better predict the market than the market can predict itself. So, the state could have argued, why use Willis's second-best system when the best system is readily available? Why not use the market to set wages?

This argument would have served the state in three ways. First, it would have required Willis to explain further the underlying rationale of his job evaluation system and eventually to admit, as all job evaluators must, that although job evaluation is an attempt to remove sex bias from the market evaluation of jobs, the process requires subjective judgments at many stages (in selecting the jobs to be evaluated; in describing those jobs; in evaluating the skill, effort, and responsibility required by them; in deciding the maximum number of points available on each factor; and on and on). Willis certainly could have defended the subjective judgments that he and those working with him had made, but he could not have denied forever that subjective judgments were made.

Second, the argument would have provided support to the state's principal defense in the case, that paying market wage rates was legal and acceptable. The state could have pointed to Willis's use of the market as a "frame of reference" for his job evaluation study and argued that it should be equally acceptable for the state to use the market as its "frame of reference" in setting wage rates.

Third, the argument would have weakened indirectly one of the central tenets of comparable worth and of Helen Castrilli's lawsuit: that the market wage rate for female-dominated occupations is discriminatory. If that tenet is true, then it was improper for Willis to use the market as the "frame of reference" for his studies. Willis's use of the market as a frame of reference implies an acceptance of the market and, hence, runs counter to the claim that the market wage rates for women's occupations are discriminatory.

But this argument was not developed by the state. It may have been because the state did not employ a job evaluation expert to assist it in preparing for Willis's cross-examination. Or perhaps, with all that needed to be done to get ready for the trial, there was no time to prepare adequately for Willis's questioning. It may have been that the state planned to make this point later when it called its own witnesses (plans that were later scuttled by Judge Tanner). Or perhaps, and this may be the most likely reason, it is just much easier to look back at a trial, as I am doing, and point out what could have been done than it is to participate in a trial and decide what needs to be done at the time. Regardless of the reasons, though, the state's questioning of Willis failed to create serious doubts about the points he made in his testimony.

Willis's testimony, however, was only half of Helen Castrilli's case. Willis testified that he had done a job evaluation that ranked jobs by the skill, effort, and responsibility required to do the jobs and then had devised a system for paying jobs on the basis of his job rankings. The pay for jobs under Willis's system differed considerably from the pay for jobs under the system that the state of Washington actually used. To win her case, though, Helen Castrilli had to prove more than that the state failed to pay jobs based on job content. She had to prove in addition that the state allowed the sex of those performing the jobs to influence what it decided to pay. She had to prove that female-dominated jobs paid less *because* they were performed predominantly by women. To prove that, Winn Newman, Castrilli's attorney, called Stephan Michelson as a witness.

Stephan Michelson is an econometrician, an expert at using statistics to analyze economic data. Winn Newman wanted Michelson to analyze the available information—information that Willis had produced and that Winn Newman had obtained from the state on what it paid its employees—and to conclude that the information proved that female-dominated jobs paid less because they were female dominated. And Michelson, of course, proceeded to testify to just that. (One need not be much of a cynic to realize that if Michelson had not been prepared to testify to that, Newman would have looked around until he found an econometrician who was.)

Michelson made his point—that female-dominated jobs paid less because they were female dominated—in a couple of ways. He began by comparing the salary the state actually paid each job to the salary the state would pay under the system Willis had devised; that is, he compared the actual salary for each job to Willis's proposed comparable worth salary for that job. To facilitate this comparison, he calculated for each job the ratio of actual salary to comparable worth salary. For Helen Castrilli's job, for example, the actual salary was about $900 per month and Willis's comparable worth salary was about $1,000 per month, so the ratio for the Secretary I, Shorthand, position was $900 to $1,000 or 0.90. If the actual salary and the comparable worth salary were the same, the ratio would be one; if the actual salary was more than the comparable worth salary, the ratio would be more than one; and if the actual salary was less than the comparable worth salary, the ratio would be less than one. Michelson testified that when he looked at his results, he found that for male-dominated jobs (jobs with more than 70 percent male incumbents) the ratio was more than one, and for female-dominated jobs the ratio was less than one. Michelson put his results in a chart (see figure 5.1), which by itself seemed to demonstrate a relationship between the pay for a job and the sex composition of that job. But Michelson testified that, if anything, the chart understated that relationship. He testified that in the absence of discrimination, one would expect about half the state's employees to be in jobs with a ratio of more than one and half to be in jobs with a ratio of less than one. And for jobs that were *not* female dominated, that was indeed the case: 49.83 percent of those employees were in jobs with a ratio below one, and 49.95 percent were in jobs with a ratio above one. (The remaining 0.22 percent were in jobs with a ratio of exactly one.) But for female-dominated jobs, 96.49 percent of the employees were in jobs with a ratio of less than one, and only 3.49 percent were in jobs with a ratio of more than one. The implication of Michelson's chart and statistics was clear: the sex composition of a job seemed to have an effect, and a pretty consistent one at that, on the ratio of the actual salary to the comparable worth salary for that job.

But Michelson did not stop there. He also analyzed the information to quantify more precisely the effect of the sex composition of jobs on salaries. He compared jobs that were ranked equally by Willis (or, as

FIGURE 5.1 Ratio of Actual Salary to Comparable Worth Salary

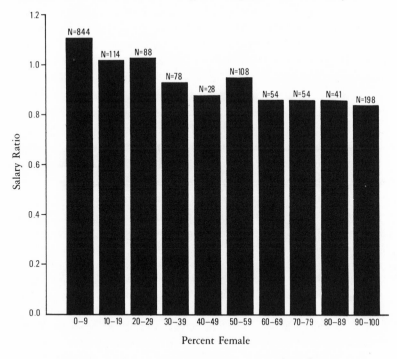

Source: Plaintiffs' Exhibit 135-B, *AFSCME v. State of Washington*, 12.

Michelson explained it, he used Willis's job evaluations to control statistically for differences in skill, effort, responsibility, and working conditions) and found that, on average, the monthly salary of job classifications in the state of Washington decreased by $4.51 for every 1 percent increase in the percentage of women in a job. There was, in other words, a significant inverse correlation between the percentage of women in a job and its pay. At the extremes, jobs held only by women paid, on average, $5,400 less per year than jobs held only by men.

Michelson then made a point that Judge Tanner repeated several times during the course of the trial. The probability that these pay disparities between male- and female-dominated jobs would occur by chance, Michelson testified, was less than 1 in 10,000.[13] Once again, the implication was clear: if the pay disparity between male- and female-dominated jobs did not occur by chance, then the state must have intended it. The difference in pay occurred because the state discriminated against Helen

Castrilli and other people in female-dominated occupations because of their sex.[14]

By the time Michelson was concluding his testimony, the trial was in its fifth day. In addition to Willis and Michelson, Winn Newman had called several other witnesses. Former governor Daniel Evans had testified about his role in the controversy; Ray Marshall, former United States secretary of labor, had testified as an expert witness about the economics of discrimination in labor markets; Eleanor Holmes Norton, former chair of the United States Equal Employment Opportunity Commission, had testified as an expert witness about the state of the law on comparable worth; and several witnesses had testified about the state of Washington's personnel policies and practices. By this time, Judge Tanner thought he had heard enough evidence, and Judge Tanner has never been one to keep his thoughts to himself. At the end of the day on September 8, with Michelson still testifying, Judge Tanner sent the parties home with a warning:

> We're going home. We're going to conclude this case. The plaintiff's case is going to be concluded. If you don't conclude it, Mr. Newman, I am going to do it for you, soon. We're getting into repetition and accumulation. . . . I don't know what you're trying to do and I don't know what the State is trying to do except avoid a conclusion. I don't understand why.[15]

One of the first principles of litigating cases is "Pay Attention to the Judge." The judge, after all, is the person who is going to decide whether you win or lose. Winn Newman knew that principle well. When court convened the next morning, the first thing Newman said was that he did not have any more questions for Stephan Michelson. The second thing he said was that he did not have any more witnesses. If Judge Tanner thought he had heard enough, Winn Newman was not one to quarrel.

Things were not quite so easy for the state's attorneys. Newman had at least had five days in which to present Helen Castrilli's case. The state had not yet begun to present its case, and Judge Tanner was already impatient, very impatient.

The state's first step was to move to dismiss the case. Basically, the state was asking the court to rule that the evidence presented by Winn Newman was insufficient to prove that the state had engaged in sex discrimination. If Judge Tanner had granted the motion, the case would have been over. The state would not even have had to present any evidence. But Judge Tanner denied the motion. The denial was pretty much expected (judges seldom grant motions to dismiss made at this stage of a case) and did not seem particularly significant at the time. Everyone except Judge Tanner thought that the judge had merely ruled that *if the state did not present any evidence,* Newman had presented enough evidence to prove discrimination. But it soon became clear that Judge Tanner thought that he had decided something else, and that "something else" was going to cause major trouble for the state.

So the state began to call its witnesses. It had a long list of witnesses who were ready to testify to two basic points. First, they were ready to testify that Willis's results were merely subjective evaluations and therefore should not be relied upon by the court as evidence of sex discrimination. (Since Michelson had used Willis's results to reach his conclusions, if Willis's evaluations could be undermined, Michelson's testimony would fall with them.) Second, the state's witnesses were ready to testify that any differences in the pay of men and women were caused not by sex discrimination but by the state's sex-neutral practice of paying the market rate for jobs.

It soon became apparent that there was quite a distance between what the state's witnesses were ready to say and what Judge Tanner was willing to hear, and it did not take the judge long to alert the state to this distance. The judge would not allow Clark Davis, one of the attorneys for the state, to direct certain questions to the first witness for the state. When the judge explained his reason for not allowing the testimony, Davis was clearly surprised.

TANNER:	Once the District Court has overruled the defendant's motion [to dismiss], the only relevant issue left in the case then is [whether there] is some legitimate, articulate reason [for the discrimination]. Isn't that what we're talking about?
DAVIS:	I believe that the defendants could still go to the question of whether a prima facie case [of discrimination] has been established in the first place.
TANNER:	What case supports that?
DAVIS:	I can't think of a case offhand, Your Honor.
TANNER:	Then I don't understand it. The plaintiff must prove a prima facie case [of discrimination]. If they do, then . . . the burden of production shifts to the defendant to articulate some legitimate reason for their action. . . . I know of no other way to try these cases.

DAVIS: If the Court is ruling [that] a prima facie case [of dis-
              crimination has been] established . . .
TANNER: I thought I did that some time ago.
DAVIS: Okay. By, I guess, by denying my motion [to dismiss
              the case]. I—is that—
TANNER: Well, you made the motion and I denied it.[16]

A few minutes later, Christine Gregoire, another of the state's at-
torneys, was questioning the state's second witness. Once again, Judge
Tanner would not allow certain questions to be asked. Once again, Judge
Tanner explained his reasons. Once again, the state was surprised.

TANNER: Apparently we're on a different wave length. I've already
              ruled [that] the [plaintiffs have] proved a prima facie case
              of sex discrimination and if I read the cases, you have to
              explain why you discriminated. That's exactly what I said
              when I overruled Mr. Davis' motion [to dismiss the case],
              that they proved a prima facie case of sex discrimination.
              Now, if I understand it, the state must say why.
GREGOIRE: We have witnesses whom I submit to you are going to
              show there is no sex discrimination in the state of
              Washington.
TANNER: Once the trial court overrules the defendant's motion to
              dismiss, the overruling of that motion for all intents and
              purposes means one thing, that the plaintiff has proved a
              prima facie case of discrimination. In reading the cases, I
              understand that . . . you must then articulate . . . some
              reasonable reason for it, not that it isn't there.
GREGOIRE: Your Honor . . . are we not entitled to rebut a finding
              of discrimination?
TANNER: Let me read you from *Gay v. Waiter*.[17] [*The judge read
              a short portion of the opinion.*] Now, as I understand it,
              once the [plaintiffs establish a case of discrimination],
              you've got to explain it; why the discrimination; not
              whether there was, but why the discrimination.
GREGOIRE: Are you ruling that the State is not allowed to rebut
              this idea that there is discrimination?
TANNER: That's the way I read these cases. If [the plaintiffs
              present a case of discrimination], you have the burden
              of explaining why, not if you did it, but why.[18]

As soon as the state began to present its case, then, Judge Tanner
made it clear that he was not going to listen to a great deal of the state's

evidence. Astoundingly, he ruled that the state could not present any evidence on whether or not the state had discriminated. He said that when he had denied the state's motion to dismiss Helen Castrilli's case, he had not merely ruled (as everyone else thought) that enough evidence had been presented to prove discrimination *if no other evidence were presented.* He had actually made a final and irrebuttable determination that discrimination had taken place. He would not listen to any evidence that might challenge that determination.

The state's attorneys were entirely justified in being surprised. First, the decision was blatantly unfair. It meant that Judge Tanner had made a final decision on whether the state of Washington had discriminated before the state had had any opportunity whatsoever to present evidence. Moreover, it meant that the state could not present a great deal of evidence to the court that any reasonable person would have recognized as relevant to the issue of whether the state had discriminated. Second, as a legal matter, the decision was unprecedented and flatly wrong. In reaching his decision, Judge Tanner relied on cases that discussed how a judge should analyze a case *after the parties have had an opportunity to present their evidence.* Those cases say, as Judge Tanner indicated in the excerpts above, that the judge should first determine whether the plaintiff has proved a case of sex discrimination and, if she has, then the judge should determine whether the discrimination is justified in any way. But Judge Tanner used those decisions not to analyze the case after all the evidence was in but to prohibit the state from presenting evidence that no discrimination had taken place. That had never been done before and, one would hope, it will never be done again. But that is what Judge Tanner did in Helen Castrilli's case.

If the state's attorneys were worried about Judge Tanner's decision to limit their ability to present evidence when they first heard it (and they were), they were horrified as the judge began to apply the decision ever more expansively. For the state's first two witnesses, as mentioned above, the judge merely prohibited the state from asking certain questions. But then Clark Davis attempted to call an expert witness for the state who was prepared to testify that the Willis studies were not reliable.

DAVIS: Your Honor, [the state proposes] to submit evidence to attack [the Willis studies].

TANNER: You're going to do that before the Ninth Circuit, I assume? [*The Ninth Circuit is the court that reviews Judge Tanner's decisions on appeal.*]

DAVIS: We anticipated doing it in this courtroom, Your Honor, with evidence that the Willis methodology is not an appropriate methodology for measuring the disparity that is purported to exist here.

TANNER: Counsel, you are going to argue that before the Ninth Circuit, I'm telling you now.

DAVIS: Your Honor, I'm not clear as to, are you ruling that we can't introduce evidence that—

TANNER: The Ninth Circuit says that it must be admissible and admissible needs to have some relevance.

DAVIS: [*Obviously not believing what he was hearing*] Let me clarify what we are talking about. We're talking about an expert who will testify that the Willis system is not adequate, is not an appropriate system for measuring the existence of disparity, does not demonstrate, does not prove the existence of [discrimination].

TANNER: I'm not interested in that witness's testimony.[19]

Judge Tanner refused to allow the state's third witness even to take the witness stand. And to the still greater horror of the state's attorneys, that stance became the norm rather than the exception. The fourth witness the state attempted to call was another expert. Once again, Judge Tanner refused to allow her to take the stand. He permitted the next three witnesses called by the state to testify but only on very narrow topics. One, for example, was permitted to testify only about the relative pay of beauticians and barbers employed by the state and another only about the disruption that would be caused by implementation of comparable worth. Judge Tanner refused to allow the state's attorneys to question the witnesses about any other matters.

After Judge Tanner refused to allow the next witness called by the state to testify at all, the state began to offer documents as exhibits, perhaps hoping that it would have more success with documents than it was having with people. It didn't.

TANNER: Specifically, tell me what you're offering that exhibit for, the SSS exhibit if that's the number.

DAVIS: JJJ and SSS is being offered.

TANNER: I have gone past JJJ. [*Judge Tanner had already refused to allow the state to admit exhibit JJJ into evidence.*]

DAVIS: SSS is offered in conjunction with JJJ. SSS—

TANNER: Does it rise or fall on JJJ?

DAVIS: Yes it does.

TANNER: Well, it just has fallen.[20]

After the state's decidedly mixed success in getting its exhibits accepted into evidence, the state (through still another of its attorneys, Richard Heath) had to ask for the court's forbearance. But Judge Tanner, as usual, was not in a forbearing mood.

HEATH: Your Honor, when we came here today we . . . brought
                [two] expert witness[es], Mr. Generette and June O'Neill.
                We had Mr. Boysen, Mr. Nordon [Nord] and we brought
                Mr. Hanson, Mr. Hayasaaka and we frankly have run out
                of witnesses that are present in the Court. We did not
                anticipate that we would go through these witnesses so
                fast and we would be—

TANNER: Mr. Heath, what was the Court's admonition to both
                parties?

HEATH: Well, Your Honor, I think it was reasonable on our part
                to at least think that some of our witnesses would have
                been able to testify, at least the experts in this case.

TANNER: More than once I told both you and Mr. Newman time
                and time again, be ready. You're not going to run this
                case in this Court at your discretion. . . . Now just because
                you told some of your witnesses for their convenience,
                they don't have to be there, that's your problem. That's
                all it could be.

HEATH: We have tried to reach several of them and they, we
                couldn't get ahold of them.[21]

So what to do? Judge Tanner proposed a deal, a deal that the state knew it did not want to accept but a deal that the state also knew it had to accept. Judge Tanner had the state list the witnesses it still wanted to call and describe the nature of the testimony for each. Judge Tanner would then rule on whether he would permit the witnesses to testify. So the state began naming its remaining witnesses and describing their testimony—and Judge Tanner began to rule, repeatedly and uniformly, that he would not permit their testimony. Seven witnesses were listed, and seven witnesses were rejected. And that was the end of the state's case in Helen Castrilli's lawsuit against the state of Washington.

It did not take long for the state to present the evidence that Judge Tanner *was* willing to hear. The state's case was over in less than two days. In all, the trial had taken seven days (August 30 and 31 and September 1, 2, 8, 9, and 14), a remarkably short time considering the importance and complexity of the case. Eleven witnesses had testified for Helen Castrilli, and five had testified for the state (Judge Tanner had refused to hear ten other witnesses that the state had tried to call). In addition to the testimony, Helen Castrilli had entered 231 documents into evidence and the state had entered 31.

The closing arguments of the two sides were all that remained before the case was Judge Tanner's to decide. But before setting the date for closing arguments, the judge held a short discussion with Clark Davis, one of the state's attorneys, and Winn Newman, Helen Castrilli's principal attorney. The discussion demonstrated that even at this point Judge Tanner still did not understand the complexity of the lawsuit.

TANNER: Let me ask you this: assuming I rule for the plaintiff, when will you be able to argue for remedy or damages and how long will it take you? I know we're talking about statistics.

DAVIS: It will take a long time, Your Honor. . . .

TANNER: Mr. Newman.

NEWMAN: Well, I don't know on that score. . . . I really haven't thought in those terms. . . .

TANNER: Is there any surprises here? Don't you already know, both of you?

DAVIS: No.

TANNER: Somebody's got the figures.

NEWMAN: My only . . .

TANNER: It's inconceivable that somebody didn't have an idea what the figures were before you filed the lawsuit, both the state and the plaintiff.[22]

The effect was not what Judge Tanner had intended. He intended to emphasize that someone must know what the damages in the case would be if the state lost, but instead the effect was to emphasize his own limited understanding of the scope and complexity of the lawsuit. Nobody even knew how many plaintiffs there were, much less the amount of money that might be involved. Nevertheless, it was this judge who would decide Helen Castrilli's case.

Two days later, on September 16, 1983, the parties presented their closing arguments to Judge Tanner. After the arguments, there was a short pause as Judge Tanner rustled through some papers. Helen Castrilli was there that day, as enthusiastic as ever.

[When there was that pause, I] just kind of felt, he's going to go for it! He's going to go for it! He's going to go! But I think I had kind of thought, OK, he'll hand down a written decision and we'll find out about it. He'll say I'm going to take all this . . . under consideration, or whatever, and you'll get my decision in a period of time and ta da ta da. So when he announced it right away! Of course, you're in a United States federal district court. You can't just jump up and give a war whoop, even though you want to. But there was a little gasp. And he knew he couldn't expect silence. But we controlled it until we got outside. Then we walked outside into a battery of TV cameras. All the press people were there. It was quite a feeling. Oh, it was.

Immediately after the closing arguments, Judge Tanner decided that Helen Castrilli had won her case. He ruled that the state of Washington discriminated against her and other people working in female-dominated occupations. And for Helen Castrilli, who had gone for it herself, it was quite a feeling; oh, it was.

6

How Much Should
a Cook Be Paid?

JULIE HAYWARD SPEAKS with the Liverpudlian accent ("scouse") that Americans know vaguely because of the Beatles. It is a hard, fast, and nasal dialect. Rhetorical questions like "wasn't it?" or "wouldn't you?" are often added at the end of sentences and emphasized with a sort of Scottish lilt in voice tone. Men are usually "blokes," and "world" becomes "wear." The strange language flows by much too quickly for Americans like me (and for many English people as well). When I spoke with Julie Hayward in the spring of 1986, she was talking—with dispatch—about principle and money. "I won the principle. I would rather have the money, too, but regardless of what happens with the money, I won the principle, didn't I, and nothing can take that away from me."

When Hayward won her case on October 29, 1984, she had won on the principle she was talking about. The industrial tribunal had ruled that her job as a cook was equal in value to the painter's, joiner's, and lagger's jobs done by men. She had prevailed on the principle that the work women do (or at least the work some women do) is equal in value to the work that (some) men do. But she did not win any money on that day. The tribunal had not heard any evidence on what Hayward and the men were paid (it had heard evidence only on whether the jobs were comparable), so it was impossible on that day for the tribunal to determine what Hayward's wages should be to ensure, as the law required, that she be paid the same as the men who were doing work of equal value. As a result, instead of awarding money, the industrial tribunal had directed Hayward and Cammell Laird to get together to decide what Hayward should be paid.

But Hayward and Cammell Laird could not reach agreement. They

70

TABLE 6.1. Comparison of Hayward and Comparator Wages

			Difference/Wk	
Factor	Cook	Comparators	Cook	Comparators
Basic pay	£103.89/wk	£126.50/wk		£22.61
Overtime	25.64/wk	27.54/wk		1.90
Sickness benefit	2,678.00/yr	910.00/yr	£16.95 (half)	
Meals	5.00/wk	—	5.00	
Meal breaks	13.12/wk	—	13.12	
Extra holidays (2)	.71/wk	—	.71	
Total difference			£35.78	£24.51
Cook's advantage			£11.27	

Source: Cammell Laird submission in *Hayward v. Cammell Laird.*

could not agree on how Hayward's salary should be adjusted to make it equal with the salaries of Brady, Cox, and Gilbert. As a result, eight months after Hayward won on her principle, the parties were before the industrial tribunal again to see whether she would also win some money.

The difficulty in deciding Hayward's new salary was caused, ironically, by her success two years before. In 1982, before the Equal Pay Regulations were enacted, Hayward had claimed that Cammell Laird was violating the fairly limited Equal Pay Act in force at that time by paying her less than it paid her supervisor. Although her claim was very weak legally, Cammell Laird agreed to settle it in 1983 by placing Hayward on staff status. That meant that although Hayward's base pay did not change, she did receive some increased fringe benefits. Her sick pay was improved; her lunch break became paid time, and the company provided the lunch; and she received two extra vacation days each year.[1] These increases permitted Cammell Laird to argue that although Hayward's *base* pay was less than that of painters, joiners, and laggers, her *overall* compensation was greater than that of the men. Hayward, the company argued, was already receiving equal pay (indeed, more than equal pay), and so her pay did not need to be raised as a result of the tribunal's decision. To illustrate its point, the company provided a table of comparisons (table 6.1).

On June 20, 1985, the industrial tribunal met once again in its offices above the Watson Prickard store to hear Hayward's claim. David Pannick, Hayward's barrister, was there again to argue on her behalf, and

Charles James was there again to argue for Cammell Laird. Everyone agreed that Hayward was entitled to equal pay, but what did that mean?

David Pannick spoke to the tribunal first. He argued that the tribunal should not consider overall compensation in determining whether Hayward was being paid equally. Instead, Pannick argued, once Hayward's work was determined to be of equal value to that of the men, she was entitled to point to any specific term in her contract which was less favorable to her than the corresponding term in the contracts of the men and to have that term amended to make it equal. For Julie Hayward, Pannick's argument meant that she should be able to point to the basic pay term in her contract and in the contracts of the men. The term in her contract was less favorable (she made £103 per week; the men made £126), so Hayward was entitled to an amendment that would make the terms equal. Hayward was entitled to £126 per week. The levels of overall compensation for Hayward and the men, Pannick argued, were irrelevant.

At first glance, Pannick's argument does not seem persuasive. The goal is to provide equal pay for work of equal value, but Pannick's approach would result in Hayward's being paid *more* than the men for work of equal value. Hayward would point to every term in her contract that was less favorable than the equivalent terms in the contracts of the men, and those terms would be made equal, but she would not point to terms in her contract that were more favorable than those of the men, so those would remain better than the terms the men received. Overall, then, Hayward would receive more pay. Cammell Laird's approach, of course, did not have this defect. Cammell Laird would compare the overall compensation levels of Hayward and the men and, in effect, balance the terms that were less favorable to Hayward against those that were more favorable to her.

David Pannick, however, could be very persuasive. The first thing he said was, let's look at the Equal Pay Regulations, let's look at what Parliament said about how to determine whether pay is equal or not. The regulations said that once a woman's job was found to be of equal value to a man's job, then

> (i) if . . . any term of the woman's contract is or becomes less favourable to the woman than a term of a similar kind in the contract under which that man is employed, that term of the woman's contract shall be treated as so modified as not to be less favourable, and
> (ii) if . . . at any time the woman's contract does not include a term corresponding to a term benefiting that man included in the contract under

which he is employed, the woman's contract shall be treated as including such a term.[2]

The Equal Pay Regulations, Pannick argued, could not be clearer. They said that equality should be determined in exactly the manner he had suggested. The regulations said that if *any term* of the woman's contract is or becomes less favorable than a similar term in the man's contract, *that term* shall be modified. It certainly would have been very easy for Parliament to have drafted the regulations differently, to have provided that equality be determined by looking at overall compensation, as Cammell Laird suggested, but Parliament simply had not done that.

Pannick also argued that his view (and that of the plain language of the Equal Pay Regulations) was supported by common sense. It would be relatively easy for industrial tribunals to provide equal pay if that meant merely that they had to equalize specific items pointed out to them by women like Julie Hayward. But if Cammell Laird's position were accepted, tribunals would have to engage in the very difficult task of assessing the worth of each term in the contracts of the men and women involved, and then weigh and balance the overall benefits against each other.

To illustrate his point, Pannick examined the comparison of overall compensation proposed by Cammell Laird in Hayward's case. There were several problems. First, the company provided Hayward, but not the men, meals valued at £5 per week. (Hayward received this benefit because she alone was on staff status.) In its comparison, Cammell Laird included this £5 on Hayward's side of the equation twice. It listed it as a separate factor under "meals" *and* it included the benefit in its calculations under the "meals breaks" factor. A second problem with the comparison proposed by Cammell Laird was that the other calculation under the "meals breaks" factor was not accurate either. Hayward, but not the men (once again, because she was on staff status), received a half-hour paid meal break each day. To calculate its value, the company multiplied two and one-half hours per week by £3.25 to reach a weekly benefit of £8.12 (the £5 value of the meals was then added to the £8.12) and the total, £13.12, was put in the "meals breaks" column). But £3.25 was the hourly rate of the men. Hayward's hourly rate was only £2.66, so the benefit of her two and one-half hours of lunchtime each week should have been £6.65 rather than £8.12.

What Pannick did not point out to the tribunal was that the problem with the "meal breaks" factor was not limited to this calculation error.

Cammell Laird placed the extra £8.12 per week on Hayward's side of the equation *as if* she actually received an extra payment each week for the free time she enjoyed at mealtimes. But that was not the case. The £8.12 she received each week (which should have been £6.65) was actually a part of her basic weekly pay of £103.89. So, in effect, the company counted the £8.12 for meal breaks twice, once under "basic pay" and once under "meal breaks." Counting the benefit twice does not seem fair; Hayward did not receive double payments for her paid meal breaks. But counting the benefit only once does not seem fair either; Hayward did get paid for meal breaks while the men did not, and that was obviously of some benefit to Hayward. This issue, then, could have been used by Pannick to illustrate the difficulty of calculating the value of benefits such as the paid meal breaks. Pannick would not have had to resolve the issue. His point would have been made by making it clear to the tribunal that comparing overall compensation levels would be very difficult, much more difficult than merely equalizing different terms pointed out by women like Julie Hayward.

There were also other problems with Cammell Laird's calculations, and Pannick kindly pointed them out for the tribunal. The remaining problems related to the company's calculations on the "sickness benefit" factor. The company calculated that Hayward's maximum yearly sick pay benefit was £2,678. If she got sick, the company would pay her full salary of £103 per week for a maximum of twenty-six weeks, minus any amounts she might receive from the government in sick pay. For the men, the company calculated a maximum yearly sick pay benefit of £910. If one of them got sick, the company would pay £35 per week for a maximum of twenty-six weeks; no deduction was made for amounts received from the government. The company then took the yearly difference in the maximum sick pay benefit (£1,768), divided it by 52.17 to determine the weekly difference (£33.89), and then decided to include half that amount (£16.95) as Hayward's weekly advantage on the "sickness benefit" factor.

There were two principal problems with the company's figures. First, the maximum benefits to Hayward would actually be considerably less than the £2,678 the company used as her maximum benefits figure. Since that payment would be reduced by any amount Hayward received from the government in sick pay, and since it would probably provide her with about £40 per week, the company's figures for Hayward were more than £1,000 too high. Second, Cammell Laird did not rationally discount the figures for the probability that Hayward and the men would actually get sick. Sick pay was available only if one was sick, so the benefit was only as valuable as it was probable that one would get sick. The company did recognize this to a limited extent; it included only half the difference in maximum sick pay benefits in Hayward's column. But even that assumed that Hayward and the men would recoup half their maximum sick pay benefits each year, that they would be sick and not work for thirteen weeks. That, of course, is not a realistic assumption. It certainly would have been possible to discount the sick pay benefits more rationally, but the company did not do that, and Pannick's job was not to suggest alternatives but, again, to point out how difficult it would be for the tribunal to make such a comparison.

In sum, then, Pannick said that the industrial tribunal should determine equal pay simply by equalizing the terms pointed out to it by women like Julie Hayward rather than by attempting to compare the overall compensation earned by Hayward and the men. He supported that claim by pointing to the language of the Equal Pay Regulations and by arguing that the alternative approach would be very difficult practically.

Charles James, the barrister for Cammell Laird, pointed to a different law and made a different practical argument to support the company's position. The Equal Pay Regulations, he argued, were based on the Treaty of Rome, which England had signed to enter the European Economic Community. Indeed, the Equal Pay Regulations were enacted in response to a decision of the European Court of Justice and were drafted specifically to bring England into compliance with the Treaty of Rome.[3] Moreover, the Treaty of Rome is superior to any national law, including the Equal Pay Regulations. Hence, if there is any conflict or inconsistency between the Treaty of Rome and the Equal Pay Regulations, the Treaty of Rome must prevail. So, James looked at what the Treaty of Rome says on the issue of how to determine equal pay:

> Each Member State shall . . . ensure and subsequently maintain the . . . principle that men and women should receive equal pay for equal work.
>
> For the purpose of this Article, "pay" means the ordinary basic or minimum wage or salary *and any other consideration, whether in cash or kind, which the worker receives, directly or indirectly,* in respect of his employment from his employer.[4]

James's argument was that the Treaty of Rome required Hayward's total compensation to be considered in determining whether she was earning the same pay as the men. Anything in the Equal Pay Regulations to the contrary was overridden by the treaty.

Pannick, of course, did not agree. The provision of the Treaty of Rome quoted by James, Pannick said, was intended to ensure that the equal pay laws enacted by member states were sufficiently broad to deal with the problem of unequal pay for women. The drafters of the treaty were concerned that employers would claim that they were complying with the treaty's equal pay requirement when they paid men and women the same salary, even though they paid men more in fringe benefits. The provision, Pannick argued, was merely intended to make clear that that employer claim would fail. The provision was never intended to limit the rights of women, like Julie Hayward, who had proved a violation of an equal pay law. It was particularly ironic, Pannick said, that James would attempt to use a provision of the treaty that was intended to ensure that equal pay laws were broadly interpreted as a means to limit the scope of the British Equal Pay Regulations.

But James added a practical argument. Pannick's approach to determining equal pay was not practical because it would lead to leapfrogging. If disadvantageous terms in Hayward's contract were improved and advantageous terms were not disturbed, Hayward's overall contract would not be equal to the contracts of the men. It would be better. The men, or other people in similar jobs, could then bring their own actions to equalize the disadvantageous terms in their contracts. This type of leapfrogging, James argued, simply could not have been intended by Parliament when it enacted the Equal Pay Regulations.

In response, Pannick admitted that his approach would permit leapfrogging, but he claimed that this was exactly what Parliament had intended when it enacted the regulations. It was not leapfrogging that would go on forever, and it was leapfrogging for a purpose. Take Hayward's case. Hayward would be able to leapfrog over the men. After her case was over, she would have a better contract than the men. At that point the men, whose jobs after all were equal to hers, would be able to make their own claim under the Equal Pay Regulations and have the disadvantageous terms in their contracts improved. But at that point, the contracts of Hayward and the men would be the same, and the leapfrogging would be over. (Indeed, it was probably over when Hayward leapfrogged over the men. When the men had their contracts improved, they didn't leapfrog over Hayward; they merely jumped alongside her.) Moreover, the leapfrogging would fulfill the purpose of the Equal Pay Regulations; it would result in equal pay for cooks, painters, joiners, and laggers. It would result in the fulfillment of the ultimate goal of the Equal Pay Regulations: equal pay for work of equal value.

The industrial tribunal listened to Pannick and James on that June day in 1985 and decided that it could not decide right away. It did not issue its opinion until September 12—and even then the tribunal could not agree. The decision was agreed to by only two of the three members of the tribunal, ironically, by the two male members of the tribunal. The female member disagreed with the decision. (It is rather unusual for the decision of an industrial tribunal not to be unanimous.)[5]

The tribunal did not award Julie Hayward the increase in basic and overtime pay that Pannick had requested. Rather, the tribunal began by saying that it approached the decision with "no small degree of trepidation." It recognized that whatever decision it reached could lead to "unforeseen complications." But a decision had to be reached, and the decision supported James's interpretation of equal pay. The tribunal relied on James's arguments—on the Treaty of Rome and on the leap-frogging problem—but the heart of its decision struck off in a new direction:

> We have no wish, and indeed we fully appreciate that it is not our function, to turn ourselves . . . into a rate-fixing body. That, clearly, was the danger which Mr. Pannick feared in his submission; that if we adopted the approach advocated by Mr. James, we should become involved in a complicated balancing act beyond our capabilities and, indeed, outside our jurisdiction. That such a danger does exist we fully realise but feel, nevertheless, that that should still not deter us from seeking to avoid too narrow a construction of the relevant provisions. It seems to us quite clear that in modern economic conditions, many of the benefits of employment are, in fact, received in forms other than cash. It may well be that, in the past, the narrower view of the term "pay," as money and nothing else, was both acceptable and, in relation to earlier times, realistic. However . . . practices and attitudes change with time. These things are not immutable, and new norms will emerge over a period of time, as to what is acceptable. So we believe it to be with pay, and that it would not now be sensible to cling to a narrow and outmoded view of that term.[6]

The tribunal, then, saw itself as accepting the modern view of compensation in accepting James's arguments and rejecting the old-fashioned view of compensation in rejecting Pannick's arguments. But in thinking that, the tribunal was muddled. In fact, Pannick and James shared the modern view of compensation. The tribunal was confused about Pannick's view on compensation because, *in Hayward's case,* Pannick was arguing that her basic pay should be increased regardless of her fringe benefits. But that did not mean that Pannick thought compensation meant only basic pay. If Hayward's situation had been reversed and Hayward had received more than the men in basic pay and less in fringe benefits, Pannick would have argued that she was entitled to an increase in her fringe benefits regardless of her basic pay. Pannick's position, then, did not at all imply a narrow view of compensation (his view of what was included in compensation was undoubtedly at least as broad as James's); instead, Pannick's position merely forwarded a procedure for deciding which parts of a broad compensation package should be increased after an industrial tribunal decides that a woman's work is equal in value to a man's work.

Nevertheless, whatever the strength or weakness of the tribunal's rationale, its decision was that equal pay under the Equal Pay Regulations required an evaluation of the total compensation received by Hayward and the men. What was the remedy, then, to which Hayward was entitled? The tribunal did not say. It ended its opinion as follows:

> Whilst not, at this stage, expressing any final or definitive view, we entertain considerable doubts [about how the company calculated sick pay], and feel that our ultimate conclusions on the point might well prove to be at variance with the [company's]. The matter requires further examination. . . . Our concluded view is, therefore . . . that we decline to make the unqualified declaration sought by Mr. Pannick, as to the terms in the applicant's contract relating to basic and overtime pay. In relation to the concept of equal pay for work of equal value we find that an employer is entitled, when dealing with the implementation of an award, to consider pay as meaning not only basic pay, and overtime pay, but also, to use the words of [the Treaty of Rome] "any other consideration whether in cash or in kind, which the worker receives directly or indirectly in respect of his employment from his employer." That, in our view, would require sick pay to be taken into account in some way, but it does not follow . . . that we would afford unqualified acceptance to the mathematical approach adopted by [Cammell Laird]. [7]

The tribunal itself did not propose to conduct that further examination. Instead, with its decision, the tribunal had volleyed the ball back into the Hayward and Cammell Laird court. They were to try again to negotiate a settlement, this time in light of the new guidance given them by the industrial tribunal.

Instead of doing that, however, Hayward decided to hit the ball into another "court." She appealed the industrial tribunal's decision to the employment appeal tribunal. So, seven months later, on March 5, 1986,

Julie Hayward's case was heard again, this time in a more elegant courtroom (one did not have to pass through a men's clothing section to get to it) in London.

From the cast of characters before the employment appeal tribunal, one would hardly have guessed that Hayward's case was the first at that level to present important "women's" issues under the Equal Pay Regulations. The courtroom was filled with men. The three judges were all men, the two barristers (Pannick and James again) were men, the two solicitors advising the barristers were men, the court's clerks were men— even the statues holding up the mantle on the fireplace were men. Julie Hayward could not be there. She was at the shipyard, no doubt serving meals to more highly paid men.

The arguments before the employment appeal tribunal were well rehearsed; the barristers merely repeated the arguments they had made before the industrial tribunal some months before. In a couple of hours the hearing was over. It took two more months, however, for this tribunal to issue a decision. On May 19, 1986, the employment appeal tribunal decided unanimously that the industrial tribunal had been right. To determine equal pay under the Equal Pay Regulations, Hayward's total compensation package should be weighed against the total compensation package of the men.

The decision of the employment appeal tribunal, even though it reached exactly the same conclusion as that of the industrial tribunal, was in a sense more damaging to Hayward's case. The industrial tribunal's decision had not been unanimous (there was a dissenting opinion); it had recognized the difficulty of weighing the total compensation packages against each other; and it had seemed to rely only minimally on the leapfrogging problem. The employment appeal tribunal issued a unanimous decision and was much more confident of its correctness. Without discussion, the tribunal rejected any notion that weighing the total compensation packages would present problems: "We reject the submission that this will pose any difficulty in practice for an industrial tribunal which is quite capable of carrying out the inquiry." While minimizing that problem, the appeal tribunal emphasized the leapfrogging problem, also without discussion: "A decision to the contrary, which would necessarily involve leapfrogging, would in the view of the industrial members of this Court result in widespread chaos in industry and inflict grave damage on commerce."[8]

Julie Hayward, two and a half years and two tribunals into her battle, had won only on her principle. She had claimed that cooks at Cammell

Laird were doing work equal in value to that of painters, joiners, and laggers, and on that point of principle she had won. Julie Hayward also claimed the right to be paid the same base wage as painters, joiners, and laggers, but on that point she had lost. Julie Hayward had won her case but had not received any pay increase as a result. Through her efforts so far, she had won a present that was beautifully wrapped in the intricately patterned paper and subtly tied ribbon of British law, but when she opened the present, there was nothing inside. Although Hayward said at the time that she was still happy with her present, one wonders if she would not have gladly changed places with Helen Castrilli, who, at about the same time, was looking into a brown paper bag and finding quite a prize.

7

A Secretary's Pay

IN SEPTEMBER 1983, Helen Castrilli also had a beautifully wrapped package. Judge Tanner had ruled that she had won her case, that the state of Washington had discriminated against her and other people working in female-dominated occupations for the state. A couple of months after Judge Tanner's dramatic oral ruling, he issued a written opinion—*American Federation of State, County, and Municipal Employees v. Washington*—which better explained the legal basis of his decision.[1]

Judge Tanner's decision was based on Title VII of the Civil Rights Act of 1964. As I indicated earlier,[2] Title VII makes it illegal for employers to discriminate because of a person's sex, but the language is quite broad and vague: "It shall be [illegal] to discriminate against any individual . . . because of such individual's . . . sex."[3] The courts, however, have defined two basic ways within that broad language in which a person like Helen Castrilli can prove that discrimination has taken place.

The first way is very straightforward. It merely defines what most people think of when they think of discrimination. Discrimination can be proved by showing that the employer *intended* to treat women less favorably than men. This is called disparate treatment discrimination.[4] If an employer looks at a female employee and says, "I am going to pay you less *because you are a woman*," the employer has clearly engaged in disparate treatment discrimination. In Castrilli's case, then, the goal was to show that the state of Washington had intended to treat female-dominated occupations less favorably than male-dominated occupations. The general problem in this kind of case, and it was certainly evident in Castrilli's, is that it is very difficult to determine the employer's true intention. The state said that even if women were treated less favorably

than men (and it contested that), the state of Washington certainly did
not *intend* to treat women less favorably. The less favorable treatment
arose because the state relied on the market to set wages, because of
history, and because of a host of other reasons, but not because state
officials at any time said, "Let's pay these occupations less because they're
female dominated." To win her case, Helen Castrilli had to prove not
only that the state treated women differently and less favorably but also
that the state did so with an intention to discriminate against women.

The courts have also defined another way in which people like Helen
Castrilli can prove discrimination. This way is less intuitive; unlike
disparate treatment discrimination, most people who are not lawyers
would probably not recognize it as discrimination. To prove it, the one
claiming discrimination has to identify a factor that the employer uses
to make employment decisions. Consider, for example, an employer that
says it is only going to hire people who are over six feet tall. The courts
have said that sex discrimination can be proved by showing that a factor
used by an employer works to the disadvantage of a significantly higher
proportion of women than of men. So if a plaintiff can show that the
height requirement eliminates 95 percent of all women but only 50
percent of all men, discrimination has been proved. In legal language,
the plaintiff has to show that the factor has a "disparate impact" on
women, so this type of discrimination is called disparate impact discrimination.[5] But a disparate impact case is not over once a plaintiff has
shown that a factor, like height, has a disparate impact on women. The
factor can still be legally used if the employer can show that it is required
to do the job. So if the employer could prove that the job required the
worker to reach objects on high shelves that only people six feet tall
could reach, the disparate impact case would fail.

In Helen Castrilli's case, Judge Tanner found that the state of Washington had engaged in both disparate treatment and disparate impact
discrimination. He pointed to several pieces of evidence to support his
finding that the state had engaged in disparate treatment discrimination—that is, had intentionally discriminated against women—when it
set salaries. First, he said, there was the long-standing disparity between
the salaries of male- and female-dominated jobs. Second, the state had
known about this disparity for a long period of time (at least since 1974,
when the first comparable worth study was done) and had done nothing
about it. Third, statistical evidence (such as the inverse correlation
between the percentage of women in an occupation and the pay for that
occupation) made it highly unlikely that the state's pay structure was

the result of chance. Fourth, there was the state's admitted failure to pay occupations on the basis of their evaluated worth—a clearly non-sex-based factor—even though the state itself had authorized and helped to formulate the study to determine evaluated worth. Fifth, there were the admissions by state officials, such as former governor Daniel Evans, that the state was discriminating against women. Finally, Judge Tanner pointed to legal history to support his finding of intentional discrimination:

> In 1888 one Nevada M. Bloomer filed a lawsuit in the District Court at Spokane Falls, Washington. She was suing certain [election officials for] refusing to receive her ballot.
>
> [When the case reached the Supreme Court of the Territory of Washington, the] only issue in the case was whether females were qualified electors under the laws of Washington Territory. One of the admitted facts was "the Plaintiff is a woman." Mr. Chief Justice Jones delivered the opinion of the Court [and in doing so] stated: "In 1852, when [the election] act was passed, the word 'citizen' was used as a qualification for voting and holding office, and, in our judgement, the word then meant and still signifies male citizenship, and must be so construed."
>
> In view of the foregoing it is apparent that discrimination against women was lawful in Washington Territory. In fact, discrimination was lawful in the State of Washington until 1971 when the State's Civil Rights Law was amended to prohibit sex discrimination. Perhaps [the State] adopted the practices and concepts of sex discrimination against women in employment as just another manifestation of centuries old discriminatory attitudes and practices of a male dominated society.[6]

For all these reasons, then, Judge Tanner concluded that the state of Washington intentionally discriminated against women when it set salaries. Indeed, he went further than he had to, and further than the evidence or reason permitted, by concluding that there was "no credible evidence in the record that would support a finding that the State's practices and procedures were based on any factor other than sex."[7] Helen Castrilli, of course, did not have to prove that sex was the *only* factor used by the state in setting wages (and despite Judge Tanner's statement, she did not and could not prove that). All she had to prove was that the state intentionally used sex as *a* factor when it set wages, and she had done that, at least to the satisfaction of Judge Tanner.

Judge Tanner also found that the state had engaged in disparate impact discrimination. He said that the state's "system of compensation" was a factor, indeed *the* factor, that the state used to set wages. He said that the evidence demonstrated that the system of compensation had a disparate impact on female-dominated job classifications; that is, those job classifications fared less well under the state's system of compensation than other jobs. And he said the state had not proved that the system was required for any reason related to doing the work the state needed done. Thus, Judge Tanner held that the state had engaged in illegal disparate impact discrimination.

Judge Tanner's decision was not the end of Helen Castrilli's case, however, not even before Judge Tanner. He had merely ruled that the state had discriminated. He had not yet decided, or indeed heard any evidence, on how the discrimination should be remedied. So on November 14, 1983, the attorneys were before Judge Tanner again, this time to discuss how much Helen Castrilli and her fellow plaintiffs should be paid. This first hearing on remedies was to determine how much they should be paid in the future; another hearing would be held later to determine how much they should collect in back pay because the state had illegally paid them too little in the past.

In the first hearing, which took three days, Stephan Michelson, the same econometrician who had testified earlier, was called as Helen Castrilli's principal witness. Michelson testified that Judge Tanner should use one of two methods for determining how much Castrilli and the others should be paid in the future. Michelson called the first method the fixed percentage remedy. Under this option the court would first identify a male comparable worth line, a line that would graphically depict how evaluated male-dominated jobs were paid in relation to their Willis job evaluation points. Then the court would identify a female comparable worth line depicting how evaluated female-dominated jobs were paid in relation to their Willis job evaluation points. Then the court would determine the average percentage difference between the two lines and raise all the female-dominated jobs by that percentage. Michelson, being a considerate person, and an econometrician, had already identified the two lines and the average percentage difference (see fig. 7.1). He had determined that the male comparable worth line, on average, was 132 percent of the female comparable worth line, so he suggested that the court raise the wages of all persons in female-dominated positions by 32 percent or eleven ranges. (Since a "range" in the state of Washington was 2.5 percent and increasing ranges worked like compound interest, an increase of eleven ranges would raise the female comparable worth line to the male comparable worth line.)

If this all seems understandable, it was because Michelson was being

FIGURE 7.1 Male and Female Comparable Worth Lines

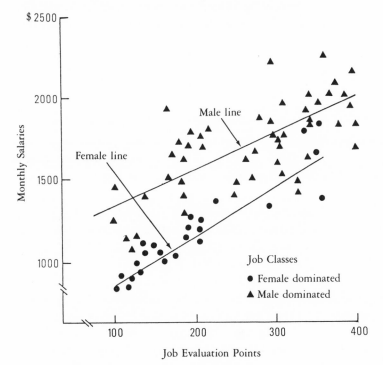

Job Evaluation Points

Source: Washington State Legislature Joint Select Committee on Comparable Worth Implementation, *Final Report*, December 1984, 9.

Note: Data points for male-dominated jobs that received more than 400 Willis job evaluation points are not included, but the "male" regression line is based on those data points as well as those indicated.

kind. He is an econometrician after all, and he had called on the technical resources of his discipline to refine his ideas. He also presented the fixed percentage remedy to the court in statistical form. This is where he discussed the "simple" formula I mentioned at the beginning of the book— $\ln(SAL_i) = b_o + b_1(EP_i) + b_2(M_i)$—but of course he discussed it in detail and with the assistance of other equally "simple" formulas.[8]

Michelson's fixed percentage remedy had advantages. One was that it would create a salary structure for female-dominated jobs that resembled the salary structure for male-dominated jobs. The male-dominated jobs, of course, did not all sit on the male comparable worth line. Instead, they were scattered around it; some were above the line and some below, but the line represented the central tendency of the salaries of the male-dominated jobs. The fixed percentage remedy would move the female-dominated jobs up so that they, too, would scatter around the male comparable worth line with some above the line and others below it.

The remedy also had disadvantages. The remedy would not correct differences in pay between female-dominated jobs. If two female-dominated jobs had the same number of evaluation points but one was being paid significantly more than the other, the fixed percentage remedy would not correct the pay difference between those jobs. Both would receive the same "fixed percentage" increase. Another problem with the remedy was that it would increase the salaries of all female-dominated jobs, even though some of them did not seem to have been adversely affected by the "sex" of the job. Clark Davis, an attorney for the state, argued that the salary for one female-dominated job was already nine ranges above the male line. Michelson's fixed percentage remedy would have raised it another eleven ranges, so that it would end up twenty ranges over the male comparable worth line—an increase that did not seem to bear much relationship to the extent to which the salary for that job had been affected by the sex composition of the job. It should not be surprising that the pay for some female-dominated jobs was not significantly affected by the "sex" of the job. Female-dominated jobs were defined as jobs containing 70 percent or more female incumbents at any time. Since many job classifications contained only one incumbent, if that incumbent was female, the job was female-dominated. But, of course, the effect of discrimination on the pay of such an occupation— particularly if it shifted between male- and female-dominated status as successive individuals became the sole incumbent—was likely to be much less significant than the effect of discrimination on the pay of an occupation such as the secretary classification, which is generally identified as a "women's occupation."[9]

Perhaps because of these problems, Michelson also provided Judge Tanner with a second method of deciding what Castrilli and the others should be paid. Under this option, the "to-the-line" option, all female-dominated jobs below the male comparable worth line would be moved to the male line. Different female-dominated jobs, then, would receive different increases, or no increase at all, depending on their current pay. Those jobs that were currently at levels below the female comparable worth line would generally receive more than the eleven-range increase of the fixed percentage remedy; those that started on the female line would generally receive about an eleven-range increase; those that started above the female line would generally receive less than the eleven-range increase; and those that started on or above the male comparable worth line would receive no increase at all.[10] This option, then, would result in a pay structure in which non-female-dominated jobs would be scattered around the male comparable worth line, while female-dominated jobs, with very few exceptions, would all be on the male line.

The state, for several reasons, was not happy with either of Michelson's options. First, the state argued, either option would result in an irrational salary structure. For example, the state had four accountant job classifications. The less difficult and lower-paid Accountant I and II jobs were female dominated, so either of Michelson's options would require the pay for those jobs to be increased and, indeed, increased to levels higher than those for the Accountant III and IV jobs, which were not female dominated. Michelson's options, then, would result in higher pay for entry-level jobs than for jobs requiring more experience and skill. Not only was this irrational, the state argued, but it would probably make it very difficult to "promote" people to the lower-paying Accountant III and IV positions.

In presenting this argument, however, the state overlooked a major irony. Castrilli had won her case primarily because the state did not pay occupations in accordance with Willis's job evaluation studies, because Helen Castrilli was paid less than campus police officers. The remedies suggested by Michelson would not only not solve that problem but in some instances would aggravate it. Michelson's options did not attempt to align jobs with similar job evaluation rankings; instead, they raised only the pay of female-dominated occupations by an amount measured not by the pay of similar jobs but by the pay of all male-dominated jobs. Male- and female-dominated jobs of equal rank on Willis's job evaluation studies would be paid equally, if at all, only by chance. The state was pointing this out, but only indirectly. A pay structure created by implementing Michelson's options would be irrational on its face. An Accountant I would be paid more than an Accountant III.

The state also argued that Michelson's options would overcompensate women. The overriding goal of the remedy should be to place female-dominated occupations in the position they would have been in if the discrimination had not occurred. But Michelson's options, the state argued, would place people in female-dominated occupations in a *better* position than they would have been in if the discrimination had not occurred. A witness for the state had testified about social science studies indicating that 60 percent of the wage gap between men and women could be explained by factors other than discrimination, 60 percent of the gap is caused because women, on average, work fewer hours than men, because they do not stay in the same job as long, because they do not have as much on-the-job experience, and so on. Michelson's options would close the entire wage gap, including the 60 percent caused by factors other than discrimination. As a result, the state argued, the remedies he proposed would raise the pay for female-dominated occupations to the level of pay for male-dominated occupations even though most of the difference in pay was not caused by discrimination.

The state's overcompensation argument was flawed, however. The argument was that (1) studies indicated that 60 percent of the wage gap between men and women could be explained by factors other than discrimination; (2) Michelson's options would completely eliminate the wage gap; and, therefore, (3) women like Helen Castrilli would be overcompensated. The problem with the argument was that Michelson's options would *not* completely eliminate the wage gap. They would eliminate the wage gap between male- and female-dominated jobs *ranked equally on Willis's job evaluation studies.* (Although, as indicated above, the options would not align *individual* male- and female-dominated jobs ranked equally on the studies, they would eliminate the wage gap *on average.*) But because a higher proportion of men than women worked in jobs that ranked higher on Willis's studies, the average pay for men would still be higher than the average pay for women. At the time of the hearing on remedies, no one knew what the average pay of men and women would be if Michelson's options were implemented (although it was clear that the average pay of men would still be considerably higher than the average pay of women). As a result, it was simply impossible to tell whether women would be overcompensated or undercompensated in comparison with the social science studies.

The state also argued that Michelson's remedies were just too expensive. The state estimated that the cost of the fixed percentage option would be $130 million per year; the "to-the-line" option would cost considerably more. Winn Newman, Castrilli's attorney, disputed the figures, arguing that either option would cost about $99 million per year. Moreover, the state's share of that additional liability would be "only" about $50 million because many people in the affected occupations were paid partly by the state and partly by other sources. Consequently, the state would not have to pay for the entire increase. Given these different estimates, one thing was clear: no one really knew how expensive either of the options would be. There were simply too many unknown variables. No one knew exactly how many occupations had been female dominated or for how long. No one knew how many people worked in those occupations. No one knew the state's share of the pay for those occupations. No one knew the precise pay increase the remedy would provide for each occupation. No one knew nearly enough to measure how much Michelson's proposed remedies would cost.[11]

Nevertheless, it was also clear that any remedy was going to be expensive, very expensive. And the expense was likely to create problems for the state; it might have to raise taxes to pay for the remedy or reduce the scope of desirable state programs. The state did not mention, of course, that the failure to provide a remedy would be equally expensive. The failure to provide a remedy would mean that people like Helen Castrilli who worked in female-dominated occupations and who had been found by Judge Tanner to be victims of sex discrimination would continue to receive lower wages because of their sex. This was truly a zero-sum game. The state's discrimination had caused a major loss. The overriding remedial issue was whether that loss should continue to be borne by the people in female-dominated jobs or whether the state, the discriminator, should begin to shoulder the burden. Viewed in this way, the state's concern about the expense of the remedy was simply irrelevant. The issue was not how much would it cost but who should bear the burden. Between the state and the people working in female-dominated occupations, the answer was clear.

The state's principal point in raising the expense of the remedy as an issue, however, was not so much to question fairness within the state as to question the effect of Judge Tanner's decision on other entities. State attorney Clark Davis argued that Washington was the first state to consider the comparable worth issue. Washington had conducted job evaluation studies to determine whether there were differences in pay between male- and female-dominated occupations; it had discovered that there were; and it had recently begun a (very modest) effort to correct some of the inequities uncovered by the studies. Davis argued that if either of Michelson's remedies were adopted, no other state or government entity would ever research the issue again: "The moral of this story . . . if plaintiff's proposed remedy is adopted . . . will be, if you see an inequity, put your head in the sand, don't look at it, don't consider it and don't ever contemplate addressing it, because you'll be sued for $130 million."[12]

For perhaps the first time in the case, Judge Tanner expressed some sympathy for the state, but it was a sympathy that was not going to help the state much: "There is no question that credit is due. The state of Washington is the first one to consider inequity of pay between males and females. . . . But the problem is they have risen up to smite you."[13] So, according to Judge Tanner, the state had acted honorably in investigating the pay levels for female-dominated jobs, but in doing so, it had proved a case of sex discrimination against itself. Davis's argument, then, was irrelevant. The state could not go back and "undiscover" the discrimination. The issue now was how to remedy the situation.

On November 30 and December 1, 1983, more hearings were held, this time to deal with the back-pay issue. How much should Helen Castrilli and her fellow plaintiffs be paid to compensate them for having been paid less in the past because of their sex? Castrilli's side did not call any additional witnesses at this hearing, relying instead on the evidence that had already been admitted at the prior hearing. The state attempted to call eight witnesses, most of them to testify about the devastating effects any award of back pay would have on the financial status of the state. In a replay of the main trial, Judge Tanner refused to allow five of the eight to testify. The other three did testify, however, one of them at quite some length.

The state's principal argument was that no back pay should be awarded. To win on this argument, the state had to overcome a very strong presumption that when an employer is found to have discriminated, it must pay back pay. The state had two United States Supreme Court cases on its side, however. In *City of Los Angeles v. Manhart* and *Arizona Governing Committee v. Norris,* the Supreme Court held that employers who had operated discriminatory pension plans did not have to pay for the past effects of the discrimination.[14] The Court said that the presumption in favor of back pay did not apply in these cases, in part because the employers had acted in good faith. The employers did not operate their pension plans knowing that they illegally discriminated against women.

At the end of the hearing on December 1, after the closing arguments by the two sides, Judge Tanner issued his decision on remedies. He rejected the state's argument on back pay. He said that in this case, in contrast to the two Supreme Court cases, the state of Washington had not acted in good faith. Rather, he said, the state knew it was discriminating against women, and it knew the discrimination was illegal. As a result, he ruled that the two Supreme Court cases did not apply and that Helen Castrilli and the others were entitled to back pay. Judge Tanner did not decide, however, how much the state should pay in back pay. Instead, he appointed a special master (basically an assistant) to hear additional evidence and then make recommendations as to the amount. (A month later, the director of the state's Office for Fiscal Management estimated that the state's liability for back pay would be $232.2 million plus $50 million for back pension contributions.)[15]

Judge Tanner also ruled that Helen Castrilli and the others should be given pay increases in the future, but he was not willing to say which of Michelson's two options should be used.

NEWMAN: May I inquire, Your Honor, as to whether you are prepared to state how you are resolving the [issue of pay increases in the future]?

TANNER: I think any [pay increase in the future] is to remedy the wrong that the Court has found, that's sex discrimination. I think that [the pay increases] should begin forthwith.

NEWMAN: I am really inquiring if you are prepared to state at this time [which of Michelson's options] you have sought.

TANNER: I said you win.

NEWMAN: I understand.

TANNER: All right. I want to put it in writing so that hopefully it will be an appealable order. I don't know. Sooner or later it's got to come to an end. As of right now, the Court's in recess.[16]

So Judge Tanner, for a while at least, was done with the case. He had decided that the state had engaged in both disparate treatment and disparate impact discrimination, and he had decided that Helen Castrilli and the others were entitled to both back pay and a pay increase in the future. He did not, however, decide how much the back pay or the pay increase in the future should be. It is likely that Judge Tanner pulled back from fully deciding the case for two interrelated reasons. First, when the testimony at the remedies stage of the trial was presented, Judge Tanner realized for the first time the extreme complexity of the case. Formulating an effective and fair remedy would take a good deal of time and energy. Second, everyone involved, including the judge, realized that the case was not likely to end in Judge Tanner's courtroom. It would certainly be appealed to the Ninth Circuit Court of Appeals in Seattle and perhaps to the United States Supreme Court. It simply did not make much sense to spend a great deal of time formulating a remedy when there was a great deal of uncertainty about whether Judge

Tanner's finding of discrimination would survive on appeal. As a result, Judge Tanner decided what needed to be decided to permit an appeal, while reserving judgment on many difficult issues that would have to be resolved if his finding of discrimination survived.

The hearings before Judge Tanner ended on December 1, 1983; on December 14 he issued his written opinion; and on January 9, 1984, the state appealed the case. So Helen Castrilli's case was headed for the Ninth Circuit Court of Appeals. But as one might expect with a case that grew in complexity with each twist, it was not headed *only* for the court of appeals. Instead, it took a detour through the Washington State legislature.

The legislature, of course, had been following the case very closely since it began. One would have expected it to, since the case represented a potential claim of hundreds of millions of dollars on the state treasury. Shortly before the trial of Castrilli's case began in 1983, about a year after the lawsuit was initially filed, the legislature passed a bill that, although it did not deal with the case directly, addressed the central issue it raised. The bill required increases in the salaries of state employees at least annually "for the purpose of achieving comparable worth"; it defined comparable worth as paying similar salaries for jobs that "require or impose similar responsibilities, judgments, knowledge, skills, and working conditions"; and it called for comparable worth to be "fully achieved" for all employees by 1993.[17] From Helen Castrilli's perspective there was only one problem with the bill. But it was a major problem. Although the legislature had established comparable worth as a state policy, it did not appropriate very much money to pursue that policy. In 1983 the legislature appropriated $1.5 million, or less than 0.1 percent of the annual state payroll, to begin implementation. At that rate, comparable worth would have been fully achieved closer to 2093 than 1993.

In 1985, while the case was still before the Ninth Circuit Court of Appeals, the legislature considered the case more directly and extended an olive branch to Helen Castrilli and her friends. And sitting on the olive branch was $41 million!

More specifically, in June 1985, the legislature authorized a special appropriation of $41.43 million for the settlement of all claims in Castrilli's case. (Actually, the amount available for settlement was slightly higher because the legislature appropriated another $3.9 million in the same bill for making comparable worth salary adjustments, regardless of whether the case was settled or not.) The legislature also said, however, that if a tentative settlement agreement had not been reached by December 31, 1985, or if the case had not been dismissed by June 30, 1986, the appropriation would lapse and the money would no longer be available. The legislature directed the governor and the attorney general to negotiate with Castrilli and the others. Any tentative settlement agreement would, of course, have to be ratified by the legislature.[18]

So a basis for beginning negotiations was set. The state and the union (on behalf of Castrilli and the other plaintiffs) formed negotiation committees, and negotiations were just ready to begin in earnest when the Ninth Circuit Court of Appeals issued its decision.

The case had been argued in the federal courthouse in Seattle on April 4, 1985. Winn Newman had spoken on behalf of Helen Castrilli and the other plaintiffs, and Christine Gregoire had argued on behalf of the state. Briefs had been filed by the parties, of course, but because this was a highly publicized and important case, briefs had also been filed by a dozen other groups such as the Eagle Forum, the Association of Washington Business, the National Organization for Women, and the NAACP. The stakes were high, perhaps not as high as some of the briefs indicated (the Eagle Forum claimed that "free enterprise, as society knows and values it today, would cease to exist" if the decision went the wrong way and that such a decision could require increased wage payments to women of $320 billion and result in a 9.7 percent increase in inflation),[19] but high nonetheless.

The case was heard, as are most cases in the federal appellate courts, by a three-judge panel. One of the three, and the one who ultimately wrote the opinion, was soon to become a household name: Judge Anthony M. Kennedy. In 1987 Kennedy was Ronald Reagan's third nominee to fill the vacancy created on the United States Supreme Court by the elevation of Justice William Rehnquist to chief justice. He was confirmed by the Senate and now sits on the highest court in the land.

Judge Kennedy was not likely to be overly sympathetic with Helen Castrilli's case. Although there was not a great deal of opposition to his nomination to the Supreme Court (the Senate voted unanimously to confirm him), the opposition that existed focused on his attitude to issues of sex.[20] When Judge Kennedy heard Castrilli's case, and for two decades before that, he was a member of the Olympic Club in San Francisco, a club that had never had any women members and that later was sued by the city of San Francisco for "invidious discrimination." (Judge Kennedy resigned from the Olympic Club in 1987 shortly before

President Reagan nominated him to the Supreme Court, presumably because the American Bar Association has a policy of recommending against the confirmation of people to judicial positions if they are members of such clubs.) In addition, Judge Kennedy did not have a good record of hiring women. He had hired thirty-five law clerks between his appointment to the Ninth Circuit Court of Appeals in 1975 and his nomination to the Supreme Court in 1987. Only five had been women. (None had been African American or Hispanic.) Although Judge Kennedy's hiring practices were probably not covered by Title VII,[21] if they had been and if the Supreme Court guidelines for deciding whether an employer has discriminated had been applied, Kennedy might have been found in violation of Title VII.[22] From what is known about his hiring practices, it seems likely that he discriminated against women in hiring law clerks.

On September 4, 1985, the three-judge panel of the Ninth Circuit Court, in an opinion written by Judge Kennedy, reversed Judge Tanner and held that the state had not engaged in illegal discrimination against Helen Castrilli and the others.[23] The decision was very broad. It firmly rejected the claims in Castrilli's case and, if followed by other courts, it would make it virtually impossible for *any* plaintiff in *any* case to win on a comparable worth claim. The decision was also noteworthy because it was wrong. The case was incorrectly decided not so much because of the Court's clear opinion on the legal viability of comparable worth claims broadly considered (although I disagree with that) as because of the Court's holdings on narrower, more technical issues of discrimination law.

Judge Tanner had decided that the state had engaged in both disparate treatment and disparate impact discrimination.[24] Judge Kennedy said that neither had occurred. On disparate treatment discrimination, which requires a showing of an intention to discriminate, Judge Kennedy said two things. First, he said that "job evaluation studies and comparable worth statistics alone are insufficient to establish the requisite inference of discriminatory motive." Statistics and studies are relevant, he said, but whether they prove intentional discrimination or not depends on the existence and strength of "independent corroborative evidence of discrimination." Second, Judge Kennedy said that the independent corroborative evidence of discrimination presented in Castrilli's case was not sufficiently strong to prove intentional discrimination. He noted that the individual plaintiffs, Helen Castrilli and the eight others, did not testify in the case, so there was no evidence that there were specific acts of discrimination against them. And, he said, the other "isolated" incidents of discrimination presented in the case did not "justify an inference of discriminatory motive by the State in the setting of salaries for its system as a whole."[25]

In reaching those conclusions, Judge Kennedy, and the other two judges who joined in his opinion, ignored well-known United States Supreme Court cases that, had they been followed, would have required a different result. In a 1977 case, *Teamsters v. United States,* the employer-defendant in an employment discrimination case claimed that statistics alone should never be sufficient to prove discriminatory motive. The Supreme Court flatly rejected the claim: "We have repeatedly approved the use of statistical proof . . . to establish a prima facie case of . . . discrimination in jury selection cases. . . . Statistics are equally competent in proving employment discrimination."[26] The Supreme Court also explained its reason for rejecting the claim: "In many cases the only available avenue of proof is the use of . . . statistics."[27] Thus, when the ninth circuit held that "statistics alone" were insufficient to prove employment discrimination, it was in direct conflict with a Supreme Court holding on the issue. Moreover, since statistical proof is often the "only available avenue" for proving a comparable worth case, the ninth circuit's result also flouted the Supreme Court's reason for reaching its decision. It very well may have been that the statistics in Castrilli's case were not sufficiently accurate or reliable to prove discrimination; if Judge Kennedy had said that, his decision would have been defensible. But he did not address the accuracy or reliability of the statistics. Instead, he said that statistics alone were insufficient to establish a case of discrimination, and that was simply wrong.

Judge Kennedy also said that the independent corroborative evidence of discrimination in the case did not justify an inference of discrimination. If he had been free to decide the case based on his own view of the evidence, that would certainly have been a defensible position. But the United States Supreme Court had decided earlier in 1985 that that was not what a court of appeals was supposed to do. Instead, in *Anderson v. City of Bessemer,* the Supreme Court said that a court of appeals was to defer to the district court's assessment of the evidence unless that assessment was clearly erroneous, unless it was illogical or implausible.[28] In this case, then, Judge Kennedy and the other two judges for whom he was writing should have upheld Judge Tanner's finding of discrimination unless they found that his conclusions were illogical or implausible. But the court of appeals did not explicitly decide that Judge

Tanner's evaluation of the evidence was illogical or implausible. It would have been quite difficult to come to that conclusion when Governor Dan Evans had admitted both when he was governor and again during the trial that the state *had* discriminated against female-dominated occupations when it set wages. Judge Kennedy's decision, then, was also wrong in this respect, because it did not defer to Judge Tanner's decision to the extent required by the Supreme Court.

Through Judge Kennedy's opinion, the ninth circuit also held that Judge Tanner had erred in finding that the state had engaged in disparate impact discrimination. Judge Tanner had held that the state's "system of compensation" had a disparate impact on persons working in female-dominated occupations. Under the state's system of compensation persons in those occupations received less than persons in other occupations, and that result was not required for any reason related to doing the work the state needed done. The ninth circuit did not find that the state's system of compensation did *not* have a disparate impact on women. Rather, it held that the disparate impact theory of discrimination was simply not applicable to the state's system of compensation. Judge Kennedy said that the theory was applicable only to "specific, clearly delineated employment practice[s]." The state's compensation system included labor surveys, agency hearings, administrative recommendations, executive actions, and legislation. It was not, in Judge Kennedy's opinion, sufficiently specific to be subject to disparate impact analysis.

On the one hand, this decision was not clearly wrong; it did not directly conflict with Supreme Court cases, as the decision on disparate treatment discrimination did. On the other hand, the Supreme Court had never indicated or even hinted that the disparate impact theory should be limited to specific employment practices. So in that respect, the decision was unprecedented (though other courts and most predominantly the ninth circuit itself in earlier decisions had begun to carve out this limitation on disparate impact theory).[29]

In addition to being unprecedented, Judge Kennedy's decision on disparate impact theory was also troubling because the judge announced an important and in this case outcome-determinative distinction between specific and nonspecific employment practices but did not provide much guidance on how to tell the difference. We know from Judge Kennedy's decision in the case that he did not view Washington's complex system of compensation as a specific employment practice. But what if the plaintiffs had used disparate impact theory to challenge only one part of that system—say, the labor surveys. Would the labor surveys portion of Washington's system of compensation have been a specific employment practice? Perhaps, but the labor surveys themselves were composed of many employment practices. Jobs were selected to be benchmarks, decisions were made about which employers to survey, questions were drafted to be used in the survey, and so forth. Perhaps the labor surveys were also nonspecific employment practices, and each of the components was a specific employment practice. But, of course, each of these components of the labor survey process also had components that could be identified as employment practices, and the components of the components had components, and so on ad infinitum. At what point does an employment practice become specific? Judge Kennedy told us that it is very important to know the answer to that question, but he failed as a tutor.

Most important, Judge Kennedy's decision on disparate impact theory was troubling because he did not indicate *why* the theory should be limited to specific employment practices. A couple of possible reasons immediately come to mind, but neither of them is particularly convincing. First, it may be that the judge thought disparate impact cases based on nonspecific employment practices, such as compensation systems, would simply be unmanageable—the statistics required would be too complex and unreliable. But to say that disparate impact analysis cannot be used to attack nonspecific employment practices for that reason is like saying that mathematics should be eliminated from the curriculum because it is too difficult. Proving a case of disparate impact will be more difficult when nonspecific employment practices are addressed, but the appropriate response to that is to evaluate the proof in every case to determine whether it is sufficient. Prohibiting disparate impact analysis entirely is overbroad; it means that the theory cannot be used even in situations in which reliable statistics could be presented.

Judge Kennedy may have exempted nonspecific employment practices from disparate impact analysis for another reason. Perhaps he wanted to protect the state (and other employers) from having to justify elements of the compensation system (or other nonspecific employment practices) that did not have a disparate impact on women. For example, assume that one part of the compensation system used by the state—say, the market survey—had a disparate impact on female-dominated occupations, but that none of the other parts of the system did. That would probably mean that the compensation system as a whole had a disparate impact, and if disparate impact analysis of the entire system were permitted and the plaintiffs could prove that the system had a disparate impact, the burden would shift to the state to justify the entire system even though only one portion of the system had a disparate impact. Judge Kennedy may have thought that is unfair. But is it? One is certain when a system has a disparate impact that at least one element of that system has a disparate impact. It is possible (although not necessary, because *every* element of a system *could* have a disparate impact) that other elements of the system do not have a disparate impact. The exclusion of nonspecific employment practices from disparate impact analysis, then, would permit the possible presence of nondiscriminatory elements of a system to shield from attack elements that certainly have a disparate impact. Now that seems unfair. A reasonable solution to this problem, if it is one, is to permit plaintiffs to attack nonspecific employment practices. If a disparate impact can be shown, the burden should shift to the employer to isolate those elements of the system that do and do not have a disparate impact and to justify those that do—or, if the employer cannot isolate the elements, to justify the entire system. This solution makes sense because the employer has greater access to the relevant information and should thus be in a better position to isolate elements that have a disparate impact,[30] and because it avoids the anomaly of permitting the possible presence of innocent elements of a system to shield from attack elements that have a disparate impact.[31]

At any rate, the week before negotiators were about to begin discussing settlement of the case, Judge Kennedy on behalf of the Ninth Circuit Court of Appeals issued a decision emphatically reversing Judge Tanner. Although the decision clearly could have undermined the negotiations, it did not—for three basic reasons. First, the result was not unexpected. The court of appeals had issued a decision earlier in the year—*Spaulding v. University of Washington*[32]—that indicated that it would not look very favorably upon comparable worth claims. Moreover, the procedures Judge Tanner had used at the trial were so unusual and bizarre—basically refusing to allow the state to present its case—that at the very least it was thought the case would be remanded to Judge Tanner for more hearings. The court of appeals decision was perhaps more emphatic than had been anticipated, but the basic result did not seriously upset the expectations the negotiators brought to the bargaining table.

Second, the result did not undermine the negotiations because even after the court of appeals decision the case had a very long potential life. Castrilli and the other plaintiffs could still seek review in the United

States Supreme Court, and, as indicated above, they had some good grounds for arguing that Judge Kennedy's decision should be reversed. It would take a year or more for the case to be heard and decided by the Supreme Court, and as one possible result, the Supreme Court could reverse the court of appeals and remand the case all the way back to Judge Tanner for a new hearing in which the state would have a fair opportunity to present its case. In that event the whole process would be started anew. Thus, there was still quite a bit of uncertainty about the ultimate fate of the case in the courts, and the negotiations provided an opportunity to end the affair.

Third, the negotiations were not undermined, because the decision, although emphatic, could not slow the considerable political momentum that had been building for a negotiated settlement. The new governor, Booth Gardner, was strongly in favor of a settlement, as was Jim McDermott, an influential state senator who had sponsored the legislation calling for negotiations. (Helen Castrilli did not share this enthusiasm. She was "very disappointed" that the case might be settled, because she still thought it could be won in the courts: "I believe totally in the comparable worth issue, and when you feel so strongly about something, you expect the court to also."[33])

But to say that the decision did not undermine the negotiations is not to say that it did not *affect* them. As George Masten, the chief negotiator for Castrilli and the plaintiffs, succinctly told me, "The decision changed the balance of power in the negotiations."

Another factor, too, affected the balance of power as the negotiations began. Winn Newman, who had been the lead litigator in the case, was not on the negotiating team for Castrilli. Indeed, shortly after the court of appeals decision, Newman was dismissed from the case entirely, and another law firm was hired to represent Castrilli and the others. Unsurprisingly, no one wanted to talk with me about this, but it seems quite clear that Newman was dismissed for an amalgam of reasons, including his lack of commitment to settlement negotiations, internal union politics, differences over appeal strategy (whether to appeal to the Supreme Court or seek a rehearing before the Ninth Circuit), and personality factors. The dismissal led to a disagreeable episode in which Newman challenged his dismissal by filing motions in the court of appeals and in Judge Tanner's court. (That challenge presented some interesting legal issues, but Newman eventually abandoned it.) Regardless of the reasons for the dismissal and the subsequent challenge,

TABLE 7.1. Sample Wage Structure before Implementation of Comparable Worth

Male 1	$1,000
Male 2	900
Male 3	800
Female 1	700
Male 4	600
Female 2	500
Female 3	400
Male 5	300
Female 4	200
Female 5	100
Average male weekly wage	720
Average weekly wage for all jobs	550
Average female weekly wage	380

the episode forced Castrilli's side to enter the negotiations without the assistance of one of its principal and most knowledgeable actors. The balance of power, then, was with the state as the negotiations began.

The negotiators were given considerable flexibility in fashioning a settlement. In essence, the legislature had provided $41 million but had left to the negotiators all the details about how the money should be distributed. They were very important details. To illustrate and to make this discussion of the settlement negotiations more comprehensible, assume that the state had only ten jobs, that each job was sex segregated, that each job received the same number of Willis job evaluation points, and that the weekly wages for the jobs were as shown in table 7.1.[34]

Now assume that the legislature sees a problem here and appropriates $500 to address it. Before it can decide how to distribute the $500, several difficult issues have to be resolved.

First, what is a fair wage in this situation? If the problem is viewed as one of sex discrimination, a fair weekly wage is probably $720: the female jobs should be paid the same average weekly wage as the male jobs. Establishing the fair weekly wage by considering *only* the pay of male jobs provides a goal that is free of sex discrimination; considering the pay of female jobs would incorporate any sex discrimination against those jobs into the goal. If that is how the problem is viewed, the Female 1 job would get a raise and the Male 5 job would not. But if the problem is viewed not as one of sex discrimination but simply as a fair wage issue irrespective of sex, a fair weekly wage is probably $550: because all these jobs received the same number of Willis job evaluation points, they should all be paid the same. If that is how the problem is viewed, the Male 5 job would get a raise and the Female 1 job would not.[35] Obviously, the resolution of this issue would also affect how much money it would take to resolve the problem. The $500 would be inadequate in either event, but it would take more money in the long run to raise the average weekly wages to $720 than to raise them to $550.

In the settlement negotiations, this issue was addressed by discussing where the comparable worth line, the line defining what a fair wage would be, should be set. At the remedies stage of the hearings before Judge Tanner, Castrilli's principal witness, Stephan Michelson, had argued that the comparable worth line should be set at the *male* comparable worth line—at $720 in my example. The legislature had indicated in the bill providing the $41 million that it preferred the line to be set at the "average actual" comparable worth line—at $550 in my example. On this point the state prevailed. The goal, under the settlement, would be to raise wages to the average actual comparable worth line, to $550 rather than to $720. (More precisely, the goal was to raise wages to within two salary ranges—that is, within 5 percent—of the average actual comparable worth line. To simplify this discussion, however, I'm going to talk in terms of raising the wages to the average actual comparable worth line.) This meant that occupations analogous to Female 1, which were paid more than the comparable worth line to begin with, would not receive any of the $500. People working for the state as nursing care consultants, school food services supervisors, and Librarian IIIs would not receive any increase in wages from the settlement, even though the occupations were female dominated.

Another issue was, who should benefit from the settlement? Castrilli's lawsuit alleged sex discrimination and was filed on behalf of female-dominated job classifications. Should only those job classifications (Female 2, 3, 4, and 5 in my example) be entitled to share in the $500, or should other jobs below the comparable worth line (Male 5 in my example) also be permitted to share in the settlement? Once again, the issue in a sense was whether the settlement should be viewed primarily as addressing sex discrimination (in which case only the female jobs should benefit) or whether it should be viewed primarily as addressing more general inequities in the state's wage-setting process (in which case the male job should also benefit). Once again, the settlement eventually reached viewed the problem not as one of sex discrimination but as one of wage inequities. All jobs below the comparable worth line, not just female-dominated jobs, would be permitted to share in the settlement,

TABLE 7.2. Sample Wage Structure after Implementation of Comparable Worth

Male 1	$1,000
Male 2	900
Male 3	800
Female 1	700
Male 4	600
Female 2	550
Female 3	550
Male 5	550
Female 4	550
Female 5	550
Average male weekly wage	770
Average weekly wage for all jobs	670
Average female weekly wage	580

to receive wage increases out of the $500. (More precisely, of course, all jobs two ranges or more below the comparable worth line were entitled to share in the settlement.) Thus, people employed by the state as mental health specialists would receive a wage increase from the settlement even though 89 percent of them were men.

A major issue in the negotiations, or rather a major set of issues, was how to distribute the money available. In my example, the $500 is insufficient to address the problem fully. It would take $1,250 to raise the wages of all the occupations to $550, the level established as a "fair wage." That is, $450 would have to be added to the wage of Female 5, $350 to Female 4, $250 to Male 5, $150 to Female 3, and $50 to Female 2, for a total of $1,250. But, of course, even $1,250 would be insufficient to address the issue *fully*. First, the legislature would have to agree to spend not only $1,250 once to equalize the wages, it would have to agree to spend an additional $1,250 *every week* thereafter. Second, even if the legislature did that, it would not have provided any remedy for the low wages these occupations had received in the past; it would only have "corrected" the problem from the date of the settlement forward. Third, even with respect to future wages, the problem would only be lessened, not corrected, because once the wage increases were made, the "fair wage" would go above $550. Table 7.2 shows the wage structure after $1,250 is used to address the problem. Unless the pay for the high-wage jobs is reduced, the problem will not be corrected (that is, all jobs will not be paid the "fair wage") until all the jobs are paid $1,000, because the "fair wage" changes as wages are increased.

TABLE 7.3. Sample Effect of Base Wage Increases on Comparable Worth

| Job | 1/1/85 Salary | 1985–90 Increases | | 1/1/90 Salary |
		Comparable Worth	Base Wage	
Female 2	$500	$50	$ 50	$600
Male 4	600	0	100	700

The negotiators in Helen Castrilli's case, then, had to address these issues in deciding how to distribute the $41 million. One of the issues they considered first was the change in the fair wage as wage increases are made. The problem arises only if the fair wage is reassessed after each wage increase. Recognizing this, the negotiators "solved" the problem by setting the fair wage as the average actual salary of state jobs as of January 1, 1985. The fair wage, then, would always remain the same. In a narrow sense, this solved the problem. The goal would stay the same as wage increases were made. The state would not be shooting at a target that was rapidly moving away from it. But in a broader sense, of course, this solution was sleight of hand. Even if the goal of bringing all occupations up to the fair wage was achieved, the ultimate goal of paying female-dominated occupations the same as comparable male-dominated jobs would not be met. Because many more male-dominated than female-dominated occupations were paid more than the fair wage to begin with, female-dominated occupations would continue to be paid less on average than male-dominated occupations that had the same number of Willis job evaluation points. This is illustrated by table 7.2. Because more "male" jobs than "female" jobs were paid more than $550 to begin with, the average wage of "female" jobs continues to be less than the average wage of "male" jobs even after $1,250 is used for wage increases. This is not to say that the situation has not improved. The average wage of "female" jobs is closer to the average wage of "male" jobs after the $1,250 is used than it was before.

The decision to set the fair wage as the average actual salary of state jobs as of January 1, 1985, created another problem as well. It made it very difficult to predict the effect of the program on the ultimate goal of paying female-dominated occupations the same as comparable male-dominated jobs. To illustrate, consider the Male 4 and Female 2 jobs in table 7.3. Before implementation of the comparable worth program, Male 4 was paid $600 and Female 2 was paid $500, even though the work of the two jobs was rated as equivalent by the Willis study. Female 2 would receive $50 of the comparable worth monies, so after implementation, *if everything else remained the same,* Female 2 would receive $550 while Male 4 would continue to receive $600. Implementation, then, would significantly narrow the wage gap between the two jobs.

The problem is that everything else would *not* remain the same. The comparable worth increase was based on the salaries for the jobs on January 1, 1985, but the normal state process for determining wages would continue to function. As a result, if the base wage rate for the Male 4 job increased at a faster rate than the base wage rate for the Female 2 job, the comparable worth increase might not narrow the wage gap very much at all. For example, if implementation took five years and during that time the base wage rate for the Male 4 job increased $100 while the base wage rate for the Female 2 job increased only $50, the Female 2 job would remain $100 behind the Male 4 job even after implementation of comparable worth (see figure 7.4). Likewise, if the base wage rate for the Female 2 job increased faster than the base wage rate for the Male 4 job, the gap between "male" and "female" jobs would close more quickly than anticipated under the comparable worth program. The decision to base the comparable worth increases on the salaries of January 1, 1985, then, made those increases static within a wage system that was otherwise dynamic. As a result, it was impossible to predict the actual effect of the comparable worth program.[36]

Another important issue dealt with by the negotiators was the back-pay question. Should workers in low-pay occupations be paid something because they received low pay in the past, or should the increase in wages apply only in the future? The issue of back pay presented two major problems. First, the funds available ($41 million) were insufficient even to correct the problem in the future. If compensation was also made to occupations paid too little in the past, the insufficiency of the available funds would become even more severe. Second, back pay would present a whole new set of issues: How far back should the back pay extend? What steps should be required to find the people who had worked in low-pay occupations in the past, many of whom had retired or moved on to other employment? How should the $41 million be divided between back pay and future wage increases? And so on. For these reasons, the negotiators decided not to provide any back pay in the settlement.

The decision not to include back pay created losses. Obviously, people who had worked in low-paying occupations for the state but had since left would receive nothing, even though they had suffered the same wrong the settlement was attempting to correct. Ironically, those people often seemed more deserving of money from the settlement than the people who would actually receive it. For example, a woman who had become a secretary in 1940 when the employment options for women were quite limited and who had worked for the state since then until her recent retirement would receive nothing, while a newly hired secretary would benefit.

Less obviously, the decision to exclude back pay created losses for the state; it meant that in the long run the settlement would cost the state more than it would have if back pay had been provided. Consider my example. If the state uses the available $500 entirely for wage increases in the future, the cost to the state will be the original $500 *and* $500 each week from that time forward. But if the state uses $250 for back pay and $250 for future wage increases, the cost to the state will be the original $500 but only $250 each week from that time forward. In other words, the money used for back pay would be only a one-time payment, but the money used for wage increases in the future would be added to the wage base and would have to be paid by the state over and over again. Nevertheless, the decision was made not to include any back pay in the settlement.

Although the negotiators were getting close to a settlement, other major issues had yet to be resolved. One issue was how to distribute the money among the occupations below the comparable worth line. Should all occupations below the line receive the same increase, or should those far below the line receive a greater increase than those relatively close to the line? In my example, should Female 4 and 5 receive greater increases than Female 2 and 3? Intuitively, one would think that they should, and that is what the settlement provided. During the first year of the settlement agreement, those occupations seven or more salary ranges (a range, once again, is 2.5 percent) below the comparable worth line would receive wage increases to bring them to within six ranges of the line. The salaries of occupations one through six ranges from the line would receive increases from the settlement sufficient to move them up one range. As a result, an occupation that was far below the comparable worth line would receive a large increase. For example, an occupation twelve ranges below the comparable worth line would receive an increase sufficient to move it up six ranges, to bring it to within six ranges of the line. Occupations only one through seven ranges from the line would receive only a one-range wage increase.

Another major issue was how quickly the $41 million should be spent. The legislature did not address this question directly when it provided the money, but it was a very important issue. The speed with which the money was spent would have a direct effect on when comparable worth could be achieved and on the total cost of the settlement to the state. Consider my example again. If the $500 was spent *in one week* to increase wages in the future, about half the problem could be corrected. That is, it would have taken $1,250 to raise those occupations below the comparable worth line ($550) to the comparable worth line; $500 would permit almost half of that gap to be closed. But if the money were paid out more quickly, the gap could be closed more quickly. If the $500 were added to the wages of the low-paying occupations in half a week (and the state then paid wages based on the new wage base from that date forward), the money devoted to the problem would, in effect, be $1,000 per week. The gap would close more quickly, but only because the state would have to devote more money to the problem.

This same calculus applied to the settlement negotiations in Castrilli's case. If the $41 million available for the settlement was spent over a year, some of the wage gap could be closed and the cost to the state would be $41 million for that year and $41 million for each year after that. If the $41 million was spent in one week, the wage gap could, in all likelihood, have been eliminated, but the cost to the state would have been $41 million for that *week* and $41 million for each week after that.

The $41 million was spent in about one year. (It is a bit difficult to calculate precisely, because the settlement began at the end of one fiscal year and overlapped into the next.) The settlement also committed the state to provide a new $10 million every year for the next six fiscal years to be used solely for the purpose of comparable worth. The $41 million, then, would not be sufficient to close the wage gap, but the $60 million in new money over the next six fiscal years would be sufficient to implement comparable worth as the term was defined in the settlement agreement, that is, to bring all job classifications to within two ranges of the actual average comparable worth line as of January 1, 1985. (The definition was narrower than a purist might have liked it to be because it raised job classifications up to only the "average actual" comparable worth line rather than to the male line, because it did not bring job classifications all the way up to the "average actual" line and because the comparable worth line did not move up as wage increases were made.)

The total cost of the settlement was estimated at $482 million. That total was substantially more than the $101 million that one would get by adding $41 million and $60 million. The $101 million figure included only the new money to be devoted to comparable worth increases. The $482 million figure also included money that would be necessary to meet the higher wage base. For the first year, then, the cost would be about $41 million. For the second year, there would be $10 million in new money, but the total cost would be $51 million—$10 million in new money and $41 million to cover the increased wage base from the previous year's increase. For the third year, the total cost would be $61 million—$10 million in new money and $51 million to cover the increased wage base from the previous two years' increases. And so on.[37]

The reported total cost, however, was deceptively high for several reasons. First, the cost *to the state* was considerably less than $482 million. A significant portion of the total cost would come from funds outside the normal state budget process, for example, from funds received as patient fees at state hospitals and from funds received from the federal government as its share of joint programs. The total cost to the state's normal budget process was estimated to be $280 million. Second, the $482 million figure was the *estimated* cost of comparable worth implementation at the time the settlement was announced. In June 1986, after the state had made the first payments under the settlement, the state made another estimate of the likely total costs. At that time, the state estimated the costs to be $362 million, $120 million less than the original estimate. Six months later, in December 1986, the state made yet another estimate of the total costs, and this time it arrived at a figure of $389 million—$27 million more than the June 1986 estimate but still considerably less than the original estimate. Third, the $482 million figure was a noncontextual, accumulated total. The cost of the settlement seems more reasonable when it is broken down into yearly amounts and put into some context. The state dedicated the largest amount of new money to comparable worth implementation in fiscal year 1987: $25.2 million of new money was dedicated for that year, or less than 2 percent of the annual state payroll. The $10 million of new money dedicated for each fiscal year from 1988 to 1993 constituted less than 1 percent of the annual state payroll. In sum, $482 million is a lot of money, but when the figure is put into context, it begins to sound manageable.

So a settlement was reached. The goal would be to bring all occupations in the state to within two ranges of the average actual comparable worth line (as of January 1, 1985) by 1993. All occupations more than two ranges below the comparable worth line would be entitled to a wage increase under the settlement (even if they were male dominated), and no occupations above the comparable worth line would be entitled to a wage increase under the settlement (even if they were female dominated). The settlement would be prospective only; no one would be entitled to any compensation for working in an occupation below the comparable worth line in the past. Occupations far below the line would be given larger initial increases than occupations near the line. The total increases for affected occupations over the entire implementation period would range from 2.5 percent to 44 percent. Approximately 70 percent of the state's 48,000 civil service workers would receive an increase.[38] The total estimated cost of the settlement over the seven-and-a-quarter-year implementation period was originally estimated at $482 million.[39]

When the legislature had extended the $41 million olive branch to Helen Castrilli, it had said that the money would disappear if a tentative settlement could not be reached by the end of 1985. The two negotiating teams, and Helen Castrilli and the other individual plaintiffs in the case, put their signatures to the ten-page document that described the settlement on December 31, 1985. Two other steps were required before the case could be considered formally settled: the Washington State legislature and Judge Tanner had to approve the settlement.

The legislative approval was relatively easy. The legislature requested and received clarifications of certain matters and then ratified the settlement agreement on January 31, 1986.

The approval by Judge Tanner was more complicated. Helen Castrilli's case was a class action; she sued not only on her own behalf but also on behalf of everyone else who worked for the state in an occupation that was female dominated. Before a class action is settled, the federal rules of civil procedure require that everyone in the class be notified of the proposed settlement and given an opportunity to object. Before Judge Tanner could approve it, then, a notice describing the proposed settlement had to be prepared and mailed to everyone who had worked for the state in a female-dominated occupation since 1980. Those people had to be given an opportunity to object to the settlement. (Notice of the proposed settlement was also printed in newspapers throughout the state and through public service announcements on radio and television.)

So a notice was prepared. It briefly described Helen Castrilli's lawsuit and the proposed settlement, listed the job classifications that were or had been female dominated, and explained how to file an objection. But a surprising thing happened when it came time to count how many copies to distribute. When Castrilli had initially filed her lawsuit, she had estimated that the class she was representing contained about 15,500 people, but when it came time to print the settlement notices, the state's estimate, which of course was based on much better information, was 59,700! Hence, 70,000 notices were prepared. (When I visited Richard Heath, one of the state's attorneys in Tacoma, he gave me a couple of copies; he had a few leftovers.)

Objections to the settlement were filed, but in comparison with the number of people in the class, the objections were few in number. A total of 286 objections were filed, or approximately one for every 200 notices. Seventy-nine objectors wanted the settlement to provide back pay. Most were people who had retired or who were no longer working for the state for other reasons. They would receive nothing under the settlement. Twenty-six objectors complained about the number of Willis job evaluation points that had been assigned to their jobs, and 179 objectors did that in a more indirect manner by objecting to the alignment of their jobs as compared with other jobs. These persons were not objecting to the settlement so much as to Willis's assessment of their jobs. The settlement provided for a review of the Willis job evaluation studies, so although not all of these objectors would be satisfied, at least their concerns would be addressed by the process established by the settlement.

On April 11, 1986, a hearing was held before Judge Tanner to consider the objections. The hearing was short. Three objectors appeared to voice their concerns directly, and Judge Tanner briefly questioned the negotiators on the back-pay issue. At the end of the hearing, he indicated that he was going to approve the settlement.

On April 14, Judge Tanner issued a written order of approval. He said that in reaching his decision he had considered the risk, expense, complexity, and likely duration of further litigation; the amount offered in settlement; the stage of the proceedings; the experience and views of the attorneys for the two sides; the fact that the state was a party; the reaction of the class members to the settlement; and (Judge Tanner is a lawyer, after all, who likes to cover all the bases) all the records and files in the case. He found that the required notice had been properly supplied to class members, and he concluded that the settlement as a whole was a fair, adequate, reasonable, and complete resolution of all the claims. He approved the settlement and dismissed the case.

So Helen Castrilli's case ended in Judge Tanner's courtroom on April 14, 1986, a month before the employment appeal tribunal's decision in Julie Hayward's case. By the spring of 1986, Julie Hayward had won a major legal victory, the first comparable worth victory in England, but had not received any money as a result. She had a beautifully wrapped package, which, when opened, turned out to be empty. Helen Castrilli had just the opposite. In the end, she was left with a tattered brown paper bag, but inside there was a pleasant little gift. Castrilli had lost her case. As a strictly legal matter the final result, the court of appeals decision, would stand for the proposition that comparable worth cases could not be won in the United States. Nevertheless, Helen Castrilli and thousands of her co-workers received wage increases. On April 30, 1986, Helen Castrilli looked at her paycheck and, thirteen years after it all began, finally saw what she had been looking for all that time. She received $106 that month as her share of the comparable worth settlement.

8

A Cook in the House of Lords

TWO YEARS AFTER Helen Castrilli first saw the results of her lawsuit in her paycheck, and more than three years after Julie Hayward had first won her case before the industrial tribunal, Hayward was still attempting to translate her victory into an entry in her checkbook. Her journey in pursuit of that goal had been long and varied. She had begun by walking through the men's clothing section of the Watson Prickard store to reach the hearing room of the industrial tribunal in Liverpool. She had traveled through two levels of appellate courts: the employment appeal tribunal, located in a modest building in a small square off Lower Regent Street in London, and the court of appeal, located in the massive and ornate Royal Courts of Justice in the Strand. At each stage, her claim that she should be paid more was rejected. (Her appeal in the court of appeal was dismissed on March 5, 1987.[1]) Finally, in February 1988, Julie Hayward found herself walking to a hearing that one reached not by passing through sundry men's clothes offered at retail but by passing under the vaulted ceilings of the Palace of Westminster. Her claim that she should be paid about £20 more each week had finally taken her to the highest appellate court in England. Julie Hayward's case was to be heard by the House of Lords.

The House of Lords is a peculiar institution to Americans.[2] Its judicial functions are performed by the lord chancellor and several lords of appeal in ordinary, commonly known as law lords. (The maximum number of law lords is eleven but the number can be increased by an order in council.) But unlike the United States Supreme Court, the House of Lords is not exclusively a judicial body. The House, even in its judicial capacity, is still very much a part of Parliament. Its judicial proceedings are conducted in Westminster (and on rare occasions in the chamber of the House of Lords itself), and its members who serve as judges are entitled to vote on bills and to participate in legislative debates in the full House. Indeed, the lord chancellor, who is roughly the equivalent of the chief justice of the United States Supreme Court, also serves as the speaker of the House of Lords (sitting upon the Woolsack when the house sits as a legislative body), is a member of the government, and normally is in the cabinet.

Still, the judicial and legislative functions of the House are separated to a degree. By convention, the law lords do not contribute to legislative debates in matters of political controversy, and the lay lords do not hear judicial appeals. The convention against the participation of lay lords in the judicial business of the House is especially strong. No lay lord has been permitted to vote on a judicial matter since 1844, and the last lay lord who attempted to take part in a judicial hearing was simply ignored.

The House of Lords is also a peculiar institution to Americans because, in contrast to the practice in the United States Supreme Court, not every judge sits in every case. Instead, cases are heard by "appellate committees" of five judges.[3] Even more peculiarly, no one outside the House of Lords knows how the five judges to serve on a particular appellate committee are selected.[4] But there is virtually no suggestion that appellate committees are selected to influence the outcome of cases, and that certainly did not happen in Julie Hayward's case.

Hayward's case was heard by an appellate committee that consisted of the lord chancellor, Lord Mackay of Clashfern, and four law lords: Lord Bridge of Harwich, Lord Brandon of Oakbrook, Lord Griffiths, and Lord Goff of Chieveley. With one important exception, the appellate committee selected to hear Hayward's case was typical—typical, that is, of the type of committee one would expect in the House of Lords. The appellate committee was not typical of the committee Julie Hayward might have hoped for in the best of all possible worlds. The committee members (with one exception) were unlikely to have had much personal acquaintance with workers in canteens and shipyards and people who, like Julie Hayward, had left school at sixteen. These judges had all gone to public schools (which are roughly equivalent to private schools in the United States), and four of the five had spent time at Oxford or Cambridge. Nor were they likely to be overly sympathetic to women's causes. They were simply not of that generation. The ages of the lord chancellor and law lords on the appellate committee ranged from sixty to seventy-three; sixty-five was the average. And of course all the judges were men.

That perhaps should not have been significant, but Julie Hayward's case had already been presented to nine other people in three other tribunals: the industrial tribunal, the employment appeal tribunal, and the court of appeal, each consisting of three people. Eight of the nine were men, and all eight had supported Cammell Laird's position. The ninth was one of the lay members of the industrial tribunal in Liverpool. She had voted to raise Julie Hayward's pay.

In one respect, though, the appellate committee in Hayward's case was atypical. The presence of the lord chancellor on the committee was a surprise. Because of all his other responsibilities, the lord chancellor rarely hears judicial appeals. Thus, the very presence of the lord chancellor on the committee was unusual. But it was the presence of *this* lord chancellor that was perhaps especially significant. Lord Mackay of Clashfern was a new lord chancellor; he had held the position for less than a year. He was an outsider to the London establishment, a Scot and the first member of the Scottish bar (although not the first Scot) to become head of the English judiciary. But it was Lord Mackay's background, rather than these other peculiarities, that seemed significant to Julie Hayward. Unlike the vast majority of law lords, he was not a product of the landed gentry but the son of a humble railroad worker from the Scottish Highlands. Lord Mackay of Clashfern, although he had gone to public school and taught at Cambridge, knew about the lives and concerns of people like Julie Hayward.[5]

At 11:00 A.M. on February 15, 1988, the lord justices who were to hear Hayward's case appeared one by one at the end of a short hallway leading to the parliamentary committee room in the Palace of Westminster where the hearing was to be held. Julie Hayward and a small group of spectators stood at the other end of the hallway behind the teams of lawyers representing her and Cammell Laird. The lord chancellor and law lords each paused before entering the room and bowed to the assemblage at the other end of the hallway. Bows rippled through the assembled group in return. The robed and wigged barristers at the head of the group returned each bow promptly in a competent and practiced fashion. The less uniform and slightly self-conscious bows of the solicitors standing behind the barristers came a second later. The remaining members of the group nervously eyed each other as they either bowed halfheartedly or waited too long to decide and missed the moment. Then the group followed the judges into the committee room.

The parliamentary committee room was small but elegant with its four gold chandeliers and its large windows overlooking the Thames.

The judges sat behind a semicircular table at one end of the room, with the lord chancellor in the center chair. In contrast to the formality of the bowing ceremony, the table was not elevated at all (when the barristers rose to speak, they would look down at the seated judges) and the judges were dressed in ordinary business suits.

Facing the judges were two rows of seats with tables for counsel and two rows of seats for spectators. The barristers for Hayward and Cammell Laird were in the first row of seats, behind tables that were separated by a lectern. David Pannick was there for Julie Hayward and Charles James for Cammell Laird, but neither would make their sides' submission to the appellate committee. At this level they were being led by more experienced counsel who would make the submissions, by counsel who had "taken silk": that is, had become queen's counsel (and hence were entitled to wear gowns made of silk). Anthony Lester was the queen's counsel for Julie Hayward, and Lord Alexander Irvine was the queen's counsel for Cammell Laird. The solicitors for the two sides and other barristers (probably pupils) were seated in the second row and a small group of about fifteen spectators—including Julie Hayward—in the remaining two rows of seats.

The issues before the appellate committee were the same issues that had been before the employment appeal tribunal. What did it mean to say that Hayward had to be paid the same as painters, joiners, and laggers? Should Hayward's wages, which were lower than the men's wages, be increased without regard to other parts of her compensation, such as sickness benefits, that were more favorable than the men's? Or did equality mean that Hayward's total compensation package should be valued and made equal to the total compensation package of each man? The positions of Hayward and Cammell Laird with respect to this gordian knot had matured in the two years since the decision of the employment appeal tribunal, but neither side could yet claim to be Alexander the Great.

The Equal Pay Act, as amended by the Equal Value Regulations, still said that where a woman's job was found to be of equal value to a man's job, "any term of the woman's [employment] contract [that is] or becomes less favourable to the woman than a term of a similar kind in the [man's employment] contract . . . shall be . . . modified [so] as not to be less favourable."[6]

The outcome of Hayward's case in the House of Lords depended primarily on the meaning of the word "term" in this section. Hayward, through her barrister, Anthony Lester, claimed that "term" meant any discrete, contractual promise. Thus, Hayward's basic pay, her overtime rate, her sickness benefit, her vacation pay, and the other elements of her employment contract were all separate "terms." The language of the Equal Pay Act permitted her to point to any one of those terms and have it improved if it was less favorable than the comparable term in the employment contracts of the men. In contrast, Cammell Laird, through its barrister, Lord Alexander Irvine, claimed that the word "term" contemplated not an infinite variety of terms in every employment contract but only two "terms" in each contract—one term concerning pay and one term on other subject matters. So if Hayward wanted the term concerning pay in her employment contract improved, she would have to show that that term, which would include *all* the elements mentioned above (basic pay, overtime pay, sickness benefit, vacation pay), was less favorable than the term concerning pay in the employment contract of the men.

The issue was not an easy one. The word "term" was not defined in the Equal Pay Act. Indeed, although the word had been in the Equal Pay Act since the act's initial enactment in 1970, no prior case defined the word or even, in Lester's phrase, "came within 100 miles" of defining it. One reason for this lack of authority was that until the Equal Value Regulations became effective in 1984, the Equal Pay Act applied when men and women were doing the same work—when men and women were working as secretaries or when men and women were working as janitors. Because they were doing the same work for the same employer, the pay structures of the men and women being compared were almost always very similar. After the Equal Value Regulations went into effect, the Equal Pay Act began to be applied to situations like Julie Hayward's in which the men and women being compared were doing work that, although of equal value, was very different in kind. The work of a female cook could be compared to the work of male painters, joiners, and laggers. In these situations the pay structures of the men and women might be quite different, and so it became necessary, as in Hayward's case, to determine how to analyze and equalize such disparate pay structures.

Partly because of this lack of authority and partly because lawyers just talk this way, the debate in the House of Lords quickly turned into a duel of hypothetical examples, with their lordships directing questions to Lester and Irvine: *"How, Mr. Lester, would you equalize the wages of a man and a woman doing work of equal value if the woman received £10,000 per year and the free use of a company car while the man received £15,000 per year but no car?"*[7]

"Since the 'term' relating to basic pay and the 'term' relating to the use of a car are probably discrete contractual promises, the woman should be able to point to the term which is less favorable to her—the basic pay term—and have it increased without regard to the term relating to the use of a car. If the employer wants to argue that the woman is paid less *because* she has a company car, the company can do that under section 1(3) of the Equal Pay Act[8] by proving that the availability of the car explains the difference in basic pay and that the difference in pay structures did not result from sex discrimination. This argument, however, is not available to Cammell Laird in this case because Cammell Laird failed to present it when it should have and, as a result, the company waived the defense and cannot raise it now."

"What would happen, Mr. Lester, if the man then brought an action under the Equal Pay Act?"

"If the man then brought an action, the work would still be of equal value, so he should be able to point to the term which is less favorable to him—the term relating to the use of the car—and have it applied to him without regard to the basic pay term, assuming of course that the employer still could not succeed under section 1(3)."

"That is not, I take it, the result you would reach, Lord Irvine?"

"Certainly not. That result is nothing short of bizarre. The woman ends up with £15,000 per year *and* the use of a car—and so does the man. If that's the proper result, the statute should be named the Enhancement of Pay Act, not the Equal Pay Act."

"How would your interpretation of the Equal Pay Act apply to this case?"

"Both the man's employment contract and the woman's employment contract contain two 'terms'—one relating to pay and one relating to other matters. Basic pay and the use of a car are both elements of one term, the term relating to pay. Thus, the industrial tribunal should determine whether the value of the woman's term relating to pay (£10,000 per year plus the value of the use of the car) is less than the man's term relating to pay (£15,000 per year). If it is, she's entitled to an increase in her term relating to pay to bring the total value of that term to £15,000 per year. Neither the woman nor the man would be able to leapfrog over the other."

"Mr. Lester says that section 1(3) of the Equal Pay Act gives the employer an opportunity to prove that the woman's lower pay is explained by the car.

Cammell Laird has waived the section 1(3) defense in this case, but doesn't that defense solve the leapfrogging problem in our hypothetical problem?"

"Not at all. Assume the employer presents a defense under section 1(3). The employer testifies that the reason the woman is paid £10,000 and the man is paid £15,000 for work of equal value is that the woman also has a company car. On cross-examination, the employer is told that the use of a company car is worth only £3,500 per year. The employer responds that yes, that may be, I never figured it out exactly, but nevertheless the car is the reason I paid the woman £5,000 less per year. Should the employer succeed with his section 1(3) defense? Regardless of how my learned friend would answer the question, the result under his analysis is less satisfactory than the result under our analysis. If the section 1(3) defense succeeds, the end result is that the woman receives the equivalent of £13,500 per year for her work (£10,000 in basic pay plus £3,500, the value of the company car), while the man receives £15,000 for his work. The man and the woman are not paid equally for work of equal value. If the section 1(3) defense does not succeed, the end result is that the woman is paid £18,500 per year (her basic wage would be increased to equal the man's and she would retain the use of the car). The man would also be entitled to that amount if he brought an action under the (if this is the result) 'Enhancement of Pay Act.' The result under our analysis is both simpler and fairer. The industrial tribunal would value the single term relating to pay of both the man and the woman. The man's term is worth £15,000, and the woman's term is worth £13,500. The woman is entitled to an increase of £1,500 per year."

"And you think, Lord Irvine, that this would be more than an isolated problem?"

"This problem would not be isolated; it would be rampant because it is built into the structure of my learned friend's analysis. Consider a very simple case. A man and a woman are doing work of equal value. The man works forty hours per week and earns £40. The woman works thirty hours per week and earns £30. If each employment contract contains two 'terms,' as my learned friend contends, then the woman should be able to point to the man's £40 'term' and have it included in her contract, and the man should be able to point to the woman's thirty-hour 'term' and have it included in his contract. Or assume that the woman is paid a basic wage of £100 per week for her work, while the man is paid a basic wage of £70 per week plus £30 per week as a productivity bonus. Under my learned friend's analysis, the woman would be able to point to the man's productivity bonus 'term' and have it included in her contract, and the man would be able to point to the woman's basic wage 'term' and have it included in his contract. This type of leapfrogging is absolutely astonishing, but it is what my learned friend would require, and it would occur often."

"Is it necessary, Lord Irvine, to solve all of these conundrums to resolve this case?"

"It would be extremely welcome, your lordship."

"From your earlier discussion of the basic wages-car example, Mr. Lester, it is clear that your analysis accepts leapfrogging. Do you agree that it would occur often?"

"Certainly not as often as my learned friend claims. Consider his example of a man earning a £15,000 salary and a woman earning a £10,000 salary with a company car worth £3,500. When my learned friend says our analysis is flawed whether or not the section 1(3) defense succeeds, he sets up a false dichotomy. He says, 'Look, either the defense succeeds and the woman earns £13,500 per year and the man £15,000, or the defense fails and they both earn £18,500. Either result is unacceptable.' The section 1(3) defense, however, is more flexible than that. It can be used to justify *part* of the pay disparity between the man and the woman.[9] Thus, when the employer proves that the woman is paid less than the man because she has a company car (and, although my learned friend neglects this, that sex discrimination is not the reason that the man is paid in money and the woman in money and car), the employer has succeeded with his section 1(3) defense but only to the extent of the value of the car. So the employer has justified £3,500 of the difference in pay between the man and the woman. The industrial tribunal should order the employer to pay the woman £1,500 more per year. Both the man and the woman would then earn £15,000 per year. There would be no leapfrogging."

"But from your position in this case, Mr. Lester, it is clear that your analysis accepts leapfrogging. You argue that Miss Hayward should be able to point to her basic wage and have it increased without regard to the parts of her employment contract that are more favorable than those of the men."

"That's true, our analysis accepts leapfrogging under certain circumstances, like those present in this case. But, of course, my learned friend's position also accepts leapfrogging. Consider a situation in which a man works under an employment contract that provides for £10,000 per year and contains a clause that the employer guarantees the man a job; the man cannot be made redundant. A woman doing work of equal value works under an employment contract that provides for £15,000 per year but does not include the job guarantee provision. How would one provide a remedy in this case under my learned friend's analysis? Under his analysis, there are two 'terms' in each contract that must be made equal, a 'term concerning pay' and a 'term concerning matters other than pay.' Thus, to equalize the 'term concerning pay' in each contract, both the man and the woman should be paid £15,000 per year. To equalize the 'term concerning matters other than pay' in each contract, both the man and the woman should have the job guarantee provision included in their employment contracts. My learned friend's position, then, also accepts 'bizarre, absolutely astonishing' leapfrogging."

"You have submitted, Mr. Lester, that the result in the car-money example would be the same under your analysis and Lord Irvine's analysis and that leapfrogging would occur under both analyses. Why, then, should we prefer your analysis to Lord Irvine's?"

"You should prefer our analysis because it is the analysis Parliament has required. The portion of the Equal Pay Act that we are interpreting contains two provisions. The provision labeled with a little i [i][10] says that if 'any term' of a woman's contract is less favorable than a term in the man's contract, it shall be modified so as not to be less favorable. The provision labeled with a double little i [ii][11] says that if the woman's contract does not contain a 'term' corresponding to a term benefiting the man, the woman's contract shall be treated as including such a term. The first and more obvious point from this language is that the words 'any term' and 'term' support our position. Those words in common usage, which must be how Parliament intended them to be read since it did not define them in the act, mean what we say they should mean. Each discrete contractual promise is a 'term': basic pay is a 'term'; overtime pay is a 'term'; vacation pay is a 'term,' and so forth. My learned friend's position, that there are only two 'terms' in each employment contract, does violence to the common usage of the words of the Equal Pay Act. The language of the Equal Pay Act also supports our position, or rather undercuts my learned friend's position, in a second, more subtle way. The (ii) language, once again, says that if the woman's contract does not include a provision that is in the man's contract, the woman's contract should be read so as to include it. That language makes sense under our analysis, under an analysis that contemplates a great many 'terms' in most employment contracts. But under my learned friend's analysis, employment contracts have only two terms. Since it is virtually inconceivable that an employment contract would not have a 'term concerning pay,' the (ii) language could apply only to the alternative term—to the 'term concerning matters other than pay.' There is no indication that Parliament intended such a limited application for the (ii) language, and there *is* an indication that Parliament intended a broader application of the language. Earlier in the statute, the Equal Pay Act says that 'terms' can be modified under the Act 'whether [they are] concerned with pay or not.'[12] Thus, the (ii) language supports our position because our position, unlike my learned friend's position, does not require an artificially narrow scope of application for that provision."

"Given the language of the Equal Pay Act which Mr. Lester has just so ably described, Lord Irvine, could you not have done better than Parliament if you were intending to draft a provision to permit comparisons only between two 'terms' in each employment contract?"

"I find it irresistible to accept your lordship's compliment that I could have done better, but I must say in response that never has an issue of construction been litigated in which it could not have been said that the drafting could have been better. Moreover, the problems with the drafting do not present problems solely for our position. Consider again the (i) provision to which my learned friend referred. The provision says that any term of the woman's employment contract should be compared to a 'term of a similar kind' in the man's contract. Our analysis sits better with that language. Our analysis compares 'similar' terms in the two contracts. My learned friend's analysis compares not 'similar' terms in the two contracts, but the *same* terms in the two contracts. His submission is that basic pay should be compared with basic pay, overtime with overtime, and so forth. Perhaps my learned friend should also be complimented on his ability to improve Parliament's drafting."

The debate before the appellate committee of the House of Lords continued in this polite, almost academic, manner for more than two days, in sharp contrast to the hour that is generally allocated for debate in cases before the United States Supreme Court. At the end of the hearing, on February 17, 1988, the lord justices on the appellate committee bowed, accepted bows in return, and left the room. Julie Hayward's case left with them. It was now entrusted to five men in the Palace of Westminster, the hallowed birthplace of the common law and the English legal system—a long way indeed from the often hot and steamy canteen on the River Mersey where the case had begun.

The formal decision in Julie Hayward's case was delivered in the Chamber of the House of Lords in the Palace of Westminster. At 10:30

A.M. on May 5, 1988, the five law lords as the appellate committee reported to themselves as the House of Lords and "voted" on the outcome. Each judge stood up, the lord chancellor first and the others in order of seniority, and voted on the appeal "for the reasons given in my printed speech." The printed opinions or "speeches" had been distributed to the parties shortly before the formal ceremony announcing the decision.

The lord chancellor voted in favor of Julie Hayward. In his printed speech he said that although

> there is no definition of the word 'term' in the legislation . . . I am of opinion that the natural meaning of the word "term" in this context is a distinct provision or part of the contract which has sufficient content to make it possible to compare it from the point of view of the benefits it confers with similar provision or part in another contract. . . . It appears to me that it would be natural to compare the appellant's basic salary as set out in her contract with the basic salary determined under the men's contract.[13]

The lord chancellor elaborated on the point a bit to answer one of the problems Irvine had raised with that construction of the Equal Pay Act. Irvine had claimed that that construction of the act would lead to an absurd result when applied to a man working forty hours per week for £40 and a woman doing work of equal value for thirty hours per week for £30. The lord chancellor's construction, Irvine had claimed in the hearing, would permit the man to have the woman's more favorable term (the thirty hours per week term) included in his contract and the woman to have the man's more favorable term (the £40 per week term) included in her contract; both the man and the woman would end up working thirty hours per week for £40. The lord chancellor responded to that problem, without mentioning it directly, by emphasizing the importance of viewing "terms" in a form that makes them "capable of being compared."[14] In Hayward's case, the lord chancellor said, "the natural application of the word 'term' to this contract is that it applies . . . to the basic pay, and that the appropriate *comparison* is with the *hourly* rate of basic pay."[15]

But what about the other problems created by the lord chancellor's interpretation? What about the man earning £15,000 per year and the woman driving a company car and earning £10,000 per year? Or the woman earning a basic wage of £100 per week and the man earning a basic wage of £70 per week and a productivity bonus of £30 per week? The lord chancellor had hinted at his ultimate response to these problems in the hearing when he had asked Irvine whether it was necessary to

solve "all these conundrums" to resolve the Hayward case. The lord
chancellor wrote in his opinion:

> While one can envisage difficult examples, in the ordinary case such as the
> present no such difficulty arises and in my opinion it would be wrong to
> depart from the natural reading of the words Parliament has used because
> of the difficulty in their application to particular examples especially when
> those examples do not arise in actual cases.[16]

The lord chancellor responded similarly to the issue of how section 1(3)
of the Equal Pay Act should be applied in situations in which an employer
claims, for example, that a woman has a less favorable term than a man
in her contract because another term in the woman's contract is more
favorable than the man's. Both sides had discussed the issue at some
length in the hearing, but the lord chancellor, while expressing some
doubt that an employer would be able to succeed with such a defense,
said that since the issue did not arise in Hayward's case, he preferred
"to express no concluded opinion . . . on the meaning and effect of section
1(3)."[17]

Lord Goff of Chieveley also filed a fully considered written speech in
the case. He voted in favor of Julie Hayward, too, and for reasons that
were quite similar to the lord chancellor's. While the lord chancellor
thought the "natural" meaning of the word "term" in the Equal Pay
Act supported Hayward's position, Lord Goff relied on the "common
sense" meaning of the word:

> In my opinion, the words ["term" and "a term of a similar kind" in the
> Equal Pay Act] mean precisely what they say. You look at the two contracts;
> you ask yourself the common sense question, is there in each contract a term
> of a similar kind, i.e., a term making a comparable provision for the same
> subject-matter; if there is, then you compare the two, and if, on that
> comparison, the term of the woman's contract proves to be less favourable
> than the term of the man's contract, then the term in the woman's contract
> is to be treated as modified so as to make it not less favourable. . . . I feel
> that [Irvine's and] the Court of Appeal's attempt to introduce the element
> of overall comparison placed [them] firmly, or rather infirmly, on a slippery
> slope; because, once [they] departed from the natural and ordinary meaning
> of the word "term," [they] in reality found it impossible to control the
> ambit of the comparison which [they] considered to be required. For almost
> any, indeed perhaps any, benefit will fall within "pay" in the very wide
> sense favoured by [them], in which event it is difficult to segregate any
> sensible meaning of the word "term."[18]

Lord Goff, like the lord chancellor, did not respond to all the problems that had been raised in the hearing, and, again like the lord chancellor, he expressed doubts about whether some of those problems would ever arise.[19]

Lord Goff, however, did respond more explicitly than the lord chancellor had to the leapfrogging problem. He admitted that his construction could lead to leapfrogging, to a situation in which both a man's contract and a woman's contract would be upgraded to bring them into line with each other. But, he said, there were two different answers to that problem. First, he said, the problem could be avoided under section 1(3). Lord Goff said he saw "great force" in the argument that an employer, under section 1(3), should be able to avoid paying an increase to a woman paid less than a man under part of her employment contract if the woman is paid more than a man under another part.[20] On this point, the speeches of the lord chancellor and Lord Goff seemed to be in conflict. The lord chancellor had said that he was "presently of the view that section 1(3) would not provide a defence" in the very situation in which Lord Goff saw "great force" to the argument that the section would provide a defense. But neither the lord chancellor nor Lord Goff discussed the section 1(3) defense in detail because it was not an issue in Hayward's case, so the view of the House of Lords on that point remains uncertain.[21] Lord Goff's second answer to the leapfrogging problem was that if his construction of the Equal Pay Act—which permitted leapfrogging—did not reflect "the true intention of Parliament, then the appropriate course for Parliament is to amend the legislation to bring it into line with its true intention."[22]

The issues on which the lord chancellor and Lord Goff disagreed were, of course, irrelevant to Julie Hayward. They were not issues in her case. The lord chancellor and Lord Goff agreed that Julie Hayward was entitled to a raise in her basic pay, even if her employment contract was more favorable than the contracts of the men in some other respects.

The other three law lords did not file considered speeches of their own. Instead, they all filed speeches indicating that they agreed with the speeches of their "noble and learned friends the Lord Chancellor and Lord Goff of Chieveley." On May 5, 1988, in the Chamber of the House of Lords in the Palace of Westminster, Julie Hayward won her case in the highest court in the United Kingdom.

Like two weary boxers who continue punching after the final bell, Hayward and Cammell Laird did not end their bout immediately after the decision in the House of Lords. The settlement negotiations extended through the summer of 1988, and there was even another hearing on minor issues before the industrial tribunal in Liverpool.[23] But by the end of the summer, Julie Hayward had been awarded her gold medal. Cammell Laird agreed to pay Julie Hayward the same as painters, joiners, and laggers in the future; she received an increase of about £25 per week in her basic wages. In addition, Cammell Laird paid Hayward about £5,000 in back pay for the time since January 1, 1984 (the date the Equal Pay Regulations became effective) during which she had been improperly paid less than the men. Julie Hayward no longer had to talk about winning only on principle. Like Helen Castrilli two summers before, she was now able to see the results of her efforts in every paycheck. But unlike Helen Castrilli, she had also succeeded in marking a route through the legal maze that others could follow.

PART TWO
COMPARABLE WORTH:
THEORY, PROMISE, AND LIMITS

9

The Antidiscrimination Principle

THE CASES OF Julie Hayward and Helen Castrilli are interesting stories about brave women, but they are more than that. They are also case studies of the struggles of two societies to come to grips with the comparable worth issue. In this latter role, as case studies, they have the potential to improve our understanding of the comparable worth issue and perhaps even to refine our understanding of the two societies. I use the Hayward and Castrilli cases in this discussion as reference points for a consideration of the general theory of comparable worth and for an evaluation of the promise and limitations of comparable worth in practice.

A natural first question, using the two cases as reference points, is what is comparable worth? One would think that an issue that former president Ronald Reagan called "cockamamie"[1] and that the European Economic Community required its member states to implement[2] would at least have a relatively clear and commonly accepted definition. But that is not the case. Instead, comparable worth is the UFO of public policy issues. It is a major issue even though people do not know exactly what they are talking about.

The common understanding of "comparable worth," in both the popular press and in much of the scholarly work on the issue, is that it requires equal pay for jobs that are of "comparable value" to the employer. Value to the employer is defined in terms of the skill, effort, and responsibility required to do the job. Thus, if an employer employs cooks and painters and the two jobs require equal amounts of skill, effort, and responsibility, then the employer, according to this understanding of comparable worth, should be required to pay the cook and the painter equal wages.[3]

Julie Hayward's case, at first glance, seems to confirm this view. Hayward attempted to show that her job as a cook was comparable in value to the jobs of a painter, a joiner, and a lagger. She did that by proving through the job evaluation procedure that her job and the others required equal amounts of skill, effort, and responsibility. Her claim, then, was that she should be paid the same as the painter, joiner, and lagger.

The common understanding of comparable worth, that comparable jobs should be paid equally, clearly arose from cases like Julie Hayward's (and Helen Castrilli's). On the surface, the plaintiffs in almost every comparable worth case, people like Julie Hayward, seemed to be claiming that they should be paid the same as men because their work is equal in skill, effort, and responsibility to the work of the men. On closer examination, however, Hayward's case demonstrates that the "equal pay for work of comparable value" principle is unsatisfactory as a definition of comparable worth. The principle is at the same time too broad and too narrow to describe the Hayward case.

The principle is too broad because it indicates that *all* jobs of comparable value must be paid equally. But it was clear in Hayward's case, and it is clear in comparable worth cases generally, that it is sometimes permissible for an employer to pay jobs differently even though they are of comparable value. After Hayward had proved that her job required the same skill, effort, and responsibility as those of the painter, joiner, and lagger, Cammell Laird attempted to prove that even if the jobs were comparable in value, Hayward and the men did not have to be paid the same, because any difference in pay was based on a factor other than sex. Any difference in pay, Cammell Laird argued, was caused by the collective bargaining agreement. For procedural reasons, Cammell Laird lost this argument, but it is clear under the Equal Pay Regulations that if an employer can prove that a difference in pay is based on some factor other than sex, the employer can pay jobs differently even if they are comparable in the skill, effort, and responsibility required to do them.[4]

The "equal pay for work of comparable value" principle is also too narrow. When the European Court of Justice held in 1982 that the United Kingdom was not in compliance with Article 119 of the Treaty of Rome, it said that the job comparison approach was "merely one of several methods" of proving a violation of the article's requirement that men and women receive "equal pay for equal work."[5] The European Court of Justice, then, would permit Julie Hayward to prove a violation of Article 119 by comparing her job to other jobs (as she did) or by using one of several other methods.[6] The European Court of Justice did not say what other methods it had in mind. I suggest some later, but the point here is that the "equal pay for work of comparable value" principle is too narrow because it encompasses only one of many possible ways of proving a comparable worth violation.

These insights from the Hayward case, then, permit a powerful critique of the common understanding of comparable worth. According to that understanding, comparable worth means that jobs must be paid equally if they are ranked equally by a job evaluation study. The understanding is insufficient because it would find comparable worth violations in situations in which none exists (it would find a violation even if Cammell Laird could prove that a pay difference between equivalent jobs was based on factors other than sex) and because it would not find violations in situations in which violations do exist (it would not find a violation where a claim was proved by a method other than job evaluation).

The insights are important, however, not only because they permit this critique but also because they point the way to a better understanding of the theory of comparable worth. The Hayward case indicates that showing jobs to be of equal rank on a job evaluation study is only one of many ways of proving a comparable worth violation. The common understanding of comparable worth, then, mistakes a means for an end. Hayward (and Castrilli) used job comparisons as a means to prove a comparable worth violation, but the violation itself consisted of something else. The other insight from the Hayward case is that the something else is sex discrimination. Cammell Laird would have won in Hayward's case if it could have shown that the difference in pay between Hayward and the painter was based on some factor other than sex. Sex discrimination, not job comparison, was the ultimate issue in the case. This conclusion is reinforced by Helen Castrilli's case, in which sex discrimination was even more obviously and more directly the ultimate issue. Castrilli did not have a law, like the one relied on by Julie Hayward, that explicitly contemplated the use of job comparisons as evidence. Title VII, the law relied on by Castrilli, said only that sex discrimination was illegal. Castrilli's task in the lawsuit was to show by whatever means she could that her pay was depressed because of sex discrimination. She used Willis's job evaluations as her primary means, but her goal was to prove discrimination.

A discussion of the theory of comparable worth must begin, then, not with job comparison but with the antidiscrimination principle,[7] the principle that commands employers not to discriminate because of sex.[8] Comparable worth is one application of this principle.

The antidiscrimination principle is very widely accepted, yet at the same time it is not found in pure form in any statute or law. There are scores of different laws prohibiting discrimination in the United States and Great Britain, and all of them are based on the antidiscrimination principle.[9] All of them, at their core, command employers not to discriminate on the basis of sex. All these laws, however, also limit the antidiscrimination principle in one way or another. Most of them, for example, permit very small employers to discriminate, and all of them permit any employer to discriminate in certain limited circumstances, although those circumstances vary from one law to another. The antidiscrimination principle, then, is a sound starting point—indeed, the necessary starting point—for articulation of a theory of comparable worth that might apply under any legal regime. The precise outlines of the theory, though, may well vary depending on the specific limitations on the principle contained in a particular law.

Beginning with the antidiscrimination principle, however, does not mean beginning merely with the command to employers not to discriminate. The principle is the starting point for all of discrimination law and has been applied to a wide variety of other issues. There is a rich body of experience refining the bare command to employers. This body of experience can be drawn upon to improve our understanding of comparable worth.[10]

Our understanding of the analytical structure of a comparable worth case, for example, can be improved if we compare it with the structure of a simple and uncontroversial case applying the antidiscrimination principle. It is well accepted that the antidiscrimination principle does, and should, prohibit an employer from refusing to hire a person because of her sex. In such a case, a woman who is not hired must prove that the employer's hiring decision would have been different but for her sex.[11] She must prove that she would have been hired if she were male. But of course she is not male, so her task is to create an inference of discrimination, an inference that the employer would have hired her but for her sex. The woman can rely on many types of evidence to create this inference of discrimination. She can rely on overt discriminatory statements by the employer.[12] Or she can attempt to create the inference by comparing her qualifications with those of the person (preferably male) who actually was hired; if her qualifications are better, the inference is that the employer hired the male instead of her because of sex.[13] Or the woman can point to the employer's hiring record over a period of time; if the employer has hired only males for a long time even though a significant number of women have applied for job openings, the inference is that the employer discriminates.[14] Regardless of the evidence she relies upon, however, her ultimate burden is to prove by a preponderance of the evidence that the employer's decision would have been different but for her sex.[15]

The structure of a comparable worth case mirrors this simple case perfectly. In her case, Helen Castrilli claimed that her wage rate as a secretary would have been different but for her sex and the sex of others working as secretaries. Castrilli attempted to prove that her wage rate would have been different if the "sex" of her occupation had been male. But, as in the simple case, the sex of the occupation was not male, so Castrilli's task was to create an inference of discrimination, an inference that secretaries would have been paid more but for the occupation's sex composition. Like the woman in the simple case, Castrilli relied upon many different types of evidence in her attempt to create this inference of discrimination. She relied on overt statements by the employer (former governor Evans's admission, for example, that the state had discriminated). She compared the job of secretary with that of campus police officer, a male-dominated job that paid more. As in the simple case, she was attempting to create an inference that the wage difference was caused by the sex of the people in the two occupations, not by any differences in how difficult the two jobs were. She also pointed to the state's wage-setting practices over a period of time, attempting to show that the state regularly paid workers in female-dominated occupations less than workers in male-dominated occupations of equal difficulty. The goal, once again as in the simple case, was to show by a preponderance of the evidence that the state's wage-setting decisions would have been different but for the sex composition of the secretary job.

The structure of the two cases, then, is the same. In the simple case, the woman compares her actual treatment with the treatment she would have received had she been male. One cannot know for certain how she would have been treated had she been male, but the woman presents evidence that permits a judge or jury to infer how she would have been treated. If she proves by a preponderance of the evidence that she would have been treated differently as a male, she proves a violation of the antidiscrimination principle. In Castrilli's case, Castrilli compared the wages of secretaries as a female-dominated occupation to the wages secretaries would have received as a male-dominated occupation. Once again, one cannot know for certain how secretaries would have been treated as a male-dominated occupation, but Castrilli presented evidence that permitted Judge Tanner to infer how they would have been treated. Judge Tanner found that Castrilli had proved that secretaries would have been paid more had the occupation been a male-dominated one. He found a violation of the antidiscrimination principle.

But beyond these similarities between a simple discrimination case and a comparable worth case, there are also differences. Perhaps most obviously, the simple case considers discrimination based directly on the sex of a person, while in Castrilli's case the discrimination was based on the sex composition of an occupation, on the "sex" of the occupation. This apparent difference, however, is not significant, certainly not as a matter of theory. In theory, every individual woman in a female-dominated occupation is claiming that her wages are lower than they should be because of sex discrimination. Every woman in a comparable worth case, then, is in the same position as the woman in the simple case. One speaks of discrimination based on the sex of the occupation in a comparable worth case not because of theory but because of very practical proof problems. In the same way that one cannot decide whether a coin is balanced by flipping it only once, an individual woman in a comparable worth case cannot prove discrimination. The discrimination can be proved only by looking at how the employer has treated groups of women (and groups of men).[16] If it can be proved that the employer discriminated against a group of women, against a female-dominated occupation, the inference is strong that every individual member of that occupation suffered the discrimination. Even on this practical level, however, comparable worth cases are far from unique.[17] Even in my simple example of discrimination, the woman relied on group evidence to prove discrimination. She pointed to the employer's record of hiring women over a period of time to create an inference that the employer discriminated against her. That type of evidence is very commonly used in discrimination cases. Once again, then, comparable worth is not a radical or even an entirely new application of the antidiscrimination principle. Comparable worth merely applies well-accepted refinements of the principle to a new area.

The extent of the employer's responsibility for the discrimination is another apparent difference between a simple discrimination case and a comparable worth case. In the simple case, the employer has a great deal of control over the hiring decision. The employer is responsible in a direct sense for the decision not to hire the woman because of her sex. In a comparable worth case such as Julie Hayward's, the employer is less directly responsible for the discrimination. Cammell Laird did set Hayward's wages but under fairly stringent constraints. Cammell Laird was constrained by the market rate for cooks' wages (if it paid less than the market, it would have trouble hiring good cooks; if it paid more than the market, it would suffer competitively) and by Hayward's union (Cammell Laird had negotiated Hayward's wages with her union, which had agreed to them). If employers are less responsible for comparable worth discrimination, perhaps the courts should be more hesitant in holding employers liable for it than for other types of discrimination.[18]

Once again, however, the difference in employer responsibility is more apparent than real. In many simple cases, employers are no more directly responsible for discrimination than Cammell Laird was, and yet the courts hold them liable. Assume in our simple case, for example, that the employer operates an exclusive all-male club and that a woman applies for a bartender's position. In that situation the employer might decide against hiring the woman not because of his desire to discriminate but because he fears that he may lose customers who want the club to remain all male. Despite this constraint on the employer's action, the courts would almost certainly hold him liable for refusing to hire the woman because of her sex.[19] Thus, in simple cases, the courts hold employers liable for discrimination even if the employer is not solely responsible. Comparable worth cases would merely require the same result.

There is another sense, too, in which employer responsibility may be different in the simple case and in a comparable worth case. In the simple case, the employer consciously decides not to hire the woman because of her sex. Whether he does so because of his own desire to discriminate or because he was catering to his customers' desire to discriminate, the decision to discriminate was consciously made. In Hayward's case, Cammell Laird did not consciously intend to pay Hayward less because of her sex. Hayward was able to prove that she *was* paid less because of her sex, but the low pay resulted from the market wage rate for cooks, from negotiations between Cammell Laird and the union, and from a number of other factors. The low pay was not the result of a conscious decision by Cammell Laird to pay Hayward less because she was a woman. The implication is that employers are more responsible for conscious decisions to discriminate in simple cases than for unconscious decisions that result in discrimination in comparable worth cases and, as a result, courts should be more reluctant to hold employers liable in comparable worth cases.

This distinction between conscious and unconscious discrimination, however, also fails to distinguish comparable worth cases from other types of discrimination cases. The courts regularly hold employers liable for unconscious discrimination in simple cases. One of the two major theories of discrimination—the disparate impact model discussed earlier[20]—holds employers liable for discrimination even if they have no intention to discriminate at all, conscious or unconscious.[21] Moreover, even in disparate treatment cases in which discriminatory intent or motive is the determinative legal issue,[22] the courts may for practical reasons hold employers liable for unconscious discrimination.[23] A disparate treatment case can be proved by showing only that an employer treats men and women differently;[24] no direct evidence of conscious discrimination is required.[25] These results are not uncontroversial, but for our purposes we need not debate whether employers should or should not be held liable for unconscious discrimination. The point here is that comparable worth cases are no different from other discrimination cases in holding employers liable for unconscious discrimination. Comparable worth cases reach the same result on that issue as other types of discrimination cases.

Although this discussion of employer responsibility fails to distinguish comparable worth cases from other discrimination cases, it does provide insights into the scope of the antidiscrimination principle. The principle operates most directly to discourage employers from satisfying their own desires to discriminate. In my original example, the antidiscrimination principle makes it illegal for an employer to refuse to hire the woman because he does not want to have any female employees. The antidiscrimination principle, though, has a much broader application than that. It also operates to discourage employers from acting to satisfy the desire of others to discriminate. In the all-male club example, the principle applies to discourage the employer from acting to satisfy the discriminatory desires of the club's customers. If an employer has an all-male work force with a desire to remain all male, the principle would apply to discourage an employer from catering to the discriminatory desires of his employees.

Comparable worth cases depend on this broad application of the antidiscrimination principle. Often, perhaps usually, the employer in a comparable worth case is acting not on his own desire to discriminate but on the desires of others to discriminate. Workers, for example, are usually concerned about how their wages relate to the wages of other workers for the same employer,[26] and their notions of a fair relationship may be influenced by discrimination. As a result, if an employer pays male employees (say, painters) more than female employees (say, cooks) to satisfy the painters' discriminatory notion of what a fair relationship is between painters' and cooks' wages, the employer violates the anti-discrimination principle. He has catered to the discriminatory desires of his male employees. Or if an employer pays the "market" rate for cooks (the wage rate that other employers are paying cooks) and that market rate results from discrimination by the other employers—whether it is direct or a result of catering to the discriminatory desires of their employees or customers—the employer would violate the antidiscrimination principle. This is certainly a broad application of the antidiscrimination principle, but it is precisely the application that is made in other well-accepted types of discrimination cases.

As the antidiscrimination principle is applied more broadly, problems associated with remedying violations of the principle become more difficult. In the simple case, if the employer refuses to hire the woman because of his own desire to discriminate, it seems fair to require the employer to compensate the woman, to give her a job and to pay her for the wages she lost. But should the employer be required to compensate the woman himself when he has refused to hire the woman because of his customers' desire to discriminate? If he is, then those who harbored the objectionable desire to discriminate (the customers) avoid liability, while the employer who did not have a desire to discriminate bears the entire burden. Nevertheless, the cases require the employer to provide compensation, regardless of the source of the desire to discriminate.[27] The reason for that result is primarily practical. The cases are between an employer and a woman who is claiming discrimination. The customers, or whoever else might be the source of the desire to discriminate, are not parties. As between the employer and the woman, it is clear that the employer should bear the burden of the discrimination; he has at least participated in the discrimination to some extent (even if that was "only" to cater to his customers' discriminatory desires), while she was a completely innocent victim. The employer, perhaps, should be permitted later to recoup the costs of compensating the woman from his customers, but employers simply have not filed those cases—for fairly obvious reasons.

This same type of remedial problem arises in comparable worth cases, and once again the result should be the same as in other types of discrimination cases. In Hayward's case, for example, Cammell Laird might have claimed that it did not have any desire to discriminate against cooks. Any discrimination against cooks arose because painters had discriminatory attitudes and made sure, with the help of their union, that they were paid more than cooks, or because Cammell Laird relied on the market and other employers discriminated against cooks so the market wage rate for cooks happened to be low. As a result, Cammell Laird might have claimed that it would not be fair to hold the company liable for discrimination when the source of the desire to discriminate lay elsewhere. But the case was between Cammell Laird and Julie Hayward, and between those two, Cammell Laird should bear responsibility for the discrimination. As in other cases, perhaps Cammell Laird should be permitted to recoup its costs from others, but that process would come later and in other cases.

In summary, the Hayward and Castrilli cases guide us toward a theory of comparable worth. The theory, generally stated, is that wage rates and other employment practices are illegal to the extent that they would have been different but for the sex composition of an occupation. In the usual case—like Helen Castrilli's—people working in a female-dominated occupation will claim that they would have been paid more but for the fact that most of the people in that occupation were women. Job evaluation studies will often be used as proof, but other types of evidence—such as overt discriminatory statements or economic studies—are also relevant. To the extent women like Helen Castrilli can prove they would have been paid more but for the sex composition of their occupation, employers should have to compensate women, just as they must in other types of cases even though the employer may not be the source of the desire to discriminate.

In theory, then, comparable worth is not an unwarranted and dangerous extension of the antidiscrimination principle. Rather, it is in the mainstream of antidiscrimination law. The antidiscrimination principle encompasses comparable worth, just as it encompasses the simplest and least controversial of discrimination claims. Comparable worth, in theory, should be as widely accepted as other applications of the antidiscrimination principle.

10
The Effect of Comparable Worth on the Wage Gap

COMPARABLE WORTH HAS become an issue in the United States and Britain (and around the world) because of perceptions of wage discrimination against women. Helen Castrilli looked out her window and thought she saw discrimination, and Julie Hayward thought she heard it when she talked with her friends. The two women began their cases because of these perceptions of wage discrimination. In a broader sense, perceptions of wage discrimination are based, in large part, on the wage gap between men and women. It is a simple and undisputed fact that men earn more than women. For decades before 1980, full-time working women in the United States earned about 60 percent of what full-time working men earned.[1] Since 1980 the ratio has gone up significantly, for reasons that are still unclear,[2] but women are still paid only about 65 percent of what men are paid.[3] Men also earn more than women in Great Britain, but there the percentage has fluctuated a bit. Since 1945 the ratio of female-to-male wages has been as low as 58 percent (in 1968) and as high as 71 percent (in 1977 and 1978).[4]

These wage gaps, of course, are not peculiar to the United States and Britain. They are found in virtually every country in the world (see table 10.1 for examples),[5] including socialist and Third World countries, and are the single most important reason that comparable worth has become a major issue worldwide. Comparable worth promises to address wage discrimination against women and, indirectly, to narrow the wage gap between men and women. But the extent to which it can narrow the wage gap is very difficult to assess. The wage gap is an unruly beast. Comparable worth's promise to tame it may be impossible to keep.

The wage gap is usually summarized by a single number. As men-

TABLE 10.1. Female-Male Wage Ratios in Selected Countries, 1980

Country	Ratio
Australia	75%
France	71
Germany	72
Israel	78
Italy	83
Japan	54
Netherlands	71
Sweden	90
Soviet Union	70

Source: Jacob Mincer, "Intercountry Comparisons of Labor Force Trends and of Related Developments," *Journal of Labor Economics* 3 (Jan. 1985), table 3.

tioned above, for example, the wage gap in the United States has been about 40 percent for decades.[6] (Even though the current gap in the United States is about 35 percent, I use the 40 percent figure because most of the research on which this discussion is based was conducted when the gap was 40 percent. It is unlikely that using the 35 percent figure would significantly change the analysis.)[7] But that single number masks as much as it reveals. The wage gap, and the ability of comparable worth to close it, can be better understood when it is viewed as a composite of a number of wage gaps, instead of as a single number. There is a wage gap caused by discrimination, another one caused by differences in the amount of time worked, and so on. Comparable worth proposes to close only one of the wage gaps, the gap caused by one type of sex discrimination.

One of the smaller gaps contributing to the composite 40 percent wage gap is caused by differences in the amount of time that men and women work.[8] The 40 percent figure compares the annual earnings of full-time male and female workers.[9] Men, however, spend more time working each year than women do.[10] Men work more weeks each year, and they work more hours each week (they accept more overtime hours, and they more often have second jobs). Thus, the composite wage gap, in effect, compares women who work thirty-five hours per week with men who work forty hours per week. If the female-male wage ratio is adjusted to compare men and women working the same number of hours, the ratio is about 72 percent.[11] Stated another way, about 30 percent of the composite wage gap between men and women (or 12 percentage points of the 40 percentage point difference) is composed of the wage gap caused by differences in the number of hours worked.[12] This portion of the composite wage gap, then, is not caused by sex discrimination, at least not very directly, and would not be addressed by comparable worth.

Another portion of the composite wage gap may be caused by differences in the productivity of men and women. Employers legitimately pay more for workers who can produce ten widgets per hour than for workers who can produce only eight per hour. If men are more productive than women, if they can produce more widgets per hour than women, a portion of the composite wage gap may be caused by that, rather than by sex discrimination. Although this seems like a productive way to analyze the composite wage gap, it is very difficult to measure productivity. How does one compare the productivity of a secretary like Helen Castrilli with the productivity of a campus police officer? Or the productivity of a cook with that of a painter?[13] Economists have dealt with this problem by looking not at productivity directly but at the skills people bring to jobs. The assumption is that people who bring more skills to a job are more productive. Measuring skills is no easy task either, but at least some crude estimates can be made. People learn skills in school, so more education should mean greater skill. People also learn skills on the job, so tenure in a particular job and length of time in the labor market generally should also mean greater skill.[14]

Economists who have attempted to measure the relative productivity of men and women in this way have found that men as a group are more productive than women as a group—in fact, quite a bit more productive. A number of studies indicate that about 40–45 percent of the composite wage gap between men and women (or 18 percentage points of the 40 percentage point difference) is caused by this difference in productivity.[15] Hence, another wage gap contributing to the composite wage gap is caused by this factor rather than by discrimination.[16]

Still another portion of the composite wage gap may be caused by differences in the working conditions of the jobs held by men and women. Helen Castrilli worked in an office that was heated in the winter and cooled in the summer. The campus police officers often worked outside, in the rain or snow. If the two jobs were exactly the same in every other respect (which they were not), the state, it seems, should have been permitted to pay the campus police officers more to compensate for this difference in working conditions. (Recall that one of the state's criticisms of Willis's job evaluation studies was that they did not give sufficient weight to differences in working conditions.) Economists, once again, have studied this factor. They have found that women disproportionately hold jobs with better working conditions, and that this factor explains another 2 to 4 percentage points of the composite wage gap.[17]

So far, then, the composite wage gap appears to be composed of several smaller wage gaps. Although all of the numbers are subject to considerable uncertainty, a gap of about 12 percentage points is caused by differences in the amount of time worked by men and women; a gap of about 18 percentage points is caused by differences in the productivity of men and women; and a gap of 2–4 percentage points is caused by differences in the conditions under which men and women work. None of these factors are caused, very directly at least, by discrimination. As a result, even if all of the remaining wage gap is due to sex discrimination and even if comparable worth were to correct all of that, only about 5 to 10 percentage points of the wage gap between men and women would be eliminated.

Comparable worth, however, would *not* eliminate all of the remaining wage gap, for several reasons. First, comparable worth directly addresses only that portion of the wage gap that results from the practice of paying too little for work that has become identified as women's work.[18] Therefore, comparable worth would not correct for all of the wage gap attributable to sex discrimination but only for that portion due to this particular type of sex discrimination. The studies indicate that if this type of discrimination—wage discrimination against female-dominated occupations—were eliminated throughout the economy, the wage gap would close by perhaps 5 or 6 percentage points.[19]

Even those fairly modest figures, however, may overestimate the effect of comparable worth on the wage gap, because comparable worth would not correct for this type of discrimination throughout the economy. Comparable worth would correct only for discrimination between employees of a single employer. Helen Castrilli compared her wages with those of other employees of the state of Washington; Julie Hayward compared her wages with those of other employees of Cammell Laird. But some portion of the wage gap is caused by interemployer, not intraemployer, wage differences between men and women workers. Women tend to work for lower-paying employers than men and in lower-paying industries.[20] Because comparable worth does not address wage differences *between* employers, a wage gap would persist even if all employers paid their own cooks and painters equally, because women work disproportionately for employers and industries that pay cooks *and* painters less. A study that accounts for this factor estimated that the implementation of comparable worth would close the wage gap by only 3 to 6 percentage points.[21]

Comparable worth would not apply throughout the economy for another reason, too. Comparable worth is limited by the reach of the laws upon which it is based. In the United States, the reach of comparable worth is limited by the reach of Title VII of the Civil Rights Act of 1964, which applies only to employers with fifteen or more employees.[22] Only about 20 percent of all employers in the United States employ that many persons (although those employers do account for 85 percent of all employees in the United States).[23] As a result, any portion of the wage gap attributable to small employers would not be corrected by comparable worth.[24] A study that attempted to adjust for this additional limitation on the ability of comparable worth to affect the wage ratio estimated that comparable worth would close the wage gap by only 1 to 2 percentage points.[25]

This sort of analysis has led one influential commentator—Paul Weiler of Harvard University—to reject comparable worth as a legal doctrine worth pursuing. He estimated that comparable worth, even if broadly implemented and universally enforced, would close the composite wage gap by only "two or three percentage points." With such a limited potential return, he said, "we should be leery about embarking upon such a novel and risky venture."[26]

But the promise of comparable worth is not so limited as this analysis would suggest.[27] In fact, the effect of comparable worth on the female-male wage ratio is likely to be much greater than "two or three percentage points." Moreover, even if that estimate were correct, it would not undermine the importance and viability of comparable worth as a legal doctrine.

The estimate of 2 or 3 percentage points is an underestimate. It defines only the minimum effect of comparable worth. The actual effect, although very difficult to predict with precision, is almost certain to be greater. The two or three percentage points estimate was obtained by viewing the wage gap as a composite of a number of small wage gaps. Several of the small wage gaps are not caused directly by sex discrimination, and others would not be directly addressed by comparable worth. When those wage gaps are subtracted from the 40 percent composite wage gap, the remaining gap is quite small. Ironically, however, viewing the wage gap as a series of unconnected small gaps can be as misleading as viewing the wage gap as an undifferentiated gap of 40 percent.

The small wage gaps have dynamic relationships with one another. A change in any one of them is quite likely to cause change in some or all of the others. Comparable worth would create a change in one of the wage gaps—the one caused by sex discrimination. Even if the change in that wage gap were only 2 or 3 percentage points, as predicted by Weiler, the change would be likely to cause changes in the other gaps contributing to the composite wage gap. Therefore, an assessment of the likely effects of comparable worth on the wage gap must consider both the direct effect of eliminating the gap caused by discrimination *and* the indirect effect of that gap on the other gaps that contribute to the composite wage gap.

Consider, for example, the indirect effect of comparable worth on the wage gap caused by differences in the amount of time men and women work. Men earn more than women in part because they work more hours than women in the paid labor market. The number of hours one works, however, is affected by the amount of pay one receives. A decision to work is a decision to allocate more time to work and less to nonwork activities such as leisure or household tasks.[28] As an economic matter, a person—male or female—should decide to work only if the money (or other form of compensation) received for working exceeds the value that person places on having time for nonwork activities. If comparable worth increases the pay of women and the value of nonwork activities stays the same, one would expect women to work more hours. The pay for working should exceed the value placed on nonwork activities more often. Because comparable worth would not increase the pay of men, the allocation of time between work and nonwork activities for men should stay about the same. As a result, the difference in the amount of time worked by men and women should narrow and with it the wage gap caused by that difference.[29]

Comparable worth may also affect the portion of the wage gap caused by differences in the productivity of men and women. Men are more productive than women, at least as measured by the skills men and women bring to their jobs. But skills do not come free. Rather, people invest time or money or both to acquire skills that are valued by employers. People invest in schooling to learn skills, or they invest time in a job to learn a skill. The level of investment one is willing to make depends to some extent on the return one expects on the investment. As an economic matter, a person should be willing to make an investment in better skills only if he or she expects to make enough money with the skills to pay for the investment.[30] Thus, a person who expects to earn more in the future should be more willing to invest in acquiring skills. It makes sense, then, that men are more productive than women. Because of the wage gap, men expect to earn more than women in the future, so they are more willing to make investments to acquire skills. Comparable worth, then, should tend to narrow differences in the productivity of men and women. Because the portion of the wage gap caused by discrimination would be eliminated, there would be less difference in the expectations of men and women about future earnings and hence less difference in their decisions to invest in skills.[31] Once again, comparable worth should result indirectly in a narrowing of the composite wage gap by narrowing the portion of the gap caused by differences in productivity between men and women.[32]

As these examples illustrate, comparable worth should have an indirect effect on all the other wage gaps. For several reasons, however, the dynamic relationships between the small wage gaps make it difficult to predict the overall effect of comparable worth on the composite wage gap. For one thing, comparable worth may often cause the other wage gaps both to narrow and to widen. The wage gap caused by differences in time worked, for example, may narrow as discussed above, but it may also widen if women are paid more—employers, for example, may attempt to reduce the work hours of the more highly paid female workers.[33] The net effect of comparable worth must be determined by weighing the uncertain narrowing effects against the uncertain widening effects.

The dynamism of the relationships between the wage gaps also makes it difficult to predict the effects of comparable worth. Comparable worth will narrow the wage gap caused by discrimination, which may narrow the wage gaps caused by differences in time worked and in productivity. Narrowing the wage gap caused by differences in time worked, though, should also narrow the gap caused by differences in productivity—and vice versa. Calculating the total effect of comparable worth involves considering the effect of changes in each of the wage gaps on each of the other wage gaps over time.

Finally, predictions are difficult because our knowledge of the relationships between the wage gaps operates principally on a theoretical level. The wage gap in the United States has been quite stable, so the effects of changes have been difficult to test empirically.[34]

Despite these difficulties, there is some empirical evidence that efforts to eliminate the wage gap caused by sex discrimination would close the composite wage gap by more than 2 or 3 percentage points.[35] Several

TABLE 10.2. Female-Male Wage Ratios in Selected Countries, 1960–80

Country	Ratio		
	1960	1980	Change
Australia	59%	75%	16%
Netherlands	60	71	11
New Zealand	70[a]	79[b]	9
Sweden	72	90	18

Sources: Jacob Mincer, "Intercountry Comparisons of Labor Force Trends and of Related Developments," Journal of Labor Economics 3 (Jan. 1985), table 3; Equal Pay Implementation in New Zealand (Wellington: P. D. Hasselberg, 1979), 16, table 1.
[a] 1972
[b] 1978

countries have attempted to eliminate the wage gap caused by sex discrimination. Although the efforts in each of the countries have varied and the efforts in the countries are different in significant respects from the methods of implementing comparable worth that might be undertaken in the United States and Britain,[36] the efforts in every case have closed the composite wage gap between men and women by more than 2 or 3 percentage points.[37] In the four countries that "come closest to subscribing to the comparable worth theory,"[38] the reductions in the wage gap ranged from 9 to 18 percentage points (see table 10.2).[39] Several studies of the experiences of these countries indicate that narrowing the wage gap caused by sex discrimination also tended to cause a narrowing of the wage gaps caused by other factors.[40] The broad implication from the foreign experience is that even if the wage gap caused directly by sex discrimination is only 2 or 3 percentage points, the effect on the other wage gaps of eliminating that gap creates a total gain of considerably more than 2 or 3 percentage points.[41]

The 2 or 3 percentage points estimate of the likely effect of comparable worth on the composite wage gap, then, is an underestimate. It considers only the direct effect of eliminating or reducing that portion of the wage gap caused by sex discrimination. Eliminating that gap, however, would also close the composite gap indirectly because of its effect on wage gaps caused by other factors. Although it is very difficult to predict the extent of these indirect effects, the evidence from other countries indicates that the overall decrease in the wage gap would be substantially greater than 2 or 3 percentage points.[42]

Comparable worth would be worth pursuing, however, even if the low estimate were accurate. The 2 or 3 percentage points estimate is an estimate of the effect on the entire economy of eliminating the wage gap caused by sex discrimination. But as Helen Castrilli's case illustrates, the effect on particular workers may be much greater (or much less). In Castrilli's case, based on Willis's assessment of the effect of sex discrimination on wages, some female-dominated occupations could eventually receive wage increases of 40 percent or more, while others—such as nursing care consulting and school food service supervising—would receive no increases. One consequence, then, of rejecting comparable worth because its effect on the entire economy would be minimal would be to deny relief even to people whose wages are quite severely depressed because of sex discrimination.[43]

This consequence is unacceptable. It is unacceptable to permit severe discrimination against one group because other groups suffer little or no discrimination. Discrimination against African-Americans, for example, would not be acceptable even if it could be shown that the discrimination had only a minor effect on the national economy. In our society, race and sex discrimination are too distasteful to permit that result; the antidiscrimination principle is too important to be limited in that fashion.[44]

Indeed, the argument that comparable worth should be rejected because it would close the overall wage gap by "only" 2 or 3 percentage points misconceives the primary thrust of comparable worth as a legal theory. The goal of narrowing the wage gap between men and women is merely a by-product of the central goal of comparable worth, the goal of eliminating discrimination based on the sex composition of occupations. One corollary of that central goal is discussed above—comparable worth can be valuable and worth pursuing even if it would have only a limited effect on the overall wage gap, because it permits isolated but severe discrimination to be addressed. Another corollary—relevant in the United States, where the overall wage gap has been closing during the 1980s—is that a narrowing of the wage gap does not necessarily mean that the central goal of comparable worth is being achieved. The wage gap may be closing for reasons other than a reduction in discrimination based on the sex composition of occupations, leaving the central goal of comparable worth as distant as it was before the wage gap narrowed.[45] Or it may be that even though the wage gap is closing in part because of a reduction in discrimination, the discrimination is not receding evenly; in that case, comparable worth could serve to extend and speed the closing of the gap.[46]

There is another reason that comparable worth would be worth pursuing as a legal doctrine even if the estimate of 2 or 3 percentage points were accurate. The estimate is crucial only if the law is viewed solely in instrumental terms, only if comparable worth is solely a mechanism to increase the relative pay of women by reducing sex-based wage discrimination. But comparable worth is more than that. All legal doctrines are more than that. Comparable worth and other legal doctrines are also an expression of public values, of societal ideals.[47] Just as *Brown v. Board of Education*[48] generated and nurtured a commitment to racial equality that far transcended the narrow instrumental effect of the decision, an acceptance of comparable worth as a legal doctrine would recognize sexual equality as an important societal ideal and value. Comparable worth is justified as a statement of the goal and of our commitment to pursuit of that goal, even if it is incapable of coaxing a recalcitrant reality into line.

11

Practical Limitations

THE CASES OF Helen Castrilli and Julie Hayward were both based on the same simple premise: it should be illegal to pay women less because they work in female-dominated occupations. The premise is firmly based in the antidiscrimination principle, and it promises, if widely applied, to close the female-male wage gap by at least 2 to 3 percentage points and perhaps by much more. One of the clearest messages from the two cases, however, is that that simple premise is very difficult to apply in practice.

Job evaluations, the most important evidence in most comparable worth cases, are a major source of these difficulties. They certainly were for both Helen Castrilli and Julie Hayward. A major issue in the two cases, as in almost all comparable worth cases, was the extent to which job evaluation studies can be relied on as proof of discrimination.

The use of job evaluations in comparable worth cases is not troublesome as a matter of theory. Theoretically, a plaintiff in a comparable worth case first evaluates male-dominated jobs (or, at least, non-female-dominated jobs) to determine how the employer compensates the relevant job factors for those jobs, to determine, for example, how the employer compensates high levels of skill or adverse working conditions. The compensation structure for male-dominated jobs, whatever it might be for that particular employer, is used as the basis for comparison on the assumption that the structure for male-dominated jobs is not affected by sex discrimination. The plaintiff then examines female-dominated jobs to determine whether the employer compensates job factors for those jobs in the same way. Theoretically, then, comparable worth does not affect the compensation structure for men at all. It accepts it as a given. What comparable worth requires is that the same compensation structure used for the male-dominated jobs also be applied to the female-dominated jobs.[1]

The practical problems with using job evaluations in comparable worth cases, however, are numerous. Willis's job evaluation in Castrilli's case was fairly typical. Willis first defined the job factors to be evaluated: (1) knowledge and skills, (2) mental demands, (3) accountability, and (4) working conditions. He assigned a maximum number of points each job could receive on each factor. Then he described and evaluated each of the benchmark jobs to decide how many points it should receive on each factor. The points the job received on the four factors were totaled, so in the end each job received a ranking indicated by a single number. Willis used that number to determine how much jobs should be paid.

Reliability is a major practical problem with job evaluations, such as Willis's. Reliability is consistency. If job evaluations were done repeatedly on the same jobs, would the results be the same? There are many points in the job evaluation process when decisions might be made which would change the ultimate ranking of the jobs. First, the number of job factors may vary. The Midwest Industrial Management Association uses eleven factors in its evaluation system; the federal government uses nine; and Willis in Castrilli's case used four. Second, the maximum number of points assigned to each factor may vary. In Castrilli's case the state claimed that Willis effectively undervalued "male" jobs by assigning too few points to the working conditions factor. Willis himself now assigns more points to that factor than he did for the Washington State studies. Third, the descriptions of the jobs being evaluated may vary. Willis used surveys and interviews to develop his job descriptions. Other evaluators might use different techniques. Finally, and most obviously, the number of points assigned to each job on each factor (within the predetermined maximum) may vary. That assignment was made in Washington State by a committee. A different committee might have made different judgments; even the same committee probably would have made slightly different assignments if it had evaluated the jobs a second time. With all of these possibilities for unreliability, it should not be surprising that the studies that have been done have found that job evaluation studies are not very reliable.[2]

The attempt to translate job evaluation points into wage rates poses another practical problem. Willis used a statistical technique known as regression analysis to do that. He took the actual wages paid to each occupation in Washington and the job evaluation points his study had assigned to each job and, using regression analysis, determined how much the state would pay each job if it based its wage decisions on his job evaluation. He found that each job would be paid $518 plus $2.51 times the number of job evaluation points received by the job.[3] The practical problem is that Willis's mathematical formula is not the only formula that could have been used. Henry Aaron and Cameran Lougy of the Brookings Institution list *twenty* formulas that could be used to translate job evaluation points into wage rates. All of them are acceptable from a statistical standpoint (although some, of course, are more acceptable than others), but they yield different results, sometimes strikingly different results. Aaron and Lougy applied their formulas to the data from Washington State and found that certain registered nurses, for example, would receive a 15 percent wage increase under one formula and a 68 percent increase under another.[4] Even if the job evaluation points themselves were reliable, then, translating them into wage rates would present practical problems.

These practical problems are significant. If job evaluations are not reliable and if job evaluation points cannot be translated into wage rates, the principal form of evidence in comparable worth cases is undermined. In a broad sense, the issue is whether the problems are so severe that comparable worth should be rejected as a legal theory, or whether the problems can be dealt with short of rejecting comparable worth. (As a theoretical matter, of course, it is absurd to reject comparable worth as a legal theory simply because one type of evidence that might be used to prove a violation is unreliable. As a practical matter, however, job evaluation studies are such important evidence in comparable worth cases that if they could not be used, the development of comparable worth would be severely hampered.)

The potential unreliability of job evaluation studies poses two questions. First, should plaintiffs be able to use job evaluations at all as evidence of sex discrimination in comparable worth cases? Second, if they can be used as evidence, what should the standard of reliability be? What weight should courts give to job evaluation studies?

If the first question is viewed in context, the answer is clear. Job evaluation studies should be available as evidence in comparable worth cases. All cases in litigation—not just comparable worth cases—are decided on the basis of incomplete information and in the face of uncertainty. Cases are often decided on the basis of somewhat unreliable evidence because even though unreliable, it is the best evidence available.[5] The issue of whether somewhat unreliable evidence should be admissible, then, is faced every day in the legal system. Generally, such evidence is admissible, and the job of the decision maker is to consider it along with the other evidence in the case and to decide how much weight should be given to it.[6] Job evaluations in comparable worth cases should be treated the same way. They should be admitted as evidence but scrutinized closely to determine how much weight they should be given.[7]

The precise weight to be given job evaluations in comparable worth cases is not so easy to define. Current law on this issue in Britain and the United States is illustrated by the Hayward and Castrilli cases. In Britain, the job evaluation is given nearly conclusive weight; the standard of reliability is determined solely by the job evaluation expert who is appointed in each case. As in Julie Hayward's case, the expert applies his or her own notion of reliability in conducting the study. That notion is then subject to only very limited judicial review. The expert's evaluation can be overturned only if he or she has "gone badly wrong."[8] In the United States, in contrast, job evaluations are given very little weight; they are held to such a high standard of reliability that they are deprived of all evidentiary value. In Helen Castrilli's case, the Ninth Circuit Court of Appeals held that job evaluation studies, no matter how reliable, were insufficient to prove a violation of the antidiscrimination principle.[9]

Even though the weight given to job evaluations in the two countries is diametrically different, a similarity in the approaches of the two countries guides us, if not to the appropriate weight to be accorded job evaluations, at least to the appropriate *process* for determining that issue. The approaches of Britain and the United States are similar in that the primary decision makers—the industrial tribunal in Britain and the district court judge in the United States—are not permitted to decide what weight is to be given a job evaluation study. In Britain, job evaluations are presumed to be reliable as a matter of law; in the United States, they are presumed to be unreliable as a matter of law. As a result, in both countries, all job evaluations are treated as equally reliable or unreliable, and more fine-tuned standards for assessing reliability cannot be developed.

The primary decision maker in comparable worth cases should determine the weight to be placed on job evaluation studies. A principal role of the decision maker in lawsuits is to weigh the evidence presented, and job evaluations are simply one type of evidence in comparable worth cases. As cases are decided over time, as some reject job evaluation studies because of unreliability and others accept them, standards of reliability will develop. The standards will develop out of a careful examination of a wide variety of evaluations in a wide variety of situations. The standards, then, will undoubtedly be richer than any simple legal rule can be. It is likely that the standards will recognize that some evaluations are fairly reliable and others less so. It may be that the standards will demand different degrees of reliability, depending on the strength of other evidence of discrimination in the case.[10] Even if the standards ended up being the same as the current standards, however, this process for determining standards is preferable. It would permit job evaluations to be assessed in the way that other evidence in lawsuits is assessed, and it would permit standards to be developed in the context of several rich factual disputes instead of at the rarefied level of abstract legal doctrine.[11]

Aaron and Lougy agree that litigants should be able to use job evaluation studies in comparable worth cases and that the studies should be given some, but not conclusive, weight. They argue, however, that the studies should be used only to determine whether discrimination exists. Because of the problem of translating job evaluation points into wage rates, Aaron and Lougy argue that job evaluations should not be used to set new wage rates after a finding of discrimination.[12] They do not explain, though, how courts are to establish new wage rates when the old ones are shown to be discriminatory. If the courts cannot rely on job evaluation studies, presumably they will either have to leave the wage rates unchanged (which would be unacceptable, because it would mean the rates that have been declared discriminatory would continue) or change them on the basis of other evidence, which is likely to be as unreliable as the job evaluation studies. Once again, the solution is not to exclude the evidence but to recognize its shortcomings. After a court has decided that a wage structure is discriminatory, it should decide upon the new wage rates by looking at both the job evaluation study—including alternative ways of translating the points into wage rates—and all other available evidence. That solution is not perfect,[13] but litigation is not designed for a perfect world.[14]

Determining the appropriate role for job evaluation studies, however, does not begin to exhaust the practical implementation problems of comparable worth litigation. The multitude of problems that remain range from relatively narrow issues of procedure[15] or statutory construction[16] to issues that go to the very heart of this type of litigation.[17]

The cases of Julie Hayward and Helen Castrilli, though they do not provide much guidance on how these issues should be resolved technically, can place the issues in broad perspective.

Helen Castrilli's case was typical of comparable worth cases in the United States. It was very large, with an estimated 15,500 plaintiffs at the beginning and nearly 60,000 at the end. And it was very expensive. The attorneys' fees for Castrilli's side alone were more than $1 million. The procedures in the United States permit class actions; they permit plaintiffs to join together to pursue complex cases. In that way, the costs of the lawsuit can be spread out over a large number of people. In Castrilli's case, of course, the union paid for the suit—another mechanism for distributing the costs among all those who might benefit.

The size of comparable worth cases in the United States permits the parties to litigate vigorously the complex issues raised. If there is a problem with the reliability of a job evaluation study or with the statistical analysis, the parties can, as they did in Castrilli's case, bring in experts from Washington, D.C., and Texas to assist the court in resolving the problem. Vigorous litigation will help resolve the difficult issues in each particular case and should result in the development of better guidelines for future cases. Standards by which to determine the reliability of job evaluation studies, for example, are more likely to be correct if the parties have sufficient resources to ventilate the issue fully.

The size of comparable worth cases, however, also creates problems. A single employee and employees of small employers may not have the financial resources to challenge discriminatory wage rates.[18] Small employers whose employees are represented by a union may not have the financial resources to oppose the union in a comparable worth case even if their wage rates are not discriminatory. Moreover, size increases the complexity of cases that are very complex in any event. This was especially evident in Castrilli's case during the settlement negotiations.[19] The procedures in the United States, then, favor large cases and a thorough consideration of the issues raised by comparable worth, even though that approach has significant shortcomings.

Great Britain, as Julie Hayward's case illustrates, has opted for procedures that balance the considerations in almost exactly the opposite direction. England has established a procedure designed to be quick, simple, and inexpensive.[20] It is designed to permit individual employees such as Julie Hayward or small groups of employees to challenge their wage rates. The referral to a nonexpert "expert" (who is paid by the government) and the limitations on challenging the expert's report[21] permit the cases to be handled more efficiently. The procedures also result, however, in a less carefully considered decision. Inquiries into the reliability of job evaluation systems, for example, are extremely limited in the normal case in Britain; the industrial tribunal is to uphold the expert's evaluation unless he "has gone badly wrong."[22] Consequently, the decision in an individual case is more likely to be wrong and the guidance provided to future cases more limited than in the United States.

The widely divergent procedural approaches of the United States and Britain do not result from differences in the general goal of comparable worth litigation. In both countries the general goal is to achieve the substantive goal of comparable worth—to eliminate wage discrimination based on the sex composition of occupations—with a high degree of accuracy and at the lowest possible cost. The general goal, however, contains internal conflicts. There is tension among the goal's three factors—achieving the substantive goal, with accuracy, and at low cost. The divergent procedural approaches arise because the two countries reconcile the conflicts within the general goal differently.

Evaluating the approaches of the two countries in an attempt to determine the optimal procedural approach is very difficult, perhaps impossible. Consider, for example, the goals of accuracy and low cost. A decision that an employer engages in this type of sex discrimination is more likely to be correct if more money is spent to investigate the employer's wage-setting practices, to evaluate the reliability of the job evaluation, and so on. The goal of accuracy, then, is in direct conflict with the goal of low cost. In the abstract, it is difficult to determine the appropriate balance between them.[23]

The problem of determining the appropriate balance, however, is not limited to abstract considerations. Finding the appropriate trade-off between accuracy and cost is difficult even as a practical matter. It is not clear, for example, which of the two procedures we have considered—the American or the British—is less expensive and which more accurate. On the cost side, the American procedure permits plaintiffs to pool their resources, so more money is likely to be spent in a single case. The costs to plaintiffs in Castrilli's case were more than $1 million; in Hayward's case, about £50,000. But the cost *per person* may be less in America than in Britain. Castrilli's case involved, at a minimum, some 15,000 plaintiffs, so the cost per person was much lower in her case than in Hayward's.

The accuracy issue presents the flip side of this analysis of costs. The American procedure is likely to be more accurate if the focus is the entire plaintiff group; it permits a more careful examination of the employer's wage-setting practices in general and of the overall reliability of the job evaluation. The British procedure, however, is more likely to be accurate if the focus is on any particular plaintiff. The job evaluation in Hayward's case examined only her job and the jobs of the men; hence, it was more likely to be accurate than the evaluation of Castrilli's job, which was considered only as a very minor part of a much broader job evaluation.

The most important goal of comparable worth litigation, of course, is to further the substantive goal of comparable worth: to eliminate wage discrimination based on the sex composition of occupations and, by doing that, to narrow indirectly the wage gap between men and women.[24] The Hayward and Castrilli cases shed some light on the ability of comparable worth litigation to further that goal.

The cases indicate first that, despite the hopes of people like Helen Castrilli, litigation by itself is unlikely to have a significant *direct* effect on the overall wage gap between men and women. The recoveries in these cases were simply too small to have a meaningful effect on the overall wage gap. That is obviously true in Julie Hayward's case, in which the recovery extended only to Hayward herself, but it was also true in Washington State. In fiscal year 1987, the year in which the settlement required the largest infusion of money ($25 million), the new money added, at most, 1.5 cents to the average weekly paycheck of full-time working women in the United States. A change in the overall wage gap from the Washington State settlement can be detected only if the gap is calculated to three decimal places.[25] When those limited effects are combined with the high costs of the two lawsuits—which means that only a very limited number of such suits can be brought—the unavoidable conclusion is that comparable worth litigation can have only a very minor direct effect on the overall wage gap.

The effect of litigation on the wage gap, however, is not limited to wage changes that are the direct result of litigation. Litigation may also have a deterrent effect. It may encourage (or not encourage) employers who are engaging in this type of discrimination to eliminate it without litigation, either unilaterally or through discussions with their employees or unions. Thus, the substantive goal of the law may be pursued in the shadow of the law as well as in its direct glare. The procedures used to enforce the law may affect the length of the law's shadow.[26]

The effect of the British and American procedures on the shadow of the law is not clear, but neither seems likely to provide much shade.

British lawyers looking at the American procedure argue that it creates no shadow at all for small, nonunionized employers. Those employers have no incentive to comply voluntarily with the substantive goal of comparable worth because the expense of litigation virtually immunizes them from suit.[27] American lawyers looking at the British procedure argue that it creates only a very short shadow even for large employers. Because employees cannot group together to sue large employers, the employers may decide to litigate individual cases as they arise rather than to make broader, voluntary changes in their wage-setting practices.[28] These doubts about the deterrent effect of comparable worth litigation are supported, if not confirmed, by the broader experiences of the two countries. The female-to-male wage ratio in Great Britain has not improved since the Equal Pay Regulations became effective in January 1984.[29] In the United States, although the wage ratio has been improving,[30] no one contends that comparable worth lawsuits have been a contributing factor.[31]

To say that litigation alone is not likely to be an effective mechanism for narrowing the wage gap between men and women caused by discrimination, however, is not to say that the wage gap cannot be effectively addressed. It can be narrowed, but litigation is too subtle an instrument to do the job. Blunter instruments can be and have been effective.[32] In Australia and Sweden, significant reductions in the wage gap have been achieved, not through litigation, but through other approaches.[33] Even in Great Britain and the United States, where comparable worth litigation has garnered the most publicity, other approaches seem to have been more effective in closing the wage gap. In Great Britain, a substantial reduction in the wage gap occurred in the mid-1970s largely because of an across-the-board requirement that the wage rates applying to female-only job classifications be raised to the lowest wage rate applying to other job classifications.[34] In the United States, increases in the minimum wage correlate with decreases in the wage gap,[35] so policies affecting low-wage occupations generally may provide effective and inexpensive mechanisms for addressing the problem. In addition, political pressure at the state and local level to increase the relative wages of female-dominated occupations in the public sector seems to have had some effect in that sector,[36] and one would expect some spillover into the private sector.[37]

Comparable worth litigation should not be viewed, then, primarily as a mechanism for closing all of the wage gap between men and women caused by discrimination. Litigation cannot, in all likelihood, bear that heavy a burden. But comparable worth initiatives in a variety of forms can play a significant role in achieving the central goal of comparable worth—eliminating or reducing discrimination based on the sex composition of occupations—and, in so doing, can have a significant indirect effect on the wage gap. Litigation, as one of those initiatives, can perform a valuable role in this process by supplementing the broader efforts to narrow the gap. Litigation provides a rifle that can target instances of this type of discrimination that might be missed by the shotgun approach of the other initiatives; it can provide a remedy for those whose wages are severely depressed by this type of discrimination but who are not helped by the blunter instruments used to address the wage gap.[38] In addition, litigation provides a forum for making important statements of public values and societal ideals.[39]

Even within this more limited role, the practical problems of comparable worth litigation—problems with the reliability of job evaluation studies and with defining appropriate procedures—are very significant. But they do not support the conclusion of some that comparable worth litigation should be abandoned. To abandon it would tell those who suffer the most from this form of discrimination that they have no remedy, and no hope. And it would deprive our society of an important avenue for making statements about the importance and scope of the antidiscrimination principle, about our determination to eradicate sex discrimination from the workplace. Moreover, none of the practical problems with comparable worth litigation is unique. They are all problems that arise whenever the courts must deal with uncertain evidence and complex litigation.[40] Comparable worth merely provides another opportunity to strive for the best solution in an imperfect world.

In sum, practical implementation problems require comparable worth to be pursued with caution. The reliability of job evaluation studies and the extent to which various procedures minimize cost and maximize accuracy and accomplishment of the substantive goal require intensive study, both inside and outside the litigation process. The problems do not, however, justify abandonment either of comparable worth as a discrimination theory or of comparable worth as a litigable issue. The road is rocky, to be sure, but it is passable, and the destination warrants the journey.

Afterword

COMPARABLE WORTH IS a simple idea. People should not be paid less because they work at jobs that have become identified as "women's work." Comparable worth cases begin with simple observations. Helen Castrilli looked out her window and saw men who were being paid more than she was, even though their work was easier than hers. Julie Hayward talked with her friends and discovered that she was being paid less than men who had the same training as she had. But once the cases begin, this simple idea and these simple observations become all but lost in a complex maze of statistics and procedures.

This complexity should be expected. Many lawyers and economists are interested in comparable worth, and if there is one universal truth, it is that the complexity of an issue increases in direct proportion to the number of lawyers and economists dealing with it. Indeed, if anything, this book understates the complexity of comparable worth. It considers directly only topics related to comparable worth litigation. It does not consider the many and varied efforts by state and local governments in the United States to implement comparable worth without litigation.[1] It does not consider, except very briefly, the efforts by other countries to raise the relative pay of women.[2] It does not consider the possible noneconomic consequences of comparable worth, such as decreases in fertility rates and family stability.[3] It does not discuss in detail the economic models—such as the human capital, dual labor market, and internal labor market models—that can be used to describe and predict the effects of efforts to eliminate this type of discrimination.[4] Comparable worth is a complex issue, and comparable worth cases reflect merely one part of that complexity.

The normal path, then, of a comparable worth case or of any serious consideration of the issue is from simplicity to complexity. That is as it should be. The complexity is necessary to understand the ramifications of a doctrine that, if implemented, would begin by changing wage rates but would also have much broader effects. The doctrine would be likely to have an effect on how many hours women work, on the education they receive, on how their families are structured, and so on. In dealing with this complexity, however, we must not lose sight of the simple underpinnings of comparable worth. The simple underpinnings provide a theoretical base for the idea. They permit us to see comparable worth as an application of the antidiscrimination principle which does not differ in significant respects from other, well-accepted applications of that principle. The theoretical base, in turn, facilitates a more satisfactory evaluation of the promise and limitations of comparable worth.

Julie Hayward and Helen Castrilli relied on the simple underpinnings of comparable worth when they filed their lawsuits. Although the lawsuits followed the normal path toward complexity, this book has used the experiences of Hayward and Castrilli to maintain contact with those simple underpinnings while dealing with the complex issues raised by the cases. The cases, then, have improved our understanding of comparable worth by forcing a consideration of the complex issues while focusing our attention on the reason those issues are important. The reason the issues are important is as simple as Helen Castrilli looking out her window or Julie Hayward talking with her friends. It is as simple as paying a secretary less than a campus police officer and a cook less than a painter. Comparable worth may have consequences that are undesirable, and it may be difficult to implement broadly and inexpensively. But to the extent we think it important to treat people such as Castrilli and Hayward fairly, it is also necessary.

Notes

INTRODUCTION

1. In 1987, women constituted 45 percent of the civilian work force in the United States. The proportions of women employed in the occupations listed in the text were as follows:

Secretaries	99.1%
Cooks	50.1
Child-care workers	
Private households	96.9
Other child-care workers	96.0
Nurses	
Registered nurses	95.1
Licensed practical nurses	97.0
Teachers of young children	
Elementary school teachers	85.3
Kindergarten and preschool teachers	98.4
Librarians	85.6
Telephone operators	92.2

U.S. Department of Labor, Bureau of Labor Statistics, *Employment and Earnings* 35 (Jan. 1988): 181–85. For more information on occupational segregation in the United States, see Women Employed Institute, *Occupational Segregation* (Chicago: Women Employed Institute, 1988); U.S. Department of Labor, Women's Bureau, *Time of Change: 1983 Handbook on Women Workers* (Washington, D.C.: U.S. Government Printing Office, 1984), 51–63. For similar though less detailed information on Great Britain, see Equal Opportunities Commission, *Women and Men in Britain: A Research Profile* (London: Her Majesty's Stationery Office, 1988), 36–38.

2. Steven L. Willborn, *A Comparable Worth Primer* (Lexington, Mass.: Lex-

ington Press, 1986), 18, table 1–5. For more detailed information on the inverse relationship between the proportion of women in an occupation and pay for that occupation in the United States, see Jane Bayes, "Occupational Sex Segregation and Comparable Worth," in *Comparable Worth, Pay Equity, and Public Policy*, ed. Rita Mae Kelly and Jane Bayes (Westport, Conn.: Greenwood Press, 1988), 22–30; Willborn, *Comparable Worth Primer*, 18–25; Donald J. Treiman and Heidi I. Hartmann, eds., *Women, Work, and Wages: Equal Pay for Jobs of Equal Value* (Washington, D.C.: National Academy Press, 1981), 52–62. For information on the effect of job segregation on female earnings in Great Britain, see EOC, *Women and Men in Britain*, 47.

3. For a recent review of the economic literature on this issue, see Morley Gunderson, "Male-Female Wage Differentials and Policy Responses," *Journal of Economic Literature* 27 (March 1989): 46–72.

4. Some people, particularly feminists, use the word "sex" to refer to differences between men and women that result from biology, and "gender" to refer to differences that result from socialization and acculturation. See Leslie Bender, "A Lawyer's Primer on Feminist Theory and Tort," *Journal of Legal Education* 38 (March–June 1988): 14–16; and Robert Stoller, *Sex and Gender: On the Development of Masculinity and Femininity* (New York: Science House, 1968). The distinction is not uniformly accepted, even by feminists. See Catharine A. MacKinnon, *Feminism Unmodified* (Cambridge, Mass.: Harvard University Press, 1987), 263 n.5. In most cases I use the term "sex" rather than "gender" because I generally use it when referring to laws that prohibit discrimination, and those laws generally use the term "sex." See Title VII of the Civil Rights Act of 1964, as amended, 42 U.S.C. §§ 2000e–2000e-17 (1982); and Sex Discrimination Act 1975, c. 65, as amended.

5. My use of the term "comparable worth" requires some explanation. Some contend that the term has never been adequately defined; others (including me) contend that it has been misinterpreted, in part because of its derivation. See E. Robert Livernash, ed., *Comparable Worth: Issues and Alternatives*, 2d ed. (Washington, D.C.: Equal Employment Advisory Council, 1984), 8–10; Willborn, *Comparable Worth Primer*, 3–5. I use the term with reference to the issue I have identified in the text: whether workers in female-dominated occupations are paid less because of the sex composition of their occupations. This use makes the term narrower than—indeed, a subset of—the term "pay equity." Pay equity, as I use it, refers to the correction of *any* inequities in pay, while comparable worth refers only to inequities caused by discrimination against female-dominated occupations.

Even this limited definition of the term "comparable worth," however, is broader than its derivation would suggest. The term derives from perhaps the most common method for proving this type of discrimination: demonstrating that persons working in a female-dominated occupation are paid less than persons working in a male-dominated occupation even though the work of the two occupations is of "comparable worth." My use of the term, however, encompasses not only that method but also other methods of attempting to prove that a female-dominated occupation suffers discrimination because of its sex composition. The term, for example, encompasses attempts to prove this type of discrimination through economic, historical, or anthropological analysis.

A final word of caution: this note defines "comparable worth" as I use the term in this book. Others may define it differently.

6. U.S. Commission on Civil Rights, *Comparable Worth: Issue for the 80's* (Washington, D.C.: U.S. Commission on Civil Rights, 1984); Michael Levin, "Comparable Worth: The Feminist Road to Socialism," *Commentary* 78 (Sept. 1984): 13.

7. Howard Kurtz, "Justice Dept. Opposes Nurses' 'Comparable Worth' Lawsuit," *Washington Post,* Aug. 16, 1985, sec. A.

8. Comparable worth is required by Article 119 of the Treaty of Rome, the principal formative document of the European Economic Community. Office for Official Publications of the European Communities, *Treaties Establishing the European Communities* (Luxembourg: Office for Official Publications of the European Communities, 1973), 205–575. The Treaty of Rome can also be found in U.N. Treaty Service, "Treaty Establishing the European Economic Community," Nov. 23–Dec. 13, 1957, 298 United Nations Treaty Series 11. For a discussion of Article 119, see pages 17–19 below.

9. Convention No. 100 requires ratifying countries to "ensure the application to all workers of the principle of equal remuneration for men and women workers for work of equal value." "Convention Concerning Equal Remuneration for Men and Women Workers for Work of Equal Value," Art. 2, § 1, 165 United Nations Treaty Series 303. The convention can also be found at International Labour Organisation, *International Labour Conventions and Recommendations, 1919–1981* (Geneva: International Labour Office, 1982), 42–43. As of 1986, the convention had been ratified by 104 countries, including such major industrial countries as Canada, France, Japan, the United Kingdom, and West Germany. The United States has not ratified the convention. See M. J. Bowman and D. J. Harris, *Multilateral Treaties* (London: Butterworths, 1984), 170.

10. The ratio of female-to-male median annual earnings of year-round, full-time workers ranged from 56.6 percent to 63.9 percent from 1955 to 1981. The average of the ratios for those years was 59.8 percent. Women's Bureau, *Time of Change,* 82.

11. From 1981 to 1987, the female-to-male ratio of median annual earnings of year-round, full-time workers rose from 59.2 percent to 65.0 percent. Bureau of Labor Statistics, Current Population Survey (unpublished tabulations).

It is important to recognize that female-to-male wage ratios are quite sensitive to the definitions of "workers" and "earnings" used. For example, the female-to-male ratio of median *weekly* earnings of full-time workers in 1987 was 70.0

percent, compared to the 65.0 percent ratio for the median *annual* earnings of full-time workers. Bureau of Labor Statistics, Current Population Survey (unpublished tabulations). The same definitions of "workers" and "earnings" must be used to evaluate changes in the ratio over time. In the United States, annual earnings are generally used for this purpose because that data series extends further back in time.

Because of this sensitivity, international comparisons of wage ratios are also hazardous. Compare, for example, the definitions of "earnings" from the U.S. sources discussed in this note with the definitions of "earnings" from the sources on Britain reported in notes 13 and 14 below.

12. A. Zabalza and Z. Tzannatos, *Women and Equal Pay: The Effects of Legislation on Female Employment and Wages in Britain* (Cambridge: Cambridge University Press, 1985); P. Z. Tzannatos and A. Zabalza, "The Anatomy of the Rise in British Female Relative Wages in the 1970's: Evidence from the New Earnings Survey," *British Journal of Industrial Relations* 22 (July 1984): 177–94; A. Zabalza and Z. Tzannatos, "The Effect of Britain's Anti-Discriminatory Legislation on Relative Pay and Employment," *Economic Journal* 95 (Sept. 1985): 679–99.

13. From 1943 to 1972, the female-to-male ratio of average hourly real earnings of adult full-time manual workers in Britain ranged from 58 percent to 62 percent. From 1973 to 1977, that ratio rose from 61 percent to 71 percent. Since 1977 the ratio has been fairly stable, with a slight downward trend. See Heather Joshi, Richard Layard, and Susan Owen, "Why Are More Women Working in Britain?" *Journal of Labor Economics* 3 (Jan. 1985): S158. The British experience is reported similarly in EOC, *Women and Men in Britain*, 45–47; and in Robert G. Gregory, Anne Daly, and Vivian Ho, "A Tale of Two Countries: Equal Pay for Women in Australia and Britain" (Australian National University Centre for Economic Policy Research, Discussion Paper No. 147, 1986), 2.

14. This figure compares the average gross weekly earnings, excluding overtime, of full-time employees on adult rates. See EOC, *Women and Men in Britain*, 47.

1. SECRETARIES AND CAMPUS POLICE OFFICERS

1. The 1974 Willis study is publicly available in U.S. Congress, House Committee on Post Office and Civil Service, *Pay Equity: Equal Pay for Work of Comparable Value—Part II: Joint Hearings before the Subcommittees on Civil Service, Human Resources, and Compensation and Employee Benefits*, 97th Cong., 2d sess., 1982, 1486–1524.

2. The 1976 Willis study is publicly available in ibid., 1525–80.

3. State statute has historically required and still requires the Higher Education Personnel Board and the Department of Personnel to conduct market surveys to determine the "prevailing rates" and to propose salaries for state

employment that "reflect" those prevailing rates. Wash. Rev. Code §§ 28B.16.100(16), 28B.16.110, 41.06.150(17), 41.06.160 (Supp. 1988).

4. There would, of course, have been several steps between a study demonstrating that female-dominated positions were consistently paid less and liability for violations of the sex discrimination laws. Nevertheless, a continued focus on sex discrimination would have increased the *risk* of liability for the state. It would, for example, have increased the visibility of the discrimination issue, thus making it more likely that a plaintiff would surface. In addition, it would have provided, at state expense, well-tailored evidence of discrimination that would otherwise have been very expensive for a plaintiff to compile, thus increasing the likelihood that a lawsuit could have been mounted. Although there were undoubtedly multiple reasons for the shift in focus (for example, the Washington Federation of State Employees supported the shift because it meant that more of its members might be eligible for wage increases from the exercise), the risk of liability was also undoubtedly one of them.

5. The data for Willis's regression analysis consisted of the job evaluation points for the 55 benchmark jobs and the weighted average monthly salaries for those jobs. The range of possible total job evaluation points was 0 to 600. The actual range of points in 1976 was 81 to 472 for the benchmark jobs and 81 to 573 for all the jobs evaluated. The range of weighted average monthly salaries was approximately $450 to $1,850.

6. Because Willis's comparable worth line represented a sample consisting of only the 55 benchmark jobs, the gains and losses would probably not have offset each other exactly when the pay for *all* jobs in the state were recalculated. Rather, there would have been a slight gain or a slight loss to the state, depending on how representative the 55 benchmark jobs were. Still, because this option would have offset increases in pay to occupations above the line with decreases in pay for occupations below the line, any loss to the state would have been less than under Willis's option (described below); indeed, the state might have enjoyed a net gain.

7. Act of May 26, 1977, c. 152, §§ 2, 10, 1977 Wash. Laws 560, 564, 570, codified at Wash. Rev. Code §§ 28B.16.110(5), 41.06.160(5) (Supp. 1988).

2. A NEW RECIPE FOR A COOK

1. The Equal Pay Act 1970, c. 41, as amended.

2. *O'Brien v. Sim-Chem Limited,* [1980] Industrial Cases Reporter 573, 578 (House of Lords); *Arnold v. Beecham Group Ltd.,* [1982] Industrial Cases Reporter 744, 750–52 (Employment Appeal Tribunal); *England v. Bromley London Borough Council,* [1978] Industrial Cases Reporter 1, 4 (Employment Appeal Tribunal, 1977).

3. The use of job evaluation studies in British industry was growing during the 1970s. Neil Millward and Mark Stevens, *British Workplace Industrial Relations*

1980–1984 (Aldershot, Eng.: Gower, 1986), 253–59. That trend, however, did not extend to workplaces in which large proportions of women were employed. "There was a strong tendency for workplaces to be *less* likely to have job evaluation schemes the *larger* was the proportion of women who were employed. It is clear that systematic job evaluation was markedly less common in circumstances where a relatively large proportion of the workforce was female. Two-thirds of establishments with 1,000 or more people had job evaluation schemes where fewer than 30 per cent of the workforce were women. Only one quarter of such establishments had schemes when the female proportion of the workforce rose to over 70 per cent." W. W. Daniel and Neil Millward, *Workplace Industrial Relations in Britain* (London: Heinemann Educational Books, 1983), 205.

4. Linda Clarke, "Proposed Amendments to the Equal Pay Act 1970—I," *New Law Journal* 133 (Oct. 1983): 936 ("For many women, the Equal Pay Act is a dead letter"). See also P. L. Davies, "European Equality Legislation, U.K. Legislative Policy and Industrial Relations," in *Women, Employment, and European Equality Law,* ed. Christopher McCrudden (London: Eclipse Publications, 1987), 33 ("By the early 1980s it had become clear that the original [Equal Pay] Act had largely shot its bolt").

5. Office for Official Publications of the European Communities, *Treaties Establishing the European Communities* (Luxembourg: Office for the Official Publications of the European Communities, 1973), 312. A slightly different version appears in U.N. Treaty Service, "Treaty Establishing the European Economic Community," Nov. 23–Dec. 13, 1957, 62.

Article 119 was added to the treaty at the insistence of the French to ensure that countries that protected women's rights did not suffer competitive disadvantages and to further the social objectives of the EEC. Evelyn Ellis, *Sex Discrimination Law* (Aldershot, Eng.: Gower, 1988), 183–84.

6. "Council Directive of 10 February 1975 on the Approximation of the Laws of the Member States Relating to the Application of the Principle of Equal Pay for Men and Women," *Official Journal of the European Communities* 18, no. L 45 (1975): 19–20 (emphasis added).

7. Commission of the European Communities, *Report of the Commission to the Council on the Application as at 12 February 1978 of the Principle of Equal Pay for Men and Women,* COM (78) 711 (Brussels: Commission of the European Communities, 1979).

8. For a brief review of the compliance activities of the other EEC member states, except for Portugal and Spain, see Janice Bellace, "A Foreign Perspective," in *Comparable Worth: Issues and Alternatives,* ed. E. Robert Livernash (Washington, D.C.: Equal Employment Advisory Council, 1980), 137–72; Commission of the European Communities, *Community Law and Women* (Brussels: Commission of the European Communities, 1983), 6–30.

9. *Commission of the European Communities v. United Kingdom of Great Britain*

and Northern Ireland, [1982] Industrial Cases Reporter 578, 598 (European Court of Justice).

10. *Statutory Instruments 1983,* No. 1794. The regulations amended the Equal Pay Act 1970, c. 41. The government decided for procedural reasons to amend the Equal Pay Act through regulations instead of through amending legislation. See Steven L. Willborn, "Equal Pay for Work of Equal Value: Comparable Worth in the United Kingdom," *American Journal of Comparative Law* 34 (Summer 1986): 424–25.

11. Equal Pay Act 1970, c. 41, as amended, § 1(2)(c).

12. *Statutory Instruments 1983,* No. 1807. These regulations amended Industrial Tribunals (Rules of Procedure) Regulations 1980, *Statutory Instruments 1980,* No. 884, and Industrial Tribunals (Rules of Procedure) (Scotland) Regulations 1980, *Statutory Instruments 1980,* No. 885. The two sets of procedures, one for England and Wales and one for Scotland, are substantially the same. Because Hayward's case arose in England, citations here are to Industrial Tribunals (Rules of Procedure) 1980, as amended by Industrial Tribunals (Rules of Procedure) (Equal Value Amendment) Regulations 1983, hereafter cited as Procedural Rule.

13. David Pannick, *Sex Discrimination Law* (Oxford: Clarendon Press, 1985), 105. See also Davies, "European Equality Legislation," 34–35. (The Equal Pay Regulations "implement the equal value principle in a pretty grudging fashion.")

14. *Parliamentary Debates,* Commons, 6th ser., vol. 46 (20 July 1983), col. 480.

15. Motion of Lord McCarthy, *Parliamentary Debates,* Lords, 5th ser., vol. 445 (5 Dec. 1983), cols. 886–90, *approved,* ibid., cols. 929–30.

16. *Parliamentary Debates,* Commons, 6th ser., vol. 46 (20 July 1983), cols. 479–500.

17. *New Law Journal* 133 (Aug. 1983): 690.

3. A SECRETARY FILES . . . A LAWSUIT

1. Warren Fanshier, *History: Western State Hospital* (n.p., 1968).

2. 42 U.S.C. §§ 2000e–2000e-17 (1982).

3. For articles on the legislative maneuvering that resulted in the addition of "sex" to the list of prohibited categories of discrimination, see Michael Evan Gold, "A Tale of Two Amendments: The Reasons Congress Added Sex to Title VII and Their Implication for the Issue of Comparable Worth," *Duquesne Law Review* 19 (Spring 1981): 453–69; Robert Stevens Miller, Jr., "Sex Discrimination and Title VII of the Civil Rights Act of 1964," *Minnesota Law Review* 51 (April 1967): 879–85.

4. This was the view of at least one member of the House of Representatives at the time. *Congressional Record,* 88th Cong., 2d sess., 1964, 110, pt. 2:2581 (remarks of Rep. Edith Green).

5. Heil Hoover, "Sex and Nonsense," *New Republic,* Sept. 4, 1965, 10.

6. The amendment may also have been approved because Congress thought sex discrimination was wrong or, somewhat illogically, because Congress was concerned that white women would be placed at a disadvantage vis-à-vis African-American women without the amendment. See Gold, "A Tale of Two Amendments," 453–69.

7. 42 U.S.C. § 2000e-2(a)(1) (1982).

8. H.R. 8898, 87th Cong., 1st sess., 1961; H.R. 10226, 87th Cong., 2d sess., 1962; H.R. 11677, 87th Cong., 2d sess., 1962.

9. 29 U.S.C. § 206(d) (1982). For a discussion of the legislative history rejecting the "comparable skills" language and substituting the "equal work" language, see *County of Washington v. Gunther,* 452 U.S. 161, 184–88 (1981), Rehnquist, J., dissenting.

10. Shortly before Helen Castrilli commenced her action against the state of Washington, the U.S. Supreme Court decided a case that bolstered her position on this issue. In *County of Washington v. Gunther,* 452 U.S. 161 (1981), the Court decided that the application of Title VII to sex-based wage discrimination claims was not limited to claims that could meet the "equal work" standard of the Equal Pay Act. Although the Supreme Court certainly did not embrace comparable worth as a theory of liability under Title VII, 452 U.S. at 166, 180–81, it did reject the dissenters' interpretation of Title VII, which flatly rejected comparable worth as a viable legal theory. 452 U.S. at 193, 203–4, Rehnquist, J., dissenting.

11. Under Title VII, a federal lawsuit is permissible only if the plaintiff has a right-to-sue letter. 42 U.S.C. § 2000e-5 (1982). The letter basically confirms that the plaintiff has satisfied the procedural steps that are required before a lawsuit is commenced. For a general description of Title VII procedures, see Charles Sullivan, Michael Zimmer, and Richard Richards, *Federal Statutory Law of Employment Discrimination* (Indianapolis: Michie, 1980), 265–361.

12. In 1986, for example, Judge Tanner had held that conditions at the Washington State Penitentiary constituted cruel and unusual punishment in violation of the Eighth Amendment to the U.S. Constitution. See *Hoptowit v. Ray,* 682 F.2d 1237 (9th Cir. 1982) and *Hoptowit v. Ray* 753 F.2d 779 (9th Cir. 1985) (reviewing Tanner's unreported decisions in the Washington State Penitentiary case).

13. For the text of Disciplinary Rule 7-104, see Thomas Morgan and Ronald Rotunda, *1988 Selected Standards on Professional Responsibility* (Mineola, N.Y.: Foundation Press, 1988), 57–58.

4. PAINTERS, JOINERS, LAGGERS, AND A COOK

1. This problem was not as severe for the union as it would have been twenty years earlier. Beginning in the 1960s, a number of "individual" em-

ployment issues (such as redundancy, unfair dismissal, maternity rights, and race and sex discrimination) were placed within the jurisdiction of industrial tribunals with the active cooperation of trade unions. See Jon Clark and Lord Wedderburn, "Modern Labour Law: Problems, Functions, and Policies," in *Labour Law and Industrial Relations: Building on Kahn-Freund,* ed. Lord Wedderburn, Roy Lewis, and Jon Clark (Oxford: Clarendon Press, 1983), 173–98. Thus, the resistance of unions to legal intervention has waned, certainly with respect to "individual" rights such as those forwarded by Julie Hayward, and perhaps even with respect to "collective" rights. See Lord Wedderburn, "Labour Law: Autonomy from the Common Law?" *Comparative Labor Law Journal* 9 (Winter 1988): 219.

2. David Pannick, *Sex Discrimination Law* (Oxford: Clarendon Press, 1985).

3. Industrial tribunals are always composed of three members, a legally qualified chair and two lay representatives. The chairs are appointed by the lord chancellor and must have had seven years' experience as a solicitor or barrister. One lay member is selected from each of two panels, which are compiled by the secretary of state for employment after consultation with representative organizations of employers and employees respectively. Industrial Tribunals (England and Wales) Regulations 1965, *Statutory Instruments 1965,* No. 1101, § 5.

Although industrial tribunals with a female panel member decide in favor of applicants more often than all-male panels, women are underrepresented on industrial tribunals generally and there is no requirement that panels in equal value cases have a female member. Evelyn Ellis, *Sex Discrimination Law* (Aldershot, Eng., Gower, 1988), 39. For a good description and evaluation of industrial tribunals, see Linda Dickens et al., *Dismissed: A Study of Unfair Dismissal and the Industrial Tribunal System* (Oxford: Basil Blackwell, 1985), 52–84.

4. Equal Pay Act 1970, c. 41, as amended, § 2A(1)(a).

5. The requirement that the job evaluation expert compare jobs "in terms of the demands made . . . (for instance, under such headings as effort, skill and decision)" is found at sec. 1(2)(c) of the Equal Pay Act 1970, c. 41, as amended. The requirement that the expert "act fairly" is found at Procedural Regulation 7(3). For discussions of the lack of guidance provided to job evaluation experts in the Equal Pay Act, see Erika Szyszczak, "The Equal Pay Directive and U.K. Law," in *Women, Employment, and European Equality Law,* ed. Christopher McCrudden (London: Eclipse Publications, 1987), 67–70; Steven Willborn, "Equal Pay for Work of Equal Value: Comparable Worth in the United Kingdom," *American Journal of Comparative Law* 34 (Summer 1986): 435.

6. Some unions in Britain have attempted to create quasi-class actions by having large numbers of women file equal pay claims simultaneously. The Manufacturing, Science and Finance union is backing equal value claims by over 1,300 speech therapists, and the National Union of Mineworkers is backing

claims by over 1,000 canteen workers. Nevertheless, in theory, these are joint individual actions rather than class-based claims.

7. It was possible, although unlikely, that the case would not have ended even had the job evaluation expert found that Hayward's job was not equal to the jobs of the men. The industrial tribunal has the authority, in narrow circumstances, not to admit the report of a job evaluation expert into evidence or to reject the report after it is admitted into evidence. If the job evaluation report is rejected or not admitted, the tribunal will normally commission a report from another job evaluator. See David Pannick, *Sex Discrimination Law* (Oxford: Clarendon Press, 1985), 117–18; Willborn, "Equal Pay for Work of Equal Value," 436–38. This has happened in at least one case. See "Equal Value Update," *Equal Opportunities Review* 13 (May–June 1987): 19–20, discussing *Davies v. Francis Shaw & Company (Manchester) Ltd.*, in which the tribunal commissioned a new job evaluation report after refusing to admit into evidence a job evaluation that found an applicant's job not equal in value to the job of a comparator.

8. Report of the Independent Expert at ¶¶ 7.5–7.6, *submitted to tribunal in, Hayward v. Cammell Laird Shipbuilders Ltd.*, [1985] Industrial Cases Reporter 71 (Industrial Tribunal, 1984).

9. Dillon ranked Hayward's job as equal to Gilbert's, even though his analysis indicated that the job of cook should be ranked *higher* in value than the job of lagger. Dillon assumed *sub silentio,* then, that the Equal Pay Act 1970 requires equal pay when the woman's job is rated as equal to *or* higher than the man's job in value. Later cases that directly addressed this issue agreed with that assumption. *Brown v. Cearns & Brown Ltd.*, 6 Equal Opportunities Review 27 (1985) (Industrial Tribunal); *Wells v. F. Smales & Sons (Fish Merchants) Ltd.*, 2 Equal Opportunities Review 24 (1985) (Industrial Tribunal). The European Court of Justice subsequently held that Article 119 of the Treaty of Rome should also be interpreted in this way. *Murphy v. Bord Telecom Eireann,* Case No. 157/86 (Feb. 4, 1988): "Article 119 . . . must be interpreted as covering the case where a worker who relies on that provision to obtain equal pay . . . is engaged in work of higher value than that of the person with whom a comparison is to be made."

10. Procedural Rule 8(2C).

11. *Hayward v. Cammell Laird Shipbuilders Ltd.*, [1985] Industrial Cases Reporter 71, 77 (Industrial Tribunal, 1984).

12. Ibid., 77–78.

13. Ibid., 80.

5. A Secretary's Case Is Heard

1. Paul Andrews, "The Court of First Resort—Judge Tanner Champions

Underdogs and Fields Criticism," *Seattle Times/Seattle Post-Intelligencer*, Feb. 2, 1986, *Pacific* magazine, 5.

2. Transcript of trial at vol. 1:21, *American Federation of State, County and Municipal Employees v. Washington*, 578 F. Supp. 846 (W.D. Wash. 1983) (No. C82-4655).

3. Ibid., 5:91–92.

4. "Federal District Judges: The Best and the Worst," *American Lawyer* 5 (July-August 1983): 111–12. The study has been criticized, however, because it relied primarily on interviews with lawyers and prosecutors and because all the "best" judges were white males and three of the eleven "worst" judges were either African-American or female. But see cases in which the court of appeals has taken the unusual step of reversing Judge Tanner and remanding *to a different judge* because of Tanner's adamance in making erroneous rulings. *United States v. Larios*, 640 F.2d 938 (9th Cir. 1981); *United States v. Doe*, 655 F.2d 920 (9th Cir. 1980); *United States v. Ferguson*, 624 F.2d 81 (9th Cir. 1980).

5. Andrews, "Court of First Resort," 9.

6. Transcript at 1:3.

7. Ibid., 1:15.

8. Ibid., 1:149.

9. Pages 8–14 above describe Willis's job evaluation procedure. You may want to review those pages before reading the next few paragraphs.

10. When he was asked how many jobs he had evaluated, Willis responded "about 200." He had actually evaluated 206.

11. See pages 9–10 above for a discussion of the state's salary survey process.

12. Mark Aldrich and Robert Buchele, *The Economics of Comparable Worth* (Cambridge, Mass.: Ballinger, 1986), 58. See also Henry J. Aaron and Cameran M. Lougy, *The Comparable Worth Controversy* (Washington, D.C.: Brookings Institution, 1986), 28–29.

13. These are the results of Michelson's regression analysis:

$$\text{MINSAL} = 331.81 + .879\text{CW} - 4.512\%\text{F} \qquad R^2 = .88$$
$$t = 84.65 \quad t = 38.05 \qquad N = 1607$$

where MINSAL is the minimum salary for each job, CW is Willis's proposed comparable worth salary for each job, and %F is the percentage of women employed in each job. Plaintiffs' Exhibit 135-F.

14. It should be noted that Michelson's statistics did not *prove* in any conclusive sense that female-dominated occupations were paid less because of sex discrimination. Statistics can never prove such a causal relationship. Rather, they can only reveal and quantify relationships and indicate the likelihood that the relationships would occur by chance. See David Barnes, *Statistics as Proof* (Boston: Little, Brown, 1983), 31, 392–95. Michelson's statistics revealed and

quantified the relationship between the sex composition of occupations and their pay and indicated that it was unlikely that that relationship would occur by chance. The "implications" of Michelson's statistics, as I call them in the text, go beyond the statistics. They are the logical and legal conclusions Newman wanted Judge Tanner to reach based on Michelson's statistics.

15. Transcript at 5:125–26.
16. Ibid., 6:142–45.
17. 694 F.2d 531 (9th Cir. 1982).
18. Transcript at 6:161–65.
19. Ibid., 7:9–10.
20. Ibid., 7:108–9.
21. Ibid., 7:114–15.
22. Ibid., 7:135–37.

6. How Much Should a Cook Be Paid?

1. I discuss this earlier case more fully at pages 21–22 above.

2. Equal Pay Act 1970, c. 41, as amended, § 1(2)(c)(i–ii).

3. I discuss the enactment of the Equal Pay Regulations on pages 17–21 above.

4. Office for Official Publications of the European Communities, *Treaties Establishing the European Communities* (Luxembourg: Office for the Official Publications of the European Communities, 1973), 312 (emphasis added). A slightly different version appears at U.N. Treaty Service, "Treaty Establishing the European Economic Community," Nov. 23–Dec. 13, 1957, 298 United Nations Treaty Series 11, 62.

5. About 95 percent of all decisions of industrial tribunals are unanimous. Linda Dickens et al., *Dismissed: A Study of Unfair Dismissal and the Industrial Tribunal System* (Oxford: Basil Blackwell, 1985), 70. In cases involving discrimination issues, the rate of unanimity is even higher, about 99 percent. Alice Leonard, *Judging Inequality: The Effectiveness of the Tribunal System in Sex Discrimination and Equal Pay Cases* (London: Cobden Trust, 1987), 72.

6. *Hayward v. Cammell Laird Shipbuilders, Ltd.*, No. 5979/84, slip op. 8 (Liverpool Industrial Tribunal, Sept. 12, 1985).

7. Ibid., 8–9.

8. *Hayward v. Cammell Laird Shipbuilders Ltd.*, [1986] Industrial Cases Reporter 862, 873 (Employment Appeal Tribunal).

7. A Secretary's Pay

1. 578 F. Supp. 846 (W. D. Wash. 1983).

2. See pages 26–27 above.

3. 42 U.S.C. § 2000e-2(a)(1) (1982).

4. The most important cases on disparate treatment discrimination are *McDonnell Douglas Corp. v. Green*, 411 U.S. 792 (1973); *Teamsters v. United*

States, 431 U.S. 324 (1977); *Hazelwood School District v. United States,* 433 U.S. 299 (1977). For a general description of this type of discrimination, see Charles Sullivan, Michael Zimmer, and Richard Richards, *Federal Statutory Law of Employment Discrimination* (Indianapolis: Michie, 1980), 16–33, 60–67.

5. The most important cases on disparate impact discrimination are *Griggs v. Duke Power Co.,* 401 U.S. 424 (1971); *Watson v. Fort Worth Bank and Trust,* 108 S.Ct. 2777 (1988). For a general description of this type of discrimination, see Sullivan, Zimmer, and Richards, *Federal Statutory Law,* 33–60.

6. *American Federation of State, County and Municipal Employees v. Washington,* 578 F. Supp. 846, 866 n.11 (W.D. Wash. 1983).

7. Ibid., 866.

8. A footnote in the plaintiffs' brief to the Court on remedial issues read as follows: "A simple method of calculation is to calculate the natural logarithm of each benchmark salary, *ln* (SAL_i), where SAL_i is the mean salary in the ith benchmark. Using a standard linear regression computer program, calculate:

$$\ln (SAL_i) = b_o + b_1 (EP_i) + b_2 (M_i)$$

where EP_i is the evaluation points of the position, and $M_i = 1$ if the position is a "male" job and $M_i = 0$ otherwise. The program will estimate b_2. Calculate:

$$P = e^{b_2 + (1/2)_v}$$

P = percentage increase from female to male jobs.

e = the mathematical number e.

v = the variance of the error term (mean square error) in the regression. A new female job salary, $SALF_i^*$, would then be calculated:

$$SALF_i^* = (P) (SALF_i)$$

where $SALF_i$ is the current salary in the ith female job."

9. Despite Davis's example, however, even in job classifications with only one incumbent, the "sex" of the classification seemed to have an adverse effect on women. In Washington at the time of the trial, there were 530 job classifications with one incumbent. The incumbent in 100 of the classifications was a woman; in the other 430 classifications, the incumbent was a man. Where the pay was reported and there was a difference between the pay suggested by the Willis studies and the actual salary, 72 percent of the classifications occupied by women were paid less than the Willis studies indicated they should be paid, while only 41 percent of the classifications occupied by men were paid less. Plaintiffs' exhibit 134-A.

10. The fudge word "generally" is required in this sentence because the "fixed percentage" remedy proposed raising female wages by the *average* per-

centage difference between the male and female comparable worth lines. As a result, a female-dominated occupation that rested on the female comparable worth line would be eleven ranges below the male comparable worth line only if the difference between the lines *at that point* was the same as the average percentage difference between the lines.

11. Estimates made after the trial indicated that both the state's and Newman's figures may have been too high. The director of the state's Office for Fiscal Management estimated in January 1984 (after the decision by Judge Tanner, but before the court of appeals decision and settlement) that it would cost about $63 million per year to raise the wages in female-dominated jobs to the comparable worth line. Helen Remick, "Comparable Worth in Washington State," in *Comparable Worth, Pay Equity, and Public Policy*, ed. Rita Mae Kelly and Jane Bayes (Westport, Conn.: Greenwood Press, 1988), 229. Later, variability in the estimates of the cost of the settlement was another indication of how difficult it was to make accurate cost estimates. See page 107 below.

12. Transcript, 11:135–36.

13. Ibid., 11:135.

14. *City of Los Angeles v. Manhart*, 435 U.S. 702 (1978); *Arizona Governing Committee v. Norris*, 463 U.S. 1073 (1983).

15. Remick, "Comparable Worth in Washington State," 229. The back pay estimate was probably low because it considered back pay only to September 1979 and did not include any interest.

16. Transcript, 13:110–11.

17. Act of May 22, 1983, c. 75, §§ 3, 6, 1983 Wash. Laws 2071, 2074, 2078, codified at Wash. Rev. Code §§ 28B.16.116, 41.06.155 (Supp. 1988).

18. Act of February 27, 1985, c. 6, § 702, 1985 Wash. Laws 2310, 2378–80.

19. Amicus brief of the Eagle Forum Education and Legal Defense Fund at 35, 37, *American Federation of State, County and Municipal Employees v. Washington*, 770 F.2d 1401 (9th Cir. 1985) (No. 84-3569).

20. For critical reviews of Judge Kennedy's record, see Robin Olinger Bell, "Justice Anthony M. Kennedy: Will His Appointment to the United States Supreme Court Have an Impact on Employment Discrimination?" *University of Cincinnati Law Review* 57 (1989): 1037–71; Molly Yard, "Under Anthony Kennedy, Justice for Some," *St. Louis Post-Dispatch*, Jan. 29, 1988; Charles Williams, "The Opinions of Anthony Kennedy: No Time for Ideology," *ABA Journal*, March 1, 1988, 56–61.

21. See *Williams v. McClellan*, 569 F.2d 1031 (8th Cir. 1978).

22. The Supreme Court has indicated that an inference of discrimination may arise if there is a difference of more than two or three standard deviations between the number of persons hired by an employer and the number of persons one would expect the employer to hire in the absence of discrimination. *Hazelwood School District v. United States*, 433 U.S. 299, 308–9, n.14 (1977). From 1975 to 1987, five of thirty-five, or 14 percent, of the law clerks hired

by Kennedy were women. In the absence of discrimination, one would expect female law clerks to be hired in proportion to their numbers in the pool from which Kennedy hired—the pool of graduating law students during that period. From 1975 to 1987, women constituted 31 percent of graduating law students (this percentage was calculated from unpublished tabulations provided by the American Bar Association Section of Legal Education and Admissions to the Bar). There are, then, 2.13 standard deviations between the number of women Kennedy hired and the number one would have expected him to hire in the absence of discrimination. Stated another way, based on this information, there is a less than one in fifty probability that the low proportion of women hired by Kennedy was the result of chance. Consequently, an inference of discrimination may be appropriate, but more information would be needed to make a definitive judgment.

23. *American Federation of State, County and Municipal Employees v. Washington*, 770 F.2d 1401 (9th Cir. 1985).

24. For a discussion of Judge Tanner's decision, see pages 82–84 above.

25. *American Federation of State, County and Municipal Employees v. Washington*, 770 F.2d 1401, 1407–8 (9th Cir. 1985).

26. 431 U.S. 324, 339 (1977).

27. Ibid., 340, quoting *United States v. Ironworkers Local 86*, 443 F.2d 544, 551 (9th Cir.), *cert. denied*, 404 U.S. 984 (1971).

28. 470 U.S. 564 (1985).

29. *Spaulding v. University of Washington*, 740 F.2d 686, 707–8 (9th Cir.), *cert. denied*, 469 U.S. 1036 (1984); *Carroll v. Sears, Roebuck & Co.*, 708 F.2d 183, 188–89 (5th Cir. 1983); *Pouncy v. Prudential Insurance Co.*, 668 F.2d 795, 800 (5th Cir. 1983); *Heagney v. University of Washington*, 642 F.2d 1157, 1163 (9th Cir. 1981). See also *Antonio v. Wards Cove Packing Company, Inc.*, 810 F.2d 1477 (en banc), *on remand to panel*, 827 F.2d 439 (9th Cir. 1987), *cert. granted*, 108 S.Ct. 2896 (1988). The en banc opinion in *Antonio* overruled *Spaulding* and *Heagney* and declined to follow *Carroll* and *Pouncy* in deciding that disparate impact theory is applicable to subjective employment practices; the opinion reaffirmed the cases, however, in limiting disparate impact theory to specific employment practices.

30. Access to the relevant evidence is one of the major factors traditionally used to allocate the burden of proof. See Fleming James and Geoffrey Hazard, *Civil Procedure*, 3d ed. (Boston: Little, Brown, 1985), 324; Edward Cleary, "Presuming and Pleading: An Essay on Juristic Immaturity," *Stanford Law Review* 12 (Dec. 1959): 8–14.

31. In a later case, a plurality of the U.S. Supreme Court indicated that the "specific employment practice" requirement should be imposed in disparate impact cases and that the burden of "isolating and identifying the specific employment practice" should be imposed on the plaintiff. *Watson v. Fort Worth Bank and Trust*, 108 S.Ct. 2777, 2788 (1988). A majority of the Supreme

Court has not yet ruled on that issue, but since the plurality opinion commanded the support of four justices and Justice Kennedy did not participate in the case, it is very likely that the plurality's position will become a majority position next time the issue is presented. The Supreme Court did not respond to the arguments presented in the text or indeed provide any reasons at all in support of this part of its decision.

32. 740 F.2d 686 (9th Cir.), *cert. denied,* 469 U.S. 1036 (1984).

33. "Pay Ruling Won't End Dispute," *Seattle Times,* Sept. 5, 1985, 1.

34. For a good discussion of remedies in comparable worth cases, see Ruth Gerber Blumrosen, "Remedies for Wage Discrimination," *University of Michigan Journal of Law Reform* 20 (Fall 1986): 99–161.

35. Both results—that the fair wage is $720 or $550—make important assumptions that I do not discuss in the text here. They both assume, for example, that the number of job evaluation points the jobs have received is, or at least can be, accurate (the settlement provided for a review of the Willis methodology); and that it makes sense to base wages on job evaluation points, either as a way to counter sex discrimination ($720) or because job evaluation points provide a standard of fairness for evaluating wages irrespective of sex discrimination ($550). These assumptions present important issues that I discuss later. See pages 147–51 below. Although the assumptions were made by the settlement *sub silentio* and, as a result, perhaps should have been dealt with explicitly in the settlement agreement, they were not. I do not discuss them here because I am now focusing on the issues the negotiators explicitly resolved in the settlement negotiations.

36. Although it was impossible to predict the *actual* effect of the program, the program was *likely* to narrow the gap between the average wages of female- and male-dominated jobs in Washington and do so in a way that disproportionately benefited persons working in low-wage, female-dominated jobs. Nevertheless, at the conclusion of the program, significant disparities would remain between male- and female-dominated jobs at every level. Helen Remick, "Considerations in Long-Range Implementation of Comparable Worth," in *Politics and Practice of Pay Equity,* ed. Ronnie Steinberg (Philadelphia: Temple University Press, forthcoming).

37. It should be noted, once again, that I have used the $41 million figure to avoid confusion. One would not, however, end up with a total of $482 million if one continued with the analysis in the text, because the initial appropriation was spread over two fiscal years. As a result, the settlement predicted that at the end of fiscal year 1986, $12 million would be used for comparable worth increases. In fiscal year 1987, $25.2 million in new money would be used for comparable worth increases and $12 million to cover the higher wage base from fiscal year 1986. In the succeeding six fiscal years, $10 million in new money would be dedicated to comparable worth increases each year and additional money to cover the increased wage base. In fiscal year 1988, then, the total would be $47.2 million—$10 million in new money and $37.2

million to cover the increased wage base from fiscal years 1986 and 1987. If one continued with this more precise analysis, the total would be $482.4 million.

38. Helen Remick, "Comparable Worth in Washington State," in *Comparable Worth, Pay Equity, and Public Policy,* ed. Rita Mae Kelly and Jane Bayes (Westport, Conn.: Greenwood Press, 1988), 231.

39. For a good discussion of the Washington State settlement and implementation problems in comparable worth cases generally, see Remick, "Considerations in Long-Range Implementation of Comparable Worth."

8. A Cook in the House of Lords

1. *Hayward v. Cammell Laird Shipbuilders, Ltd.,* [1988] Queen's Bench 12 (Court of Appeals, 1987).

2. For discussions of the House of Lords acting in its judicial capacity, see Alan Paterson, *The Law Lords* (Toronto: University of Toronto Press, 1982); Robert Stevens, *Law and Politics: The House of Lords as a Judicial Body, 1800–1976* (Chapel Hill: University of North Carolina Press, 1978); Louis Blom-Cooper and Gavin Drewry, *Final Appeal: A Study of the House of Lords in Its Judicial Capacity* (Oxford: Clarendon Press, 1972); R. J. Walker and M. G. Walker, *The English Legal System,* 3d ed. (London: Butterworths, 1972); R. M. Jackson, *The Machinery of Justice in England,* 6th ed. (Cambridge: Cambridge University Press, 1972). For a general comparison of U.S. and British legal processes, see Henry Abraham, *The Judicial Process: An Introductory Analysis of the Courts of the United States, England, and France* (New York: Oxford University Press, 1975).

3. Although this is not the practice in the U.S. Supreme Court, other U.S. courts, most visibly the courts of appeal, do sit in "committees," or "panels" as they are more commonly called in this country. Stephen Wasby, *The Supreme Court in the Federal Judicial System,* 2d ed. (New York: Holt, Rinehart & Winston, 1984), 42–43.

4. The American Bar Association recommends that judges be randomly assigned to cases "to avoid any suspicion [that] manipulation . . . could affect decisions." American Bar Association Commission on Standards of Judicial Administration, *Appellate Courts* (Chicago: American Bar Association, 1977), 91. But see John Martin and Elizabeth Prescott, *Appellate Court Delay* (Williamsburg, Va.: National Center for State Courts, 1981), 66–67 (many state courts that use panels do not use random assignment procedures).

5. For a brief history of Lord Mackay of Clashfern, see Alan Hamilton, "Calculations of the Outsider," *London Times,* Oct. 29, 1987, 12.

6. Equal Pay Act 1970, c. 41, as amended, § 1(2)(c)(i).

7. This is a stylized version of the submissions to the House of Lords. Lester and Irvine did not debate directly. Instead, Lester presented Julie Hayward's case for slightly over one day of the proceeding, then Irvine presented Cammell Laird's case for slightly less than one day, and then Lester rebutted Irvine's

submissions for approximately one hour. The judges asked probing questions during each presentation. No transcript was made, so the quoted passages in the text are not verbatim quotations but rather are taken from my notes. They are intended to convey in a succinct manner primarily the main substance and, to a lesser extent, the mood of the presentations.

8. Section 1(3) of the Equal Pay Act 1970, c. 41, as amended, provides that the employer need not pay a man and a woman doing work of equal value equally with respect to "a variation between the woman's contract and the man's contract if the employer proves that the variation is genuinely due to a material factor which is not the difference of sex and that factor . . . may be . . . a material difference [between the woman's case and the man's case]."

9. This point by Lester illustrates the difficulty of the issues in the case. David Pannick, who had represented Julie Hayward in previous stages of the case and who was being led by Lester in the House of Lords, had earlier written that an employer should not succeed with a defense under section 1(3) if he can justify only a part of a disparity between a man and a woman. David Pannick, *Sex Discrimination Law* (Oxford: Clarendon Press, 1985), 111. Thus, Irvine, in a sense, was relying on authority provided by Hayward's counsel to make his point, and Hayward's counsel responded by repudiating that authority.

10. Equal Pay Act 1970, c. 41, as amended, § 1(2)(c)(i).

11. Ibid., § 1(2)(c)(ii).

12. Ibid., § 1(2).

13. *Hayward v. Cammell Laird Shipbuilders, Ltd.*, [1988] 2 All England Law Reports 257 (House of Lords).

14. Ibid., 261: "However, one has to take account of the hours to be worked in order to earn this money and I think this consideration points to the importance of the provision in question being one which is capable of being compared from the point of view of the benefit it confers with a corresponding provision in another contract to see whether or not it is more beneficial than that provision."

15. Ibid. (emphasis added).

16. Ibid.

17. Ibid., 263: "Since in the nature of the dispute between the parties [section] 1(3) has never been in issue in this case I prefer to express no concluded opinion about its construction but I am presently of the view that [section] 1(3) would not provide a defence to an employer against whom it was shown that a term in the woman's contract was less favourable to her than a corresponding term in the man's contract on the basis that there was another term in the woman's contract which was more favourable to her than the corresponding term in the man's contract. At the very least for [section] 1(3) to operate it would have to be shown that the unfavourable character of the term in the woman's contract was in fact due to the difference in the opposite sense in the other term and that the difference was not due to the reason of sex."

18. Ibid., 266.
19. Ibid., 267.
20. Ibid., 266.
21. Indeed, because of the brevity of the discussion in the two speeches, it is not even certain that the lord chancellor and Lord Goff disagree. The lord chancellor said that he was currently of the view that section 1(3) would not provide a defense, but he went on to say that "at the very least" section 1(3) would provide a defense only where the unfavorable term in the woman's contract was in fact due to the difference in the opposite sense in the man's contract and only where the difference in the contracts did not result from sex discrimination. Ibid., 263. If the lord chancellor would interpret section 1(3) in that manner when he reached a "concluded" view, and if that was the manner in which Lord Goff would interpret the section 1(3) defense—he indicated in his speech that the defense would apply only when the difference in the contracts did not result from sex discrimination, but he did not discuss the "in fact due" element of the defense suggested by the lord chancellor—then perhaps there was no conflict in the speeches.

In a later case, the House of Lords again addressed the scope of the section 1(3) defense. In *Leverton v. Clwyd County Council,* [1989] 1 All England Law Reports 78, a woman paid £5,058 per year was performing work of equal value to that of men paid between £6,081 and £8,532 per year. The House of Lords held that the employer had successfully presented a section 1(3) defense by proving that because of differences in working hours and holiday time, the notional *hourly* pay was £4.42 for the woman and £4.40 for the men. Because the differences in annual pay disappeared when converted into hourly pay, the House of Lords was willing to infer that the difference in annual pay was "in fact due" to the differences in hours worked, even though there was no specific evidence of a causal relationship between hours worked and pay. Ibid., 86.

Although they predate the most recent developments, good discussions of the significance of the section 1(3) defense in equal value cases can be found in Evelyn Ellis, *Sex Discrimination Law* (Aldershot, Eng.: Gower), 44–53, 56, and Pannick, *Sex Discrimination Law,* 105–14.

22. *Hayward,* [1988] 2 All England Law Reports at 267.
23. *Hayward v. Cammell Laird Shipbuilders, Ltd.,* No. 5999/84 (Liverpool Industrial Tribunal, Sept. 12, 1988).

9. THE ANTIDISCRIMINATION PRINCIPLE

1. Howard Kurtz, "Justice Dept. Opposes Nurses' 'Comparable Worth' Lawsuit," *Washington Post,* Aug. 16, 1985, sec. A.
2. Comparable worth is required by Article 119 of the Treaty of Rome, the principal formative document of the European Economic Community. See Office for Official Publications of the European Communities, *Treaties Establishing the European Communities* (Luxembourg: Office for Official Publications of the Eu-

ropean Communities, 1973), 205–575; or "Treaty Establishing the European Economic Community," Nov. 23–Dec. 13, 1957, 298 United Nations Treaty Series 11. For a discussion of Article 119, see pages 17–19 above.

3. For examples of scholarly work that have adopted this understanding of comparable worth, see Mayer Freed and Daniel Polsby, "Comparable Worth in the Equal Pay Act," *University of Chicago Law Review* 51 (Fall 1984): 1078 n. 1; Comment, "Equal Pay, Comparable Work, and Job Evaluation," *Yale Law Journal* 90 (Jan. 1981): 657–80; Donald J. Treiman and Heidi I. Hartmann, eds. *Women, Work, and Wages: Equal Pay for Jobs of Equal Value* (Washington, D.C.: National Academy Press, 1981), ix, 1–2, 69–70; *The Comparable Worth Issue,* a BNA Special Report (Washington, D.C.: Bureau of National Affairs, 1981), 1.

4. The Equal Pay Regulations permit an employer to continue to pay different wages to a man and a woman doing work of equal value if the employer can prove that the difference "is genuinely due to a material factor which is not the difference of sex." Equal Pay Act 1970, c. 41, as amended, § 1(3). In the Hayward case, the employer might not have been successful with that defense even if it had overcome its procedural difficulties. The collective bargaining agreement might not have been construed as a "material factor"; even more likely, it might not have been seen as free of sex discrimination. But see *Reed Packaging Ltd. v. Boozer and Everhurst,* 21 Equal Opportunities Review 24 (1988) (employment appeal tribunal held that separate pay structures and collective bargaining agreements justified a pay disparity). Nevertheless, the Equal Pay Act clearly contemplates situations in which equal pay is not required even though the work is of equal value, for example, where there are seniority differences or shift differentials between the workers. See *Shields v. E. Coomes (Holdings), Ltd.,* [1978] Industrial Cases Reporter 1159, 1170 (Court of Appeal).

5. *Commission of the European Communities v. United Kingdom,* [1982] Industrial Cases Reporter 578, 597 (European Court of Justice).

6. Some in Britain have claimed that the Equal Pay Regulations, which were enacted by the Thatcher government in response to the European Court of Justice decision, are insufficient to bring Britain into compliance with Article 119 because they permit Hayward to prove her case *only* by comparing her job with other jobs. See Linda Clarke, "Proposed Amendments to the Equal Pay Act 1970—I," *New Law Journal* 133 (Oct. 1983): 936; Linda Clarke, "Proposed Amendments to the Equal Pay Act 1970—II," *New Law Journal* 133 (Dec. 1983): 1130; Linda Clarke, "Equal Pay for Work of Equal Value," *New Law Journal* 134 (Feb. 1984): 177.

7. For insightful general discussion of the antidiscrimination principle, see Paul Brest, "The Supreme Court 1975 Term, Foreword: In Defense of the Antidiscrimination Principle," *Harvard Law Review* 90 (Nov. 1976): 1–54; and Owen Fiss, "A Theory of Fair Employment Laws," *University of Chicago Law Review* 38 (Winter 1971): 235–314.

8. The antidiscrimination principle usually commands employers not to discriminate on the basis of a number of factors in addition to sex, factors such as race and religion. The principle as applied to the comparable worth issue, however, is usually directed to sex discrimination, and so that is all that I discuss here, even though the theory should be applicable to other forms of discrimination. See Julianne Malveaux, "Comparable Worth and Its Impact on Black Women," in *Slipping through the Cracks: The Status of Black Women,* ed. Margaret C. Simms and Julianne Malveaux (New Brunswick, N. J.: Transaction Books, 1986), 47–62; Judy Scales-Trent, "Comparable Worth: Is This a Theory for Black Workers?" *Women's Rights Law Reporter* 8 (Winter 1984): 51–58. Cf. *Bazemore v. Friday,* 478 U.S. 385 (1986).

9. There are two principal national laws prohibiting sex discrimination in both the United States and Britain. In the United States, they are Title VII of the Civil Rights Act of 1964, as amended, 42 U.S.C. §§ 2000e–2000e-17 (1982); and the Equal Pay Act of 1963, 29 U.S.C. § 206(d) (1982). In Britain, they are the Equal Pay Act 1970, c. 41, as amended, and the Sex Discrimination Act 1975, c. 65, as amended. In addition, in the United States the vast majority of the states have at least two laws prohibiting sex discrimination, and there are also many local laws prohibiting sex discrimination. See Virginia Dean, Patti Roberts, and Carroll Boone, "Comparable Worth under Various Federal and State Laws," in *Comparable Worth and Wage Discrimination: Technical Possibilities and Political Realities,* ed. Helen Remick (Philadelphia: Temple University Press, 1984), 238–66; EEOC Procedural Regulations, 29 Code of Federal Regulations § 1601.74 (1988) (listing fifty-eight local laws that prohibit sex discrimination).

10. I focus here on mainstream approaches to the antidiscrimination principle, the disparate treatment and disparate impact models of discrimination. There are other approaches to discrimination law, including the "dominance" approach of Catharine MacKinnon. See her *Feminism Unmodified* (Cambridge, Mass.: Harvard University Press, 1987), 32–45; and *Sexual Harassment of Working Women: A Case of Sex Discrimination* (New Haven, Conn.: Yale University Press, 1979), 101–41. I do not discuss those other approaches here, not because they are unimportant or because they do not apply to comparable worth but because they are not yet accepted in the mainstream of antidiscrimination law; my primary point here is that comparable worth, at least in theory, *is* in the mainstream of current antidiscrimination law.

11. Even if a woman cannot show that she would have been hired "but for" her sex, she can prevail if she can show that sex was a motivating or substantial factor in the hiring decision. *Price Waterhouse v. Hopkins,* 109 S. Ct. 1775 (1989). For our purpose, however, the subtleties of causation in discrimination cases need not be explored.

12. As one would expect, this type of evidence is quite rare. See *Gates v. Georgia-Pacific Corp.,* 326 F. Supp. 397, 399 (D. Ore. 1970), *aff'd,* 492 F.2d 292 (9th Cir. 1974) (direct evidence of discrimination "is virtually impossible

to produce"). Nevertheless, there are examples of overt discriminatory statements in the case law. See, e.g., *Wetzel v. Liberty Mutual Insurance Co.*, 508 F.2d 239, 258 (3d Cir.), *cert. denied,* 421 U.S. 1011 (1975) (women claiming employer channeled them into certain jobs and men into other jobs pointed to recruitment brochures that described the female-dominated job as "Fit for a Queen," while asking applicants to the male-dominated job if they were "the right man" for the job); *Butta v. Anne Arundel County,* 473 F. Supp. 83, 87–88 (D. Md. 1979) (employer told white applicant that he would prefer to hire a black person); *Hodgson v. First Federal Savings and Loan Association,* 455 F.2d 818, 821–22 (5th Cir. 1972) (interviewer wrote "too old" on notes of plaintiff's interview).

13. See, e.g., *Kinsey v. First Regional Securities, Inc.*, 557 F.2d 830, 837 (D.C. Cir. 1977); *Aikens v. U.S. Postal Service Board of Governors,* 665 F.2d 1057, 1060 (D.C. Cir. 1981), *vac'd on other grounds,* 460 U.S. 711 (1983); *Wright v. Western Electric Co., Inc.,* 664 F.2d 959, 964–65 (5th Cir. 1981). Cf. *Texas Department of Community Affairs v. Burdine,* 450 U.S. 248, 258–59 (1981) (evidence that plaintiff more qualified than person hired is probative of discrimination but not necessarily dispositive). See generally Mack Player, "Applicants, Applicants in the Hall, Who's the Fairest of Them All? Comparing Qualifications under Employment Discrimination Law," *Ohio State Law Journal* 46 (1985): 277–312.

14. See, e.g., *Teamsters v. United States,* 431 U.S. 324 (1977); *Hazelwood School District v. United States,* 433 U.S. 299 (1977).

15. See *Texas Department of Community Affairs v. Burdine,* 450 U.S. 248, 256 (1981) (plaintiff's "ultimate burden [is to persuade] the court that she has been the victim of intentional discrimination"); *United States Postal Service Board of Governors v. Aikens,* 460 U.S. 711, 715 (1983) ("the ultimate factual issue . . . in a Title VII case is 'whether the defendant intentionally discriminated against the plaintiff' ").

16. Group evidence is necessary to prove a violation of the antidiscrimination principle, or of a statute like Title VII that implements the antidiscrimination principle with broad prohibitory language. Group evidence is necessary to isolate sex from the myriad of other factors that might explain a wage difference between an individual woman and man. (In very rare circumstances—for example, when the employer makes overt discriminatory statements—group evidence may not be necessary.) The law, however, can be structured so as to permit individual women to prove discrimination in comparable worth cases. The British Equal Pay Act 1970 creates a strong presumption of discrimination if a woman can prove that her job is equal in skill, effort, and decision to that of a man. Julie Hayward, of course, is an individual woman who was able to prove discrimination under that law.

17. See, e.g., *Teamsters v. United States,* 431 U.S. 324, 357–62 (1977) (proof of discrimination against a class creates a rebuttable presumption that

every member of the class was subject to the discrimination); *Franks v. Bowman Transportation Co.*, 424 U.S. 747, 772–73 (1976) (where discrimination against a class has been proved, employer bears burden of proving that individual members of the class were not victims of the discrimination).

18. This was one of the rationales Judge Kennedy relied upon in deciding Helen Castrilli's case. *American Federation of State, County and Municipal Employees v. Washington*, 770 F.2d 1401, 1407 (9th Cir. 1985). The rationale has also been used in other important comparable worth cases in the United States. See *American Nurses' Association v. Illinois*, 783 F.2d 716, 720, 722 (7th Cir. 1986); *Spaulding v. University of Washington*, 740 F.2d 686, 708, *cert. denied*, 469 U.S. 1036 (1984).

19. Employer attempts to appeal to customer preferences to justify discrimination have been rejected by the courts except in very narrowly defined circumstances. *Gerdom v. Continental Airlines, Inc.*, 692 F.2d 602, 609 (9th Cir. 1982), *cert. dismissed*, 460 U.S. 1074 (1983) (customer preference for thin stewardesses did not justify airline's strict weight requirements); *Fernandez v. Wynn Oil Co.*, 653 F.2d 1273, 1276–77 (9th Cir. 1981) (reluctance of Latin American and southeast Asian customers to conduct business with a woman did not justify company's failure to promote woman to an international marketing position); *Diaz v. Pan American World Airways, Inc.*, 442 F.2d 385, 389 (5th Cir.), *cert. denied*, 404 U.S. 950 (1971) (customer preference for female airline stewardesses did not justify airline's discrimination against men); *Wilson v. Southwest Airlines Co.*, 517 F. Supp. 292, 298–304 (N.D. Tex. 1981) (customer preference for female airline stewardesses did not justify airline's discrimination against men even when airline used female sexuality as a marketing strategy). Compare, *Kern v. Dynalectron Corp.*, 577 F. Supp. 1196, 1200–2 (N.D. Tex. 1983), *aff'd*, 746 F.2d 810 (5th Cir. 1984) (preference of customer for Moslem pilots justified employer's religious discrimination because pilots were required to fly to Mecca in Saudi Arabia, where non-Moslem pilots, if caught, are beheaded); *Backus v. Baptist Medical Center*, 510 F. Supp. 1191, 1194–95 (E. D. Ark. 1981), *vacated on other grounds*, 671 F.2d 1100 (8th Cir. 1982) (customer preferences against male labor and delivery nurses justified discrimination where personal privacy interests were strong); *Fesel v. Masonic Home of Delaware, Inc.*, 447 F. Supp. 1346, 1350–51 (D. Del. 1978), *aff'd*, 591 F.2d 1334 (3rd Cir. 1979) (preferences of female nursing home residents, based in privacy concerns, justified discrimination against male nursing aides).

The courts have also been generally unreceptive to a related employer defense, that the discrimination emanates from other employees rather than from the employer. When employees discriminate through their union, Title VII provides a direct cause of action against the union. 42 U.S.C. § 2000e-2(c)(3) (1982). Thus, rather than providing a defense to an employer, employee discrimination that comes through a union permits a plaintiff to sue both the union and the employer under Title VII. See, e.g., *Howard v. Internal Molders*

& Allied Workers Union, 779 F.2d 1546 (11th Cir.), *cert. denied,* 476 U.S. 1174
(1986). Also see generally Charles Sullivan, Michael Zimmer, and Richard
Richards, *Federal Statutory Law of Employment Discrimination* (Indianapolis: Michie, 1980), § 2.14. Similarly, employers have been found liable for co-employee
racial and sexual harassment where the employers knew or should have known
about the harassment and failed to take corrective action. *Barrett v. Omaha
National Bank,* 726 F.2d 424 (8th Cir. 1984); *DeGrace v. Rumsfeld,* 614 F.2d
796 (1st Cir. 1980); *Martin v. Norbar, Inc.,* 537 F. Supp. 1260 (S.D. Ohio
1982). But see *Smith v. Rust Engineering Co.,* 20 FEP Cases 1172 (N.D. Ala.
1978). For a discussion of this issue from an economic perspective, see James
Ragan, Jr., and Carol Tremblay, "Testing for Employee Discrimination by
Race and Sex," *Journal of Human Resources* 23 (Winter 1988): 123–37.

For an important early discussion of employment discrimination emanating
from employees, customers, and the market, see Gary Becker, *The Economics of
Discrimination,* 2d ed. (Chicago: University of Chicago Press, 1971), 55–100.
One of the important points Becker makes is that "market" discrimination is
merely the summation of the individual discriminations of employers, governments, employees, and customers (pp. 84–100). The market incorporates the
discrimination of individual actors in the market and translates them into an
overall discrimination rate. Thus, employer attempts to defend in comparable
worth cases by arguing that they pay market wage rates (see the cases cited in
note 18) should be treated the same as appeals to employee or customer
discrimination.

20. See page 82 above.

21. *Griggs v. Duke Power Co.,* 401 U.S. 424, 432 (1971) ("good intent or
absence of discriminatory intent does not redeem employment procedures" that
have a disparate impact); *Teamsters v. United States,* 431 U.S. 324, 336 n.15
(1977) ("proof of discriminatory motive . . . is not required under a disparate-
impact theory"). See also *Watson v. Fort Worth Bank and Trust,* 108 S.Ct. 2777,
2784–85 (1988).

22. *Teamsters v. United States,* 431 U.S. 324, 336 n.15 (1977) (in a disparate
treatment case, "proof of discriminatory motive is critical"); *Texas Department
of Community Affairs v. Burdine,* 450 U.S. 248, 253 (1981) (in a disparate
treatment case, the ultimate issue is "whether the defendant intentionally discriminated against the plaintiff"). This conception of disparate treatment discrimination may be too narrow. For example, it would fail to sanction a
personnel manager who, although harboring no overt prejudice, always hires
white persons, perhaps because she feels more comfortable working with them.
See Brest, "In Defense of the Antidiscrimination Principle," 14–15.

23. The Supreme Court has recognized that the issue of conscious or intentional discrimination is "elusive" and "sensitive and difficult." *Texas Department of Community Affairs v. Burdine,* 450 U.S. 248, 255 n.8 (1981); *United
States Postal Service Board of Governors v. Aikens,* 460 U.S. 711, 716 (1983).

Also see generally Paul Brest, *"Palmer v. Thompson:* An Approach to the Problem of Unconstitutional Legislative Motive," in *Supreme Court Review,* ed. Phillip Kurland (Chicago: University of Chicago Press, 1971), 95–146; and John Hart Ely, "Legislative and Administrative Motivation in Constitutional Law," *Yale Law Journal* 79 (June 1970): 1205–1341. As a result, the Court permits a judicial finding of disparate treatment discrimination even in the absence of direct evidence as to the employer's state of mind (see text below).

24. *Teamsters v. United States,* 431 U.S. 324, 336 n.15 (1977).

25. *United States Postal Service Board of Governors v. Aikens,* 460 U.S. 711, 717 (1983).

26. See James Annable, *The Price of Industrial Labor* (Lexington, Mass.: Lexington Books, 1984). See also Arthur M. Ross, "Orbits of Coercive Comparison," in *Unemployment and Inflation: Institutionalist and Structuralist View,* ed. Michael J. Piore (White Plains, N.Y.: M. E. Sharpe, 1979), 94–111; and Arthur Ross, *Trade Union Wage Policy* (Berkeley: University of California Press, 1948) (wage expectations of union members depend on comparisons members make with other groups of workers).

27. See cases cited in note 19 above.

10. THE EFFECT OF COMPARABLE WORTH ON THE WAGE GAP

1. See introduction, note 11.

2. The reasons for the increase have not yet been adequately explored, but they have important implications for the comparable worth issue. One way of approaching the issue is through the human capital model, the dominant paradigm used in the United States to explain the earnings ratio between men and women (see note 14 below). The basic hypothesis of the human capital model is that earnings can be explained in terms of the endowments (human capital) that workers bring to the labor market, such as education and work experience. The combined earnings equation of men and women that is derived from this theory can be written as follows:

$$E_i = \sum_{j=1}^{n} \alpha_j^M x_{ij}^M + \sum_{j=1}^{n} \alpha_j^F x_{ij}^F + u_i$$

where E_i is the log of earnings of the ith person and x_j are human capital variables. The superscripts refer to whether the individual is male or female, and u_i is an error term.

This equation permits the increases in relative female earnings to be decomposed into two components, a portion due to increases in the relative human capital endowments held by women and a portion due to increases in the relative return to those endowments (i.e., a relative increase in the female coefficient). If, as is likely, a portion of the increase in relative female earnings is due to a relative increase in the female coefficient, that increase can be decomposed into a portion due to changes in the occupational mix of men and women and a portion due to other changes.

The reasons for the relative increase in female earnings during the 1980s, as disclosed by this type of analysis, would have important policy consequences with respect to the comparable worth issue. Differences in the returns of men and women to their human capital endowments (i.e., differences in the coefficients in the equation) have traditionally been interpreted as evidence of sex discrimination. Alan Blinder, "Wage Discrimination: Reduced Form and Structural Estimates," *Journal of Human Resources* 8 (Fall 1973): 436–55. If the increase in relative female earnings has been caused by relative increases in female human capital endowments, the increase in relative female earnings does not indicate that the sex discrimination addressed by comparable worth theory is easing. If comparable worth was worth pursuing before the increase in relative female earnings, it should still be pursued. If the increase in relative female earnings has been caused by a relative increase in the female coefficient, the implications for comparable worth depend on the reasons for that increase. If the relative increase in the female coefficient has been caused by changes in the occupational mix of men and women, the increase in relative female earnings does not indicate that the sex discrimination addressed by comparable worth theory is easing. (Although it may indicate that other forms of sex discrimination are easing— such as discrimination restricting women's entry into certain occupations—it does not indicate that the discrimination addressed by comparable worth theory, discrimination in wage setting, has eased.) Once again, comparable worth should still be pursued. But if the relative increase in the female coefficient has occurred for reasons other than changes in the occupational mix of men and women, the inference is that the sex discrimination addressed by comparable worth theory has eased. Perhaps the problem that comparable worth addresses can also be addressed with some effectiveness through market forces.

As indicated above, this type of analysis has not yet been done. Nevertheless, it is highly unlikely that differences in the returns of men and women to their human capital endowments have been wholly eliminated by the increase in the female-to-male earnings ratio in the 1980s. Instead, it is very likely that significant differences in returns still exist and that comparable worth will remain an important issue into the foreseeable future. See note 45 below.

3. See introduction, note 11.

4. See introduction, note 13.

5. Ratios in the table reflect the hourly wages of all workers except for Australia (weekly wages of full-time workers), France (annual wages of full-time workers), and Italy and Sweden (hourly wages of manufacturing workers). Jacob Mincer, "Intercountry Comparisons of Labor Force Trends and of Related Developments: An Overview," *Journal of Labor Economics* 3 (Jan. 1985): S6.

6. Although this discussion of the wage gap uses figures from the United

States, the analysis should apply equally well in Great Britain and most other industrialized countries.

7. If one uses the 35 percent figure as the total wage gap and the high estimates of the effects of time worked, productivity, and working conditions on the gap, a gap of about 7 percent remains after adjusting for those factors. If the low estimates of the effects of those factors are used, a 10 percent gap remains from the original 35 percent. Both numbers fall within the estimated range using 40 percent as the original wage gap. See page 140 below.

8. This analysis of the constitutive elements of the wage gap relies heavily on Paul Weiler, "The Wages of Sex: The Uses and Limits of Comparable Worth," *Harvard Law Review* 99 (June 1986): 1779–94. In essence, between pages 138 and 141, I am reporting on (and in some respects supplementing) his analysis of the wage gap and the effect of comparable worth upon it. Later I criticize that analysis. See pages 141–46 below.

9. See, e.g., U.S. Department of Labor, Women's Bureau, *Time of Change: 1983 Handbook on Women Workers* (Washington, D.C.: U.S. Government Printing Office, 1984), 82; and June O'Neill, "The Trend in the Male-Female Wage Gap in the United States," *Journal of Labor Economics* 3 (Jan. 1985): S94.

10. More precisely, men spend more time than women working *in the paid labor market* each year. If *all* work is considered, including housework and child care, it is likely that women work as much or more than men. Victor Fuchs, for example, has calculated that in 1983 the average man worked 1,667 hours in the paid labor market and the average woman 929 hours, but the average woman worked 2,383 total hours, including housework and child care, to the average man's 2,287 hours. "Sex Differences in Economic Well-Being," *Science* 232 (April 1986): 460.

11. The 72 percent figure is based on June O'Neill's analysis of 1983 data. "Male-Female Wage Gap," S96–S97. See Weiler, "Wages of Sex," 1781 n.196. That result, however, is subject to quite a degree of uncertainty. Several researchers report that even as full-time workers women on average work fewer hours per year and per week than men. See, e.g., Susan E. Shank, "Women and the Labor Market: The Link Grows Stronger," *Monthly Labor Review* 111 (March 1988): 6–7; Earl Mellor, "Investigating the Differences in Weekly Earnings of Men and Women," *Monthly Labor Review* 107 (June 1984): 25; and Malcolm Cohen, "Sex Differences in Compensation," *Journal of Human Resources* 6 (Fall 1971): 442–43. But determining the extent of the disparity in hours worked and calculating the effect of that disparity on the wage gap are quite difficult. See, e.g., O'Neill, "Male-Female Wage Gap," S93 n.2, S96 n.5 (discussing two ways in which the data on hours worked are uncertain), and compare Cohen, "Sex Differences in Compensation," 443 (using the higher of two possible hourly rates to calculate the effect of hours worked on earnings because many of the extra hours worked by men were at overtime rates) with

Mellor, "Differences in Weekly Earnings," 25 (men are generally not compensated at overtime rates for extra hours). Because of these difficulties, estimates of the effect of this factor on the wage gap vary dramatically. O'Neill estimates that it explains about 30 percent of the wage gap between men and women (pp. S96–S97); Cohen, about 20 percent (pp. 443, 446); and Mellor, about 9 percent (p. 25).

Figures from Great Britain also indicate that the "hours worked" factor contributes to the pay gap. In 1986 the female-to-male ratio of average gross weekly earnings in Britain was 66 percent. Men worked an average of 3.6 hours of overtime each week, however, and women an average of 0.8 hours. If overtime payments are subtracted from the earnings of both females and males, the wage ratio is 71 percent. Thus, overtime pay alone accounts for about 15 percent of the wage gap. Considering overtime alone, however, does not exhaust the probable contribution of the "hours worked" factor. Men worked an average of 38.2 nonovertime hours in 1986, and women an average of 36.5 nonovertime hours. Thus, differences in hours worked also contributed to the wage gap of 71 percent based on nonovertime pay. Department of Employment, *New Earnings Survey 1986* (London: Her Majesty's Stationery Office, 1986), A14–A15.

12. I explain changes to the wage ratio in terms of two different but related types of percentages. To illustrate, if a factor such as hours worked changes the female-to-male wage ratio from 60 percent to 70 percent, I can describe this either by saying that the factor changes the wage ratio by 10 percentage points or by saying that the factor explains 25 percent of the wage gap (i.e., 10 percentage points of the 40 percentage point wage gap). I cue the reader to which description I am using by using the term "percentage points" when I am using the male wage as the base and simply the word "percent" when I am using the wage gap as the base.

13. Researchers have recognized the difficulties of measuring productivity directly. See June O'Neill, "Earnings Differentials: Empirical Evidence and Causes," in *Sex Discrimination and Equal Opportunity*, ed. G. Schmid and R. Weitzel (New York: St. Martin's Press, 1984), 71; and Donald J. Treiman and Heidi I. Hartmann, *Women, Work, and Wages: Equal Pay for Jobs of Equal Value* (Washington, D.C.: National Academy Press, 1981), 17.

14. This, of course, is the human capital approach, in which productivity is measured indirectly by quantifying and analyzing the investments workers have made in their "human capital," i.e., in factors such as education and work experience. In the very large literature on this approach, perhaps the most important seminal works are Gary Becker, *Human Capital*, 2d ed. (New York: National Bureau of Economic Research, 1975); Jacob Mincer, "The Distribution of Labor Incomes: A Survey with Special Reference to the Human Capital Approach," *Journal of Economic Literature* (March 1970): 1–26; and Theodore Schultz, "Investment in Human Capital," *American Economic Review* (March 1961): 1–17. Although I agree with Weiler that the human capital approach

can be useful in analyzing the wage gap, there are also very significant theoretical and measurement problems with the approach. For a brief review, see Treiman and Hartmann, *Women, Work, and Wages,* 18–19. Weiler seems unaware of or unconcerned about these limitations. See, e.g., Weiler, "The Wages of Sex," 1790 ("Modern econometric analysis enables us to test the actual importance of female representation in influencing the wages paid for a particular job relative to other jobs"). See also note 27 below.

15. To reach this conclusion, Weiler relied on research that assigned 44 percent of the wage gap to human capital factors. Weiler, "The Wages of Sex," 1783 n.202, citing Mary Corcoran and Greg J. Duncan, "Work History, Labor Force Attachment, and Earnings Differences between the Races and Sexes," *Journal of Human Resources* 14 (Winter 1979): 3–20. The Corcoran and Duncan study explained as much of the wage gap as any studies of this type, and more than most. See Steven L. Willborn, *A Comparable Worth Primer* (Lexington, Mass.: Lexington Books, 1986), 13–15, table 1–3 (listing fifteen studies of this type which explain from 0 to 45 percent of the wage gap).

16. Factors such as time worked and productivity, of course, may not be independent of sex discrimination. Because of discrimination, women may be offered fewer work hours or given unequal access to productivity-enhancing activities, such as on-the-job training. See, e.g., Benson Rosen and Thomas Jerdee, "Sex Stereotyping in the Executive Suite," *Harvard Business Review* 52 (March–April 1974): 45–58; Mark Sieling, "Staffing Patterns Prominent in Female-Male Earnings Gap," *Monthly Labor Review* 107 (June 1984): 29–33; and Benson Rosen and Thomas Jerdee, "Influence of Sex Role Stereotypes on Personnel Decisions," *Journal of Applied Psychology* 59 (Aug. 1974): 9–14. For this and other reasons, the economic analyses may overestimate the amount of the wage gap that can be explained by factors other than discrimination. See note 32 below. These other types of discrimination would not be addressed very directly by comparable worth, however; they would be better handled by other applications of the antidiscrimination principle. See Weiler, "The Wages of Sex," 1781–82.

17. Weiler, "The Wages of Sex," 1783–84; Randall Filer, "Male-Female Wage Differences: The Importance of Compensating Differentials," *Industrial and Labor Relations Review* 38 (April 1985): 426–37. See also Christopher Jencks, Lauri Perman, and Lee Rainwater, "What Is a Good Job? A New Measure of Labor-Market Success," *American Journal of Sociology* 93 (May 1988): 1322–57; Robert McLean, Wayne Wendling, and Paul Neergaard, "Compensating Wage Differentials for Hazardous Work: An Empirical Analysis," *Quarterly Review of Economics and Business* 18 (Oct. 1978): 97–107. For general discussions of compensating wage differentials, see W. Kip Viscusi, *Risk by Choice* (Cambridge, Mass.: Harvard University Press, 1983); and Viscusi, *Employment Hazards* (Cambridge, Mass.: Harvard University Press, 1979).

18. This is not to say that this type of discrimination is unimportant or

insignificant. To the contrary, it is a major way in which sex discrimination is manifested. Women are expected to care for the young and the old and to perform other work in the home, without direct compensation. This has several consequences. First, it depresses the wages for the salaried equivalents of such work; for example, the wages of child care and nursing home workers. See Donald R. Williams and Charles A. Register, "Regional Variations in Earnings and the Gender Composition of Employment: Is 'Women's Work' Undervalued?" *Journal of Economic Issues* 20 (Dec. 1986): 1121–34. Second, it infects technical job evaluations, which then serve to reinforce the low wages for women's work. See Mary Witt and Patricia Maherny, *Women's Work: Up from .878* (Madison: University of Wisconsin-Extension, 1975), 11 ("the *Dictionary of Occupational Titles* systematically—though not purposely—discriminates against virtually all nondegreed, people-oriented women's jobs"; most seriously devalued are "the salaried derivatives . . . of homemaking and mothering"). Third, the effort expended in work at home makes it difficult for women who do work in the paid labor market to expend the same effort there as men do. See Gary Becker, "Human Capital, Effort, and the Sexual Division of Labor," *Journal of Labor Economics* 3 (Jan. 1985): S33. Despite its significance, however, this devaluation of the work women do in the paid labor market is only one of the ways in which sex discrimination is manifested.

19. For representative studies, see Mark Aldrich and Robert Buchele, *The Economics of Comparable Worth* (Cambridge, Mass.: Ballinger, 1986), 94–99 (job segregation accounts for about 15 percent of the wage gap); Paula England, "The Failure of Human Capital Theory to Explain Occupational Sex Segregation," *Journal of Human Resources* 17 (Summer 1982): 366 (job segregation accounts for 4.6 percent of the wage gap); Patricia Roos, "Sex Stratification in the Workplace: Male-Female Differences in Economic Returns to Occupation," *Social Science Research* 10 (Sept. 1981): 216 (job segregation accounts for 13 percent of the wage gap). For discussion of the studies on this issue, see Elaine Sorenson, "Effect of Comparable Worth Policies on Earnings," *Industrial Relations* 26 (Fall 1987): 233–36; Aldrich and Buchele, *Economics of Comparable Worth*, 84–101.

20. For discussions of this phenomenon, see Weiler, "The Wages of Sex," 1792–93; Treiman and Hartmann, *Women, Work, and Wages*, 39–40.

21. George Johnson and Gary Solon, "Estimates of the Direct Effects of Comparable Worth Policy," *American Economic Review* 76 (Dec. 1986): 1123.

22. 42 U.S.C. § 2000e(b) (1982).

23. *The State of Small Business: A Report of the President* (Washington, D.C.: U.S. Government Printing Office, 1988), 62–63, 90–91.

24. Until 1986, Great Britain also had a "small employers" exception. The British law applied only if an employer (defined to include any associated employers) employed more than five persons. Sex Discrimination Act 1975, c. 65, § 6(3)(b). The exception, however, was repealed in 1986 in response to a

decision by the European Court of Justice. Sex Discrimination Act 1986, c. 59, § 1(1). See *Commission of the European Communities v. United Kingdom,* [1984] Industrial Cases Reporter 192 (European Court of Justice, 1983) (blanket exclusion of small employers from coverage of the British Sex Discrimination Act violates EEC law).

25. Johnson and Solon, "Direct Effects of Comparable Worth," 1123. This estimate assumes that the comparable worth mandate would cover 40 percent of the jobs in the economy. The validity of that assumption is difficult to assess. Although Title VII's scope of coverage extends to 85 percent of the jobs in the economy (see note 23 above), one would expect the practical effect of a comparable worth mandate based on Title VII to cover a substantially lower percentage. Robert Smith estimated that the comparable worth policy would apply to between 8 and 23 percent of full-time female employees in the United States, would not apply to 21 percent of full-time female employees, and would probably not apply to 56 percent of full-time female employees. "Comparable Worth: Limited Coverage and the Exacerbation of Inequality," *Industrial and Labor Relations Review* 41 (Jan. 1988): 235. Although Weiler's analysis uses economics to predict the effect of comparable worth on the wage gap, others using markedly different analytical frameworks also doubt the ability of comparable worth to cause significant change. See, e.g., Barbara F. Reskin, "Bringing the Men Back In: Sex Differentiation and the Devaluation of Women's Work," *Gender and Society* 2 (March 1988): 58–81.

26. Weiler, "The Wages of Sex," 1791, 1794.

27. Weiler's analysis is primarily an economic analysis of the likely consequences of comparable worth. Therefore, one could challenge it by questioning the underlying assumptions of law-and-economics analysis, especially as applied to labor markets, and the assumptions of the human capital approach to wage determination. I have chosen not to do that here but rather to argue that even within Weiler's set of assumptions, his conclusions do not follow. For articles that question the application of economic concepts to legal issues, see Duncan Kennedy, "Cost-Benefit Analysis of Entitlement Problems: A Critique," *Stanford Law Review* 33 (Feb. 1981): 387–445; C. Edwin Baker, "Starting Points in Economic Analysis of Law," *Hofstra Law Review* 8 (Summer 1980): 939–72; C. Edwin Baker, "The Ideology of the Economic Analysis of Law," *Philosophy and Public Affairs* 5 (Fall 1975): 3–48. For works that question application of the concepts of neoclassical economics to the labor market, see Glen Cain, "The Challenge of Segmented Labor Market Theories to Orthodox Theory: A Survey," *Journal of Economic Literature* 14 (Dec. 1976): 1215–57; Peter Doeringer and Michael Piore, *Internal Labor Markets and Manpower Analysis* (Lexington, Mass.: Lexington Books, 1971). For a discussion of the limitations of human capital analysis, see Treiman and Hartmann, *Women, Work, and Wages,* 18–19.

28. Those of us who have chased a two-year-old for a few hours (or, as in my house, a one-year-old *and* a two-year-old), or cleaned toilets or washed floors,

recognize that it is not very accurate to describe the performance of household tasks as "nonwork activities." I use the term here merely as a shorthand way of referring to all activities that one might substitute for work in the paid labor market.

29. This notion of how men and women allocate time between work and nonwork activities has been well developed theoretically. See, e.g., Reuben Gronau, "Leisure, Home Production, and Work—The Theory of the Allocation of Time Revisited," *Journal of Political Economy* 85 (Dec. 1977): 1099–1123; and Gary Becker, "A Theory of the Allocation of Time," *Economic Journal* 75 (Sept. 1965): 493–517. Empirical evidence tends to support the theory that increases in relative wage rates also operate to increase the amount of time women spend in the paid labor market. See Mincer, "Intercountry Comparisons," S26–S27 (experience of ten countries shows significant positive correlation between rate of married women's labor force growth and increases in female-male wage ratio). But see note 33 below.

30. Becker, *Human Capital,* 71–88.

31. See Lois Shaw and David Shapiro, "Women's Work Plans: Contrasting Expectations and Actual Work Experience," *Monthly Labor Review* 110 (Nov. 1987): 7–13.

32. This type of analysis can also be used to mount a more basic attack on economic analysis of the wage gap: "Suppose . . . that men and women have the same basic productivity, but that discrimination reduces the earnings of women 10% below their market productivity. Given the advantage of specialization, such discrimination would induce a sexual division of labor, with most women specialized to the household and most men specialized to the market. As a result, earnings of the average woman would be considerably less than those of the average man, say only 60%. A decomposition of the 40% differential would show that sexual differences in investments in human capital explain 30 percentage points, or 75%, and that only 25% remains to be explained by discrimination. Yet in this example, the average earnings of men and women would be equal without discrimination, because there would be no sexual division of labor. More generally, discrimination and other causes of sexual differences in basic comparative advantage can be said to explain the *entire* difference in earnings between men and women, even though differences in human capital may appear to explain most of it." Becker, "Human Capital, Effort, and the Sexual Division of Labor," S42.

33. The wage gap caused by differences in time worked may also widen in response to higher relative wages if the female labor supply curve is backward bending. See Jennifer Roback, *A Matter of Choice: A Feminist Critique of Comparable Worth by a Skeptical Feminist* (New York: Priority Press Publications, 1986), 33–38; George Hildebrand, "The Market System," in *Comparable Worth: Issues and Alternatives,* 2d ed., ed. E. Robert Livernash (Washington, D.C.: Equal Employment Advisory Council, 1984), 106.

34. The increases in the wage ratio in the 1980s may soon make it possible to test empirically the relationships between the various wage gaps, but that has not yet been done.

35. In addition to the foreign experiences discussed below, see the study by Elaine Sorensen which, based on an analysis of job evaluation studies in Iowa, Michigan, Minnesota, Washington, and San Jose, determined that comparable worth would eliminate 28 percent of the national wage gap. "Effect of Comparable Worth Policies on Earnings," *Industrial Relations* 26 (Fall 1987): 227–33.

36. For general discussions of the experiences of several of these countries, see Janice Bellace, "A Foreign Perspective," in Livernash, *Comparable Worth,* 137–72; Willborn, *Comparable Worth Primer,* 77–96.

37. Consider, for example, Mincer's table of wage ratios from 1960 to 1980 in "Intercountry Comparisons," S6, table 3. The table provides 1960 and 1980 wage ratio data for five countries from the European Economic Community plus Australia, Japan, Sweden, the United States, and the Soviet Union. The EEC countries (which are subject to the equal pay mandate of the Treaty of Rome), Australia, and Sweden have attempted to eliminate the portion of the wage gap caused by sex discrimination. The wage gaps in those countries declined by 7 to 18 percentage points between 1960 and 1980, with an average decline of about 11 percentage points. The decline appears to have been fostered by the public programs designed to deal with the wage gap rather than by general worldwide trends, because the wage gaps in the other countries in Mincer's table declined by 0 to 8 percentage points during the same period, with an average decline of about 3 percentage points. The decline in the wage gap in both the United States and the Soviet Union during that period, as reported by Mincer, was zero. Much more comparative research is necessary, of course, before we can reach these conclusions with a high degree of confidence. (It should be noted that in Mincer's table Britain showed an 18 percent increase in the wage ratio from 1960 to 1980. That increase was attributable largely to Britain's implementation of its Equal Pay Act. See A. Zabalza and Z. Tzannatos, *Women and Equal Pay: The Effects of Legislation on Female Employment and Wages in Britain* (Cambridge, Mass.: Cambridge University Press, 1985); A. Zabalza and Z. Tzannatos, "The Effect of Britain's Anti-Discriminatory Legislation on Relative Pay and Employment," *Economic Journal* 95 (Sept. 1985): 679–99; P. Z. Tzannatos and A. Zabalza, "The Anatomy of the Rise in British Female Relative Wages in the 1970's: Evidence from the New Earnings Survey," *British Journal of Industrial Relations* 22 [July 1984]: 177–94. The increase was not at all attributable to Britain's efforts on the comparable worth issue. The Equal Value Regulations did not become effective until January 1, 1984.)

38. Bellace, "A Foreign Perspective," 170.

39. These ratios reflect the weekly wages of full-time workers for Australia, the hourly wages of all workers for the Netherlands, the hourly wages of

nongovernmental workers for New Zealand, and the hourly wages of manufacturing workers for Sweden. Mincer, "Intercountry Comparisons," S6, table 3; and *Equal Pay Implementation in New Zealand* (Wellington: P. D. Hasselberg, 1979), 16, table 1.

40. See, e.g., Heather Joshi, Richard Layard, and Susan Owen, "Why Are More Women Working in Britain?" *Journal of Labor Economics* 3 (Jan. 1985): S154 (women have tended to increase their relative investment in education since the increase in relative female wages); Joop Hartog and Jules Theeuwes, "The Emergence of the Working Wife in Holland," *Journal of Labor Economics* 3 (Jan. 1985): S235 (increases in women's wages contribute substantially to increased rate of participation in the labor force by married women); Siv Gustafsson and Roger Jacobsson, "Trends in Female Labor Force Participation in Sweden," *Journal of Labor Economics* 3 (Jan. 1985): S256 (increases in women's wages, due in part to dramatically decreased sex differentials, are the most important explanation for increases in the labor force participation rate of married women); R. G. Gregory, P. McMahon, and B. Whittingham, "Women in the Australian Labor Force: Trends, Causes, and Consequences," *Journal of Labor Economics* 3 (Jan. 1985): S306–S308 (since the large increases in relative wages, women have increased their investments in education and the length of their uninterrupted job tenure).

41. More detailed study would be necessary to state this with a high degree of confidence and to quantify the effect of closing the wage gap due to sex discrimination on the wage gaps caused by other factors.

42. It is unlikely that there would be a decrease in the wage gap in this country equivalent to the decreases in table 10.2 if the only strategy used to reduce the wage gap were litigation. See pages 154–55 below. But given the many nonlitigation approaches to the issue currently being pursued in the United States (see chapter 11, note 36 below), it appears that litigation will not be the only, or perhaps not even the most significant, method of addressing the wage gap. As a result, the decreases in table 10.2 would appear to be possible.

43. A similar response can be made to another argument that has been forwarded for rejecting comparable worth. Robert Smith ("Comparable Worth," 238) notes that a comparable worth policy would have only limited coverage and argues that the women to whom the policy would apply are better paid than the women to whom the policy would not apply. Because comparable worth would help more highly paid women, Smith says the policy would "tend to exaggerate earnings inequality in society." His argument seems to be that because a comparable worth policy would not be available to all who suffer from this form of sex discrimination, the policy should not be available to anyone. A more acceptable conclusion from his premises would be that the coverage of the comparable worth policy should be broadened to encompass as

completely as possible everyone who might suffer from this form of discrimination. Smith's argument fails for another reason as well: his conclusion that a comparable worth policy would "tend to exaggerate earnings inequality in society" is wrong. Although a comparable worth policy may increase the variance of earnings of women, the variance of earnings in society overall (and in particular the variance of earnings between men and women) would decrease. For a consideration of the same argument in a slightly different context, see Richard Freeman and James Medoff, *What Do Unions Do?* (New York: Basic Books, 1984), 78–93.

44. Denying relief to people whose wages are quite depressed because of sex discrimination is also unacceptable from a practical standpoint. A practical argument could be made that comparable worth should be rejected because it is difficult to confine it to severe cases of discrimination, and as a result the cost of applying comparable worth in all cases does not justify the benefits that would flow to people whose wages are severely depressed because of sex discrimination. The argument is unconvincing, because litigation should be quite successful at confining comparable worth to severe cases of discrimination. Women like Helen Castrilli and Julie Hayward, and all potential plaintiffs in lawsuits, make their decision to litigate by balancing the potential gains from the lawsuit against the costs of the litigation, discounted by the probability of success. See George Priest and Benjamin Klein, "The Selection of Disputes for Litigation," *Journal of Legal Studies* 13 (Jan. 1984): 1–55. The costs of comparable worth litigation are quite high. Castrilli's case cost the plaintiffs well over $1 million to litigate. The plaintiff's expenses in Hayward's case, which involved the wages of only one person, were over £50,000. These costs should decrease to some extent over time, because many of the legal issues that needed to be litigated in the early cases will have been settled. Comparable worth cases will always be factually complex, however, so the litigation costs will undoubtedly remain relatively high. The plaintiffs' probability of success at trial, over time, should approach 50 percent. Cases in which the plaintiffs' probability of success is significantly greater than 50 percent should, in most instances, be settled before trial, and cases in which the plaintiffs' probability of success is significantly less should, in most cases, not be pursued. As a result, with high litigation costs and a probability of success approaching 50 percent, plaintiffs should litigate comparable worth claims only if the potential gains from the lawsuit are fairly high; that is, they should litigate only if the extent of the sex discrimination is fairly severe. The balancing process used by a plaintiff to determine whether a lawsuit should be filed, then, should operate to filter the more significant cases from the less significant. The argument that comparable worth should be rejected as a legal doctrine because it could not be confined to cases of severe discrimination is unconvincing. Indeed, since comparable worth lawsuits produce public goods (see page 146 below), the problem is more

likely to be that too few lawsuits will be filed than that too many will be. Mancur Olson, *The Logic of Collective Action: Public Goods and the Theory of Groups* (Cambridge, Mass.: Harvard University Press, 1965), 30–31.

45. See note 2 above. From preliminary studies, it seems likely that the current reduction in the wage gap has resulted not from a reduction in wage discrimination against female-dominated occupations, but rather from progress made by women in other occupations and from reductions in the real wages of men. James P. Smith and Michael Ward, "Women in the Labor Market and in the Family," *Journal of Economic Perspectives* 3 (Winter 1989): 10–14 (wage gap reduced because women are increasing their human capital relative to men); Victor Fuchs, *Women's Quest for Economic Equality* (Cambridge, Mass.: Harvard University Press, 1988), 64–67, 82–83 (women who have improved their position are white, young, unmarried, and well educated); National Committee on Pay Equity, *Briefing Paper on the Wage Gap* (Washington, D.C.: National Committee on Pay Equity, Sept. 18, 1987), 4 (one-quarter of reduction in wage gap from 1979 to 1986 caused by fall in real wages of men).

46. See generally John Donohue, "Is Title VII Efficient?" *University of Pennsylvania Law Review* 134 (July 1986): 1411–31; and Donohue, "Further Thoughts on Employment Discrimination Legislation: A Reply to Judge Posner," *University of Pennsylvania Law Review* 136 (Dec. 1987): 523–51. See also Richard Posner, "The Efficiency and the Efficacy of Title VII," *University of Pennsylvania Law Review* 136 (Dec. 1987): 513–21.

47. Owen Fiss has been an important proponent of this view: "The Death of the Law?" *Cornell Law Review* 72 (Nov. 1986): 1–16; "Out of Eden," *Yale Law Journal* 94 (June 1985): 1669–73; "Against Settlement," *Yale Law Journal* 93 (May 1984): 1073–90.

48. 347 U.S. 483 (1954).

11. Practical Limitations

1. Carin Ann Clauss, "Comparable Worth—The Theory, Its Legal Foundation, and the Feasibility of Implementation," *University of Michigan Journal of Law Reform* 20 (Fall 1986): 18–34.

2. See Donald J. Treiman, "Effect of Choice of Factors and Factor Weights in Job Evaluation," in *Comparable Worth and Wage Discrimination,* ed. Helen Remick (Philadelphia: Temple University Press, 1984), 88; Donald P. Schwab, "Job Evaluation and Pay Setting: Concepts and Practices," in *Comparable Worth: Issues and Alternatives,* ed. E. Robert Livernash, 2d ed. (Washington, D.C.: Equal Employment Advisory Council, 1984), 59–62; Donald J. Treiman and Heidi I. Hartmann, *Women, Work, and Wages: Equal Pay for Work of Equal Value* (Washington, D.C.: National Academy of Sciences, 1981), 69–82; Donald J. Treiman, *Job Evaluation: An Analytic Review* (Washington, D.C.: National Academy of Sciences, 1979), 34–39, 40–43.

Even if job evaluations produced consistent results, their use in cases designed to identify and quantify sex discrimination would present problems. Job evaluation in these cases is used in an attempt to produce a ranking of jobs that is independent of sex. But sex bias can creep into the job evaluation procedure through a number of cracks. For a brief discussion, see Steven L. Willborn, *A Comparable Worth Primer* (Lexington, Mass.: Lexington Books, 1986), 65–66. For a discussion of the implications for comparable worth, see Donald P. Schwab and Dean W. Wichern, "Systematic Bias in Job Evaluation and Market Wages: Implications for the Comparable Worth Debate," *Journal of Applied Psychology* 68 (Feb. 1983): 60–69.

For a review of job evaluations in Britain under the Equal Pay Act 1970, see "Evaluating the Role of the Independent Experts," *Employment Opportunities Review* 24 (March–April 1989): 17–19.

3. For a more complete description, see pages 11–13 above.

4. Henry J. Aaron and Cameran M. Lougy, *The Comparable Worth Controversy* (Washington, D.C.: Brookings Institution, 1986), 29–36.

5. This is especially true in cases involving discrimination. The determinative factor in most discrimination cases is the state of mind of the employer. Since direct evidence of a discriminatory state of mind is seldom available and the employer's statements about his state of mind are not reliable (the employer has incentives to be less than truthful), most cases are decided on the basis of circumstantial or statistical evidence that creates, or fails to create, an inference of a discriminatory state of mind.

6. The rules of evidence prohibit litigants from using certain types of evidence that are particularly unreliable; that is a principal reason that hearsay, for example, is generally inadmissible. I. Daniel Stewart, "Perception, Memory, and Hearsay: A Criticism of Present Law and the Proposed Federal Rules of Evidence," *Utah Law Review* 1970 (Jan.): 1–39. Well-done job evaluation studies, however, do not fall into that category. They should be admissible under the rules of evidence, Federal Rules of Evidence, rules 702 and 703; see generally Edward W. Cleary, ed., *McCormick on Evidence*, 3rd ed. (St. Paul, Minn.: West, 1984), 641–50; and the courts, recognizing this, have admitted them into evidence, often without objection, as in Helen Castrilli's case.

7. A good general model to follow would be the use of statistical evidence in discrimination cases. Statistical evidence, like evidence relating to job evaluation studies, is relevant to the issue of discrimination but difficult for laypersons to understand and subject to various types of distortion and misinterpretation. See generally David Kaye and Mikel Aicken, *Statistical Methods in Discrimination Litigation* (New York: Marcel Dekker, 1986); Thomas Campbell, "Regression Analysis in Title VII Cases: Minimum Standards, Comparable Worth, and Other Issues Where Law and Statistics Meet," *Stanford Law Review* 36 (July 1984): 1299–1324; David Baldus and James Cole, *Statistical Proof of Discrimination* (Colorado Springs, Colo.: Shepard's, 1980). Despite these problems, the courts have generally been very open to the use of

statistical evidence. The U.S. Supreme Court has held that questionable statistical evidence should be admitted but scrutinized closely to determine its probativeness—*Bazemore v. Friday,* 478 U.S. 385, 400–404 (1986)—the approach suggested here for evidence relating to job evaluations. More generally, the Supreme Court has emphasized the useful role that statistics can have in discrimination cases and indicated that evaluating the probative value of statistics can best be done on a case-by-case basis. *Watson v. Fort Worth Bank and Trust,* 108 S.Ct. 2777, 2789 n.3 (1988).

8. *Hayward v. Cammell Laird Shipbuilders, Ltd.,* [1985] Industrial Cases Reporter 71, 78 (Industrial Tribunal, 1984).

9. *American Federation of State, County and Municipal Employees v. Washington,* 770 F.2d 1401, 1407 (9th Cir. 1985).

10. Once again, the analogy to judicial treatment of statistical evidence is apt. The standards of reliability for statistics in discrimination cases have been developed (and are being developed) through an examination of the use of statistics in a great many cases. The standards are as rich and detailed as the cases in which they were developed. See *Watson v. Fort Worth Bank and Trust,* 108 S.Ct. 2777, 2789–90 (1988); Campbell, "Regression Analysis in Title VII Cases," 1300–1301 n.7.

11. The case-by-case approach to the probative value of job evaluation evidence "incorporates a strong tendency toward [an] efficient outcome" that is lacking in the current per se approaches in the United States and Britain. See George Priest, "The Common Law Process and the Selection of Efficient Rules," *Journal of Legal Studies* 6 (Jan. 1977): 81.

12. Aaron and Lougy, *Comparable Worth Controversy,* 29–36.

13. Remedies in comparable worth cases may affect the competitive position of employers. If the remedy over- or undercorrects for discrimination, the employer would be at a competitive disadvantage or advantage vis-à-vis its nondiscriminating competitors. Indeed, even if the remedy accurately corrects for discrimination, an employer could be placed at a disadvantage if its competitors engage in sex-based wage discrimination but have not yet been sued.

14. Discrimination cases often present remedial problems even more severe than those present in comparable worth cases. Two ready examples involve school desegregation and court-ordered affirmative action. See, e.g., *Swann v. Charlotte-Mecklenburg Board of Education,* 402 U.S. 1 (1971); *Local 28, Sheet Metal Workers' International Association v. Equal Employment Opportunity Commission,* 478 U.S. 421 (1986). The remedies in those areas are not perfect, either, but the decision makers, like decision makers in comparable worth cases, are attempting to fashion acceptable responses to unacceptable situations. The decision makers are certainly not precluded from considering relevant information, as Aaron and Lougy suggest should be done in comparable worth cases.

15. For example, there may be problems with who is entitled to bring comparable worth lawsuits, *American Federation of State, County and Municipal*

Employees v. County of Nassau, 664 F. Supp. 64 (E.D. N.Y. 1987); with defining and managing the classes created, *Wetzel v. Liberty Mutual Insurance Company,* 508 F.2d 239 (3d Cir.), *cert. denied,* 421 U.S. 1011 (1975); and with determining the relevance of employment practices that predate the enactment of Title VII, *Bazemore v. Friday,* 478 U.S. 385, 395–96 and n.6 (1986).

16. For example, there may be problems in determining whether a woman who claims equal pay works in the same establishment as the man with whom she seeks to compare herself. See Erika Szyszczak, "The Equal Pay Directive and U.K. Law," in *Women, Employment, and European Equality Law,* ed. Christopher McCrudden (London: Eclipse Publications, 1987), 62–66; Michael Rubenstein, *Equal Pay for Work of Equal Value* (London: Macmillan, 1984), 51–54.

17. Crucial implementation issues include the burden imposed on plaintiffs to prove a prima facie case (see note 23 below), the scope of the employers' "genuine material factor" defense (see David Pannick, *Sex Discrimination Law* [Oxford: Clarendon Press, 1985], 105–14), and the availability to employers of a "market" defense. See *American Federation of State, County and Municipal Employees v. Washington,* 770 F.2d 1401, 1407 (9th Cir. 1985).

18. Every comparable worth case in the United States, to the best of my knowledge, has been filed as a class action and against a large employer. See, e.g., *American Nurses' Association v. Illinois,* 783 F.2d 716 (7th Cir. 1986); *American Federation of State, County and Municipal Employees v. Washington,* 770 F.2d 1401 (9th Cir. 1985); *Spaulding v. University of Washington,* 740 F.2d 686 (9th Cir.), *cert. denied,* 469 U.S. 1036 (1984); *Lemons v. Denver,* 620 F.2d 228 (10th Cir.), *cert. denied,* 449 U.S. 888 (1980); *Christensen v. Iowa,* 563 F.2d 353 (8th Cir. 1977).

19. See pages 100–108 above.

20. In Great Britain the authority to handle equal pay cases and other industrial matters has been given to industrial tribunals rather than to the courts. The tribunals were formed with the hope that they, at least relative to the courts, would be cheap, accessible, free from technicality, quick, and expert. See *Franks Committee on Administrative Tribunals and Enquiries* (London: Her Majesty's Stationery Office, 1957), ¶ 406. For a brief review of the history of the establishment of the tribunals and a critical assessment of their efficiency, see Linda Dickens et al., *Dismissed: A Study of Unfair Dismissal and the Industrial Tribunal System* (Oxford: Basil Blackwell, 1985), 3–11, 182–221. See also Jon Clark and Lord Wedderburn, "Modern Labour Law: Problems, Functions, and Policies," in *Labour Law and Industrial Relations: Building on Kahn-Freund,* ed. Lord Wedderburn, Roy Lewis, and Jon Clark (Oxford: Clarendon Press, 1983), 173–84 (industrial tribunals depoliticize collective activity, tend to convince workers that industrial conflict is abnormal, and substitute law and litigation as the normal way of resolving industrial disputes).

21. See pages 40–41 and 46–48 above.

22. *Hayward v. Cammell Laird Shipbuilders, Ltd.*, [1985] Industrial Cases Reporter 71, 78 (Industrial Tribunal, 1984).

23. In the United States the courts in comparable worth cases have emphasized accuracy to a great extent, at the expense of both the "low-cost" factor and the "achievement of the substantive goal" factor. This emphasis on accuracy—and a narrow version of accuracy at that—can be seen most readily by comparing comparable worth cases with discrimination cases that do not involve comparable worth. In the latter a plaintiff can successfully present a prima facie case by demonstrating that an employer treats men and women differently. The plaintiff need not show that the employer subjectively knew of the difference in treatment or that the difference in treatment resulted from the employer's desire to benefit men at the expense of women. See, e.g., *Teamsters v. United States*, 431 U.S. 324 (1977); *Hazelwood School District v. United States*, 433 U.S. 299 (1977). In one of the two most influential comparable worth cases to date, Judge Posner of the Seventh Circuit Court of Appeals held that proof of a disparity between the wages of men and women is not sufficient to make out a prima facie case and that even proof of an employer's knowledge of such a disparity is not sufficient. The plaintiff must prove in addition that the disparity was "motivated at least in part by a desire to benefit men at the expense of women." *American Nurses' Association v. Illinois*, 783 F.2d 716, 722 (7th Cir. 1986). This enhanced focus on accuracy in comparable worth cases raises their costs by making them more complex and factually dense, and makes it less likely that the substantive goal of comparable worth will be achieved because it will enable some employers who engage in this type of discrimination to escape detection.

24. I must reemphasize that the goal of narrowing the wage gap between men and women is merely a by-product of the primary goal of comparable worth, the goal of eliminating discrimination based on the sex composition of occupations. See page 145 above.

25. These figures are based on rough calculations. I calculated the female-to-male wage ratio for full-time workers in the United States from 1986 data in the Bureau of Labor Statistics's Current Population Survey and then added $25 million to the overall income for women and recalculated the wage ratio. (In at least three respects, this overestimates the effect of the settlement on the wage ratio: (1) the $25 million figure comes from the estimates of the future costs at the time of the settlement, and the actual costs turned out to be substantially less; (2) it assumes that all of the $25 million went to women when, in fact, a portion of it went to men; and (3) it assumes that all of the money went to full-time workers when, in fact, some of it went to part-time workers.) The unadjusted female-to-male wage ratio in 1986 was 69.212 percent; the adjusted wage ratio was 69.215 percent.

26. See generally Robert Mnookin and Lewis Kornhauser, "Bargaining in

the Shadow of the Law: The Case of Divorce," *Yale Law Journal* 88 (April 1979): 950–97.

27. See note 18 above.

28. See Alice Leonard, *Pyrrhic Victories: Winning Sex Discrimination and Equal Pay Cases in the Industrial Tribunals, 1980–84* (London: Her Majesty's Stationery Office, 1987), 29–32, 50 (cases heard by industrial tribunals seem to have only limited effects on employees other than the applicant). For a general critique of the procedures for equal value cases in Great Britain, see Bob Hepple, "The Judicial Process in Claims for Equal Pay and Equal Treatment in the United Kingdom," in McCrudden, *Women, Employment, and European Equality Law,* 143–60.

29. The female-to-male ratio of gross weekly earnings of full-time adult workers in Britain was 66 percent from 1983 to 1987 and 67 percent in 1988. The female-to-male ratios of gross hourly earnings of full-time adult workers for the years 1983 to 1988 were 74, 73, 74, 74, 73, and 75 percent respectively. These statistics are all from the Department of Employment's New Earnings Survey. The statistics for 1983 to 1986 are reported in Department of Employment, *New Earnings Survey 1986,* Pt. B (London: Her Majesty's Stationery Office, 1986), B29–B32, and those for 1987 and 1988 in "The Pay Gap," *Equal Opportunities Review* 22 (Nov.–Dec. 1988): 24.

30. See introduction, note 11.

31. The major reason for this, of course, is that comparable worth lawsuits have been so unsuccessful. See, e.g., *Colby v. J. C. Penney Co.,* 811 F.2d 1119, 1126 (7th Cir. 1987); *American Nurses' Association v. Illinois,* 783 F.2d 716, 719–23 (7th Cir. 1986); *Lemons v. Denver,* 620 F.2d 228 (10th Cir.), *cert. denied,* 449 U.S. 888 (1980); *Christensen v. Iowa,* 563 F.2d 353 (8th Cir. 1977).

32. In addition to their effectiveness, these blunter instruments may be preferable to litigation as mechanisms for addressing the wage gap because they apply broadly and simultaneously to employers and, as a result, are less likely than litigation to affect the competitive position of employers. See note 13 above.

33. In Australia, significant reductions in the wage gap were achieved when governmental wage-setting boards ended their historic discrimination against female-dominated occupations. See S. Deery and D. Plowman, *Australian Industrial Relations,* 2d ed. (Sydney: McGraw-Hill, 1985), 308–11; Robert G. Gregory and Vivian Ho, "Equal Pay and Comparable Worth: What Can the U.S. Learn from the Australian Experience?" (Discussion Paper No. 123, Centre for Economic Policy Research, Australian National University, July 1985) Daniel J. B. Mitchell, "The Australian Labor Market," in *The Australian Economy: A View from the North,* ed. Richard E. Caves and Lawrence B. Krause (Sydney: George Allen & Unwin, 1984), 185–87. In Sweden, significant reductions were achieved primarily through the collective bargaining process. See

Robert J. Flanagan, "Efficiency and Equality in Swedish Labor Markets," in *The Swedish Economy,* ed. Barry P. Bosworth and Alice M. Rivlin (Washington D.C.: Brookings Institution, 1987), 143–49; Willborn, *Comparable Worth Primer,* 93–95; Bellace, "A Foreign Perspective," 160–61.

34. Sections 3 and 4 of the Equal Pay Act 1970, c. 41, required that collective bargaining agreements and orders of wages councils be amended to ensure that "terms and conditions [that apply only to women] are not in any respect less favourable than those of all persons of the other sex to whom the agreement [or order] applies." Although the sections were later repealed (Sex Discrimination Act 1986, c. 59, schedule, pt. II; Wages Act 1986, c. 48, schedule 5, pt. II), they seemed to be a major explanatory factor for the large increase in relative female wages in Britain in the mid-1970s. See A. Zabalza and Z. Tzannatos, *Women and Equal Pay* (Cambridge, Mass.: Cambridge University Press, 1985), 7–9, 37–48; P. Tzannatos and A. Zabalza, "The Anatomy of the Rise of British Female Relative Wages in the 1970s: Evidence from the New Earnings Survey," *British Journal of Industrial Relations* 22 (July 1984): 186–93; P. L. Davies, "European Equality Legislation, U.K. Legislative Policy, and Industrial Relations," in McCrudden, *Women, Employment, and European Equality Law,* 44.

35. Between 1956 and 1981, there were increases in the minimum wage in twelve of the twenty-six years and none in the other fourteen years. The wage gap narrowed in eight of the twelve years (or in 66 percent of the years) in which there was an increase in the minimum wage. It narrowed in only five of the fourteen years (or in 36 percent of the years) in which there was no increase in the minimum wage. My source for the years in which the minimum wage was increased was various issues of *Statutes at Large;* my source for the wage gap between 1956 and 1981 was U.S. Department of Labor, Women's Bureau, *Time of Change: 1983 Handbook on Women Workers* (Washington, D.C.: U.S. Government Printing Office, 1984), 82.

36. There have been a large number of state and local initiatives on the comparable worth issue. For summaries, see Diana Stone, *Pay Equity Sourcebook* (San Francisco: Equal Rights Advocates, 1987), 461–74; and Mark Aldrich and Robert Buchele, *The Economics of Comparable Worth* (Cambridge, Mass.: Ballinger, 1986), 41–42, 64–69. Although no definitive study has been done, the efforts seem to have had some effect on the wage gap. Gregory and Ho, "Equal Pay and Comparable Worth," 16, 25–27 (wage gap is smaller for employees of state and local government—27.1 percent—than it is in the aggregate—38.7 percent—and for private sector employees—34.6 percent).

37. There are undoubtedly a number of similar, broad-brush approaches that could be tried in an attempt to close the wage gap. One commentator has suggested labor law reform that would encourage unionization and thus permit the problem to be dealt with through the collective bargaining structure;

voluntary affirmative action by employers (especially large governmental employers) on the pay gap; and an extension of contract compliance requirements to include a pay equity component. Paul Weiler, "The Wages of Sex: The Uses and Limits of Comparable Worth," *Harvard Law Review* 99 (June 1986): 1797–1806. Another has suggested child-centered policies, such as parental leave and subsidized child care, which would help women participate more fully in the labor market. Victor Fuchs, *Women's Quest for Economic Equality* (Cambridge, Mass.: Harvard University Press, 1988), 130–38, 145–52. Tax policies could also be used to enhance the position of working women. See Laura Ann Davis, "A Feminist Justification for the Adoption of an Individual Filing System," *Southern California Law Review* 62 (Nov. 1988): 197–252; Gary Burtless, "Taxes Transfers, and Swedish Labor Supply," in *The Swedish Economy,* ed. Barry P. Bosworth and Alice M. Rivlin (Washington, D.C., Brookings Institution, 1987), 188–92.

38. See pages 144–45 above.

39. See page 146 above.

40. For example, the problems with the use of job evaluation studies as evidence in comparable worth cases are similar to problems that arise in many areas of the law. I have already alluded to the similarities with the use of statistical evidence in discrimination cases (see notes 7 and 10 above), but the analogy can also be made with many other areas of the law that use statistical evidence. See, e.g., *McCleskey v. Kemp,* 107 S.Ct. 1756 (1987) (criminal law); and David Barnes, *Statistics as Proof* (Boston: Little, Brown, 1983), 33–34 (listing cases in several areas in which statistical evidence has been used, including torts, contracts, environmental protection, antitrust, trade practices, and tax).

AFTERWORD

1. See, e.g., Diana Stone, *Pay Equity Sourcebook* (San Francisco: Equal Rights Advocates, 1987), 461–74; Mark Aldrich and Robert Buchele, *The Economics of Comparable Worth* (Cambridge, Mass.: Ballinger, 1986), 41–42, 64–69; Virginia Dean, Patti Roberts, and Carroll Boone, "Comparable Worth under Various Federal and State Laws," in *Comparable Worth and Wage Discrimination,* ed. Helen Remick (Philadelphia: Temple University Press, 1984), 238–66.

2. See chapter 10, notes 35–41, and chapter 11, note 33, with the relevant text.

3. Jacob Mincer, "Intercountry Comparisons of Labor Force Trends and of Related Developments: An Overview," *Journal of Labor Economics* 3 (Jan. 1985): S20–S22; Robert Michael, "Consequences of the Rise in Female Labor Force Participation Rates: Questions and Probes," *Journal of Labor Economics* 3 (Jan. 1985): S117–S146.

4. For an attempt to predict the effects of comparable worth using a neo-

classical model, see Victor Fuchs, *Women's Quest for Economic Equality* (Cambridge, Mass.: Harvard University Press, 1988), 125–29. For a general review of the economic models, see Donald J. Treiman and Heidi I. Hartmann, eds., *Women, Work and Wages: Equal Pay for Jobs of Equal Value* (Washington, D.C.: National Academy Press, 1981), 13–68.

Select Bibliography

There is a great deal of literature on comparable worth, and I do not intend to provide a complete bibliography of it here or even a complete record of all the sources I have consulted in preparing this book. Rather, I offer the following list as a guide to the most significant sources for those who wish to pursue the topic further. More detailed references are available in the notes.

INTRODUCTION TO COMPARABLE WORTH IN THE UNITED STATES

Aaron, Henry J., and Cameran M. Lougy. *The Comparable Worth Controversy.* Washington, D.C.: Brookings Institution, 1986.

Blumrosen, Ruth G. "Wage Discrimination, Job Segregation, and Title VII of the Civil Rights Act of 1964." *University of Michigan Journal of Law Reform* 12 (Spring 1979): 399–502.

Gold, Michael Evan. *A Dialogue on Comparable Worth.* Ithaca, N.Y.: ILR Press, 1983.

Livernash, E. Robert, ed. *Comparable Worth: Issues and Alternatives.* 2d ed. Washington, D.C.: Equal Employment Advisory Council, 1984.

Remick, Helen, ed. *Comparable Worth and Wage Discrimination: Technical Possibilities and Political Realities.* Philadelphia: Temple University Press, 1984.

Treiman, Donald J., and Heidi I. Hartmann, eds. *Women, Work, and Wages: Equal Pay for Jobs of Equal Value.* Washington, D.C.: National Academy Press, 1981.

Weiler, Paul. "The Wages of Sex: The Uses and Limits of Comparable Worth." *Harvard Law Review* 99 (June 1986): 1728–1807.

Willborn, Steven L. *A Comparable Worth Primer.* Lexington, Mass.: Lexington Books, 1986.

INTRODUCTION TO COMPARABLE WORTH IN GREAT BRITAIN

Ellis, Evelyn. *Sex Discrimination Law.* Aldershot, Eng.: Gower, 1988.

McCrudden, Christopher, ed. *Women, Employment, and European Equality Law.* London: Eclipse Publications, 1987.

———. "Comparable Worth: A Common Dilemma." *Yale Journal of International Law* 11 (Spring 1986): 396–436.

O'Donovan, Katherine, and Erika Szyszczak. *Equality and Sex Discrimination Law.* Oxford: Basil Blackwell, 1988.

Pannick, David. *Sex Discrimination Law.* Oxford: Clarendon Press, 1985.

Rubenstein, Michael. *Equal Pay for Work of Equal Value.* London: Macmillan, 1984.

Willborn, Steven L. "Equal Pay for Work of Equal Value: Comparable Worth in the United Kingdom." *American Journal of Comparative Law* 34 (Summer 1986): 415–57.

RELEVANT STATUTES

Equal Pay Act of 1963, 29 U.S.C. 206(d) (1982) (United States).

Equal Pay Act 1970, c. 41, as amended (United Kingdom).

Equal Pay (Amendment) Regulations 1983, *Statutory Instruments 1983*, No. 1794 (United Kingdom).

Industrial Tribunals (Rules of Procedure) (Equal Value Amendment) Regulations 1983, *Statutory Instruments 1983*, No. 1807 (United Kingdom).

Sex Discrimination Act 1975, c. 65, as amended (United Kingdom).

Title VII of the Civil Rights Act of 1964, 42 U.S.C. §§ 2000e to 2000e-17 (1982) (United States).

RELEVANT CASES

American Federation of State, County, and Municipal Employees v. Washington, 578 F. Supp. 846 (W.D. Wash. 1983), *rev'd,* 770 F.2d 1401 (9th Cir. 1985).

American Nurses' Association v. Illinois, 783 F.2d 716 (7th Cir. 1986).

County of Washington v. Gunther, 452 U.S. 161 (1981).

Hayward v. Cammell Laird Shipbuilders, Ltd., [1985] Industrial Cases Reporter 71 (Industrial Tribunal 1984), *reh'g on remedial issues,* No. 5979/84 (Liverpool Industrial Tribunal, Sept. 12, 1985), *aff'd on remedial issues,* [1986] Industrial Cases Reporter 862 (Employment Appeal Tribunal), *aff'd,* [1988] Queen's Bench 12 (Court of Appeals, 1987), *rev'd,* [1988] 2 All England Law Reports 257 (House of Lords), *reh'g on remedial issues,* No. 5979/84 (Liverpool Industrial Tribunal, July 20, 1988).

Spaulding v. University of Washington, 740 F.2d 686 (9th Cir.), *cert. denied,* 469 U.S. 1036 (1984).

ECONOMICS

Becker, Gary S. *The Economics of Discrimination.* 2d ed. Chicago: University of Chicago Press, 1971.

————. *Human Capital.* 2d ed. New York: National Bureau of Economic Research, 1975.

————. "A Theory of the Allocation of Time." *Economic Journal* 80 (Sept. 1965): 493–517.

Corcoran, Mary, and Greg J. Duncan. "Work History, Labor Force Attachment, and Earnings Differences between the Races and Sexes." *Journal of Human Resources* 14 (Winter 1979): 3–20.

Filer, Randall. "Male-Female Wage Differences: The Importance of Compensating Differentials." *Industrial and Labor Relations Review* 38 (April 1985): 426–37.

Mincer, Jacob, and Solomon Polachek. "Family Investments in Human Capital: Earnings of Women." *Journal of Political Economy* 82 (March–April 1974): S76–S108.

O'Neill, June. "The Trend in the Male-Female Wage Gap in the United States." *Journal of Labor Economics* 3 (Jan. 1985): S391–S116.

Tzannatos, T., and A. Zabalza. "The Anatomy of the Rise in British Female Relative Wages in the 1970's: Evidence from the New Earnings Survey." *British Journal of Industrial Relations* 22 (July 1984): 177–94.

Zabalza, A., and Z. Tzannatos. "The Effect of Britain's Anti-Discriminatory Legislation on Relative Pay and Employment." *Economic Journal* 95 (Sept. 1985): 679–99.

————. *Women and Equal Pay: The Effects of Legislation on Female Employment and Wages in Britain.* Cambridge: Cambridge University Press, 1985.

INTERNATIONAL COMPARISONS

Gregory, Robert G., and Vivian Ho. "Equal Pay and Comparable Worth: What Can the U.S. Learn from the Australian Experience?" Discussion Paper No. 123. Centre for Economic Policy Research, Australian National University, July 1985.

Mincer, Jacob. "Intercountry Comparisons of Labor Force Trends and of Related Developments: An Overview." *Journal of Labor Economics* 3 (Jan. 1985): S1–S32.

JOB EVALUATION

Beatty, Richard W., and James R. Beatty. "Some Problems with Contemporary Job Evaluation Systems." In *Comparable Worth and Wage Discrimination: Technical Possibilities and Political Realities,* edited by Helen Remick, 59–78. Philadelphia: Temple University Press, 1984.

Schwab, Donald P. "Job Evaluation and Pay Setting: Concepts and Practices." In *Comparable Worth: Issues and Alternatives,* 2d ed., edited by E. Robert Livernash, 49–77. Washington, D.C.: Equal Employment Advisory Council, 1980.

Schwab, Donald P., and Dean W. Wichern. "Systematic Bias in Job Evaluation and Market Wages: Implications for the Comparable Worth Debate." *Journal of Applied Psychology* 68 (Feb. 1983): 60–69.

Treiman, Donald J. "Effect of Choice of Factors and Factor Weights in Job Evaluation." In *Comparable Worth and Wage Discrimination: Technical Possibilities and Political Realities*, edited by Helen Remick, 79–89. Philadelphia: Temple University Press, 1984.

———. *Job Evaluation: An Analytic Review.* Washington, D.C.: National Academy of Sciences, 1979.

Willis, Norman D. *Washington State Comparable Worth Studies, 1974 & 1976.* In U.S. Congress, House Committee on Post Office and Civil Service, *Pay Equity: Equal Pay for Work of Comparable Value—Part II: Joint Hearings before the Subcommittees on Human Resources, Civil Service, and Compensation and Employee Benefits.* 97th Cong., 2d sess., 1982. Serial No. 97-53: 1486–1580.

INDUSTRIAL TRIBUNALS IN BRITAIN

Dickens, Linda, et al. *Dismissed: A Study of Unfair Dismissal and the Industrial Tribunal System.* Oxford: Basil Blackwell, 1985.

Leonard, Alice. *Judging Inequality: The Effectiveness of the Tribunal System in Sex Discrimination and Equal Pay Cases.* London: Cobden Trust, 1987.

———. *Pyrrhic Victories: Winning Sex Discrimination and Equal Pay Cases in the Industrial Tribunals, 1980–84.* London: Her Majesty's Stationery Office, 1987.

Wedderburn, Lord of Charlton, Roy Lewis, and Jon Clark, eds. *Labour Law and Industrial Relations: Building on Kahn-Freund.* Oxford: Clarendon Press, 1983.

Index

974.

Steven L. Willborn is a professor of law in the College of Law at the University of Nebraska. A graduate of the University of Wisconsin Law School, he is the author of *A Comparable Worth Primer*. He has written extensively on discrimination law and employment rights.

974006

WESTMAR COLLEGE LIBRARY

214487

REMOTE K 1770 .W55 1989 / A secretary and a cook

K 1770 .W55 1989
Willborn, Steven L.
A secretary and a cook
                    (89-1191)

DEMCO

W9-CCT-188

The Melancholy Fate of

· CAPT. LEWIS ·

The Melancholy Fate of

· CAPT. LEWIS ·

A Novel of Lewis & Clark

MICHAEL PRITCHETT

UNBRIDLED BOOKS

This is a work of fiction. Names, characters, places and incidents either are the product of the author's imagination or are used fictitiously, and any resemblance to actual persons, living or dead, business establishments, events, or locales is entirely coincidental.

Unbridled Books
Denver, Colorado

Copyright © 2007 Michael Pritchett

All rights reserved. This book, or parts thereof, may not be reproduced in any form without permission.

Library of Congress Cataloging-in-Publication Data

Pritchett, Michael
The melancholy fate of Capt. Lewis: a novel of Lewis & Clark / Michael Pritchett.
p. cm.
ISBN 978-1-932961-41-6 (alk. paper)
1. High school teachers–Fiction. 2. History teachers–Fiction.
3. Lewis, Meriwether, 1774-1809–Fiction. I. Title.
PS3566.R583M46 2007
813'.54–dc22

2007021533

1   3   5   7   9   10   8   6   4   2

Book design by SH • CV

First Printing

❋⸙ ⸙❋

"If we could have got a person perfectly skilled
in botany, natural history, mineralogy, astronomy,
with at the same time the necessary firmness of
body & mind, habits of living in the woods & famil-
iarity with the Indian character, it would have been
better. But I know of no such character who would
undertake an enterprise so perilous."

—Thomas Jefferson, 2 March 1803

"The appearance of the work, which was announced for publication nearly three years ago, has been retarded by a variety of causes, among which the melancholy fate of Captain Lewis is already known and lamented by the nation."

—Nicholas Biddle, prospectus,

expedition journals, 1814

"It is with extreme pain that I have to inform you of the death of His Excellency Meriwether Lewis, Governor of upper Louisiana who died on the morning of the 11th Instant and I am sorry to say by Suicide."

—James Neelly, 18 October 1809

The Melancholy Fate of

· CAPT. LEWIS ·

I.

"...conceipt that he heard me coming on..."

✿ "... About half are dead!" Clark said to his visitor, this Washington Irving, who was nearly as old as he himself. What did they want him to say, and why keep coming year after year when he only said the same things again? Everyone wanted to look into the matter, and always went away unsatisfied with his rote answers.

"I saw him once," this Irving, a famous writer in his own right, said. "At Burr's trial. I didn't know who he was at the time."

Clark waited for a question. Maybe these visitors just needed to talk about Lewis, and of the pain they felt, a flat, empty sense of having missed their own time.

"I wrote a story once, about a man who falls asleep and wakes up in the future," Irving said, having got distracted, no longer taking notes. "A man who goes to investigate a strange thunder in the mountains and encounters some dwarfish men."

Clark raised his head and fixed his gaze on this Irving. "How am I to answer?" he asked. "You wish me to say I heard phantom artillery? What if I did?"

They sat in Clark's study, and he could see out the window to the vegetable garden with one eye, Irving with the other. Clark rather didn't care if he spoke of it now, or never did again, if this fellow remained forever or got swallowed by the earth.

"Just anything, then, or something about Lewis, or the slave, or the Indian girl," Irving said.

"Is that all anyone wants to know?" Clark asked, wishing for a lot of crows, or a bombardment, to come level the house. True love vanished, and then one simply wondered. People came asking all the wrong questions and Clark refused to hint at the right ones. "He predicted his death to Aaron Burr's daughter. Surely you know that much."

"So many of your party are dead so soon," Irving said. "In my late tour of Europe, I met a Mrs. Shelley, an author of tragical romance."

Clark waited, on guard for the question, if there was one. This man's obscure pain or loneliness made him impatient. Clark blew out through his nostrils.

"Forgive me," Irving said, "but I no longer know if America is my country or not. The venom of the reviews of my books I cannot describe. I've given up stories for history."

"He was convinced I was coming behind to save him," Clark said. "I was far away."

"Is't true he was murthered?" Irving asked quickly, head down, one dark eye, one brow darting up to nab his quarry.

"No, of course not! He had a cousin who murdered in a temper, then did himself in. The Lewis's suffer a strain of madness," Clark said. "So too the whole human race!"

Irving, with his gray-black head, thick and wild hair and charcoaled, crazed brows, had the shipwrecked air of men who strike the limits of their talent too soon. Clark got no pleasure from thwarting him and wished to think of a thing he hadn't told yet.

"But why, then?" the fellow asked.

"How shall I answer?" Clark answered. "Sometimes I think it *was* murder, but a strange, imprecise sort. He seemed unable to live on water, food and air as though denied his proper nutriment on this earth."

O, it was impossible, but impossible, to tell it! Words made everything worse. Nothing ever hit the mark.

"What about women? Did he court? Have affairs?" Irving asked.

Clark shook his head. Always looking in the wrong places, these sleuths.

"Every woman loved Lewis, and no woman did," Clark said. "For how does one love what is not there? I sometimes think we made him up. He represents something we want in the world, and his own ideas about himself be damned!"

"Court-martialed for dueling," Irving said. "Advocated the slaughter of the Arikara Nation." Reading from his notes.

"Acquitted of any wrongdoing," Clark said. "And wrote the Indian policy that restricted white settlement to the Missouri's shore."

"Did you never suspect Neelly, who turned up later with Lewis's guns? Or his valet, Pernia, who showed up actually wearing his clothes?" the upstart asked.

"No, never," Clark said. "But then, I knew him. Never was there a better."

"He had enemies, though," Irving said, flipping back through the pages of his notebook toward the start.

"None so formidable as himself," Clark said. "If he thought it were better to die to bring about a better age, to hasten its coming, he might die."

"I have something here about a Mandan chief—Big White, was it?— who was literally years getting home from Washington," Irving noted.

"A sad case," Clark said. "By the time he was back, nobody believed he'd lived in a marble city filled with white people. Lately, he is said to doubt it himself."

"What of Janey?" Irving asked.

Clark looked across with a jerk of his chin, then a casual recrossing of his gouty, swollen, tender legs. "Dead these twenty years," he said.

"Her son and daughter?"

"The son a lawyer, briefly, now is a mountain guide. Her daughter dead from fever."

"The husband, then?"

Clark's head and feet pained him with the coming rain. "O, lively as he ever was and drawing a handsome pension at the Mandan Indian Bureau, God help us."

"Anything more you wish to add?" Irving asked, looking disappointedly through the meager notes.

"Only that Janey's dying, and Theodosia's vanishing with her ship and crew, and the great comet and earthquake of a generation ago all coincided with the murder of George, Lilburne's butter-fingered slave," he said. "Several years ago, the second and third presidents of our country expired together, on the precise day of the fiftieth anniversary of our union."

"What can that mean?" Irving asked.

"Nothing," Clark said, and waited for the demonstrated effect. Perhaps now he would go away. Perhaps now they'd all go away and let him die. "A pity about your bad reviews," he added.

Irving could not meet his eye. "Yes, thank you. No life is without its painful reflections," he said. "But what of this rumor, by the way, that your slave York is in fact not dead but has made of himself a Crow chief in the Colorado territory?"

"He is dead," Clark said firmly. "Of yellow fever in Tennessee. But write it any way you wish."

"Do you think your friend ever had any lover? What about Burr's daughter, this Theodosia?"

Clark sighed and peeled dead skin from his thumb's pad. "Write it however you wish."

"What about the girl? The interpretess?" Irving asked. His lamp-lights now glowed full hot as he regarded Clark and a red, like burns, wounded both his cheeks.

"Impossible. And if you write that, I'll sue," Clark said.

Irving seemed poised toward one more inquiry, but was warned by Clark's tipping his chin down an additional degree as if to reach out and seize him. Which he would do, Clark feared, and with a strange cry, too, a hysteric sob. It seemed he had, in some way, become Lewis after his death, as though the absence of one required he play both parts.

"I do sometimes think the president was a kind of diabolic rationalist, a madman of empiricism," Clark said. "And Lewis his re-animate creature."

Clark felt it clearly, at last, that same helpless hysteria that Lewis must have known, the wish to get up and shove this Irving over in his chair. He was at last starting to see exactly how mad Lewis had been, and in which directions. "So what did really happen between you and Mrs. Shelley?" he asked suddenly.

"Nothing at all. We met one night at the opera. But I saw something there, back of her eyes, and chose not to investigate," Irving said.

"You should know that my servant York was a very great dissembler, shape-shifter, and liar. A regular Baron Münchhausen. He probably started that Crow chief story himself."

"We will never know," Irving said, noting something on his little "reporter's" pad.

"I freed the fellow, and then he has the nerve to return to me later and damn his freedom to my face, saying it is nothing of the sort, and worse than his shackles had been," Clark said. "Imagine the cheek!"

"You were Lewis's dearest friend," Irving said abruptly. "Did you feel responsible?"

Clark lurched inside and fleered sideways, but outwardly knew he appeared unfazed and innocent of even the faintest blush. The room tried to turn over on its edge, then righted itself. Irving shewed no sign of having seen. "One always wishes to have done one more thing for a dead friend," he said. It was this Irving's last attempt to unseat him, last and best, and had failed, Clark was fairly convinced.

Irving paused over a lengthy note to himself. The mantel clock ticked off the instants left until death.

"One felt responsible for Lewis," Clark added, taking himself by surprise. "And wished to be like him and liked by him. Without the help of others, and guidance and temperance, he would perish, one felt fairly sure. He blundered blindly toward great things, and believed you'd help him, and e'en depended on 't. He saw our potential, but fought back despair brought on by keen, sensitive perception of the problem and its scope."

Irving wrote that. They both listened to the clock. "Are you familiar with *Gulliver's Travels?*" Irving asked.

"Yes," Clark said, looking up. "I seem to recall . . . early in our journey . . ."

"Those people believed that Gulliver's watch was his god because he was constantly checking its face, as if for reassurance," Irving said.

Clark waited for a point, then understood that was it.

"What about the all-water route?" Irving asked.

"For all we know, it is still out there, waiting for discovery. And the Northwest Passage, too," Clark said.

"Do you truly think that?" Irving asked, pen paused.

"I am not certain that I ever did think it, or that it mattered to me," he said, looking upward for the answer. "My friend asked me to join him, in triumph or in ruin."

He was at last pleased by something he had said in the interview, and resolved to end it.

"Or both," Irving said.

"Or both," Clark concurred.

"Do you know," Irving said, "that an angel of the Lord has recently appeared to a man in upper-state New York on four separate occasions? And that he has found, buried in the woods, some heretofore unknown books of the Holy Scriptures?"

"In New York?" Clark said. "Well, that sounds unlikely, does it not?"

Irving sat still and stared at the black, waxed floor planks as though he were wishing it to be true, as if wanting a new faith to go along with his return to the new continent. Clark felt embarrassed, like he had disappointed a younger version of himself. "This new age is confusing," Clark said. "In a way, one misses the Spanish and the unquestionable right of conquest. Lewis would disagree, but where is he now? Do you see him here or there? When a man speaks too long and loudly for the Enlightenment, it seems the world must kill him."

Clark was aware of saying things he never ever had, so this must be the last person who would come asking.

"But why?" Irving asked, as if waiting earnestly, erectly, to know.

"Very simply, this must not be the actual world, but something merely painted on its surface," Clark said. "Otherwise, life would matter and we would take every measure to preserve it. Instead, we recklessly chance everything. And if not slaughtered that time, we do it again. The notion that life is precious is the greatest lie of our age. What matters are the passions, the thrilling lusts of rage, desire, and hatred. Nothing else is actually here."

Irving was writing quickly, trying to get it, note for note. "Do you have it, then?" Clark asked. "Are we finished?"

"Yes, I believe so . . ."

" . . . cutting himself from head to foot . . . "

At long last, Lewis had come to the place, a hollow by the side of the road, an inn simple as that which snubbed Mary. O, here, finally, was the large house with milled boards! And a cabin of roughcut timber, a barn with a trotting-horse weather vane and honeysuckle on the post box. Also, an arbor, some limestone steps, and a dirt lane between house and privy.

The smokehouse door was propped with a stone, flies swirling 'round glazed hard rinds of hams. His gown was dry, despite attempts to drown in the river. Now only Pernier knew, and what he knew nobody else ever would, because of his marked silence. Pernier took the horses under a tree and waited there, staring at the ground, apparently having one of his philosophical discoveries. Pernier was wise, poor, and free. But if he ever left Lewis, he must simply take up with another great person.

The keeper's wife greeted them, and liveried the horses. Then showed him the place. "Pernier and I like to sleep under the stars, except in bitter weather," he said. "Yet your inn is fine as any like it in the world."

No doubt, she brewed a weak coffee and larded rather than buttered the morning cake. But was honest, good, hard as bricks if tried, in all ways a credit to her kind. She offered her bed. "I have not gone near one in years," he said, panting and holding his head. "A bed is the shape of a grave."

He would rest on the hard floor in the buffalo robes, the ones that were his bed in Her wilderness.

Trees overarched that road thickly to the east, more sparsely to the west.

He sought a vantage point in order to look back. The clouds, spread across the horizon, were true anvils, purple-black and full of rain. They blocked the sun. The rays broke forth in ev'ry direction, illumining random pieces of ground. The picture shimmered, as if trying to collapse altogether. He'd come far, but could not see a road. A heaviness in his sight promised a sleep e'en the trumpets of Judgment wouldn't break. There was no joy in anything, except the evening, the sweetest he'd known.

He sat bitterly shaking in the lengthening gloomy light. That lady brought her sewing out and sat in her rocker. Her nimble hands, separate from her intent, still form, tried to restore order to a chaotic void. It wasn't the chair which rocked, but the world that moved while she stayed in place. She was the center. O, Copernicus, revise your formulae, for a new body stands still in the heavens!

He'd never felt content as just himself, and was not now. He'd started as an industrious eldest son, wonder boy, who ran the farm and its indentured blacks. Yet all along, he'd been indentured, too! For being great only meant labouring under a great yoke. But what was wrong with the world could not be righted from this side, the living side, of it.

Lewis guzzled his whiskey, mind tumbling and staggering while he drank and drank and stayed perfectly sober. The lady in the center. Her chickens scratching in the dirt, her horse kicking in the barn, as her sun plunged into her Pacific whose waters lapped along her vast, impious soul. But he'd seen what Columbus never did! Yet it would not help finish her sewing by dark.

Wishing to speak to her, his mind was a tangle. Pacing outside the cabin, he was trying to outrace fate, seeing the open door and blanching, stumbling away. He'd produced no true accounting. But how could he tell one story while holding back another? If only, when he'd come back to the world, the world had been there. But it was nowhere. This lady rocking, just miles from where she was born, was now the whole thing. Columbus, dying of the syph in the tropics, knew this at the end.

When Lewis was a boy, they'd said the world revolved at furious speed. So he tested this by leaping into the air—and coming down in the same place.

That lady's eye was on him. She looked up to plot his trajectories toward and away from her. She knew distresses of the soul, how to recognize the signs in cows, pigs and men. He needed to speak to her with his knotted, poor tongue. His servant, Pernier, attended all from the shade of a flow'ring crab. And knew and knew, and said nothing.

Clark would catch him up, Lewis was sure. Clark would not let him perish alone here. He simply had to last a bit longer. Still, all was in readiness for his crossing over.

And they had toiled so furiously upstream, while this place, o'erreached by trees, struck by hard lines of radiant light, blindly waited. Locust Hill, snowy mornings, his dogs, Mother's face. That sad monster called boyhood. Lewis's throat constricted, and swallowing became impossible. In the end, a body simply outlived its usefulness.

He was now in for the worst. The heart beat and beat and need run itself out.

O, to see his Janey again! For hers was a soul so grim, stoic, and resolute. *We are sent to keep one other person alive. And not 'til the end do we know which one was ours, which was the one we were sent for.* All of one's good was displayed in a moment. But not 'til the end did one know *which* moment.

Wishing to speak to that lady, he saw she was just now occupied with the memory of a dead child, and turned away. By not marrying, he'd at least been spared that!

Night now came crashing and breaking in pieces, shards and motes of black.

Her cow's lowing fell quiet. Her dog barked. That lady would wish him a good night, if only he could approach her. Pernier attended with dark and somber look. The lady knew! O, she knew his plight, even with her little ones tucked in bed, her chicken dinner simmering on the stove, bubbling tiny curls of bloody feathers. Her cribs were full to the very top, for winter.

"A pleasant evening—" he croaked, at the apogee of his orbit.

"Yes, Captain?" She brightened, for here was conversation.

O, dismal! O, painful! Reflections swarmed to goad him away from her, for she was comfort and aid. Any instant, he'd beat his head and cry out and be truly insane. He just managed to break off with a smile. With a slight bow, going his way politely while a din, a gnattering of demonic flies, resounded by his ears.

He began to circle and chant. Looking west, where ev'ry hope went to die.

The clouds with weak gold light along their bottoms were seeing the world's end. The world: the thing for which he'd never stop fighting. But why was it all designed? *God, please end the world, and let us all awaken in the next!*

A cardinal said, again and again, Am I alone? Where are you?

But O, for an earth made the way they'd believed! With one long river top to bottom and shore to shore. Which prov'd the creation was not for Man, who was only cast-away in it.

No, tonight the planet was only a lonely outpost in a forgotten corner. The garden was dismantled quickly now. As for Tom, he'd wonder when he saw the notes. "But these are mere facts," he'd say. "Where is the woolly mammoth? Where is the Northwest Passage, the ten Lost Tribes?"

Tom had called him the fittest person. But not 'til that moment did he comprehend what he'd been fittest for. Meanwhile, from her screaming nightmare, Janey had waken'd gasping, crying over her children, who fled a world desp'rate to kill them. Like her, they'd be abducted over and over, held captive and raped, and raped again, over and over.

The dark was heavy as iron on leaves and branches. And through the crushing weight, the night stars began to press. Venus was out, naturally. He had but a moment left. And yet that lady did not leave, for summat was very wrong with her guest. But she was not afraid. A natural thing was happening, like a birth. She was a great lady on a par with his mother, or Janey, or F., or Theo, or L. B., or the madwoman who'd scarified herself in a horrible manner.

Twice had he tried for that embrace, the dousing of the fire that burned in his ev'ry nerve. In constant tremor, with flashes of wildfire, he suddenly heard the growl of his familiar.

The new world was coming on behind him. Light broke the clouds open and spread all around. Pernier was silent and forbore it all, foresaw every moment.

Falling to his knees by a beautiful arbor, the o'erreaching branches stretch'd tendriled fingers, and dead milkweed pods and vines clung fast to a limestone wall. A part of him he'd got cut off from felt such joy. How he should love to feel it! Perhaps it was not too late to feel! But a nameless, bottomless thing said there was nothing. An explosion threw up colours to the west, and the sun fell in the sea, making clouds from the steam. Slowly, two worlds ground their way into each other, like lovers, and eras'd his time. The road came loose and the columns toppled. He could not stir from there unless that lady came forward to release him. Everywhere about Heaven, Sergeant Floyd was asking and looking for him, in increasing alarm.

Now, streaks of light broke into shrill rockets and screamed in ev'ry direction. Each note flow'd and spark'd, did tricks in the air, like countless swallows of gold whiskey, red wine, green absinthe. The earth was shaking, and the universe vibrat'd and flick'red at such velocity as to appear solid. New sensations arrived nowhere and meant nothing. He'd come so far, but could not stir the final step. To stink in the body and bowel, to not be able to flee the stench of fear. Meanwhile, his enemies smiled, trading satisfied looks.

Probably, he'd ended that day on the beach, where Janey scorned him. He had never returned after all.

The evening lasted, and that place grew in space, pushing out to form the sides of his universe. This widening in a lost track dead-ended here. It seemed he'd always seen it, in his mind's eye. And that lady was awaiting his crossing. Through it all, a whistling of wind acrost a hollow-mouth'd bottle. Something hurtled toward him. That bullet which missed him on the Maria's! On a flick'ring plain, in his squirming mind's eyes, he embrac'd Janey, dirty skin and animal musk. Stinking, with ripp'd nails, scarred knuckles, rough hands and chapped rasping lips, teeth yellow at the root, he nursed at those small brown dugs, worked a rough nipple into his mouth which let go a flow of thick yellow cream. And as he clambered up, his spunk came.

Wishing not to ever forget the distant bright world, sobbing after it already with longing, he went in the cabin, loaded the pistol and shot himself in the skull. Then, lying on the floor, he shrieked forth, "O, Madam! Give me some water, for I am so strong and it is so hard to die! . . ."

why did I come down in the same place

3.

"...why did I come down in the same place? ..."

B ill Lewis was, that moment, saying something to someone, and looked up to find the dim, surprised faces of his class. He was at the chalk-board with the chalk in hand, the squealing tip having slid down in a crooked line, like its author was interrupted by a seizure. Richard, in the back row, had his hand up with a question. The room was full of maps. And globes. The silence, impatient, had undertones of anguish. The faces were those of lovely young women, interrupted here and there by the duller male. "Are you all right?" Joaney asked. She was quite plainly big, pregnant, hugely ready to give birth. Her hard, thrusting belly crowded the desk.

He stepped back and looked. It wasn't his handwriting exactly, but he had clearly written it. His hands didn't seem familiar.

"Mr. Lewis, you want me to get the nurse?" Joaney asked. "You're sort of white."

He felt a little sick, full in the bladder, trembly as if for want of food. It seemed this scene kept happening, or had happened before. The roll was open on the desk: Pete, Jeff, Chris, Bethany, Joaney, Rebekah, Natalie, Skyler, Tremaine, Richard, etc. It was all pretty American. Maps looked back at him from all sides. Maps accused him and confronted him. It was all his fault, but what was? One boy was black. One girl was Asian. Richard was still waiting and Lewis happened to glance at his last name, Mercutio. "Richard, your last name is really Mercutio?" he asked. Laughter pressed him and held him in one place. "Your question was?"

"Were they queers?" Richard asked.

"It's like they loved each other," Joaney said. "The way they sound in their letters."

"It doesn't mean they were queers," Skyler, his one Asian girl, said.

"Oh yes it does," Richard said.

Lewis felt himself starting a bad sweat, shirt soaked through to his jacket, cold rivulets running on his skin. "Finish reading the chapter," he said. "I'll be right back."

Then down the hallway, long and empty and lined with steel lockers, and he turned in at the door marked BOYS with bumpy green glass in the door, a room lit by transom windows. Cool, tiled sanctuary with pissoirs on the wall, floor done in squares of yellow Italian marble. He turned his wedding band on his finger. To wash his hands, he twisted a handle, which produced water. Someone else came in, wearing a tag that said "Hildebrandt, Psychology," a balding guy with glasses, whom Lewis seemed to recall liking. And not being liked in return. The guy urinated with a heavy long sound and Lewis bumped out of that dripping place with the writing crammed into the mortar lines between tiles.

Looking for a window, he went up a stairway and gazed out on a little village, a church steeple, some small houses and brick storefronts. And, moving briskly by, curious vehicles with no visible means of locomotion. His ring was burning, so he teased and moved it with his thumb. It could be anyplace, Virginia, St. Louis, Georgia, Washington. He tried to breeze back in casually, but his class wasn't having it. "Well, did you make it?" Joaney asked.

"His pants are dry," Skyler said. "Close call, though, definitely."

Sometimes he wasn't sure what to do for his kids. He learned their names and then simply stayed with them, stuck it out for as long as required. They had a restless wish to go, to be gone, to keep going. Joaney had a special power in the room, and was its queen. "Are we doing anything today?" she asked. The last thing he could remember . . . He gazed hastily at his arms. There'd been cuts, slashes. He touched his breastbone and temple. He was thirty-five. No, he was *forty-five*. As a boy, he'd leapt into the air and landed, saying, "If the world turns, then why did I come down in the same place?" But no, wrong again. The explorer Lewis did that, not him. He felt a heartsickness, a homesickness, like during that terrible winter, when he was freezing and starving on a barbaric, desolate coast. Except he hadn't. That was that other Lewis again. By the light in the windows, it was just now September. Hugely with child, Joaney blinked at him. "What was I saying?" he asked her.

"You were saying how Jefferson sent him because he couldn't find anyone actually qualified who'd be stupid enough to go," she said.

"Jefferson had half-white bastards all over the place," Richard said.

"Tom's wife had died. It totally crushed him," Lewis said. "I'm not sure we can understand it now. Your heart was a crypt by the time you were thirty-five, already full up with dead parents and spouses and children and siblings." Only Joaney and T, for Tremaine, nodded their heads. Lewis saw that he'd written the names of several of Lewis's hopeless conquests on the board, "girls of the neighborhood" he'd tried to court and marry.

"What about Sacagawea?" Joaney asked.

"Her name meant 'bird-woman' in Hidatsa, the tribe that stole her away from her family," he said. "In Shoshoni, it meant 'boat-launcher.' Like Helen, she'd apparently launched a lot of boats."

At eye level, when he turned, was suddenly a map of North America, and some wag had pasted a little arrow pointing to his town: YOU ARE HERE. Good to know. He was right where the Kanza or Kaw met the Missouri, smack in Osage territory.

16

So where were the native faces? He couldn't find even one. And the fierce eyes looking back warned him to be careful of what he wanted to know, how badly he needed to find out.

"Why'd he do it?" Joaney asked.

Skyler had jewels sparkling in the side of her nose, and both earlobes, and an eyebrow. Under the clock was a very good copy of Clark's map of the Missouri, its course and tributaries. Mozart suddenly started to play, but it was hollow, false and tinny. Richard dug hastily into his bag and brought up a little device. Lewis snatched it, and faces turned eagerly to see what sport he'd make of Richard. He shook the thing. He pressed its numbered face, making it squawk and object like a parrot. "Jesus, take it easy!" Richard said, grabbing it.

Joaney's eyes, like the Mona Lisa's, followed him everywhere, head turning on the long, elegant stalk of her neck. "The Bible, if one counts all the begats in Genesis, dates creation at 4004 B.C.," he said. "That's the kind of pre-Darwinian era Lewis lived in. The world was still young. Everything was fairly new, from the Republic on down. Even if you'd made bad mistakes, it wasn't too late to fix them. The trouble was, somebody was going to rush past you and grab up everything good, if you didn't hurry."

"Just answer the question," T, for Tremaine, demanded, his only black kid.

This must've been what Jefferson meant when he said, "History will not be kind to us." T asked the question as a command, but now his lip slightly quivered, as if his whole being trembled before the answer.

"He was way in debt," Richard said.

"He drank like a fish. He ate opium pills like they were TicTacs," Skyler said.

Lewis was dizzy, and dropped suddenly into the chair he'd apparently placed there for the purpose. He might be sick. His color, he assumed, was not good. "What can I offer except facts?" he said. "Born the same year as the Boston Tea Party, at age five he lost his father, who caught pneumonia one night in the rain, dodging a British patrol. Not much education. Passenger pigeons are extinct now, but their migrations once blotted out the sun. The family motto was *Omne solum forti patria est,* which means 'It is best to die for one's country.' Or it might mean 'To a brave man, all earth is his country.' On his mother's side, the motto was *Force and counsel,* but they were Welsh. Jefferson called Lewis's grandfather the most sensible man he ever knew. Lewis shot a bull at full charge at age nine. He was head of a household at thirteen, with two thousand acres and twenty-eight slaves. He learned herbal medicine from his mom."

For some reason, Bill now got out his wallet, taking out the first item, a likeness of himself on a card with a bunch of numbers. "Everyone was related to everyone else. For example, Sergeant Floyd, the only one who died, was Clark's cousin. Lewis was related to Jefferson. The Randolphs, Hearsts, and Lewises all intermixed bloodlines too often, and it was blamed for the many suicides in the family. Robert Penn Warren wrote a poem about Lilburne Lewis, who chopped up one of his slaves with an ax, then killed himself. Is this helping?" he asked. "Is this what you want to know?"

They nodded, waiting for more. Just in time, the bell rang. He didn't think he could stand, so he simply sat smiling and nodding as they filed out. "Don't forget the field trip!" he said.

Alone, with his picture in his hand, he knew he hadn't really answered their questions, not the big ones anyway. He felt that familiar lightness in his throat, craving for the cigarette, which he hated and loved and wanted and needed. It kept something down that was trying to bubble up in him, riot in him. The cigarette held it at the bottom of his throat.

He felt as alive as ever in his life, sitting there, but must've gotten up too quickly, because he saw darkness, then met the floor with a painless crash, thinking, *Oh, a header! A face plant, a canvas nap.*

Bill was helped up the steps and in the front door with Emily's arm around him, having left the ER after a CAT scan for his head, a butterfly bandage for his brow. Emily'd left her BD (behavior-disordered) and LD (learning-disabled) kids with another teacher for a while, to care for him.

He couldn't do the wraparound staircase to get upstairs and gingerly explored his way to the couch, getting onto it like it might tip or go shooting away. She heated chicken soup, with its slight tang of tin can, and brought a bag of frozen peas and a throw. He ate, with her watching him in alarm. He balanced the peas on his head and looked out at her from underneath.

"Maybe I should cancel this float trip. It's just two days away," she said.

"No, no. I plan to be floating the river, one way or another," he said. "Don't spoil it."

"What if it's a brain tumor?" she asked.

"Don't you need to get back to work?" he asked.

She used to be an actress, strictly amateur, and they'd met because he used to write little melodramas for the local playhouse. But they gave it up years ago, when she gave birth to Henry, and they decided to get married because they were "in love" as Emily always liked to say it, with both words in quotes. At some point, she'd stopped saying it.

"When Henry gets home, tell him there's a sandwich in the fridge, and that he's to eat all of it, and drink all the milk," she said, going to the hall mirror and pulling on her hair, giving it a few warning tugs. And out the door she went, back to face the kid who was making her life a living hell that week, old what-was-his-name? Dennis, that was it. Recently, he'd dived down a laundry chute, trying to kill himself on the concrete floor below, but instead got stuck and ripped flesh off both arms.

As soon as he heard her pull away, he got up, balancing the peas on his head, got his cigarettes from the drawer, Camels, with the matchbook tucked in the cellophane wrapper, and went grimly out to the sunporch and closed the door, holding his frozen-pea hat with one hand, sitting in the porch swing. As he lit the first one, his hand shook because he needed it. Smoke blew back in his eyes and smarted and caused tears. He pulled at the smoke, drawing it, that suction of lip and tongue, how it caused the tip to come to life, burn, a supersonic stream of air passing backward through the dried, treated, shredded, compressed, rolled tobacco, its nicotine released as a vaporized cool blue jetstream. And nothing leftover but ash. He used a soda can for an ashtray since Emily refused to buy one. Drawing on the cigarette was like sucking at the straw of life, taking it in, tasting it, mulling it around, getting soothed by it, using it up, then blowing it out, that moment just a memory now.

It was about tobacco, this story he was trying to tell. The Virginians needed land for their cash crop, and lots of it, because tobacco sucked all the nutrients out of the soil and gave back nothing. You had to have all the land you could grab. And no matter how much you had, it probably wasn't half enough to make it in tobacco. The expedition carried 130 rolls of pigtail tobacco as a trade item. When they got west of the Rockies, the tribes had never seen tobacco before, but turned on to it, gradually.

Didn't seem that long ago. But when Jefferson offered a bounty to anyone willing to try for the Pacific, he offered it in pounds, one thousand British sterling pounds, not dollars.

Lewis and Clark weren't even the first ones. In 1793, when Lewis was just nineteen, a guy—a British subject—made it all the way. And on a rock overlooking the Pacific, he wrote, "Alexander Mackenzie, from Canada, by land, the twenty-second of July, one thousand seven hundred and ninety three." An English sea-captain saw the message and sailed all the way around the Cape of Good Hope up to Boston, his story finding its way back to Jefferson. Which'd scared Tom to death, that Britain might try to snatch up all that land.

Henry came in at 3:20 and looked down on Bill where he lay on the couch, whistled at his injury, then got his sandwich and came back to keep him company. While Bill watched, Henry disassembled the sandwich, tearing crusts off the bread, breaking it into hunks, ripping the bologna into strips, folding the cheese into little squares, then working on each pile, meat, then cheese, then bread. Policing his meals was now their side occupation after Henry had fainted at school. Bill was less shocked by it than Emily, but he himself had been a very anxious, worried, neurotic kid. So he tried to be patient with the eating business, having grown up in a time when adults didn't know what to do with a nervous boy.

Back then, you had the good sense to hide anything different about you, and to pretend to be unfazed by what happened to you, regardless. You just tried to have a place in things, even if your place was terrible, on the bench, last in the pecking order.

The explorer Lewis had written letters to his mom from the army, saying he loved it, that they had "mountains of beef and oceans of whiskey" and he felt able to share it with the "heartiest fellow in camp." His mom probably cried when she read it, because it showed he was an oddball, with difficulty making friends, and so grateful just to belong. But soon he was in fights. He was offering to kill people at dawn, and being court-martialed (acquitted) for dueling, then getting transferred elsewhere.

Bill didn't want Henry's boyhood to be like that, broken on the bitter rock of experience, because those boys never grew up but just got older, and many didn't even do that. They went to pieces before everyone's eyes, on the five o'clock news.

Bill also wanted to know and be close to his son, but Henry always sat down about a foot farther away than seemed necessary.

"So what were you thinking about," Henry asked, "when it happened?"

"What, are you my shrink now, Hen? Is that the sort of stuff your shrink asks you? Stuff like that?"

"I guess. Pretty much."

He shifted the peas to see Henry better. "I guess just the usual things, to answer your question. Lewis and Clark. Lewis's suicide."

"Oh, uh-huh." He nodded. "Why'd he do that?"

"He owed a fair sum of money. He couldn't find a good woman. It ran in his family. You pretty much take your pick."

"How much money?"

"Only about six hundred bucks. Which was not that much, even by their standards. So it's a mystery."

"Why didn't Clark loan him the money?" Henry asked, chewing with great concentration. Bill had a suspicion he counted his chews, and swallowed when he got to a certain number.

"It wasn't so much the amount. He'd written checks with the War Department's checkbook, and they suddenly refused to pay, left him holding the bag."

"Why?" He was cross-legged on the floor and now pulled one knee up into a single-lotus and went on working the sandwich.

"I dunno, Hen. He'd come home to a different world. Jefferson wasn't president anymore. Maybe they wanted to shut down anyone from the romantic old world so as to usher in the tougher, harder modern world."

"Typical," Henry said.

Bill shrugged. "I think it all follows from something the Spanish called the primary right of conquest. Your rights derived from your ability to attain them, by whatever means at your disposal. The ends justified the means."

He was talking from under his crown of peas. "Anyway, Lewis's main job on the expedition was to keep a document of the trip, but he had trouble with it and stopped four times, once for eleven whole months."

"What was wrong?" Henry asked. He was working on the milk now, a swallow at a time.

"He suffered from a tendency. Sensible depressions of the mind," Bill said. "Say, would you reach me that other pillow, old buddy, old pal?"

"Sure." Anything to lay off that milk a minute. It was very odd. As a kid, Bill had eaten whatever was put in front of him. His dad used to challenge him to eat seven hot dogs or nine pieces of chicken, and he always did it, and never puked after. He'd eat his food and his dad's, too. But then, his dad had sort of eaten vicariously through Bill, because of his severe ulcers.

"How'd he do it?" Henry asked.

"Shot himself. Once in the head, then the chest. When that didn't work, he cut himself, sort of head to foot, with a straight razor."

"I couldn't cut myself," Henry said. "I might be able to hang myself, though."

"Henry, old boy, I hope you never have to work it out," Bill said.

His son made him feel interesting. He was the kind of kid who wouldn't want you to think you were boring, who wanted the people he met to feel good about themselves. Bill even felt guilty sometimes, having a son and liking it, too, like it was something he didn't deserve.

Similarly, Jefferson and Lewis had almost been father and son, working alone together a lot in the president's house. Lewis even delivered Tom's first state-of-the-union address to Congress. Lewis always showed great presence of mind when in physical danger, people said. Others said less flattering things: that he was bowlegged, stiff, graceless, and awkward, that he reminded you of Napoleon. And Lewis did, in fact, sign "Citizen" in some of his letters, after the French custom of the time.

"There are always the murder theories, of course," he said. "He was slightly mixed up with a traitor named Aaron Burr and his daughter Theodosia. Lewis even predicted his own death to her, in a letter."

"But you don't think it was murder," Henry said, nodding. Henry worried about him, Bill knew, and seemed to know when he was down and wondering about the point to things. Much as he tried, Bill had difficulty reciprocating. It was just hard for him to picture what Henry—a modern boy—thought about during a given day. Public school had not changed, was still filled with threat, profanity, violence, obscenity and in-your-face sexuality. But in his own schooldays, it'd never occurred to him to borrow a gun from home. Now, if you had trouble at school you just killed everyone, staged your own massacre. Nobody understood it, but this harmless-looking thing, a public school, was actually driving some people insane. In the privacy of their minds, some kids were made nuts by it. And adults had little control over it, that shadow-world called adolescence.

Henry was an inch from triumph over the glass of milk. The color was leaving his face as he worked.

"We have a reliable account from people at the inn, what he said, what he did, the order of events," Lewis said. "He said he wanted to rob his enemies of the pleasure."

The blood gradually came back to Henry's face, but it was clearly taking all of his will to beat this thing. He carried his plate and glass away, and pretty soon Lewis heard him above his head, in the bathroom. He strained to hear if Henry was getting rid of the food, their other fear, but couldn't hear a thing in that old plaster-walled house, soundproof as a vault. You could commit murder in any room.

Bill stayed on the couch, thinking. It was supposed to be this big secret. When Tom asked for the money from Congress, he lied and said they wanted to explore the Mississippi. He didn't want the Spanish or British to guess the truth, that he was about to grab up the whole thing, sea to shining sea.

It was a suicide mission. When Tom gave his instructions to Lewis, he didn't say "*when* you elude the dangers and reach the Pacific." Oh, no. He said "*should* you elude the dangers, & etc., etc." He wasn't sure they'd even come back.

He must have fallen asleep. Emily's voice suddenly woke him. "Lewis, what is this?" she asked. His eyes popped open. On the floor was a sizable, long shipping box. "Please don't tell me that's what I think it is."

"It's not. I swear."

"Because it looks to me like the UPS man just left a gun at my house."

In fact, that was what it was, or at least a replica of one.

"You promised me, Bill. You said we would never ever keep a gun," she said.

"It's not. It's just a replica of one that Lewis carried," he said. "It won't fire. You'd need powder and patches and ammo."

"It doesn't feel like any replica. It's heavy, just like a fucking gun," she said.

She went upstairs to take off her work clothes, and he sat up, a little dizzy from so much sleep. As he tore away the strapping tape, Henry and Emily appeared in the doorway, then moved into the room and sat on the sofa before him and the box. "Don't worry," he said. "It's not addressed to Pandora."

"I'd like to see it, please," she said.

He ripped away plastic and Styrofoam, exposing a solid maple case, flipping the antiqued-brass latches and prying up the lid. It was astonishing, pretty, as it lay in its custom red-velvet rest, solid walnut stock, octagonal barrel, polished brass flintlock mechanism and ramrod, a bead of real gold as the front sight.

"Okay, so it's a gun," she said.

"It's just for show," he said, lifting it out, hefting it. "Here, Henry, you want to hold it?"

"Now, why would he need to hold it?" she asked, then looked at Henry. "*Do* you want to hold it?"

"Yeah, give it here," Henry said, and knelt down to take it. "Wow, are they always this heavy?" He put it to his shoulder correctly and aimed, closing one eye, squeezing the trigger. As he did, Lewis got a sudden gut-wrenching shock to his nerves that it might somehow fire, and Emily saw his expression.

"Just a replica, huh? Give it back to your dad, Henry," she said.

They sat over the gun for a moment. It was interesting how there seemed to be four people in the room now, like the gun *was* someone. And even after he'd wrestled the gun upstairs to his office and thrust it harmlessly away, into a closet, it still felt like somebody was there.

They weren't talkative during dinner. When he did speak, Bill had the sense the gun was listening, and knew they were aware of it, feared it.

Which was strange because, as a kid, Bill often handled guns and never feared them. It was people you had to watch out for, what they suddenly did to you or said to you when no one was looking.

Emily was trapped, he knew, between respecting his book research and looking out for Henry. Women could be their own worst enemies in this regard, taking any male endeavor more seriously than their own.

After dinner, Bill went to his office under the stairs as usual, to sit and ponder.

The thing was, Lewis was supposedly helping found a new order of man in the New World, and was an agent of the Enlightenment. He called the expedition Voyage of Discovery, and his party members the Corps of Volunteers for Northwestern Discovery. It was strictly scientific. On the other hand, the money came from the War Department. Which meant they'd use military hierarchy and army discipline, with flogging for most offenses, and shooting for desertion.

He invited Clark, his favorite ex-commander, who'd taken early retirement due to health problems. Clark was at home doing not very much and probably wondering if he was finished, done for, washed up at thirty-four. Then came Lewis's letter, which said, *Hey, pal? How's it going? Howzabout joining me on this crazy mission we're unlikely to ever return from?*

Clark's affirmative reply went out in the next day's mail.

Lewis had waited 'til the last minute to invite him, so either he was sure of Clark's reply or he didn't have anyone else to ask.

What was Lewis told to prepare for in the West? Woolly mammoths and giant sloths, cannibalism and polygamy, a light-skinned race of "Welsh Indians," a mountain of pure salt and the ten Lost Tribes of Israel. They asked him to study suicide among the savages. For instance, did they ever do it from heartbreak in love? While he was at it, he was supposed to find an all-water route to the Pacific Ocean and, if it wasn't too much trouble, the Northwest Passage.

Bill was in bed early, with Emily already there, but not asleep. They lay there—together but not touching, not talking but conscious. Then she gradually left him and he was awake in the house, and so was It. Meaning his oldest adversary, Depression. That siege engine of mental illness.

Creeping in through his teens, twenties, and thirties, now it was always over him. And sometimes the illness set down so hard, he thought seriously about doing IT, that it might be best for everyone if he did, and saved them from a prolonged, drawn-out crash and burn. He and Emily were newly married the last time it hit hard, and had a tiny baby. Naturally, she'd wanted him to shake it off and pull through, but she'd also needed to look out for Henry. Bill lost his college-teaching job along the way, and now they got by on two secondary-ed salaries, hers from a special-ed position. They'd probably never ever retire.

And while Lewis the insomniac lay awake, maundering all of this, he knew that Lewis the explorer was lying in his grave in Tennessee and not worrying about a single thing. Not the least thing.

4.

"...we fear something amiss..."

Shoving off from St. Charles, Missouri, May 1804; Observing the Manitou figure-painting on a rock; York nearly losing an eye by having sand thrown in it; Seeing the gilded clouds; A snake dances on its tail in the river; Recalling the woman shot the first day.

❋ In fact, he never rested, and even now crawled on hands and knees through a tunnel of redbud branches. He looked around for the river, relying on it to guide him. The foliage was thick and lush, the height of summer. Squirrels dropped things or plummeted to earth themselves. A French *engagé* fired a gun at some game on shore.

Amid shouts and cheers, they'd shoved off. Now they made their wavering way, having left behind just everything, all of their loved ones. Somewhere, young women were tearful. He felt the hard fact of forty days' provisions with no place to replenish anything but water, meat, and firewood for three years. An unlimited letter of credit meant very little now; there was nobody up here to honor it. No Indians either, the wise ones having cleared out, having vanished in a half instant into the shade of towering immense black or green trees.

They'd met one Daniel Boone, and dined on deer brisket and yams at his large rustic French-style house, and received a book from him on loan, which was his fireside reading while blazing the Kentucky trail: *Gulliver's Travels*. Lewis was grateful to have it, but more so to be quickly on their way.

Because he was very, very late. Possibly too late to reach the Pacific in time to seize the continent from the British. A Canadian had etched his name on a rock above a bay on the Pacific, then somehow a decade had got by. Lewis was just thirty, but already ten years too late, it seemed. He was in a bad patch.

At the next rise, he stood a moment, thinking of Pierre Chouteau's half- breed daughter a few stops back, a most decent-looking female. And he was already keeping a secret from the men: Captain Clark's commission was not that of a captain at all, but of a lieutenant. Which gave him an awkward edge on his older friend, who'd been dying in domestic comfort when the fateful letter had arrived.

He felt observed. When commander, somebody was always watching, even watching you think. The president had tried very, very hard to turn up someone better. But nobody with the right qualifications, in botany, anthropology, astronomy, geology, zoology, and medical science, ever appeared.

The mission was almost certain to fail on account of weather, illness, starvation, and Indian attack. Also, he suffered desp'rate bouts of anger at God, for making him fatherless, and the eldest male child, and his family's only hope. Sometimes he even hated Him, and resented being left down here in the dark in so many ways. Why couldn't God just love him, as he seemed so freely to love and bless so many who didn't deserve it? He even enjoyed defeating God, in little ways, like pressing down a trigger to end the life of some dumb, beautiful creature He had made. And then destroying and ripping it, with strong white teeth, God's handiwork.

That morning, they'd met a tribe who gave them watermelons for roast meat and did not believe it when he said the U.S. had possession of their lands. It made him very cross, their cool insolence. He saw red. He saw stars. For some reason, he recalled his empurpled rage in the school-yard, at six, when a mentally-defective boy tore the picture he'd drawn for his mother's birthday, when he'd tried to kill the boy with a rock.

In the river the day before, he saw, on a rock projecting out over the water, a painting of a strange figure, the Manitou, their Zeus, and Michi-manitou, their Hera. The Nations were, in their polytheism, strangely touching and backward. But he had his own backwardness, his own clumsy wrongness. For instance, something about the crudeness of the men made him very dull and ugly inside, festering and impure. He was not happy among them, and sometimes felt a stinking misery. That was the sadness again. And yet he loved to see the little "kids" in the villages. If only they need not become adult men and women. And many would be dead when they came back, so where was the point in liking them? Yes, today he was in a bad patch.

By evening, he'd found his way back to camp, following smells of corn cooked in grease, and pan-bread, boiled salt pork, and Indian meal cakes which gusted down the channel into his nostrils, tender and red from hay fever.

At sunset, the clouds suddenly caught flame all along their bottoms, and burned like a wildfire turned upside down. O, what madness the sky could display! Its violence and lurid feeling never lasted, though. It was turning gilded and innocent again, the last ember going out. Each day, something in him flared up and wanted to cry out to those colours, as tho to a parent, "No, don't leave! Don't go! Don't leave me here among these awful people! O, take me with you, for they want to undo me, and harm me to death, and ruin me!" Though what exactly was being done to him, and by whom, he could not name. A game of some sort was being played against him. In truth, he wasn't deemed worthy to command this expedi-tion, but only available for the trip.

As he stood 'neath those clouds, facing the prairie, he felt the pressure and presence in those meadows and woods and fields of the ones who were coming. Though not yet born in haylofts in Europe, though not yet landed, still puking over the gunwales in the middle of the Atlantic, he saw all around him their ghostly houses and livestock and fences, privies and gardens.

Some of the things he'd already seen were beyond the pale. Nobody would believe it if he reported ten thousand pelicans carpeting an island. No, he could only report the plainer facts, like Clark's negro York nearly losing an eye from having sand thrown in it. Yes, how plain, how very straightforward human behavior was, after all, and never any surprises. But what about the snake who'd swum up under a deer hung over the river to drain of blood, the one who wouldn't stop dancing on his tail in the water and leaping at the fresh meat? The one he'd had to kill.

What was the use in telling the truth, though, since none could hear it?

What about the swimming swans and their whiteness? What a joy they brought, a joy so boundless. Then they'd shot one, and the corpse looked just like a bride killed on her wedding day in her white wedding clothes.

What was more, on the way down the Ohio, he'd shot a woman in the head. No, he hadn't actually aimed and pulled the trigger, but he'd let the airgun, primed and ready, out of his hands for a moment, and a green French *engagé* had touched her in the wrong place, and the ball felled an innocent woman who'd been out strolling along the shore. The scalp wound gushed blood in vivid helpless warm gouts and he tried not to touch it but her blood got on his shirt and soaked through to his skin, and was hot like pissing oneself and gave an unspeakable tender horror as it made the fabric heavy. But he had no other. So he wore her blood, hot at first, then warm and very wet. It was terribly intimate, like holding a dying lover and having her blood splash onto you from her consumptive lung, from her abruption in childbirth. And the smell, even now, made him lightheaded to recall, how raw, like beef.

Maybe he fell in love with her. She struggled up out of his arms babbling, then looked at him as if he'd been indecent. Maybe a desire was in
her eyes to slap at or hit him, though she held her bloody scalp instead
and got clear of him, muttering in French. He loved her. It sometimes
happened to him like that, stunningly. She seemed suddenly beautiful.
But her mouth twisted in insult: he was wrong, unnatural. And there was
God again for you! God and His jokes! *I will make you handsome, but also
somehow offensive to women.* He never had the remark ready on his
tongue, to cloy and soothe and entice their interest. How he loved a moment of their company, while his own was treated as clumsy, stupid. How
dare he show up at their side! His very presence made blood pour from
their heads.

He needed to withdraw, with apologies, though he should have
stayed, to care for her poor head, to help her through her delirium and
drain the swelling from the infection, her head grown pregnant from his
penetration. He should have found a way to make her love him, and etc.
But no, he had the mission and must depart. He never saw her again.

5.

"...reason to believe he hath deserted..."

A man is sun-struck; A catfish breathes out of water; The incident of the feathers; The passing of Great-Spirit-Is-Bad Creek; Reed returns with a curious object.

✳ Within a few days, a man had fallen asleep on guard duty and needed disciplining. Pleading his innocence until sentencing, which was one hundred lashes, he confessed, and got fifty instead. A man was then sunstruck while poling and walked off the deck directly onto the water, and was hauled up, sputtering and raving. Lewis bent over him as he lay dripping on deck and blocked the sun from the private with his body. He peered closely at the wet red-and-white whiskers, the bloodshot whites of blue eyes, the green spider-veins in his cheeks, the pustules scattered over his skin in lines like volcanic eruptions.

"What year is it, Private?" he asked.

"Fi'ty-eight ought eight, sir?" the man said.

Lewis's mouth fell stunned, open, at that answer. "Do you know where you are, sir?" he asked.

"I don' know nothin'. Nothin's familiar," he said, gazing side to side, then looking Lewis in the eye. "But you I know, sir! I know you from that hell!"

"What hell would that be?" Lewis asked. The fellow shook his ragged red locks and blinked fiercely. Lewis went a few steps away and got the medical kit, taking out a tiny metal tin of niter and making the man swallow some. In a few moments, a door behind his eyes seemed to swing shut, and a plain light came back to them.

Which disappointed Lewis obscurely. In fact, he was suddenly quite low, and threw the niter back into the kit. He had loved that French girl with the wounded head, but would never ever see her again. She'd heal and marry and the brute could never properly love her—not the way he already did!

"Explain, please," Clark said, "the business of the year. The fellow was not even close and yet wants to go back to his post."

"He meant *anno mundi*. World year," Lewis said. "He counts from the time of creation, reckoned as the year 4004 before Christ."

"Peculiar," Clark said.

Lewis shrugged, for the Indians believed that the world was all an illusion, a mere shadow cast by the real one, and that one must know how to dream with eyes wide open in order to enter into and live in it. There were other worlds, without a doubt, but his own experience of them was second-hand and anecdotal. Never had anyone managed to seize hold of the least thing while visiting in those nether realms and bring it back, not a unicorn hair, not an angel's wing, not e'en a speck of fairy's shite.

As for this world, his world, it was strange and often unhappy. For Clark already had his girl, his wife-to-be, and likelihood smiled on all these plans. Lewis awaited the woman who would pine and sulk, weep and yearn and die with his name on her lips, make a riot for worms, lie stiff and gaunt and mere bones still longing for his touch, become dust, feed a crop, and then be ruminated by livestock.

Past noon, dark clouds moved in and the wind rose and whipped the trees, and the sunlight was all sucked away with the air, as in a cataclysmic eclipse or some other doom. The sky got angry and purple and boiled, with a state approaching panic among the men on deck as the crafts bucked and thrashed in the swells, and barrels tossed like balloons up into the air. He felt strangely at home in this element, and stayed busy by saving the sextant and compass and writing desk from going overboard, though he was wet through and aching, with shivers and rattling teeth.

In a minute or two, the clouds moved on like arrows shot overhead, out of view, and the river became as smooth as glass.

Ashore the next day, walking, he saw wild plum and cherry, two kinds, and brown hazelnuts and green gooseberries. It grew stealthily quiet and quieter. He found himself in a deeper part of the woods than he'd realized. Slowly the quiet and the mildness and lack of weather made him pause, be still. He grew aware of an increasing need to turn around, to go in search of fellows, company. His heart fairly flooded with blood suddenly and his extremities drained empty, and dark places pounded in his vision. He turned carefully, on shaking legs. For should he break and run, should he even show haste, insanity would be upon him and he would fall off and down and down into the burning exploding chaos of the lunatic, the asylum inmate.

None knew how close he came at such moments, and his whole motive was to keep any from finding out, which meant a life in double harness, both suffering under it and never letting it show.

He did not sleep well that night, and during the day was asleep each place he paused to rest and indeed was never fully awake. Whenever they wanted to meet the tribes, they set the earth ablaze and made a great black smudge against the sky. The Pawnee and Otoe who came looked sorry they had, and gazed in alarm on so many "cloth men" marching through their territory.

The men caught some white catfish and threw them on the deck, where they lay, breathing outside the water, and croaking like a person suffering apoplexy or aphasia, like enchanted men trying to recall the rudiments of speech. It seemed that wherever he looked along the shore, some animal, deer, elk, beaver, possum, thrust forth its head and gazed with affronted, somber eye. Or a man went to chop wood only to have the trunk become like India-rubber and the ax rebound, blade sinking deep into his knee.

Throughout the next dark and rainy morning, the river sizzled as if boiling.

Around a bend, in all directions, trees four feet thick lay on the ground, snapped off as if by the detonation of a bomb. Then a fierce little lion, with striped fur and snout, and teeth like a wolf, fought them to the death with two balls in its back, and was called a *blaireau* by the French *engagés*. (And how odd that the men moved around Lewis and talked with each other, and yet sensed nothing amiss. Nor had anyone ever, except of course Mother, who knew him best.) Next, they brought out the airgun for the first time since the accident, and fired it. Which astonish'd the tribes, since it made no explosion and needed no powder, no flint or spark.

In the morning, it was discovered Reed hid his things outside camp the night before, collected them, and departed. Sergeant Floyd came to Lewis's tent with the news, red-faced, in a fury, white spit in the corners of his mouth, and shaking.

"Take two men and locate him, and shoot him on the spot," Lewis ordered, not meeting Floyd's white-eyed gape.

Clark, standing nearby, said nothing in poignant disapproval. But if the policy lacked compassion for the souls of the flock, Lewis reasoned, it at least kept it together in one place. And since his own commanders had done thusly, so would he, too.

The next day, a white feather came tumbling and rolling over and over in the current. Lewis sighted it at a quarter mile, while talking to Clark about the desertion, and could not look away from it. It approached. He reached and snagged it, nearly going overboard, saved by Clark, who'd guessed his action a moment beforehand.

Clark's man York came to see what prize, golden treasure, and Lewis gave it him, all unconcerned. And noted more feathers rocking on the flood, a dozen, no more. Then the river was white with feathers, shore to shore, the water turned to feathers and the boats pressed upward in a fast, rasping current of feathers. Sergeant Floyd, at the helm, turned. "Captain—!" His face was fevered and red, and an orange flume hung down from above his head, surrounding him. Lewis glimps'd it from the corner of his eye, but it vanished when looked at straight.

Clark allowed the feathers to tumble, rush, and bump under his submerged palm. Lewis didn't try to estimate the number, because none could possibly believe him.

Then they passed out of it, blanket changing to a veil, then a loose-woven net, and at last the river again. Sergeant Floyd held his side at the place where they wounded Christ the Lord. And a sudden flush afflicted Lewis. An all-over blanching, a sinking of the organs, nauseated terror and blackness at the edges of his sight. For York's hand no longer gripp'd the feather! But no, there it was in the other, which now made a gesture as if to discard it. Lewis's dry voice, like wood ripping, broke out: "No, I will have that, York!" The men all looked at him, and at York. York looked into Lewis's eyes, appraisingly. "If you do not mind, York, I will have that," he said again, lowering his voice. "For the articles and specimens." York, a remarkable example of his kind, noted something amiss in this (Lewis knew), but gave it over.

Later, Lewis would count this as the first day he was certain that the thing which gripped him in times past was laying hold once more. (And he would remember this event again, this incident of the feathers, when Floyd died.)

"What on earth—?" Clark said, turning to see the flood of feathers though it was already gone around the next bend.

"What, Clark? Have you not seen two miles of feathers before? How doth it compare, in your opinion, to the talking fish of day before yestiddy?"

But they were sent to find marvelous things: mastodons and saber-toothed lions, the ten Lost Tribes of Israel, and a river running deep and clear to the Pacific through a neat cleft in a tiny row of pebbles called the Rock Mountains. He was to look for Hebrew hieroglyphs and try out Yiddish words on the tribes. And one question in particular continued to revisit him: Was suicide (and especially suicide from love) as common among them as in white, polite society? His mind hung up on that inquiry. He examined it with vague and advancing dread.

His hand had still not lost the feel of Tom's, of the president's. O, why had he put himself in this absolutely gorgeous position to fail, and as publicly as one possibly could? Meanwhile, he continued to feel at odd moments the very thing he'd felt since early boyhood, powerful, wrenching, and inexplicable. He had a strange, malignant affliction: an inability to act in his own best interest. Sometimes, he behaved without right regard for his own safety and was called "brave," and sometimes without caring for others, which was termed "passionate."

Around the next bend, they met a tribe wearing coyote pelts, all afraid of what had just transpired across the river: four hundred Mahar wiped out by the smallpox. Clark listened to the account with his intelligent scowl, in skins newly fitted from head to foot, soft deer hide with fringe, tailored to his form, with red beard, and his large red head all woolly and topped by a beaver-skin chapeau. Clark leaned on his rifle barrel, with a no-nonsense set to his mouth, and worked his eyes about. "What is that place called now?" he asked.

"They call it The-Great-Spirit-Is-Bad Town, roughly," the French *engagé* said.

"And a good name for it," Clark said. "Did you hear that, Commander?"

Lewis, carefully separate by several yards, nodded. "Indeed. But why not call it There-Is-No-Great-Spirit Town? Why not catch the sentiment closer to the head?"

"A savage is not so quickly made an atheist," the *engagé* said.

Clark wore a badge, like a little flag, turned up on the brim of his cap with a royal-red center and plumes, fanning straight up into the sky, of green, blue, and yellow, giving him the look of a rustic sergeant major.

"Why insist? In the face of tangled wilds stretching over the whole earth, why say that an order exists tho 'tis invisible?" Lewis asked. "Is it not cowardice to demand that a thing be thus-and-so simply because 'twould be lovely if it were?"

The *engagé* doffed his hat and withdrew and Clark watched him departing and set and reset his lips in various shapes. "Is everything all right, Lewis?" he asked.

"How could everything not be *all right?*" he asked. "I am on the excursion of a lifetime. If I am not loved by those I command, I am at least obeyed by them. I am healthy, fit, and in the prime of life, don't you know?"

"You rarely have a rough word for these people, that is all."

"I find their faith childish today. I lack patience for it when we are thus far behind in our own programme," he said.

"I thought you were happy with our pace. I had no idea." He angled the regal head in a dubious way to see Lewis better, and to register concern and doubt.

"How can I be happy with this pace when we are ten years late?" Lewis asked. "We are finished before we've begun!"

Moreover, the whole nation saw how tardy they were, and that the prize itself, left languishing thus long on the rocky Pacific coast, was of doubtful value by now. And though he was only midway through life's journey, as the saying went, the chance in his hands to make up for it seemed blown apart, lost, which gave his heart a pain and relentless desperation.

Just then, cries went up, and the search party issued in a body from the woods, pulling Reed, the deserter, along by a rope wound 'round his wrists. They all looked sore and beat, but the hunters were grinning and not contrite at having ignored his orders to put Reed to death.

"O, for God's sake!" he cried. "What is that man doing back?" For all knew about the order—it was all they talked about since its issue.

"Are you stupid?" he asked them, coming up. "Are you really so dull as this? You spare this criminal?"

The men made no answer but simply stood 'round with smiles and averted faces, like bad boys ashamed of their species.

"O! Tie him to a tree! Only do not make me look at him."

And so Reed sat on the ground in hobbles just within the trees and looked at no one and said nothing, eating furiously of anything thrown near him, for all the day and late into evening. Finally, when he was all but hidden in the shadows, the firelight reaching only one part of his face, a single eye, Lewis came into the thicket to talk to him. Reed breathed rather hard and showed his ordeal in his sunken eye and cheek. He stank powerfully and gave off a heat and humidity and seemed to faintly steam and tremble in the night air.

"Ugh! You stink!" Lewis said, to which Reed made no sign, as if deaf or sleepwalking. "Come, let's hear your reasons, man. I want to know them."

"Don' have none, Cap'n," he said, though his jaw hadn't actually seemed to move. His eyes were wide, surprised, as if unable to contain something they'd seen. He rocked slightly and even grunted, sotto voce.

"What is the trouble, Reed?"

"Ah'm sick and need ta shit!"

He was holding his hands tightly together, and seemed to have an object concealed.

"Reed, what do you have there?" he asked.

"Dunno what 'tis," he said. "I foun' it!"

"Let me have a look at it or I'll keep you from the latrine," Lewis said. Squinting, biting his lip, the man was suffering and not trusting him. Then he opened his hand and let the object roll down the little incline onto a patch of sand, where it stopped.

"What on earth?" he said. "Is it a ball? It appears to be a made thing."

"Never seen nothin' like it," Reed gasped. "Foun' it in a creek bottom!"

At first touch, its pebbled, desiccated, dimpled surface felt like bone. It had lain underwater for a positive age, it appeared, for its outside dented under thumbnail pressure, but sprang back when let go. Its curious chevron marking was of India ink, mostly worn away.

"Two hunnerd an' eighty-eight," Reed said. "I counted 'em."

"It 'pears to have suffered a pox epidemic," Lewis said, nodding. "May-be 'tis ivory. Sometimes ivory will develop such pits as these."

"They was more," Reed said. "I jest grabbed the one."

"Could you find the spot again?" Lewis asked. My, but it had an uncanny feel, like nothing he'd put a hand to before.

"Might could," Reed said, grimacing.

"I can have you shot for your crime, Reed," he said.

Reed shook his head. "I don' care, Cap'n, I surely don'."

"What do you mean you don't care? You want to live don't you?"

"I don' know," he said, eyes tearing, getting a very long, hangdog face. "I might jest run off again. I might throw myself in the river and drown. I don' think I want no more o' this. Even if I do get to the Pacific, when I get back home, I won' be nobody else but me and have to go right back to plowin' or detasselin'. It makes you sore and sick jest thinkin' of a twelve hour day in the sun, breakin' your back, and for what? So you can make jest enough for next year's seed! I tell ya, it ain' worth it! I wish those boys'd shot me. I told 'em to go ahead and do it, but they wouldn'! This here's hard work jest to get back someplace where more work's waitin'! I jest a-soon you killed me, Cap'n."

Reed chewed his way through this lengthy sermon like he was eating a cord-load of firewood.

"No, I've seen this, Private," Lewis said. "This sorrow you purport to suffer is nothing but a fever, and I have a touch of it myself lately. And here is the cure! The guard will take you to the latrine, and then we shall see to you!"

Reed was led away, hobbling in his deer-hide shackles. With the air rather improved, Lewis sat examining the ball of bone. He tried it with his teeth and made a respectable gouge. It tasted of nothing, the river. He started up suddenly and called out for Sergeant Floyd and instead got Sergeant Pryor, as Floyd was on sick call with pain in the lower gut.

"Sergeant, I want a rather gorgeous beating for this man," he said. "He is not only guilty but disaffected in spirit. I want him to forget his former self and the woman who gave him birth. Make it sudden and cruel and have it duly repeated until we achieve some measure of correction. D'you understand me?"

The sergeant saluted and rushed off, shouting out names and giving orders to take arms with green switches, nine to a man, or tamping rods, and a gauntlet was duly assembled, toward which Reed was herded and his ankle hobbles cut. In double line, the men stood jostling each other for room, and grinning at Reed and slapping switch bundles on the palm or a meaty thigh, and calling out to him in brute tones, in apt mockery of the Sirens calling sailors to join them below, for a frolic, and to be cut to ribbons amidst the coral. Driven by a kick to his posterior, Reed waded among them and greeted a hail of blows that almost turned him around. The blood sprang out from his skin and in amazement he discovered pain, and fled forward down the line and out, on his face in the grass. And was made to rise, whence it happened again, with more violence and a blow that all but broke his nose, the men applying blows of fatal force if done with a medium stick of kindling. Reed's skin turned from red to black as the wounds gathered dirt and grime. He fell out the far end of the tunnel on one knee, and was picked up and tossed back in, and at last made sounds, and his eyes flew open wide as they could go, and he cried out with all the amazement of Caesar stabbed by Brutus, that any world no matter how dread could invent such agony. He lay panting on his face and was bodily raised up and turned about, the men now worked into a rather awful furor, their cheeks and eyes blazing like those of fiends, and their bodies slick with sweat and flecked with Reed's blood and other filth. Reed, enraged but crying out in pain too, gave a bellow and rushed headlong in, and was met by four square walls of brutal punishment that had no other aim but to end his life, to batter the soul free of the body or else pound it deeper into hiding. He ended on his naked back on the bank of cocklebur and, unconscious, was examined by the sergeant, who pronounced it at last sufficient.

6.

" . . . a double spoken man . . . "

On Saturday, Bill and Emily floated the river, a relatively clear tributary that eventually met the Missouri, and was best navigated in the fall, after the July rainy season. It wound past one edge of the zoo, an open-air theater, Bill's usual golf course, and the head of a trail he'd once gone up on a long Boy Scout hike. They were headed out into the deeper woods east of town, Emily splashing him with her oar whenever he got hypnotized by the tiny whirlpools in the current and let the canoe turn ass-end downstream.

"Wake up, Lewis!" she cried. Another couple, whom they didn't know, a skinny guy maybe ten years older than his red-headed wife, and a second pair named Jasmine and Leslie, were also along, having signed up, like he and Emily, without knowing the others. They all laughed a lot, at anything, he noticed, while he and Emily were not quite so merry. Henry was with friends for the weekend, so they were free to act like a childless couple, cursing like sailors if they felt like it. Lewis'd come prepared for some woodsy frolicking with three Trojans zipped into his fanny pack, and some airline-sized fine whiskeys to enhance Emily's natural proclivities. She liked it in the woods. "Like bears," she told him. "I feel like a really hot lady bear in the woods." For him, it went a bit beyond that. Everything worked better, his senses, bowels, hard-ons, etc. He slept more and snored less. He also felt a creeping sadness and a constant crying feeling in the back of his throat, like he would at last grieve something he hadn't yet. His balls ached.

They floated easily through the afternoon in clear, blue-sky weather, above the leaf-caked bottom, with the shadows of alligator gar, prehistoric monsters with dagger-lined jaws, passing like torpedoes under the canoes. And the blunted hulks of paddlefish hung in deep water, cruising with mouths open a foot for microscopic prey, some going a hundred pounds or more. The air was crisp like a green apple. He watched the other man and woman, Pablo and Rita, to see what was going on with their lives that particular weekend. Bill made up a drama, that Pablo wanted a baby but Rita wasn't sure. They sometimes struggled with their canoe, he noted, and it wandered shore to shore.

Bill was trying to write a book about the famous Lewis, but had tried before and never finished, chucking it in disgust. Emily admired the attempts, like you admire someone who's been struck by lightning but still ventures out. As for Jasmine and Leslie, no need to fabricate. They were gay, and that was probably drama enough for anybody. Every one of them had been married before, he wagered. He and Emily had. Yet here they were again, having plunged like polar bears into those freezing, ice-choked waters, like it was nothing. The other guy, Pablo, didn't look Latino, white hair shaved to a fuzz over his scalp, tan and athletic, and heretic-skinny with bulging John Brown eyes. Rita was just Rita thus far, a pretty redhead.

They took the easy bends in the river. It was starting to gall him all over again that he'd picked Lewis as his subject. So the country was celebrating the expedition. Two hundred years! Woo-hoo! And you say the hero blew his brains out after? Hot dog! But what else could one add to that, so long after the fact?

Maybe it *was* just a story about a bunch of white guys setting off to oppress people of color. But many in the crew were only half white. Peter Cruzatte was half Omaha, and George Drouillard half Shawnee. Sacagawea was Shoshoni and her husband half Otoe. Or maybe Paiute, he could never remember. He'd surely get it wrong. What he'd come to believe about the expedition would screw with the facts, causing unconscious omissions, errors. They didn't allow married men to sign on, which indicated just what they were getting into. Private Frazier, it turned out, was a fencing master, and sort of a throwback since gunpowder had made swordplay obsolete. Naturally, the one guy who died on the trip, Sergeant Floyd, signed up to rid himself of chronic health trouble. It worked! Lewis told his mom not to worry about him going, that he was just as likely to die at home. Which could be read different ways.

Whiteness was a big preoccupation. In fact, whenever they met a light-skinned Indian, it always excited them like they'd found proof of something. The ten Lost Tribes of Israel? Or was it something else? The darkest member of the party had the least power, and that was Clark's slave, York. And Clark was treated like Lewis's equal, but he wasn't. He was called "Captain" by the men, but wasn't. And Lewis promised Clark he'd fix it, but it was actually Bill Clinton, forty-second president, who finally did.

Jasmine and Leslie drifted up beside. Jasmine, in an Aussie bushmaster hat, smiled at him. "So what do you do?" she asked.

"History," he said. "I'm a historian, of sorts. I teach high school. And this is my wife, Emily. She works with the learning-disabled and the behaviorally disordered, which is how she got me."

"Funny. Leslie's a PE teacher. I don't know what I am," Jasmine said, with a laugh. "A kept woman, I guess."

"Bill's writing about Lewis and Clark," Emily said, paddle across her knees, squinting back at Jasmine.

"Oh. So I guess this is research for you," she said. "So tell us something interesting about those guys."

"Um, okay," Bill said. "At the very end of the trip, Clark makes a promise to Sacagawea that he and his fiancée will take her little boy, Jean, and raise him as their own. Without consulting the fiancée, of course."

"Whoa, that is interesting. So, in your book, you'll say he was Clark's bastard?" Leslie asked pleasantly, making a sun shade with her fingers, grinning at him.

"Actually, she was already pregnant when she joined them. But she had another baby right after, and the Clarks took that baby too."

"I bet the fiancée was pissed beyond reason," Jasmine said.

"So, a little native action on the side, huh?" Leslie said. "A little squaw action."

"I heard all those guys died of syphilis," Pablo said, pulling their canoe abreast with vigorous paddle strokes. "Weren't they all dead before they were thirty-five?"

"I guess that's somewhat true," Bill said, "although—"

"When you get done writing about them, I'll tell you who else would make a great buddy story," Pablo called back to him. *"Hitler and Eichmann!"*

Bill shrugged, letting that go, dragging his paddle and allowing Pablo's canoe to get ahead in the line. He mostly didn't mind when people talked smack about the captains. Something about the subject was provoking. Even the most civil people said things they hadn't planned to say. Ahead of them, Pablo continued loudly, "So where are the Indians on this trip, anyway? Somebody point out a Native American for me."

"But Lewis was just a patsy, wasn't he?" Leslie asked him, moving the canoe in behind his. "I mean, all those guys thought they were enlightened, didn't they? And weren't they really just Chapter Two in a final solution against nonwhiteness?"

47

He shrugged again, and noticed he was becoming spiritually blank, losing the ability to know his feelings. They kept paddling, though the current was taking them where it wanted and at its own speed. He never knew what to say. Not that he wanted to defend the captains but, after all the research, he felt like he knew them. It was a symptom of the depression, too, a tendency to freeze up and not be able to really reach other people, or yourself. And though they called and called to him, he made no answer, and could make no answer.

They swung around a bend, and their outfitter's teenaged employee was there as promised, waiting to help them unload the canoes and portage them to a trailer. He'd pitched the tents, stacked the firewood, even started the fire. Two propane stoves waited on a table and the coolers full of "provisions," on ice, rested underneath. They didn't have to do a thing, having paid a lot not to. But still they complained about how easy it all was, and how lavish. Russ, their teenaged cook and valet, furrowed his brow at their guilty remarks but said nothing. One whole cooler was full of wine, and Russ pulled the corks and poured the icy-cold stuff into real glasses. He was starting to smile as he handed them out.

Bill rallied after his first glass, and found he was able to enter the moment again. Emotions were such tricky, roller-coastery things anyway, and his were worse than usual. For instance, he'd got fixated on Rita over the past several miles. How serious she was! And how little she smiled or talked, and how private she was with her expressions, her eyes. Rita was having a different experience of the river than the rest, it seemed. And Bill noticed. If there was an unhappy woman nearby, he always knew it. Pablo wasn't doing anything about it, nor did he seem aware. But Bill often felt this, that other men were waiting for him to step in and help them out of these puzzling situations—so he did. He didn't even mind, and did it with one hand tied behind his back.

As for Rita, some kind of darkness was trapped around her. She wasn't comfortable with these strange women. She was afraid they'd figure out . . . something. He couldn't pick it up from where he was and got closer. "Rita, how's the wilderness treating you?" he asked, setting his pack down near her.

"Better," she said, holding up her wine.

She sat on her duffel, casting nervous glances around at Emily, Jasmine, and Leslie as they unpacked with one hand and gulped their wine with the other. Rita sat knock-kneed, slump-shouldered, arms crossed over her breasts, like a girl at camp on the first day. A great mystery about how to be happily female was closed to her. Wasn't everyone afraid of these strange women? Didn't anyone realize the bad things that happened when they didn't like you? He wished Emily would come over and talk to her, but they always used man- rather than zone-coverage when socializing. "So . . . are you writing a book or something?" she asked.

"You could say that. It's about Lewis and Clark. Actually Lewis, mainly. But somehow Mary Shelley and Washington Irving and a whole bunch of people have gotten into it."

She nodded, drinking. They already knew each other, somehow. She looked over at Pablo, because he was the real mystery, Bill could tell, the true other, even though she showered naked with him and ate with him and picked out dining room chairs with him. And yet this stranger seemed so familiar to her, like they'd known each other before. So what was love? You struggled so hard to know the beloved. And then some weird guy you talked to for five minutes finally got you to relax. Her brow worked on this mystery. She needed to get it worked out before she and Pablo went ahead with this baby they'd been talking about, not after. And that was Bill's generation, all right, always figuring it out ahead of time. For his own parents, there'd been nothing to figure out.

As for the captains, they were told, basically, *Pull this off, and you'll enjoy happiness, prosperity, and honor forever after.* The sky was the limit, thanks to the Revolution. In fact, Lewis was given an unlimited letter of credit, carte blanche, to finance his expedition. He took his first step westward on 30 August 1803. And almost killed a woman that same day. That Lewis, the historical Lewis, was also a soft touch with the ladies, mentioning the beautiful wives of friends met along the way, and the striking looks of Pierre Chouteau's half-breed daughter. Practically a feminist ideal, at least for the day, Lewis noted how women were treated among each tribe, and cited the worship of male and female gods, both Manitou and Michimanitou.

When Bill got up, Rita stood and came along with him and was smiling. Emily was already well into her second glass of wine. She'd wanted to come but didn't like being parted from Henry just now. And Lewis didn't know what to do for her exactly, but no man was a prophet in his own country. So he came up behind her and put his arms around her shoulders and she held them, and looked out into the undulating current of the river, unctuously snaking away and away oh so endlessly. "I just know he hasn't eaten," she said. "Some mother. I can't even feed my own child."

"He'll eat when he's ready," Bill said.

"He's starving before my eyes! My little boy is hungry and where am I? Drunk, and about to eat a steak."

"It's got to be some girl," he said. *"Cherchez la femme."*

"Did he tell you that?" She stiffened slightly in his arms.

"No, but doesn't it always come down to that? I mean, doesn't it?"

She shook her head, whipping his face with her brown hair, and worked loose, pushing him away. "No, I don't like you anymore," she said. "Go away."

So he watched Russ turn the meat and poke the potatoes. It got dark. Jasmine and Leslie did some kissing up against a tree.

As a young man, Lewis had surely had conquests, a few. But after the expedition, he had no luck with women. And even the deepest research into these liaisons went nowhere, and uncovered nothing. Clark was always trying to set him up, but he fended off most of it, and started calling himself a "widower with rispect to love," whatever that meant. Nothing, post-expedition, came easily to Lewis. Not like it did for Clark with his new bride and family, a house in St. Louis, a position as super-intendent of Indian affairs, and promotion to brigadier general.

They gathered around the fire with their glasses, to eat the steaks with-truffle butter that Russ doled out from a margarine tub, and roasted-rosemary potatoes, and one hell of a nice trifle for dessert: custard, ba-nanas, strawberries, walnuts, cognac, all layered in a dark-chocolate cup you could pick up and eat. Emily ate barely half her steak, and mulled one bite of potato in her mouth, then spat it into her napkin. But nobody turned down a refill on wine. Soon her eyes were on fire from the inside, and a high basted color came into her face. She laid her head on his thigh and gazed into the fire.

"Didn't they eat a lot of dog on the trail?" Leslie asked.

"Lewis preferred it to anything, but Clark wouldn't touch it," he said. "They were hungry in the winter. One time, they ate their candles. An-other time, starving dogs crawled into camp and ate up their moccasins."

"I know it's supposed to be a proud moment, or whatever, but I find the whole thing kind of sad," Rita said.

"I agree. Like with the buffalo and everything," Jasmine said. "How they were all gone in just a few years."

"No, I mean everything about it," Rita said. "Every last thing."

"I bet they got a lot of action on the trail," Pablo said.

"If the captains did, somebody cut it from the accounts," he said. "The men hooked up frequently with the native women and that was treated as no big deal. Except for this one time, when somebody's hus-band caught his wife coming in late and stabbed her three times."

"Sounds like a big deal," Emily said.

"True," he said. "But don't some diplomatic practices do terrible vio-lence to the individuals involved?"

Jasmine, who was tough, nodded matter-of-factly. Of course, women were generally tough now, in the new century, and had few illusions. The male-dominated power structure was toppling more easily than expected.

Men were letting women into everything now, pulling back every curtain sort of sheepishly to reveal . . . ta-da! . . . nothing much, a box of *Playboys*, a few French ticklers they'd bought one time at a truck stop. Surprise. No dripping female corpses hanging from the rafters. Oh well.

Russ topped up their wine. Emily's breathing on Lewis's thigh was causing a slow-glowing tumescence to develop. Pablo gave Rita a back rub as she sat with her forehead on her knees, and she was groaning.

"Lewis killed himself, didn't he?" Leslie said, with her sort of bulging eyes on his, an anxious expression. "Do I remember that or am I making it up?"

"That's tragic," Rita said, with eyes closed to better feel Pablo's hands.

"Please. That's not tragic. Tragic is wringing hands and tearing clothes," Pablo said. "Tragic is everybody laid out dead at the end on a bloody stage."

In the firelight, his face was almost medieval, bearded, wild-eyed and monk-like.

"Maybe tragedy isn't that obvious now," Bill said. "Maybe it's quieter and it hides better."

"A busful of kids going over a cliff," Rita said. "That's tragic."

"That's horrible," Bill said. "It's a catastrophe and a disaster, but is it tragedy? Does it show agency on the part of the hero?"

"It does if it's your kid on the bus," Emily said quietly.

"But traditionally, the hero has to choose death," he said. "And in fidelity to something bigger than mere survival."

"Who's going to call up some kid's mother and tell her her kid's death doesn't qualify as tragedy?" Emily asked. "Who, Bill?"

"By that logic, Bill," Rita said, "the death of a child could never be a tragedy."

The wine had loosened his tongue, and his voice was ringing clearly against the iron dome of the dark sky. He'd forgotten he wasn't in class. He'd actually been trying to say something about Lewis, but doing it drunkenly. Facts rose up in his head, joining with other facts, making exciting new designs for the book or pointless ones: The French *engagés* were used to six meals a day, and found two meals barbaric; on the very first day, they passed a creek named for a Spaniard who'd killed himself at its mouth.

He finally answered Rita. "But it's not me saying these things. It was Poe who said that art, in order to be art, has to be beyond such things. Amoral."

"Dope fiend," Jasmine said. "Sour little man."

"I liked his one story," Russ said, "about the heart trapped under the floor while it's still beating." So now the hired help, least among them, had come to Bill's aid.

"Look, never mind," Bill said. "I'm just a history teacher."

"I want to read your book," Pablo said, "even though you just gave away the freaking ending!"

Bill shrugged, smiling, with that dark and familiar feeling, of nothing being any use. What good was a thing if it made people awkwardly quiet, if it caused them to suspect you had no heart? Why open your mouth if it only caused people to more carefully watch you?

"Bill, read us something," Emily said, "from the journals."

His copy of the journals did happen to be on top of his pack, full of Post-Its, swollen up to twice its size. He read the entry for Lewis's thirty-first birthday, in which he chided himself for living selfishly thus far in life and resolved to live for humanity from then on.

"Poor guy," Jasmine said. "Nowadays, we just join the Peace Corps."

"And at thirty-five, we come crawling back to our desk jobs, and thank God on our knees for flushing toilets," Pablo said.

Bill held the book. The expedition truly got under way in May 1804, with three cheers from the small party on shore at St. Charles, Missouri. They soon met Daniel Boone, then turned north along with the river just west of what'd become Independence. Mormon holy land. Harry Truman's birthplace. They just missed a detachment of Spanish troops sent up from Santa Fe to intercept them. But the really weird part was who'd sent it: one General James Wilkinson, chief of the U.S. armed forces and Spanish spy known as Agent 13. He'd later be linked to a plot by Aaron Burr, Tom's vice president, to divide the union, seize the western U.S. and Mexico, and set himself up as emperor of a new nation called Burrania, with his daughter Theodosia by his side. And if anything about this filial tie seemed improper, then that explained the "despicable opinion" Alexander Hamilton voiced about Burr, and why Burr called Hamilton out in July 1804 and killed him.

It was all kind of crazy, how it all intersected, with Lewis in there somewhere, too, corresponding with Theo within a month of his death.

Bill read aloud from a part where Lewis went out hunting, a day he got chased by a grizzly, almost pounced on by a lynx, and charged by three buffalo, all within an hour's time. Which rattled Lewis so, he thought it must be an enchantment or a dream. It read uncannily like Dante's encounter with the lion, the leopard, and the starving she-wolf in *The Inferno*.

"Would we like this guy?" Pablo asked. "Would we invite him to pull up a stump?"

"I don't know," he said. "A friend of his said he was stiff, bowlegged, without grace, and that he reminded you of Napoleon."

"Sounds like my ex," Leslie said ruefully, blinking at the fire.

"Sounds like everybody's ex," Rita said.

"I've got more about Lewis and the Virginians, from various sources," he said. "Washington Irving wrote a story in which he called them—let's see here—'a pack of lazy, louting, dram-drinking, cock-fighting, horse-racing, slave-driving, tavern-haunting, sabbath-breaking, mulatto-breeding upstarts.'"

By now, the dark had come down all the way, like a lid, and they were fully lubricated. Russ watched the fire, and them—Bill noted—in wonder edging toward alarm. His job forced him to rub up against a white-collar world that scared and disgusted him by turns, and would send him right into forestry. "I thought they were heroes," Russ said. "I mean, that's what I was taught."

"How come he never married?" Rita asked. By now, she was looking fairly gorgeous in the firelight. And just why did women have to be so beautiful? Why did the desire for them not only not diminish with time but actually get worse and worse? In fact, it hurt so much, sometimes you wanted to hurt them back. Meanwhile, Emily lay on him. But was clearly thinking of Henry, her worries only blunted by the wine. And Bill didn't know a single trick or joke or caress to snap her out of it.

"Maybe he seemed doomed," he said. "He had his chances, but maybe he scared them all away."

"I don't buy that," Jasmine said. "Doomed is sexy as hell. Doomed means you won't hang around and get fat and boring."

He nodded. It certainly was a mystery, not unlike the New World itself.

They passed a bluff that burned perpetually, eternally, 24–7, and stank of sulfur and brimstone. And long stretches of grass so finely manicured, you could play ninepins on them, like the little men in that Washington Irving story. Enormous flocks of white cranes flew high above. They knew so little about how the world worked, they were relieved to see storm fronts moving west to east, just as they did in Virginia. They were alive at a time when there were migrations of green and yellow parrots so vast that, flying at sixty miles an hour, it might take two full days for a flock to pass overhead.

"Tell us something shocking," Rita said. "Something we wouldn't know."

"Lewis had a servant named Pernier with him when he died. That guy killed himself, too, about six months later," Bill said. "He did it in the snow outside the White House. With laudanum." He had to be careful now and hold himself back or he was going to fall into her eyes. But you always wanted a Rita, or a Diane, or a Laura. And you simply went on and on wanting her, and she probably didn't exist. Probably. Even when you thought you'd found her, as soon as you married her, she ceased to be. That thing about her died.

About twenty years after the expedition, as Clark was fading, he received a visitor, America's most elegant pen, Washington Irving, who'd fled to London, away from the terrible reviews of his books, where he gave up storytelling for history. There, he'd come very close to a fling with the widow of the poet Percy Shelley, but was scared off by something in her eyes, her gaze. He wanted to write a "Where are they now?" about the expedition, and to find out why so many were dead so young, why Lewis had killed himself, & etc.

Which brought up other strange intersections, that Irving sat at Burr's defense table during his 1807 trial for treason as his legal counsel, and saw many noteworthies there, including General Wilkinson, Lewis, and Theodosia Burr. And in fact, Lewis and Theodosia were seen dining together in the evening, and going out riding in the afternoon. So they all kept turning up together.

Probably, Clark told Irving about the strange artillery they'd heard in the Black Hills, like a six-pounder firing at a distance of three miles. And maybe Irving remarked about Rip Van Winkle hearing just such a sound in the Catskills before meeting those grim, silent little men. Which may have reminded Clark of Spirit Mound in South Dakota, where he'd gone to see some fabled little men or devils, eighteen inches high with grotesque enormous heads, and blowguns that killed at great distances.

"What else? Anything else?" Rita asked.

"Always something else," he said to her. "A guy named Peter shoots Lewis while they're out hunting together and then denies repeatedly that he recognized Lewis was his target."

"There it is," Pablo said. "The Christ metaphor."

Eyes looked back at Bill's out of the dark, with Rita's beauty in the firelight sort of stopping his heart. God or Someone seemed to love to torment mortals by placing His most ideal visions within view but not within reach.

"Now tell them the great irony," Emily said.

"He kills himself for nothing," Bill said. "The government bankrupted him by refusing to pay the expedition expenses. But then, three years after he was dead, they called it a simple misunderstanding and paid them."

"But tell the thing about his assistant," Emily said. "This'll make you cry."

"Oh. Naturally, when Lewis gets the job as Jefferson's secretary, somebody else gets passed over for it," he said. "So, when Lewis is later made governor of Louisiana, guess who his assistant is? The guy's brother!"

Groans and laughter. "And after Lewis's suicide, it was the assistant's fault, everyone said, for undermining Lewis and generally making his job a living hell," Bill said.

Pablo watched him with glittering mistrust in his possibly Cuban American or maybe Argentinian eyes. Life was about who did the best tricks for the women's pleasure. There wasn't anything else: if you had that, you had all the marbles.

Russ at last said his good-nights and got in his truck and drove away. Leslie watched him go and said, "I think my heart is broken."

"I'll make you forget him," Jasmine said.

"Man, the values out here are strictly Kennedy-era, aren't they?" Pablo asked. "Twenty minutes out of town and we're back in pre-Elvis times."

The evening was winding down, Rita sitting in Pablo's lap, Leslie and Jasmine in the grass thigh to thigh, and Bill looking forward to eight hours of drunk, dreamless sleep. "So, anybody see a Native American around here?" Pablo asked. "What's the story, Bill?"

"I don't know," he said. "They arrive in a village just after a miracle has occurred: a wildfire has burned straight over a half-breed boy and he's survived it without even a burn. The old men of the tribe credit his half whiteness with saving him, when actually it's his quick-thinking mom, who threw a wet buffalo hide over him. I mean, if you want reasons, that could be one."

"I want to read your book, Bill," Rita said, just as she and Pablo were getting up. Before he could say anything, Pablo yanked her into a tent. Emily helped him up, then pushed him into theirs.

On the sleeping bag, she wriggled out of her jeans and underwear and threw them in his face. As she leaned back on her elbows, knees together, the triangle of her pubis, Battery of Venus, as Lewis called it, was dimly visible. He reached for the fanny pack, but she stopped him and pulled him to her. "You don't need that," she said. Which caused his hardness to suddenly falter, to fade. "Oh, *merde*. I said the wrong thing again, didn't I? That's me, all right," she said.

"I'm drunk is all," he said.

"Or not drunk enough. Still reasoning. Lewis never stops reasoning," she said, then turned over, putting her rump to him, and covered her head with the pillow. He pulled the other sleeping bag over them, over her nakedness, and touched his forehead to her back between her shoulder blades, and thought of Lewis.

As gifted as Lewis was as an explorer, he could be rash and unforgiving as the Old Testament God. When a man deserted, Lewis ordered him run to ground and shot on sight, which the men wouldn't do, returning him to camp instead. He had a man flogged for saying mutinous things, a private whose name happened to be New-man. As plentiful as game was, they were terrified of starvation, and killed everything in sight, even hawks, ravens, eagles, and swans. They ate coyotes. Early in the journey, unbeknownst to them, the nation's third vice president called out the first treasury secretary and shot him dead. Odd, all right, and about to get odder.

Trying to sleep next to Emily, he thought about Lewis's grave, which was located not a hundred yards from where he'd died that night in

Tennessee. For a long time, there hadn't been a marker, just some split rails thrown there to keep the pigs out.

Where Bill was with the book, they'd just passed a creek called *l'eau que pleure,* or "the water which cries," and Sergeant Floyd was about to take ill and die. And then Lewis would almost poison himself to death, tasting a mineral sample for purity. They'd pass the grave of Blackbird, a Mahar chief, known for his magical ability to cause his enemies to sicken and die. Of course, the magic was arsenic, which he'd purchased from a trader.

Trying to sleep against Emily, he ran the facts as a sedative, and thought about time, and sitting in meetings at school waiting for someone to make their point. He wanted to hurry everything, but didn't know why, because there was no hurry, and nothing to get to but that last item on the do-list: get buried.

Before he could work it all out, he was asleep.

much astonished

at my black

servant

7.

"*... much astonished at my black servant ...*"

On Tuesday, after signing six kinds of waivers and releases, Bill piled his class onto a short bus. Then they rode a long way downhill, down and down into the woods, and past the zoo, heading for a specially-restored acre of glade wilderness, nature the way the captains saw it, not this confusing jumble of vines and shrubs hijacked from all over the globe. His class wandered over it, slipping on the rain-slick limestone outcrops, the girls in thin sandals with no tread and handmade ponchos.

The one he really felt for was Joaney, pregnant as a beluga, cheeks red as a pomegranate, taking mincing little steps, pausing to hunker down and gasp, glaring at him. Richard followed him close, nodding in disbelief to everything Bill said, like he made it up as he went. Which he did, sort of. And Skyler, his one Asian girl, who was crushing hard on Richard (who was pretty clearly gay), kept laughing at anything the kid said in desperate fuck-me fashion. Bill's only black kid, T, kept sitting down, looking perplexed at the exertion. But he was a big guy, and climbing a hill was a serious matter for him: he just wanted to know why. He liked to call Bill "Doc" and didn't turn things in on time, or format them properly. Sometimes he didn't do the work at all.

In the book last night, Bill had dealt with such incidents as Clark's slave York almost losing an eye from having sand thrown in it. Why it was thrown, or who threw it, wasn't mentioned. Lewis said York sometimes frightened the tribes badly by making himself "more terrible" than they wanted him to, growling and rolling his eyes and acting like a wild animal. York told the kids he was a cannibal, saying he used to live exclusively on the flesh of children. They tried to wash the blackness off him by wetting their fingers and rubbing. When they couldn't, they dubbed him "the Raven's Son."

Now, centuries later, York's experiences in the New World were influencing T's, and in surprising ways, including what he turned in and what he didn't.

Lewis stood up on a rock to address the class. "Daniel Boone blazed trails through country like this," he called out. "And at night, around the fire, he'd read aloud to everyone from *Gulliver's Travels*."

Joaney put up her hand, very cute. "Is that the one with the talking horses?" she asked. "And the giants and the Lilliputians and the Yay-hoos?"

"That's it," he said. They took turns standing up on the rock overlooking the Little Blue River, Skyler and her sweet china-doll looks, and pregnant Joaney, and gay Richard, and T.

"At the end of that book, Gulliver makes a terrible discovery," Bill said. "He realizes he's not a higher-order creature like the talking horses but the lowest of the low. He's a Yay-hoo. And when he gets home, he sees how his wife and kids are also Yay-hoos and the sight of them sickens and disgusts him."

"I think that happened to *my* dad," T said.

"Yeah, mine, too," Joaney said.

"Yours, mine, and ours," Bill said. "That's everyone's father in that story."

"So izzat what happened to Lewis?" Richard asked.

"Maybe," Bill said. "After he got back, he never slept in a bed again. Couldn't go near one."

"He did too much drugs," Skyler said. "Bed spins."

"He was in some sort of trouble," Bill said. "When you're in trouble, you'll shove anything in your mouth you can, even poison. Anything to get some relief."

They all stood observing that truth from above the yellow-and-green woods, the brown, curling road and the trickly, shiny creek.

"Who died?" T asked. Did he mean, why was everyone so sad all of a sudden? Joaney looked awfully blond, and curly-headed, and had her prenatal glow, like she was being shot through a Vaselined lens. He worried he was in love with her. Or maybe with Rita, from the float trip.

"Floyd's the only one who died," Lewis said. "Though possibly two others during the winter of 1803. Over half were dead by 1832. Sacagawea only survived six more years, Lewis only three."

"He poisoned himself?" Skyler said, turning Vietnamese eyes on his, her looks a legacy of French colonialism, and the twenty-year American nightmare, domino theory, & etc.

"That was earlier," Lewis said. "He stuck some cobalt in his mouth on the trail, and it almost killed him."

"He's trying to do himself all the way, isn't he?" T said. "Right? Right from the start." He was peering toward the cataract below, and the riffles downstream.

"Maybe so. He and his horse are constantly rolling over cliffs. He's shot at three times and hit once. A grizzly tries to eat him. In a way, even agreeing to go was suicide," Bill said.

"He's like some kinda circus geek," Skyler said. "He'll eat anything. Nothing disgusts him, not even syphilis sores."

"What's with the feathers?" T asked, slinging a stone, whipping it sidearm. Bill could only shrug.

"I think the whole thing is a crack-up," Richard said. "Lewis tells the tribes the whites have possession of their country, and they totally ignore him."

"Jefferson called the tribes his red children," Bill said.

"Right. The great white father routine," T said.

They moved on to the zoo, so he could show them a California condor, largest American bird. The men had shot one on the beach with a wingspan of nine and a half feet. But when they got to the cage, Bill couldn't return the bird's mortified, sidelong gaze; it reminded him too much of the old man's dead eye in Poe's "Tell-Tale Heart."

Joaney held the small of her back, and they passed the big cats, monkey island, the sea-lion tank, and the African veldt. "They were told to expect mastodons and saber-toothed tigers," he said. "They believed in Manifest Destiny, and Providence, and a river running east to west across the continent."

"It's called magical thinking," Skyler said. "Little kids grow out of it by about fifth grade."

They ate lunch at a corn-dog stand, and Bill wound up with Joaney at his table. No longer a child, she had to sit with the grown-ups, and was picking all the breading off her corn dog and eating only that, dipped in mustard.

"I'm gonna quit after," she said. "Everyone says they'll have the baby and come back, but it's a lie. You can't come back."

"What'll you do?" he asked.

"*Do*? What'll I *do*? That's real funny, Mr. Lewis. I won't *do* anything. I'll be somebody's mother. I'll live in my gramma's old house. I'll get some crap job."

When he didn't reply, she said, "I don't need a man. I'm very independent."

"I'm sure you are," he said. The clouds crossed the sky rapidly now, tinged in soft circusy colors, tumbling over each other like masses of pink and blue cotton candy. Richard sat with Skyler, and had her bent over his lap like she was giving him head, while he probed her scalp and she squealed and winced.

Joaney, looking around, said, "This place is kind of crummy, isn't it? It's sort of had it."

"It was nice when I was a kid," Lewis said.

"When was that?" She laughed, winking at him. She was putting on a brave face, and he suddenly knew she wasn't still in school for his class, but for the company. It was sort of shocking, like learning the head cheerleader has a morbid fear of crowds. He got up to see about Skyler and Richard. Richard pulled back her hair with some delight to show the swelling on her neck, a grotesque lump red as a little sun, stuck full of hairs like darts.

"Somebody do something," Skyler said. "Can't you see I'm diseased!"

Before Bill could say anything, Richard had taken out his pocketknife and stabbed the "ugly imposthume," to use the nineteenth-century term. Skyler jerked, but T had come over to help hold her, pinning her arms to her thighs. The gory contents drained into Bill's napkin. It bled some, then wept a clear serum. "Ugh. Aren't you grossed out?" Skyler asked.

"I guess not," he said.

Then they all got back on the bus, his class, skinny kids and tall ones, or heavyweights. Some were distraught-looking, or expressionless, clear-skinned or acne-ridden to an almost desperate state. He looked right past the healthy ones, seeing only the distressed, terrorized, and despairing. And recalled the Indian women Lewis had seen, so far gone with syphilis they'd passed into a state beyond suffering, nearly divine. The captains saw other strange sights: a couple of boulders that were in fact a pair of star-crossed lovers turned to stone by the gods, so they might always be together, their faithful dog by their side. When grieving, many of the people cut off fingers and toes, or ran arrows through their arms.

Also, in a particular lake dwelled a monstrous amphibian with horns like a cow's—which Lewis never actually saw. Nor did he see the snake reported to gobble like a turkey, or the band of murderous little men, eighteen inches high, with blowguns and gigantic heads.

In the seat ahead, Skyler kept fingering the new hole in her head. T sat next to her, massive, immovable, refusing to cooperate until he heard a good reason why. As for Clark's slave, York, he'd asked to be freed after the expedition, or at least to be near his wife. Clark refused at first, then tried beating him, then finally hired him out for hard labor. Though Clark at last relented, with urging from Lewis, who couldn't bear to see a loving husband denied the comforts of marriage.

The bus now hugged the river, which looked exactly the way the captains had seen it, except for billboards, bridges, city skyline, power plants, barges, levees, dredgers, and a little airport with planes leaping off the end of the runway and banking hard right, heading west. And the river had a deep V-shaped channel now, so it couldn't spread and wander five miles wide and three feet deep anymore. "Lo," he said to the class, "the major artery of a teeming nation." But it wasn't really true; rivers hardly mattered now. And the fabled Northwest Passage, found at last by Amundsen in 1904, was utterly impractical thanks to the Panama Canal.

Lewis knew it, too, and long before they'd reached the Pacific: there was no all-water route, no great river stretching shore to dazzled shore. He noted it matter-of-factly, just the same way he wrote, "Shields killed first buffalo," on the 3rd of August, 1804.

"So what about Sacagawea?" Joaney asked. "What's her deal?"

"Stolen from the Shoshoni by the Hidatsa in an attack in which her family was slaughtered. Or, taken from the Hidatsa by the Shoshoni, then later stolen back. And eventually purchased by a Touissant Charbonneau, French guide and interpreter," he said.

"I bet they raped the crap out of her," Skyler said. "You know they did! Why else do you take somebody?"

"Then you had to cook and clean for the asshole who stole you and raped you," Joaney said.

"Sounds like my mother's life," Skyler said.

Joaney shifted her big stomach using both hands, like it was a big rock she was stuck under.

"Hey, why'd the Indians have to go and dig up Sergeant Floyd?" Richard said.

"Oh. Well, this chief wanted to put his son's body in with Floyd's," he said. "That way, he'd go to the white man's Heaven."

"I think that's sad as shit," T said. "But I know black people like that."

"Sometimes, we identify with a thing in order to handle being swallowed up by it," he said. For some reason, he glanced down between Joaney's parted legs, at her Battery of Venus clearly outlined by her stretch pants.

Bill thought of the falling-out with the Sioux, who tried to exact a toll from the party before allowing it to proceed upriver. And how Lewis got so furious, and called the men to arms. Fortunately, a wise chief intervened. But Lewis never forgot or forgave it, calling them the "vilest miscreants of the savage race" and telling the whole country to treat the tribe as criminals and outlaws.

Joaney suddenly groaned and sat forward, a tiny muddy puddle now down between her shoes, silvery and reflective like sperm or a snail's track. She grabbed his hand. Skyler looked over the seat at the floor, and nodded to T, who nudged Richard. Then they just stared at poor Jo, like some hapless family band, perplexed by this event, unsure whether to make a sacrifice, dance, or pray. Bill slipped away and spoke to the driver, then came back and took Joaney's hand.

"Tell me some things," she said.

"Like what?" he asked.

"I dunno, but goddammit, make it quick!"

He started talking, about how they found the backbone of a "fish" forty-five feet long, just lying out in the middle of a field. And how the tribes ran gangs of buffalo over cliffs, like Jesus stampeding the herd of swine into the sea. He told about Martha F., whom Clark named a river after, and whose true identity remained a mystery, a woman lost to time. And about the meat ration, which was barely adequate at nine pounds per man per day.

He told her Lewis's favorite dish was dog, any style. He got her to half groan about George Shannon, who kept getting lost and running out ahead of the party. Sure that he'd been left behind, he raced out so far ahead that only a chase team of hunters on fast horses could catch him. Afraid of running out of things for her, he strayed into the taboo, such as Lewis's talk of the "Battery of Venus," whether the women displayed or concealed it. He talked desertion and mutiny, and about Newman, who was disbarred, and the deserter, Reed, who had to run the gauntlet four times while the men bashed him with their pencil-thick brass tamping rods. "What'd the Indians. Think of that?" she gasped.

"They thought it was barbaric," he said. "But when Lewis told them the reason, they agreed that examples were necessary, even in the best families."

Joaney nodded, breathing fast, staring ahead. She was into something hard and reliable now, and it had nothing to do with him.

"Did he help her?" she asked. "I mean, when she needed it the most?"

"He tried," Bill said. "Lewis was mostly into bloodlettings and strong laxatives. He got her a drink made from crushed rattlesnake tail, and possibly that helped."

She nodded, panting. Even in extremis, he found her very lovely and dear, her skinny arms and legs, her swollen breasts and big stomach that would deflate into a pucker, her knock-knees, her lithe wrists and ankles, her long neck and dark brow, and her aloneness, and her need, and then her aloneness again. The bus gusted up into the hospital drive and he got down to help the nurse with the wheelchair, and then got back on the bus though it tore him up to leave her there. What a mystery it all was. And what an awesome race of creatures, splendid creatures, women were.

At home, he told the story to Emily and Henry at dinner. Instead of calm family time, their dinners had turned anxious, with Henry constantly stirring through his food as if for a dead mouse. Emily didn't have too much to say about it except that Joaney ought to have had someone with her, that he should've at least stayed a little while, and what was the matter with people anymore, anyway?

In his office later he couldn't work, thinking about Joaney, and about Lewis's command of herbal cures, how he would've known about purple cone flower, for instance, that it was good for madness and delivered real results in rabid dogs. Lewis hadn't done much for Sergeant Floyd, who'd died with such grace that it sounded made up. He'd calmly announced that he was "going away," as if on vacation, and asked Lewis to write a letter for him. How romantic. So where was the crying and the pleading? Where was death's sting? And could Lewis's account really be trusted? The main thing Tom asked for was a daily record of the trip, and yet Lewis wrote in fits and starts, leaving poor Clark to somehow fill the gaps. Of course, certain things could be checked out, like Sacagawea giving birth during a total eclipse of the moon. It was a difficult birth, but Indian women pregnant by white men suffered more in labor, as if they'd displeased the gods.

In bed that night, Bill tossed and turned, and Emily mashed a pillow down on her head. At that moment, for all he knew, Joaney was not only in pain but all alone as well. O, what a world it was, and what a life!

8.

"...the residence of deavels..."

He poisons himself; Sgt. Floyd dies; Killing the first buffalo; A visit to a residence of tiny Christian devils; Geo. Shannon missing; York makes himself more terrible than they wish; A man confined for mutinous expression.

❀ Reed lay without moving all the night long, for Lewis got up to check that he was breathing and not dead. For reasons he couldn't fully fathom, he would not mention the carved ball to Clark or its 288 bumps, divisible by the twelve months or twelve disciples of Christ. Nor did Reed appear to recall finding it. And in a day or two, the private took up the old objects and implements of his former life as if by habit and was good and obedient as one might hope. Through a painful canal, he'd got new birth back into the tribe, and remember'd a purpose in the midst of his agonies there.

Days passed, and their visits to tribes along the way fell into a pattern of savage surprise at so many white faces and so much weaponry. One could scarce wish the situation reversed. Exchanging diplomatic half truths about aid on one side and obedience on the other, they kept on the move. He was never alone, but had the unlucky, rare gift for loneliness with a fellow human by his side. And wondered if God had a reason for making each mortal so singular and so painfully aware of the fact. And what'd become of his wounded French mistress? Where was she and did she touch her scar and think of him?

As he looked about, he seemed to see his life had already happened. He'd no great love like what lay before Clark, simple, easy for the taking. This job was prearranged before his birth, for the president was already his relative. He then stumbled on a grassy outcrop of what looked to be purest cobalt, weathered to a delicate creamy orange—and broke off a morsel. Having suddenly an awful hunger for that element, he thrust it into his mouth, while some distant part of him exclaimed, *Poison! Poison! Spit it out!* Like his mother shaking him the time he'd swallowed that one-cent piece.

His eyes and nose now burning, he stumbled toward the river, throat convulsed shut, tears scalding his face. With stung and puffy lips and swollen tongue, he could not even cry for help, and fell face first into the water and gurgled and sucked down mud and weeds. Somehow, Clark was now upon him and shaking him, asking not just what he'd ingested, but why. The grappling felt angry, and Lewis could not tell whether Clark was trying to push him deeper into the water or haul him up out of it. Clark spluttered and started into questions he could not finish. "Why did you—? What on earth were you—? What is the meaning—?" But the pure mineral had burned out his faculties and, as Clark dunked him, up seemed down, the sky was under him, the river above. What was more, he wished that it might never ever stop. Then abruptly he needed air and began to fight. He and Clark had each other by the neck and rose up each choking the other and the streaming drops appeared to fly sideways off their bodies. He let Clark go and was thrown or fell back into the water and there decided to rest. O, how lovely was a river! He would simply drift. Soon, though, his lungs missed the airy, chaotic world and he broke free again with the help of a multitude of male hands and voices. He waited to be pulled to pieces by those hands, but was lifted instead.

Later, it was night, and he lay alone in the grass. And then it was morning, and a mouse's shadow jerked along the outside of the tent. He followed it as far as his eye could reach. God surely hated him because he was still alive, feeling bludgeoned, butchered, and skinned. Clark was talking to him. They'd been conversing and he'd dozed. "—as for what was in your mind, I cannot presume," he said, and was waiting for Lewis's answer.

"I wish to call it accident," Lewis said.

"Lewis, you do not take careful care!" Clark snapped.

My, he sounded alarmed! But that was Clark, with a body full of reliable anger and outrage that broke out as easily as his sweat.

"Something's amiss," Lewis said, holding his head. "I want to eat a yard of earth. I could chew rocks or eat dung. Some element is lacking in me."

"How are you now?" Clark asked. "And have you heard? Sergeant Floyd is dying."

"Somehow, I knew that he was," Lewis said. "I must see to him." He tested a foot on the ground. He sat up, temples pounding.

"That seems hardly wise," Clark said. "And useless, too, for he will not last the night."

He was up already, and staggering off with Clark still talking, bursting out of the tent, finding a friendly tree to lean on while the rollicking earth settled. Going tree by tree, and not believing a thing was real 'til he'd touched it, he found the right tent and slipped in. Floyd, on his back, with that singular look of the dying, those thousand-mile eyes, greeted him and then said, "I am going away."

"Are you, then? Are you sure that's a sound idea?" he asked.

"Please write me a letter," Floyd said, through wet mutton-chop whiskers. Lewis smiled, and nearly made a joke about letters of reference to Saint Peter. He felt they were brothers at this moment, sharing their nearness to death. For Lewis felt his own life would end any moment, though it was curious how it persisted and hung on. A little after he took the letter down, Floyd died.

At dawn was a solemn little ceremony, a yawning shallow trench, prayers, a lively pitching of fresh earth into a hole, onto Floyd. The men looked to Lewis to say something. Finally he knelt and put a hand on Floyd's cold forehead and said, "Ah, Floyd, you whom we invited with us on our expedition. And now you go and leave us out of yours!"

That task done, Floyd entombed, enshrined in limestone, all desire abandoned him. He felt trumped by death. The men waited on him in dismay, with searching looks, until at last he gave an order to load boats.

Later on, they saw the first buffalo and Private Fields shot and killed it. Lewis walked out and stood by, his mouth yet aching from the mineral, burnt lips stinging, tongue still thick and hard to work. Was there any hope of getting to the Pacific without some slight desire to do so? Clark joined him, to toe the cooling animal.

"This before us is the first buffalo, Clark," Lewis said, with difficulty. "The very first one."

"And a very grand fellow indeed," Clark said. "A tasty-looking morsel."

"I am not making myself clear," Lewis continued, and wiped his eyes, which cried tears, for some reason. "I must not be well. I simply wish to say that here at our feet lies the first buffalo. I cannot say more than that, though I apparently feel a great deal about it."

But O, feeling! What a nuisance, bubbling up so suddenly and irresistibly. Why was it so excessive, so contradictory? He must be going out of his mind, or perhaps he already had, years ago.

Farther on, a group of Sioux came up on foot and bade them pay a visit to their town, using signs. Later, they escorted Lewis to a large hill that appeared man-made. He was told, through interpreters, that it was the home of little Christian devils, eighteen inches high, with freakish large heads, whose blowguns could kill at great distances.

He burst out laughing, certain the interpreters had got it wrong. The Indians, blankets on their shoulders, feathers tied in their hair, scowled, and their chief made a sign, a single finger drawn away sharply from the mouth, twisting and turning, for an untrustworthy person. Lewis choked back the untimely mirth, which only doubled its intensity, finally biting his tongue 'til he tasted blood. Then they soberly investigated the hill, but no little demons were about.

Nevertheless, the place had an airless, doomed, and motionless sense, and was gusted with dry, hot winds, the grasshoppers singing at a steep infernal pitch. Its chest-high grasses were full of currents and whisperings, making it palpably a region of spirits and bad medicine.

"Something awful occurred here once," he said to Clark. "Certain places on earth have this about them, this dark sort of dread."

He'd seen it all before, he was sure of it, as if he were repeating this same journey over and over, endlessly, like an inward-turning circle, as though his life had got loose from the mainstream and was caught in an eddy. They walked down from this "spirit mound." There would be a road up to it one day, just there. He traced the path with his finger. One day, he'd come up it. In fact, he'd already done so.

The next day, he and Clark walked out ahead and found, in ev'ry hollow and thicket, ev'ry knoll and copse—ready for the picking and eating with wild juices running down chins and fingers stained red—grapes, plums, and blue currants. Each thing that was new, they named, and with the naming of each lark, wren, and blackbird, he could see a time coming when all things would be named, and none cared about the natural world disappearing, because new methods of valuing, unimaginable now, would arise and determine what was good or ill.

When they made camp, Shannon was missing. This man, with the poorest sense of direction ever, was forever losing his way, even going to the latrine. This time, he'd utterly vanished with two U.S. government horses, as though he'd stumbled off that plane of existence. But the man had a genius for finding hidden places, doors in hillsides, folds in the garment of time. And was never far off, for they found signs of him all over, a warm ash pile, a half-gnawed rabbit skull, a hastily buried turd. But he remained hidden. Did God so love George Shannon? And could there truly be a bearded old man in the sky? Or was He only a scapegoat for all man could not answer? If so, then enormous lies were being told, and defended with torture by black-clad tonsured craven bullies. Now and then, the tribes caught one of these, these missionaries, covered him in soot, pulled off his skin, lashed him to a tree, then put the tree in some rapids.

That next morning, the object was to shoot one of the gazelles or antelopes they'd seen, like an animal of the Serengeti. They ambushed him, and Lewis sat stroking the coat of bright yellowish silver, reddish-brown and a leaden gray, and looked into the emptied eye, of a deep sea green. Then they wanted a female for comparison, but too late—those animals moved over the plain more like flighted birds than quadrupeds. Clark killed a prairie wolf, lean, distant figure loping forever on the edge of life. It gave Lewis a strange pain to watch it fall and lie still.

Often and often, he had to pause and wonder whether honour, glory, dominion, and renown could still be his. The plain they skirted was as close-trimmed and neatly cultivated as a beautiful bowling green and bore the appearance of man's handiwork. But what purpose to mow broad swaths up and down the prairie, and then lay them head to head? He counted eighteen of these features, all carefully arranged on a piece of land.

Several miles above them, Drouillard was riding upriver as hard and fast as he could go. And though he nearly killed a horse in the bargain, he'd at last overtake Shannon and bring another of his insane flights to a close. George had been quite crazy for days, trying to catch a party that was not there. And afterward insisted he'd heard their voices ahead, and smelt their horses, cooking, and latrines, but could find them nowhere. Shaking, clothed in rags, peppered with cockles, he rubbed one eye, then the other, deranged by lack of sleep. Nature played such sport with this man, making him think north was south and up was down.

That night, the men came 'round to be stabbed, cunningly wounded, by Lewis. And Lewis was only too happy to oblige, for few things did he hate more than a festering boil. A poultice of sugar and soap might suffice for some, but give him the lancet and the needle, white-hot from the flame. His readiness to pierce and puncture elevated him in the men's eyes to a place not far from godhead, for they respected only agony and copious bleeding.

A day or so after, they met a party of Sioux and went ashore to palaver. But within a very few minutes a horse had gone missing, and then sundry small articles as well. Lewis, standing under a huge, leafless tree, shielded his eyes to look up from the river at the chiefs on the ridge with the sun behind their feathery heads.

"I'll have you know we are not afraid of Indians!" he shouted up to them, knowing that the words meant nothing, that his tone carried all his meaning. "When Indians steal from us, we kill them! Isn't that so, Commander?"

"O, yes!" Clark said, standing in the sun, a hand on his sword, a second tiny figure they looked down at. "We have possession of your country! And we only deal fairly with those who are fair to us!"

The chiefs, blanketed, thin, squinting, and as wrinkled as raisins, expressed consternation and shock, anger, and outrage with a long retort, and so Lewis had his answer. He and Clark turned and walked down the hill, and with them flowed a body of two hundred warriors, and women and children, the entire village. He wondered, with a bitter curiosity, if it was almost over, if his slaughter would be next. Some young men got to the bateau and seized its line. Clark drew his sword. Lewis cried, "Men, take arms!" And then waited for the Almighty. But a doddering old chief limped into the shallows and took the rope from the young men, and indicated that taking him on board would avert a massacre. So they were allowed to escape, and put the old sinner ashore a few miles above.

That night had everyone in bad spirits. At the next village, they were skittish, and every sparrow's fall was possibly a slaughter commencing. Those women, decorated with the scalps of defeated enemies, danced. Many had flint- and iron-pointed arrows run through their arms in grief for loved ones recently fallen in battle. So, apparently, did love hold sway with those people. But hatred did, too.

Lewis, reflecting on what had almost happened, had a bitter night. His sorrow acted like claws curved backward, and the more he struggled in its grasp and tried to escape, the deeper it dug and faster it held. His sentiments were crafted like a thousand tiny gold fishhooks into which he'd blundered, and now he attempt'd not to panic or resist. He got down and prayed with his head to the earth for it to be lifted, and was surprised there by Clark. "Are you ill, Lewis? What's the matter?"

"Nothing at all. Merely resting."

Clark stared and angled his head in that interrogative Irish way, and frowned as he did when a thing was irrational.

"Lewis, what was in your heart, making that call to arms?" he asked.

"Nothing. Curiosity to see how it would fall out," he said, standing and feeling foolish about the dirt on his knees and his brow, making him appear like some sort of Catholic.

"But to fight rather than to bargain—?" Clark said.

"But Clark, I didn't choose it!" Lewis protested. "I never choose a thing to do or say but what is thrust on me by my station, rank, training, situation, time of day, even the position of the sun. In effect, no choices appear to me at all but always the one course as though it were already writ somewhere. As though all this were occurring in God's head, and He were setting it down, and rapidly, with no hesitation or crossing out."

"Would you prefer some crossing out?" Clark asked with a worried smile, slapping dust out of his beaver hat.

"I do not prefer at all," Lewis said. "I cannot resist a bit in these traces. They are snug and double."

Clark plainly didn't care for his answers and didn't pursue them. The tribe later walked them out to see two large boulders with a third smaller, purported to be star-crossed lovers turned by the gods to stone, side by side for eternity. And their dog. "Romeo and Juliet," Clark said.

"Though I can't help but think of the Gorgon, Medusa," Lewis said. "And of Lot's wife, also."

That evening, they confined a man (Newman) for mutinous expression, and sentenced him to seventy-five lashes. Lewis was curious to see an actual mutineer and visited him where he was shackled, finding a character with long blond hair and a rosy face, a regular cherub, but sunk into sullen study of his right shoe.

"What's the game, Cap'n?" he asked.

"What? There's no game, Private."

"Sure, this here, the whole thing, is it. I'm just askin', what's the rules so we can all play and that'd make it fair."

"I'm sorry you think so, for it will make the thrashing useless unless you see we are not about play and sport," Lewis said, wincing at some shooting pains in his skull.

"Once more, sir. What game are ya playing on me? For I on'y said, to a few fellas, we should refuse to man-haul these boats above ten hour a day."

"Aye, the men might listen to such a young, devilishly handsome fellow, and that is why, as of this moment, you are disbarred," he said.

"Whuh! O, no, sir," Newman said, casting forward onto his knees and trying to rise in the hobbles.

"O, yes. You are disbarred, Newman, and stripped of rank, and are now an ordinary teamster," he said, rather relishing the blood rising in the fellow's face, soaking his skin to the roots of his hair, the outrage, the sputtering shock at such a punishment.

"I'll desert!" he said.

"Yes, do. And then I can hang you outright, you stupid upstart," Lewis said.

Newman's lip trembled and his color went as he saw it was no jest. "Wha'd I ever—why, Cap'n? I never done harm. I on'y made idle chat about the hauling!"

"I know what you are, man, better than you know yourself, and here is how to deal with you," Lewis said, grinning. "I simply came to see if you are what I suspected, and you are."

"I ain't no harm, Cap'n. I on'y shot off my mouth to the others. They're against me, is all, and have been all along! Don'tcha see?"

Lewis walked off, away from the bereft, hysteric voice, the pleas. Poor, handsome, craven creature. Though he'd enjoy the lashing of such a man.

Walking out, he noted that this nation's houses were eight-sided, eight being the number of candles in a menorah and the days of Hanukkah. But he could espy no other Hebrew features that might identify one of the ten tribes. In an hour, just at sunset, the beating commenced and the stroke and Newman's cry rang across the prairie. Suddenly, it stopped in the middle, the chief coming forth and staying the whip, crying out at such cruel treatment.

"Tell him we are making an example of this man for challenging my authority," Lewis said to the interpreter. "Tell him that, if there are kindnesses at all between white people, it is lashing that makes them possible."

The chief listened to the explanation and then, showing himself a sensible man, said examples were useful from time to time, and withdrew to let the beating resume. Newman at last fell on the ground, overcome by his wounds, and was beaten there to the count of twenty-five, then left.

"... they gave him four girls ..."

A half-white boy survives a wildfire; Sacagawea and her husband
join the party; A man stabs his wife three times; Sgt. Pryor's shoulder replaced; York with frostbite on his p—; A visit from men dressed
as women; S. gives birth.

❧ The next day, they were under way early, the tribe anxious to consult
a prophetic boulder about an impending war with their enemies. The
men parted company with those tawny damsels, of marked esteem, and
agreeable in nature. Lewis wondered briefly about a Miss G— H— and a
Miss J— L— back at home, but could not believe in their existence.
Surely those ladies had already lived, been loved, died, and were now remember'd on headstones under spreading shade trees. The clouds
steamed like ships on a harbor, casting shadows on herds of buffalo
streaming in rivulets o'er the plain.

Then several days and nights of relentless freezing drizzle, during which
the romance was all expunged and the real expedition got under way.

In the next village, the chief had two little fingers off in grief for a dead son, and the old men were sitting and talking with a miraculous half-white boy, recently spared horrible death in a wildfire that burned straight over him. His mixed ancestry, particularly the lightness of his skin, was credited for his salvation (never mind his quick-thinking mother who threw a wet hide over him). So the president's dream of one nation, united sea to sea, was being born, coming into real vitality all around them. Yet Lewis was in quite as gloomy a frame of mind as ever, and wondered whether humans were really better than the previous drowned race, of which Noah was the last. It hardly took a prophet to guess the shape of this landscape one or two hundred years hence. Unease found him every few instants and his heart was tight. The pleasant evening mysteriously excluded him; he could not experience its joys.

Later, a man came into camp, quite French, traveling with two wives, and petitioned to join the party as interpreter, a Snake-talker no less. He was the very thing they needed to get over the Rock Mountains, which grew in size with each passing day, throwing their long shadows on the surface of every eye. They talked with him, and he kept referring to their "mysterious journey" ahead. Clark spoke to him first on the matter, and Lewis stood glancing across the ravine toward the littler of the two women, one who plainly didn't belong to her station in life, and was estranged, and showed no fear or hope. She awaited her fate at a distance of three dozen paces, which was just near enough. He couldn't see her well, but well enough.

Suddenly taking Clark aside, Lewis said, "My impression is of a man but ill-suited for his occupation. Methinks the smaller wife is somehow key in his employment and is the real translator."

Clark did not look at the fellow, nodding. Direct, easy, red-headed, and military, Clark was suspicious of words when acts were possible, and trusted Lewis as more intuitive than he.

Lewis walked up to the fellow, in his red Flemish cap, with a nose, prodigious organ, all pox'd and pimpl'd, that had apparently been made slapdash by a blind artisan who was missing several fingers. With short legs, a concave chest, long arms, simian hands, and crude, blocky feet, he hunched rather than stood. Rough strips of cloud above them had spread apart, showing the stars. Mr. Charbonneau, or "Mr. Charcoal," as he was called, crooked forth a dirty little paw to shake. Here was one more foreigner who could not do it properly, and was not manly.

"As to terms," Lewis said. Which instantly made hatred boil in the hollows of the piggy eyes. Lewis stated a handsome price, twice what that fellow was worth, and yet the rage only seemed to double. Such crude hands as those had surely poisoned out of revenge, had bludgeoned a sleeping enemy to death. He breathed a miasma of indigestion through broken teeth and, in utter and complete disgust, gave his hand anyway. Lewis dared to glance again. The neatness of her outfit. The eyes illumined from behind and blazing into the growing night.

"It is good to at last meet a Snake-talker," Lewis said.

"Where is the fucking pig who says otherwise?" the fellow demanded, then laughed. In the lowest of rustic scenes, such creatures were made, Lewis knew, and for the rest of their lives sought relief for their crude condition, and ultimately found none.

But she! She was daughter to the God who incinerated Sodom. He looked to find her once more, and saw only where she had been. The fellow turned quickly to see where Lewis's eyes had gone, but Lewis shut them and ducked away.

Later, he lay unable to sleep, eyes open, feeling immured in the cracks in time, watching floating columns of apparitions—Northern Lights—dancing on the tent. When he closed them, her face glinted in the dark, self-evident, essential, perfect. Then suddenly, the oxish stare of the husband intruded, divining all, observing his observing, and he was wide awake again.

· · ·

In the morning, he witnessed a serious farewell between the old wife and the new, looking long and earnestly in each other's faces, for this was maybe the last time they'd set eyes on each other, this side of death. Then the old wife was gone, and without so much as a backward glance at her husband.

Lewis felt it had happened before, yet everything had changed. Now he had someone, one whom he was able to watch without needing his eyes. He saw her with his mind's seeing-organ, and noted so many things about her: her sportive willingness to journey, the wry silent witness she was to a large party of men. Also, formed last by God, her labours were now heavier after the departure of the old wife, even though her belly showed that she was far gone with child.

In the following days, he knew her proximity, direction, and activity every moment. If ever asked her whereabouts, he could answer without looking up—but never dar'd.

That night, near 10 P.M., the dark erupted into shouts of anger and a woman's cries of pain. He and Clark forced a way through the mob and found a lady bleeding on the ground from three deep knife gouges, and her husband, smeared with the warm life of his beloved, with three privates sitting on him. It seemed she engaged in sport with the men, and the husband caught her, coming in late.

"You see, Clark?" Lewis asked. "This bedroom diplomacy does violence to souls unsuited to it."

"'Tis puzzling," Clark said, shaking his head. "To a savage, jealousy is generally thought impractical."

"O, 'tis the least practical thing in the world," Lewis said. "Please to tell the men to turn in."

After Clark did, Lewis stayed a while and stood where he could not be seen and watched the bridegroom sitting half naked in the bloody snow, gasping and blowing and spitting red from having bitten his tongue in anguish. Behold, the angry forlorn cuckold. He seemed not to care whether he froze to death, lost in wonder. *Why, little one? Why do you do this to me when you know I love you?* Or words to that effect, while her blood dried on him. Ah, love. Lewis at last withdrew to his own bed, but lay too agitated to sleep, tossing and remembering his French mistress, being bathed in her gushing blood.

The next afternoon, Sergeant Pryor, a mere youth with twinkling blue eyes, curly locks, and smooth, high forehead, got his hand wrong in a rope, helping to raise a mast, and the violent wrench tore his shoulder from its socket, and he fell on the deck and writhed and kicked, and was sat upon by three of his fellows while a fourth tried to draw the arm out straight. The first try failing, Pryor all but bit his own tongue off and blood dribbled out of his mouth. "Goddamn you men! You butchers! You filthy, lazy, worthless wretches!" he cried. "You have been against me! I know you do not respect me! But I am . . . agh! . . . your sergeant, you stinking filth!"

On the second try, the joint ground in the socket, then jumped out again. Pryor kicked out and would have screamed could his jaws unclench, which they could not. With eyes squeezed, leaking tears, he espied Lewis, and blinked and made guttural growls and gnashed his teeth. "I see them! The lights about your head! Look above your head!" he said.

At the third try, Pryor seemed to go unconscious for a moment, and went limp as if dead, in a contorted, tortured pose. He slowly opened his eyes. "O, yellow pack of miscreants! You vile, disobedient demons! I at last see you! I see what ye really are!"

On the fourth attempt, at the pop of the shoulder going fully home, Pryor dropped dead away and was left where he was, the men walking off muttering about what a pip Sergeant Pryor could be at times, though not so bad, after all, as some officers.

Lewis waited nearby, curious, with never an inkling that the sergeant could be so wild and vindictive. Pryor opened his eyes and glanced about, seeming not to see him at first. He looked around expectantly, then his face dulled with disappointment. "Everything is . . . as before," he said.

"And how should it be, Sergeant?" Lewis asked.

"A bright flame played about your head," he said. "All this—" he gestured at the woods, "—was of the most variant hue and brilliance. Each blade of grass was a bit of fire."

Lewis stared the sergeant in the face, for Floyd had actually emanated some sort of orange flare from the crown of his head, while the feathers came down the river. And then, very shortly after, expired from no certain cause.

"Never mind, Sergeant," he said. "You will be your old self in a day or two."

Pryor nodded, but didn't look relieved at this news.

Over the long winter days, when she was in the hut, he was careful to be elsewhere, and worried he'd be discovered by his avoidance of her rather than the contrary. The temperature in the Mandan village fell and fell, until it seemed they had found a place on earth without limits. But it at last stopped, at 72 below. York went out hunting, and from dragging buffalo carcasses into the wind, got frostbite on his feet and p—.

One night, above the wind, they suddenly heard a most terrific wailing, a concatenation of shrill female voices, lifted in a fever of ritual song. With lanterns raised, Lewis and a few privates ventured forth to peer out at a party of squaws just within the woods. Charbonneau somehow materialized at his elbow. "Berdachers," he pronounced. "Do ya know what they are?"

"They are females," Lewis said.

"Only in manner and appearance. Dem're witches. Able to change form and fornicate with men. There's nothink like a night with a berdacher, but a man kills hisself in the morning. Better keep an eye to your sodjers."

He glanced at the flickering French eye beside him, the thick, wet lips, thrust tongue, and rolling white, like something atop a cathedral. Each night, she laid her small, perfect head beside that visage.

"These men are confined to quarters after dark," he said. But as soon as he'd got it out, the husband crooked a finger forth with a laugh.

"Dere he goes! Catch him, boys, catch him! Tie him to a tree!"

In fact, a man had set out and was halfway to the woods, trying to reach that dark band of white-faced furies, when he was overtaken and tackled and forcibly retrieved.

"Shackle him," Lewis said. "And if you must, sit on him all night, but keep him indoors!"

He watched that they did this, but when he turned back he no longer saw the husband, that face of the hell-born *agoniste*, or the berdaches.

The next night, the Nation got up a huge medicine dance to bring the buffalo back north in the spring, and they gave this man, the one who tried to run, a seat of honor at the feast and four maidens, for the good luck it would bring the tribe.

Then came a total eclipse of the moon, and much chanting and singing.

Lewis suddenly received Charbonneau, who came to his tent to show him a red rising on his tailbone. "Either you are sprouting a tail," Lewis noted with some relish, "or you have an abscess forming. Let it rise 'til you cannot bear it, then summon me."

And indeed 'twas strange, this general epidemic of boils and abscesses, so that every man suffered some such complaint, almost as tho they drew near to some invisible disruptive force, disord'ring their flesh.

"O, one other thing," the husband said before departing. "It seems her time is nigh."

Lewis gaped at the milky, insolent blue eyes, one and then the other, before the meaning at last dawned on him. "Sir, do you mean your wife is giving birth? This moment?"

"Aye, these twelve hour, ever since the moon come up," he said blandly, and clumsily loaded a pipe.

As if at a signal her voice, in transports of agony, sounded high and clear above the songs of the dancers. "My God, you might've said something before! She is in distress."

"She 'as me worried, 'at she 'as," the fellow said.

Lewis went to the hut and found her there with a woman of the village, midwife, arriving just in time for a terrible sight of her gray skin, and to feel of her icy hands and feet, and to hear her scream instead of making the healthful grunt and bearing down of a successfully labouring woman. Her throat seemed to rip, to be torn in two. She continued this way for another hour, and he left her and attempted to go about business elsewhere. But her cries awakened ev'ry nerve he had and worked them like an iron file on harp strings, like a hurricane in a dry field of rye. He found no refuge anywhere, and heard it when it wasn't there, while the sergeants queried him on various things. He was helpless inside it, like a child at the hands of a fiend. At last, he stumbled into the hut for the medicine kit, found dried rings of rattlesnake tail, crushed them fine, mixed with water, and ran. And though the midwife viewed 't suspiciously, he held it to her lips and she drank with a tender awful trust in her eye, and fiery hands grasping his.

Within ten minutes of his departure, from the suffocating confines of the maternity ward, she delivered a healthy boy, whose cry he perceived from where he had fallen, face foremost, in the snow.

Then, a few days later, she walked out for the first time, mother and child rivaling each other for radiance in the spring light. He did not dare go near her nor dare to stay away and so glanced only a moment at her prize.

The husband, standing some distance from her and appearing heedless, was in fact very carefully observing this visitation (Lewis knew), devouring each detail of his expression and hers with starved attention.

Lewis felt the moment, like ev'ry moment since Creation, was formed of iron and bolted on ev'ry side. And knew he had a dog at heel now, and a shade by his side, which was the husband, who was waiting and watching for some particular sign, some telltale glimmer in her eye or his to give him cause to act, to pounce.

But how? When had he made the slip and put that bloodhound on his scent? No, it wasn't possible. He'd not made the least error, never an imprudent glance. No—the fellow awaited evidence. Lewis was sure of it, or almost certain, moving carefully away from the little gathering, out of the fellow's sight.

10.

" ... she brought forth ..."

In the morning, before school, Bill and Henry walked Bosco, their boxer. Bosco was everything a dog shouldn't be, nervous, anxious, polite, tongue-tied, tentative on a leash, and never pulling or barking or prancing but just worried, with those awful wall-eyes, always sure you would push him into traffic. Henry had picked him out immediately from the line-up at the pound. Bill sometimes compared Henry to himself at the same age, and wasn't thrilled by the marked similarities. At least Henry still showed faith in a few things—he wanted to try out for baseball—whereas Bill had given up on most things by then, and barely believed the sun would rise.

"Let's hurry it up, shall we?" Bill said, still thinking about Joaney's rough night and wanting to make a private call.

"Okay, sorry, Dad," Henry said.

"For Christ's sake, don't be sorry. And stop being so nice and polite all the time," he said. "They aren't handing out awards for it, don't you know?"

"God, what's eating you?" Henry asked. Then he took off with Bosco before Bill could answer, making the dog run, Bosco looking back to see what was chasing them. Bill felt a sort of tidal surge pushing him from behind, and he was trying to keep his head above it. The thing about depression was that it sucked at you and dragged on you, like some slowly revolving vortex. You were haunted by a certainty, each and every moment, that the wheels were coming off.

After class, Bill stopped by the hospital and bought a bear in a bow tie holding a bunch of Mylar balloons. He almost got on the elevator, then backed away and had it sent to her room. For all he knew, her baby-daddy, Tommy, was up there, playing the television too loud, hogging the bed, checking on the scores.

The doctor's office called that evening with the results of his CAT scan. It was the tech, Jenna, whom he remembered like you remember a dream-lover. "Guess what?" she said. "We have to do it again. There's a shadow on the screen, so maybe you moved."

"What kind of shadow?" he asked. "Like a tumor-shadow?"

"Actually, it looks like two scans or like a double exposure or something," she said. She seemed to be chewing gum.

"How on earth does that happen?" he asked.

"I don't know. Unless you're possessed or something," she said. "Otherwise, we have to do it again."

"Again? Well, I'll have to think about that, Jenna," he said. "I'll be in touch."

The dinner table that night was charged with a lot of impacted feelings. Neither he, Emily, nor Henry knew how anything was going to turn out, especially if Henry wasn't going to eat and Bill was going to be sneaking off to make private calls. There was a chance, too, that he'd stop sleeping like the last time he tried to write a book. He just might lose his grip on reality again and collapse, wind up in the hospital.

Henry sought him out later in his office, and appeared to be in some sort of inarticulate distress, shrugging when asked what he wanted. So Lewis took him around the house, and they fixed anything they found that was broken or out of kilter, too squeaky or not squeaky enough. Then, when Henry seemed no better off, they headed out to rake, and in a wind so stiff it made Bill's whole body hurt, from ears to hands to knees. He talked because Henry encouraged it by asking lots of leading questions. Like he was just trying to keep his father talking. Like it would stop them both from slipping into some dangerous state—shock or coma or death.

"They met every kind of tribe you could think of," Bill said. "Tribes far neater and cleaner than white people. Tribes with no idea of personal hygiene. Tribes with everything flipped, so the women had short hair and the men had long hair and did all the cooking. Tribes with no land and no home, who lived on the run from their enemies. Tribes so hungry they'd fall over each other for a bucket of raw deer guts. Tribes with so much to eat they burned their leftovers to keep warm. Tribes that stole them blind. Tribes that crossed mountain ranges to return little items they'd left behind. Tribes that price-gouged them over a handful of roots, even when they were starving. Tribes that gave up their own horses so the party could eat, and asked for nothing in return."

"Was Lewis a good guy or a bad guy?" Henry asked. "Do you admire him and stuff?"

"Actually, of the four physical assaults recorded, white on Indian, Lewis did three," he said. "After the expedition, three tribes are singled out as malicious troublemakers, worthy of extermination: the Teton Sioux, the Arikara, and the Great Osage. And one of the first to point the finger is Lewis."

"Are you serious? What a jerk," Henry said.

"And yet he also decrees that white settlers must be kept from crossing the Missouri onto Indian land," he said. "On the other hand, if you were having a little card game in your room, and you didn't invite Lewis, he might just burst in and offer to kill you, pistols at dawn and all that. In other words, he'd rather be court-martialed than excluded. He'd just as soon shoot you as be left out."

"Yeah, why not?" Henry said, which seemed to refer to something that'd happened to him, jaw muscles working, eyes remote. "I mean, why the hell not?"

"Listen, Hen. Is something bothering you?" he asked. "Is somebody at school bothering you?"

Henry shook his head. "What about Jefferson? Did he like Lewis?" he asked.

"No, I don't think he did like him. But I do think he loved him. Lewis aggravated everyone. He had his own reasons for everything he did," Bill said. "And Tom flip-flops on Lewis. First he says Lewis wasn't really qualified to lead the party. Then, later, he boasts that Lewis was the perfect choice. Finally, after Lewis kills himself, he says he isn't surprised."

Henry's eyes in that light, with the sun shrouded by the October clouds, were about the blue of a cutting torch, of a fighter jet's afterburners. If push ever came to shove between him and Emily, Bill realized, he didn't know for sure which way Henry would go. Sometimes Henry's gaze frightened him.

"Can you finish this up?" he asked, and Henry nodded.

Bill went around behind the garage and smoked four cigarettes, because at least once a day he needed to be alone with and face up to his old adversary. Smoking. He hated it, but wasn't completely ready to let it go. He drew carefully on each puff, smoking the marrow out of each one, feeling the drug spreading through him and turning every switch to "on." The true savor of life, whatever one was able to get out of it, was about this: holding each moment carefully and long, and concentrating. He got a funny, buzzy feeling in his chest from the drug, like it was full of moths, and his heart beat hard, maybe too hard.

Bill'd now been to a lot of the key spots and landmarks along the trail, but still didn't know why Lewis had done it, not really. Lewis started out from Harper's Ferry, Virginia, where they would catch and hang John Brown in 1859. Then he'd ended up in Tennessee, in a little inn on a dark night by the side of a road used by highwaymen and boat pilots walking home from New Orleans.

He stood by the garage knowing that an awful sorrow had lifted from him for quite a while—but it was threatening again. Happiness, or something close to it, must have been his for a time, but it was slipping. And how deep and how long a struggle he had before him, he didn't know. Whatever his inner demon was, It was escaping, and whatever had held It at bay was failing. Doors to where the bad stuff lived were opening, releasing the sort of stuff Kurtz babbled about in *Heart of Darkness*.

Mostly, Bill felt himself wanting to go . . . he didn't know where, just away. His heart was full with the need to depart.

By his foot, a brick sat on top of an inverted bucket, which sat on a second brick, and he lifted them, replaced the cigarettes and lighter, then restored the pail, set the first brick on it, and went in the house.

On Thursday after school, Bill pulled up outside Joaney's little two-bedroom bungalow, a small, run-down cottage with a gravel drive. He sat there, and pictured himself from a bird's-eye view, sitting there, his car a blue dot on a snaking black road.

Women always liked him. In him, women seemed to see the one they couldn't manage to save, a father, a brother, a first love. It was as if, with him, they were getting a second chance.

As for the male world, he avoided it. Coming at him from that region was a sort of cosmic feeling of dislike and mistrust. It was mutual.

Joaney greeted him in sweatpants and a t-shirt, a blanket over her shoulders, and one hand placed carefully on her cheek, which she kept there and would not take away. "You don't want to come in here," she said. "I'm sick." But she stood aside anyway, inviting him.

He stepped in—and caught his breath in surprise. Her house *stank*. It was wood rot and mildew and backed-up drains and clogged gutters, wet plaster, sodden insulation, and rusted nails, all mixed up with fruity potpourri, incense, and air freshener.

All the same, she couldn't look bad to him, even ill, the tight corkscrews of her lemony-blond perm in wild abundant shocks on her shoulders. And she kept that hand on her face, like she'd just said, "Oh, my stars!" or "Holy shit!"

Right after Sacagawea gave birth, she too was ill, and Lewis declared it an "obstruction of the menses," whatever he thought that was, and crafted a device to fit her "region," a poultice designed to draw out infection. Very soon, she got better. But then relapsed because she ate a particular root, the "white apple" which Lewis had warned her husband not to let her have. So for the second time she was deathly ill, and again Lewis nursed her back from the brink, and again the husband was the culprit. Lewis also noted how her husband worked her too hard, and polluted her body with venereal diseases, and was abusive. At least twice more, she almost died. In both cases, the husband could be seen cowering helplessly, unable or unwilling to come to her aid. The husband's only apparent skill was cooking a sausage made of sweet meats stuffed into a buffalo intestine, which was boiled, then fried in bear grease. "Janey," on the other hand, did everything well, bringing Lewis rare specimens of plants, witching up roots of all kinds with nothing more than a pointed stick, speaking five languages, and serving as a guide through Snake Indian territory where only she'd been before.

From the covered porch, Bill stepped into the living room. About a quarter of the ceiling had simply fallen in, from a terrible roof leak. The ragged hole gaped above pans arranged to catch rainwater. She pointed him to a chair, its seat consisting of a board and a pillow. She sat across from him on the ancient nubbly green couch with its shot springs. A sheet over a wooden cable-spool was her end table. Even her lamp was cracked. She sat in evident pain, but managed a smile. "Jack's asleep," she said. "Gawd, he was big as a house."

She removed the hand to adjust her blanket, but put it right back, protecting what appeared to be a shadow under her eye, a reminder that the baby-daddy lurked somewhere nearby, around town. A pretty desperate scene. And he was just making it worse, sitting there and staring at it, able to do exactly nothing for her. In one way, she was just Joaney, his student. But in another, she was the golden one, the dark-eyed one who always danced out of his reach, who ducked his kiss, and stood him up. The light coming through the window behind gave her a slight glow. As for the house, one window showed real leaded glass in solid oak framing, which hinted at what a lovely little Craftsman it had once been.

As for the explorer Lewis, what a hard, bitter winter he and the party suffered, in North Dakota among the Mandan Nation, with the endless fields of snow acting as a huge reflector dish to create a second sun in the sky. The men taking frostbite, York even getting it on his penis, the mercury at night dropping into hell, 72 below. But they'd had to go out anyway and kill all they could, slaughtering up to three thousand pounds of meat in a single day. Which barely replaced the calories they burned killing and dressing it out. Not to mention the strangeness of the season, with men dressed as squaws coming around at night, trying to lure them with unearthly, ululating falsetto songs. Around the fire at night, for diversion, Clark mentioned some "rough conversation about boys." And Lewis recorded a Mandan creation myth, about the tribe's origins in a garden beneath a lake, which they'd climbed up out of on a long grapevine. But the vine broke when a big-bellied woman tried to climb it, so that half the tribe fell back in. When those from the above-tribe died, they moved down to the lake and lived with the below-tribe, just as they did in the upper world.

"Have you got kids, Mr. Lewis?" Joaney asked.

"I have a son who's fourteen. We won't have any more, it doesn't look like," he said.

"That's prob'ly for the best," she said, with a slight smirk. "I mean, given your age and all." On the floor, by her bare toes, was Shelley's *Frankenstein* with a butter knife marking her place, assigned reading for his class.

"Lewis'd been dead nine years when that came out," he said, nodding at the book. "Mary had this big crush on Washington Irving."

"You mean the guy who wrote 'Rip Van Winkle'?"

"That's the guy," he said. "At the trial of the traitor Aaron Burr, Irving sat at his defense table as one of his attorneys. Burr's daughter, Theodosia, was at the trial, and so was Lewis, and they were seen together, going riding together, though she was married."

"That's real interesting," she said. "I sort of wish I'd finished it."

"Yeah, when Irving gets back to the U.S. from living abroad, one of the first people he looks up is Clark," he said. "He wants to track down some living members of the expedition."

"I like the voice of it," she said, touching the book with her bare toes. "I like the way they talked back then. And how the monster does whatever it feels like."

"Something about us is so horrifying, we don't want to own it," Bill said, still trying to teach her. "Or maybe we can't. Irving and Shelley almost had an affair. But then Mary gave him a look at the opera one night that scared him about half to death."

"Some look," Joaney said.

He wanted to tell her more, about a tree the Mandan used for ceremonies, tying cords to the branches, then punching them through their flesh, and hanging there, suspended in air. And about this group of young Sioux warriors whose motto was "No retreat." When Lewis met them, only four of the twenty-two founding members were still alive. The day the party left there, in the spring, was about the happiest of Lewis's life. He said he loved their several canoes as much as Columbus ever did the *Nina*, the *Pinta*, and the *Santa Maria*.

But his last daily entry in the journal came just weeks later, on 23 May 1805. At about this time, they named a creek "Roloje" because it came to Clark in a dream. Sometimes they had to club animals out of their way just to walk down the trail. The deer were the largest they'd seen and had a drain by the eye, which gave them "an aspect of weeping." They named everything. York's name was given to a dry riverbed, a fact too ironic not to be true. As they traveled up, they kept hearing an artillery, a bombardment. The Spanish had heard those noises, too, and said it was the bursting open of rich veins of silver. But could that really be true? Could the conquistadores really have been that greedy, childlike, and delusional?

"So what happens to Sacagawea?" Joaney asked, shivering in her blanket.

"She dies."

"Well, duh!" She rolled her eyes.

"She lasts about three years after Lewis," he said. "Or maybe she lives on. Women keep coming forward, claiming to be her, right through the Civil War."

The heat and cold of the room, steam registers and a dripping ceiling, and the mildew were making him dizzy, and his eyes kept fluttering in a funny way. How strange it was that Janey had gotten picked for this trip, which meant she had to march straight back to where her family was massacred. Of course, the inner life didn't matter much back then—unless it was your own. The Enlightenment was supposed to change that, but maybe it really didn't.

"You don't seem like a teacher," she said. "You're like anybody else."

"Yeah, that worries me sometimes," Bill said, "but what can you do?"

"You're a worrywart," she said. "So what should I call you, Mr. Lewis? You're not really my teacher now."

"My folks called me lots of things. Bill, Mac, Buddy. They couldn't figure me out," he said. "It's very strange how we wind up in one family and not another, one marriage and not another, you know?"

His mind wouldn't hold a line of thought. After a rain, the party had watched the entire river change from mud-brown to the color of claret wine. No party in recorded history had traveled so far or so long with so little modern medicine and so little loss of life. But Lewis gave his all to whatever he attempted, and inspired the same in others. Like it didn't matter to him if his life ended disastrously soon, because of X. To understand him, you simply solved for X.

"I'll try and call you 'Bill,' I guess," she said, then touched Shelley's book with her toes. "So would she have known what happened to Lewis? Could she, like, read about it in the paper?"

"Janey? Maybe she knew. It's hard to say what we know about her, though," he said. "So many claimed to be her."

"Why not?" Joaney said. "If you'd been kidnapped, and raped, and your family was killed, you'd think, 'Shit, I must really *be* somebody if all this shit is happening to me!'"

"So where's this Tommy in all of this?" he asked.

"Don't know, don't care," she said.

He nodded and glanced once more at her ceiling, and made up his mind to at least do something. As for his motive, there weren't going to be any awards handed out at the end of life, anyway, no prizes. "Look, don't worry," he said, standing up.

"Oh, okay. If you say so," she said grimly, and limped to the door behind him, holding a place low on her tummy. He gave her a card with his cell number, and she waved good-bye to him with it.

Then, driving straight to the nearest superstore, he bought everything he could think of, diapers, formula, wipes, cranberry juice, a heating pad, and a bunch of chemically activated hot compresses for "applying intense heat to localized areas." They came in sizes, so he simply had to guesstimate how large it needed to be. Doubling back, he snuck all the bags onto her porch and pulled quickly away, heart beating like it would come out his mouth.

It wasn't too far into the expedition before somebody tried to kill the husband. He couldn't swim, which might seem peculiar for a waterman. And when the white pirogue swamped one day, he panicked and abandoned the rudder. Spilling her into the river along with their baby. Not only did she have to save herself and her infant, she also grabbed a lot of small, precious navigation tools. Peter Cruzatte stuck a loaded musket in the husband's face and told him to take up the rudder or die on the spot.

So the whole affair, the entire quadrangle, Lewis-Clark-Janey-and-the-husband, was almost settled right there. Lewis said life would no longer matter had the white pirogue gone down. But the husband took up the rudder at last. And while his reputation never recovered, his wife had shown the calm and fortitude of the bravest man. The white pirogue, which suffered more mishaps, was apparently possessed by some sort of evil *genius loci*, Lewis said.

At school the next morning, he dropped into the front office, and the "admins," Candy and Elaine, seemed to look at him differently. Or he imagined it. When he asked for Joaney's file, they stayed frozen where they were, looking above his head and to the right as though the answer was there. "Is she coming back?" Elaine asked.

"No, I doubt it. May I have the file, please?"

"She's kind of spoiled," she said, bending to pull open a cabinet.

"She's in pretty bad straits right now," he said. "Her ceiling just fell in."

"My car door fell off this morning," Candy said. "My husband just tied it back on with a rope."

"At least you have a husband to tie it on," Elaine said.

"Thanks," he said, accepting the folder. "I'll bring it right back."

"You'd better," Elaine said. Then he felt them watching him leave the glassed-in office. When he'd gotten about a hundred feet down the hall, he glanced back quickly. They were still looking.

"...thretened to shoot him instantly..."

Shoving off from the Mandan village, April 1805; The peril of the white pirogue; His watch won't run; Naming Bird-Woman's River and the Judith River; "A most unbelievable stench"; The husband pursued by a grizzly; Three animals block his path; He shapes a device to her region.

❀ Just past supper, Lewis sat with Clark in the tent, when the fellow and his mistress, with baby on her back, came calling. The husband, not meeting Lewis's eye, was in some way agitated, scowling then grinning then shaking his head, and Lewis felt unaccountably nervous and afraid. The fellow entered wagging a finger, and cast down the paper bearing his mark. "I no longer like you!" the fellow said. "No, sir! No, sir! I am not satisfied! 'll not be used thus. 'll not! 'll cross back over the river!"

"What are you saying?" Lewis asked. "We gave our hand on this already."

The man wagged the finger, pacing about in furiously annoying fashion. "No, sir! For you never said who you were!"

"We made it clear what and who we are," Clark said. "You are impertinent."

Lewis saw the man's cunning now, the ploy, to agree to certain terms, then return later and make veiled accusations and claim abuse, cry foul, to bluff the other into some concession. And might have argu'd or thrown the man out had she not looked pale, miserable, embarrassed at these frequent scenes since her recent marriage. "Name your new terms," Lewis said quickly.

This stunned Clark into silent, indignant study of his own right foot.

Charbonneau shook the finger at Lewis with a raucous laugh. "He knows I am right!" he said to Clark. "That is why you must me pay one U.S. dollar for each day's service . . . one whole and entire U.S. dollar for each day's suh—!"

"Done," Lewis said. "I shall draw it up and bring 't you to approve."

Clark, looking doubly stunned, was only able to look and hold his tongue in his head, for this bordered on madness. Lewis well knew it, but at that moment would pay double that sum to get her back home, off her feet, and out of the night air. He had known, even before the fellow spoke, that whatever fight ensu'd was already lost.

After they were gone, Clark said nothing for several whole minutes, his most poignant form of rebuke.

"Please say something," Lewis said. "Your silence is most awful."

Clark shrugged. "Without a Snake-talker, we are lost," he said.

"We must have a Snake-talker." Lewis nodded. "Nothing can be allowed to come before 't. 'Tis why I have an unlimited letter of credit from the president."

"Mostly, I hate to see that fellow win," Clark said. Which might have settled it. But a question, a scowl, remained on his face, showing his surprise. Something was here that he could not understand.

．　．　．

They shoved off early the next morning, the gates of the known world closing after them, and their two small crafts and six canoes.

A woman who'd formed a particular attachment to one of the men followed along the shore for over an hour, clearly big with child and falling down frequently, while making piteous entreaties in her tongue to travel whither he may go. And certainly Dido was no more bereft over the loss of Aeneas. But at last she fell behind, and they only heard her for an hour or so more, calling his name.

Soon, they passed into country that had burned, with boiling springs charged with sulfur that stank richly of brimstone as if new-erupted from the bung of hell. God promised Noah the fire next time, and it appeared that here He was making good on the bargain. The place smoked and stank and was sooty, throwing a black smudge miles across the sky that obliterated the sun. Some white cranes, crying like disembodied souls, passed up the river, heading deeper into confinement.

When put ashore, though, Janey proved able to make an Eden of any place. Using her sharp-pointed, root-witching stick, she rapidly filled her skirt with dirt-dusted fruit. And came and shewed it to him, as if to prove what a gifted housewife she was. He ate from the bounty a crisp, juicy specimen, marked plainly with her thumbprint. They picked wild onions and cooked them with the meat. When they heard frogs, it seemed no human ever heard a frog-song before.

But the next afternoon found Lewis alone and by the river's edge, shaking, infuriate, unable to speak or think. Unmoving, his legs were too weak to stir another step. He simply looked about himself at all of his belongings, his pack and gun and horn about him in the grass, hands and arms empty of burden for a change, still trembling.

Several moments before, he'd witnessed a horror, and everything he'd ever done had flashed before his eyes. The husband had been at the rudder of the white pirogue, with she sitting amidships with her infant, and

Lewis following along on the shore. Then a gust came up suddenly and flipped the boat onto one side. The husband, in an instant, went from apparent calm to magnificent panic and threw the rudder the wrong way, tipping her and the baby into the current. Peter Cruzatte, at the helm, began shouting in every known language, English, French, or Savage, for Charbonneau to recover the rudder, but to no avail. She, with her baby, was in the river, and precious tools and instruments were in the current all about her—*and she was gathering them one by one* whilst keeping herself and the baby upright! Lewis threw off his pack and gun as if to swim for it. Luckily, Peter took up his rifle and thrust it in the fellow's mouth. "The rudder! The rudder! You pig! You filth!" he cried.

Meanwhile, from shore, from every man and officer, came such a cacophony of commands and countermands as was never heard. The husband at last tumbled backward in surprise onto the rudder arm and swung it, and the pirogue righted itself. In the meantime, he'd done nothing for his wife and child. Nor would any be sorry for Peter killing him, including possibly the creature's own bride.

Lewis was now mastering himself gradually, but the scene had left a sympathy on him that was not off yet. He stood wondering if time were really passing, as he watched the clouds. Perhaps these events had already happened, and he was trapped inside some author's story, immured forever in the pages of a dusty book, under a corner of a shaky wardrobe in the maid's room. And what sort of girl was she, pretty or plain? He rather liked them plain, but loved them when they were lovely. His pocket watch, he noted, ran only a few minutes at a time, then stopped. And hadn't it often been said, about a man soon to be killed in battle or drowned at sea, that he could not keep a watch running?

That country was varied and deep, of redwood, gooseberry, chokecherry, honeysuckle, and willow. He'd begun walking again when a buffalo calf lost from its mother took him up in a sportive, friendly way. Lewis let him get quite close, then wheeled and struck him across the snout with his gun barrel, and sent him bawling away, nose streaming blood. And now able to recognize those who meant him harm.

The men killed a bear, which took ten shots, and he sliced open its gut, revealing fish, roots, wild fruit, and animal flesh of several kinds, along with fragments of Jonah, Daniel, and Abednego. And, despite all these marvelous items digested, Mr. Bear himself was about to be chewed and swallowed.

He now took to calling her Janey, because it was a piece of impertinence to ask a wife her name before her husband offer'd it. She had a quick eye for anything that white men did or valued, Lewis saw, and was careful, critical, and silent in her anthropology of them.

The buffalo viewed their approach, these naked, two-footed creatures, dressed up in their hides, without horror. In the background, the wolf tended to any creature feeling sick or lame or out of sorts. One grabbed your flank and the other your snout and they gently wrestled you down. And if they espied you watching as it happened to another, they merely winked, as if to say, O, do not worry, my son—for you are next!

Everywhere, they sought news of a river running to the setting sun, but none could they find. The landscape ran forever in infinite parallel lines, as though predestined for roads and canals. The plague of boils continued apace, until Job himself might have been moved by the men's condition.

Lewis was always ill. And so far as he knew, always had been. Most didn't realize it, for he was vigilant not to let them. Surely there was a reason for creating him thus afflicted. Or so he reasoned. But to see too much order in the world was to find human faces in the bark of every tree, and to enter the mad world of signs and whisperings. And yet, clearly, here was design: the grizzly, who would happily *rend* one in pieces, could be *render'd* into eight gallons of useful oil. And, here and there, entire seams of coal lay in plain sight on the cliff face.

On the other hand, they watched geese flutter up in the air and fall down again, over and over, having lost their flight feathers in a gale. So

God was the master, patient, disinterested, and man was all alone in his endless self-regard.

The next afternoon, they passed a handsome river fifty yards in width. After it was gone by, he said to Clark, without turning his head, "If we knew her name, then that could be her river."

Clark, as he copied some of Lewis's writings, shrugged and said, "O, well, now. She is called *Sah-cah-gah-way-ah*. It means 'birdwoman,' I am told."

He started to jerk up to see Clark, then managed not to move. "How long have you known?" he asked.

"O, for days. Her husband gives her two epithets: in Hidatsa she is 'bird-woman,' but in Shoshoni, she is 'boat-launcher.'"

"O, no, she is not!" Lewis said, with a laugh.

"I am only repeating," Clark said, puzzled, bemused. "Where is the joke in that?"

"'Tis an ancient one," he said. "Our Janey, a launcher of ships!" And he gave one more loud bark of joy, though Clark only shrugged and smiled.

"Be careful, or she may hear you," he said, nodding.

In fact, she heard all, Lewis was sure, whilst rapidly stripping bark from roots with her strong little hands, and need'd no knife, tearing with fierce nails. Lewis approached and, in loud French, greeted her. "*Bonjour*, Madam!"

"*Bonjour*," she said softly, and did not look up, and increased her pace.

"We name a river for you," he said, in awkward phrase, in that strange language emanating from the back of the tongue. "Are you happy?"

She looked at him sharply, giving one hot glance, swatting flies from her face, going on with infuriate zeal. She stripped faster if possible, skin flushed with restrained furor. For how could anyone be so stupid? Who would tender the gift, then shout it aloud before the camp? She tore a nail, and angrily thrust it in her mouth, glaring past him. Understanding came, but too late as he bowed and backed away. He was wet all over and faint. Something cheerless ran riot through him.

And day by day, those Rock Mountains grew larger and took up more of the sky. They were able to spy creatures, tiny white dots with immense spiral horns, unaffected by Newton and idling on sheer, featureless faces, that gambol'd with an ease resembling flight.

The next morning, they passed another likely, lovely stream. Clark thoughtfully studied it for a time. "I should call it the Judith," he said seriously, pushing his lips out, and taking on meechingly. Lewis turned quickly to bite back the smile.

So they'd named their ladies and their streams, though Clark did not, could not, see that. Lewis felt unknown, unexplored, his own best friend and gender a mystery to him. For he'd never loved any girl back in that Virginia neighborhood, those tepid, ingrown, and frustrated spirits, distracted with trifles, fearful, self-centered, suffering fantasies of impossible, ideal loves, and suffocating in their small circles, their afternoon "coffees," with the dull lustre in their eyes of monks in their cells.

Then, later that afternoon, a gory spectacle. About one hundred buffalo, pursued to their deaths, having plunged a long way down, now rotted in a heap at the foot of a cliff. The stench, so deplorable, brought Legion to his mind, that demon exorcised by Christ out of a man and into a herd, then into the sea. In the foreground, a wolf tugged at the grisly guts. Lewis was caught there; he could not look away. The whole scene, it was his illness. Spread from shore to shore and stinking to Heaven, and there for all to see.

Thus caught up in nauseate horror, he missed the sudden, passionate act as Clark grabbed up a spear and threw it, and the wolf fell dead.

Before Lewis had recovered from it, 'round almost the next bend, they were greeted by a very different but still alarming sight, of elegant ranges of tall buildings, parapets, statuary, and galleries, all ancient, all ruined almost beyond being what they were.

"What am I seeing, Clark?" Lewis asked. "O, help! Can such things be?"

"What is it, Lewis?" Clark said. "I see only some natural features. A landscape."

"Of course. As do I," Lewis said.

The next morning, she went about collecting moccasins from the whole party, over three hundred pair, so as to sew on "double souls," as Clark recorded, for the rough terrain ahead. In the afternoon, the husband surprised a grizzly in a patch of berries, discharged his gun into the ground by his foot, and ran headlong, bawling, straight for the men, who at last shot and killed it. An occurrence of a few moments that delivered Lewis many, many days' worth of joy.

Suddenly one day, they rounded a bend, and the Missouri forked into two rivers. But which to choose? Which the right course? For to select wrongly now meant the whole party lost in the mountains, starved, dead. All the party, to a man, liked the northernmost stream the best. But he knew they were wrong. Lewis climbed to a height, gaz'd at a trident of waterways, returned to camp, and said to them, "No! 'Tis the southernmost route, for that is the one our hearts least wish it to be; it kills all hope of the Northwest Passage."

Even Clark argued. In the end, Lewis was forced to oppose everyone, and could not even say how he knew.

The next day, he looked about and did not see her, and could not feel her, and knew something was amiss. Then came the husband to report pain in her lower regions, in walking, and in "going pish," as he said in his blunt, artless way. Lewis called on her, and found her in a high, hot, dry fever. "How goes it with you, my lady?" he asked, in French, but she made no answer, watching him from deep inside herself, motionless, the effort of speech beyond her. He bled her, and she received his wounding with a complete and provoking trust, only moving her eyes, which flicked here and there.

"You are ill, and you are ill," he said. "Pray, do not die. For I can find none like thee in this whole entire country." He spoke in English and if she did not understand, she never shewed the least sign. He felt anxious that she answer, and may have driven the knife too deep, as the warm gouts of her blood leapt forth in almost jolly manner, into the pan. He'd come because he needed something from her, this woman. For they could, with a word or touch or glance, draw out the poison from a man. And if he could not see her every day, yes, every day, the poison stayed. Burning in his veins, it built to a fatal level. He could not neutralize it. And wasn't it cruel, how God put humans on earth unable to salve their own wound, so they must rely on each other? What god locked away such conditions as these, such roarings in the loins, such beastings in the throat, in the finite human body?

He left her after bandaging her arm. "When I leave you, I will think of nothing else but this. Please do not slay me by getting worse, Janey girl." Whether she comprehended, he couldn't say. But small details as that did not lessen his feelings. Understanding would come.

Now, the trouble was, he couldn't stand any company but hers. After shifting restlessly about camp for a time, emotion building to exquisite levels, he took his rifle and spear and climbed up above the Great Falls, the grandest sight he had beheld until seeing her blood leaping into that dish. The broad extensive and fertile plain he walked on was made of straight lines with sandstone outcrops regular as fenceposts, an unnerving, cultivated look. If he stared too long at a knoll or copse, it became the collapse of a barn or house, away off in the blue distance, away across the hazy reaches of that vista.

A buffalo suddenly walked up over the embankment, and he shot it straight on, so that it slumped forth with blood pouring from its mouth, and settled in a hapless position, a sad look on its brute, shaggy face. "All the same, I cannot pity thee," he said over it.

Standing there, he forgot what sort of world it was, and neglected to instantly reload. A movement to his right, noticed too late, and a grizzly larger than the largest buffalo was coming up at a run, shoulders level with his head. Breaking away toward the creek, he dropped the useless gun and pack and powderhorn (shedding everything in fact but the spear!). And plunging into the water to his waist, he turned and presented that "bayonet" to his pursuer. The fellow pulled up short, and blew out an astonished gust of air as if to say, "But I am a man, too! I was like you, before stumbling on this uneasy spot, this too-too-cultivated plane!"

Lewis stayed in the water, 'til the enchantment relented, and the bear was gone. Gathering up what he'd discarded in his flight, he next looked over and saw a lionish little gent flanking and observing him curiously. He threw up his arms at it. "Away! Get thee behind me!" But the creature only crouched, preparing to spring. Lewis hurried, and had just reached the buffalo and was reloading when three more crested the hill. They charged, forcing him to withdraw as fast as he could go, the entire afternoon so bedeviled that any moment they'd curse him in human voices and vow revenge.

Returning near suppertime, he found her no better. He was growing suspicious of an obstruction of the menses, of an infection blocking its monthly progress downward. Mixing peruvian barks with a white rising-flour, he fashioned a device for drawing the poison, of a shape and size approximate to her region. And was, by the time it was completed, trembling, wet from exertion.

He brought it to her. Suffering in the heat and dark, the quick life of her spirit visible only in the reddish eyes, she took it in her fingers with a terrible softness. She instantly apprehended, as women always did, the benefits of such an object. He looked aside as she placed it. It would take time for his remedy to creep with ineluctable speed up her dry, inflamed canal and into the nest of disease.

Leaving her, he went straight to the river and dropped into its icy shallows.

For a whole day, she was out of her senses. She rambled in tongues and did not know anyone, her eyes strange and on fire. Every human face had a horrible aspect, and all were trying to kill her. She fought heroically to escape and was at last staked under a hide, to protect her from herself. He at last administer'd doses of barks and opium, and within another day, she was free from the grip of death.

"You gave us a respectable fight, Madam," he said to her. "One of my men is still nursing a cracked rib. I prithee, do not attempt to die again."

She would say nothing to him and only studied him as though she recognized his face. He, too, was a resident of that hell she'd so recently escaped.

"Stolen from your family, bought and sold as goods, laying your face by a gargoyle's each night, no wonder you fight to escape," he said. "That is how it is, and I understand. You are teaching God to take care: if He trifles with you further, down you shall go and break His handiwork to bits."

She again made no sign, but he felt her understand. He looked out the tent flap toward the sunset and sighed, not wishing to be parted from her yet. "What do we suppose, Janey? Do we imagine that if we find the garden again, we'll be admitted this time and allowed to remain, these thousands of years of wandering a misunderstanding after all?"

The next day, she walked out for the first time, and display'd the might of her physician for all to see, and demonstrat'd that only one possessed a true feeling for those most mysterious and little-known recesses in her. Then retired for the rest of the night.

In the morning, small brown grasshoppers were swarming the plain and the grass appeared to writhe like green snakes under their armored jaws. Clark was busy making the first map ever of these eternal estuaries. Lewis was e'en seized by a little hope, for a man who'd saved her might manage to live himself. And so went forth to take the head of the advance as they continued up. Though a single image continued to annoy and bother him, of the husband loitering outside her tent that morning, watching him. And of a quantity of white apple on a plate of bark by his foot. The one thing not needed just now, such a powerfully astringent fruit.

"Mr. Charbonneau," he'd said, approaching.

The husband raised up the gargoyle face hopefully, suspiciously. The fellow who'd panicked in a rapid and nearly cost them everything, supplies, gunpowder, and the journals. Disgrace, failure, had grazed so near that Lewis had almost let Peter blow the man's heart out.

Lewis did not wish to address him, for a strange look was on his face. The unnatural fellow had designs, that was plain. And Lewis knew not what, but wasn't it always the same thing and hadn't it always been, for all of his days? The awful fellow would have him.

"Is your wife stirring?" Lewis asked.

"As still and cold as stone," he said.

"Please, can you spy that fruit there by your foot?" Lewis asked.

"This? D'ya mean this?" the fellow said, as though he never saw it there.

"She must not eat of it," Lewis said.

"This stuff here?" He kicked it. "'Tis all she eats."

"But not today," Lewis said. "I cannot stay and look after her."

"O, you cannot, can't you? You would not stay, even for a little while? I have a little tobacco, good twist. For I might like and would talk to ye about summat—"

"I must go," Lewis said, the vague good of the morning now completely expunged. The man was one of those rioting over the lawless earth, ruled by no principle but seizure, every one a little Napoleon, a bent distorted creature.

She was in his thoughts all the day, though, and he was guilty. No wonder God wiped them out before, for they were all but helpless against passion.

All the day long, until the afternoon had waned, and the sun fell ahead of them and the crickets came out, he forced himself away. But with the last light, he rushed back to her, almost running, arriving before supper. He was greeted by a strange silence, the lifting of heads, murmurs and looks over shoulders. None would say it; they simply stared. "What, man, what? Did I die day before yesterday?"

"The Indian woman, Cap'n. In truth, she's poor. I say she's a-dyin'," Sergeant Gass said.

He ran. And there, on the bark platter just outside, lay only a few of those apples. The husband was nowhere about, which was lucky indeed. He went in and found her staring, as before, hot and fevered, pulse thready, far away inside herself. And gave her an emetic and she brought forth all in several violent heaves. Clark appeared, and stood watching Lewis from the tent flap with the self-same gaze as the men before. What did they expect him to do? And why stare, like her death was predicted by a gypsy?

"Where is he?" he asked Clark. But Clark was steadfast, head tipped forward, mouth set, a mulberry branch in his hand which he carried like a baton, smacking it into his red palm.

"Here he is," Clark said, the husband appearing out of the woods, walking slowly and casting his eyes about him. He'd done it all right. He came closer, and began to pull sad, doleful faces, shaking his head in a complete mockery of regret, like an elephant swaying its great trunk. It was true, then; he would dispatch his own wife, and he'd do it to harm Lewis unto death. Clark, sensing something, withdrew.

"You needn't speak," the fellow said sadly, "for none can chastise me as I have already done myself."

"I cannot make you out!" Lewis said. "And I think you false, sir! I gave you the simplest charge!"

Charbonneau covered his face with his hands, leaving only his eyes to peek up above the fingertips, and then gave a long, grievous moan, as of a lost soul locked in a tomb. Though his eyes lost none of their glint.

"O, spare me the dumb show," Lewis said.

"Aye, Monsieur Cap-tan," the thick lips mumbled. He took away his hands and stood frowning and shrugging as if supremely bored.

"At the least, think of your son!" Lewis said.

The milky blue occluded eye blinked at him, aping ignorance. None was ever so wicked as the seeming fool. "Who can tell a woman what to do?" he said, with more jerks of the shoulders, more shrugs. "Not her husband."

"Now she is nearly dead," Lewis said. "Your own wife."

Charbonneau stared at the ground. "When I was a little fellow, I had—*a friend,*" he said. And the way he used the word "friend," with such insouciance, revealed an actual sentiment. The filthy thing actually felt, and wished to recall his little school days. He'd been a boy! He'd had a friend! His memories were obscene.

"You remind me of him," he added, stinking of rancid fish oil, with which he soaked his beard to defeat the lice. The cracked red lips got licked and licked again by a prehensile tongue.

"I don't care what you had," Lewis said. "You look to your wife! I am about to take measures!"

"*Measures,* he says." The fellow shook his head. "Measures? For that little whelp?"

"She is not—" Lewis began. "She is the only necessity. I—we— need her."

The man shivered on the brink of some passion, whatever ugliness lay at his depths, but held himself back. The blue eyes, heavy-lidded, flicked and rolled. Despite himself, Lewis was almost touched. Forever loving the one most despised by the rest. Because he himself was not easily liked. Not like Clark, whom men loved at first sight. Clark looked the part, where he himself had the brief upper lip, ghostly skin that never tanned or coarsened. But Lewis hated to be liked, was made helpless by 't, and always returned the affection, regardless.

"A Frenchman has no friends," the husband said. "I cannot even trust you, which means I have nobody here!" And appeared to get actual tears in his deep eyeholes, which didn't fall but glittered there!

"Come, come," Lewis said, disgusted, moved.

"I care more than I am credited for," the fellow said. "She was dying when I found her in that village! She was badly used!"

His right eye now worked at the hollows and features of Lewis's face, like a cat's paw inside a hole in a wall.

"Then look to her," Lewis said. "Speak to her. Ask after her health and the progress of her labours. Be a bit generous. Kind."

The man's eye got cold and colder, then black, and was finally a bit murderous and dim, like a coal dying in the fire. He gave Lewis one more miserable longing look, and went away.

Now he knew the husband, a type of hopeless beast, parasitic, the kind who had no choice but to steal the beloved, to take hostages, because none would come otherwise. Ironically, he then used to death what he stole, as his food. Then simply found another host. If to be evil was to consume others in order to survive, then he was.

And Lewis knew such creatures, for one was at large in him now, and always had been. One that ruined each good moment. One that made him eat the ore. One that drove him into solitary pursuits so it might eat him in peace and quiet.

His thoughts turned back to her and, strangely, to America herself. Whom the conquistadores had also tried to sack and rape. And when she wouldn't surrender her treasure, they fell to wandering in her, heartbroken and lost, and got swallowed up by her, and finally were vomited forth again, broken in body, atheist, riding their horses to the sea and making away for home on any ship.

Lewis stayed near her all day. He dozed fitfully. And when he awoke in the evening, and looked around at the men, they appeared somehow larger, their hands loutish and huge, each eye a lantern with a piercing beam, each infected pore sprouting a dark hair and bulging with white seed, the skin of their noses stuffed with oily blackheads. He felt awakened and alive, but how did anyone bear it? No wonder blindness was common among the tribes, for even ordinary sights now caused him to whinge and look away.

The men began to cling to him. Tho slip away Father might try, to wench and fight and drink, his terrible children always found him. Crowding 'round him, they ushered the old fellow, teetering, home, where they locked him safe and sound. Tho he shuddered at the touch of their greavy hands and loud games, and hated to watch living things seized by them, torn limb from limb and pushed down gaping maws, still they crowded closer, shrieking, "Don't you love us, Father? O, don't you love us? Don't you? Don't you, Father?" And God help him should he say no.

The next afternoon, they found themselves, tiny and creeping, moving along the shoulder of a mountain. He'd got separated from Clark and Janey, and the husband, who were higher above. He was observ'ng a cloud, grinding along a peak. As it did so, its belly was ripped out of it by a crag, and it dumped its load of rain in a violent torrent into the valley far over their heads. The cloud was gutted, and the downpour stopped. They thought nothing of it except that they'd avoided a soaking.

Next, abruptly, all birdsong ceased. And down the ravine came everything in creation: an exploding mass of mud, water, rocks, and over half the mountainside. In a moment (Clark said later) they were hip-deep in a boiling and trying to scramble up out of its reach. The husband was of course quickest. Janey with babe in arms was mired to her waist. Clark scarcely got out of a cleft that was suddenly fifteen feet deep in water. The husband, wet and crouching helplessly, could do nothing for his wife. The babe's clothing and litter were torn away downhill. Clark just managed to catch a bit of her sleeve and pulled her up behind him, while driving that cringing fellow with insults and blows. Finally they were safe on a ledge and the flood was a trickle, already stopping. Lewis would hear it in several versions, by many authors, some of whom were not there.

Each time he heard about that man's failed courage, Lewis felt something, a twinge. It was unmistakable fellow-feeling, and over that miscreant's paralytic terrors. He bit his own cheek in despair. O, why? Why was that fellow his? Why was all of distressed humanity his, even the pox-iest cheek, the most palsied hand? Whomever he wished to put far from him he was crammed closest to. One could never bury such shame deeply enough. The husband was a coward. And for the male, no awfuler hell exist'd than to have "quailed" at the moment of crisis, before wit-nesses, not once but several times.

Back at camp, he saw the husband. For the first time, Lewis looked through the seeming utter indifference, and saw a man—a fellow in supreme trouble with himself. Unable to rest anywhere, without friends, this man's self-regard clung by its fingernails to a ledge above swirling annihilation.

"...we being the first white persons..."

A sumptuous repast and dancing, 4 July 1805; Discharges of a strange artillery; She recognized the country; Firing guns and hallooing for her people.

On 4th of July, they feasted on bacon, beans, suet dumplings, and buffalo beef, and toasted the twenty-ninth birthday of the nation with the last of the whiskey, and heard discharges of that unaccountable artillery, like a six-pounder firing at a distance of three miles. "'Tis the bursting of rich veins of silver in these hills," Clark said drily. "So a Spaniard says."

"Yes, and where are the Spanish now?" Lewis asked. "Do you see them, here or here? Their ghosts wander forever through our forests at night. They abandon their black forts, taking nothing, leaving behind only smallpox, venereal disorders, a mistrust of whites, Christianity, and mission bells."

"Do you suggest the earth is made of just earth, dear Lewis?" Clark chided.

"And winds and sleets, hungers, fevers, and pustulous disorders," he said. "In this world, the weak swimmer survives because he doesn't know how to fight the currents. The strong one drowns!"

"Yes, but don't trouble yourself over 't, Lewis," Clark said. "You mustn't trouble over anything."

Lewis did not look up, but knew he must change his tone for Clark's sake.

"Look at the sunflower in bloom," he said, as they continued along a path, "their fierce yellow faces glaring and bobbing in gentle mockery above our heads."

Clark canted his bright red head and smiled. "But we're nourished by this lion of the meadows, and he is delicious in puddings mixed with water and bone-marrow grease."

Lewis shrugged, trying to appear calm, looking up very carefully for a species of white sheep they frequently saw, with the horns of a centaur, and the face of a dean of men. Any moment, he expected this entire enchantment to end and fire to rain down.

They were moving beside cliffs that stood over them 1,200 feet tall, beside which they were but moving specks of dull color. Now and then, imperceptibly, or so he believed, he allowed his eyes to find her in a canoe, a privilege he denied them for a quarter hour at a time.

"Look at her, Lewis," Clark suddenly said, jarring him. "We enter the region from which she was stolen as a girl. Here her family was sacked and murthered before her eyes. And yet, can you say she betrays the least emotion? Or anything at all?"

Lewis turned an eye to her, as if surprised to see her there. "No, sir, I could not. But can we be judged by how we appear? If so, then who shall 'scape whipping?"

Clark didn't answer.

"Clark, you're old-fashioned!" Lewis cried, clapping him on the shoulder. "You think there's more to us than meets the eye! Next you'll say we have a soul!"

"Well, what should I believe, then?" Clark asked.

"I don't know," Lewis said, frowning at a sharpness in his thoughts. "As for me, I want to trust in the Enlightenment, but it often seems so much philosophy."

And this appeared to trouble Clark, as though he were uncertain what his friend might think of almost anything. Lewis felt a more complete fraud than ever.

"Dear Clark, I think we are of the dirt," Lewis said, "but are not the dirt itself. We cannot fly to Heaven but maybe we can win the way. Don't ask how."

They paused at midday and went ashore on an island thick with wild onion, crisp, sweet, and mildly flavoured, so that one puzzled at the daily misery of mankind. With such bounty possible, why did God not eliminate want?

Soon, he and Clark were joined by the husband, who idled unhappily nearby. "There 'tis, Monsieurs, Cap-tans," he said, nodding, voice rather trembling and full of bitterness. "You see it, do you not? The headwaters of the Missouri!"

"O ho!" Clark said, smiling at Lewis, not hiding a mocking, insular wink. "So we surpass your mark! A little bird tells me you were the first white man to venture thus far."

"That may be," the fellow said, turning his head to spit juice. "You have not heard it from me."

"No, a small bird chirped it in mine ear," Clark responded, with a full-knowing smirk at Lewis. But Lewis could no longer smile over the petulant, childish, jealous, and quarrelsome man, a man so fearful, who suspected everyone of misliking and plotting against him. A man the gods seemed intent on doing mischief.

On the other hand, this same fellow made her stagger under hundred-pound loads if he could arrange it. And gazed after her, and sighed, and coveted his own wife, who he possessed but did not have.

As for her, she remained the hero of her own story, Lewis saw that. Her eyes flashed suddenly straight into his, skewering him in one place, blinding, the sun exploding into view from a cloud. She was his, all right. But not he, nor any, could have her. Thus, things in the world continued apace, and some went mad, while others were born mad, and still others were simply alive in mad times.

Now and then, he went out looking for her people and found none, only the footprint of a man with inward-turning toes. He fired his gun and hallooed, but could receive no sign. He rested for a while at the river's edge and watched the fisher at his post, stock-still, while the little fishes drifted amid his legs, and his immense eye grew 'til it reflected the whole world and the sky. Two things were clear: streams gave up all they were to rivers, and humans were on their own regarding murther and sin.

The fisher bird struck a lightning blow—and missed.

And now Shannon was lost—again. "This man—goddamn him!" Lewis said. "These wood nymphs so make love to him, he purposely loses his way! They drown his cries with kisses. They smother the report of his gun with their crushing thighs and turn him all around!"

The husband, however, was not lost, and constantly beside him. It seemed the fellow suspected him of tampering with her soul and so was constantly there, watching, calculating. If he could not get the prize, he would be sure Lewis didn't, either! Among the Nations he had medicine, too, as the most lowly, miserable, and deformed always did.

As for himself, Lewis felt alive again. His dingy, ragged spirit had ceased to move until she'd looked on 't. Now, he grew sensible, most sensible, to feeling. The cormorants were suddenly jet-black as any in Dante's verse. And the light at sunset shredded his nerves like the pealing of iron bells. He praised the meat, and was able to smile and laugh, while his other part jerked in hell. He looked about him now, and wondered if others understood, that this seeking across the earth would soon come to a whimp'ring end.

When he needed to speak with her, he was careful never to go alone, always bringing Clark, too. "Madam, please teach us a word to bring your people near," he said in English, and—when she looked annoyed by that tongue—halting French.

She kept her brutal forthright eyes, bright daggers, sheathed halfway and averted. And said something very soft.

"I could not catch it," Clark said.

"*Tab-ba-bone,* I think she said."

She nodded and smiled, as if to her familiar, not to either of them.

Before he walked out again, Drouillard, sign-talker, shewed him "shakes-out-a-blanket," a universal sign for come sit and *parlais-vous.* Then they walked far and far inland, but saw no sign of any Nation. He got out ahead and was just about to turn them back, when a single brave on a horse leapt into view and stopped. For a moment, he dared not breathe. As he began calling out and signing, using her word, the fellow hung there for a horrified instant. Then whooped, kicked his horse, and vanished like he'd never been. When he looked behind, here came those two damned privates! They were coming on the run, though he'd ordered them to keep back. Lewis threw his rifle at their feet.

"You are the greenest goddamned idiots ever to enlist!" he shouted. "As dull as a fool is, none has ever approached the stone-deaf, dumb, blind, thick-skulled stupidity of you two! You are a sin on four legs! The harm you do by breathing is unforgivable! You amount to exactly nothing, you sad, stinking pigs!"

They received this in open-mouthed wonder, and he mimicked them to their faces. "O! Here is you! A cow is clever beside you. I'd like to stomp you in hob-nailed boots!"

So far, they'd heard nothing out of him of that sort, and froze. He might tomahawk them both, and they would meekly bleed and die.

He prayed for it to pass. He walked in large circles and begged himself to stop and gradually he did. And stood panting and staring into the trees where the brave had gone. Neither the word nor the sign had worked. Nothing worked as it ought in this strange place. Even his watch misbehaved, and the chronometer started and stopped.

Not knowing what he was doing, he plunged ahead into the woods, and ran madly, coming out into a clearing where three women mixed with a stick in a pool of water. *"Tab-ba-bone!"* he cried. One of them sprang, fleet as a deer, into the woods and vanished, with his plea ringing after her. "No, wait! *Tab-ba-bone! Tab-ba-bone!"* The other two were wailing, and kneeling with bowed heads, praying to be quickly destroyed. As he tried to sign with and reassure them, sixty riders issued out of the trees on excellent horses with Spanish brands.

He was made to remove his moccasins, like Moses at the bush, and brought before the One Who Never Walks, Cameahwait, a chief. Like many faces on this journey, he'd seen this one before. Later, Drouillard caught him up and conversed heatedly with those people without a single word uttered on either side.

Lewis could only stare at the creek, at this water which ran downhill westward, and suddenly knew why he was gazing so. This trickle went all the way to the sea. He stood and shook. For there was no all-water route, no endless river. A moment so sweet was suddenly bitter, then sweet again, then bitter. Could he really endure this? He saw, dreadfully, that he could.

When at last she caught up, he looked her over very carefully. The magic word, so called, had driven these people from him. But she looked past him as though seeing a ghost. Muttering something coarse and low in her tongue, she rushed forward and fell on her knees before the chief, clasped his hands, then his naked legs, bumping her forehead on his thighs like a child. Lewis might have died of confusion without Drouillard there, who began to laugh and exclaim and strike his forehead. "What is the matter?" Lewis asked. "What is it?"

"A miracle. He is her brother! And here come the sisters!"

Now two more fools crashed into the scene, grappling each other, at first not believing her, not embracing her, and looking on at her abandoned display from a distance. He almost went forward to knock their heads together. Life, for them, had continued here apace while hers had been raped and sacked.

Clark looked on with a scowl, for he hated all excess of emotion. "Thank God you're here," Lewis said. "If they do not embrace her, I shall kill them all."

Clark carefully smiled, just as if Lewis had said he loved watermelon.

Then the sisters returned her embraces and saved their plump hides. Her brother made a lengthy speech about the event, this first visit to the neighborhood by the first of the fabled white people.

That night in the tent, he listened as the ghosts of conquistadores, which sounded like gulls, floated on the winds overhead. Little Pomp, her baby boy, often watched him from his board, with the suspicious gaze of a Chinese emperor. As for Lewis's outburst earlier, it was now legend among the men. And whatever Clark knew of it, he need not worry; he had his prize, his *amour,* and the men loved him to boot.

As she lay near, Lewis felt the easy yoke of their attachment, and joyed in it grimly. His love was real and was also returned! It was! No, it was! The least thing he cast her direction came back to him ten-fold.

In the morning, he stood looking at all the Spanish brands on most decent-looking horses. For ev'ry power had tried for this corner of the world, French, Spanish, British, and now American. Each one had courted her hard, reached out to possess her, and always, always lost her.

"We must make ourselves weak and harmless," he told Clark later as they lay opposite ways on the ground. "These people are starving, so we must seem even more worthy of pity."

"Would not a show of strength be better, in all cases?" he asked.

"You should listen to me, Clark," Lewis said, "for I know about starved, incapacitated things."

Clark merely grunted.

"She failed us today. She tried to prevent us," Lewis said.

"What?" Clark asked. "How?"

"By teaching me a word of warning instead of greeting," he said. "Is that wrong of me to think?"

"You never say a thing against her. This is the first."

Lewis turned around and fumbled in the dirt between them with a stick, scratching shapes. "The Spanish are vacating this place, and are no penetrating force. We are the new landlords. The dream of our age, to sail in ships around the earth, drops away."

"Lewis, do not count us out yet!" Clark said with a short laugh. "There is still the Pacific!"

"But the things we've seen, Clark," he said.

And was visited again by the ghoulish sight, those starving people, grabbing up every part of the steaming guts of a fresh-killed deer. As substances exuded from lips, they shoved intestine in their mouths and squeez'd it empty with the other hand.

"All is not peace and love, dear Lewis."

"When I close my eyes, all I see is those people, mauling each other for a piece of raw gut," he said.

"Her brother the chief is a considerable fellow," Clark said.

"And talks with her husband, thus I fear something there," Lewis said.

"Such as?"

"I know not. But he cracks the whip over her suddenly, and keeps her at endless chores, and the filthier the better."

"He is most careful to be always idle," Clark said.

"He is jealous," Lewis said, pressing too hard and breaking the stick. "He is like any mutt with a bone."

"I think you admire her," Clark said, lowering his eyes. "And where is the harm in that?"

Lewis vigorously rubbed out the thing he'd been drawing, which was that monster or god he'd seen painted on rocks, that awe-filled Manitou.

"No, Clark, you mistake me," he said. "I regard all in my charge exactly the same. Admiration is a luxury I may not afford."

Clark turned over onto his back. Lewis reached up and jerked the flap, blocking out starlight and firelight alike.

13.

"...for striking his woman..."

His thirty-first birthday entry; the last of the sugar; treachery uncovered and a massacre foiled.

✤ In the morning, she was the first thing that greeted his sight. And he was glad. Simply to rise one more day knowing that she existed, at work near the fire. Adam was not more happy to awake and find Eve. By now he could not recall the time before, his past. She combed her eyebrow with her thumb, and that image got etched on the face of time. Then, on the heels of that sensation, a gloom unlike any, without bottom, like he'd fallen to the foot of a hill where no people were, and was too far down for God to see.

As he walked out to see the chiefs, he was joined suddenly by the husband. "Ah, yes. Good morning, sir," Lewis said. "I trust you slept."

"The second chief says you are spies for their enemies, the Pakhees," the fellow said. "You're to be killed."

"Are you joking?" Lewis asked, looking closer at him. "Is this how one says good morning?"

"This is no jest," the fellow said, stopping him and leaning in, breathing that fish-oil stench on him, his beard fairly dripping.

"Nor am I amused," Lewis said. "I am in no mood."

So, suddenly dizzy, alarmingly upset for the hour, he broke off from the fellow and went straight for the second chief and fairly threw his rifle into the man's arms. "Tell him he may keep that for now," Lewis shouted, for all to hear. "And to shoot me if he suspects me. Tell him it is disgrace among white people to entrap others with falsehoods."

He did not wait for translation, but walked on. All morning, a phrase from the president had kept dancing through his thoughts, over and over, in an inane, and circusy way: "History will not be kind to us, history will not be kind to us, history will nary be kind to us, fa-la, la-la-la, la-la-la-la," like some idiotic carol.

Later, in the tent, he penned his thirty-first birthday entry. Now that they were arrived there, he felt strangely below her in station, a mere citizen in her wise government. For she was back among her royal family, a sister to the chief, and shining the brightest amid all her relations. She confined her expression and emotion, but was clearly able to feel for the first time in years and in a plain and splendid way. She was queen in all but title. Tho the true nobility never insist'd on titles.

Before dinner, a fellow with feathers tied in his hair and bright bits of pink quartz swinging on strings from his deer-rib buckler, with vermilion on his cheeks, approached and opened his hand. There, neatly arranged in a circle, six pieces. Seashell! Lewis offered his knife, but the fellow shook his head.

"You have been to the great water?" he said, signing along with himself. "You have journeyed to the stinking lake?" The fellow frowned sadly. No. No, never. And never would, either, that face seemed to say.

At dinner, he sat by Clark, aware of her at her meal nearby. Little Pomp was at his dinner, too, from her rather fulsome breast. He told about the shell, which excited Clark. "Then let us move up our departure."

"No, I'd rather we lingered. A day or so more," Lewis said, too quickly.

"But why?" Clark said, angling his face toward him. That huge head, the barbaric red beard, rather crowding its way into his vision. "Come, now, a reason. We have plenty of horses now."

"I'd rather they were a few more," he said.

Clark chewed a bite of meat, and looked at the fire, and shewed clear suspicion, for—again—something was here he didn't understand.

Just then, the husband turned and struck. Slapped her so hard in the face that she toppled straight over in surprise, Pompy going with her. In a blink, the fellow was already striding away.

All blood had gone from Lewis. He saw stars and black spots, and found himself on his feet, his supper in the dirt, unable to master his voice, or make a move. Clark saw, too, and got quickly past him. Meanwhile, she had righted herself, and looked to Pomp, come unfastened from the tender brown dug. "I'll see to this," Clark said, going for the husband.

"You must," Lewis managed faintly, the blackness pounding in his eyes. Though mussed a little, she shewed not a tear, and would not dignify the act by touching the offended spot, the imprint of those grubby fingers still plain in her flesh.

The husband, standing apart, was looking no less mystified than if rebuked for breathing air. In a moment, Clark was back. "They quarrel," Clark said. "He does not love the tone of her retorts."

"He will apologize," Lewis said.

Clark lowered his chin and worked Lewis with his stronger right eye. "Come, Lewis. He is her . . . he will not apologize."

Lewis shifted around him and in four strides met the fellow at the edge of the firelight. The husband snorted in amazement, at not one but two official audiences in an evening. But could not appear entirely surprised, for a second light lurk'd in the glistering eye. He aped casualness, and lit a pipe, shakily, on the edge of emotion, fingers twitching around the firematch. He'd wanted this audience, had made love to this occupation. "A good deal of trouble for a little whelp," he said, watching Lewis's face.

"What do you want?" Lewis asked.

"I want for nothing, Cap-tan."

"What are you about, then? What do you hope to gain?"

"I know not what—"

Lewis advanced again, turning to the side so none would see or hear the poisonous whisper: "Whatever harm you think you can do, do it directly. Do it to me. Try anything you wish. But do not pursue this method, I warn ye."

Devious, cowardly intelligent, a seething hate back of the eyes, the fellow scratched his neck with dirty fingers. "Cap-tan, I—"

"Do not lie! You plan to see me undone."

Black-gummed, the red mouth punished the pipe stem clamped in its jaw. Within the shuddering ring of firelight, the scene unmade and remade itself in millionths, with every flicker. The fellow was maddened, suspicious, unable to decipher Lewis's furor. They balanced on the edge of a discovery of one another—he felt it—but the fellow lacked a piece of the puzzle.

Lewis should have seen it coming, he knew. For she was among her own people, now, with a new tone in her voice, which the swine must crush before it took root. Should he kill this husband? Make the bones in the pig-knuckled hands crack and splinter, turn that hog's mouth to jelly, shatter the chalky teeth? And with that creature screeching and blubbering, bleeding from every opening, blinded, then shove a musket up his arsehole and blow him inside out? What if he did not? The man was harming her to death.

Tho, gradually, Lewis recalled the mission. It valued the life of each one equally, except deserters. So he could do nothing. For all he knew, his secret was halfway out already, and a favorite joke among the men. *Thus proud be, you Virginian pioneers! You raised your boys up straight, with jaws of iron, able to drop over dead with the words to save themselves clamped in their teeth!*

"I dunno what you are speaking of," the fellow said at last, grimly chawing the pipe stem like a ruminating cow.

"I will be plain," Lewis said quietly. "Apart from our large family, I cannot restrain you. But while we are together, you will observe that we do each other no harm!"

He had to withdraw then and conceal how debilitated he was, how tremulous. In the tent, he tried to calm himself by writing but was gripped by such cold furor that the ink seemed to freeze in the pen.

Then, through the night, he practiced the art familiar to him now, of floating in the quicksand of the madness, of willing without willing, of moving without action, of treading water without any outward, or inward, gesture. He'd studied on it long, through many hours of affliction.

Through a disastrous adolescence, awkward, without grace, into a chilly, melancholy adulthood, he'd studied it. He had no idea what was meant by happiness. What was this happiness? How? Where? Had he met anyone happy? As for the regard of his fellows, why should he want it? For look at the harm they caused, and the manure they talked.

Spirits sounding like gulls cried over his head as he lay wrestling, and he awoke more tired than the night before.

Around camp, he watched the elderly, dreams visible in their eyes. They drifted through days or whole epochs, without speaking, hardly shifting or taking nourishment. They appeared to know a world very different, and perhaps could not find this one real. He met a woman with a shell about her neck which was as curled into itself as the human ear, with a hidden recess no faith or science could help him observe.

It appeared their women could share in conversation. They wore their hair short while the men's tresses were long and flowing. Also, those people were insistent to examine their rifles; polite, but insistent.

Thus far, only one thing was certain: she'd suffer at that man's hands for all her days and it needed death to release her. Lewis now saw that his attentions to her, and theirs to each other, would shorten her life.

As for those people, they were kind, excessive, poor, and dirty. Also, their honors accorded from bravery in making war. How could there ever be peace if honor followed only from war?

So he settled on one unhappy thought, then another.

Then her brother came near and shewed him a prize in his palm, an indifferent gray lump of matter. Clark and Drouillard, tarrying nearby, also had a look. "What 'tis, then?" Lewis asked.

"The last of our sugar," Clark said. "Can you believe it? She's had it all this time, a piece tucked away for emergency."

"Yes, but tucked where?" Lewis said. "She's been dunked ten dozen times."

Cameahwait put it in his mouth and consumed it with great concentration.

"Does he even realize?" Lewis asked. "Do you believe he has any idea at what price, how many near-drownings and maimings? Just so *he* might spend a sweet moment?"

"I don' have signs for that, Cap'n," Drouillard said. "'Tis beyond me."

Later, Lewis visited the nearby village, but could not remain long. All about him, those people kept beating their foreheads, wringing their hands, and weeping in a most piteous manner. And since it were easier to remove the cause—his skin—he departed. Meanwhile, from precipices far above, those white, goatish creatures with human faces looked down on him.

He arrived back in camp, and found Clark grimly awaiting. Lewis was suddenly reminded of his mother, telling him his father was dead.

"Who is it?" he asked, chunk of ice in his guts. "Who's lost?"

"We are," Clark said, unsmiling, pale-faced. "Or almost were. For I just have it from the husband, or actually from her, the news of a massacre. They want to kill us for all we possess."

"What's this? Then sound the alarum! Why do we tarry?" He swung his pack to the ground and seized his powderhorn.

"No need, for the plot is foiled," Clark said. Closeup, Lewis smelled the wild onion on his breath, and saw the grime worked into the crow's feet of Clark's eyes, which were, just now, an unlikely blue. "But wait for more. Her own brother knew and it had his blessing. And the husband heard many hours ago. My God, if it weren't for Janey . . ."

"That man!" Lewis ground his teeth and cast down the rifle and horn. "That sorry work of demons trussed up in skin! I am through with the folly of Mr. Charbonneau, Clark! What more does he want? Everything is his ten times over!"

"I'll be deuced if I know," Clark said. "Or why she is contrite on his behalf."

"Where is the brother?" Lewis asked.

"O, here he comes now," Clark said. And indeed Cameahwait approached, with entourage, and Drouillard capering forth to interpret.

"How did you plan to get away with this?" Lewis demanded.

Drouillard made the signs and said a word or two of Shoshoni. Cameahwait, with a look of defeated, starved consternation, made a sign from the top of his head and it swirled like a whirlwind.

"He says he is insane, Cap'n," Drouillard said. "Watching his people starve makes him mad. He is sorry, too, I believe."

Cameahwait, trembling, a bright blanket on his shoulders, stayed straight, as if awaiting the next stroke of his doom.

"Tell him his plan is shortsighted," Lewis said. "For if he kills us, he will never see another white man so long as he lives."

Cameahwait made no sign, expression rigid with hunger, eyes burning with starvation-fever, hollow and red.

"He understands a fair bit of English, Cap'n," Drouillard said.

"I tell you, Commander, I am through with this husband!" Lewis said. "He must be kept out of my way."

And left the brother there, understanding too well all of the man's motives. But what were hers? For, had a massacre resulted, she would at last 'scape the husband and the white people. And rejoined with her family, and restored to her rightful place, she might live happily always. Instead, she saved them all.

It was hard to grasp what it meant, as he walked faster and faster back to camp. Unless she loved! She might've saved herself! Unless she loved. At the least, it didn't disprove that she did love.

As for him, he most definitely loved. And for so long hadn't a girl of his own, as Clark so easily did, as other men so easily did. The sweet abiding face by his, the breath of clover, a sympathetic touch and caress, a gentle creature with eyes shining in his. And yet, and yet . . . a log sank peacefully to the bottom of the mill's pool, until the chain suddenly tightened, hauling it lurchingly, violently backward, unnaturally and against gravity, then dragg'd it to the spinning saw. So his mind suddenly cracked-the-whip, and he recalled his actual circumstance. Her bruised cheek.

Clark then hove into view the way he did, with that cautious smile which perpetually asked, *Is my friend mad today or sane? Must I eventually confine and shackle him, and is today that day?*

"I want out of this vicinity, Clark. We leave tomorrow," Lewis said.

"But what of those few more horses?" he asked, smiling in that provoking, patient way.

"Give them my spare rifle," Lewis said, hurling it down. "If these people want our guns so badly, give them mine!"

He watched her that next morning, forced again to say good-bye too soon to her family, which she'd lost, then found, and now lost again. It was dragging lead for her to depart, to have the spear torn out of her side once more. The mosquitoes in his ears were his familiars, and there they gnatter'd. The pores of a man's nose, stuffed with blackheads, shocked his left eye, and a deer gasping on the forest floor, all cancerous lumps and tumors, assaulted the right. Creeks dropped right out of the sky, from high up on the cliff wall.

That afternoon, he rolled a hundred yards down a hill, under his own horse, which ended upon his writing desk, all smashed and broken. He wondered, as he gathered up the pieces, what he might have done and accomplished in life, against lesser handicaps.

Then, in the next village, they met a very light-complected tribe, and he excitedly tried out Hebrew words on them. To no avail.

she was taken prisoner

14.

"... she was taken prisoner ..."

In the morning, Bill smoked behind the garage for a much longer time than usual. When he was done, because it was Saturday and Emily wanted to go on a picnic, he gassed up the hybrid, and got it washed. All the while his stomach was full of nails and broken glass, feeling both icy and molten, from an unaccountable, immense anxiety. Meanwhile, the sun was shining on a perfectly benign cool-warm October morning, and people were out using squeegees on windshields and reading tire gauges. SUVs rolled quietly along the leaf-strewn streets on soft rubber treads.

From home, once the hamper was stowed along with blankets and cameras, the vid-rec, a huge cold bottle of wine, they headed out toward the zoo.

Slowly the boulevards gave way to parkways, and the grid of town dissolved into curves, and they were swallowed up by the woods. He felt ill with excitement. Life wasn't just life when you had someone, when you loved someone, and he suddenly did. What he wanted was to be alone with the feeling, but instead he'd keep a stiff, sweaty upper lip through the day. He'd wait it out. And feel crummy this way, and wrong, and elated, and bad, all the while.

Emily'd been married before, to Lawrence, who was long gone and living in Melbourne, or somewhere. Bill had seen some of the pictures, and they sure had looked like a happy couple.

A few more sweeping right-hand turns, and they were going down and down to the picnic area, the long, shady creek, the sandy parking lot, and those charcoal grills, so antique nobody knew what they were for. People rested their coolers on them, and tied matched pairs of basenjis to the posts. So crazy, so primitive. But, as a kid, he'd cooked on them, and squirted on tons of flaming carcinogens, too, like there was no tomorrow.

It rained, a light patter of drops on the canopy of branches. But it wasn't serious; nobody paid any attention. He used to come with his parents, Lloyd Charles cooking hot dogs and his mom in dark glasses, flipping through a magazine. Quite a bit of that home feeling with the past came to him now, along with lightheaded unease and stomach-dread at being down here again.

As for the famous Lewis, he said the grandest sight he'd beheld was the Great Falls of the Missouri River, which was now mostly under a reservoir in Montana, because the grid ran on power, not postcard scenes. When Lewis wanted to talk to some chief, it crossed five languages: English to French to Mandan to Hidatsa to Shoshoni. Then back. The process needed, at least, Drouillard, Sacagawea, and her husband. Which meant they must have gotten it wrong, hilariously or dangerously wrong sometimes.

Also, naming was a big part of the job, and even Adam and Eve would've blanched at cataloging all the birds, plants, insects, and bodies of water the captains met. Between them, they named rivers for four women: Clark called the Judith River after his intended, Julia Hancock, and Martha's River after a woman lost to history. Lewis named Maria's

River for his cousin and Bird-Woman's River after "the interpreter's squaw."

Bill now looked about, both loving and hating the picnic grounds. Emily thought being a grown-up meant you forgave the past and moved on. But who really did? Who ever got over learning about death, or the conditional nature of love? Yes, baby, I love you; now here are my conditions.

They found a table across from a shelter, near the creek. In his family, they'd done a lot of things outdoors. At any mention of camping, they liked to laugh and say, "Well, we're Lewis's, aren't we? We invented it, didn't we?"

The creek itself was just a trickle, a toy creek, just a good place to set up army men and stage a little war. Emily laid out their lunch under a big cedar tree on a soft bed of needles, lobster-tail on brioche, radishes in crème fraîche, warm slices of Gruyère on apple, and strawberry-banana parfait for dessert. Spread along the bottom of the woodsy picture before them was flowing water, which found its way to the Little Blue River, and then to the Missouri, and so forth and so on.

Emily started having a little wine. Then he gradually noticed that she was having a lot of wine, so he decided that he would, too, keeping up with her cup for cup. They weren't looking at each other or talking very much. Henry messed around by the creek, hunting crawdads under rocks just like his father and his father's father before him.

They finished the wine. Then Emily pulled him up and they marched, in crooked fashion, down to the creek, jumped it, slipped on the mossy rocks and got their feet wet, then started up the limestone uplift fault on the other side. It was formed one day when a giant dropped his stone deck of half-shuffled cards, and then grass grew on it. It wasn't hard climbing, sort of like an angled staircase in a building, post-earthquake. But there was loose pea-gravel, and the ledges they sometimes clung to were dripping from the rain, so they were often close to a slip, which could've turned into a bad fall, a crippling injury, even death.

On the trail, the real Lewis had taken a lot of tumbles over cliffs, with a thousand-pound horse bouncing right along with him. And broken his writing desk to pieces in just such a spill. In August of 1805, he'd turned thirty-one, and written the oft-quoted birthday message, resolving to stop living so selfishly, to start living for Mankind with a big "M." He'd frequently noted the howling of wolves around them. And how the Black Hills, in the evening light, with their soft sandstone cliffs, looked like "a thousand grotesque figures." Or like ancient ruins of temples and colonnades, with statuary and fountains. Before they got to the Great Falls, in Montana, he'd been ready to send a small party home with some artifacts and papers. But the mission was so delicate and fragile, he decided not to, afraid it might all come down with a wheezing crash. He felt himself under a spell, he said. One day, he walked out alone and in less than an hour met a grizzly, a lynx, and three buffalo, and each one tried to kill him. When they came to a fork in the river, with no idea which was right, the lady or the tiger, Lewis had to choose—and chose correctly.

Now, Bill and Emily kept going, though it wasn't like them to climb things. But since she'd started it, he'd keep his mouth shut and simply try to stay with her. It was good for her to get away from Henry now and then, anyway, take a breather from his diet, and planning it, and puzzling over what to do.

They came out between two leaning rocks, on a promontory above the picnic area. Their thirteenth anniversary was coming up. So the outing was partly an observation of the event, he suddenly understood.

His stomach felt light and unsteady, like he was in clear-air turbulence. She gave him a direct look of unsurprise, eyes half closed, and clapped the wet sand off her hands.

"What's the matter?" he asked.

"I don't know, Bill. What's the matter with you? You're the one who's being weird."

Every lover knew these exchanges by heart, the ones you entered into, the things you said when you began to face up to, confess, the difficulty.

But there wasn't anything. Or maybe he didn't need to say it. The problem was already out in the open. And her voice had dropped into a register he'd heard before. One time, Lawrence had called drunk from Sydney, collect, saying he was in bad trouble: he'd gotten married and needed money. And she'd honest to God sent him some money, but not because she still loved him. She said.

But Bill's problem was the kind you didn't confess in a long marriage. There was no vocabulary for it. And her anger wasn't anything she could vent because there wasn't anything to accuse him of. Yet. She shook her head, with a little smile. "Jesus, God. Can we really keep having these things?" she asked.

"What things? Which things?"

"These *anniversaries!*" she said, like it was dirty. "Thirteen in a row. Jesus Christ."

She sat down on a large, flat-topped, upthrust chunk of limestone, in profile to him. It was sort of dreadful, what happened in time. Sometimes when he looked at her, sometimes right in the middle of saying something to her, her beauty, its integrity and wholeness, did a terrible, disconcerting thing. It dissolved, deconstructed, into its several dozen parts. To his eye, she was no longer discernible, accessible. He couldn't remake her by an effort of will. Suddenly he'd have no idea what she looked like, with people saying she was beautiful, and him looking and looking, unable to see. In fact, it was doing it to him now. Life was at it again.

The other thing, lately, was how she looked at *him*. For instance, if she happened to see him at a time or place she hadn't prepared to, her face flashed anguish, followed by aggravation, a struggle to recover, then a troubled smile. It took about four nanoseconds, but he never missed a phase.

She bent down and picked up a large rock and stood up with it. Then, with a sudden pivot, she heaved it as hard and as far out into space as she could, with a drunk and angry grunt. They operated on similar sets of assumptions about life, how it was likely to go. She expected to have to endure, to persist desperately at things that were probably temporary. He knew this about her. And he expected to have to struggle and hang on, too, and for things to be temporary, and then end disastrously.

She turned back and looked at him deadpan, like she was trying to see him better by making herself empty. They had shifted and were no longer looking down the tunnel together, but facing each other from opposite ends. "I guess it's just our time," he said, with a thick tongue, making himself say it.

"Our time for what?" she asked.

"Our time of life, Em . . . to, um, to be together, Em."

She kept staring. He wanted to say something more about it, like he hadn't known he'd live this long, or that clinical depression made it tricky to plan ahead. But before he could launch into it, she started down, this time taking the back way, to his relief, the easy zigzagging trail. Though he arrived at the bottom all the more drunk and dizzy.

Then, at the creek, she suddenly lost it. A torrent of reds and oranges went down into the creekbed, the gourmet lunch, the wine, the sorrow of thirteen years of imperfect wedlock, her fears about Henry, about him dying, and etc., etc. Henry came walking up. "Jesus. What's the matter?" he asked.

"Nothing, Hen. Everything's fine," Bill said. "Your mom's a little sick."

"Who threw that big rock down?" he asked.

"I did," Emily said hoarsely.

"I thought one of you fell or something. Are you guys fighting?" he asked.

Bill waited for Emily to answer, and looked back up at the top of the pinnacles behind them.

"No, we're not fighting," she said, and went ahead down the trail, toward the parking lot. Bill didn't know what to say, so he simply walked along with Henry.

"Is everything all right?" Henry asked again.

"It's fine. Don't worry." He patted Henry's shoulder lamely. They took the turns in the trail.

"So how's your book coming, Dad?" he asked. "I've been meaning to ask you."

"Too soon to tell," he said.

"You think it'll maybe make a lot of money?" he asked, as they descended around and around on the hairpins toward the picnic area.

"No, I don't think it'll make much at all," he said. "I really don't expect it to make any. Even if it comes out all right."

Henry then looked at him, in some surprise. And as they walked along a little farther, he felt Henry reach an epiphany, like he understood something about his father, and his own life and future that he hadn't 'til right then.

It was very burdensome and awful and troublesome to be a father. Or maybe to be a human being. People, especially your children, kept looking at you like there was one more thing they thought you'd say or do. And once again, you hadn't said it, hadn't done it. You'd held it back. It was something they really needed, too, though for the life of you, you didn't know what it was. Like that. That's how he felt with Henry.

The famous Lewis had his troubles, too, of course, forced to deal with Charbonneau, a real high-maintenance type, like a teenaged boy. Somebody who constantly needed saving from himself. But much less likable than Henry. A poor schmuck who was twice chased by grizzlies and had to be saved by the men. The closer they got to her old tribe, the more he sort of clung to Lewis and asked to walk along with him. Why? What was he up to? What did he want? Lewis's mood shifted about then, as they got closer to her people, and he was suddenly gloomier than ever before.

Recently, he'd stood astride the Mighty Missouri, one foot on either shore of a trickle. He knew he'd failed: there was no all-water route. And a man he despised would not let him be. Lewis asked Janey for a password, a word to call out, so she taught him to cry, "Stranger!" She left him tramping up and down the countryside, calling out a warning. Why? What was she up to?

Finally they found her people, and Lewis said she showed no emotion. But Clark said she laughed and sucked her fingers, meaning she'd been a child in those woods. The women had short hair and "an equal share in conversation." The chief was her long-lost brother. The husband she'd been promised to was still alive! And looked her up and down, then said he had enough wives. The party had no food, only berries. So she reached in her bag and gave away her emergency ration, a lump of sugar, to her newfound brother. A happy occasion.

A night or two later, the husband clobbers her at dinner. Lewis had some difficulty recording it because the ink kept freezing in his pen. Soon a plot was hatched, then exposed, to slaughter them all and steal the rifles. What was more, her brother and her husband knew, yet said nothing. So it was Janey who had to expose it, going straight to the captains with the truth.

Riding home in the car, the picnic a flop, Bill thought how he hated his position—being the one making other people miserable. The problem was, how he felt was not how anyone wanted him to feel. Nobody on earth could seem to help how they felt, and that's why it was all a big mess, the whole thing entirely out of hand.

Then, the next morning, driving to school, he seemed to be doing better. The feeling wasn't there, or at least it wasn't as strong. And then someone cut him off as he was merging and he had to stand on his brakes. He found himself leaning on the horn and leaning on the horn and for several seconds wondering if he was going to be able to let off as it went A-A-A-A-A-A-A-A-A-A-A-A-A-A-A-A-A-A-NGH! That howl said something a buried part of him could not. Which got him to school feeling much worse than ever, so he had to just sit there and try to calm down.

The famous Lewis was happy when they left her tribe, as happy as he'd been that one day the previous spring, when he was first going forth with her into the Black Hills. The men were happy, too, and they danced at night to Peter's fiddle. Also, they met two very merry chiefs, laughing well into the night, because they expected to be massacred at dawn.

Lewis was always very nineteenth century, very cute and Victorian about how he worded things, calling the vulva "the Battery of Venus" and "those parts that propriety hates to mention." They kept the rough stuff offstage, the Victorians. They tried, with the very best intentions in the world, to keep things pleasant.

So what happened? Bill often wondered. In 1966, Steve McQueen starred in *The Great Escape,* a war movie in which hardly a drop of blood is shed. Then, just four years later, he made *Bullitt,* in which a guy is blown to pieces against a hotel-room wall with a 12-gauge pump, the whole thing shown in live action and Technicolor. What happened? In '66, Bill was a happy nine-year-old. And then, just four years later, a jaded and angry thirteen. In 1806, Lewis was toasted at presidential dinners in his honor. Just three years later, he was dead.

So the school day passed, period after period, and he did the first half of Shelley's *Frankenstein* six times, getting better each of the first five, and then losing his place, missing his timing, and badly bungling the last one, actually bringing one of his smart girls to tears by jeering at her definition of "hubris."

After school, he thought he was headed home. But then he missed his usual turn, and then another. He watched himself doing it, feeling that he was two people. One really loved nineteenth-century writing, while the other could appreciate a well-shot, slow-motion bloodbath. There was a value, after all, in really seeing what bullets did to the body.

As he drove, quasi-aimlessly, he thought how happy Lewis must've been in 1803 and 1804, when he was getting ready to go and using that unlimited letter of credit to buy supplies. The best thing that'd ever happen to him was just starting, success still possible. He'd been too busy to think much or ask himself lousy questions, like whether the British hadn't already stolen this prize he was chasing.

The clown-prince was Shannon, who got lost twice, with his unerring instinct for the wrong direction. A guy who just knew he'd been left behind, when in fact he was miles ahead.

Were the captains getting any on the trail? And if not, why not? And if so, how was it kept out of five different accounts? And was that why Lewis was buying them up as fast as he could? Of course, it was easier to believe chastity of Lewis than it was of Clark. Clearly, Clark lived more in his body than Lewis.

Somewhere up above the Mandans, a woman came to the fire circle one night brandishing a knife and acting as if she would "scarrify herself in a horrible manner." She had a lot of small trinkets, and was handing them out. Then she sang a little song about having nothing more to give. And cut herself to ribbons and ate the blood, went stiff, toppled over, passed out.

Which was just what Lewis would do in a few years' time, by the side of a road in Tennessee.

In a few minutes, he'd arrived at Joaney's, the car knowing where they were going all along. He worked there all evening, putting back her ceiling. It meant first uncovering about half the roof, pulling off the rotten decking, and reshingling. That was two nights. Then he moved inside and chopped away all the bad plaster, all the black mold, and took it in wheelbarrow-loads to the curb. He next had to drywall and mud all of it, and sand and paint it smooth. Another three nights.

He liked doing this for her, which increased the guilt of not going home until it was burning in his throat. It was like being twenty again, with that endless energy and worry and fear. She made tuna sandwiches and they ate them at her rickety kitchen table. He carved up all the wet, stained, stinking, antifreeze-green carpeting and hauled it out of the house. One fix led to another: the leaky steam radiators had softened the joists, so he "sistered" them and rebuilt the floor.

But the most terrible secret awaited in the basement. The sump pump was broken and years' worth of rainwater had ebbed and flowed down there, under a lot of crap furniture, and *National Geographics* going back to the '30s, and bamboo fishing poles, carburetors, canning jars, ax heads, and panoramic murals of Yellowstone, Mount Rushmore, and the Grand Canyon. So now he dragged and hauled and bagged and smashed until the basement was empty. He took apart and cleaned the pump and it gurgled to life and sent stinky black water splashing out into the sideyard, where it drained away.

That was his weekend. On Sunday evening, her scented candles and potpourri at last got the upper hand.

Meanwhile, he'd been listening as she took care of Jack, his howls of hunger and wetness and perplexity at this place he'd recently landed, this useless body he was trapped in. He didn't speak the language yet and nothing was familiar except her smile and her naked boobs and the wooden cage where he slept.

When he heard pounding, though, he'd get quiet, Joaney said, as if trying to figure out what it was. Something was down in the basement tearing the house apart.

Joaney brought him down to show him. "See, look, you big goofball. Don't be so worried all the time. It's just Mr. Lewis, fixing our house."

So far, no Tommy. But that didn't matter: Bill was fixing Tommy's wagon for him, whether he ever showed his face or not. He was fixing it good. Tightening a bolt in a new joist, he'd even say it, under his breath, "Fixing your wagon, Tommy. Feel me fixing it, my man? I'm fixing it sooo good."

The best news, though, was that Joaney wasn't limping anymore, or going pee every five minutes.

And working with his hands was always good, because it freed him to think about the book. In Sacagawea's tribe, Lewis noticed how much longer the girls' heads were kept in wooden presses than the boys. At least two times, the party experienced the loaves and fishes, when a small quantity of roots and berries was somehow enough to feed them all, and more. They enjoyed delicacies of the region, such as roasted hyacinth blossoms. Then, west of the Divide, their diet changed from lean elk to fatty salmon, and everyone was sick. They got caught in flash floods and hailstorms and got pelted with stones the size of golf balls. The tribes who'd never seen whites before assumed they'd dropped out of the clouds. When they met the Nez Percé, they had no trade goods for food and were starving. So the tribe just went ahead and gave them all the horses they could eat. Lewis struggled to find words for how this made him feel. The party again heard rumors of a great river running toward the setting sun. And it was crazy how, every time the all-water route was dead in Lewis's heart and he gave it up, a whisper revived it again.

Bill kept working, replacing washers and refitting seals on all her faucets, then taking up her leaking toilet and scraping out the soft wax gasket, and seating it on a new one. "Doesn't that disgust you, handling my toilet?" she asked. "I mean, I go poop there."

"What disgusts me is a bad job," he said. "This seal was never right and it's leaked for years."

"God, I was so sick last week, Mr. . . . I mean, Bill," she said. "And do you want to know something? What really helped were those heat thingies you brought me. Those babies really put the heat right where the, uh, problem was, if you know what I mean."

His head was down behind the toilet, so she couldn't see his blush. He knew exactly what she meant. She meant that, as far as her experience of men went, he was the first to really understand her southern region.

"You really know how to take care of things," she added.

"I like to be a help," he said. "There's more I can do. Your porches are falling off. If you really fix things, I mean fix them all the way back to the start, they'll never trouble you again."

"I should do that to my life," she said, tugging at a peeling edge of the daisy-patterned wallpaper.

"I guess we all should," he said. "In the end, I guess we have to."

"What's your wife think about all this?" she asked.

"All of what?"

"About you coming over here all the time." She nodded at his white-gold wedding ring. He examined it, too.

"The main thing is to get your house fixed," he said.

"So she's not mad? She won't be waiting for me some night in the parking lot?" she asked, shifting Jack, fixing his sock so the turn-down was the same on both sides.

"I don't see why she would," he said, and flipped the valve open, water sputtering and farting and gasping its way upward through the house. He straightened. A bead of water quivered on the right lens of his glasses. "But if it bothers you, my being here . . ."

"It doesn't bother me," she said. "I've got enough to think about. I can't worry about *all* the peculiar shit that goes on."

At a certain point, Bill knew, if you read all of the journals, start to finish, the husband's many mishaps and brushes with death began to look suspicious. Lewis even implied intent, that the husband was doing it on purpose. Not long after leaving the Nez Percé, they saw the ocean. The first place they stood was Cape Disappointment, a wind-blasted and lonely north Pacific beachhead. The men thought the captains named it because of how cold, wet, and hungry they were when they all got there. Actually, it was a Captain Gray, of the *Columbia*, who'd sailed for months to get there, then couldn't find a way over the sandbars. And more die of heartbreak over the all-water route. And then some more.

Bill chose to disappear. Having grown too familiar at Joaney's, he packed up every tool, each screw and nail, the least crumb of sawdust, and cleared out. This time, she didn't see him to the door, and they set no date for his return. He didn't even try to catch the screen door, letting it bang shut behind him.

But he could never seem to go home. It was only a mile or so to Emily's special school. He always gazed at apartment complexes, ones where the units were brand new, very simple affairs with new carpet, appliances, paint, tile. The sort of place you wound up if your marriage failed, a locale within the upper ring of man-hell. He drove by, he looked and, there but for the grace of God, kept going.

Sometimes on Saturdays, he liked to drive around town. He did it to feel lonely, to know nobody and have nothing. Like some sort of ordeal of solitude. Like Steve McQueen in *Papillon*.

The thing about life was how hard it tried to take your soul, and not with a crisis but by persistence, repetition day after day after day. It was the depression, how it was there the moment your eyes opened in the morning, ready to take you on again. It went on and on. And then some more it went on. Then some more.

It'd probably be great and welcome to snap. But at some point came the hard realization, the very rough one, when you realized you could probably go on. You could live a long, long life. And never go to pieces, and always keep it together but only through a constant struggle, a day-by-day kind of thing.

Sometimes he actually stopped and gazed long at those apartments. But today he just wanted to drive by, and to think about Lewis. There'd been four episodes of violence between a corps member and a Native American, and the culprits in three cases were Lewis, Lewis, and Lewis. (1) He threw a puppy at someone. And threatened them with his tomahawk for dropping it (the puppy) into his dinner of roast dog. (2) He shot a guy. (3) He struck a man several times who tried to retrieve an iron oarring from a boat they were burning in order to keep his tribe from having it. Lewis never did lay hands on the husband, but did "sharply rebuke" him for mistreating his wife.

On the other hand, Lewis had run the first democratic election on American soil to include a woman and an African American, a vote to decide where they'd spend the winter. They celebrated Christmas 1805 with nothing but spoiled elk meat and cold water. It's at last there that Clark refers to Lewis in the journal as his "particular friend." Janey makes Clark a present of two dozen white weasel tails, which he regifts as a coat for Lewis. They meet a freckled, red-headed Indian, apparently the bastard son of some shipwrecked English or Spanish sailor.

Naturally, Lewis has lots of time that winter to gaze out on the Pacific in all its moods. And to conclude that, with all the nations visiting that shore, there must be some sort of way station out there, some halfway point between there and Japan, to aid in the crossing.

The next afternoon, Bill hurried over to Henry's school to catch him before he got the bus. When the kid came out, Lewis was sorry to see that he wasn't in the company of several buddies or some cute little ninth grade girl. No, he was quite alone, his son. And often looked strained right after school, as if severely tested by it, flapping along in his clothes, a scarecrow. He came straight to the car and got in. "I didn't expect you," he said warily. "What's going on?"

"I just hadn't talked to you for a while, Hen," Bill said. "I thought we'd grab a burger."

He raised his eyebrows: it wasn't part of his diet, and would probably annoy his mom. "I'm just surprised to see you," he said. "So let's go. People are looking at you, Dad."

He clutched his book bag to his chest like a flotation device, nodding ahead, rubbing insomniac eyes, wearing a couple of bulky shirts and a pair of oversized corduroys. They went to the Colossal Burger, the original one built in the '30s, now in the parking lot of a corporate tower, like a little oasis of art deco and last remnant of *that* America, the one with the streetcars, and Pretty Boy Floyd gunned down at the city's Union Station in broad daylight, and the Thompson submachine gun, and burgers wrapped in wax paper with lots of onions and mustard, no cheese, and malts in tall fountain glasses.

To Bill, these things meant something, but nothing very real. To Henry, it was just a place he'd liked since he was small. They ordered hamburgers and Cokes, onion rings and French fries and malts, squirting the ketchup and mustard out of red and yellow plastic bottles. The burgers were loaded up with pickles, the juice and grease making the wax paper see-through, like wet parchment. Henry did his usual, tearing the sandwich in half then quarters then eighths then sixteenths. He pulled the fries in half, too, as though to make it all smaller and less trying. "Dad, how's your book?" he asked.

"Oh. You asked me before about that. It's going, I guess," he said.

"I can't wait to, uh, read it, I guess. When it's published, I mean," he said. "I'd never do anything like that, write a book, unless someone was making me."

"It'll be a while before you do anything that's your idea," Bill said. Then he wondered if anyone ever did anything that was their own idea. "People say they're doing what's best for you right now, but what they mean is, what's best for the regime. It keeps everything running."

Henry just stared past him, as he did when his dad talked in this particular way, nodding very slightly, like he was listening to a talking bush.

"Strike that last line," Bill said.

"No, I like to hear stuff like that," he said, trying to peel a husk from a French fry and remove the pulp. "I really do." Then he chewed it, and kept on chewing, and chewing some more, until Lewis thought he'd have to make him swallow. It was alarming. Because if you couldn't chew up and swallow the world, it chewed up and swallowed *you*. All he could do was sit in pained silence, waiting for the saving moment when Henry finally did it, throat convulsing. And Henry clearly couldn't help it. He had to mash every bite very small so it could pass, like the opening in his throat had shrunk.

And how maddening and even frightening for him, Bill guessed, to have to work so hard for just a little nutrition.

But Bill was noticing something else, too, how one by one, one by one, all the boy-children were coming down with what used to afflict only the girls, disorders, neuroses and hysterias, manias, syndromes and complexes once thought female by their very nature. Surprise! Nurture had a role after all.

"So, how've you been feeling, Dad?" Henry asked. "Any more dizzy spells?"

"Not to notice."

He nodded and sipped nervously at the shake, which sank maybe an eighth of an inch.

"This is dinner, kiddo, so do all the damage you can," Bill said.

"Yeah, I know," Henry said. "I just—" He hesitated, and sat forward as if to cough or sneeze. Then Bill realized Henry was trying to get hold of himself, and was now teary-eyed. "It's just that [swallow]. Nothing . . . tastes very good, Dad. It's like food isn't [harder swallow] I dunno . . . like what it used to be. Like everything tasted a lot better when I was little . . ."

"I'm sorry, Hen. How's the biofeedback coming along? Is that helping?" he asked. "And what about your meds?"

"I can't really tell," he said, getting a napkin from the polished chrome dispenser and blowing his nose.

"Are you bothered at school?"

"Sometimes. But the more trouble I have," he laughed angrily, snorting into the napkin, "the more girls talk to me! In fact, two of my friends sort of cat-fought over me today, because they both want me for Sadie Hawkins!"

Lewis shook his head, and looked at his watch. "I have to hand it to you, Hen. When you have a problem, it's a doozy."

Henry noticed his gesture. "I'm taking too long," he said.

"No, you're fine," Lewis said.

"It's like it's not even me they're fighting about," he said plaintively. "It's like it's something I was born with, like a birth defect!"

Bill was going to say there were worse things, but he couldn't really think of anything worse than being thirteen, fourteen, and fifteen. "One of my students, her boyfriend is hitting her," Bill said. "Who knows, he may eventually come after me."

"God, that's horrible!" Henry said, throwing down a French fry, as though his problems were minuscule next to that. "What are you going to do?"

"Life will go on," he said. "Life goes on."

"It sure does," Henry said, biting a fry with a little burst of fury, chewing and chewing.

"Ol' Lewis got in and out of a lot of tight spots," Bill said. "It seemed like half his men, and all of nature, and the War Department, too, were out to get him."

"Is that why he did it?" Henry asked.

"People have come back from worse," he said. "He could've seen it through."

"Are you going to say for sure in your book? Why he did it?" He sorted through the fries left on his plate, discarding them one by one for various reasons. Meanwhile, Bill's meal was gone, devoured, every bite, the ketchup mopped up and both glasses dry. Henry had lost whatever poor momentum he'd had. He hadn't eaten that much, and Lewis felt it as another personal failure.

"I'm not sure what I'll say. Maybe I'll say life works out according to its own crackpot plan," he said.

On the way home, Henry apologized several times for not eating more. And Bill felt no better, like taking Henry out was supposed to boost his own spirits, like *he* deserved something extra out of it.

For some reason, his thoughts turned to Janey, who'd been continually working to feed the party, finding lots of "white apples" and another licorice-tasting root, using nothing but a pointed stick and her instincts. Lewis's plant descriptions started to get very sexy, too, with corollas swelling and anthers rising and pollen bursting. Pretty inspired stuff. And everywhere they went, Lewis saw wives and daughters prostituted for a fishing hook, given into marriage for a canoe. He also found that the tribes which were familiar with white commerce, who did lots of trading, were much less charitable than their "more pleasing Clatsop friends" who lived near the fort. A turquoise bead, or "chief bead," was the currency, and those people gave up "their last mouthful" to get just a few. Lewis wanted a seal pelt, but had nothing to trade. Janey had a girdle of blue beads she wore every day, and gave it up just like that, so he could have it. Not unlike the unfaithful wife who gives Gawain her green girdle in the bawdy old tale. So Janey was steadily divested of all she possessed, to please her men. Eventually, even Pomp and her daughter, Lisette, would leave her to go and live with the whites.

That next afternoon was Sunday, and when the phone rang, showing a number Bill didn't know, it turned out to be Pablo—Pablo from the float trip—calling. "Hey, how are things with you, Bill?" this guy, bankruptcy lawyer, who looked white but had a Spanish name, unaccountably, wanted to know. "How's it coming with that book?"

"Oh, fine. Real good," Bill said.

"Is it finished yet? Is a book ever really finished?" he asked, from way down the line, maybe from inside his car, probably a Jag, or a desktop speaker.

"Gee, I hope it will be. Maybe someday."

"Hey, I don't know if you ever go a baseball game, but there's one Thursday night, just a minor-league thing, and I wonder if you'd like to go," he said. He emphasized the phrase "minor league," meaning no way would he ask Bill to a major-league game, with all the doping and the crazy salaries. But minor-league ball was still okay.

Dismayed that Pablo was calling him, and had taken some obscure interest in him, and was possibly even trying to be friends, Lewis didn't know what to say. Probably the guy was up to something, and Bill just wasn't discerning enough to figure it out.

"Yeah, why not?" he said. "We should do that." Then, after he'd hung up the phone, he yelled, "Damnit! Goddamnit!"

He waited until bedtime to tell Emily. "So you see I'm caught now," he told her, grinding the heels of his hands in his eyes. "I'm screwed tight with no room to maneuver."

"Why do you say that? I think it could be good for you," she said. She was sitting up in bed to smear cream on her feet, between her toes.

"But what could he possibly want? Who am I to him?" he asked, wadding a pillow against his face.

"Maybe he likes you. Maybe he's got a thing for historians." Their bed was opposite Henry's and on the same wall as Henry's, so they did their talking sitting up near its foot while taking care of any moisturizing, manicuring, or flossing.

"I'll have to beg off somehow," he said.

"But why? You know he won't ask you again. I swear, you're so peculiar."

The next day, he called Pablo back, at his bankruptcy law office. When Pablo picked up on the other end, he didn't sound at all surprised or disappointed or wary that it was Lewis calling. "Hey, Bill. What's going on?"

"You know what, Pablo?" he said, "I, uh, well . . . I just wanted to say thanks and all for inviting me to the game. But I don't know, uh, . . . I can't remember what time it starts."

"Six-thirty, buddy," Pablo said. "Can you make it?"

"Oh, sure. Sure, I definitely can," he said, amazed as he listened to himself saying the exact opposite of what he'd called to say. "Listen, thanks again for inviting me."

"Okay, Bill. See you Thursday, then," Pablo said. And now he did sound disappointed in Lewis, as though he was actually hoping Bill was calling to cancel. Because if Bill was actually coming now, really planning to show, he had no choice but to do the awful thing Bill was just asking for. In fact, he'd made it so easy, it wouldn't even be much fun. And here he'd thought Bill was smarter than that, too smart to fall for the oldest gag in the world. Oh well.

After he'd hung up, Bill tried to figure out why he said yes. Sifting his own motives to the bottom, he guessed he owed something to Pablo because he'd made eyes at Pablo's wife, Rita, and she made eyes back.

Which got him thinking about Lewis when the expedition was over, and he was back home in Charlottesville, where well-meaning friends like Clark could hook him up with blind dates. Historically, at least six or eight women were linked to Lewis, including Theo Burr, who he saw at her father's trial for treason, in Richmond in 1807. It was all intertwined, with Washington Irving as one of Burr's attorneys, who'd later know the poet Percy Shelley's widow, Mary, who was daughter to the first feminist, Mary Wollstonecraft. Burr would try to seize Mexico and set himself and Theo up as emperors of a new nation called Burrania. After Lewis was dead, Mary wrote this crazy book about monsters and the dangers of the rational age.

A few years after Lewis did the deed, another Lewis, a cousin named Lilburne, also shot himself. It seemed his wife had recently died and, when a slave named George accidentally broke her favorite water pitcher, he chopped his head off with an axe. And almost got away with it, too, but while he was disposing of the body, burning it, the New Madrid earthquake struck, knocking down the chimney.

Then, about a year later, Theodosia vanishes too, off the Carolina coast during a storm, she and her crew seized by pirates and forced to walk the plank. Though another story has her spared, placed in a dog collar, and forced to service the entire crew. Later, *Frankenstein* appears, then Irving's *Tales of a Traveller*. And Irving's reviews were so awful, he abandons America, and storytelling, and turns to writing history, in

London. He couldn't escape so easily, though. The reviews kept coming, forwarded to him by some "evil genius."

On his return to America, Irving then went to see Clark, to learn what became of that destined detachment of men. O, to have been a fly on the wall of that meeting room! What might Clark say, after all, about Janey, and what could Irving surmise? What reason did Clark give for raising her children? Did Irving smell a rat? Was Clark reluctant to discuss Lewis's death? Or did he wax sentimental? Clark was the sentimentalist, all right; something in Lewis burned colder. He lived in his head. And yet he'd led them all the way to the Pacific and back. He'd lost only one man, and it wasn't even his fault. In short, he'd stolen fire from the gods, and then had to pay and pay.

The next day, after school, Bill decided to drive out east of town, taking one of the back roads behind his old elementary, where the road surface changed from nice asphalt to crummy chip-and-seal. He pretended to himself that he had no purpose, just out for a drive. But he held the address of a Donna Cormier, pronounced "Core-me-yay," in his pocket. She might refuse to see him, even if he could find it, but anyway he'd give it a try. It seemed Joaney's birth name was actually Cormier, but she used her foster one, Pfeffercorn.

He started out in the early evening, making the turns away from the nicer suburbs toward the zoo and the little bits of remaining woods and the Blue River. What was it that drew him to make the trip? It always called him back, that low end of town, like, unconsciously, he was still after something down there. A car sat in the driveway, a red Honda, and he rolled up and stopped across the street. He shut off the engine, then sat and waited and watched, like a killer with a plan. The land was parceled out very strangely, into pie-pieced lots, huge oblongs or tiny slivers. How arbitrary and brutal it all was, like amateur butchering. The Cormiers' small wedge narrowed as it went back and back, into the woods. They had a rickety swing set, a shed, a one-level house, a yard of mostly dirt, grass trampled almost to death by kids and dogs. The covered porch was lined with potted cactuses and begonias. The screen in the door bulged from small kids ignoring the handle and planting both hands, bursting through with all their tiny might.

So Joaney had half-siblings, then, and was a first-marriage baby. He went up to the door, feeling he had a pretty good idea of who would answer, what she'd be like, and rapped on the frame. A woman's shape came at him out of the dimness, unlit cigarette in her hand, in a midthigh pink dress, barefoot, bra strap peeking out on one shoulder, and much too young to be Joaney's mom. But it was her, all right. She too had the bulb at the end of her nose and was faintly broad-shouldered, and her pretty, heavy bosom thrust straight forth. She put the cigarette behind her leg, in a girlish pose, like he was the truant officer, hair in a modern, sleek, and modest Farrah.

"Yes?" she said, with fear or nervousness in her eyes, and her nostrils quivered. Was he there to say that the terrible thing she feared had finally happened? She braced herself, almost swelling to meet him. And was familiar to him. Maybe she'd come to a back-to-school night? She seemed to know him, too, and pushed open the screen door, stepping out to show she didn't fear her destiny, having no illusions left about it.

"I just got home," she said, sitting down in a white metal chair.

"I know," he said.

"How do you know? Have you been spying on me?" she asked. "You're Bill Lewis, right? From up at the high school?"

She had pink shiny lips and little sparkles in her blush. Her eyes were the same disturbing, intense blue as Joaney's.

"Joaney's going through a bit of a hard time," he said.

She nodded at the chair across from her, and he sat in it, then stared at her cigarette. She crossed her legs, bounced her foot, and tipped her head to keep from squaring her eyes to his.

"So you say your name's Bill?" she asked.

"Uh, right. Did I forget that? Bill Lewis."

"Oh, I know what it is. I'm messing with you. I know you." Her nostrils got red and her eyes clouded.

He hoped she'd tell him how, because he couldn't quite place her.

"What are you doing here?" she asked, and smirked. "I must be in big trouble."

"No, not at all. This isn't official," he said. "Nobody knows about this."

"Oh, a secret. Why's it so secret, Bill?"

"I'm just trying to help Joaney through this tough place she's in. She seems so cut off," he said. "No family or friends, for whatever reason."

"She doesn't want my help," she said, pushing her hair over her ear as if to hear him better. "Plus, she's got that boy, old what's-his-name. Jesus, she has a baby."

"It's hard for her now," he said. "I'm the only one checking up, and who am I? Her old teacher, that's all." Making himself look away from those Joaney-eyes.

"I tried to keep her. Don't think I didn't," she said, and flicked an ash. "People think you won't do something, but the truth was, I couldn't. I was post-partum, and I mean, certifiable. And I just never got better. If I made you swallow a knife and then run a mile, how far do you think you'd get?"

"Not very far," he said.

"And people would say, 'Oh, you're fine, Donna. Everyone gets the blues. Get up.' And I'd say, 'But it's like a knife in me.' And they'd say, 'What knife? Where's a knife?'"

"So you care about Joaney?" he said.

"I'm remarried, Bill. I've got two little kids now, with Reuben." Her eyes came back to him, wandering over his tennis shoes and white-collar hands. "I'm not even sure what her foster parents did to her," she added.

"Did what to her?" he asked.

"You don't know about all that? About Ted and Annette?" she asked, eyes widening.

"No, I'm her teacher. I'm helping her fix up her house," he said.

"Joaney learned too much at too young an age, that's her problem," she said. "What a mess. Ted almost went to jail."

"She's like my best student. Always did the extra credit. I gave her *Don Quixote* to read and she finished it in a week."

"Plus, she's gorgeous, isn't she?" she said, grinning, suddenly showing how lovely she was herself. "Poor Ted, the poor guy. Nearly destroyed his marriage."

He kept staring at her almost-spent cigarette. "Would you mind?"

She jumped as if seized by surprise and delight and extended the pack. "God, I'm so rude. I didn't even think."

They both lit up and he sucked hard at the first flare-up, pulling, pulling on the nicotine stream with some urgency. He gazed around. The "something more" he always looked for over here was nowhere in sight. His eyes closed on the first cool, funny rush of the drug. He suddenly felt very close to Joaney's mom.

"Boy, you really needed that one, didn't you?" she laughed. "Are you trying to quit?"

"I guess I was," he said. "Maybe since yesterday."

"So are you in love with Joaney?" she asked. She straightened her chin to his, with intensity in her voice and eyes. Why was she trying to provoke him?

"No, I'm not," he said, "but I am deeply, deeply concerned for her. And I'm very upset and worried and scared about her and how she's living."

She smiled; he amused and bemused her. Starting to say one thing, she flicked an ash, reconsidered, and tipped her head away again, the better to see him. "We went to the same grade school, you know?" she said. "I was Donna Strayhorn, but you would have known me by Ray, spelled R-A-Y, my middle name."

He had to sit back and look at her again. "Holy, holy Christ! You are? You're Matty Strayhorn's little sister? Jesus, how's he doing? Where in the hell is he now?"

"Oh, Matt's been gone a long time, over twenty years," she said. "He went in the navy and we never saw him again. I can't believe you didn't see the obituary. People get busy, though. Time marches on. Of course, Matty was never a very happy sort of guy."

"Good Christ! My best friend. You know everything about me," he said.

"Oh, hardly. I know we both come from broken homes," she said. "But all my little friends did. That's just how it was."

"How about that?" he said, trying to connect the cute, funny, cruel little girl he now dimly remembered to this middle-aged woman.

"It was hard on Matt, when my dad left," she said. "You couldn't do anything for him. It was like God and the Blessed Virgin Mary had called it quits. Like someone left him in the woods for the witch to find."

"I guess it was all pretty bad," he said. "I don't think about it much anymore, tell the truth."

She gave him a candid, disbelieving stare and blew smoke straight up. "He was just crazy about that old Pinnacle Park. Do you remember? Where we all went that one day on that Boy and Girl Scout hike? To climb up those ledges and stand up on top? Do you ever wonder why they made us do that? Anyway, Matt called it his 'cosmic place.' I thought that's where they'd find him one day, with a broken neck, but I guess he fooled me."

Bill tried hard to feel something for Matt, or remember something good about him to chime in with, but only recalled a desperate kid, far too broken to fix, a kid who'd sell his own sister for a beer or a dime bag of pot.

"Remember all the séances and stuff you guys did together, how you both loved cemeteries? You guys were so morbid, you have to admit."

He nodded uncertainly, trying to remember séances.

"Remember how you guys were going to get a house together?" she said. "How you used to go through the Sears catalog like a couple little lovebirds and pick out all your furniture?"

He nodded faintly, and grinned a little, not because he remembered, but because he knew she'd confused him with someone else. Another friend of Matt's.

"You remember, don't you?" she teased. "I thought you would. Boy, I sure do. Boy, do I. I've never forgotten one little thing, though I've certainly tried."

He nodded and continued to stare at her. The crazy coincidences of life were sure interesting. Though even more stunning was how they failed, finally, to make a pattern.

"So are you going to tell Joaney we talked?" she asked. "Are you spying *on* her or *for* her?"

"I don't know, Donna. I'm assessing the situation," he said.

"I see you're married," she said, glancing down. "I wouldn't go screwing up my marriage."

"No, you're right about that," he said.

"Not that it matters much these days," she said. "Most of that Puritan stuff is dead now and good riddance."

"I guess so," he said, pinching out the cigarette. "When I married Emily, though, we did traditional vows."

"Oh, Reuben and I said 'til death do we part and all that," she said. "The old vows prob'ly do give us too much credit. But the new ones maybe don't give us enough. Maybe."

He nodded. She was looking at him in a different way now, with almost a straining forward in her eyes, a hunger. Would she embrace him as a way to reach out for and grab at something she'd lost along the way, back in the past? He had to admit he wanted a few of those moments back, too, a chance to grow up right. He glimpsed the panorama of his life, and wondered, perhaps as she did, why it'd turned out this way and not another? In what parallel universe was she his wife? She had to be wondering what Matt's long-lost friend Bill was doing on her porch now.

"Speaking of Joaney," she said, "I remember she used to do this thing to me when she was little, where she would just sit and study every freckle and blemish on my face, like I was the best book she'd ever read. A man won't do that. It takes a little kid to really show you to yourself."

He nodded. Time to go.

"Bill," she said, "would you give Joaney something?"

And went inside for it before he could answer. He stood, and looked across to a woods where Joaney may have explored as a girl, from the porch where she'd played and danced and sung dumb little songs and been happy. That is, until the day the child services people came. Until she awoke the next day in a strange house, having wet the bed. And then always needed a light to sleep by, and was constantly terrified that something even worse was about to happen. Bill could just hear the social worker now, telling Donna she'd be fine, that pretty little white girls were easy to place. And then Ted, her foster dad, and how he became steadily deranged by her beauty. To reach out for her was wrong, but the world was full of so much worse, rape and murder and starvation. It was a lot of things. Probably she'd looked like his very first crush. Also, he'd gotten to that place you did, where you hated everything, and sold real estate because you couldn't swing the loan for the bakery. In his arms, she'd felt right for the first time in years, felt safe and protected and loved. And then, discovery and disaster, shame and scandal.

Donna returned with a tiny ziplock bag, and in it, a man's gold wedding ring. "My dad's," she said, ushering him toward his car. "Now, Reuben'll be here any minute with my boys and he'll be furious when he knows I gave you this."

"I'm so sorry about Matt," he said, scuffling his big cross-trainers in her gravel drive.

"So how come you never left town?" she asked, stopping, giving a shrug, hugging herself with both arms.

"I guess I don't know," he said. "I'm writing a book."

"Really? About what?"

"It's about these two friends. They go off on this long trip and . . . well, that's about all I've got so far."

"Maybe one should get married and be happy, and the other one should drink himself to death," she said. "Wouldn't that be a good story?"

She gave one more wave from the porch, pink dress, golden clipped wings of hair, deep blue eyes full of Viking history and *Beowulf*, and women daubing their men's cheeks with their monthly blood as the war drums thundered.

He headed home, treasure in his shirt pocket, thinking, *O, Ray! From that long-ago time in your green uniform and little white gloves and merit-badge sash! And, O, Matt! Dead in the navy; at last you found enough booze to drown that demon.*

It was an Ishmael moment, all right, a real "And I alone am escaped to tell thee!"

"...the Battery of Venus..."

"Made as if to scarrify herself in a horrid manner"; Crying and wringing their hands; Bones for the depth of four feet; Heads of female children in the press; Great joy in camp! The ocean in view!; Cape Disappointment.

✻ Walking all day in the rain and as wet and cold in every part as he'd ever been. They were down to the portable soup, carried in hard cakes like lye soap, which needed boiling for an hour to dissolve. Earlier that day, his pack horse fell in the river and away went all of his winter clothing in a muddy, ice-studded instant.

He loved her, and in doing so loved even her misery, a moment of which was more fine than hours of his loftiest feeling. They proceeded on, for the human will was so great that it gladly stripped its own last shred of meat from its own last bone to gratify a passion. Did God care, and did it matter? And why had his first ancestors risked the happiness of the entire race for some puny knowledge?

Later, the Shoshoni scout said they lay two sleeps, then five sleeps, then five more from that great body of bad-tasting water, "the stinking lake." And though he loved, there was no all-water route, no Northwest Passage, and every explorer's fondest wish was now expunged. He'd survive just long enough, it seemed, to see every fancy in the heart of man decay and die.

They commenced, all the same, to build canoes. Boiled roots, their only food, now made every man ill, and the days were suddenly very hot. Watching her, in a brutal midday light, he saw her newborn grief, for she'd been torn from her family twice. True, she loved him, but none could know 't. And had died before his eyes four times now, while that sorry creature yelped and cring'd.

In the next village, they found dogs—and were only too eager to buy and consume several on the spot. For no flesh was sweeter than that of man's little brother, due to his close devotion and trusting nature.

After dinner, a loud quarrel between the Fieldses and the husband, who was knocked down twice over a simple card trick, played on him in jest. Lewis let Clark sweep in to restore the peace, and no great matter, for only a Frenchman had been mussed.

A bit later, a woman feigned madness or went mad. She began behaving strangely, offering up some little trinkets one at a time. Then, singing that she'd nothing more to give, produced a knife and rubbed it along cheeks and eyes, nose, ears, arms. Which seemed all in play. 'Til suddenly her blood sprang from all these points and ran dripping from her fingers. She rouged her cheeks with the blood, and ate some of it, then went rigid and fell like a post on the ground, and shook. Lewis started up as if to help, then got away from the scene, for it had an uncanny horror. He'd seen this sight before! Clark pretended not to see him go, then came along, after a time. They stood watching her from afar, who was now reanimate and upright, being tended by her saner sisters.

"That lady," Lewis said, "gives me the strangest pain."

"The mad will always be with us," Clark said, nodding, trying not to look in his friend's face.

"Ask me what separates us from them," Lewis said, "and 'll tell thee. We are merely sane for longer times between fits."

"She seems harmless now," Clark said.

"I don't begrudge her anything," he said. "Nor does she resent my slightly greater share of sane-time."

Unluckily, he glanc'd in Clark's face, and knew that whispers of madness were now pursu'ng the expedition along its last leg. The captain, it was said, was unwell and altered. In point of fact, he was, but it was *love*.

The next stream was log-jammed with dying fish, and one might walk across on their backs and stay dry. Those people ate all they could, and dried it by the ton, and burned the rest as firewood, but still fish rotted everywhere.

In the clear water, when he passed o'er it in boats, he saw salmon swimming at a depth of twenty feet. Then a cloud covered the sun, and *ach!* He was suddenly, sullenly, face to face with that peculiar, odious fellow with the dumb expression. No, he did not love that fellow much, tho perhaps she did.

There, the savage men took equal share in hide-scraping and fish-gutting, like women, and Janey glared in disgusted contempt, pulled faces and held her nose, and scornfully laughed. With more eloquence in a frown than all the books of the Bible. There, the women generously exposed the Battery of Venus. But she would not be so whorish as that. O, yes, everything about her pleased him to the bottom.

They proceeded into lonely immensities, over endless deeps of icy water, and saw shores darker, more rocky, than any god could conceive. At night, his heart woke him, racing, like it would shake into pieces or stop all at once. He wished hard to be glad, but could not feel joy 'til he knew she was his.

Going ashore at a village, people were crying and wringing hands and banging heads on the ground. Then, seeing her, they stopped (for women didn't travel with war parties!), allowing him and Clark to come in alone. This time, a strange sight pulled him up short. "What's here? Tell me my eyes are wrong!" Lewis said, gazing down. "O, please, Clark! O, help!"

"Indeed," Clark said. "Well, by God now. I will be hanged. Blankets!"

"Clark, if those are blankets, then a battleship is a boat," he said. "If those are blankets, I am the queen of England! A machine made those blankets. Those are steam-loomed blankets. Don't you see? White commerce hath encircled the world!"

And there was more: twenty wooden houses after the European frame-style. British cutlasses, and teakettles. An Indian man in a round bosun's mate's hat and jacket.

All that night, the gulls mocked sleep with their cries. In the morning, they took to the boats, entering a region of mists and fogs, drizzling mild rains warm as pish, and miasmas and haunts and creeping damps. Two chiefs from the local tribe encamped with them, and were very merry far into the night. Lewis, out walking in the dark, encountered Drouillard, and the husband.

"Please to tell me, Drouillard," Lewis said, "what do these old vultures laugh about all night long?"

"They laugh from a rumor," Drouillard said. "They laugh because they are dead or think so, for the band below means to overrun and massacre us. We'll see at first light."

And the husband grinning and nodding, scratched his beard with long simian fingers, stood by, with not the least grace to recommend him. Yet gazing hopefully, and waiting, waiting to be addressed kindly. It might have touched Lewis were it someone or something, were it anything, else. For hope was written o'er that sad creature, that lowly flesh, which dreamed it could possess the female spirit one day. If only Lewis would show him, for Lewis seemed to know what women were. Tho what that sad sack of flesh really wanted, what he awaited, red lips quivering, body well-wrought as a stump, what he yearned for was nothing less than love.

So a sign was what the husband wanted, a glance was all he wish'd, a chance, a nod from the newer type of enlightened man. The creature awaited anything at all, a hint, a flicker.

And could Lewis grant it, they might safely navigate the moment. Such an eternal instant, it lasted less than a half second. Lewis knew what he had to do. With the husband standing there rigid as Lot's wife. For Lewis only need shift a little to show the man mercy. To say, *I bend. I am malleable toward your cause.* Instead, he would not yield.

No, he would love and love and never confess, and hate and hate and never give in; his spine was a redwood, his neck a Roman column!

"Good night, Private," he at last said to Drouillard. With not one word to that fellow, the look of cold horror breaking out in those features almost boyishly, then growing hideous in bitter, acid rage.

There, Lewis said inside. *Now he knows what God has done to him.*

"G'night, Cap'n," Drouillard replied, with a glance at the husband, whom the commander had snubbed for some odd reason. The husband was now leaving the scene, and was, if possible, even more hunched, blocky, and shambling, with chin lowered, fists tight.

Lewis was not even happy. So he'd trampled on the hopes of a lesser, stupid, violent man. Walking to the tent, he came upon trees ornately carved into animal faces, stacked atop each other. They rose up at him suddenly, like nightmares lifted whole from his mind.

Morning came again. By now, the brows of all the men were wasted and haloed with their privations, while Janey's grace and esteem kept on blessing every act, and made straight every stroke of their oars and axes.

Outside a village, six wooden vaults of advancing age were in a row, the newest filled with bones four feet deep, the oldest a heap of dust.

He found the world contemptible, and wished to look away. For one, the heads of all the female children were in the press. And for another, all were clamoring after those blue-glass "chief" beads, and ready to part with their last mouthful for only a few. The fog, heavy as milk, yellow and smoky, was too much for the weak, cool sun. A skunk-stench of bogs pressed on all sides, as well as the cries of brants, cranes, storks, gulls, pulvers, and cormorants black as any in Dante's hell.

A woman in the markings of the Snake Nation seemed to await them on shore, and they stopped and accosted her. Janey took her woodland sister by the wrists, and spoke. Now the woman started as if struck! And pulled away, answering with a string of rude, nasty gibberish and scowlings. Frowning, Janey tried again. This time, a throwing-away gesture of disgust with both savage arms, and each stepped back from the other.

"O, strange indeed!" Clark said. "They cannot converse." Indeed it was the case, and Janey's bewilderment very hard to observe. (In fact, he might needs kill this creature if a tear formed in Janey's eye.)

And now, for the first time, her eye sought his in the broad light of day. It accused him of having made this Babel, where her powers had now failed her. O, how he loved her then! For at last she suffered his handicap, of not knowing what people meant by the feelings they said they felt.

Later, those people stole his tomahawk pipe and the husband's cape, and that fellow's ranting over its loss very nearly touch'd the pleasurable. Lewis might've laughed, but a boundless gray gloom was all about them, the earth covered with a mirror of silver water. From its other side, something was trying to emerge. He stretched forth his eyelids to be first to see. Then nothing appeared.

A clamor of seagulls overhead, a cacophony of cries and diving white shapes, distracted the party, and freed him to take a look around. Suddenly, she was there, too, upright and splendid. He stared and she stared, for this had never happened before. And what a sweet intercourse of looks it was, that none other observed for that single eternal instant. Then, momentarily, the clattering, noisy throng moved on.

Though wet, cold, and disagreeable, he joyed in every discomfort, for it was like being human again and well. Now and then, a man vanished and was not seen or heard of for a whole day, then two. Lewis would just start grieving when the shout went up and the private strolled into camp, laughing. Everything had a rare portent. Clark went out walking and counted seventeen striped snakes. Each place they were, the women wore a girdle or thin tissue of pounded cedar bark, behind which the Battery of Venus was still visible to the penetrating eye.

They blundered into view of the ocean!

Up went a cheer from the men, and his own hands flew up into the air. His own voice shouted and shouted until it began to fail and tear.

"What do you say now, Commander?" Clark asked, grappling him and grinning, with skin as brown as a savage's, and teeth brilliant like a cannibal's.

"O, I am happy. These must be tears of pleasure."

All the moment lacked was her little hand on his arm.

The rain came then, in volleys of needles, and the wind howled. Shortly, they saw why the first whites there had called it Disappointment. On that black shelf, they huddled, with the men sleeping in bedding wet and rotten, and sucking cold water lashing on all sides.

When it was not pouring rain, they explored a coast and found a village of thirty-six good houses, all abandoned, unaccountably. They heard the cry of strange birds, and saw peculiar green flashes in the sky. As a boy, he'd amazed all who knew him by not feeling cold, going barefoot in the snow until his own blood lay in his footprints. He seemed inhuman, and could not show fellow feeling. But if he was not like man, he was not like woman, either.

He worried she'd take ill again in that rough climate. Yet she daily proved that God and women persisted even in the most savage places.

In the evenings, with the surf pounding the shore like it held a grudge against it, he sat with Clark, fiddling with the lock on his gun.

"Clark, look here," he said, pointing at the spare locks. "What do you notice?"

"They are all similar, quite," Clark said.

"Nay. They are not similar at all, not at all. Look closer! They are identical down to the last detail!"

"Ah, so they are. The same smith must have fitted them," Clark said.

"Nay, wrong again. For I saw those fellows at their work. They have a system by which each lock is touched once by each smith, who performs his one skill and passes it on."

"How remarkable. How efficient," he said.

"It is completely new and produces more locks faster and cheaper, but of indifferent esteem."

"Faster and cheaper is good," Clark said.

Lewis frowned at the locks, laying them beside each other one by one. No, he'd failed to say it. Something was not right. He felt he should despise the locks, but on what grounds? He ought to destroy them, but that was mad, and sabotage.

"Somehow, I hate them," he said. "They gleam with a rational brutality. They are ugly, as the rational is ugly, I want to say. But if I say so, my dear Clark, I will think so. And then I will be mad, don't you see?"

Clark's eyes grew remote and worried. "Lewis! I know you are a rational creature and—"

"And what?"

"I know you can take this—this wild mania of yours—in hand."

"Sometimes, Clark," he said, looking down and arranging and arranging the locks, "I am in its grip, nearly, and only stay safe by being perfectly still and not breathing so it does not know where I am." Tears rose to his eyes and a whole apple filled his throat.

"If you hate the locks, then hate them," Clark said. "Or for Christ's sake, love them! You try too hard to govern your passions. If you hate, hate. If you love, then goddammit, love! Or you will certainly go insane."

"I do hate, Clark," he said. "I hate most horribly. Dare I say it? Are we friends?"

"Yes, you may say it, Lewis. And I am not just a friend. I am—your particular friend. Do not forget that, all right?" he asked, taking Lewis by the shoulder. "Truly, you are a fool at times."

"I know. But I truly hate, Clark. Also, I truly love. And why should I have to deny it?"

"And why should you?" Clark asked. "I have declared my love, so why should you not shout your own from the rooftops?"

"There are reasons," he said. And tasted sorrow once more, a downward dip of the vulture-wing. Of course he would not tell, for he could not.

"Clark, one more word," he said with a rapid glance. "Her husband . . ."

"That man," Clark said, shaking his head.

"Yes." Lewis nodded. "He has a nettle stuck deep in his innards, incurable and long-festering. He is bent on the misery of the created world."

"He is unhappy, sorry, and unpopular," Clark said. "In natural gifts, he is totally lacking."

"Yes, unhappy to distraction," he said. "The most meager insult, in such a soul, is pounded and worked by that damned spirit into an awful weapon. He sees himself standing alone against a tide of spies, enemies, and assassins."

"He has the charge of a remarkable woman," Clark said.

"All he has is that," Lewis said. "He is nothing but a dirge, a ribald ditty, against her great soul. And knows it."

"He is hard with her," Clark said tersely. "Demanding, certainly."

"Which is why he needs a special charge," Lewis said. "Not to lie with her again. Not 'til we are parted."

Clark's red face darkened. Dismay took it over. "What? A charge to do what?"

"Clark, he has made her ill twice, and twice she nearly died! He is a disease in boots!" Lewis said, face averted, hunched on his stool, almost crippled with terror at being so nearly naked and exposed, heart staccato.

"But—a marriage, Lewis? You're tampering in a marriage?"

"You call that a marriage?" Lewis cried. "That! You call that thing a husband?"

Clark sat still for a moment. Then, after a little while, shook his head once, and vigorously.

"No, Lewis. I beg you," he said. "She is a wife. Moreo'er, she is *his* wife, and must, by wifely arrangement, acquiesce time to time."

He was trying to get his face into Lewis's eyeline, bending his head.

"I see," Lewis said.

"Do you?" Clark asked. "I hope so, my dear Lewis. For we mayn't disagree, not on this point."

Lewis groaned, then waited, still and mute as a post. Clark was looking at him, and in a way that showed he knew: his friend's state was precarious and bore watching.

"Lewis, what are you thinking?" he asked.

"I am just musing," Lewis said. "I am thinking the world is kind to give us a role in the plot that destroys us."

Clark scowled and looked away.

"And now let me test you, my friend," Lewis said. "Do you not feel a lonely joy steal o'er you? Don't you? When you stand on this cape against an ocean more big than the sky?"

"Yes, I do, Lewis," Clark said. "I do feel that."

"Well, I do not," Lewis said. "And further, I confess to not feel most of what others feel. As I grow older, I care where I shouldn't and don't where I should, and my horror of this never gets less. Good night."

They set to building the fort. And the deer that came to look were different, with darker, deeper bodies, shorter legs, and larger eyes, and thrust their heads out rudely, and accused them with their female faces.

He tried, in his imagining, to envision a world in which she was not, now that she was all he could see. At night, he went on his knees and prayed to God, "O, transform our state! Why can't You curtail this suffering?"

Now, wherever she was, the husband was also. He watched her labour for his dinner, and made droll little comments ("My girl, you do wear yourself so!"). And that cavity in his face was never idle, always licking, chewing, spitting, muttering.

The neighborhood got emptier, as though the tribes knew something and were departing. She often slept apart from that fellow, as if the yoke of his government was grown weaker. He was seen talking to himself in the forest, making strong points and backing them with sound reasons.

Using their fingers more often now, he and the men tore their meat and champed it, grinning. Lewis was surprised when she did the same, because she was not raising them up to her excellent ways, but being dragged down by theirs.

He sometimes caught her baldly looking at his back, brutally forthright, a question burning in those tiny forges called eyes. He wondered at it in a sort of helpless furor. For why did women place hope in impossible things? When would they ever quit yearning after lovely, doomed notions?

Until the fort was built, the sea came right into camp at high tide and mouthed them in its jaws, and toss'd tree trunks at them two hundred feet long, which they dodg'd without remark.

He'd arriv'd, but nothing had changed. No Miss ——— awaited his sail on the horizon. The lovely world was all covered over by a drear, wave-swept pentimento.

A trio in a canoe paddled by with a gig and basket they had clearly just stolen from the party. Forced to stop and give it up, they fled, and he cried after them across the bay, "IF YOU STEAL FROM US, WE WILL KILL YOU! BY GOD, IF YOU STEAL FROM US, WE WILL KILL YOU ALL!"

The ocean, day by day, was more big than the sky. This private vessel of his, this body, vibrated, shuddered, and creaked. Proceeding forth had been his remedy before, but now he had no place to proceed to, no step to take except drowning. With a continent at his back, he was out of room.

And she was wherever his eye fell, the husband not two paces from her. She'd asked that the new camp have potatoes growing near it, and with a bow and a lowering of his head—very far to get beneath hers—he'd said, "Yes, lady. *Por vous,* all the potatoes in the universe."

It scared him if she chanced to address him, because of the risk she took, doing so before others. Mostly, they'd graduated to no words, and a more easy and graceful intimacy with a woman he had never known. And didn't understand why she risk'd it with rude speech. But never start'd from her, and always let her go away first.

The next day, he found Clark awaiting him in the quarters, with the journal open on his knees to another of Lewis's blank pages. No, he was not keeping it up. For how could he write and still hide the truth?

"You're angry, I see that," Lewis said. "But this gap cannot be bridged, not by any pen, not even Thompson's."

"Each day, Lewis," Clark said, grimacing and not lifting his eyes, "each and every day, I study the tremor of a hand, the quality of a smile and try to know: Do I entertain hopes or fears?"

"You mustn't entertain at all," he said. "'Tis why I need you so. You provide the stroke before mine can be missed."

"I do, but for how long?" Clark asked. "Two need to make this poem."

So Lewis took the notebook from Clark, opened it, and read the first line. "'O, how horrible is the day!' That is well writ, sir, and better than I can do. Your eloquence is enough!"

"I wish I could joke," Clark said, taking the book back.

"One day, you will know why," Lewis said. "Or try searching your suspicions, for you know already!"

Then Lewis walked out a long way, out to the cape's hem, and watched Calypso close up as she tumbl'd in fury over Odysseus's escape, and roil'd the corpses of dead men through her fingers, sifting, sifting, vainly wishing one was his. In those deep blue-gray inlets, she wove black seaweed necklaces to decorate their reechy forms.

That night, an old bawd brought six girls to camp. And then led them away in cold and black-eyed fury, stiff and upright rage, when the captains refused! One with a tattooed name, "J. Bowman," on her upper arm. Lewis had no qualm with carnal lust (in others) but was not prepared for the force, or the number, of such offers in this locale. From then on, the gates were locked.

Out walking, he wander'd, to tire the demon. But 'round a turn in the trail, there she was. As if she knew—of course she knew—his nightly route. She stood before him, held her baby, and stared him into oblivion. "A pleasant evening, Madam," quoth he. "Are ye well? How is your baby? *Très bien, les enfant?* Do you know that I love you and always shall?"

She gestured for him to come with her, with some urgency. He did. She indicated they should sit, by the fire.

"You wish me to sit? Very well. Now what? Ask me anything. You will find me very candid and most agreeable."

She disrobed, throwing away her cape, placing little Baptiste and his backboard nearby. And sat down before him. And pulled up her skirt, stopping near the hip. He might've toppled had he not spied it, that ugly imposthume, just above her midthigh. Tying off her dress there, placing her hands behind her, waiting.

"Oof, you are right. A bump most terrible. *C'est horrible.*" He took the lancet case from his breast pocket, a handkerchief. "Yes, it appears awful. An infected and ingrown follicle," he said, grinning, his hands starting to quake. "There will be blood and other matter. *Sangre beaucoup!*"

She nodded and made a move with her chin, as with a knife.

"You want I should stab you, Janey? A very hard thrust? So it shall be. Anything *por vous.*"

He thought to look for the husband, but saw just a few men loitering not far away. And heated the lancet on the fire. And, loving her, took time to wipe the soot from the blade. He offered her leather. "To bite on, Janey? Like so? No? No? That's my girl. Steady now."

She was not afraid outwardly and did not move. When he'd laid the point against a promising spot, her eyes invited him. *Do your worst,* those eyes said, with a daring, reckless look, a vigorous nod. The lancet jumped into her and came to rest, sunk to the hilt. Her lower lip drew down, showing her teeth, eyes losing focus, while she felt the bright, jagged intruder. A little blood leaked and dripped. Now for the heartless maneuver. The twisting in the wound, the sound coming from her, eyes tearing, chin lifting in surprise. Did he love hurting her and having her at bay? Yes, and yes. For how dare she be exquisite and drive him to this? One silvery trickle of bloody juice and he let the blade come free, tears now marring and mottling her face. 'Twas a good wounding, and wept a clear serum. He was wet through his clothes, to the roots of his hair. She untied her skirt, and reached for Baptiste. "How now, Madam? Will it do?" he asked. "I have struck you and you will heal. As for me, I know not."

She left the place without a backward glance. Lewis looked 'round, and saw the husband after all, proud, vain, and egotistical, his devious cunning glinting out. And nursing some grievance with a demoniac patience.

And yet, he is mine, O, all mine, Lewis knew, awfully. *Even the least of these is mine.*

Later, they were at their fire, she and the husband. And Clark, for some reason, sat with them. He was insistent that Lewis join them, too. She sat back rather farther from the fire, produced an object, and held it forward.

"She's got summat for you," the fellow said, addressing Lewis.

"Oh? What is this, then, Madam?" he asked.

"'Tis bread, Cap'n," the thing said. "She's saved it for you."

"O, my God, Clark, it is in fact bread!" Lewis said. But could not take anything from her hand. He tried, then waited, then again tried. For if he did, if he ate from her fingers, it would be out. Clark took and ate it immediately.

"How does it taste?" The husband frowned, disappointed. "Good, eh?"

"It is wet, it is sour, and the best thing I have had in weeks!" He offered the last bit to Lewis, and Lewis shook his head, grinning, almost laughing aloud, O, utter fool. For he could not take it; his best friend must have it instead. It was her last good thing, and had lain against her skin for a time.

Then, careful not to notice the refusal, careful not to remain, she left, and he went to bed.

Or tried, body storming all night long. For his was a heedless, careening drunkard of a body, not to be trusted. Several times, he walked out and shook the gate of their fort, and worried o'er the wrath of those women, turned out for pimping.

The next day was Christmas, celebrated with water so cold it made the lips red and sour elk positively green with spoil. Clark's gift from her, two dozen white weasel tails, became a coat for Lewis. Thus, all along the way, this was how they'd work it, with no thing coming to him straight from her hand, and no witnessed intimacies.

And every night came a visit by his three o'clock hound, black dog, making him flee the tent to tremble 'til dawn under a blanket by the fire, that bone-shaking cur, growling fiend.

Then the whale, like a monster from his very own deeps. Washed up in the night, 102 feet long, and the village buzzing like a hive of ants going out to parse a fallen mouse. "How good of God, sending us a whale to swallow, eh, Lewis?" Clark asked. "Poor Jonah, he got it wrong way 'round."

Next, the country emptied of Indians, who laid claim to all this Leviathan and did not share.

Late that morning, Drouillard came to see him, pale and unhappy. It seemed he was out tracking game when a snake crossed his path. "It means death, Cap'n, to the one who saw it. Or may-be to another!"

"But why tell me, Private? Am I a gypsy?"

"Help me, Cap'n! 'll do whatever you say."

"Heavens, man! Keep it to yourself!" Lewis said. "Omens are the last things we need just now, well or ill."

16.

"... (Damned rascal, son of a bitch..."

*She thought it very hard; "Damned rascal, son of a bitch";
Except a wife, with whom it is equal; Begged of me to take out the
bad fire; Kill them all and set fire to their houses; An excellent
subject for electricity.*

✤ Each night, he had the same dream, in which he was awake and
lying in the bunk, with his body senseless, paralyzed. Buried alive inside
himself, he struggled hopelessly to break free. And only could, finally,
with a great wrenching of his soul.

How he looked forward to day, labor and suffering, and hated night
and rest! But in the light, when he stared hard at things, they appeared
to wobble and shift beneath his eye, as if about to lay open a deeper
truth.

"One should, day by day, grow stronger, of greater cheer, less afflicted," he said to Clark. "But I am more beleaguered here the longer we
remain."

"You are pursued, and all night long," Clark agreed. "Soon, 'll be sleeping in the compound."

"What troubles me is we're covering up the world that was here," Lewis said, touching the bark of a nearby tree. "'Tis there but no longer visible. What was undiscovered we have uncovered and changed its face."

"Shh. Everything is all right, Lewis."

"If you say 'tis," Lewis said. "But having not slept in so long, I feel the light with the hairs on my head. I sense the world that will come to crush this one, and can almost make it out."

Clark shook his head, clucked his tongue. "Yes, but look liveliest now, for we have now to see the Leviathan whale. Who shall I pick for our party? And do you know that someone new has petition'd to go?"

Lewis hesitated. Then said, "We will bring Drouillard, and York, and the Fields. Now, let's be on our way."

Clark blinked at him. "That is all, then? Just those?"

"Yes, Clark. Just those. Why? What's the matter?"

Clark scratched his shaggy red head, disturbing the nits not drowned by the bear grease he combed into it. "Nothing, not 't'all," he said. "But someone has been most insistent to go. You yourself said how few are her pleasures."

"Clark, this is no holiday inn!" he said. "'Tis the army."

"I know, Commander," Clark said. "And please to refrain from the matrimonial tone." With right eyebrow up in hurt irritation.

"She may go another time," Lewis said. "But not today."

But why? he himself had to wonder. To exclude her. And why? Because it was time to face hard fact: in no real world could he love her. The first denial was now past his lips.

He turned. There she was, not ten feet away, holding Pomp in his litter, and clearly primed for excursion. And several paces behind her, that miscreant.

"Yes, Madam?" he said, in a terrible voice, a most officious voice. She colored as if struck. Then, starting toward him, features a deep red, spoke loudly and angrily, in French, about what a fine thing it was to haul a baby thousands of miles and then be denied admission to amazing wonders: the monstrous fish, the endless, stinking body of bad-tasting water.

Nobody could say a thing. 'Twas the longest speech she'd ever uttered. Men working nearby simply stopped and raised up, to gawk at the miracle. A few Clatsop women making a canoe at the shore walked up and stared, awaiting the bolt of lightning that must destroy her for speaking thusly to a white man.

"She wishes to know why," said the husband then, as if the whole world had not heard her, "she says 'tis a hard thing to come so far and not be tolerated to see the monstrous fish and the stinking lake!"

"I know what she said," Lewis said quietly, his face, ears, and throat all painful and hot.

No, none could mistake it, or her tone, of a woman used by a man and then deceiv'd, cast aside. And he could say nothing. He who commanded all could not make a sound. O, a lovely scene! And what a fool he'd been for weeks and months! For she was only guilty of hope! Why shouldn't he steal her from that creature? She'd already been stolen twice!

"Will you not answer her, Cap-tan?" the husband asked. "Answer her, now, and I will translate."

It was shocking, truly. All were pretending not to comprehend. She'd tasted enough bitter to o'erflow the sweetest pool. And he the clear source of that evil brew. She had dreamed, as only young women can, of impossible things, of laying her head by one not so lawless, stupid, devious, and immoral.

"Your answer, Cap-tan?" the fellow said with glee. "She awaits thee."

"Please answer her in every language you know," Lewis said. "Please tell her we die if we ever stir a step without her."

"'Tis fancy, but 'll try to come near it," he said, nodding happily and kneading his left hand vigorously with his right.

. . .

The trip was made and surviv'd without incident. Later, he sat among those people 'til night. Tho cheerful, they were never gay. He listened as they spake of the most intimate marital acts in the frankest terms. A woman's chastity was simply not practical, in their view, with benefits deriving from sharing her sex.

As low as events brought him, he sank lower still. For the husband had made no such demands of her so far, but it now occurred to him that nothing could prevent 't. Lewis almost laughed out bitterly: each time one reached the end point of horror, a new one appeared.

He went to see Clark in the tent.

"What is wrong, Lewis? You are positively fish-coloured," Clark said.

"Never mind. I am worried for her," Lewis said, glancing out the tent flap.

"Lewis, you'll think me hard, but here we are! Safe! Not that I want her harmed, but aren't such worries behind us now—?"

"These people will prostitute a wife for a fishing hook," he said. "Her health is already precarious."

"But after the way she treated you yestiddy," Clark said, almost scornfully, "how doth she remain in your high regard?"

"What are you after?" Lewis said. "What do you mean?"

"I only seek your thoughts," Clark said. "As always."

"I've said it before. We must give him a charge. She is in our employ, as U.S. interpreter and army scout."

Clark studied on the problem, brow hunched. "And how would one phrase that exactly?"

"That he must not endanger her, and by that I mean 'go in' to her, as the Bible says," Lewis said.

"You will have to do this, Lewis, for I cannot," Clark said.

In the next days, she wouldn't look toward him, nor sit or walk near him. She was precisely like a woman deceived in intimacy who has delivered her abuser's name in public. And he could ask no pardon, for they'd not ever spoke to begin with! To the degree she had opened (O, she had, and he had joyed in her freely!), now she was just that tight closed, their holy union torn apart and trampled.

And that sorry man, without graces or talents, was the sudden object of all her devotion. Her hand was on his arm, shoulder, or thigh, and she leant in subjected female manner, indulging him now with kisses and caresses as tho to make up for a long separation.

Lewis walked about pressing a place near his heart, praying the hand that crushed it would finish him or relent. And the men were now anxious to include him, shewing him all their tricks for mixing baits, which required slicing the scrotum of the male animal, pressing the testicle into a mortar, mincing fine, then crushing with nutmeg, cloves, cinnamon, and a drop of whiskey. He sat with them, moved by their anguish, which was the terror of boys for an ailing father, or believers for a fallen idol.

Trying to swallow what had happened was like ingesting a whale, gullet distended hugely to accept what it cannot. For days, the rain blew sideways or in circles like a tortured ghost. Those people knew just two phrases of English—*You damned rascal! You son of a bitch!*—and those words rang out all about him.

One night, a man from elsewhere made designs on Private O'Neal's blanket. And would've killed him if not chased off. So, despite their advances, human beings still murthered over trifles.

Lewis was thinking of marriage, of children and love, how they'd never been the easy matters for him they were to Clark. In fact, all his thoughts of those pale, corseted creatures a-waiting back home left him cold. O to be that sort who saw a universe in a grain of sand!

On and on, he and the party kept clinging to that shore like crabs on a shelf. When it was not raining, they stumbled and weaved 'mongst its caves, fens, bogs, and dens. One night, a chief told him a story of a river running all the way to Spanish-held land. He gazed straight at this sincere fellow. Then laughed. For would it never end? The lies, and the lies, of secret rivers and passes? O, to be the lowliest buzzard skimming five miles o'erhead, and know the truth! But he no longer cared. Here was the water that matter'd, for she had stepped in it.

Now there was nothing, outside her regard. At night, Pompy suck'd at her breast, a most intent, thralling silence in the flick'ring gloom. They'd spanned a hard, wicked continent, but nothing compared to her fury and desolation at being so deceiv'd. All that was gone. Everything was gone. They'd never even speak of what was never formed in acts, his lips mauling hers, his hands gripping the fat and oily-sweet dugs, her thighs hotly clutching his rushing hips.

During the day, he and the men pursu'd the elk in the wood, and were dreadful, all trussed up in the skins of their quarries, with noise sticks spitting smoke and deadly cinders.

One morning out of spite, in a narrow-choke of spawning fish, he stood and struck two dozen onto the bank with blows of his open hand. And at night, set up rows of dried small fishes and burned their bodies like candles. He did not sleep. Then spent each long day in a duel with the creeping sun, to stay sane 'til sunset.

Clark sought him out in the evening, with news. "You see that the Chinooks are returned from trading by the shore," he said.

"Yes, and how awful," Lewis said. "For after their visits, every man comes down with the venereal."

"Expect an epidemic shortly." Clark laughed.

"I have a diff'rent idea," Lewis said. "Let us disbar any man who comes admitting such condition." He looked at Clark with a carefully even smile.

"That is, um, perhaps severe, Lewis," he said. "My God, you know they won't obey!" He glanced into the dark and close-set depths of his friend's eyes.

"Then let us disbar them, each and every one," Lewis said. "If they cannot act like men, 'll do it gladly. Every single last one."

"We will have mutiny and the Chinooks down on our heads," Clark said.

Lewis thought to press the point. Then suddenly no longer cared for it. "On another subject. We need canoes."

"What with? There is nothing left," Clark said.

"I have a uniform coat, and a half roll of tobacco. What is a canoe worth?" he asked.

Clark chuckled and removed a cocklebur from his beard. "A canoe is worth one wife," he said.

"A wife?"

"Or a daughter," Clark said. "Depending."

"Depending on what, for God's sake? The quality of the canoe? Or the daughter?"

Hysteria perched on the edge of that Pacific scene, creeping up closer to him now, and again a bit closer.

"Be careful, Lewis," Clark said. "Honestly, you worry me."

"Summer is coming, Clark, and I've strength for only one 'run' out of this place. The passes will open for a moment, and we must dash through the gap," he said.

Clark nodded, sucked his gums thoughtfully.

"O, and Clark?" Lewis said.

"Yes? What?"

"The first man who comes to me with a certain complaint is disbarred," he said. "Tell the men."

Clark went forth to give the hated order. The trip was changing him, Lewis could see, and he left the tent a grimacing, misanthropic, melancholic despiser of life. Lewis counted the tailfeathers of a hawk killed that morning, and found it was nineteen. Was God in the evens or the odds, the wholes or the primes? The bone-ball's bumps numbered two-eighty-eight. Each moment, the world kept up this chaotic clamor, which only she had ever silenc'd.

He slept that night, but dreamed two long planks were clamped to his skull, with painful cords, and at each turn in the trail caught fast in branches and crotches of trees. And awoke crying and knowing: he'd had her dream. Tears filled up and blocked his sight.

He wrote a list of all their names and nailed it to the gate. To those crying people, he gave certificates of good conduct. It ought to've been sweet, parting from that coast with its dreads and night sweats. But he felt instead like his own first ancestor, heading east toward a wasteland, to pursue its few rough joys.

At the next village, those women's bubbies were down to the waist, the Battery of Venus plain for all to see. Now she kept herself back inside her eyes as they toured disgusting scenes. And saw dirty, naked wretches, insensible to their own horror. And ate the dried "candle-fishes" and sometimes a meager dog. The huckleberry vine crawl'd over everything at night, but lay quiet and innocent by day. They marched out directly toward the rising sun, light burning their cheeks and lips. And even killed the eagles, the hawks and falcons, little cannons hurling ore fresh from the earth's belly, for a hot, smoky death. Nature now lacked principles, and rubbed up close, and open'd wide its glist'ring eye.

Very hungry, they came upon a little band just as starved. But who owned an indifferent piece of elk they'd not trade at any price. So Clark threw a fire-match into their fire that smoked and sparked in a weird way.

"There! Then take this bad fire," he said. "I leave it to harm and afflict you evermore!"

Then those people wailed and tore their clothing, and wrung their hands, and banged their heads. With a magnet concealed in his opposite hand, he made his watch turn and cavort weirdly. Beside themselves, they threw the elk-meat into his arms and begged him to go. Thus, this New World justified new tactics, tricks they'd been too ashamed to try before.

"A hungry human can do without principles," Clark said, slicing off pieces of elk-beef.

"Nor do I argue," Lewis said, chewing. "In just a few short years, look what we have seen: Beauty struck across the face by Truth, his fingerprints visible for an hour afterward. And Beauty crying out vengeance while Justice stands and bows its head."

Clark paused, then gestured with his knife. "Is that Mount Saint Helens I see, weakly smoking in the distance?"

"The very same infernal beauty. Another famed launcher of boats!" he said.

In the next little *"ville,"* a tomahawk, stolen from them on the voyage out, was espied by Private Colter and snatched back.

Farther on, good old Seaman, Lewis's Newfoundland dog, went missing, as did an ax. Lewis strode in among their houses. "LISTEN, YOU PEOPLE!" he said. "I AM NOT AFRAID OF INDIANS! STEAL FROM ME, AND I WILL KILL ALL OF YOU AND SET FIRE TO YOUR HOUSES!"

But then later, they sat down and ate sweated wild onions and roasted hyacinth blossoms at their fire. Lewis watched her accept a hyacinth into her mouth from the husband's dirty fingers, her lips forming a most obscene O.

And wasn't he himself to blame? Hadn't he been the one to lead them to the sea, and never let anything turn him? And Janey was lost now, o'er a fortress wall. She'd not signal to him from its battlements, ever again.

He ministered to those people and their pustular disorders. Ah, the breathtaking grandeur of the body's afflictions. The chief's wife, a sulky bitch, needed camphor for her back. And tho he helped her, she hated him, and suddenly matter'd more to him than all the rest together. He'd taken much care to please her, and could not!

Careful not to be alone, careful not to tarry, the madness yet pursu'd and worked at him from ev'ry way. Clark, he knew, was looking after him and keeping him in sight. They tried to get horses to cross over the Divide, but those people would take nothing in trade, not even canoes. "I have not seen the like," Clark said. "What do we do?"

"Let us burn every canoe."

"Until they relent?" Clark said.

"Regardless."

They never did give in, but only stood by astonish'd at so much spiteful waste. A fellow loitering nearby put forth a hand and touch'd an iron oarlock. Lewis, on him with a piece of kindling, surpris'd him with blows which laid him out flat. Sergeant Gass saw and would probably write it, Lewis knew. And panting, seeing red, was happy his men were so many. For if the fellow died, they'd need a massacre to escape.

That night, the husband somehow "overlooked" tying his horses and lost two. In the morning, hearing the news, Lewis was dizzy, sick, and murderous.

"I am out of patience with the folly of Mr. Charbonneau," he said, holding his head. "What will we do?"

"She has her trousseau," Clark said. "That is, her leather clothes. Probably worth one middling horse."

"And a good thing she produced the heir," he said. "For he reduces her to nothing, the clothes on her back."

They pressed on, and everywhere desp'rately talked of horses, where to find horses, how to get horses. The tribes attended their pleas with one ear only, whilst feting, and dancing, and passing side to side, shoulder to shoulder. 'Til Lewis felt they were laughing at his haste and fear. 'Til he thought he'd kill them or go mad.

"And why this crazed insistence?" he said to Clark. "Do you see how we look? Why not antelopes? Why not white whooping cranes? What are we on about, after all?"

"I'm sure they don't know," Clark said.

"Not at all! Unconcerned, they pass to and fro dancing!"

Meanwhile, she and the husband stood together like man and wife, his arm about her brief waist in grand luxury, and hers draped in similar fashion, and twining her small fingers about the thick, hairy hilt of his knife.

He returned to his occupation of sores, bloods, and swellings. The increasingly tender, hot edges of his soul stung and whinged. At night in his bed, he yearned after marriage like a young girl aching for love. During the day, he hid himself from Clark and the men. One might as well say it: Clark belonged to the men, and he did not. Add it to the list of things not granted him by God.

Then the next little band had a Shoshoni hostage. She and Janey fastened, one to the other, and took each other by the arms. Like two little castaways, they talked intently, in low voices with anxious glances, on matters too easy to surmise. (*What was your band? Who was your father and mother? Who is your husband? Are you very unhappy? Have you tried to escape?*) Here they'd found a most desolate and desperate-seeming young woman. And here she must remain, with no improvement in her state and perhaps feeling more bitter than ever.

Janey was clearly bothered, at leaving the poor girl, and Lewis was made happy by her sadness. And then, self-despising, fell down lower than ever. He sat watching hundreds of those people dance, coming to hate all humanity. In two great circles, one inside the other, the dancers turned in opposite directions, in a vision like Ezekiel's.

In that place, he saw the House of Coventry, where a woman must go each month, and not eat or cook or walk with others, after the ancient Hebrew custom.

He waited long to see effects on Janey from that Shoshoni prisoner. Would she soften? Would she yield? No. Hard-hearted girl! She'd shun him forever.

They were waiting and waiting to cross through the pass. He drew a diagram in the dirt with a stick. "The river, just here, is our silver cord which we have unraveled, and now must reel up again," he told Clark. "The Minotaur is dealt a mortal blow but he is not yet dead and takes a side passage, here, to cut us off. I think we are cut off."

"Lewis, we will be all right," he said. "You must be still."

"I am like vermin in the terrier's jaws, Clark. And God is the terrier."

"These people think we are gods with all our medicines," Clark said. "I only wish they worked so well."

Lewis threw his stick away, eyes blackening. "O, do not pretend you are troubled. Let us not pretend anything at all. Deceive them all you can, for our need is still great," he said.

He stared forth. At dinner, someone threw a puppy in his plate to mock his tastes. Lewis got up with his tomahawk, and had to be restrained, Clark's arms around his.

Now he saw that ev'ry conquest was mere license for more. Turning over in the dark of its underwater cavern, his soul tumbl'd like an unborn animal in the womb, blind, upside down, using its hooks to cling and grope along.

"I still think of that inmate in the last village, their Shoshoni prisoner," Lewis said, "and her harrowing plight."

Clark sighed and thrust his thumbs in his belt and stretched his feet to the fire. "To an Indian woman, one man is like another," he said. "She will be all right."

Lewis sat forward, elbows on knees, to see Clark plainer. "You mean to say they never form particular attachments? No particular attachments at all?"

"Perhaps it has happened," he said, shrugging. "Anything is possible. The test of all attachments is fidelity, is it not?"

"But suppose she loved another, not her husband? Would she not need to admit them both?"

"Ah!" Clark said. "I see your point. A married woman must acquiesce. So, my answer is yes, she receives only her husband and lover."

Lewis lowered his eyes. "But what if the lover were absent? If he were in prison, say?"

"Then she must only rarely accept the husband, and only when pressed," Clark said. "But how could one prove it but by observing her every day?"

"Yes," Lewis said, keeping his face cloaked in a shadow, to hide the glimmer of sublime pain there. For he'd watched every moment for two long years, and never did she take up another! None knew his hopeless and inward exultation. None would ever know.

All the next day, the women pounded roots, with a sound like a nail factory. The House of Coventry stood up there, exercising its power o'er the scene like a temple, with its bloody rituals carried out in secret.

They needed meat, and tried to assemble goods to trade for horses. But when the chief heard of this, he was adamant: they must take all they needed.

From afar he observed her, heart flat and slack, as she played with Pomp. She sang him little songs and pulled him to her, then suddenly shoved him over. The little fellow, enchanted at all she did, lay upended, laughing, and never shewed pain or alarm. Indeed she might throttle him and never erase the love-struck fixity of his gaze. Bowled flat, he arose and assaulted her—with a kiss.

As for her little captain, if she would but glance, give a single inch, he would fly the thousand miles to her side.

The next day, Sergeant Gass shewed him a slide-top box she carved for his Christmas. Then the husband came with Pomp, a large profundity rising on his neck. Lewis tried to play their grizzly game, in which a finger thrust into the bear's den (Lewis's fist) yielded a "bite" from his thumbnail. Today, tho, Pomp made no sound, his tiny digit mauled to the bone. The prideful husband, lord of the U.S. Army tent that protected his head, looked finally humbl'd. "My wife says to stab this creature. Use your trusty little knife and kill it," he said.

"Does she truly?" Lewis said, avoiding the piggy eyes, those almost hidden declivities in his face. "In fact, 'tis so involved with the babe's throat, I dare not."

The husband sighed heavily and coloured darkly, started to say one thing, thought better of it, choked, and started again. "Will you not even try? For the boy's sake?"

Lewis threw down the lancet in the tray and got up. "No, sir, not for any sake. Not for Mary herself! For it would do no good, and his screams would kill your wife besides. And who will carry your pack for you then?"

Such hate then blazed forth from the husband's face that the air curl'd and waver'd o'er him. Lewis wished he had not said it, but there it was.

He waited as the fellow somehow mastered himself. And not through strength but rather cunning, the husband showed his ability to await the proper moment to pounce. For he had a capacity to lie in ambush, and had survived thus far on that.

"I will make him a poultice," Lewis said finally.

"A poultice? A poultice!"

"That is what I said, sir. Of boiled onions. It draws the infection."

He made it up and fastened it to the squirming, hot child with many windings, and his father carried him away. She would be so unhappy, in sorrow and misery. Lewis cringed in self-disgust at the thrill of pleasure he felt, for she suffer'd.

"You've done all you could," Clark said. "None could fault you."

He felt obscure rebuke in the remark and looked at Clark's face. "You are wrong, sir. I fault myself. The demon attacking him needs air and light to survive. And here is my wager: that this devil has dived too deep after this child's life and will suffocate to death one instant before Pomp does."

"An awful wager," Clark said.

"True. But no marvel on earth compares to suffering in children. It is the only proof of God I know."

Clark stared at him. "*Escusez-moi?* How proof?"

"Do you not see 't, Clark?" Lewis said. "If even the innocent suffer, then this place must be a trifle amidst the eternal life of the soul. If this life were really real, only a monster could conceive 't or live happily in 't."

"Still," Clark said thoughtfully, "would you dare tell that lady? Would you say her little boy's sufferings are a trifle 'mongst the stars? Why, those eyes could strike a Christian dead!"

The next day, they found a chief in a village paralyzed and lying on a board. Lewis made him sit under a tarpaulin with water poured on hot rocks below, producing a violent sweat. After he recovered use of his arms and one leg, Lewis relented (but wish'd he had electricity and means to apply it: the fellow was an ideal subject).

The ugly imposthume on Pomp's neck matured, ripened, then cracked and wept like a large female breast. The strain of his illness shewed on her and she would not eat. And although a sharp blow would, in a gory instant, discharge the contents and speed healing, Lewis could not, for Pomp's screams would make her finally insane.

Now robbed of an intercourse unlike any he'd known, a union beyond all his history with her sex, his soul began to go ranging. And was away from him as often as not. The only remedy being a certain type of biting fly, tenacious beyond description. When he wanted, he let them light on him very thickly and, in those bright sensations, was sane again, whole, and in the world.

Desperate to eat, they cut the buttons off coats, traded for a colt, and ate him down to and including his marrow bones. Lewis shot a bird to find an omen and counted twelve tailfeathers, even and divisible. Had God hid a message in His handiwork, and would he ever recognize it?

The husband was about more frequently, as tho with a question he could not spit out. Lewis felt shadowed by a creature who lived outside the reach of God's blessing.

And then it finally dawned on him, and he started to laugh.

"How good it is to hear you laugh, Lewis!" Clark said. "I feared you might never again."

"Now I see it, Clark," he said, nodding toward the husband's shambling form. "I've been too hard on him, don't you see? He lives outside her special regard. He is her husband in name only, and cannot receive her actual charms."

"I'll wager he receives some of them," Clark said.

"But he has never once entered the citadel itself," Lewis said. "Never once has he addressed the saints there!"

"I await the joke," Clark said.

"But there it is. The supremely majestic injustice. He is called her husband but is not."

"And why do you care, Lewis, what that man doesn't enjoy?" he asked. "Why pay him any mind at all?"

"He is always about me. He hands me a knife before I need it," Lewis said. "He assists me with a girth strap, and kicks my horse when he tries to swell."

"Well, what does he want?" Clark said, looking toward that lone distant figure across camp, forever at the edge of life.

"I don't care," Lewis said. "I preferred his pigheaded arrogance to this new game."

"Ask him," Clark said. "Otherwise, your mind will plague you."

"O, I certainly will, Clark. For only a madman lets a thing tease and bother. And mad I certainly am not!" He got up in play-haste and play-offense to hide his actual anger.

"Do not even joke, Lewis," he said. "We are almost home free."

"Indeed? Are we, then?" Lewis said, and left the tent.

The next day, Lewis was out gathering specimens and that fellow played his usual trick, stepping out of a shadow by the trail and falling into step with him easily, like a close friend. "So, Cap-tan—" he said, as though to resume a chat momentarily interrupted.

"Yes, sir? You've a question of me? Please ask it, for I am waiting." Lewis looked about for someone, anyone, a witness, but the woods were strangely empty just then.

"A simple question. I do not wish to perturb you," he said, grinning appraisingly, and wrapping himself in a self-loving embrace with both arms.

"Ask it! For I am desperate for both the question and my answer."

"Well, sir, this is the question," he said, winking. "What thinkest thou of my state?"

Lewis glanced, then looked away. "I do not understand you."

"I simply wan' ta know, sir, does it please you? Dost thou love my condition? Do you enjoy 't?"

"Mr. Charbonneau—" he said, careful not to give him his whole eye, and not to slow, still searching the woods for any human face.

"You walk too fast," the fellow said. "Please slow down, for you tire me, Cap-tan."

Lewis slowed a little, and looked on the man. O, he was miserable. It rolled off him like a stink, this exile he suffer'd from human intimacy. Like skunk-water in a rotten log, he was stagnated and forsaken, a failed work of God's hand, left here on the fringes of hell to hide the botched job. God was apprentice'd at making this man. Loving him was a test of love itself. Lewis ventured a second look and saw more brutality and lies, the red mouth, a hateful eye, a crude, obscene excuse for a nose.

Well, 'twas easy to love the smooth cheek, the strong chin, the shining eye! The true test of the human, of the real enlightened soul, was to somehow exalt this creature. *He is one of mine, one whom I answer for. I must not shudder.* But where was it written that he must account for one and all? And how did these creatures always know? They came unerring, like tugs in a harbor, straight for him, their misery and barbarity laid at his door. Like this fellow, hanging here, pining for the captain as if for his beloved, at a bend in the trail.

"Nothing so unhappy as a human being, eh?" the fellow asked. "I hate to walk alone. I don' like the forest."

Lewis stopped at a red stretch of mud and took up a handful. "It compacts in the hand, like a soft port-wine cheese."

"Satan tempted our Lord to turn stones to bread," the man observed helpfully.

"I wish to God he would tempt me," Lewis said. "I would change the mountains to beef and the oceans to whiskey."

The fellow shook his finger at him and clucked his tongue. "So ye are God now! You should not take on so."

The wind was riffling some blue heads of quamash in bloom and made the whole meadow move like a body of water. Ahead was the broad spreading river, some marshy, endless flats and muddy, sandy basins. He was tired of resisting this endless game and longed to fall as prey. "The world we are finding, we are destroying," Lewis said. "One sees a thing for the first time only once."

"You are too deep for me, Cap-tan. But if you say so."

Lewis was giving in, though an almost dead part of him wanted to turn and smite that snake-like head. The fellow fix'd him with a grin that made his plan clear: either they'd reside together in the skies, or kick jointly in hell. And how to resist this diabolical design when Lewis's senses were failing him, one by one, like horses in an overworked team?

But for the first time, Lewis had seen the Minotaur, locat'd the beast. Now, how to surprise and kill it?

"What a disappointment we must prove," the fellow suddenly said.

"To whom?" Lewis asked, placing his feet carefully in the trail.

"O, women," he said simply. "First they endow the most unpromising fellow with rare possibility. Then, their hopes dashed again and again, they settle into family life, awaiting the champion who does not ever come."

"Sir—" Lewis began.

"I could be a friend to you," the fellow said. "Or an enemy."

"Now he threatens me." Lewis laughed. "Is this how you make friends?"

"In truth, I never knew how," the fellow said, in a quite unguarded way. "For none would e'er teach me!"

Lewis shuddered and quickened his step. "Too late for that," he said.

The husband was now deathly quiet at his shoulder, hurrying to keep up, a red flush in his face like a port-wine stain. His mouth opened and closed like a magical fish talking. "I almost give her to you," quoth the creature, finally.

Lewis hurried faster. "No, sir. No more. O, leave me be," he said.

"No, truly. She coulda been yours," he said. "But now . . ."

"Get away from me," Lewis said, and cut straight away from him, through the woods.

"It is best she shunned you!" the husband shouted after him, through the pine-poles. "For *you* could never have left *her!*"

The man then hurled curses after him, in French, for a long mile. He got back to camp wet through, shaking, and fevered. His heart hammered and a huge icicle hung from his gullet, piercing his guts.

The world, at times nearly magical when he was a boy, was in fact *hell*. In the tent, he lay with his face to the wall. He closed his eyes so tight, and wished so hard for oblivion, he passed out.

Somehow, the next day, the mission went on. They all got up at dawn to totter after it, in rags, starving. He rattled as he walked, with cracked leather bladders in place of his lungs. The men gave their penetrating attention to his every trifling utterance; they worried for this their father, since many had never had one.

Now, when she struggled in the deep snow and fell down with Pompy, others had to aid her, for he stayed back. Which surely was noticed and caused gossip. They staggered along a road only evident because Indians could follow it, and ate their only ration: bear's oil poured over roots. She'd located these deformed, knobby gentlemen, and he ate them unwashed, along with her fingerprints in smears of bitter yellow earth.

He went forward because he'd told Tom he would. As ever, life was a matter of saying yes since saying no was impossible. And the talons of his predicament gripped sharpest if he ever tried to escape or resist. So he somehow had to wait and wait, until its attention wandered elsewhere.

He now knew why she'd known him, why they'd known each other at a glance: their dilemmas were much the same.

In those mountains, they were cold, wet and numbed one moment, and plunged into smoking springs and boiled red in baths of liquid fire the next. One day, he looked 'round and saw they'd cross'd the ranges again. So the trip wasn't fatal after all, far from it. It had a divine effect of opening his eyes.

And what he saw was plain: he needed that man gone. Someone need scout Maria's River north of there, and though it led straight to the land of the godless Blackfeet, he resolved to send himself. Also, nobody else was suitable.

"I am for the Maria's," he told Clark, whom he'd found at a stump-table on a mossy earth chair.

"O, are you, then? For a lady?" Clark asked with impertinent grin.

"For the president," he answered, and scowled and stared.

"I am jesting," Clark said. "I am headed for a lady, as you know, and happy, and wish you'd choose happiness, too."

"Are you so sure I haven't?" he asked.

Clark positively clapp'd hands for joy. "O! Tell me, then! Who is it? Do I know her? Is she from the neighborhood?"

"No, not from the neighborhood, and that is all! I am not like you. I am not—forthcoming."

"Give me her first name, at the least," Clark said, putting down the pen and cracking his knuckles like a teamster. "At least her initial."

"It is 'J.' Are you extremely well pleased? It is 'J.'" He coloured brightly, he knew.

"Extremely well," he said. "Does the lady know?"

"I'll never tell," Lewis said, looking down at the ground, up at the sky, left and then right to keep rapacious blue eyes from seizing his. "My ladies aren't like yours, Clark. Mine never fade or coarsen, bloat or wither."

Sensing a stalemate, Clark said, "Then I am, too, for the Maria's."

"No, you are not. You must see them safely home," he said.

"And what will you do there, then? Get murthered by the Blackfeet?"

197

"There are worse things in life than death, Clark," he said, looking askance. "I think I may say that now. Madness, for one."

"Lewis, we are almost home. You must take heart now, if ever in your life!" Clark smacked the stump with his hand and was quite suddenly empurpled, face blooding up.

"I'll try," he said. "Though from every thicket, copse, and tree, animals thrust their heads at me. White buffalo and horned sheep, doves, wood-peckers, cranes, and more with no name at all! And yet I'll try."

"You should ask Janey for their names," Clark said. "That girl knows a name for all things under the sun."

"No, I will not, Clark. I shall not e'en approach near her," he said. And Clark frowned, but never asked to know why.

Up early in the morning, he went for a stroll. Composing his thoughts. Alone at camp's edge, trying not to think, he saw a fox killed by the hunters lying still in the grass. He stepped closer to her, a vixen, with her genitals so placed she must lie on her back to conjoin, like a woman. And for several moments, froze above the curl of her dainty lip, the ar-ticulated poignance of an extended paw. He expected her release from enchantment as she lay concealed in the grass curled nose to tail, and dead, tho soft and warm through all her limbs. All about was bright day and not a breath of wind. The madness was very close and waiting. Curi-ous, nameless, ready to seize him should he stand too still or move away too hasty. It took infinite effort to make no efforts at all. He was nearly caught by the deathless eye. But at last made away. Mad, it would seize him. Mad, he would bolt. But sane, he escaped and ran straight into Clark.

"O, Lewis, you are shaking," he said.

"You may not touch me," Lewis said. "I am all right, but not to be touched. And must be on my way at daybreak."

"But how? How will you manage in your . . . state?" Clark asked.

"'ll do what the mad always do, Clark. No matter what depths it reaches, 'll be deepest still."

"But that is so dreadful," Clark said. "What's to be done?"

"Go by the Yellowstone River, just as we planned," he said. "I'll meet you some morning. And take that man with you."

"The husband? Yes. But—"

"O, and do not worry about me," Lewis said, watching a host of mosquitoes swarm from the grass to drink his blood, which they'd do as soon as the terrible sun rose. Now they alighted on him thickly and he welcomed each sting.

"How do I manage that?" Clark laughed, so unhappily.

"You must try. Even the deepest abysses have ledges to catch on," he said.

The mosquitoes that night were so thick, one could not speak a word, or draw a breath. One ate and drank them. He looked about himself and saw his expedition had grown horns and cloven hooves, had turned poxy and ripe, smeared with dirt, ash, and grease and was torn and swollen. They had been turned back, after all. He was leaving her before her deeps were truly sounded, while her mystery was still mysterious.

All that night, the buffalo kept up a constant, tremendous roaring. "A finer mockery of male anguish I have never heard," he said to Clark, in the dark of the tent.

"What?" Clark said, nearly asleep.

"Nothing. The fellow wants his lady," Lewis said. "Wolves are about and he needs her charms for distraction."

except a wife,
with whom it
is equal

17.

"...except a wife, with whom it is equal..."

After class on Thursday, Bill saw the message from Pablo in his box, and his heart sank. Then he was surprised at his reaction, then angry, because this was always the way it went, always and always.

But it turned out Pablo was only calling with a change: a third guy would join them, somebody named Derek. Bill didn't like it. He could hold his own with one guy. But adding another, and at the last minute, that sounded like trouble. He wished he still had the good sense to cancel, or not show at all.

Leaving school late due to detentions, kids he'd had to chastise, he killed time just driving around town. Finally he made the turn that led to the highway, and then out to the minor-league park. New but not fancy, it was a period re-creation of a small, old, farm-team stadium. It seemed these strange rendezvous kept repeating in his life. He kept going to his own doom, lamb to the slaughter. He kept getting knocked down and not staying down, like in a fistfight where people are shrieking at you, *Get up,*

Bill! Jesus, get up! And you did, until it got very bad, until at last it was just boring, and people were saying, *All right, Jesus, stay down, Bill. Don't show your agony. Stop crying, for Christ's sake.*

Yes, America could forgive you many things, but not a failure to entertain. Fall, yes, die, sure, but keep it interesting.

He met Pablo and Derek at the "will call" window. They were wearing their ball caps and baseball jackets, waiting flat-footed in tennis shoes and jeans. Pablo was his same self, heretic-skinny and tan, with that starved wild look, and Derek was heavy, a jowly face, vigilant, with ready, trouble-making eyes. They held programs already. Derek kept a folded mitt under his arm. "So you're a Lincoln Cavalier?" Derek said. "You look familiar."

"Sure. I went to Lincoln."

"Derek didn't go to Lincoln," Pablo said. "But maybe you guys met someplace else."

"Yeah, maybe you kicked my ass in junior high," Bill said. "Just about everybody did."

Soon they'd found their way inside, to seats, with Pablo in the middle, and Bill to his right. Now Bill sat looking out on a familiar landscape, of doubt and suffering and pain. It was plain dirt and grass, a diamond of chalk, making him think of masonic ritual and torture. The sacrifice fly. He'd gone out for all the teams, but it never worked out: he'd been run over at first, flattened at second, knocked ass-over-teakettle playing catcher at home. The diamond had not changed, and he hadn't forgotten its paganish feel, its Druid-like lines drawn with pulverized stone. With bleachers surrounding it on three sides and a fence marked "400" painted green, ten feet high. A couple of guys in outfits, cap brims low, with just shadows where their eyes should be, loosened up out there.

Pablo lifted his glasses up from his chest and read the program soberly and carefully, wearing a bright-pink polo. He looked at Lewis over the steel frames, grinning in his affable, cadaverous, John Brown way, the face of the bankruptcy lawyer. Derek, it turned out, had misappropriated funds, and now taught companies how to keep a lookout for guys like him.

As they waited, Bill noticed his own rising, vague impatience shading toward annoyance and disdain and restrained fury. Which was all mixed up with sympathy for the boys in the stands, all the gawky, uncoordinated, and despairing boys. Why did they go on and on building them, these monuments to shame? If the terrorists wanted targets so badly, then why not this?

It was early and warm, late-summer evening, with the cicadas keeping up a throbbing in the nearby trees. The lights, up on poles, all kicked on with an audible chunk. The metal roof hung up overhead somehow, thank God, with lightweight cables, crisscrossing braces. The netting which protected the crowd from foul-backs suddenly ended right where he was sitting. He'd have to watch it, then, and look alive out there. Soon they had cold beers, $5 each, and spicy Polish sausage rolls, $4 each. The moths and flies were out in numbers, dive-bombing the banks of lights.

As for Pablo and Derek, they were in a sidebar, something private. So he ate the sausage roll and drank the beer while the game got under way. He lived in America, where blatant evils like genocide, apartheid, and secret government experiments were mostly declassified now, out in the open. Mostly. But evil itself, wrong, had simply gone down lower, under the radar, underground. Shape-shifted, transformed, it was now hiding in plain sight. If you were lucky—untouched, undamaged, uncrippled by its effects—you never knew it was there.

Bill was thinking back now to the baseball strike, the day they'd shown all those stadiums on the 6 o'clock news, sitting empty and dark. And how jubilant he'd been. How he'd wanted to go out and dance in the streets. How he'd whistled all day, his spirits buoyant as hell. It had ended, of course, but some fans—they said—never went back. And if even one stayed away, even one, it meant there was hope.

Checking the scoreboard, Bill noticed a kid from Brazil was pitching, a kid with a Latin first name and a German last name. Pablo and Derek stopped talking for each wind-up and delivery, then picked it up again, keeping their sidebar just below his hearing. Though he could not care less. He was already at a baseball game, so nothing worse could happen.

"Anything wrong, Bill?" Pablo asked, sipping his beer.

"Not at all. I've just noticed that our pitcher is a Nazi," he said. "See? Latino with a German last name. Here before us, we have a grandchild of Nazis, whose SS grandpa fled to Brazil after the war."

Derek looked at him with high, earnest eyebrows, glasses on top of his bald head, like maybe he thought he was Swifty Lazar or something. "Is he kidding?" Derek asked, nudging Pablo.

"No, Bill never kids," Pablo said, and grinned at him uneasily. "That's one of the great things about Bill."

"Sorry," Bill said. "But I just can't help thinking. I mean, what about the Jews in the stadium tonight? What would *you* think if you saw a Brazilian pitcher with a German last name?"

"Bill's one hell of a good historian," Pablo said, glancing at Derek. Derek shrugged as if to say, *Hey, a bitter, morbid, hateful intellectual. So what else is new?*

"I don't mean to get us off on a moral discussion," Bill said. "At least with this league you don't have the salaries and the doping, the gang rapes, the speedballing."

Meanwhile, the boy from Brazil walked the next three batters. When he gave up a home run, he was gone by the third inning. Bill decided to shut up for a while, and bought the second round of beers. He took part in the wave when it came around, to show he wasn't a complete prick or truly bad sport. Which made him angry all over again, having to prove it.

"I've been thinking of your book," Pablo said in the middle of the fourth. They were down by three runs and already onto their third pitcher. "You've got a tough nut to crack there. Heroes don't kill themselves. Heroes get the girl."

Derek, listening in, nodded sagely. So they'd apparently talked about him beforehand and reached consensus about his book.

"Well, Jesus didn't get the girl," Bill said. "Hamlet didn't get the girl."

"Isn't there mounting evidence that Jesus *did* get the girl?" Derek said. "Or do I have my history wrong there?"

Just then, a foul tip came back. It came right for Bill, then clipped a skinny cable and soared into center when it should have hit right between his eyes.

Bill watched it dribble to a halt in the grass, like he'd just witnessed the thwarting of divine justice. This could be good for him, Emily had said. He didn't see how. Women either knew something extra, had a special knowledge or insight, or did not. And if not, then he'd wasted a lifetime believing something untrue.

So what should he do? What should you do when what you think is true abandons you? He really wondered. In *La Divina Commedia,* in the dark wood, when he faced the three beasts, Dante's Beatrice let him down. It turned out she was just a dead shade herself. That was when God sent him a messenger, a Virgil. Bill looked around but saw only Derek.

"I dunno how I feel about old Lewis and Clark," Derek suddenly said. He glanced at Pablo, as if they'd debated whether he should say this (with Pablo advising against). "I mean, they were just glorified errand boys, weren't they?"

"No, they *wished* they were errand boys," Bill said. "It was far worse. They were *patsies.* They were just stooges for the Enlightenment, which never even happened."

That brought a pained silence. "But they're your subject, Bill," Pablo said with a cautionary glance, a nod of encouragement that said, *Get up, Bill! Jesus, get up!*

"Like I have a goddamn clue what my subject is!" Bill laughed. "If you want the truth, I'm probably writing about this." And he nodded out at the diamond, with a slight chin-lift to include what lay beyond, which was all of it, America.

"Baseball?" Pablo laughed.

Bill shook his head. No, no, not baseball. Or yes—baseball. Because for every kid who was helped by it, two more were crushed by it, and lost their faith over it and felt lower than batshit because of it. It was a scourge on the culture, and he'd personally rather hand a kid a pistol, a crack pipe, than a baseball glove.

"No, I hate baseball," he said. With a distinct feeling of being watched.

He turned and saw that the woman behind and above Pablo had over-heard and was looking down on him like at a bog-smear on a slide.

"Bill, what the hell?" Pablo asked. "Why didn't you say so, if that's how you feel?" Beside him, Derek hunted diligently through his popcorn, shaking the box, shaking his head.

"Look, I said I wanted to come, and I wanted to," he said. Distracted by the little girl walking down the stairs past him, carrying a funnel cake balanced on a paper plate like a huge gold wedding ring on a little silk pillow.

"But I feel like I forced you."

"No, Pablo, you didn't," he said. "I'm having a good time." And he was, for some reason, or as good as he ever did. Despite the fact that sport should be wiped from the earth. And with it, all games based on physical prowess. Because every last one made excuses for the strong to go on and on victimizing the weak.

"I just didn't know, Bill," Pablo said.

Derek, tipping his head back, was shaking popcorn into his mouth.

"I don't expect you or anyone to cater to me," Bill said.

"Nevertheless," Pablo said, "no more baseball for Bill."

As Pablo turned away, he felt himself slipping. A silence, filled with a smell of roasted peanuts and cotton candy, and the sounds of the crowd, enveloped and engulfed him, and he couldn't drink anymore from his half-empty cup. He was shaking all over and afraid of losing it there, that he wouldn't keep control, no, not at all, this time. He hadn't even meant to say most of it (but would be damned if he'd take it back!).

He noted some new stats flashing for the batter coming up. And what caught his attention was the poor guy's average, which was low-low, 180, and only 19 runs batted in, and no home runs. Now, here was a schmuck who wasn't going anywhere, whose big-league dreams were taking him straight back to the Sears Automotive Center. Who, after a couple of pitches, caught just a little piece of a slider and sent a high bouncer straight to the shortstop, and got thrown out cold with twenty feet to spare, his dream dead before he'd even limped back to the dugout.

The organist then played a few sprightly chords, an elegy to a soul jerking at the end of its rope. Lewis glanced around at people talking to each other, or heading off to the concession, or draining a beer. They hadn't even seen it. The only real event of the evening, an exit from the human stage, and they'd missed the whole thing.

"So where's it at with the book?" Pablo asked, eyes on the field. Derek slightly bending an ear to hear his answer. Yeah, this ought to be good.

"I've come to the place where Jefferson, Frankenstein, and Mary Shelley are in it," he said.

"I'm not sure I follow," Pablo said. "Now Frankenstein's in it?"

"Long story," Bill said. "But Lewis knew the daughter of the traitor Aaron Burr, and Burr used to visit Mary's folks when he was in London and talk them up about the virtues of democracy while secretly plotting the overthrow of his own government."

"But isn't *Frankenstein* fiction?" Derek said.

"Well, yes," Bill said.

"Then you've lost me," Pablo said.

"I think they're the same, Jefferson and Frankenstein," Bill said. "Both are these so-called enlightened types. But, in the long run, they're guilty of overreaching, and hubris, and maybe much worse."

"That would make us the monster, then, wouldn't it?" Derek said. "You're saying America is the monster and Jefferson brought us to life?"

The woman in the row behind suddenly dropped her beer, which hit the ground, warm contents exploding over the back of Pablo's seat and head. Then she was hurrying away up the row, with her husband looking after her in surprise.

The stale, warm beer landed on Pablo and ran down the front of his beautiful silk baseball jacket, like something unspeakable. Anyone could see, just by Derek's face, that the wrong person just got wet. So that made two times that divine justice had missed Bill that night. "Hey, I'm real sorry about that," the husband said, and maybe he was. But Bill no longer knew what was what.

"I have to go," he said, getting up with two innings left.

"Yeah, let's go," Pablo said. "They're down too far. It's too late."

Bill's shaky legs would just barely carry him. They threaded their way back the way they'd come in, through arched corridors and iron turn-stiles and along curving walkways of stone. At the end, Pablo shook his hand, as did Derek. But Derek did it in a special way, like saying good-bye to a doomed man. Later he could say, *Hey, I even shook the guy's hand. It was that very night.*

"So maybe golf next time," Pablo said to him.

"Yeah, just give me a call. Anytime," Lewis said, smiling, sweating, his palms clammy, his pulse thready. And wondered why in God's name he'd said it, since there was nothing he despised more than golf unless it was baseball. He doubted he'd make it to his car, done in as he felt.

"Hey, Bill, I'm just curious. Will there be anything funny in the book? Did the captains ever have a laugh?" Pablo asked.

"Oh, there's loads of funny stuff," he said. "Lewis gives out laxatives for everything. If you come to Lewis with a spear in your chest, first he bleeds you and then he gives you a laxative."

So he'd leave Pablo laughing, at least. And as Pablo was turning to share the joke with Derek ("Hey, did you hear what Bill just said? He just said . . ."), Bill bolted toward his car.

The attendant met him halfway across the lot, a sweet-looking, dark-haired girl dressed all in black, which meant she represented the angel of death. She showed him to his row and punched his ticket and waved as he drove away.

As he pulled out, he saw a dark sort of pounding in the edges of his sight. He needed another CAT scan; something was wrong. He felt so strange, like he'd been diverted into a sidestream, some eddying, endless cycle of déjà vu. And now his bad feeling about the night, projected outward, had become the bad night itself. He remembered a time, long ago, when some older kids got hold of him and a friend of his and beat the piss out of them for fun, something to do. So that, too, was America or maybe just boyhood, people always needing to knock the crap out of you, and trap you alone where you couldn't cry for help. Why? Because of a meanness and a cruelty, crawling at the bottom of America or the human soul. It was buried deep, and nobody wanted to look at it. Oedipus hadn't wanted to, either, and had to gouge out his eyes. Lot's wife *did* want to look, but then couldn't handle what she saw.

Anyway, so long to Pablo. Pablo, adios! And Bill did wish, as he aimed the car, that he could just die now, or sometime soon. Because if he did, maybe he'd be reborn as something whole and not so damaged and banged up.

With shaky hands and rubbery legs, thinking nothing good could come from driving in this shape, he kept going. Might as well. Because even if you didn't feel that good, even if you seemed to be dying, in fact, duty required that you go on and on. Keep showing up, bring home the bacon, hang up your coat. Be ready with a joke.

In his last weeks of life, as Bill well knew, Lewis headed for Washington, leaving from St. Louis for a showdown with the War Department over his rejected drafts. But he must not've known what he'd do when he got there, because he never did.

Something happened on that far Pacific shore. He got into an altercation with her, over some dumb little trip to the beach. She demanded to look at the ocean and the gigantic fish. It was the only recorded instance of her anger.

Later, at a ceremony in which young men offered their naked wives to the older men, the ladies stretched out on buffalo robes in a field and served as "the reward of impudence." Had Janey ever partaken in such sexual adventures? Lewis didn't say.

Often they couldn't write or sleep, eat or breathe for the mosquitoes. More than once, the mere sight of the party sent whole villages into panics, wringing their hands and banging their heads on the ground.

The rules changed on the road home. Now, when they were hungry, they used deception and terror to make people give them food. At night, by the fire, one of the French *engagés* danced on his head. The tribes asked to hear a white song, so the party sang two that all knew by heart, which greatly affected the listeners. Twice they saw the cuckoo bird.

Then, very strangely, Lewis divided the party into five small groups, giving each a different course home. This after he'd noted, and repeatedly, that the one thing keeping them safe from a massacre was their large number.

In a way, it was Tom's fault. He'd insisted on knowing if any river flowed into the Missouri from north of 50 degrees latitude, giving the U.S. claim to part of Canada.

It was Blackfoot territory, which Lewis entered almost alone, knowing that a trespass there would probably mean a fight. Nor was he surprised when it happened.

Also, very curiously, when Bill compared this part of the account to Dante's and Virgil's narrow escape from the centaurs in the seventh ring of *The Inferno*, they were the same in many particulars.

Bill sifted the scenes as he drove, running events forward, then back, changing the order, trying to calm down. He was headed in the general direction of home. Something said he wouldn't get there. As he took the woodsy curves, the clouds pointed in straight lines west above the railroad tracks and the fields, above the loneliness and solemnity of the scene. Maybe a hobo in the Depression had looked on this same vista, and wondered why he had no place, no wife, no house, no work. With nothing but his shame and heartbreak to keep him company, that guy had just kept going, toward the sound of a train's whistle.

Bill had done it again, and knew it. He'd thought he could do what he clearly couldn't, write a book. "Stupid! You're stupid!" he said.

The car never veered but simply hugged and then jumped the curb. Little trees, saplings, began to slap the bumper and hood and mirrors. The brake under his heel just gave, a marshmallow. "I'm checking out!" he yelled—or perhaps only thought he had. As he plowed all the way in, the trees were eating up the car, chewing it like teeth.

Then there was just darkness. And ticking of bits of dirt as it trickled down off the embankment onto the hood.

On hands and knees, someone, maybe him, was then scrabbling up a wet, weedy hill, with tiny trees springing up from under and hitting them, or him, in the face. Bill fended off the blows as best he could. Over his shoulder, down the hill, some sort of wreck was shimmering through the close-set trunks.

The moon was up, too, when he made the top of the hill, over this scene. In his grasp, clutched tight like love letters, was a sheaf of pages, rolled, dirty, wet, but still in his hand. So at least he'd saved something. Up here, where he'd crash-landed, were fences of diamond-wire, or milled lumber. The parcels of land were cuneiform or oblong, hacked apart by a madman or blind man in the unmistakable manner of people, then stitched back together with rusty wire. Some of the houses were just shanties. But one was familiar and he clambered over its lattice fencing and up the steep backyard. As he rounded its corner, a young woman, strikingly blond, a baby in her arms, gaped at him from the front step. "Mr. Lewis!" she said. "What the hell? Where did you come from?"

"Down there." He pointed.

"Oh, my God! Is that your car? Did you have a wreck? I thought I heard something."

"I'm a mess. My clothes," he said.

"Well, Jesus Christ! Come in before you fall in, you poor thing!"

He followed Joaney, across the very porch he'd shored up and re-floored, into a house he knew as if he'd built it himself. He collapsed into the wreck of her couch, into the comfort of its smelly pillows and cushions. But he wasn't there long, falling away from her almost that instant.

The next thing he knew, a quilt settled over him, and she was there. "God, I thought you were in a coma or something. What's happened to you?"

"I don't know. I mean, I don't know if I can tell you."

"And what the hell is this?" she asked, holding up the wrinkled, torn, soiled baseball program he'd been clutching during his climb up the hill. So that was what he'd so heroically saved from the accident scene.

"I was at a ball game," he said.

"And just what were *you* doing at a baseball game?"

"This guy. Invited me," he said, feeling very oddly that he'd somehow misled her and betrayed her trust. He'd presented himself as a loner, someone like her.

"What guy? I didn't think you knew any guys. I didn't think you knew anybody at all. And don't take this wrong, but I didn't think you *had* any friends," she said. She tossed down the program with a certain contempt.

"Don't worry. Those guys may be a lot of things, but they are not my friends."

"Oh, so now it's *guys,* as in more than one. So how many was it? Five? Six?"

"No, no. Just two. And one of them I didn't even know, never even saw him before. The other I met on a float trip."

"You don't even look like yourself," she said accusingly. "I didn't even recognize you at first, all banged up and looking so crazy."

He didn't know how to answer and simply shrugged.

"So did they win or lose?"

"Lose," he said.

"It's just as well," she said, her manner and her tone changing, softening. "What'd they do to you exactly? How'd you get in this condition?"

"I don't know. I'm not sure they did anything at all. I had some sort of episode and ran my mouth. I couldn't seem to shut up. We left early."

"Not early enough, if you ask me," she said. She stood before him with Jack in her arms, rocking side to side. Jack's eyes were squinched shut tight but he wasn't quite asleep and kept peeking out at the world, then clenching them.

"Listen, Bill. I called Emily," she said.

He sat upright and put a hand on the coffee table for balance. "You did? You called my . . .? What? But how did you get that number?"

"I looked it up. Isn't that what you always said? Look everything up, see the truth for myself?"

By his watch, it was almost midnight. "Uh-huh. And how'd she sound?" he asked.

"I hate to tell you, but she didn't act all that surprised. Not about hearing from me, or about you having a wreck, or anything. Like she's gotten used to crap like this."

"She has," he said. "Anything else? What'd she say exactly?"

"That she'd talk to you when you got home. And not to worry about calling. You're in big trouble, basically."

Jack now opened his eyes to see who was talking. Could it be his father, for instance? Then he kept moving his head around as if to see somebody behind Lewis, someone Bill was hiding behind him. She at last took him into his room and put him down in his crib, and Lewis could hear him demanding, in his primitive tongue, why he now had to go to sleep when he was finally wide awake?

"Now tell me, really," she said, returning and sitting down in the pillow-board chair. "What happened to you? Really?"

"Stupid, that's me. I let some guy I hardly know close to something I care about."

"Ha! Me, too!" she said. "That's how I got Jack."

He tried to get up, and couldn't. Dizzy.

"I'm going to fix you something, but then you have to go," she said. "You're in luck, because I just went to the store." So she boiled up some noodles, and fried a steak, and mixed mushrooms and cooking sherry and beef boullion with the cubed, rare beef, and created a wonderful little stroganoff, which she ladled onto the pasta. He ate two plates with bread and butter and a lettuce-and-tomato salad with balsamic vinegar. He drank two glasses of milk and two of red wine and, by that time, was starting to feel a little better.

"You're doing better with my name," he said "You called me Bill."

"I'm trying," she said.

"You can really cook, by the way," he said.

"Oh, I can do everything," she said. "I just can't keep a man. There's something terribly wrong with me."

"Not from where I sit," he said.

"No, I'm a mess. Something one of ya'all did to me along the way, or being a foster child, or something. It screwed me up. I can tell by how people act when I enter a room. Pity and fear. But for the grace of God, there goes Joaney."

"I just don't see it," he said.

"So are you feeling any better?" she asked.

"Yes, I am," he said. "On the other hand, I think something's wrong with me, too. I feel like there's no Santa Claus. And what's more, I think there never was one."

"Santa Claus was invented by Coca-Cola," she said.

"By the way, Jo, I saw your mom," he said.

She swallowed and put both hands down where he couldn't see them. "You what? How would you have done that?" she asked.

"I guess I sort of looked her up in your file. And then I kind of dropped in on her one day, after work," he said.

"Oh, my God. When the hell did I say you could do that?" she asked. "Oh, my God. What in the fuck is the matter with you?" She got up from the table and moved to the sink, regarding him from there, arms crossed.

"It turns out we know each other," he said. "Or at least we knew each other, way back in the day. It's a long story."

A last, lone June bug wobbled along the edge of her porch-door screen, in the light. Bill'd gone overboard with the fixture in that room, which took four forty-eight-inch bulbs and made her appliances and counters wincingly bright white. She turned and directed hot water onto the dinner dishes and then mixed them in the sink, with fervor, like she was making hash.

"And did you think about how I might feel?" she asked. "No, you didn't, because people never do! So now you're acting just like her, the person who gave me away to Teddy and Annette!"

Her mouth was pinched hard as she mashed the dishes in the scalding water, hands turning red-red like claws.

"I'm sorry, Jo. We talked about your Uncle Matt, mainly. I kind of knew him. We were in the Boy Scouts."

"That doesn't make this your business," she said. She stopped washing and pinched her upper lip with two fingers, studying the islands of suds.

"Jo, I'm sorry," he said.

"Oh, God! Don't be sorry," she said. "I'm so sick of men apologizing to me."

"But I am," he said.

"That's your problem, then. So what else have you done without telling me, hmm?"

"Nothing. That's all," he said.

"So here's a question for you," she said. "Maybe you won't know, but I'm curious. When Sacagawea saw *her* family again, what did she do? For instance, did she try to kill them? Did she ask them why they didn't save her from being raped and raped? And sold? And enslaved?"

He returned her gaze, careful not to look away. "So it was like that?" he asked. "Being a foster kid? Like that?"

"No, not exactly," she said. "But to a certain degree, yeah, it was." She clasped both hands in a dish towel. "And it only has to be that way a little bit to mess you up a lot."

"Lewis said she didn't show any feeling toward them at all," he said. "Nothing at all."

"No, why should she? Why show your feelings to people who won't help you?"

"There's something else, too," he said. "Her husband hits her, right in front of her family and everyone."

"I don't know about that. She was probably getting out of line," she said. "She was remembering herself as a girl, before she got messed up so bad."

Joaney put a hand back into the smoking water and pulled the plug, and he picked up a dish towel and started to dry. "Her tribe actually cooked up this plan to kill everyone in the party and steal all the guns," Bill said. "Her brother was even in on it."

"Oh, don't tell me," she said. "Let me guess. She stopped it! She saved them all." Before he could finish the first dish, she jerked the towel out of his hands and wouldn't give it back.

"Yeah, that's pretty much it," he said. "She got the truth out of her husband, and then went to the captains and told the whole thing. And Lewis confronted her brother, who said he was very sorry but his people's slow starvation was driving him insane."

"Maybe she didn't do it to be nice," Joaney said. "Maybe she identified with white people to such a degree, she didn't know what was good for her."

"If Lewis knew her motive, he doesn't say."

"Listen, Bill," she said, pointing at him, "I don't plan to see Donna, if that's what she's after. I tend to stay away from people who tend to sell me down the river."

"She gave me this," he said. And they paused there awkwardly, together, caught and exposed in the bright space of the kitchen with the blackness outside the windows, the yellow walls, and newly varnished cabinets. He held up the tiny clear bag. She almost didn't reach for it, then did.

"Was Tommy ever a good guy?" he asked. "Does he have any skills?"

"He's not bad with his tongue," she said. "That's really about it."

His head was clear, at last, but now he felt such a blankness. He wanted to stare at everything and comprehend the hidden quality under its surface. He couldn't seem to blink.

"He works at the same school your wife does," she added. "For a while, I thought we were a little project you guys were working on together. You know? Like, let's fix Joaney and Tommy."

"Did I know that? Maybe you told me and I forgot."

At last the wrecker he'd called came, with backing lights flashing. The operator affixed a cable and dragged his car backward up the slope with saplings and weeds bristling from the wheel wells and bumper like mouthfuls it had foraged from the ditch. They stood on the back deck, watching. He seemed to be hovering, viewing his accident recovery from the vantage of the afterlife.

"You still haven't told me," she said. "Who were you out with?"

"A guy named Pablo. His last name's Garcia, but he doesn't look Latino."

"Oh, I know who you mean. They always quote him in the legal pages, with his picture. Sort of a scary little fucker?"

"That's him," he said.

"What about your book?" she asked. "How's that coming?"

"I don't know." He headed down her back steps.

"What the hell's that mean?"

"It means maybe that's over now. Maybe a crash is a sign."

He waved and jumped her fence, heading down to meet the wrecker operator, with his baseball program—retrieved from her kitchen trash—

rolled into a tight baton which he beat against his thigh. Maybe Lewis, the real one, didn't want him telling this story after all. It wasn't all good news, by any means. All his life, the guy had been like a tricky firearm, liable to go off in someone's face. He'd invited the destruction of three tribes, the Teton Sioux, the Arikara, and the Great Osages. Then again, he wrote a policy that called for keeping whites out of the West. Then again, he'd self-destructed at an early age. He'd gone off in his own face.

Bill didn't want to leave, but felt he must. And yet, in going home, felt he was observing some very old custom, so gone, so ancient, so nearly dead. Like he was making himself suffer in an archaic way, rolling in barbed wire, scourging with nettles.

He got up in the cab with a kid who didn't seem to believe his story of losing control, and wouldn't even comment on the notion of trees eating a car. When the wrecker turned toward home, it was toward Emily, the new enemy of his happiness. Just as he was hers. The war between the sexes went back and back, all the way. It was a bloody trench war, with mere inches of ground traded back and forth, enormous body counts, and never any lasting peace.

Anyway, he wouldn't talk to Emily tonight. Maybe she suspected an affair, and maybe he did, too, but she'd never ask. She'd wait him out.

The quiet kid next to him made turns with one hand and talked on his radio with the other. Bill felt his thoughts drift to Pablo, and then past him, to his wife, Rita. What might she be doing that night, at that instant? Were she and Pablo happy, in love? Could she be tempted away?

Then he was treading upward, through the dark house; it creaked in all the usual places as he climbed the staircase past Henry's room. The structure was listening, interrogating silently, and wanted to know if he was true, if he would last. Henry, too, was probably awake, and wondering if his father would last, if he would go the distance. Bosco, in the basement, listened without barking, knowing his sounds.

Emily, probably not asleep either, was hearing him clumping closer and closer to his prison, his cell. He was out of breath from being quiet, but at last lay panting in his place, in the dark, and she lay motionless beside him. He tried to sleep on his own, and then began running the scenes of the book.

Lewis, with a very small party, was now on his way up the Maria's River, straight into the teeth of the Blackfeet. Before long, they'd meet a party of warriors outnumbering them two or three to one. Encamping together for the night, they'd smoke and talk, Lewis making the usual promises of new trading posts and inviting them to come and trade with him.

But this night was different. Instead of showing gratitude at the offer, their headman would say nothing. It was clear what was coming. Then they bade each other good-night and all went to sleep. Usually troubled by insomnia, Lewis slept very soundly that night, not waking 'til a warrior actually had his rifle in his grasp. A fight ensued, with one Blackfoot stabbed to death and another shot and killed.

Bill turned over. O, love! O, marriage! What was it, after all? A financial convenience. A binding contract. Meanwhile, love (nobody told you) went away. It simply departed, and left you high and dry, together and alone, separate, inside a house. It left you with nothing but a lot of furniture. Plus this boy.

All the real Lewis ever wanted was to be married, like Clark. But had he lived, had he married, he would be here one night, too, with his wife, and out of love. Shocked to discover that love somehow got used up, faded away.

Bill gradually noticed someone else awake in the house, patiently waiting to be recognized. Was it the gun? A gun never just existed, after all; a gun waited and waited to be used. Was it America herself, so deadly at night, with her child-killers, her child-rapists, out cruising her streets? She had so many unwanted, for whom killing was a reflex to pain, like a dog biting its own broken leg.

He suddenly felt himself joined with those millions, that faceless multitude of unwanted. He sought the places he might be wanted that night, in Joaney's life, in Rita's. He'd have to go against Pablo, but that was all right. Doing harm to another man was always all right. Were the situation reversed, he'd do it to you. Anyway, if you wanted fire from the gods, you didn't just ask to borrow a cup. You fucking well stole it!

Bill turned over, himself again, and knew what was still awake in the house. It was his anger, and his bitterness, and then his anger again. And he clutched it, for whatever consolation it could bring him, and fell asleep.

"...(Damn you, you have shot me! ..."

*Howling around them; As if the fates were against him; Stabbed
the Indian to the heart; Felt the wind of his bullet; "Damn you, you
have shot me!"; He offered to take his little son.*

When next he arose, just at dawn, he did not quite believe the sight
gradually revealed, of at least ten thousand buffalo, stretch'd to the horizon on every side.

Soon, they were ready to go, to make a try at the Maria's. And who
else was there to send him off but that man? He made Lewis a sign, a lift
of the chin, and a pinch of the nose, as a promise or assurance of some
sort. But Lewis did not mind, for he was not expecting to be back. His
dog, which had howled all night from the stings of insects, tried to come
to his heel but Lewis ordered him back.

Very briefly, he bade farewell to Clark. And Clark unaccountably
shook his hand, as his best attempt at expressing any feeling, from worry
to regret. "Have we been introduced?" Lewis joked. "How do you do, sir?"

But then regretted it, and saw too late by Clark's expression that he thought Lewis would not be back.

"O, goddamn it, Lewis!" Clark said, and jerked away.

That will be mine, Lewis thought. If we never meet again, and parted this way, that will be mine to carry, forever.

Just outside camp, he counted twenty-seven wolves on a single buffalo carcass. The small party marched out into a level, lush plain, like a shaved bowling green, and all that was missing from it was its army of gardeners.

The country they moved through—desolate and beautiful as Heaven (and twice as empty)—was not their object, so they could not remain. Having left canoes behind at a fork, they proceeded straight forth into the land of that vicious, lawless, and abandoned set of wretches known as the Blackfeet. All through that day, the wolves were with them as quick flashes in the trees. The undergrowth framed the faces of many strange animals.

That evening, several wolves walked right into camp—enchanted conquistadores seeking the company of other men—only to have flaming sticks thrown into their surprised, civilized faces.

In the morning, he was sitting to *parlais* with Drouillard when the chronometer suddenly stopped. Drouillard glanced about for the cause of Lewis's expression and at last spied it.

"Has it stopped?" he asked.

"Yes, Private."

"How d'ye know, sir? I never heard it," he said.

"I always hear her," Lewis said. "Nor is there a moment when I am not carefully listening for her. And though she is not ticking now, I hear her still."

"Wot makes her stop?" Drouillard asked, bending closer to peer, but not reaching down to touch.

"My desperate dependence on her," he said, "for she knows that without her I shall lose my place on the globe."

"There, Cap'n! *Voilà!* She is going again."

"So she is. She's driving me mad by stopping longer each time." They sat for more moments as she ticked off the instants of eternity.

"I hear her now, Cap'n! How peculiar that I couldna' before," he said.

"Yes, and how lucky you could not," Lewis said, tucking it in his pack. "Be careful or it might become your job, to listen for her always."

So they continued their upriver march. And the deeper their penetration of that forbidding place, the more confirmed Lewis felt that the husband was up to a dreadful thing. That fellow would use this time apart to lay and prepare his scheme, of a thing too horrible to imagine and beyond Lewis's power to discern.

The river they followed was no broad, gentle flow like that alleged to run through the Northwest Passage, but a boiling and a-twisting in a cataract, like the terrible Styx.

Drouillard, scouting ahead, was exposed and in the open. Then suddenly, out of the white aspen poles, were born a dozen Blackfeet on excellent horses. Lewis felt unsurprised. Spying the scout and then their small party, those fellows rode straight down like a landslide, dexterously leaping their horses over fallen timbers. The men were ready to bolt (Lewis felt that) but did not show it. Meantime, the cold, unmoved, and immovable one inside him did nothing, made no inward change.

Now speaking in tongues to each other and in sign to the white men, they agreed to repair together to a place to sit and palaver. Lewis produced medals—heads of the president—and tied them about their necks. He made the usual speeches, about fine trading houses soon to appear downstream. It was nearly night. The little valley had a most foreboding gloom, a chilly and hopeless anticipation. He awaited an answer, but their headman replied nothing at all.

All understood, and at the same instant, the meaning of this affront. Coming shortly was a fight to the death. A trance state overtook the party in which every man (Lewis knew) looked toward the fire and thought and felt nothing.

"We shall talk more in the morning," Lewis said, and he promptly lay down in his bedroll, to which all followed suit. A curious calm had come to him. For the first time in weeks, he was in his right mind, thinking clearly, and seeing plainly. A spell of some kind had fallen on the camp, for already several were snoring within just feet of their enemies. This same drowsiness now overtook him. What was more, he felt safe in this, and confident that not a thing would fall out 'til dawn.

Then, at three or four, he came suddenly bolt upright. His sleeping mind had work'd until the thing fell out at last, full-bloomed like a pois'nous ruby-red and glistening flower. At last! He knew the husband's plan. And O, how good and excellent and heartless it was, how likely to succeed. "O, 'tis too good, 'tis much much too perfect!" he whispered at the stars and laid his head back down. "Thank the heavens I am dead and will never live to see 't!"

The next thing he knew, it was half light, and someone prized at his rifle.

Fields, beside him, drew his knife and sat up, stabbing one fellow to the heart. He then took aim and shot another who was fleeing. Lewis, now utterly awake, leveled his rifle and fired at the same instant that a brave fired on him. And felt that hot chunk of wobbling lead, angry corkscrew, which came fleering like a swallow through his hair. Shot in the stomach, his own man lay over dead. The rest escaped.

Lewis then stood above the still forms while Drouillard burned all the abandoned weaponry, all the bows and arrows. It was a shock, not to be dead, and hard to think clearly. Fields started to take peace medals off dead necks.

"No, leave 't," Lewis said. "'Tis our calling card. And now come quickly, for we've blunder'd outside the garden and into its unprincipl'd outskirts."

They managed to catch horses, enough to escape on, and rode as by devils possessed back to the canoes. "Everything depends on our exertions at this moment!" he said. "Let us reload on the run, boys, and sell our lives dear as we can!"

They raced downstream, paddling without rest. For a time, he was nothing but a pair of lungs and arms and a tongue dry as wood, and flying at breakneck speed toward a discovery he did not wish to make, and a place he did not long to reach. And so far, no sign of a pursuit by the Blackfeet.

Before long, he heard the joyless report of a rifle ahead. While he still could, he reveled in the chance that he dream'd it, that she'd never cursed at him on that lonely shore, and the husband never witnessed 't (and God was not a fable), and he need not suspect his fellow creatures.

But when they pulled up at the headwaters of the Yellowstone, she was not about, just as he'd expected. The husband was there, however, as was Clark, and they were standing in just such an attitude, together on the bank, and had walked out together for this reunion. O, it was all so appallingly exact! He nearly fell down at how clever, at what genius it took to kill him through his friend! He was mortally weary and shut his eyes, for there was nothing on earth he wanted to see.

Clark cleared his throat to make some false, joyful utterance, but Lewis put up a hand. "No, Clark! We have no time, for we leave two dead above us and a war party not far behind!"

Thus, they all shoved off into the current and ran with it a good fifteen miles, and then at last pulled in for the night, well after dark.

Once they were settled, Clark tried very hard to come near to him. But Lewis, a moving target, was careful not to pause or be alone. Let him suffer! For he himself had been suffering ever since falling under her gaze at the Mandan town.

The husband too seemed to try to corral him into some corner or thicket, but to no avail. Only she remained aloof from him, and sat petting and prodding and poking her little son constantly, like a cat with a half-killed rat.

At last, the next morning, Clark was able to catch him unawares, and in the open. Lewis tried to break free, but Clark blocked him with his big, rude body.

"If I didn't know better, I would think you were dodging me," Clark said.

He shrugged and sighed. "Not at all," he remarked.

"O, really! Then what is the matter with you?" Clark asked.

"My familiar is tearing and ripping up the sod today, that is all. He is gnashing his teeth at the heavens," he said.

"At what? Pray tell me, Lewis."

Lewis shrugged.

"I am trying to share some excellent news, if you only will hold still," Clark said. He approached a step closer and Lewis edged away half that distance.

"All right," Lewis said, turning slightly aside, for he already knew it. "What is it?"

"It seems that I will increase our family sooner than expected," Clark said. "For our little dancing boy, Baptiste, is to come to live with us in St. Louis. His mother says so."

At the last phrase, Clark lowered his gaze, as if unable to say it straight in his friend's stolid gray face. Lewis made no sign or response.

"Lewis, I had thought—" Clark said loudly. Then, glancing about, carefully: "I had thought that you especially would be pleased at my news."

"Yes, and bully for you," Lewis said.

"Is that all you have to say?" Clark asked. "But don't you see? This way, he may grow to manhood, which he never will otherwise."

"Perhaps," he said, "tho his future is not sure. For a half-breed has twice the enemies."

"Lewis, is something in your mind? Perhaps you should say it," Clark said, squaring his frame to his friend's.

"If you really wish to know, I've been thinking of the female heart," Lewis said.

"How so?" Clark asked.

"What a veritable crypt it must be, don't you think so? Festooned with the mouldering corpses of skeletal lovers, and reeking of dead flowers," he said. "O, what a charnel house! And we its inhabitants, Clark, we its ghastly host, either sooner or late."

"O! We must be something more than that, Lewis! Please. O, help!" Clark laughed, but sadly.

"Friend, in time we are nothing but. We are a dusty corsage pressed in a forgotten album," Lewis said.

And felt mean for saying it, but would be damned if he'd be decent. Then walked away.

On the next morning, the world, to his naked eye, looked broken. Stunned into recognition of 't at last, he gaped around himself. With an ague and a shivering and oily perspiration in a wool blanket, he got up and ordered the boats loaded.

Shortly, under a cold sky, following a river that looked like the ragged, wandering course of a crow, they blundered along. The men's limping distant silhouettes ranged out ahead of him, leaving an imprint on his glaring eyeball. The boats issued out of a rocky declivity into the recently burnt hills, black and treeless, an inky landscape and a shattered plain, with smells of charcoal and pitch.

In the river, he espied a swimming buffalo. Crawling, he managed to get out ahead of it, firing on it as it scrambled out of the stream. So ruthless was that stinging bee, the bewildering world having betrayed the poor fellow again, that he could not even run but only fell over and kicked. Surprise! And that it should come on this particular morning, too.

Lewis looked on the dying animal and felt he'd arrived at the end point of wonder. There was no mystery, after all. One creature lay for another, and that was that.

19.

" ... a sertain fatality ... "

Three days earlier . . .

✤ Clark could not understand 't, why Lewis had to divide them at the Yellowstone, though it had some strong degree of purpose in 't. For one thing, he wanted to be shut of the husband. Clark did as well, but Lewis's need border'd on a strange kind of crisis.

He'd agreed, but was not happy this way, to be off alone with that man, and madonna and child. Even stranger was to be borne on that flood for a change. To go downstream and no longer ceaselessly resist the current caus'd an almost painful exhilaration. He was curiously bold inside, and even reckless with a new sensation, seriously excited, as tho things would now happen that circumstance once prevent'd. That *Lewis* had prevented. He hated to think it, but Lewis changed the tenor of a scene just by being. He made you feel the world wasn't there, and pleasure an illusion. That you were a fool for smiling. You felt you must try hard around Lewis, and must start by wiping that idiotic grin off your face.

But traveling with the husband made for a change of mood. Clark felt his own expression change to one of worldly grim humour. He was suddenly someone else now, or perhaps his actual self was at last emerging.

The husband, on the other hand, seemed a bit lost and out of sorts, as if not knowing what to do with his hands and feet.

"What's the matter, sir?" Clark asked. "Are we lost without Captain Lewis to harass and nip?" And surprised himself with his candor.

The fellow looked up with a start, then grinned, being found out. So it truly was a new expedition, then. The matter was on the table, finally, and they were out here completely on their own. What was it about Lewis, after all, that caused creatures, male and female, to form such peculiar, strong attachments, to alter their very nature in his presence?

Before long, they floated past stretches of boiling mud, sputtering hot pots filled with a rich, sulfurous reek. A hole in a rock issued a long, expectant sigh. Then out of this same bunghole fired a ringing fart of steam, a geyser of water fifty feet in the air. All about was glug-glugging of natural kettles that bubbled and stank with a fresh fragrance of hell, making him hurry past that reeking place.

The afternoon flew along, while into him crept a most insistent, aching melancholy. The journey was mostly over. The oncoming night was ushering in the end of everything. They stopped and made a camp.

"Cap-tan, we must leave you in a day or two," the husband said in the sing-song French Canadian way.

Clark nodded. The fellow was coming closer to him as he sat by the fire, as if with a subject, and Clark knew what it was. And tried, but could not rouse himself to flee, to escape, before a talk resulted. He was very tired, after all, and the world was too too simple. One could not go on and on forever, resisting. Lewis only complicated things, with an idealism that was not natural. And he thrust women up much too high. It struck Clark suddenly, with the power of revelation, that Lewis had no real insight into women. O, he had ideas of them, all right, but his notions were mostly untested. Lewis was, in fact, brittle, fragile and awkward, and determined to resist God, to pay Him back for the insult of creating him a mere man. Lewis had no use for a body and clearly hated the one he was thrust into.

"Worried about him, are ya?" the husband asked.

"If I do not see my friend, I worry," Clark said.

"The Blackfeet torture their prisoners most horrible, don'tcha know?" the fellow said. "It is luck to be killed outright."

"He has no choice in this matter," Clark said. "One does not say 'no' to kings. Or to presidents."

"My wife is very worried and afraid," the man said. "In truth she is very miserable. About the little one."

"Oh? What's the matter with Pompy?"

"Infants mostly die up here, and before five years. 'Tis a hard life for men, but hardest for women," he said, then nodded his hairy, dense, and overgrown head and licked his red lips, licked and licked them.

"Your little boy has a most ancient wisdom in his face," Clark said.

"Poor little fellow. I am going to miss him. I am going to hate to dig his little grave." Making a lively digging motion.

Then he rubbed a palsied, thick, and not cleanly hand over his scalp, with crushed black nails pointed and sharp. It reminded Clark greatly of a pig's trotter, colourless and long preserved in vinegar.

"Well? What would you have me do about it?" Clark asked, with a sudden uproar inside himself of distaste and impatience. He realized he was shaking.

The man started in comical consternation. "Why, Cap-tan! I would na' have you do anything for us. Leave us be, for we'll manage all right . . . or—"

"Or *what?*" Clark was suddenly infuriated beyond what he should be. It was Lewis's hatred of the man somehow coming into and possessing him.

"No, leave it be, Cap'n," the fellow said.

"No, I will not leave it alone," Clark said. "For you have been pursuing me all day, and for two days and two nights together, with a question. So either spit it out now or be quiet for all eternity!"

His expression changed then, at last revealing his true feelings, a ravening desire toward all life and all humanity to hasten its end.

"I don' speak lightly, Cap-tan," the fellow said hatefully. "I speak only to them with strength to do. A thing may look quite mysterious and hard. But, often and often, a thing is most simple."

Clark didn't nod. Tho, often and often, he thought the same thing.

Yet one could not say so, and especially not around Lewis, for the Enlightenment had changed that. One could not say so, even if one thought so, that the whole thing, and its Rights of Man, and its elegant logic, was a mirage. For little in the real conduct of human affairs had changed, or would ever. Those with the gold yet made the rules, and to be good was good, but a reliable gun was even better.

It was at last dusk. That hour of evening had come when it seemed the sun had gone, never to return again. Clark was so weary and very lonely, for he'd held up as long as he could. Death might be crouched 'round the next bend in the river. He hardly ever got so low, but a crow cawing in a nearby tree made him suddenly sick for life. O, what was the use in anything if, in the midst of living, one felt cut off from life itself? Life was a woman, of course, and the reason for everything. One wanted her so awfully, and to possess her so bodily. Whether one wanted to love her was a matter for debate. But to have her, in her postures, in the dark, that was the entirety of the thing.

No, tonight he'd not think like Lewis. For Lewis's great value in the world was that he did the job of pondering so many issues, leaving one free to do and act.

I will not be made into my friend! was his next thought. For this, what was happening tonight, involved Lewis not one bit. *I will not be the type who wrongly intrudes, and thrusts himself in where a wiser man won't,*

Clark thought. *And not the type who suffers at the nature of man but does nothing to improve his state on earth.* No, tonight he felt cursed by his ties to Lewis, and perversely happy they were at last apart. He'd no longer be subject to Lewis's government and its hopeless demands. Yes, tonight he'd be his own man.

"*Entre nous,*" the fellow said, "there is in fact a question."

"At last!" Clark croaked, his voice raw in his throat.

"*Oui, c'est.* And she says to ask it of you and not of him. So how am I to refuse, Cap-tan? I am only her husband, after all."

They'd come to it now, the issue coinciding exactly with the terrible moment of sunset. She'd been nearby in the woods, an insistent presence but he'd only glimps'd her. If her little boy would benefit, then all right. But it was not chiefly for her little boy that he remained, and found himself unwilling to go now, walk away. No, by all means, not only for the little boy. Thus far, he'd possessed a few women, and the more forbidden they'd been, the better.

Also, 'twas the intoxication of knowing a woman was waiting, anticipating.

She was there, close by, and she wanted him (O, yes, very, very much! For he could save her little boy!). Simply knowing she was his was quite good. It might even be enough for one like Lewis. But not for him, a flesh and blood man. Theory was fine for some things, but for nothing touching women.

Peter Cruzatte then appeared at a distance, at the very edge of the growing gloom, all decked out in his kit, eyes shadowed by his raccoon-pelt hat, leaning on his rifle in careful, erect attitude, unsmiling, waiting, as if for rituals to commence.

"There is Peter for me now," the fellow said, taking up his gun. "Good night, Cap-tan. You will see none of me before dawn. We are off to the *ambuscade.*"

The man broke from him immediately and joined Peter. And said something to Peter, in French, to which the fellow happily laughed and clapped him on the back. O, strange world! The two of them, hunting together, after Peter'd stuck a gun in his mouth to kill him.

It was the last thought left in his mind. He sat for a time, letting it get darker, curiously unable to think. Then, at some point, he was moving and toward her tent. They were the only two on earth this night, and nobody else about. He ducked his head to see into the dimness of her close abode. At first, he saw nothing. Then, slowly, the tiny white hand stretched forth in silent entreaty. Taking it, he was drawn fervently in. Before he could sit on the buffalo sleeping rug, she'd pushed him down flat with great and fierce energy. He was aware of a few things, a star among the pines, winking through a seam in the tent, and her naked legs, which he touched to know a woman's naked thighs and buttocks again. He felt the cold air as she jerked the lacings, freeing him, his member stretched up high and hot and rigid. Her white face—for it looked white in that darkness—appeared too high to be real, near the treetops. She slowly enveloped that thing in herself and holding his shoulders rocked back on her heels and made a single sound (*Angh!*), swallowing the whole of it in her. Then, very slowly, lifting, withdrew it almost fully. Then rapidly engulfed it again, so it roughly struck bottom in her. She smelled powerfully of salt, vinegar, gunpowder, and the sea. Collapsing forward on his belly now, she rested on her hands, drawing him almost out, to the tip-top endmost point, and he was stung by her short, sharp hairs. Then back in again, all the way. And again. And again. Their mouths bumped, collided, teeth against white teeth. Was she grinning? Did her black eyes seem to glitter into his with animal joy? After, he couldn't remember. She steadily drew forth his sap, in a rhythm. He felt it climb up, higher and higher. Gripped tightly in that velvet muscle, his milk pod cracked, burst, and its seed was jerked out of him like a cord with thirteen knots.

It was over, and he could not feel his heart. He was under the buffalo robe and covered, all but one watery, stinging eye that blinked at that star yet visible through the seam. He lost all sense of time, what hour of night it was, and only knew she was there, breathing beside him, and fully content, very quietly exultant. For she'd saved her little boy! Now he would surely, surely live. While Clark himself was not alive, barely working, motionless. Truly, this must be his death. It seemed he would not last the night. But slowly, sensation spread though he was buried alive under this night and this rug. He saw he'd damned himself when he answer'd the very first letter. When one signed on with Lewis, it led inevitably to this, to some awful embrace with one's own nature. Looking around him, moving one eye, he saw Pomp in his sling, wide awake, plainly returning his gaze.

He was up to the hilt in this now. They'd forced respirations from each other's lips. And empty, dry, sore, and cold, he rolled out under the side of the tent into gray twilight and dusty grass.

It occurred to him, a tad hopefully, that Lewis wouldn't come back. For he was a hero already. If dead then he passed, painlessly, into legend.

Clark found and fell into his own "rack," wet and fever'd, and didn't move until full daylight. When at last he opened one bloody eye, he saw, on a boulder across the clearing, that sphinx of a Frenchman, her husband.

He staggered out. She was not about yet. Suddenly, at a mile's distance, there came a report of Lewis's gun. Clark jumped, unaccountably panicked, and was surrounded by commotion and scrambling of hunters to fire answering volleys, like the Judgment was commencing. And how frightened the men had been, apparently, of Lewis never returning.

In a few minutes, Lewis himself appeared. He advanced up the trailhead, before his small party. The husband, gargoyle crouched on a rock, looked down on Lewis like he were being carried in on his shield, all gory. Soon, all were gathered around him, and Clark noted this peculiar difference. His going away to die, then returning, had at last won every man to his cause. One saw, by the looks on their faces, that Lewis somehow made them feel part of his perilous feat. Awkward, graceless, brittle, and remote, Lewis was, nonetheless, one of them now.

A little while later, he told Lewis about Pomp. Then Lewis came back again and grabbed his hand. "So it is true, then?" he asked.

"*Escusez-moi?*" Clark croaked, struggling not to remain in Lewis's grip. "Is what true?"

"I mean about Pompy, you fool! I cannot find her to confirm 't."

"Er, y-yes, Lewis, I told you."

Lewis held on and wouldn't let go, drawing him closer in. At the bottoms of the subterranean gray eyes was a knowing. O, yes—he knew. Of that Clark had no question, no doubt. Which was more terrible than accusation, because it meant he could not ever confess. By shaking Lewis's hand, he was forc'd to a devilish bargain: Yes, it truly happened. Yes, they'd never speak of it.

Lewis now put Clark's hand from him.

"So. You have had a good terror," Clark said.

"Clark, I tell you—I felt the wind of that bullet in my hair," Lewis said. "I am not certain it truly missed. Any instant now, I shall fall dead."

In Lewis's face was no less enthusiasm or warmth than before. And yet—and yet—wasn't there a slight difference? Wasn't the eye just a bit cool, the gaze a trifle shallow? Clark knew what he'd done then, what it meant. He'd never be certain Lewis was not changed. He'd always suspect so. They'd never be so close again, and Clark would always feel it was his fault.

Lewis turned away. O, a New World, indeed! A harder, less joyful place, in which one's eyes were opened a bit wider and one saw the rust on the bloom, the jewel-like flies clotted in the wound.

The day passed. The following morning, Lewis found himself out hunting, with Peter. They separated at a wood, taking opposite tracks, to flush the game toward one another. He was grateful to be alone, for he wanted a chance to study, in the privacy of his mind, the shuddering beauty of the husband's treachery. And found nothing more eloquent to think but, *My God! O, my God!* And to shake, and to gaze in wonder at his rifle. How did one foil such perfect villainy, after all? One thing he might do, the only thing really, was place muzzle under chin and press the trigger down with his thumb. He started to do it, to turn it. But a sudden thought rankled: What if even *that* was part of the husband's—or God's!—own scheme? A frustrated tear leaked from his eye corner.

Then, a sudden movement to his right, and he was leading a trotting elk with the sight-bead, about to press a trigger down on that life instead, when smoke and thunder erupted by him and a little volcano burst out of his hip. A wild, crazy pain made him jump in a hobbling circle, the red lava streaming down, shoe rapidly filling. Ach! At last! The magic bullet from the Maria's had traveled 'round the earth and found him. Or else it was an attack! Or else it was Peter.

"Damn you, you have shot me!" he cried. When Peter didn't answer, he hopped away at double time, calling and calling for Peter. And then, finally, at the top of his voice, cried, "Ambush!" and "Blackfeet!" and "Massacre!" Giddy, seeing stars, he found the camp and fell down on a bench. And tho he wished for anyone else, it was Clark rushing to his aid. "They have Peter," Lewis said. "You must do what you can. Save Peter!"

"Who has Peter?"

"O, the Blackfeet! Hurry or it will be too late!"

Meanwhile, he writhed and twisted under Clark's hands and his manhandling.

His trousers were ripped to expose the wound, and the crescendo of hurt made him squeeze his eyes so tight he fainted. Through the darkness, voices were saying, "Why, confound me, sir! Here's Peter. Peter! Peter! Captain, here is Peter, and he looks to be unharmed!"

He opened his eyes and indeed here was Peter, having shot him, and now looking at the ground and stepping foot to foot like a little boy needing a pish.

"Peter, you shot me!" he said.

"I didn't, sir. I shot an elk."

"You were aiming straight at me, sir. Admit it and be done!"

"I never did. I never saw you!" Peter showed signs of desperation, like an animal in a tree, going red in the face, then purple.

"You did this," Lewis insisted.

"Don't say any more," Clark commanded. So Peter fell on the ground and sat with his head in his arms.

"Clark, 'tis that bullet!" Lewis said. "Do you see? It's killed me after all."

"It passed straight through," Clark said. "You will whistle when the wind is right."

He tried to sit up, but Clark pushed him down. "No, it's all right, Clark," he said. "For here is the stroke, here the calamity. I have never felt more alive than when shot dead. The sunlight is sparkling as it rains down from Heaven."

"This is bleeding quite a lot," Clark said.

"She simply demanded her right," Lewis said. "She only asked for her right as my woman. But she was not my woman, was she, Clark?"

"Hush, be still," Clark scolded, poking near the crater. "Or do you want every ear to drink up this heady draught?"

Lewis turned his head and dark blots raced and cartwheeled in his vision, along with wars, famines, plagues, and floods. Ancient streets ran in rivers of fire.

"I cannot answer, for I am raving," he said. He twisted his eyes about to locate his gun, for the rapture was increasing and, if unable to bear it, he must find some way to cut it short. "Joy is a most awful endless feeling, like being shot upward through the clouds. I must be some new kind of Icarus, Clark. I can't walk naturally on the earth."

"Shush, Lewis. Stop or I will stop thee with my hand," Clark said.

"You'd regret that," Lewis said. "But I will be quiet, for there is so much I know. You have only to ask. Or ask my love. Ask the two now lying dead on the Maria's. Then Sergeant Floyd. Then ask the Nez Percé, all slaughtered now and gone."

"Lewis, shut up," Clark said. "Those people are where we left them. Nobody slaughters them just yet."

"Death has a thick and bitter nut-like stench," Lewis said.

"The bleeding has slowed now," Clark observed. "It is almost stopped."

Taking a maple stick and working off the bark, Clark cut it in two inch-long pieces, then thrust one in where the bullet had exited. Lewis stiffened, gagged with pain, and passed out.

A moment passed; it was the next morning, and his hope was all extinguished.

And what a supreme trick, to make him think 'twas all his doing, dividing the party, laying the groundwork for this turn. All it lacked was the husband, who'd soon come mocking. What was more, his own best friend had done the job, and done it for free.

Now, when he moved, came bright flashes of pain as of a red-hot poker in the wound. Writing especially sent spasms into the wet red canal the bullet cut through his body. He recalled the old story of a king wounded in the groin, who sought a knight to send on a holy quest, someone pure of heart, & etc.

The parallel was, if possible, too good. But what that story truly said was, when a man got wisdom, with it he got a *womb*. Some permanent wounding came, in the loins.

To get about, Lewis pulled himself and hopped, smiling ruefully at the ache in this new womb of his. It thrilled and itched at his every change of mood, 'til he longed for something to thrust in it and quell its pangs of hunger and distemper.

Clark came to him that afternoon, in the awkward, artless way that people now came and went in the post-Enlightenment world. "I have confirmed it now," he said. "Peter cannot discern a musk ox from a mountain range and has the use of one eye only." His eyes were on Lewis's dressings.

"Too late to benefit my hip," Lewis said.

"Yes. And you are bleeding again," Clark said.

"My monthly visitor," Lewis said, grinning. "Perhaps I need go to the House of Coventry."

"Is this more fever? Or plain madness?" Clark asked, tugging at the knots he'd fashioned in the dressing. When Lewis didn't answer, Clark put a finger into the blood spot, as if by accident. Or perhaps hurting him was becoming a habit.

"A bit of both," Lewis returned, whinging from the touch.

"I come with more news," Clark said. "Colter says he does not prefer to go farther down with us. He wants to go back up, in fact."

Lewis turned his head to see Colter among the men and gazed in surprise and interest, while a pain shouted through his wound. "O, is that a fact? He signed an agreement with us, but now does not prefer to honour it, eh?"

"That is it, more or less," Clark said.

"Shall we kill him? Let us kill him, Clark. Let us shoot him at dawn for a cowardly lying traitor," he said, arresting Clark's wrist. "Are you with me?"

"Do not jest, Lewis," Clark said. "Let me go."

"But what is now the matter with him?" Lewis asked. "Why is our company no longer pleasing? Does he smell a massacre on the wind? Have we become dissipated, immoral? Are we wicked in his eyes?"

Clark raised his eyes toward Lewis's, but then could not meet them. In the silence was an ugly possibility of confession. It hovered, it wobbled, and like a green infernal carrion-bird, flapped heavily away. "What do I tell him?" Clark asked.

"Tell him no," Lewis said. "Tell him nobody makes me a Judas to my own faith. The answer is no and no and no."

"Naturally. For if we were to say yes," Clark said, nodding, "others might apply, too. So I will tell him no, he cannot. Or what of this? That he must promise none go with him."

"Very well," Lewis said. "But do not let me see him. By sunrise, he must have vanished from the earth."

He said it through his teeth, biting back another jolt of anger and womb-pain. "And let me add that nobody knows their duty on this earth any longer. Here we see the start of chaos."

He went to bed and slept, and awoke in the dark, listening for what had disturbed him. And gradually heard it again, a delicate noise, forced respirations from two mouths. And leapt up as best he could and hobbled out. Then, shaking, he sat by the fire until dawn. Several passed him going to the latrine, but gave no sign he was there. For there were no secrets in a camp.

It was high time that he was out of this body, and tried to think of a way.

But no passenger could change vessels midocean. Clark was the first to come near him in the morning, with a rueful shake of the head. "Lewis, Lewis," he said.

"So you heard it, too," Lewis said.

"No, you are wrong. I heard nothing," Clark said.

"Liar. You know it was her," Lewis said. "Breaths forced from her lips despite attempts to suppress them."

"Possibly I heard—something," he said. "Call it murmur, sigh, night sound of ineffable sort."

Lewis shook his head and spat. "Bah! Only a few nights remaining and now these disgusting noises."

Clark wished to disagree, but for no reason he himself could fathom. "Perhaps she only sighed in sleep."

"Are you joking, Clark? Are we schoolboys? What I heard was woman's pleasure. What I heard was woman by man possessed!"

"What if you did?" Clark asked. "What then?"

Lewis looked into the fire. For now that he knew he'd heard it, death held no terror. If only he could suspect he hadn't heard it!

That day, they arrived back in her neighborhood, and were greeted again by the chief called the One Eye. Which meant it was time to settle accounts, and divide himself from her, depart.

Once, twice, she came near to him. She stood not six paces from him but never put her eye to his. As if to remind him what he'd lost, as if he didn't know it times a thousand.

Clark paid out $500.33 to the husband. When Lewis looked up, they were coming out of the dark tent shaking hands, conspirators. Lewis awaited the fellow's smugness. Instead, the man looked sad and anxious, thick fingers worrying buttons, with frays in his coat, a ragged cap, and a raw, unhappy, trembl'ng face.

Strange, for the fellow had won. With Lewis's own best friend thrusting the prize straight into those grubby hooks! But clearly he was sad. He sucked at his teeth and edged up to Lewis, holding the money away in one hand as if not his. They were awkwardly alone.

It suddenly dawned on Lewis that the man loved him, and never wish'd to kill him. Then, unable to have him, he'd robbed the only treasure Lewis *did* want, and made sure it went to Clark instead.

Now it was over. And the one who'd truly won was Janey, for she'd saved her little boy!

They did not shake hands. They did not say good-bye. That creature wandered off haplessly, just as he'd entered the scene, and she followed after him, without a word or glance.

Clark came out again, looking after as they departed. "That man is not much, but his son is a joy," Clark said, "and will be with us next year."

"He'll be dead next year," Lewis said.

Clark seemed to measure that statement, waited, then said, "Well, that may be. But if not, he will come east and live with us."

Lewis nodded. "Slowly, we are dispossessed of our extensive family," he said. "All that remains are letters to be written."

Clark said nothing, for he had much more to do than write. He needed to see his intended and then go ahead with his plans to be happy, have children, & etc. Lewis wished to walk away from him, but could not, and scowled deeply at the discovery that his heart was trying to overlook trespasses it should not, poor, poor heart. But what was the use in idealism? It seemed to have no part in actual living.

As for Fort Mandan, which they'd built up so industriously, it had burned—or was set ablaze—in their absence. The river was full of water spouts and whipping gales, the plain blurred by dust devils. He shuddered to recall it now: the hauling and dragging of the boats a thousand miles upriver, inch by inch. And the losses since then. Life's losses were so breathtaking and stunning, and yet not fatal. *O, why were they not fatal?*

A bird had caught his eye, flapping along ahead. It perched on a branch against a red-streaked sky. Then, as they drew near, it opened wings and glided forth 'til scarcely a speck—and alighted once more. Which it did over and over, all day long.

The river pulled them down with it, going very fast now. Far from picking the pace of their departure, they were being driven from the garden in haste. But at least Adam was allowed to keep the Queen of the Sinners by him, to sin out the days of a sinful existence on a fiery yellow plain, wracked by thirst all day, frozen stiff at night.

Along the bank, he saw a party of seven hundred Teton Sioux marching. They waved and called for him to come ashore and trade. Lewis took the helm, and stood up tall. "YOU ARE ENEMIES AND DOUBLE-SPOKEN MEN!" he shouted, then waited as Drouillard cried forth the translation. "I CONDEMN YOUR WHOLE NATION AS DEALERS IN BAD FAITH!" he yelled. Then friendly, eager expressions changed slowly to anger, hurt, and malice. Lewis seized the rudder and threw the craft sharply to starboard, into shore, and dropped over the side, hobbling up the bank with a rifle as a crutch. "YOU HAIL US IN VAIN!" he cried after them, as they fled. "YOU ARE DOUBLE-SPOKEN MEN, AND YOUR EFFORTS SHALL AVAIL YOU NOTHING!"

He clambered back aboard, with help, as they hurled their language after him.

"They change their minds," Drouillard said. "They now say white men are no use for trading but very good for killing!"

They proceeded on. By now, he hoped, she'd begun to regret her ferocity, hard-hearted creature! As for love, in the end, it left one mad—mad with longing and with grief. He'd felt the quick, sure movements of an infinitely wise spirit just once in his life, only to lose it in that country, behind him, on a shore of mud and reeds crusty with ice. Let her cast her breath upon the waters. Let her tarry there no longer, for her sullen husband awaited his supper.

The panorama of the plains was darkened here and there by cloud shadow, as the wind made currents in the grass and twenty thousand buffalo streamed up its middle. But now, when he saw something lovely, he was reminded that any soul on earth could be enlisted in one's disasters, even a best friend.

That night, they encamped on an island unseen for two years. Sitting out on the upriver end, in the middle of the night, with nothing but the coyotes cackling and laughing, one thing was certain: there would be no more women. There in the inky starry night, with crickets, he knew it. And he'd so loved women, too, and thought them all the good in life and the only proof of God.

"...Down on hands and knees..."

In the evening a dinner and ball; No all-water route; Down on hands and knees.

❧ The next day, they were again the only thing on the river. Then, from out of nowhere, a boat appeared, headed upriver. Its crew sighted some band of castaways in canoes, bearded, starved, dressed in skins, plum-faced with sunburn and windburn, red-eyed and sandblasted. All the men burst into a laughter and shouting so savage and terrible, the other party stopped poling and stooped for muskets.

"O, hullo!" shouted Lewis to the boat. "Tell me, sir, if you can. Who is now president of this country? For I must send him immediate word: *there is no Northwest Passage!*"

"Jefferson!" its captain called back after a time, and said nothing else, having no idea who it was he had found.

"Don't you know us, sir?" Lewis asked, the boats halting a dozen meters apart. "Does nobody here recollect the poor Captains, Lewis and Clark, and their Corps of Discovery?"

The man stared and then clapped a hand to his forehead. "You are overdue!" he said, "What's more, the Indians have opened the grave of your sergeant and placed one of their own in with him."

"Have they, now?" Lewis asked. "Have you any whiskey, sir? For we suffer long embarrassment concerning that item!"

And from this man, this James Airs, they got a gallon of spirit, and some linen shirts. The men got quite merry and cheerful on the whiskey ration, and were only too happy to gather up the bones of the late sergeant and rebury them.

They were truly going home. But home, that word, did not signal anything in Lewis. More than this, he could not go home, or toward anything near. For he had known much more than embarrassment, and was limping, sore, in a state of disgrace with all creation and God. He must accept a thousand congratulations, all false, and must not be ashamed, and somehow look others in the eye, and hold up his head and say, "Yes, I attacked vigorously and won a victory most pleasing to myself!"

He and Clark had fallen into a business, over the recent days, of not prying at each other with eyes or words. It was a rigid, hateful dignity of never apologizing or explaining. At bottom, it was vanity. Worse, it was poise. One must not ever be ruffled. One must never appear bothered. For it might reveal the intemperate passion of a missionary, artist, or asylum inmate. To be indifferent was ideal. Unless one lacked feeling, which was to miss the mark another way, and be monstrous.

Thus, poise was all in life, and a man rose or fell not by his uses or virtue but by being unmoved. The beauty of this discovery "increased by swallows" as Lewis downed his first drams in months. He could admit it now: how upset he'd been at seeing Floyd's grave standing open. Lord, but men were strange creatures! Like that husband, for example, who'd done everything to lock up Janey's soul and keep it from its nightly wanderings. Who'd sooner see her dead than happy.

And she! Sharing her body with his best friend just to bring him harm. O God O God! What did two people want with each other, after all?

The boats kept floating. He traveled farther and farther from her, and more of him leaked from the hole in his side, trickling into her river. His "womb" had recently closed but both ends wept a clear fluid. He woke frequently, suddenly, in the night, heart pumping in exhausted futility.

At dawn, an interpreter well known to them, one Mr. ——, came up from below, having come from Washington. With sad news that the Ricaree chief he was escorting took sick there and died.

"I am for the Ricaree villages, and there to deliver the blow," he said grimly, sitting forward on his haunches and looking in the fire.

"What happened to the old fellow?" Lewis asked. "Fever?"

Mr. —— shook his head and removed his hat, then worked it through his fingers like a rosary. "A strange thing, that," he said. "It worries me. From the first sight of that city, that immense white city, the old fellow began to shake and perspire. He took ill from that instant onward, and lasted only a few days."

"You mustn't think on 't," Lewis said. "Listen closely to me. If you are heading upriver, you can ill afford to let any matter weigh on your mind."

"I am aggravated at my own poor powers of expression," Mr. —— said. "If only you could have seen him . . ."

"Get some rest, sir," Clark said. "Start afresh in the morning with the matter far from your thoughts."

The fellow nodded but did not get up when they bade him good-night. When Lewis looked out, at just past midnight, Mr. —— was still seated, trying to uncover the hidden thing the incident was concealing from him. In the morning, the fellow forced a large share of his own provisions into their hands—whiskey, biscuits, pork, and onions—and went up in the hasty manner of one not coming back.

One by one, they encountered again those who'd watched them depart. And all these men stared in baffled surmise, as tho no room existed in the world for the existence of the long-lost corps.

That next evening, they glided past thirty-seven deer drinking at the river's edge, and not a rifle raised or a shot fired. Like soldiers after a long awful war, they regarded these former enemies 'crost a table of peace.

The direness had gone, and yet he remained gut-sick and heart-sick. Over one thousand miles lay open between her and himself. And he knew, before they'd rounded the last bend, that home was not there. In fact, he himself had gone missing, and was no longer.

And in the men's faces, he watched as confused emotion dawned. Several turned to look, to know what he'd done to them. They were divested of something, but what? They never knew, and now it was gone. In a stroke, they reached middle age.

At the sight of cows on the bank, some set up a cheering. But at the next landing, people only gawked and returned no grins or halloos.

"They look on us so strangely," George Shannon said, standing by his elbow. Lately, it was Shannon who was often there when he turned, as tho he wanted something.

"We are supposed to be starved, Private. Frozen. Buried in avalanches. Trampled in buffalo stampedes, and our throats slashed by Indians. Our bodies dashed to bits in rapids, burnt black by the sun, swept into a heap and eaten, while still kicking, by wolves and grizzlies," he said. "Frankly, one is embarrassed to disappoint them."

"They view us with a hush," Shannon said. "They are almost—Cap'n, they are almost—"

"Hateful," Lewis said. "Yes, Private, you may say it. They hate us. This merry lark of ours mocks a hard farm life of toil and effort, terror and doubt."

The villages now appeared one after the other along the bank. Or perhaps the houses and people glided by while the boats stood still. Far behind them, in her village, she was trying to tell of her adventure. "O, pshaw! No Indian woman has ever walked to the ocean. And if one ever does, it won't be you! My God, what a liar! Stop your lying and pound the meal, idiot girl."

They passed all the way back down to St. Charles, where they'd shoved off twenty-eight months before. Certain glowing figures rose up in the evening gloom. He stared and stared, and could not make heads or tails of this vision. Finally it dawned that they were actual ladies in actual white dresses. Gentlemen in evening attire, out for a stroll along the bank.

"Evening wear!" he burst out, laughing. "Coats with tails!"

"Indeed, so they are," Clark said, straining his eyes to detect the joke, smiling worriedly.

"O, please to forgive me," Lewis said. "I am not yet divested of my savage temperament."

"Never mind, for tonight is a ball in our honour," Clark said.

"Very well. I am ready to pronounce about hardships," Lewis said. "Tho' please choke me if blasphemies start to pour out."

Then he closed his eyes and awaited landing, having nothing he wished to look at. Nothing would be her.

"...that void in our hearts..."

Landing at St. Louis, September 1806; Much handshaking and back-pounding.

❀ Then, after the handshaking and back-pounding, they got rooms. Tho his door wouldn't work. Several times he was inside, only to rebound out into the hallway, then all the way down into the street. He took a walk to the tailor, but could not go in. He went around the block and tried again, his heart sweating and face beating. He walked on.

Now, was this how life would be? He'd dread his own people, and abhor towns, and be mortified at a whole way of being? And he could not go back upriver, because it was his duty not to. He was able to know this and remain unshattered for a moment at a time. He made a decision every instant not to break and run.

At the beach, unloading some two million words' worth of paper, they had to peel apart and lay out each wet page, with a rock for an anchor, and let them flutter like thousands of tiny sails. He walked up and down, asking a truce with whatever assailed him. He went to prod with a toe each sheet, each dead, dried line for any signs of life.

That night, a dinner and ball. He sat in a place of honour between Clark and a young lady, someone's eligible daughter. And wracked his brains for something to say to her. She wore yellow, with white gloves that made her cutlery slip. Perspiring, she put a hand to her forehead, then saw him see it, and took it away. She was terribly gaunt, probably consumptive, delicate and finely made. If only women were not all so miserable. If only he were not so attuned to their distress.

"The Arikara have a dance that is very like a waltz," he said at last, because she liked the dancers floating over the floor.

"Oh? Truly?" she said, glancing at him, angling her ear slightly his way. His stature as honoured guest and national hero made no great impression. She seemed impatient already.

"Yes, the young husbands dance with the wives," he said. "And then the wives remove the only garment they have, a blanket, and lie down on it, and the old men are invited to, er, lie with them, there." The anecdote was not so wrong until just past his mouth.

She gazed at or just past him. Then she was gone, with a rustle, a flutter, a jolt of the table. She exited.

They had seventeen toasts at dinner. He knew the precise number, because counting gave the frantic mind a focus. The language spoken by the toast-makers, English, seemed only distantly related to his own. At some point, he got up and said things about patriotism, and religion, and action, for he was now an authority on the latter. But whatever he'd said, it seemed they wanted it put rather better, or longer, or something else entirely. While Clark appeared jubilant, satisfied, contented, and self-assured.

Lewis got out, too, fast as he could.

Back in the room, the bed proved impossible. He wound up at last in the corner of the room, in his sleeping robe stinking of grease and soot, like an animal trapped indoors.

As often as he could in those first days, he felt of everything, all the polished floors and tables, all the spoons and knives. With eyes wide, he traced every feature of a turned chair leg, and soft-felt piano hammers, and brittle cold china cups, and sharp silver oyster forks. He could not feel enough. But as soon as his hand lifted, he'd forgot what the thing was like.

On the street, town was a loud, infernal place, full of strangely attired demons and billowing chimneys on ev'ry side. He spent a whole day writing a letter to the president, while the postmaster at Cahokia held the rider there, waiting to spur his horse at ev'ry moment. It was a lengthy missive, but could be captured in a line: *Dear Tom, We are alone on this continent, with no sign of anyone but us.*

Yet it took him days to properly say anything, as though balancing skittish birds on flimsy branches, before they startled and exploded into the sky. What exactly were the accomplishments? *Dear Tom, Thanks to us, no human can ever face west again with excited expectation. The all-water route is lost to the ages. Also, the infinite is now finite. Yr friend, Meriwether.*

O, the harm being done by this letter! And along with it went the caring of a great man, which was all one knew of God while on earth. He wrote and wrote this letter, fighting off the fugue, wiping his brow with his sleeve, swallowing back a puzzling sorrow and feeling that he must not pen its last line, that a grief would then set on him like crows on a harvest.

When he'd been a boy, they'd said manhood was the cure for this ailment. When that failed, military service was suggested. At last, a great undertaking was the thing. And now, he faced the widely offered answer to every remaining ill: marriage and children. All were pursuing it like the holy grail. In fact, at that moment, Clark was "attacking most vigorously" at the battlements of Hymen and would no doubt triumph.

Clearly, some way was needed to burn and waste a sensitive temper to hardness. If crossing a continent were not it, he must now undertake what was.

For a while, he bided his time and wrote his Indian policy. O, how little the Teton Sioux knew the fate they'd brought down on their heads, exacting that toll. They'd wonder in their graves how they'd inspired such wrath. At some point, a party must try for upriver, and return the Mandan Sioux chief, Big White, to his people. And settle the upstart Arikara, who were attempting to blockade the river.

For a time, he lived with Clark and Julia. But Julia thought the house very small and crowded, and said so in his hearing. So he stayed out 'til the wee hours, or hung fire in his office and slept on the settee. And the silence of that little room was a terror, filled by the squealing of pegs in his chair, a smell of dust and beeswax and dying flowers, the clatter of gravel under iron wheels, and the stink of frost-killed pumpkin vines.

Every now and then, in the evening, in a tavern, with a sheaf of papers under his elbow he'd not yet looked at, Clark was suddenly there. "'Tis only me, Lewis," he'd say.

"I can see who 'tis," Lewis said.

"Come home with me, sir," he said, trying to pull him by the elbow. "A comfortable bed awaits you."

"Nay, 'tis too small there," he said, drawing the elbow firmly back, so that Clark must either let go or have people say they'd scuffled in a tavern.

"Is that our book?" Clark asked, gazing at the papers under his arm. "Are you making good headway?"

"Most excellent progress," Lewis said. "Eight miles a day!"

"You are too much alone, sir," he said.

"I find everything ridiculous," Lewis said, wiping the always copious sweat from his face. "From beds to linens to chairs to locks with keys stuck into them. Have you never noticed, Clark, how obscene a lock is? With its key fitted in 't?"

"Everyone makes adjustments," Clark said. "York is so changed, I can do nothing with him."

"Truly? Have you tried beating him? Cutting off his head?" Lewis asked.

"I have tried everything," Clark said, "but that. But you, my dear Lewis, what can be done for you?"

And he leaned in closer with those pry-bars of blue, sincerely insisting.

"I fret o'er how I appear," Lewis said. "I go to dinners and toast the memory of Columbus, Cook, and Washington, and nearly add my own name to the list. I once had a pursuit on which my whole soul was embarked."

"And shall again!" Clark said.

"O, Clark. Why did we do it?" Lewis suddenly implored. "What has it accomplished, after all? Show me one soul whose lot was improved."

"That is not for us to answer," Clark said, bowing his great red mane forward, looking blindly at the table.

"Clark, the dead are talking," he said. "They demand to know: Were their deaths worth it?"

"Which dead are you referring to, Lewis? Do you mean my cousin Floyd? Tell me you don't mean those damned Blackfeet."

Lewis shook his head. He wasn't sure precisely what he meant. He'd heard recently that Tom had made him governor of the whole vast territory, an area larger than all of Europe, and awaited the catastrophic letter.

Occasionally, at the end of fruitless talks, he went home with Clark, to remain a few days. He at last embarked to go back East and see his mother, and the president. Which gave relief from the absolute famine of money besieging St. Louis, and a fraught feeling in the air. For if one could lay hold of one thousand more arpents (one felt), a little more acreage, one's fortune was made, and that of one's children's children. He'd stretched his credit all it could go and more. And still his were such tiny parcels compared to enormous lots changing hands.

"...a man of no peculiar merit ..."

Denouncing one of his own; The traveling actor; Down on hands and knees.

✿ One day, a notice appeared in the paper, of a certain Robt. Frazier, lately of the Corps of Discovery, soliciting subscribers. For he'd penned his personal accounting of a recent expedition to the Great Western Ocean, illustrated, and scientific discoveries detailed within.

Lewis was sick and left the tavern. For a whole afternoon, he did nothing, going to and fro in a daze. At last, he sat at his desk and composed a letter, denouncing the promised book as a total and utter fraud by a fellow (yes, sadly, one of his very own!) who could not possibly deliver on the promise, having no science or authority at all.

It ran in the paper.

Within days, he received a visitor in his little office foyer. And looked up from his desk to find one Private Frazier, angry, red-faced, scared, embarrassed, and dull about the eyes. In short, a man whose hopes were dashed.

"Private, come in, sit down. I think I know your purpose," Lewis said jovially, dusting a stool and placing it.

"It's just Frazier now, sir," he said, and sat, looking about unhappily, as though the answer to life's mystery might be tacked up on these walls.

They regarded each other a moment. Lewis tried to recall if the pistol in the drawer were primed as well as loaded. "Frazier, I am sorry," he said, "but no untested person is going to publish if I can help it. I know you hate and wish to kill me now. One day, you will blame ambition, not me, for this setback."

Frazier sat with legs apart, his head wagging in a peculiar manner.

"We are the world's living, Frazier," Lewis added. "Somewhere, we are emperors of a realm. But down here below, we must scrape and bow for every crust."

Frazier undid the parcel under his arm, unwrapped the pages of a healthy volume, and, setting it on his knee, looked at the fire in the grate.

"There, now, Frazier. Steady. We shall have no more ambitions, you and I," Lewis said. "Ambition makes a ruin of one nation after another!"

Leaning forward, in his new suit of plain homespun, gripping a hat, mud dried on his boots, with a scar under his eye from a fencing rapier, Frazier cleared his throat and swallowed and, hating Lewis beyond speech, waited.

Lewis opened a metal box with a japanned lid and took out money and gave it him, rising to place it in his hand. The man held it some moments, not looking down, studying the end of his literary aspirations. "Lentil soup," he then said with a dark chuckle.

"What's that?" Lewis asked.

"Esau sold his birthright for a bowl of lentil soup," Frazier said. "You must know the story, for you are educated, unlike myself."

"If you recall," Lewis said, "it was *I* who invited *you* on this adventure, Frazier. Anyway, there is another story in that book, as you know. The story of Jacob, who wrestles with an angel of the Lord. Wrestles him to a stalemate, then will not let him go without a blessing. Now you have yours. As for me, I await mine."

Frazier handed over the heavy pages. "What'll become of it?" he asked. "'Tis the only thing I ever wrote."

"Authorship is a heartache," Lewis said. "You are better off without such."

Frazier rose and then seemed not to know how to leave, like he'd placed his child in an orphanage.

"Never mind, Frazier. You will be grateful later," Lewis said, and got up.

"I look forward to your account, sir," Frazier said, a bit hopelessly. "Who knows? Perhaps one day, I may open it and find a line borried from mine, eh?"

"Indeed, sir," he said, pressing Frazier down the stairs and into the street, a firm hand on his shoulder. "With the wonders we have seen, anything is possible!"

Frazier, by his old captain's hand propelled, set off down the street with a nod and a deep-set scowl. He'd made an enemy, Lewis knew, but was relieved nonetheless.

Not halfway up the stairs, his heart dropped again. For there were many of these "diarists" among the corps, at least five he knew of, and he might need denounce and ruin them all. He picked up Frazier's book, opened the stove with his foot, and threw it in.

Then watched it burn, wondering if he was, in fact, corrupted. He was using subterfuge, and lying and concealing. And had started at a point he could not definitely recall. But the world had seemed a just place then, and now it was not. He was guided to each action in a mysterious way he could not understand.

He still felt her heart, at times, even at that distance. Just like his, it was sore-tender and rueful, and now regretted certain acts and speeches.

With no choice now, having waited too long, he must to Washington, that city in the clouds. For the president was writing to say time was passing swiftly, and lack of news about his book was being felt "most awfully."

Lewis wished to let the silence grow even more and worse. For there was gratitude for you, from the great! On top of it, he'd made Lewis governor. And as a reward, it was certainly all that Tom could do. But why, O why, had he not done less?

He set out for Charlottesville with the chief Big White, the best-looking Indian one could imagine. In a jingling, tinkling, creaking caravan, they lurched along. And in every little burg and ville, were feted with whatever poor extravagance was mustered, in a freezing church or smoky town hall, with sour cider, sorghum pies, and dry, greenish hams.

With a glass of musty brandy in hand, inevitably, an old wife in a gingham dress and bonnet, strings trailing, came for him like a pointer spaniel and fixed him to the spot with a pair of blazing blue eyes, a pointing finger, a bobbling chin. He cast about him for help, but always in vain. "You are the lead actor!" she'd say, wagging the finger scoldingly, like catching a sneak thief or other fraud.

"No, Madam, I am Captain Lewis," he said, slightly sweating, grinning. Her face then drooped and grew jowls.

"But you are the traveling actors!" she insisted. Her face got slowly gray and hard, shriveling back toward the misery of a rough, disappointed life. And now here he was, one more.

"I have been to the Great Western Ocean, Madam. I situated its longitude on maps," he said, with a half-apologetic duck of his head.

"O, have you, sir? Did you now, sir?" Now, something a bit more ominous. She seemed to grow, rather, in his sight. She was swelling up, her face taking on a brighter and deeper, warning colour.

"I am certain of it," he said. "I and my men. Five years in the planning and doing."

"And was it very dangerous for you, then?" she asked. She was coming closer. "Should I thank you, sir, for peril on my behalf, in finding out where the ocean is?"

"You—you needn't, no, Madam," he said. "For 'twas my pleasure."

"O, was it now?" she asked. "Was it indeed your pleasure?"

He said nothing, for she had backed him right against the rickety table. He was unable to retreat an inch.

"Then perhaps you know our Janus. Do you know our Janus, sir?" she asked him. "Do you?"

"I know nobody by that name," he said. "I am only passing through."

"You ought to know him, all the same," she said. "For he is only one hundred and five years old and has not stirred once from this county since the day he was born."

She fixed him with what slowly swelled up, bloomed, into a yellowish, mischievous, cruel, bitter, angry smile.

"Truly?" Lewis said. "How remarkable."

"There is none better than our Janus," she said, fluttering her fat eyes at the thought, like some stunted girl over her boyish beaux, curling grotty lashes up toward Heaven, and twisting her big farmer's hands. "For he never saw any of your tiny oceans or your little mountain ranges. And is a better man for it! *And is a better man for it!* Our Janus has lived a better life than any dirty Spaniard, better than your Columbus, dying of the syph in the tropics!"

He was positively running with sweat now. How perfectly detestable people were, and especially his own common, country people. "Madam, I don't know any Janus, venerable as he may be. My only aim was to relieve distressed humanity," he said.

Her face froze for a moment as tho he'd kicked her. Then the mouth began to work, and the wrinkled skin to color, its dried-apple surface passing from crimson to purple-black. "What d'you know of distresses?" she cried, eyes narrowing, striking his face with her dry spit. "Why, you puling little pilcher, why you mincing little gent . . . you, you chickenshit little bastard!"

He bolted, almost running out. And along with him went the final image: the apoplectic, spitting, swollen, monstrous hag, coming into and possessing that mild old dame. And could not erase her from his mind. Helpless to resist, her image coming back again and again.

It seemed such madness was in the world now, and such hate. Even in the old women, in the hunched-up farm wives who shouted forth shrill hymns about Jesus on Sunday, then went home and baked acerbic, mea-ger pies. May-be there truly was no need to look farther or see more.

He gave speeches, in every hall and in every town. And what he saw in the audience were stunned and despairing eyes of those who searched but could not find, in his face or his words, some comfort they starvingly sought.

At last, he came in sight of the fabled city, white and pillared, in greenery, with gentle hills, basins, and vales. Pale sunshine lit the stone-work, the chisel marks, and the checkerboards of farmland with clouds steaming above like ships. Here was the city where all spoke backward, in rhymes, and took their meals in blood from newborn babes. For the whitest places hid the darkest secrets.

The caravan halted after dark, at the president's house, with torches smoking and shadows trembling up its steep face. Servants in livery scut-tled here and there. The president met them, very informally attired. The strings of his vest actually hung down untied! His shirtfront exposed, his hair gathered in a samurai topknot on his head. Lewis stammered non-sense to the changed man before him, for Tom now had a hatchet face, with cadaverous smile. He let his hand be punished in Tom's larger grasp. Clearly, years of this office whetted a man to a most fearsome edge. Meanwhile, Lewis himself, he knew, was scorched, starved, frozen, and burnt by the trail.

But if Tom found his old secretary changed for the worse, he never showed it. Though Lewis had the awful dull sense that his old employer did not actually see him, that the eyes never locked, coupled, with his.

Inside, in the dining hall, they sat to a tedious dinner persisting for three hours on course after course of strange-smelling dishes, jellied meats, raw shellfish, and vegetables frozen in aspic. He was not seated by the president, having to make do with Tom's piercing looks and sharp smiles.

Now that he was there—at long last!—he wished desp'rately to be gone again. What a fool, O, what a fool! To think life was ever something different, something one wanted, lovely or profound.

He was taken by the sleeve into the study. And then made to wait alone a long time, with Clark's sooty, spotted map in his hand. Until Tom suddenly popped at him from out of the wall, from a hidden door papered over and trimmed like a riddle.

The tall man with the stuck-out belly and skinny legs came to the middle of the room and stood as if to address Congress.

"A year ago, to the day, I toasted you with French wines," Tom said.

"And I you. With water so cold it cracked my teeth and meat so green it fizzed on the tongue," Lewis said.

"I have here your letter," Tom said, "about your many discoveries and . . . and successes." He removed and unfurled a document from his pocket and gave it a shake, as one would a little animal killed for an experiment.

"O, it wasn't all success!" Lewis said, and heard his own anger. He felt badly used. He'd been sent forth to prove fairy tales, he suddenly saw. But why him? And why had the thing once burning for him in Tom's eye now gone out?

"Come, let us have the map!" Tom said, rubbing his hands together.

Lewis could not care less about the map, unfolding and kneeling next to 't on the carpet, and crawling about it on hands and knees like a schoolboy, with Tom, a U.S. president, down beside him. Tom exclaimed in his great rapture, but Lewis heard only two male voices, two hollow, false voices, ringing out rudely one after the other, echoing. Over a worn, spotty relic, stinking of the trail. He made a desperate study of the rug itself. The president spoke. "*Pardonnez-moi?*" Lewis said.

"I said we were sorry to hear of the sergeant's demise," he said. "Did he linger much?"

"No, not at all," Lewis said. "He made a very regular military death. No fuss or bother."

What hurt most was how Tom's interest had erased the distance be-tween them, once, long ago. And how badly Lewis needed that, more than ever.

"Every nation made designs to cut you off," the president said. "The Spanish dispatched a force to intercept you, but you outran them."

"We outran ourselves," Lewis said, "and met an Indian girl."

Tom almost met his eye then, but averted it. He was a god now en-snared from ev'ry direction, and could not afford a question, or an old ap-prentice. Plus, he suffer'd embarrassments in his family, over money. And other ongoing troubles: the death of the treasurer at the hand of the vice president, over the unnatural love of said V. P. for his daughter. Lewis knew her, in fact, and would see her soon.

Most troubling of all was a sudden British peace with France, demanding embargoes of both, cutting the new country off from Old Europe completely.

Tom sat back on his haunches and surveyed the expanse with a sigh. "That is it, then," he said. "That is all we have, and not a cubic yard more!"

"Not an inch," Lewis said. "Not a fraction."

"Still and all . . . it may have to do," Tom said.

Lewis said nothing to that, letting them be enfolded in that magnifying and unfurling silence. History seemed to listen. His eyes lost their focus.

*kill them all and
set fire to their
houses*

23.

"...kill them all and set fire to their houses..."

Next morning, Bill stood behind the garage, smoking bitterly, and wondering why there wasn't real beauty in life. Like Joaney, who was just there for Tommy, waiting for him to come claim her anytime he wanted. Instead, what did that big jerk do? He clobbered her, he departed.

Emily had gone in early, before he was even out of the shower. She didn't want to know, apparently, about his adventures the night before. He and Henry ate breakfast, with Henry eating about half of an egg, maybe three-quarters of a strip of bacon. Then Bill sat on the sunporch with the door open, though it was cold weather suddenly, and smoked four more cigarettes fast and unreflectively, not savoring. It was double his ration, but he was trying to feel less dead. At last his heart rapidly bumped and knocked in his ribs, arrhythmia from the rapid infusion of nicotine.

As for Rita, Pablo's wife, who was on his mind more and more, she was a counselor for young couples, using her law degree to provide divorce intervention, keeping it out of the courts. He might have to look her up in the phone book. He might need to drop in on her, out of the blue.

He went to school, and taught "Rip Van Winkle" three times before the nineteen-minute lunch break. Then, after smoking in his beat-up car instead of eating, he called Emily.

"Yes, what?" she asked.

Nowadays, you always knew who was calling, so there was no "hello."

He'd expected the tone of voice, though, and it even meant something to him that her kindness never did. In fact, when she was nice, he found himself tempted to reverse it and stir things up. He suddenly noticed how the phone had a single tiny pinhole where his voice went in.

"Hey, how's your day?" he asked, shaking his head to clear it.

"Okay. How's the car?"

"Superficial bumps and contusions. I understand Joaney called you last night and woke you up, got you all upset."

"I wasn't all upset. She said you were fine, so I went back to sleep," Emily said, through a yawn. "You sound sort of funny."

"The book has me down," he said. "The harder I stare, the less sure of it I am. I'm starting to wonder if Lewis really was scientific, truly was a rationalist, or if that's just hype. I say the Enlightenment never even happened."

"But it's in all the history books," she said.

"You see my trouble," he said.

"Bill, are we getting to why you weren't home last night?" she asked.

"But I was. Okay, I admit it was late. In my defense, I hit my head pretty hard, sweetheart."

"And what should I think about the other thing?" she asked. "The part where this young woman is telling me not to worry. 'I know he's not with you, but don't you fret, Miz Lewis: he's with me.'"

He bent his head a little lower. He was sitting in his car behind the school, having entered that zone of lovelessness the married often did. It was hard and painful, because the furniture remained but the feeling faded. And for someone like him, dependent on feeling, it was like losing both compass and map.

"I'm just trying to help Joaney out," he said. "Do you know a Tommy, by the way? There at work?"

"Mmm. There's a Tom Faryion who volunteers for us. Big shaggy-headed kid? Like a fireplug with an angel's face?"

"That's her baby-daddy. That's the one who slugged her."

"Lots of our kids do assaults," she said. "In fact, violent history is a given."

"You let people like that volunteer?" he asked.

"They need to learn a new reaction," she said. "When somebody steps up to them, they need another reflex, something other than murder."

"Yeah, don't we all," he said.

"Bill, while I have you," she said, "Henry is driving me crazy about wanting to go golfing. You haven't taken him in a long time, and he really wants to go."

"This really isn't the weather," he said.

"Just do it anyway. It might cheer him up and it'll keep me from killing him. It's him or me this week."

"You know I'll do it," he said.

He looked up, hating these conversations, and accidentally caught his own eyes in the rearview. He'd seen people on the phone, talking this way in public, sitting all alone with this exact type of look, angry, unwanted, unloved. Bitter. And now he was one of them, not different. The discovery had depth and an ache. He realized he hurt all over from the crash. *Poor guy,* he thought. And, *Poor Emily.*

Yet he hesitated to hang up, because he wouldn't truly *see* her later. She'd be masked and covered up, into her mothering role with Henry. So that old, old saying, about parting being sweet, was really true. Emily said, "Okay, I need to go. See you tonight." The words were sweet as hot pastry, because how many more times would she say that? One day, they'd be headstones on a hill, their love ancient history.

He folded the phone and sighed, thinking how much he hated golf courses. And how he'd been a disaster as a boy, everything more than his nerves could handle. Even the Boy Scouts was more adventure than he really needed, that and public school. Plus the pressure of watching enough TV every day so you knew what people were saying. And going around in a big mob of kids, which was like watching twelve TVs on thirteen channels. He'd rather face fire hoses than the human gaze. At the same time, he forced himself to go among people, rather than be alone. When he was alone, things went on in the room that he knew really weren't.

All his life, he'd had this sense that, behind overwhelming reality, something much worse was crouching. Awaiting a moment when he was alone and nobody could help him. But there was nobody to tell about it, so he hung on the periphery and avoided eye contact. He let girls make halfhearted passes at him, as they honed their skills for a real boy. By talking to them for hours, he soon knew women better than he did himself.

In college, he lost his virginity with a drunk girl after a party. And then overheard her tell her roommate about it. "Oh, ugh, you did it with Bill? Ick. I mean, he's kind of cute and everything, but yuck!"

All the same, he felt part of a couple then, and somewhat married. He followed and watched her, loving her, loving her, and not coming closer, for he was grotesque and she was essential, perfect. Other guys didn't know they were ugly, and went after the best girls, and frequently got them. But when he read Shelley in college, he related to the creature, who hated all men and was hated by them, and fiercely loved all women, but couldn't have one. And nothing on earth it wouldn't destroy to win a woman's love, including its best friend.

He'd fought to get the illness, depression, under control, all through his first brief, unfortunate marriage to ——, a woman now lost to history. And when that broke up, down he went, down and down into madness, the color sucked out of the world. Years of night sweats and panics. As much as he hated the illness, it had a perfect logic, torturing you all it could, but not quite driving you to suicide, keeping you alive for food and company. He'd learned grudging admiration for the monster, because it was absolutely hard and steely, and never showed mercy.

As for Lewis, the real one, the book now had him headed up the Maria's—and he was in a reckless mood. He'd even brought his papers with him, and big chunks of the journal. And if it came to a fight with the Blackfeet, he was prepared to die before he'd give them up. Of course, Tom had sent him knowing this about Lewis: he'd rather go too far than retreat too soon.

It meant being parted from Clark and Janey and the husband for a number of days and nights. And when they reunited, Clark was suddenly talking about adopting Pomp and raising him as his own child. And never consulted his intended, Julia, before making this huge promise.

Within a few days of Lewis's return from the Maria's, Peter Cruzatte shot him while hunting. And Lewis, still thinking of the near miss on the Maria's, cried out that the Blackfeet were attacking. Then accused Peter of doing it. Then called for all to take arms against the Blackfeet, who could not be found. When Peter reappeared, he denied shooting Lewis, then denied it again. And never did admit it or apologize.

Of the several accounts of Lewis's wounding, only Sergeant Ordway's mentioned fainting. Later came a theory that it was no accident, with Lewis "fragged" on purpose for making a bad decision, just as officers were in Vietnam.

He was in pain for many days, and writing was impossible. Colter's defection from the party—his request to not return home—happened about this same time. The captains agreed, but only on the condition that none apply to go with him.

So the party was coming apart, and still a thousand miles to go, Lewis's self-made family falling to pieces. From then on, it was nothing but good-byes until no more were left.

Now they saw swarms of brown grasshoppers destroying the plains, and multitudes of blackbirds. They met a chief again from the voyage out, who reported eight of his people killed since coming under the "protection" of their great white father in Washington. Another chief refused their peace medal, saying that white people, and all their gifts, frightened him.

A huge party of Teton Sioux again crossed their path, with Lewis shouting after them, calling them enemies and double-spoken men. A herd of thirty-seven deer slipped by without a shot fired. A sighting of cows brought shouts and cheers of joy. One by one, they met again those who'd watched their departure, who'd given them up for dead long ago.

Along the banks at St. Charles were men in evening dress and ladies in long gowns, out for a stroll. Like none of it had happened. Just as if nothing they'd done had altered the world the tiniest little bit.

Now began the worst trouble of Lewis's life. He wrote long-awaited letters, one to his mother reporting success, another to Tom with news of failure. The Northwest Passage hadn't turned up. He'd spent fifteen times his original budget. He was in dire straits, and acted like it, sinking every dime he could borrow into risky land speculations. In everything he did, he seemed to be on the run, visiting a month here, dropping in a few weeks there, never staying anyplace long, poor guy.

Bill watched the mad scramble in his mind's eye, lying in bed Saturday morning in their two-story house, his head packed under his pillow. You entered the house through an arched portico, into a rounded, domed entry. From there, it was straight up the wraparound stairs to where he lay. Or a left into the dining room and kitchen, a right into the living room.

He didn't want to give up the pillow. If it was already light out, on one of his few days off, he'd rather not know. He was keeping his eye on Lewis, in nineteenth-century St. Louis, fording mud streets, rushing to make his fevered deals, sending whatever cash he could borrow right back out the door.

It was fateful, the beginning of the end. He couldn't look away.

But then, slowly, he switched to Rita, whose very name was slender and pretty. She was becoming his new girl, and was with him invisibly through his day. Her clothes snugly hugged her, and her slacks had neat, crisp creases. She had long, narrow feet and strappy shoes and was made of lines, not too curvy, her breasts not even a handful. His bloodshot eye, naked eyeball, followed her. She was getting a cup of coffee at work, and licking her fingers because the sugar clung to them. She was putting her hair in a quick ponytail with a rubber band. She was guiding the miserable couple back to her office, no smile, just a handshake.

The invisible eyeball left her as her door swung to. Oh, it was sad, the expression on her face as she closed the door, which knew that people couldn't stay together. What did anything matter? Why was everything so heartbreaking?

Then Emily's voice flew up the stairs, and rang in the rafters. "Bill, Henry's ready to go! You're late!"

He came shambling down the stairs in a few minutes, showered, dressed in Saturday clothes, carrying his shoes.

"Listen, I invited Joaney, too," he called, as he sat tying the laces. "I hope that was all right."

Emily didn't say anything, keeping her back to him. Slender and petite before Henry, she was rounder now, her figure there but slightly vague, bottom much fuller.

"She could really use the outing," he added. He'd put in another few evenings at her house, tiling the kitchen counters in yellow and green and Pacific-island blue, using remaindered stuff or sometimes lying to her about his own out-of-pocket. Now, he needed to tear her shower down to naked studs and retile it in immaculate white.

So this thing he was doing to Tommy was acquiring sides and stories, taking on bulk and heft, and he still hadn't laid eyes on the kid. Eventually, he'd grow it so massive, Tommy wouldn't be able to undo it. Nobody would.

"What about her baby?" Emily asked. She was holding her coffee near her mouth and looking out the side window at the garden. She seemed to be studying some sort of trouble out there, wondering if it was coming in.

"Jack's coming too," he said.

"Mm," she said. "By the way, your dad called."

"Oh. Any message?"

"He just hasn't heard from you," she said.

By 10, he and Henry were standing in the pro shop at the local course. Jack in his stroller, in his porkpie hat and a pacifier, cut a Churchillian figure, as if to remind them the last "good" war was long past, almost all of its heroes dead.

It was hard to say when Bill had started hating golf courses. Probably about the time he'd started hating being a boy in America. As a kid, you were always being chased, made to feel worthless, not good enough to live. You were thrown off golf courses, cut from teams, kicked out of Boy Scouts. Eventually you grew up, but that never changed. You still got tossed out for doing too much of something or not enough, for doing it too fast or too slow, or what have you. And the golf course was the eternal, pristine emblem of that system. He couldn't drive by one without a frisson of anger.

Henry, who got nervous around most sporting venues, who chewed his nails and stayed off to one side looking glum, socks bagging around his ankles, was actually there on purpose. He was making himself take up sports, having forced a promise out of Lewis to teach him.

Meanwhile, Joaney looked good in her shorts and deep V-neck sweater and green-tinted visor. Henry was awed, and took just one look at her, then studied the sky.

"I didn't know you played," Bill said.

"Better than you," she said. "I was on the team. When I lived with Teddy and Annette."

Henry got a new expression. His mother hadn't been all that happy lately, and maybe he thought he'd seen the cause.

At the first tee, Henry led them off, taking a short backswing, knocking one right down the middle of the fairway that rolled up onto the green, then dribbled off again.

"Man, that sucks!" he cried, and thumped his club on the ground. He was a different Henry on the golf course, which was both scary and encouraging, seeing this passionate side come out.

"Easy, Hen," Bill said, and glanced around, wondering which way they'd come from, the groundskeepers and officials swooping down in their special, souped-up golf carts to kick them off. In a way, it would be welcome. But he was afraid of what he'd do, and in front of Joaney and Henry.

On a golf course, there were rules about every stinking little thing you did, and it kept Bill nervous. After each flaring shot, ricocheting off trees and yard markers, Joaney apologized for being so rusty after the baby, and Henry stalked off ahead of them. He'd chip twice and putt three times as they chopped and whacked their way along. Then race ahead to every tee, calling back at them not to take all day.

The course was a landscape of surprising violence. Now and then, a clear obscenity echoed across the terrain, over hill and over dale. When they dredged the water hazards every fall, one hundred clubs came up out of each.

Next to a green, Bill passed a guy who could've been Shannon, lost from the expedition, with his bushy beard and shaggy head and sad hang-dog face. He stood there in workshirt and pants, waiting to start the sprinklers. Separated from the party, and unable to find them, George'd apparently taken a menial job near the river, hoping that if he stayed in one place, they'd come back for him.

He smiled broadly at Joaney, showing a broken mouthful of teeth.

"Hey, darlin'," she said, like they knew each other, and walked on.

Bill stared hard at him, and the guy sort of looked, too, watching Bill from the corner of his eyes. He seemed so familiar. "Is that you, George?" he asked. "George Shannon?"

"Muh-my name's not George!" he said, whipping the hose around suddenly and stalking away.

"Do you know that guy, Dad?" Henry asked.

"I actually thought I did."

"'Cuz he seemed to know you, too."

On the next hole, the fairway flanked the Little Blue, the river that Lewis, the real Lewis, came up a short way just to get a look at the country.

Bill took out a 3-metal and walked out to the bank above the fast part of the channel. He hit a ball as far as he could downstream, and saw it make a drab little splash in the shallows on the opposite shore.

Henry stopped to watch the ball land. "What the hell was that for?" he asked.

Bill shrugged. What the hell was anything for? *Why not suicide?* was the question Camus had asked. And wasn't it sometimes the best option? Not too often, but occasionally? After all, you could only take so much, and only for so long.

As for Lewis the explorer, he'd sailed up this little river one day. Maybe he was planning it that very day. Maybe it was the furthest thing from his mind. But within five years of rounding that bend, right down there, he'd do it, in a tiny log cabin, in the middle of the night, in the heart of deepest, darkest Tennessee.

Bill and Joaney hit their next shots into the water, with Henry somehow managing to skip his across. "What a cheap crap shot!" he yelped and clubbed the ground. Joaney shrugged and laughed at her flub.

"Man, I suck at this," Henry said. But he always thought he sucked, as if he expected to be a natural at life, as if his greatness had been foretold. Bill never knew what to say. By Henry's age, he was already taking revenge on life by doing it badly, hacking and slashing, purposely not trying.

"Are we having fun yet?" Joaney asked, taking long strides that kept her ahead of him. Henry took a turn pushing the stroller with Jack.

"No, no fun," Bill said. "Did I mention I hate golf courses? They're too goddamned nice. Makes me feel like my own country is too good for me, you know? *Keep off the grass!*"

"Then what're you doing here?" Joaney asked.

"For Henry," he said. "This we do in Henry's name, amen. He likes it."

They looked toward Henry, who hit his ball, then swore, and took off after it at the hell-bent pace at which he liked to play. At least it showed determination, trying to get good at something.

Bill's next tee shot took a bad bounce, landed in a creekbed. He went down after it, while Henry stood above, glancing back now and then at Joaney and kicking his toe in the grass, worrying. And taking that usual Henry posture, working his mouth into bitter shapes, muttering to himself.

Maybe he thought he shouldn't be here with his dad and some little knock-out blond. Maybe he felt he was betraying his mother. But how could you betray your mother by just standing there minding your own goddamn business? And yet it clearly bothered him.

Bill, slipping on the mossy slabs of black slate, almost turning an ankle, hopped out of the creek, dropped a ball.

Joaney waited for him on the green, smiling, perfectly at her ease. As the only female, she was in her element. She winked. But then again, she winked at every man. What she didn't like was another woman. In class, she'd shied away from the other girls, he'd noticed, as you might from a creature you didn't comprehend.

Bill walked along, feeling like a creep, like the husband Emily couldn't manage to love right now. Meanwhile, Joaney was crazy about him. And Rita'd made eyes at him. And Henry was helpless not to love him, too.

He wondered some about his madness. Was it caused by love? Was it possible he truly loved all these women, these unattainable women, with this insane ferocity? Should he try to unwind each of his days and ways to himself? Or maybe to another shrink?

And wasn't it astounding that it was this amazingly hard just to navigate a few simple minutes of a typical morning on earth?

He wondered what his dad had wanted, calling. Since Isabelle's—his stepmother's—passing last year, Lloyd Charles called all the time, and never wanted anything in particular, just to shoot the breeze.

The strange thing about forgiveness was that sometimes Bill didn't forgive old Lloyd for their past. But sometimes he did. And he never knew, one day to the next, which Bill would answer, the forgiving or the angry one. Lloyd didn't either. Some days the past seemed long gone. But other days, he again felt fatherless and lost, his history refusing to stay where it belonged.

Then Bill looked at Henry and got a sudden flash of anger at Henry's stubborn thinness, his sensitive nature and defiant neuroses. But confronting him did no good. The kid hated food and eating, and life was just rough on people like that.

Off the next tee, Henry smashed a hot left-to-right fade that fell away into the trees. Joaney hit next, and her ball followed Henry's. Bill took his hardest swing so far, unleashing a terrible hook that dropped into the woods opposite.

He started off down the hill, away from everyone, off on his own. The trees accepted him. As he penetrated the woods, they seemed to know and take notice of him. He kicked around among their feet. He always felt watched, but had learned not to look around because nobody was ever there. The quality of silence changed and Henry's and Joaney's antic, cartoon voices dropped off. He gradually felt almost sheltered, protected in there, and didn't want to go back. It was a skinny neck of woodland that rested in an oxbow of the river. From the top of the hill, he could look down at the water and, in his mind's eye, watch doomed Lewis help to pole the boat upriver.

And doomed Lewis, from his special perspective within that tiny boat, could look up into the trees and try to figure out why he, too, always felt watched. No, he couldn't see anyone. He went back to recalling some particular "girl of the neighborhood," one he'd wanted to pin in a patch of clover but, mysteriously, never had.

It got really quiet then. Bill heard nothing, no machinery, no human voice. It was as if everything, everywhere, was suddenly gone. He broke into a cold all-over fever sweat and started walking fast, rushing hard away from a terrible feeling. Since he was a kid, there'd been moments like this. Something awful underlying the scene reached up to seize him. Throat flooding with panic, he came out of the trees at almost a run, trembling.

"Dad, what's wrong?" Henry asked.

"Not a thing, kid. I'm just fine," he said, his face covered in fat droplets of sweat. "Where's Joaney?"

Henry pointed. Then he walked off after her into the woods, at the place where she'd vanished into the trees. Jack, parked by the edge of the green, slept with little hat askew, trusting completely that his mother would come back, or that someone would, that he was safe.

Pretty soon, here they came out of the trees, walking very close together. And as they did, Henry tipped his head toward her and said something, and she looked down at her unzipped shorts and zipped them.

"That sure took a while," Bill said stupidly.

"Yeah, it did. Me and Henry are engaged now." She laughed. "As soon as he can afford a ring."

"I've got seventeen thousand dollars in the bank," Henry said.

"Darlin', I think that'll just about cover it," she said, shoving him. "You might just be the man of my dreams."

"That's for college," Bill said. Henry, for his own part, tried to be cool about it, indifferent. He stood on one foot, then the other. He wandered in a small circle.

Bill decided to treat it like a phantom, a mirage. So she'd zipped her shorts. With his very acute vision, he was always seeing stuff he wished he hadn't.

They finished the round, with Joaney totally muffing the rest of her shots. And Henry beating everyone by about thirty strokes. Jack, who'd slept as if in suspended animation, awoke halfway into the car seat and began pitching a purple fit.

"Goddamn, Jack!" she said. "If you like the outdoors, you're going to love it when we're homeless!"

"Lewis used to hunt all night," Bill said. "Barefoot in the snow, with six or seven dogs. He was only eight years old."

"Lewis, Lewis, Lewis," Joaney said, rolling her eyes.

"But wasn't he also a drunk, Dad?" Henry asked. "And a slaveowner and a junkie? And didn't he try to wipe out a bunch of Indian tribes?"

"I never said he was my hero," Bill said. "He's just a guy. He's just somebody who couldn't seem to adjust to his own time, or something."

A woman came out of the pro shop and headed down toward them. At first glance, it seemed to be his very own mother. But that simply couldn't be true.

He was blowing his life. That notion came unbidden, once again, and from wherever those cold discoveries were born. It happened whenever he thought of his folks. Whatever it was they'd dreamed for him, he was falling short.

They drove Joaney home, in his still dinged and rumpled car, with her beside him in the front seat. He felt that people in other cars, at stoplights, were looking over at them together, sort of astonished, pointing him out. Joaney put her head back on the headrest and smiled over at him, her whole white throat, her jugular with its beating pulse, exposed.

At her curb, he helped get Jack out and then watched them go up the walk together and in the door. Wanting to go in with them, maybe just to sit in there and look at all the things he'd fixed. She waved, and they pulled away. As he did, her iron-framed bed rose up in his mind, with its pink-and-black-checked quilt, and sat quietly gleaming.

He thought of the real Lewis, who never did get the girl. Unlike Clark, who cemented his engagement to Julia right away, after she'd waited three whole years for him, never knowing if he'd even come back. Lewis tried and tried, but his conquests always failed. Nor did he ever lay a finger on his sweet, sweet Janey.

As for Joaney, in that dream-bed, she was saying something to him, teasingly, while undoing his belt. "So what's hiding in here, Bill? Huh? Let's have a little look-see, shall we?" Then she was clasping him to her, like he was a crocodile that'd crawled up on her belly. She was wrapping her legs around him, saying, "Oh, yes, Bill. Oh, yes, yes."

"Call me Lewis," he whispered in her ear.

"What, Dad?" Henry asked from the seat beside him. "What'd you say?"

"Nothing, Hen," he said.

After three years, the real Lewis came back from the Pacific not knowing what to expect, what'd changed in his absence, or even whether his mother was still living. Nowadays, with penicillin and chemo, you pretty much counted on everyone to kick off in order, after about 84.2 years. So Bill'd missed out on that, that white-hot, intense kind of life and love, when you loved for all you were worth, and right now, because you might be snuffed out at any second, by a fever, a tiny scratch from a rusty nail.

As for Clark, he'd gotten just a dozen years with his sweet Julia before she was gone, dead from childbirth.

After his return, Lewis hid himself away to write the nation's first public policy on Indian affairs, which said to keep settlers out of the West, and reported how white commerce was destroying morality, forcing the tribes to steal things they needed and had no way to buy. With all the starvation and warring he'd seen on the trail, he called for relief of "those wretched peoples of America."

On the other hand, he advocated the slaughter or exile of three "outlaw" tribes. On the third hand, he recommended a half-Indian boy to West Point.

And Tom, no longer lamenting the lack of a qualified leader, now called Lewis "the fittest person in the world" for the job.

"Whatcha thinking about, Dad?"

"Nothing," he said. "That we've got to help Joaney. That I have this need to help her, right now." That was at least true. He was admitting he needed her.

"Maybe you just need another cigarette," Henry said. He shifted his skinny legs, and looked out the window, God bless him.

"Does it bother you I smoke?" Bill asked.

He shrugged but wouldn't look over. "Not that much."

"Right. Why should it bother you?" Just because his father seemed to be working on leaving the planet, and the sooner the better, like he had no desire to stick around.

Still, Bill didn't think he could just quit. Smoking was risky and intense and he looked forward to it. Some days that was all, in fact. So he was inhaling poison. The thing was, the poison wasn't intended for him. It was for something down there he was trying to smother. He made daily attacks, but it kept crawling deeper.

Some liked to insist that Lewis was murdered, Bill knew. And it wasn't that he didn't have enemies. He was against white settlement, and he knew the wrong people, like Theodosia, daughter of a traitor, like the Spanish spy General James Wilkinson. Plus, he'd been traveling the treacherous Natchez Trace that night he died, a road full of highwaymen. Plus, he owed money to everybody he knew.

But the eyewitness accounts of his several-weeks derangement were many and consistent. And the two people who never treated it as murder were his best friend, Clark, and his surrogate dad, Tom.

Still, it gave Bill pause. How could so much go so wrong all at the same time? Like God had it in for you, or something.

But it wasn't the money or the women or his job. No, whatever was wrong with Lewis was wrong from the start. He stopped writing in his journal during four long periods, once for eleven months. And never went near a bed again, curling up on the floor in the buffalo robe, from the first night of the expedition to the last night of his life.

They got home as it was starting to rain. Emily made them patty melts under the broiler for lunch, and then Henry went up to read *To Kill a Mockingbird* for class. She did some French-press coffee with sweetened condensed milk and they sat drinking it on the screen porch. Actually, he stood in the door while she listlessly swung in the small hammock with one foot brushing the floor. Though the sky was darkening and the light failing, neither made a move for the lamp. The calico rugs in the room were dirty and old. He remembered buying them in shocking detail, down to what she'd been wearing as they'd stood in J. C. Penney's.

"Bill, do you want to talk to me about anything?" she asked, not looking at him.

What he wanted was to fall down and die. Partly, it was her tone, but also it was what she was really asking. *O, how horrible is the day!* Horrible that a moment like this ever had to occur in any man's, any woman's, life! O, what did two people want with each other, anyway? What did any man deserve to ask from any woman, and what did he need to give her?

The whole trouble was how much he loved them, women. If he'd grown up among the Mandan, it would've been simple. When a boy liked women a little too well, they just dressed him as a squaw, and married him to a man. Problem solved.

"Like what?" he said at last.

"I don't know. Like how miserable you are." She pulled up the foot she'd been dangling, like drawing up the ladder to her treehouse. Then tucked up her legs and crossed her arms.

"Am I miserable?" he asked.

She laughed unhappily, and covered her eyes with her hands.

"I mean, I know I haven't been the best company lately," he said. "I know it. But what kind of a question is that? Anyway, it's this goddamn book. It's driving me crazy."

She turned her face toward his. Her hard green eyes softened just a little. "Why's it driving you crazy? What's the matter?"

"It's obvious, isn't it?" he asked. "I might not figure it out. I might never know why he did it."

"But is that really your job?" she asked. "Who says you have to give the answer?"

Just then, a sound overhead. It was Henry going into the bathroom and shutting the door, then locking it. The click of the lock was not loud, but it made her flinch, and a muscle in her cheek jumped.

Was Emily still pretty? Was she beautiful? He stared hard at her, wanting to find out. But all of the signals and readings that came back at him, as usual, were a jumble of confusion. It was getting more and more hopeless.

"In this business, you have to commit. Make your case," he said. "And once you do, you'd better have some pretty good goddamn reasons."

"So what do you have, Bill?" she asked. "What are your reasons?"

"So far, all I've got is lust."

Her eyes darted to his, then slipped to one side. Now he was talking, because lust was a subject that really interested her.

"Sounds like a good place to start," she said. "Then what?"

"Well, there's unrequited love," he said. "Possibly revenge."

She stared at him carefully, puzzling over that, then looked at her hands in her lap. "How revenge? Revenge for what?"

"Well, for instance, if you felt that someone had taken everything from you," he said, "and you were pretty sure they knew it, too, what they'd done to you, but were refusing to own up to it. Then you might do it to punish them, for both crimes at once."

Henry was running the water in the sink upstairs and it seemed he'd been running it for a long while. Just when it seemed he would shut it off, it went on some more.

"Henry, that's enough goddamn water, goddamn it!" Emily suddenly yelled at the ceiling. "Turn off the water!"

She then held her head as if it hurt to yell. From the porch, Bosco set up a frantic yelping.

"Em, are you all right?" he asked.

"Yes, I'm just losing my mind," she said. "I just never dreamed he wouldn't eat. Did you ever, in your worst nightmare, imagine that he wouldn't eat? And I thought I'd thought of everything that might happen, but not this."

They waited until Henry padded back down the hall to his room, and shut the door.

"It helps, Em," Bill said, "when we talk."

"It does? Who does it help? You? Me? Henry?"

"Actually, I was referring to myself, again," he said. "But yes, maybe Henry, too, indirectly."

"Bill, I can't do last year again," she said. "Not that and this, too."

Which meant she couldn't live through the depression Bill'd gone through the previous year, not ever again, with the weight loss and insomnia, the feebleness, so weak he could hardly sit up at the table and feed himself, eating soup by using his left hand to help his right.

"I think it's about a girl," he said.

"What's about a girl? What is?" she asked, cutting her blue eyes in at him.

"Henry," he said.

"Christ, maybe it is!" she said. "I just don't know anymore." She looked very tired all of a sudden, and sank down into the hammock, and closed her eyes. "If I fall asleep, will you please wake me in time to take Henry to baseball?"

"To what? To baseball?" He felt he'd been dreaming or in a coma, and missed a whole series of events.

"Yes, we already talked about this. I said I'd take him to sign up," she said, like it was the most ordinary thing. Bill remembered, but was in denial and still hoped it wouldn't happen. Could Henry even throw, let alone field and hit? Could he body-slam the second baseman to break up a double play? Throat-punch a catcher trying to block home plate? Fist-fight with a bean-ball pitcher in a bench-clearing brawl?

"Don't discourage him," she said warningly.

"All right, I won't," he said, and went upstairs.

He sat for a while in the little office, knowing he should call his dad back but not doing it.

About a year after the expedition, Lewis got very slow about answering Tom's letters. Then stopped replying at all. Everybody expected Lewis to edit the journals quickly, straighten each crooked line, and bring them out as a book. It made sense that he'd turn his odyssey into commerce as fast as possible, and sell it for all he could. But the book didn't come out and didn't come out, and became a mystery. And the answer was simple: he was keeping them.

In fact, even Clark had no access and hadn't a clue where they were or what was happening. It was very strange, and the answer was, Lewis was keeping them. More accurately, he was *withholding* them. Because he'd decided the world didn't deserve the book, and could never understand or appreciate what'd happened. Also, he wanted to frustrate everyone's demand that he do the right thing, get on with his life.

He was almost thirty-five. In a letter to Clark, he said he now considered himself "a perfect widower with rispect to love." As though he'd desired love at one time, but it was dead in him now. Or he'd been in love, but the lady's refusal had killed it.

He'd gotten involved again in the "Mystery School" of Freemasonry and joined a lodge. He and Clark wrote back and forth about York, who was causing Clark trouble, asking to be freed. It seemed his wife had been sold miles away, and they were living apart.

As if unable to see a man denied his wife, Lewis advised Clark to give in, to hire York out to a farm near her. Clark instead beat York and jobbed him elsewhere, saying he'd sell York at New Orleans if he caused more trouble.

Lewis found a house for himself and the Clarks in St. Louis, but was crowded out of it by Clark's relations and "took rooms" at Pierre Chouteau's. His half-brother, Reuben, now called Lewis "His Excellency" in letters to their mother. Soon Julia had her first boy, and they named him Meriwether Lewis Clark.

Bill, sitting in his office tucked up under the stairway, thought about all these matters, and really wanted to talk to Pablo's wife, Rita. He might see her again, and possibly he'd use the book as a way to do it. He might ask Pablo to read it, maybe even drop it by there himself. Though it'd sort of mean using Lewis, and Pablo, to get to her. But it felt like the obvious next step toward whatever was going to happen. It also meant Pablo might read his work. And that was okay, too, because what did old Pablo know about writing, good or bad?

Bill could dimly see what was happening. You slowly became part of the plot or scheme against you, all right, which someone else had set in motion and could not be stopped. He felt what he often did now, a futile fury, a cheated bitterness.

He drafted a note. Then he told Emily he needed to drop something off, and ducked out, heading his banged-up car toward Pablo's.

It took a little while to reach that part of town, where the houses were taller, with half-circle driveways. He found the house easier than he'd expected and parked, walked down to it, and stuffed the book into the mailbox out by the street. And then just stood there, smelling the air of those hilly lanes with little footbridges across creeks that led out to the ubiquitous tees, greens, and fairways. With nothing ugly in it if Pablo didn't care to see it.

He almost yanked the book back out of the polished brass box. For a second, he'd forgotten the plan. Was it to somehow hurt Pablo by seeing Rita again? Or was it simply to see Rita without involving Pablo? Or was it merely to bash good old, dumb old Pablo?

As for the real Lewis, it wasn't enough to withhold his own book; he'd had to shut everybody down. Of the seven diarists on the trip, only Sergeant Gass managed to slip his work past Lewis. Another one, Sergeant Floyd, was fortunately dead, so no worries there.

Still, it wasn't like Lewis *liked* being a prick. Yes, he refused to cooperate, but he always had very good, very secret reasons. He said one thing, then did another, and was contradictory and duplicitous in every way.

But it wasn't his fault, Bill knew. When a depression set down on you, crows on a harvest, that was just what you did, how you behaved. You pretended like hell that everything was great. Your perfect demeanor snowed everyone into thinking you were all right. Eccentric, yes, unpredictable, sure, but not nuts.

Meanwhile, nothing in your life seemed to be your idea. You thought about suicide the way peasants think of revolution, as a way to seize back one's country by burning it to the ground.

During the expedition, Lewis seemed to have great luck. Afterward, he had none. For one thing, after becoming governor of the territory, the brother of the guy he'd beaten out of a job once before was made his assistant. At first, they quarreled. Then, they feuded.

But it wasn't just that things went wrong for Lewis. It was that a whole *lot* of things went wrong all at the same time. And he'd just come through a very trying set of ordeals on the trail.

Also, the depressive bouts would be getting worse, each attack lasting longer, more wasting, and more dire, almost as if the more power Lewis got—being famous, and governor—the more power It got. Like he was being taken over by some separate, diabolical entity.

And whom could he turn to? Was he allowed to turn to anyone at all? The American myth of the "rugged individual" was born in the West. In fact, Lewis practically invented it.

Bill looked around Pablo's neighborhood once more, stuffed his hands in his pockets, and walked back to his car. He sat and stared at Pablo's mailbox a while, then drove home to wait.

In the den, Emily sat with her face in profile, blue from the light of the TV, eyes clouded and puffy, with an expression of annoyance or contempt, like she'd just seen a news story too terrible to be believed. He could tell she'd been crying. "I just left my book at Pablo's," he said.

"You did? *You did?* Are you sure that's a good idea? You just met him."

"I'm sure it was a horrible idea," he said. "Don't ask me why I did it."

"Your dad called again," she said. "I wish you'd just call him so I don't have to think of a story."

"I'll call him," he said.

But instead he waited, staring into space, at the problem. Things they'd been working on making happen for years were starting to fail. Or they were happening, but in the wrong order, with outcomes they hadn't foreseen. They both felt grief over it; Emily's was just more obvious. He might've cried himself, except he couldn't lately.

"I'm sorry," she said.

"What are you sorry for, Em?"

"I don't know what's wrong with me anymore. Little things set me off."

"Things will look different in the morning. That's what my mom used to say."

"I never heard her say that," she said. "By the way, you need to do the shopping for the get-together this week."

He nodded and headed upstairs. He was a bit surprised to find Henry's door open about a foot, and him clacking away on his keyboard. Lewis stopped and leaned his head in. Henry's posters were all movie stills, from sci-fi horror classics such as *The Thing, It Came from Outer Space, The Day the Earth Stood Still,* and *Forbidden Planet.*

"Who you talking to?" Lewis asked.

"Nobody. Delilah."

"Delilah? You know a girl named Delilah?" he asked.

"Yeah. She's—this girl." He sat, nose to screen, and all folded in on himself, knee up under his chin, jutting Adam's apple, lips moving as her replies snaked along under his. He was keeping one eye on her words, one on his father. A cruel god might've looked down and laughed at such intensity over a fourteen-year-old girl. God, maybe it *was* about her. Maybe Henry was showing her just how tough, how self-denying, he could be.

Bill took a long shower, standing in one he'd built from scratch, running the pipes up into the ceiling and dropping the showerhead in from above, rain-forest style. Misery—waiting for the book to be discovered in Pablo's mailbox—made him feel closer to Lewis, so he let the hot water soak his skull, and did some thinking: Where to next with this saga?

Romantically speaking, Lewis could be tied to about seven women, including (1) E. of Philadelphia, (2) a Miss C., (3) a Miss——, (4) a Miss

A— R—ch, (5) a Miss E— B—y, (6) a Letitia Baldridge, and (7) Theodosia Burr. A list that left out a certain someone.

Lewis said he considered women to be a large part of what made life "esteemable," calling them "that dear and interesting part of creation." Some of his personal ties were royal, or close to it. Theodosia's mother came from the Russian imperial court. For much of her life, Theo had expected—just any day now—to be rescued from her plain, housewifely existence and presented as empress to her subjects in Mexico City.

And Burr did try, conspiring with U.S. Army General James Wilkinson and Tennessee Governor Andrew Jackson to seize New Orleans in a military coup. But was given up by the general, Agent 13, a spy in the pay of the Spanish with too much to lose if his true identity ever got out.

Strange stuff. Like Lewis being at Burr's trial. During the long, hot days, he and Theo were both there, dining together, going out riding, like a couple.

How much of her life did Theo disclose to Lewis, and how much then got reported to Tom? Did Tom know the chief of the armed forces was a Spanish spy? Probably so. The degrees of separation were very few.

As for Theo, she worshipped her father as a god. Burr devised a special code for sending secret messages, referring to himself by the name "Savius," after the Roman emperor forced to drink poison for seducing his own son.

Lewis predicted his impending death to Theo. But why Theo? She'd have a short, hard life, with chronic bad health and multiple exotic symptoms including "womb obstruction," seeing bright flashes of light, hearing voices, and glimpsing figures passing around her bed at night. To ease her suffering, her doctors had her drink doses of steel dissolved in vitriolic acid.

Bill simply had to laugh and shake his dripping head as he shut off the water and toweled off. Because how great it must've been to be mentally ill back then. What better time to suffer a clinical depression than the nineteenth century?

Then he shook his daily pill out into his hand and swallowed it, dry.

The next day, Rita called him.

He'd just gotten home, slightly after Henry, the kid's bag sitting on the couch.

"Henry?" he'd called. Nothing. "Hey, Henry!" Silence.

Right away he got that odd prickling sensation at the back of his throat, the one constantly poking him, telling him that danger, disaster, was sneaking up. He felt the strange excitement, the lightness in the soles of his feet, the quickening pulse within his breast. He was starting up the stairs when the phone rang.

"Lewis, hi, it's Rita," she said. He was elated. Then cautious. Then afraid, like somebody could be trying to trick him. This was what life was about, what it was lived for, though, these excited, pleased feelings. But he seemed to be forgetting something very important. What was it again? Oh, right, it was Hen—.

"My God. Rita? How are you?" he asked.

"I'm fine, I guess. If I sound strange, I'm in my car. My 4 o'clock stood me up."

"Gee, that's awful," he said.

"No, it's actually wonderful," she said. "Hey, listen. I need to ask you something."

"Okay. I'm all yours. Ask me."

"Well, this is just something I was wondering." She paused. His pulse went up another notch. "Um, okay, I'm being weird. Here's the question. Did you have any fun at that old baseball game Pablo dragged you to?" she asked. And changed her voice, on the words "baseball game," to convey derision and scorn.

"Sure, it was fine," he said.

"Oh, really? Well, Pablo said you weren't yourself and he was afraid you had a bad time."

"No, I had a wonderful time," he said. "It was perfect. Right afterward, I drove my car into a tree."

"Are you serious, Bill?" she asked. "Oh, Bill. Oh. Is everything all right?"

"It's wonderful," he said.

"Really? See, I never know when to believe you. You're one of those people who seems to be kidding, but later you find out they were serious."

He could hear in her voice, in her manner, that they'd managed to forge a real connection on that very brief campout. So it wasn't just the wine or his imagination. He really heard it in her half-flirting, half-joking, half-serious tone.

"So Pablo thought I wasn't myself?" he said. "That's a riot. That's as close to the real me as I ever get. That was the actual Bill."

"He said you said that one out of three American men have their boyhoods ruined by sports," she said.

"Actually, I said *two* out of three," he said. "But to tell you the truth, Rita, I can't recall exactly what I said. I must've hit my head when I crashed."

The backwash of noise on Rita's end suddenly stopped, as though she'd been cut off. The silence in the house was full and round. His ears were just about stuffed with it.

"Bill?" she said. "Are you still there?"

"Of course, Rita. I'll never hang up on you," he said. And felt a sweat break, realizing he'd just made her a promise, the first.

"Bill, I have to tell you about your book," she said.

"Oh, God. Don't tell me you actually looked at it," he said. "I only left it there thinking Pablo might give it a glance."

"Well, I read it," she said. "I don't know how, but I read the whole thing in, like, a night. I hardly slept."

"It's only part of a book. I might never finish it."

He could just picture her. She'd gotten home, and was sitting in the quiet driveway of her tall, dramatic house, with the bushes trimmed and the grass cut, and the two-story glass entryway, the crushed-stone walk, the mission-style copper yard lamps. For whatever reason, she wasn't eager to go inside, like today she couldn't bear to hear the door shut behind her. So she'd put that moment off by calling Bill, to frustrate the house's claims on her.

"I don't know," she said, "maybe it's just the way it is with me and books. But I kept having this feeling—and don't you laugh at me—but I felt like you had written it directly to me. Isn't that crazy? Like you would write it to me personally, then leave it here for me to find. Isn't that nuts? I'm completely insane!"

"My God, that's nice of you to say, Rita," he said, "and that's just how I wanted you to feel."

He listened to her breath catch. Here was a little moment they were having together. And why wasn't all of life this way? Why wasn't every moment so rapt and so secret like this? Why couldn't your heart always pound like it was going to burst?

"What I mean is, that's how I want everyone to feel when they read it," he said. "So, in a way, I did write it to you."

"Oh. Well—I loved it," she said. "I mean, some parts might be too long, but overall it's really—it's just really—okay, yeah. I've gushed enough, I guess."

He laughed, because she'd had to give him that small slap. He'd led her on for a second there. "Hey, don't stop on my account," he said. "I know it's too long."

"Oh, right, yes," she said, with a laugh. "Much, much too long."

"Anyway, how've you been, Rita? How's it going?"

"Oh. You don't want to hear," she said. "I never do anything interesting."

"That sounds . . . you sound sort of down. What's wrong?" he asked.

"Oh. I'm sort of having a hard time. It's kind of hard for me to try to make friends with Pablo's friends," she said. "I'm just not quite enough for them, somehow. Or maybe I'm too much, I don't know." Her voice was growing faint. She'd lowered it to complain to another man about Pablo. And this was Bill now fixing Pablo's wagon for him, cooking his goose, as he did with every man he brushed up against in his life, eventually. One by one, one by one, he got around to every last one. Why? To get even. For what? It was a long story.

"Bill, I like you, and I have ever since the campout," she said. "How you just walked up to me and started talking to me, like we'd known each other forever."

They were skirting along the border of dangerous territory. But the true explorer proceeded on, didn't he? Lewis had proceeded on and on, falling over cliffs, ruining watches and losing compasses, as if unconsciously trying to prevent his own success. Or return.

Bill knew he and Rita had crossed a line. Old Pablo would be none too thrilled at this conversation, if he could hear it. Emily either, for that matter.

But it was easy, and felt so good, so effortless, being with women. It was what God created him for, apparently. He didn't bother with men because a man was just a guy whose approval he could not get. God, too, for that matter.

Though someday, somehow, he needed to get over it. He needed to stop being bitter, and cross it off the list of "Stupid Things Bill Needs to Give up on Because They'll Never Change."

"Rita, thanks a million for reading the book," he said. "I'll drop by and get it sometime, if that's okay."

"That sounds good," she said. "Make sure you call ahead so I'm— well, so one of us, at least—is here."

"I'll do that," he said. "Hey, I don't suppose old Pablo has looked at it, has he?"

"No, he hasn't, Bill, not yet," she said. "But I'm sure he will soon."

"That's okay. It's no big deal. It was just a crazy impulse anyway."

"It's so great, Bill, so, so great. You really have no idea," she said, and hung up the phone.

He stood there a moment, decompressing, slowing his heart. Then a scraping sound came from the hall above him, like Henry had listened to his end of the call, then slipped back into his room. With no time in his schedule to go over to Rita's house the next day or the next, that'd have to wait. As for Henry, the kid clearly knew something was up. But Bill felt confident in his love: Henry wouldn't rat out his own father, not even to his own mother. Which must've posed quite a wonderful, quite a terrific, dilemma for him. Or one more, actually.

Bill thought about Lewis's wound then, for some reason, when he'd gotten shot in the ass, on the way home. Something about the placement of the wound, and its timing, suggested foul play. Maybe he'd been "fragged" by his own men. After all, he'd divided them into five small parties and almost got one whole detachment wiped out. Which'd forced them to kill two Indians while on a peace mission.

On the other hand, Lewis never seemed to have choices. Tom needed to know if any tributary of the Missouri lay north of the fiftieth parallel, giving the U.S. a claim to parts of Canada. Everyone was scrambling to get their share after the new treaty with France. In other words, it was a well-meaning plan, like Lyndon Johnson's to keep communism from ruling Indochina. And led to two killings on the Maria's River and the massacre at My Lai.

Bill's dad lived in a retirement community not too far away. But Bill didn't visit often, since it always seemed like he'd just been there, or just talked to his dad, when he'd suddenly realize three months had gotten by.

It took maybe an hour to get there, to Three Lakes Estates, just off the Atchison River, between the towns of Boneparte and Genessee. Sometimes it was hard to run old Lloyd Charles down, because he hated to stay in one place for long. Plus, Bill was averse to calling ahead, since it felt like asking permission.

In fact, Bill was surprised, or confused, at having a father. He'd hardly had one as a kid and then none at all, postdivorce. Now, Bill sometimes worried that he would finally get *used* to having a father, and Lloyd would die on him.

He was embarrassed, too, because Lloyd had made rugged, tangible things all his life, bridges and levees and dams, while Bill's job was a mixture of babysitting and staring out the window. Also, his hands looked girlish when placed next to Lloyd's, pale and unscarred. Lloyd was starting to forget things, too, and repeating his stories, which always made Bill squirm.

But God never cared what you felt, only what you did. Which grieved Bill a lot and made him feel worthless. When Emily chided him for being this way about people, about Lloyd, Bill didn't know what to say. "Maybe I got knocked down in the baselines too many times. Maybe I kept getting up when a smart person would've stayed down," he'd say. "Maybe what they finally beat out of me was the milk of human kindness."

And she'd say, "But you're nice to me."

And he'd say, "Not always. Not when you're not looking."

And she'd say, "That's true."

So he drove out to Lloyd's without calling ahead, arriving around 6 that evening, thinking he'd buy him dinner. But Lloyd's three-wheeled bicycle, the one he rode all over the complex and little town, wasn't by his door.

Bill drove around until he spotted it, parked at the pro shop of all places. Lloyd saw him and waved, with some dark mirth on his face, the way he always did when his son suddenly turned up. He wore a white baseball cap and was talking with the African American Pepsi employee who was there filling the machine. Bill came up and stood, and listened to Lloyd's harangue about how the machine was acting up and how much money he'd lost in it. Bill always felt lesser around Lloyd, and the worst part was when Lloyd waited this way to greet him. "Oh, hey, Terry, this is my son," Lloyd said at last.

"*You* have kids?" Terry said, glancing once at Bill, then turning back to his work. "*You* do?"

"Well, sure, why wouldn't I?" Lloyd asked.

So they were on intimate terms, clearly, and apparently had regular talks, about the machine and the weather but not Bill. Terry didn't shake hands and they didn't say anything to each other in parting, Lloyd or Terry, as he hustled back to his truck.

"You didn't have to drive all this way," Lloyd said.

"I was taking a drive anyway," he said. "So what're you doing over here?"

"I like it over here," Lloyd said, scratching both elbows with a sort of self-hugging maneuver. "This way, I get to spend more time with Terry. And the view's better, too." He looked up at Bill from under his hat, skinny, mouthy old guy with chisel-end blue eyes. He was small through the chest and shoulders, but never *seemed* small.

"I guess it is," Bill said, "if you like golf courses." With nowhere else to sit and Lloyd not getting up, he perched on a post slightly too high for sitting.

"How's Henry?" Lloyd asked, always his first question. Bill was sort of keeping them apart, and Emily was, too, fearing that Lloyd's rocky, extreme nature might be awakened in Henry's blood by frequent contact.

It was other things, too. The divorce, the '70s, feminism. The decade settled like locusts on Bill's childhood, pitting husband against wife, father against son, son against mother, and so forth. Jesus warned everybody He wasn't there to bring the peace but to destroy it, which was true of feminism, too. There'd been a war, and the casualties were staggering. Women, it was agreed, had won. But in a war, were there ever any winners?

Just like the American South in the Civil War, Lloyd's side had lost. And, just like the South, he refused to act beaten. Which was something Bill could never understand about the South, or Lloyd.

It reminded Bill of how Jefferson had tried to reason with the Native Americans, telling the forty-five assembled chiefs not to resist white occupation, that white men were numerous as the stars and each one owned a gun. Then the tribes resisted anyway. But at least Tom could say he'd tried.

"Henry's doing fine," Bill said. "His only problem is he won't eat."

"Won't eat?" Lloyd said in alarm. "That doesn't sound so fine. Why won't he eat?"

"He won't say. I think there's a girl involved."

Lloyd waved at some old duffers going by in a golf cart, raising his hand like a small white papal figure, greeting a crowd.

"So since when do you play golf?" Bill asked.

"I don't." Lloyd grinned, leaning back so Bill saw all his lean teeth, and red gums, too. "I told you, I'm just here for the scenery."

"Don't they mind you sitting over here and not playing?"

"Well, I help the groundskeeper set his hoses. And sometimes I'll rake out a sand trap or two," he said, "if I'm in the mood." He rolled up on one hip in the chair, crossed his legs at the knee, and clasped his hands behind his head. "I'm what you call a big shot around here!" His hair stuck up in tufts above his ears, blue eyes watering in the stiff breeze. But no longer such a terror. Nor was he striving for dominance now, like he used to, in that way that'd eaten him up inside with stomach ulcers.

"What's so great about this scenery?" Bill asked. "It's artificial."

He didn't really want an answer, but did want Lloyd to know he hated everything and his life. And hated not having words to tell his dad how lousy it all was, with no freedom anywhere, no difference between his life and a jail cell.

Looking around for culprits, he saw nothing but a lot of painfully short grass an unlikely shade of green. He felt ingrown as a toenail, crabbed up, deformed. And wanted to tell Lloyd about it, that all this striving needed to stop. But didn't know how. Or if he was crazy.

"And how's Emily?" Lloyd asked.

"She's, uh . . . she could be better, I guess. She cries a lot."

He was surprised to say it, and winced, and rubbed his eyes.

"Cries a lot?" Lloyd said, blinking up at Lewis. "What's she crying about?"

"Henry, mostly. He's lost all this weight, which makes her feel like a failure."

"Well, how's that *her* fault?" he asked.

"I don't know," Lewis said. "Maybe it's both our faults. Maybe he's scared to death we'll get a divorce or some crazy shit like that."

His dad looked at him again. "So now you're getting a divorce?"

Bill, about to answer, looked over at a bushy-bearded guy with a scared, hangdog face, going by on a mower. He could swear it was him again, that same George-Shannon-looking guy from the city course.

"I don't know. But you don't seem very surprised," Bill said.

"It's the first I've heard of it," Lloyd said, crossing his legs the other way and screwing his cap down a little tighter on his white hair. "I don't think you've ever mentioned a divorce."

"It's all I think about," Lewis said, wringing his hands, hoping his anguish wasn't real. Maybe if he did comical things, pulled faces and groaned and clowned, it might stop short of tears. "I mean, just imagine what this'd do to Henry? This'd kill him."

"Oh, I doubt it'd kill him," Lloyd said. And without saying, "It didn't kill *you*," managed to imply it.

Lewis got tears in his eyes, hot like molten lead, because he wasn't so sure. Sometimes it seemed his boyhood *had* killed him. Was this really surviving? Was this life?

"Maybe, maybe not," Lewis said.

Lloyd shrugged, having always arranged his mind according to what he knew for a fact and what he didn't, and never dwelled on the latter. And was the better man for it? He was most definitely Rational Man, while Bill himself (he knew) was the newer version, Intuitive Man.

Which was best, the old or new model? And why were they forced to go along this way, with only half the parts they needed?

"I don't think marriage works," Bill said.

Lloyd nodded. "Oh, yeah? Try to imagine any of this without it," he said.

Bill tried. Without romantic love, the only truth would be that things cost money and someone had to earn it. All the titles—father, mother, aunt, uncle, son, daughter—would be swept away. As a child, you'd simply say, "That's one of my caretakers." Or, as an adult, "I'm one of his caregivers." And a five-year renewable contract with joint, shared custody of children to replace 'til-death-do-you-part.

But what about heartbreak? At some point, no matter how smooth it went, a kid was looking up and asking, "Why, Daddy?" And, "Why can't you stay, Daddy?" and "Don't leave me, Daddy!" and "Please, please, please, Daddy!" and "Is it because of me, Daddy? Am I bad?"

"To top it off, Henry wants to play *baseball*," Lewis said, pronouncing it like an obscenity.

"Yeah? So what?" Lloyd asked.

"So, he'll sit the bench. Or worse. He's not exactly an athlete."

Lloyd narrowed his eyes then, and sat forward, elbows on knees. He looked out across the grass, like he'd just thought of something impossibly sad. And was wishing, Bill imagined, for a son who was a buddy, someone he could turn to and say, "Jesus Christ, Bill, would you cheer up? God, your problems are boring as hell. I came out here to relax, not listen to this boring crap!"

They looked across that green landscape, with its delicate grays, shading toward purple in the distance. Their lives were basically two different movies of the twentieth century. Lloyd's featured the stock-market crash and Black Monday, Roosevelt, Truman and Johnson, Mao Tse-tung and Ho Chi Minh, the Boxer Rebellion and Japanese internment, Paul Newman in *The Hustler* and Steve McQueen in *The Sand Pebbles,* and the Mustang convertible. And Vegas when Sammy was headlining. The Playboy Mansion.

Bill's, on the other hand, played more like a bad drug trip, with Patty Hearst and the Zebra murders, Altamont and Attica, the fall of Saigon, Helter-Skelter and Charlie Manson, My Lai and the Watts riots, psychedelic rock, and those crummy social-activist *Billy Jack* movies.

And was America waking from her nightmare at last? Or was she only turning in her sleep, preparing to dream again?

"Look, I'm not here to make *you* feel bad, too," Bill said. Which wasn't even true; he was actually very tired of feeling bad all alone.

"I didn't know you felt that way," Lloyd said. "You should've told me."

Bill shrugged. "I got real depressed last year, Dad," he said. "I almost did the deed. Finito."

"Well, why in the world would you do that?" Lloyd said, startling and gazing up at him.

"I was depressed!" he said. "It's a disease. Like TB, polio, cancer."

"Well," Lloyd said, "the way I see it, you can't *afford* to kill yourself. You've got a family."

Bill couldn't think of what else to say. Apparently this was it, the thing he'd come to tell Lloyd in the first place.

Anyway, it was starting to get dark, with the golf carts coming in one by one and not going out again. The sky was streaky with contrails. Bill tried to see the sky from Lewis's point of view. What would he've made of these crisscrossing lines, all these crucifixes slowly spreading into thin, gauzy nothingness?

Lewis's illness followed him back and forth across a continent for three or four years. Always there, waiting for its moment. And after he'd taken the governor's job in St. Louis, and had to stay in one place and do it, it caught him.

His first campaign, to return Big White to his people in North Dakota, failed, with George Shannon losing a leg in a fight with the Arikara.

As for Mary Shelley's novel, the parallels cut every which way, with Lewis as Frankenstein and the expedition as his creature, or Tom as the mad scientist and America as his dangerous, orphaned entity.

Just as the monster always does to its creator, when the expedition ended, it seemed to take Lewis down with it.

After Shannon's injury, things start to unravel. On a short trip up the coast, twenty-five boxes of expedition artifacts go straight to the bottom. Lewis was issuing advance-copy vouchers for a book he wasn't writing. Battling his insomnia with long walks, he'd tavern-hop with friends until the wee hours. Then, in his rooms at the Chouteaus', sleep until afternoon in his buffalo robe stinking of the trail. The tone of Tom's letters changed from inquiry to accusation, saying Lewis's tardiness with the journals had made him "bankrupt" in the eyes of many.

The mystery of the journals grew enormous, and the answer was, Lewis was keeping them. He wasn't going to hand them over to a bunch of people who—he now realized—never really knew him. They could just forget it.

Along in here somewhere, Lewis took charge of a friend's thirteen-year-old son. And one could imagine the sort of advice and counsel Lewis might give a young man as he watched his own situation crumble.

God loved Lewis, one had to suppose. But whether Lewis felt that love while tumbling under the Niagara of the depression was another question. And one couldn't say, "Well, he might've been all right if such-and-such had happened, or if so-and-so had helped him." No, sorry. No way could Lewis be all right. Not with opiates and whiskey as the only medicines.

Bill left Lloyd's a little after 8 and got to Joaney's just before 9.

She let him in, without any sign of surprise, like he belonged there. She was in the middle of changing Jack on the couch, and went back to it, teasing him by wiggling his little penis between two fingers, making him arch his back and grin like a fool. Not even out of diapers and already women could make him cavort like a trained seal, poor guy, with just a touch.

He didn't even know why he was there, and simply paced around her living room, wondering what he was up to, showing up again. Well, he'd just have to watch and see what he'd do.

When the depression was bad, he suffered a feeling of dividedness from others. And when it was very bad, the divide was an abyss. You felt one false step could finish you. And one side of him was trying to survive, all right. But the other side wasn't, having had it up to here.

"So how are you? How's your book?" she asked, as if the two were one thing.

Her body, her roundish, sleepy-eyed face, sort of hung there before him. She always looked drowsy, bedroom-eyed. Her tight-fitting stretch pants, in aqua, her Lycra top, in peach, showed her trim strength. She might go out and run five or ten miles if she felt like it, at the drop of a hat.

"I'm having trouble, Jo," he said.

"What's the matter, Bill? Are you sad 'cause the hero dies at the end?" She grinned at him, then picked up a pillow and hugged it.

"No, not so much," he said. "On the contrary, I'm watching it happen. I'm not helping it along, but I'm definitely clearing away the obstacles in his path. He's got no choice and never did."

"Well, that's just what happens. It's history," she said, sitting in the chair he'd rebuilt and redone in red leather with brass studs in rows down the arms. The blond carpet he'd put in now had a purple stain in the middle.

"Yeah, but this is my version," he said. "And this sounds crazy, but I think he's doing it partly to get rid of me. He's going to end my control over him. Mine and everybody's."

She picked up Jack and put him in his pen. Then she went away, into her bedroom, and came back carrying the abridged copy of the journals he'd given her.

"I want you to listen to something," she said. "This is him, writing. 'She rested on her back, in a small case prepared for her, suspended by a universal joint. She was carefully wound up every day at twelve o'clock. Her rate of going as ascertained by myself for that purpose was found to be 15 and 5/10s of a second too slow.'"

"That's about his chronometer," he said.

"Oh, I know what it's about," she said. "But it makes my blood cold. It's like a horror movie I'm sure I've seen, about some psycho who's got a woman sealed up in a glass coffin. He's got her hung up inside it, by wires, so that she's part of a machine. Meanwhile, she's running like crazy, trying to keep up or get away, but she can't ever move fast enough. She's falling behind."

"I can't explain his gender cases," he said. "But he *is* totally dependent on her. And she *is* sort of temperamental."

She kept flipping pages, making her way to another place.

"That isn't all," she said. "Listen to this. This is about a flower, I guess. 'Veined, glossy, corinated and wrinkled . . . some of its flowerets have expanded their corollas . . . swelling as it ascends and gliding in such manner into the limb that it cannot be said where the style ends and the stigma begins . . . the anther, in a few hours after the corolla unfolds, bursts, discharges its pollen and becomes very minute and shriveled.'"

"It's sexy stuff," he said. "He gets really heated up about flowers."

"He sounds so frustrated," she said, and took the book completely out of the room with her. He gazed around at his handiwork. The floor in the dining room still needed finishing. But supposing he did that, then what? Another floor in another room? He didn't belong there. Yet he couldn't seem to get up and walk out. He searched for his goddamn feelings about it all.

Joaney was in Jack's room with him now, using pleas, then threats, then pleas again to get him to sleep. Jack would grow into a man. Henry, too. And a man was just a guy who'd try to get Bill into a corner, force him to admit he was nothing, a bit of stuff. With a man, he always failed the damn test, failed to meet some little condition. *You didn't say, "Simon Says."*

While Jack fought the good fight, Bill stepped out onto the porch and sat on the swing, its anchor-bolts sunk six inches into the joists above his head and not going anywhere. With one hand, he dialed Rita's cell number. It went straight into voice mail, with her mysterious voice and its dark, round, Scandihoovian accent. Then the tone.

"Rita. Hi, it's me, Double-u, em, Lewis, American hero, calling. Listen, I, uh, I just wanted to tell you . . . um, well, here's how things stand with the book. They just got home, which means the worst is yet to come. He's got to be governor of the whole territory. A ten-thousand-aspirin job, as the Japanese say. Plus his personal assistant is causing him grief, and is the brother of the very guy he beat out of a very plum job, being Tom's secretary. Later, this guy will confess he loved Lewis and didn't mean to drive him crazy. Anyway, that's where we are. It's the beginning of the end."

He closed the phone, marveling a little at the facility of these under-the-table dealings, sitting at "the other woman's" house calling yet a third. He was turning into a real creep, all right.

Now he noticed something. A car was idling across the street, one too nice for the neighborhood, a long blue sedan. He didn't know why, but for some reason it made him think of Ted, Joaney's foster dad, and the scandal, which'd forced her to move into a group home at fifteen. Realtors almost always drove those big Town Cars, too.

Joaney was in the living room when he went in, waiting for him. She was sitting on the couch, unsmiling, her expression held together with toothpicks.

"Who was on the phone?" she asked.

"Oh, that? That was just old Pablo," he said, pocketing it.

"You liar," she said. "Jesus, what is it with guys? If you were talking on the phone to a woman, why don't you just say, 'I was talking to a woman'? And I know you were, because you have this little voice you use with women. You even use it with me!" Her face was turning red now.

"Now, just wait, Jo," he said.

She wasn't waiting. She covered her face with both hands and burst into tears.

"Oh, hey, Joaney. Hey, look. I'm so sorry," he said, shrugging and getting up, coming near, afraid to actually touch her. "What's the matter?"

She shook her head. Then she smeared tears out of her eyes. "Bill, I'm in so much trouble! You have no idea. I'm losing my house!"

"You are? But why?"

"Because of Ted!" she cried. "Because of him and bitchy Annette. They always help me out every month. And now, all of a sudden, they stopped."

"But why?" he asked.

"I have no idea!"

"Well, what have they said about it? Is it a lot of money?"

"It's five—five hundred," she stammered. "And if I can't get it, Jack and me, we won't have any—we won't have a . . ."

She couldn't get the whole thing out and started a fit of heartbroken, end-of-the-line-type of crying, saying, "Oh God oh no oh it's so fucking useless Jesus everything is so fucking useless!"

He at last crouched down and put his arms around her, her red face hot and humid, her skin hot and damp and hopeless against his own. She looked up into his eyes, then planted a fiery, soft, and desperate kiss about halfway onto his mouth.

"Look, you don't have to worry," he said, not looking in her eyes. "I'll give it to you."

She stopped. She pushed him back, hard. "What? No, Bill, no! You can't do that!" she said.

"Oh, but I can. It'll be a loan, if that's how you want it. Just a loan."

She pushed him back again, all the way away this time. Now she was just looking at him in a very cold and appraising way. She crossed her arms, hiding her bosom from him. "So you'd do that for me, huh? Just like that? Easy as pie?"

"Yes, why not?" he said, unable to meet her eyes. "Jesus Christ, you need it, don't you? And I've got it, don't I? Jesus, it's about all I do have. Money in the bank."

She nodded, and now looked very, very disgusted with him. He'd said the wrong thing, and it was too late to take it back. He'd led her down a primrose path of hoping for something else, and suddenly just whisked it away. Bait and switch.

He wasn't sure what he regretted most, losing the gleaming vision, the quilt-covered bed, or giving up the war with Tommy, surrendering the turf. He'd really enjoyed beating the kid, too, really loved making some guy feel lost and deprived, betrayed, humiliated.

In a way, he'd been doing it to *teach* Tommy the best lesson he'd learned, that we mustn't count on things to work out. And who was better proof than Lewis, who never got to tell his side, who'd tried desperately to clear a space to tell what happened but ran out of room?

He got out his checkbook and did the deed. She took the scrap from him, not looking at it.

"Sometimes Ted—" she said.

"Ted? What about him? Sometimes Ted what?" he asked.

"Sometimes he just shows up. I don't ask him to, Bill, but he wants to talk to me. About her, you know?" she said. "We just sit in his car. I can't make him go away. I don't want to hurt him anymore, and I know he never wanted to hurt me."

"Christ, I think I just saw him," he said. "I think he was just out there."

"That's why," Joaney said. And shrugged.

"What'll you do?"

"Something," she said. "I'll tell him something. She does this, and then he stops showing up, and eventually the money starts again."

She showed him out. Then used the little flag, his check, to wave good-bye to him from her porch steps. Good-bye, good-bye. He waved, too, backing out. Well, he'd almost had her. *Almost had you, my dandelion-headed blond baby girl.* Up on her toes, waving, crying again, a little, she turned her rump to him and went inside. It was sore, sour relief, though, because now nothing would change.

Fresh out of destinations and excuses, he turned for home. The route he picked took him past places he tried not to go if he could help it,

scenes of romantic failures, boyhood defeats. It seemed he'd never gotten the girls he wanted, for a reason too awful for words, which was that
he'd lost every fight. He'd been thrown in holes and stomped on, pissed
on, made to beg for mercy. Then limped home wet, muddy, a burbling
mess. But not a drop of blood on him. Which was important, because
one tiny drop could've saved him, could've transformed him into the clas-
sically bloody, unbowed hero. But no, God couldn't spare him even that!
Not one stinking drop!

Really from that time on, if he saw any boy with any girl, he had to try
for her. Her, and all the rest.

Now, when he was almost home, a strange sympathy was born in him
for Ted. Ted parked across the street from Joaney's. Ted hanging around
where he didn't belong. Desperate to have her again, knowing it was
wrong, but trying to force these opposites together and forge a world in
which he could be happy.

"... *the fittest person in the world* ..."

Forced into solitary pursuits; Afternoons with the lovely F.;
Resigning from the army; Clark leaves him to go west to St. Louis.

✻ At every ball, every eligible lady in the whole city came to look on him, and he on them. They were strewn about the floor in bundles, like upright corn sheaves with red-rouged faces and bare shoulders, with clutch-purses, and bands about their throats. One night, when he could not make himself go to them, awkward and hating everything, a bold young woman brought her squad to him, to stand a yard away and toss out innocent questions. He thought he recalled this kind of battle, and roused himself for it. But something in his face, emotion undefined, angry distress, froze them. She stood up front with her face hidden from her subjects, and was desperate herself or would never have steer'd straight into that reef. "Your lip curls a bit too much, Governor," she said, as he smiled. "You show too much canine." The others strained forward, fanning, and turned a frantic ear but couldn't quite catch the repartee.

"I've lost the art of female company," he said. "Please leave me alone."

But she held his eye, being desp'rately mad or madly desperate, or a witch. His throat hurt and his eyes teared.

"I want to know the worst," she said softly. "Something you've never told."

"*Escusez-moi—?*" he said. A dirty limerick crossed his mind. Couples crossing the dance floor just now were looking at him and whisp'ring and laughing together at his expense.

"They say you saw the Western Ocean, and 't made you mad," she said. Her dark hair made a number of turns about her head and was held up with many black pins. Her hazel eyes large and bulging, her mouth downturned and quaking. He had to get out. He left.

Now, forced into solitary pursuits, he knew it was true. But what was he doing or not doing, saying or not saying, to cause all to know it? He walked about town, through rivulets of horse urine, his arches aching from the cobbles, mouth carefully set, mind poorly hid from the prying eyes of everybody. Tho perhaps only the insane knew him for what he was.

He paced along with every nerve alive with terror, glancing hard past ev'ry face, trying not to see what it knew. A lifetime of this could never do. And one couldn't avoid all the mad, discerning people, for they were on ev'ry corner, like churches. They raved and foamed and were ignored. Eventually, bound hand and foot and gagged, they were shut up and forgotten. He saw himself being visited in the madhouse by his mother, by his so-called particular friend, Clark, and almost bolted. Walking faster to get out ahead of the vision. *You will never have the least things he has,* a voice whisper'd to him, *the pretty young wife, the children in the yard.*

He journeyed far out into the country, along the river. As hard and as fast as he could go, downing several ales in each place he stopped, he walked and walked. Panting, still thirsty, and winded, he struck out again, and again, going until nightfall, dimly aware of the men he talked to, the hands he shook, their puzzlement and offense over his abrupt leave-taking. He got out of each place in a hurry, and never found his own street, and sleeping robe, and corner of the room on the floor, until daylight of ev'ry day.

Rising stiffly, he felt musty and creaky. Though it was past noon, the sunlight breaking in ev'ry crack could not defeat the March cold. His breath show'd on the interior air, his skull-bones shifting under the flaps of skin and pads of hair that made his face.

He looked about, the room throbbing with his weak pulse, the light red like his thin, barely-motile blood. And tried to keep busy, writing letters until dark. When the sun set each ev'ning, a strange, alarming state seized him, a certain indescribable something, a mix of panic, dread, and horror. Then he must get out, and quick, before the ceiling split and his soul caved in. It required the help of ev'ry remedy, many drams, lots of tablets, and plenty of walking to exhaust the demon.

Now, he knew a thing or two about possession. Something not himself awaken'd every night at dusk. The thing was not lying in wait along the open road, or in the woods, but did closely threaten him in those clubby taverns, and inside his rooms, especially near the bed. If only he could say for sure what it wanted! At any rate, it was too strong to keep at bay.

In Charlottesville, it let him give a speech which was, in fact, a densely coded plea for help. ("I stand before you with the fond hope that, it may hereafter be believed, I have discharged my duty.") *Because my hereafter is coming soon!*

It told him what to do and sank him down to hell if he disobeyed. Meanwhile, God didn't care and he suffered. But his familiar did care, and always pointed the way toward salvation, letting him breathe when he chose the correct path, away from life, and cut his wind to a whisper if he resisted, and rained down plagues such as insomnia, fits of dread, white-hot barrages of needles pricking every nerve's ending, and jolt after jolt from a fitful sleep all night long, like he jerked between poles of a battery.

He moved in the thrall of others and, when he needed to change locales, borrowed their wills, Tom's, Clark's, his mother's, his half-brother's. *It* couldn't stop him as long as he obeyed another. Forced to go along, in hate-filled jealousy, it lay waiting for him to try some act of his own.

Like a ball of India rubber he got tossed, St. Louis to Louisville to Frankfort with Clark, then Locust Hill to Charlottesville to Washington and the president's house with the Mandan chief Big White. And reeled back up by Tom, he went to sleep in that great "white house," and wonder'd how one escap'd what never slept.

He could move on his own, if he didn't know where he went. Tom made him governor, and Lewis used the leftover force from that mighty act to resign from the army and issue a publishing schedule for the three-volume journal (October for the first, December for the second, the third following at New-Year's) before *it* knew what had happened.

How had he got so divided? It started, he felt sure, at thirteen, when the horror of becoming head of a household, two thousand acres, and twenty-eight slaves was too much and broke him right in two. He'd seen the truth too early: except for a meteor falling on him, his whole fate was written, his life-course set by the stars eons before his birth. Unless he ran away.

He ran—but still his destiny was fix'd. And the papers now began to exhume the corpse of the Corps of Discovery to pick over what remained. He was reminded often that a Canadian, one Mackenzie, had done it first and better, with one-fourth the men and resources.

Talking with people, he watched their eyes closely to see if they knew about his mad visitor. Either none did or all did. He got sick with fever along with Tom and the whole household. And ill, very, very ill, he noticed his guest was silent, hushed, for it had a holy reverence for disease. It hated capable things, but death trumped it. For one day it, too, must die, and after a lifetime of company with a man it couldn't trust, a man it loved because it had no one else, a man who plotted against it ev'ry instant, and prayed for its death.

By drinking until he was stuporous, Lewis sometimes got the upper hand. But just as he got it, he'd fall unconscious. And opiates only made the monster stagger and stumble and wander in the underwater labyrinth of his brain, confused and homeless. God Himself pitied that thing then, and forced Lewis to let it up, back to the surface, into freezing air and scalding sunlight, to breathe.

One day, Lewis ran into Frazier again. Of all people to find on the cobbled streets of downtown. Though he didn't know it was Private Frazier, whose book he had throttled in its crib, 'til a grinning, bearded face was thrust into his. Two large hands, which could grasp a rapier handle like a baby bird, closed about his like a set of oak stocks and jerked him back and forth.

They walked together. Lewis followed the slightly mincing toes of his own boots through the streets as they moved along too quickly. Sorry about the man's book, but desperate to involve anyone he could find, he gave Frazier $50 and sent him to St. Louis.

"You must join us there, sir," Lewis said. "For we'll need everyone as we tackle this next bit of business." And wasn't sure what he meant by it exactly, but Frazier seemed glad to be directed, and took the money. Aimlessness, after all, was worse than the awfulest duty.

In the afternoon, if he hadn't been drinking, he saw the lovely F. He'd made her acquaintance through Clark, and sat with her in a courtyard, on its bench of solid marble. If he didn't tell her what he held inside, they could court, after a fashion, and she could try to look in his eyes as he dodged. When words failed, as they did, he traced a word on the marble or her white arm. Over a series of days, he wrote, "torment," "misery," "suffering," "disease," "death," "dying," "insane," and "possessed." When he at last wrote "suicide" on her flesh, she pulled away.

"Wait, no more," she said. "I don't really like that." And rubbed the spot on her arm as if burnt.

"Oh, you see? Look, now. I've given offense," he said.

"I'd rather you just told me," she said. "Would you, please, Lewis? Would you tell me what it is makes the famous so strange?"

She had dark hair and leaned forward, letting it hang down, ankles crossed under the bench. Each day—he imagined—she came here to await the world, for it was about to come through the gate, into her lap, and rub its big head 'gainst her loins and show her its fangs.

He felt sick with wanting to want her and sweated as the opportunity was lost, an awful, engulfing panic closing his throat. He scrawled one last hasty word on alabaster flesh.

"Remember what?" she asked.

"I am for Philadelphia," he said. "Just for a few days."

He was gone three months. And there, called on a dozen men. He toted up the thousands he'd need to print the book. Had his portrait done. He gave Sergeant Ordway $300 in exchange for his journal. Everywhere, he used the pronouns "us" and "we" and "our," never "I." There was no "I" anymore.

During the day, he accounted for the vast expense of the expedition, arriving at a list of 1,989 items, and where purchased.

At night, they walked—he and his friend Mahlon Dickerson, who was a black-eyed attorney, a man who found everything and nothing funny. They called it walking, though really they plunged and dove down those dark alleys between taverns, with Dickerson's braying laugh, that of a bitterly wronged ghost, chasing them. Mahlon talked of the cases he couldn't wait to try the next day and the lies being told by both sides.

Lewis truly loved Dickerson for these gusts of drunken doom he gave off. They both were about to be found out, the next day, or the next. And with Mahlon, you felt the end had arrived, and was as much worth celebrating as victory. Now you could let go, because it was all done, and never any chance for happiness anyway. Yes, Lewis was almost happy for a time. They had fits of laughter over twenty-five boxes of artifacts at the bottom of Chesapeake Bay.

And yet, still, he wanted women and was uplifted seeing a likely one on the street. He sat for another picture by Saint-Menin in the coat made with her gift of white weasel tails, a thing actually touched by her lithe, lively fingers. Now he'd appear for all eternity in her secondhand gift, the one she'd given first to Clark. Which was more than fitting and O, so very true.

In Washington in July, he moved rapidly to Locust Hill, then to Monticello by August. Going quickly, he sometimes felt a false freedom. But in truth, these were just more steps in the original errand Tom'd dispatched him on. Then came Burr's arrest for treason.

He'd heard it long after the fact, after Burr had killed Hamilton, back in '04. And later came the gossip'd reasons, with a partial truth only he and few others might know. He knew Theo, a most unsettling woman with a frank, unblinking, manly gaze. You sensed she wasn't governed by rules. Talk with her for even five minutes, and you feared she'd confess to something terrible. The rumours about her were bad as those about her father.

And now Burr was in the hands of the federal authority, after being caught on the run in Alabama and hauled back to Richmond.

Before his creature could unsay the desire, Lewis was on horseback to Richmond. (He'd surprised it by not announcing the plan to himself.) He was doing whatever impulse allowed, and unwinding a silver cord behind him in the form of endless IOUs.

He rode straight through the heat of airless afternoons. Sweating his clothes 'til they dripped, he walked them dry again. Meanwhile, the trees were like trees in paintings, motionless and flat, the dirt of the road red and fine as theatre makeup, the leaves black underneath, lemon-green on top. Not a bird cried. Now and then, from his eye's corner, a wing flashed in the primitive blue of the sky with nary an actual crow or robin or parrot to account for 't.

Terror stole in very quietly, coming toward him from one side. When it at last hit him, with a gust and a gasp, he just managed to stay on the horse. "No, I tell you, this was ordained!" he said to it. *"Fight me.* Go ahead and fight me all you wish. Stamp me out, I beg you!"

In town, he got rooms by the courthouse. Before he could flee, he sent a messenger to let her know he'd arrived. At the trial's recess, she came walking out of the building without any sense of surprise or wonder, saw him, and pointed toward a little park across from the square. She had a companion, but motioned him back and came by herself. Approaching closer and closer. He'd forgotten her jaw, strong as any man's. And her positively Trojan eyes. She hurried down a hill to meet him, stumbling over her skirts then grappling his hands and kissing him on both sides like they were meeting in France.

"I knew it!" she said. "I said it to him just yesterday, 'Lewis will come when he hears of our distress.'"

"And here I am, as if summoned," he said. "You've brought me running."

"I'm so glad. O, Lewis! You can't imagine the smallness, the pettiness of these people! Good God, who are these men?" Her brown eyes glittered into his, and leaked tears she dried with the backs of her strong hands. The plot—it was in every paper—was to seize New Orleans, then Mexico City, and set her up as ruler, empress over that whole peninsula, which they'd rechristen "Burrania." It was highly romantic, and positively eighteenth-century. It was Napoleonic, Alexandresque, a silent tragedy from French theatre.

And yet, here under his hands, Lewis held a real woman, and after so long, her arms meaty and bare, her sleeves rolled for the hard work of empire-building, her dark hair coiled off her neck, stomach and thighs pressing through the thin cotton of her dress and ready to burst its seams, her breasts as round, lively, and sportive as some musky tropical fruit.

But hadn't he said so before? Women truly were the interesting part of creation, for what else made life esteemable? She had moles—three— near her right brow, on her chin, and in the humid valley of her bosom, all black as quivering beads of coal oil on white plaster. Her arms—he still held her!—had a slippery sheen as of a fine sea mist, also on her throat, cheeks, and tops of her tremoring breasts. Suddenly, he loved her. The lawlessness of her gaze, once so alarming, was like cream on a burn. His whole self was raw and blistered and needed her touch.

As for her father, the little man in black, he was done for. Just weeks ago, a British warship seized an American frigate, and now talk of war was in every beer hall. His acts would be treated severely, most likely with death.

They smiled. Her implacable black brows remained leveled at his, and the mouth, so voluptuary, ready for kissing or retorts, was perfectly shaped for a sherry glass. She untangled him from her and brushed her skirts. "So, a bachelor still, eh? Or are you trapped in the matrimonial embrace of love?" she said.

"Recently widowed," he said.

Now that he'd looked a bit longer, greenish hollows shewed under her eyes. She'd been ill, or still was, and slightly puffed in the face from the medicines. She shook very finely. Her being reached toward him from the dark eddy turning slowly about her, her hair blown in a circle about her head by its gusts. So she was caught, still, held in thrall by the little black schoolmaster. They had him on trial, but couldn't swerve her devotion or break his spell. Ten husbands, a thousand lovers, couldn't match him. Her mother had come from the Russian court, but even a high birth couldn't save her now. Tho she did have her little boy, her one pure object. Which shewed that someplace inside, down deep, lay an unbroken, undefiled silvery course, if only she might reach 't in time.

"We can't talk here," she said. "Spies are in the bushes and behind every rock. You must come tonight—to the prison."

Then she broke away from him and dashed back up the hill and into the courthouse. He arrived there himself later, and sat behind her, making no sign of recognition. Through the trial, Lewis balanced and wavered on the hard black mahogany bench and sweated into the unmoving air, staring at the little man in the black suit, diabolic monk of a self-made order. And next to him his famous counsel, Irving, America's most elegant pen. Lewis had never seen Irving, and felt it like the lowest insult. O, that fame for writing books should ooze from any as it did from that man, like a stink! Meantime, his own book lay fallow.

Later, in the falling light, Lewis rode flat out to the Virginia State Penitentiary, a two-story whitewashed megalith, fallen idol, lying on its side. Nothing lay close to it, "stuck up" as it was, against the sky, a blind bluff. In one direction, above the edifice, spread the immense empty heavens and, in the other, an immense empty country. A sight sure to make one think hard and plainly about one's crime. The red road slashed into the hill was rude as a Mexican plantation track, rutted and un-wholesome, and lacked only a venerable burro. Lewis barked out a laugh: the little schoolmaster had his Mexican palace at last.

He felt this again when Theo opened the large double doors of the guest quarters like its mistress, its empress, in a green dress of shiny silk. The crude room, whitewashed, with pitch-pine furnishings, was the war-den's usual lodging, with a dinner table set with hand-thrown pottery dishes, crafted rudely by the inmates.

She served graciously, carved ferociously, and Lewis hardly tasted the dinner of salt-cured ham, the floury potatoes,boiled greens. In truth, the iron-red wine had scalded his throat and melted the crown of his skull so that air touched his brains. The husband was behind them in town with her son, her father busy in his cell with several lawyers.

When they'd exhausted gossip of a few shared friends, she sighed and looked at him. Then she started to cry. "O, my poor people, Lewis," she said, shaking her head.

"Your—your people?" he asked.

"The common folk of Mexico," she said, wiping her tears with her fin-gers. "I've felt they were mine for so long! I've loved them all my life! The peon farmers in their white clothes. Their wives in lace shawls bringing us armloads of flowers on holidays. I'm sick when I think what will happen to them now."

He didn't know how to answer. Even Andrew Jackson had strayed into the thick of this plot. Anything at all seemed likely to be true or to occur. The roof of the building might suddenly shoot away into the starry sky.

"And the general," she said, facing him very soberly. "I don't know if you know. A spy! But this must stay between us. *Entre nous!*"

"I'd heard rumours," Lewis said.

"His other name is 13. Agent 13. O, but I've killed you, dear Lewis! Because if he ever knew—! Or even suspected you knew and might tell the president—! You see? Already I take your life."

He nodded, eyes lowered, because this was not really news, and all well known to Tom. And not thought very important.

But life lacked urgency as it was, and particularly when one was married, and a woman, so that he hated to spoil her fears. The strong medicines she took gave her eyes a glister, a vacancy and a transport all at once. He scented roses and sulfur, a lovely brimstone, from her hair. At thirteen, she'd presided at diplomatic dinners for savages. Her mouth was droll, then embitter'd as she picked over her dinner.

"How terrible this is for you," he said, her face flick'ring in the barbaric oil-lamp light of the prison.

"To distract myself, I read the myths!" she said ironically. "If forced to choose between our own pathetic God and Zeus, I much prefer the latter." And gave a toss of her hair like a younger woman.

"I think he will return with flying colours to this country," he said, because he felt he must.

Theo scowled. "O, let's not lie tonight. I can't bear it."

He drank deeper and deeper into his glass, wishing as he always did when seriously drinking that he could fall inside and be swallowed.

"My God, that they dare to interfere with him," she said, wiping tears with her napkin. "With *him!* If they are not careful, the giant will rouse himself from his slumber and lay waste to their nation!"

Lewis attempted feverishly to eat before this vision of a black figure swollen to enormous size, wading into the middle distance over buildings, roads, boundaries, and restraints with his baby daughter standing on his upturned palm. Plunging over the horizon, the giant father at last seizes her and bites away her arms and legs.

Blinking furiously in the dim light, Lewis said, "Your father is a formidable man, and will be all right."

"O, he is no man. He is nothing like a man," she replied and pushed the food away impatiently.

"Does nobody understand?" she then said. "The world is full of accountants! And you, Lewis! You of all people know this too, too well! They are ruining everything. They are making a world you and I can't even live in!"

She raised herself to her full stature, spine straight, her white forearms bare on the table, her eyes tearing him open. They shone with a desperate affection and mauled and shoved him back in his chair.

"Don't let's lie, Lewis," she said. "I see how it is with you! And you knew me years ago, the moment we met! You saw it all. We saw it together!"

"But *what* did we see?" he said.

"That we're being done in, Lewis. They are replacing us with the latest models. My favorite story now is that of Iphigenia—"

"Are you very ill?" he asked.

"You see how I am. I spy strange flashes of light about people's faces. I feel a sinking sensation, like absence. Figures move around my bed at night. I feel that my womb is obstructed. But that is beside the point. . . ."

She lowered her eyes and let weak, forceless tears fall. He waited for her in a pained silence that vibrated with yellow shadows.

"Just to see you again, Theo," he said. "I've been so lonely. I know I should be happy, but forces are aligning to wreck my hopes. I feel as if vast conspiracies are afoot."

She regarded him, looking up. "But there are, Lewis. Here and now, in the room with us, and outside. Plans are put into quiet action, making us sicken and die and betray each other. We come to bad and mysterious ends."

"But who and why?" he asked. "How are we to know the enemy when these villains smile and smile in our faces?"

"This plane is no place for us anymore, dear Lewis," she said, lowering her voice, glancing about as if for the spies in the window-wells and listening down the chimney.

"But I'm a simple bureaucrat, Theo. I am a notary public, nothing more," he said.

"Not at all. You are the new man, Lewis. I am the new woman," she said, her eyes unearthly, mouth shaking. "We are the new creatures. But we have happened too soon. We have got out too far ahead of the others . . ." She waited a beat. ". . . and need die. We need be killed."

Her eyes turned black in the yellow-gold glow of the poor, white-washed, plastered room. He saw the lip print, very faintly red, of her mouth on her glass rim, and her smeary finger marks, too, and oily drips of wine running down the inside. She was almost grinning with some weird joy, but something else was back of her words and tears, making a silvery outline around each eye.

"Come, now, must we die?" he said. "Who would kill us?"

Her smile shivered. What a complete and robust and captivating woman she would have been! How she might've made a room seem warm and inviting and lacking in nothing. Even a poor meal would be rare, exotic fare, and even indifferent wine like the spiced, heady beverage drunk at the last supper.

"I lately feel," she said, tipping her glass to her lips, "that the end is not far."

"Whose end?" he asked. Lowering his gaze, he suddenly found himself looking back from within his table-knife's blade, and jerked. "And why? How?"

"I can't tell you," she said. "But it will be good. We can stop lying."

For a half-glimm'ring instant, the cuts and slashes, the royal rouged cheeks of the blood-gobbling madwoman flashed before Lewis and replaced Theo's living image, so that he started at the shock. A flush, start-

315

ing at his forehead, spread crazily downward to his feet. The symptoms were becoming worse than the disease. It was all he could do to remain; his color must have faded right away.

"Lewis! O, Lewis! You're frighted to death!" she said. "I've upset you."

"'Tis a spell," he said and mopped his forehead and cheeks. "I take spells, and then I'm all right."

"But you are victorious now," she scolded. "All's well that ends well. You must be so pleased."

"Excepting I am not victorious, and not a thing is well." He laughed, covering his upper face from her with a fever'd hand. "I am left owing everyone. A book about my travels wanted and long overdue. All my ready cash, signed away. And my gratitude to Tom awaited, for a job I can't do and never asked for."

She eyed him indulgently, with calm remove. She was not truly an earthly being, he suddenly saw. He calmed himself by refilling the glasses, choking the bottle two-handedly. Then drank his almost to the bottom. "I issue vouchers for a book I am not writing," he said, gasping. "I want to relieve those wretched people of America. But we are as distressed in our way as they in theirs!"

"I don't like to hear this," she said, drawing back in the shadow of the lamp's tin shade, then leaning forth, her forearms bare on the table. "Think on this, Lewis: I am a Mexican empress, tho' exil'd. You are the ruler of half a nation. Lewis! For God's sake! You and I take in the whole world when we think. Or we are lost!"

Then she sat back, erect in her seat, twisting the base of her goblet on the cloth, regarding him with squared chin and head, bust-like. She was empress, all right, but forced to live on the outskirts of those unimaginable conquests and acts. They were motionless together, unseen by any human eye. With a sense of being far out beyond the pale, he sat with Theo and viewed all time and the whole world, but was not able to get one inch nearer to 't or farther from 't.

And she was so far beyond the puny lives of women, no lover would do except the first outrageous one, his every touch and kiss like lightning strikes, burning her all black inside. She'd never last a mortal's time. But how many women could say they were *almost* empress?

"Yes, we must," he said at last. "Or we are lost."

"At the least, we must not lie," she said. "The truth is that a nation is a vast creature and it needs food. If it cannot eat one way, it will massacre its own children and eat another. It feeds on us, Lewis. It lets us live as long as it can, because it cannot eat dead flesh. The dead are its memories, and the living are its hands, to go out and get its meat. It loves us if we can feed it and never praises a word more than it must. All it does is from fear of being wiped away."

He sat, nodding in time to her voice, the voice of someone dying. A timeless voice, deeper than a woman's, like a river flowing under granite. His throat hurt and his eyes welled. People who talked this way, who lived and loved this way, were ceasing to be. Like candles snuffed one by one, all across a vast, burgeoning, sleeping, and as yet unknown continent.

"Will I see you again?" he asked.

"You will always see me again," she said. "You will always see me."

He clenched his fist to his mouth and bit down hard on his tongue, closing his eyes at the pain. What sort of world would it be? A world where no woman anywhere was lying awake all night, planning her first act as empress? Was that a world worth staying for? Was it worth it, to have a hand in its making? In truth, it wasn't up to him.

Finally he left her and rode down the hill, wet and shaking. The dawn was just empurpling the sky to the east.

Then he got away from there, to Philadelphia, taking his half-brother Reuben. Before departing, he got word from Clark about a woman in Fincastle, where Clark was. He tried to think nothing of this and to keep his mind on Theo. But it took all his restraint. He didn't want to show Reuben he was dizzy, distracted, in the grip of a thing, hearing a voice that was forcing him to cock an ear at 't. Thus, he was accident-prone, and unable to look people in the eye. Now he could strike what he wish'd as hard as he wish'd, an iron gate, a stone wall, and with a doubled-up fist. The dull pain stopped halfway to his brain.

Her name was Letitia. Clark should've known better than to utter her name, because now Lewis loved her. Without knowing two things about her, he loved her very very much. And was already her tender and eternal husband. Love, he was learning, could begin from nothing. As for Theo, she would not be had by mortal man. But somewhere—in Fincastle!— was a woman who perhaps felt excited terror at mention of his name. In her heart, she was already his wife.

As they got closer, his panic grew, jaw clenching so tight it cramped. Any number of times, he thought to turn back. Somehow, by going back now, he could save himself, his miserable life. Reuben viewed this peculiar hesitation, his talk of turning 'round, with perplexity, then mirth, having guess'd its cause.

They arrived at General Clark's (yes, 'twas *General* now) with Lewis in an exhausted, overexcited state. He could not get down from his horse.

Clark met him at the gate, observed his friend's condition, and helped Reuben unhorse him and bring him into the shade to sit and drink water.

"We have some news on that matter I mentioned," Clark said, after Lewis began to come 'round. Clark sat, shod in slippers, his tails out, his placket undone like a proper husband taking his ease in his garden at home. But his forced grin, thrust-out chin, lips just a pale line in red flesh, a tricorner handkerchief tied on his red head, shewed bad tidings.

"What's wrong? Is she ill? Is she dead?" he asked, preparing himself to don black for a year and be the most heart-rendingly-devoted, the most-widowed groom on earth.

"Worse, I'm afraid. She's gone. To Richmond with her father. She departed today, and it was somewhat . . . sudden."

"But did she know I was—?"

"She knew," Clark said, lowering his gaze and pressing his hands together at the fingertips. "She's to be engaged. I am so sorry, my friend."

"Nonsense," Lewis said, making a smile which hurt, a hideous grimace, a cadaverous wrenching of the mouth. "I wish her every happiness. Please tell her so for me, when you see her next."

"Anything. 'll tell her anything you wish," Clark said faintly, unable to look at him.

"'Tis a poor season for a marriage, anyway," he said. "We've much too much to do."

"That's the spirit," Clark said, but raised his chin suspiciously, rubbed his palms together half-heartedly. "Shall we dive into this matter together at last? Write our book?"

"Y-yes," Lewis said. "But before that, I must scribble a new Indian policy. And I need to be in St. Louis. I have needed to for some months but do not go. I have the peculiar notion that . . . that I will not ever come back."

He spoke haltingly, because the blow was still falling in a series of increasingly serious explosions. They marched closer and closer, like a barrage, so that he could not hear for the roaring in his ears. Departed? Why not call a thing by its proper name? She *fled*. And why? Because he was dreadful and the thought of his company was like a black pall coming down to crush her soul. No, there could be no more women. The only woman for him was the concubine of a vicious troll. Or daughter to an unnatural father.

"But where will you go? How can I reach you?" Clark asked.

"I'll be quite near for a time," he said, grinning in a malevolent way. "And then farther off. To be blunt, I haven't the least notion. Don't try to find me."

Clark looked at him a long moment. In his eyes were his regret and apology for the thing he'd done. A thing for which he could not ask forgiveness, or even admit. *He probably wishes I would die,* Lewis thought, *and release him from these stabs of guilt.*

He remained a few days, but was careful not to be alone with Clark, to make it impossible to get anything hidden out into the open. Let it stay buried and fester like an infected and ingrown hair. Let it swell and grow into a hard knot, and remain always thus. At least that way, one was remembered.

He had a letter, every several days, from his new assistant, Bates. Could it be that same Bates, passed over for the plum job of Tom's secretary? Or his brother? It was very unlikely, but would be just his luck.

Instead of answering these desperate missives, Lewis gaped from the window an hour at a time, at clouds tumbling against the crown of a hill, massing, then somersaulting, legging it over like sheep over a fence.

He dressed each day in mourning, feeling he'd been a husband, and a lover, but lost both occupations for liking them too well. This way, God kept the passions in check, by keeping certain types out of the business.

Writing the Indian policy, it pleased him to come and go, to be observed walking to the tailor, and for none to know he shaped their destinies forever and ever. His pen scratched and scraped away the veneer of things with a sharp point, reveal'd what lay beneath. A few strokes and a wall got erected on the Missouri's eastern shore to keep the white people out. Another, and a wall on the west bank kept the nations in.

How satisfying it was, to frustrate all white men with a single blow. But best of all, it was moral.

Tho why did his heart flood and feel sick? Because here was how a man undid himself, by moral purity. But he smiled bitterly and trembled. At the very least, he was proving it at last: the Enlightenment never happened. And hadn't Tom as much as said it? *When I consider that God is just, I tremble for my country.*

It took days to write. Through it, he suffered a relapse of malaria and shook and shivered, even in his dreams. But the fever granted reprieve from the falling sickness, and the sense of a judgment coming, and the aching for a woman, a woman, all through the night.

The most strangely foreign and bizarrely European place he ever saw was St. Louis when at last he arrived there, his horse limping. Wandering her streets were indolent Spanish nobility and idle French exiles, in ruffed collars, preparing for Mardi Gras, and the coronation of their "king" and "queen." Even a child could see it was a feudal place, a queer outpost of monarchies being toppled all around the world, a hideout, a museum piece. Or perhaps it was the shore of a second nation. For hadn't Burr seen it? That two nations might be made of this one, if only one knew where to cut?

In just weeks, Clark and his relations would land there, too. And the house Lewis found would be suddenly too small to include him. For sleep, he'd sprawl on a sofa in his office and doze in dank corners.

When the malaria lifted, his friend returned. For it loved him and wished to be near and to feed on him, always. He was nuzzled by a horror that crept closer. At night, it sat on his chest, crushing away his breath. He shunned company, lest they notice his invisible companion. He had no appetite, for he was being eaten. And thought often about the beast's location, when and where to insert the knife.

One day, he got a letter from old René Jessaume, then left it to read the following morning. First thing the next day, he slashed the wax seal, glanced and saw that René wished to send his thirteen-year-old son to apprentice. Scoffing, chuckling, about to draft his negative reply, he suddenly heard a shoe scrape on the threshold. He looked up to behold a boy. They observed each other in consternation, stiff wonder, and mistrust for long moments.

"O, for God's sake! Please tell me you are not little lord Jessaume," he said.

The boy, in a bad, roughly fitted suit of stiff wool, whose eyes looked up past him and to the right, stretched forth his chin and bent back his wrists, and wobbled in the door, as if about to fall forward on his face.

"No, no, no," Lewis said. "No, this will never do. I got your father's letter only this morning!"

"Yestiddy," the boy said, his finger in his mouth-corner, feeling a tooth.

"Beg pardon?"

"It came yestiddy. You read it jus' now," he said. "I was standin' here an' I saw you." Indolent, he dug with his thumbnail in between the front incisors. His eyes bobbled intrepidly to the right and left, touching Lewis's briefly with brown insouciance, ominous indifference.

"Boy, where is thy father?" Lewis asked.

"At home."

"And he sent you all this way? With only a letter?"

Jessaume gazed right and stretched his wrists and stuck out his lower teeth in a sort of yawn, a struggle to keep from bolting, fleeing the interview, or falling over in a faint. He grew a bit wall-eyed, like a horse smelling battle for the first time. He was shaking and about to cry, terrified of being sent away, for he'd been turned out with only a suit, a letter, a little money. And told not to come back 'til he'd made his fortune.

"So that is how 'tis, is 't?" Lewis said.

Jessaume shrugged and eyed Lewis with a lowered chin, pretending not to care that it was. With a very tired gray face, the boy panted steadily through cracked lips, his stomach jerking in and out pitifully. Lewis saw Jessaume's whole life in a moment, the days and years of unhappy perplexity. Awkward exchanges with associates he mistrusted, the better girls eluding him, one by one, for better matches. And breathless, frustrated anguish over it all, mute and sweaty with pale effort.

"O, for God's sake! Wait for me in the hallway," Lewis said at last, and Jessaume went, like a hound released from point.

Each day, then, they were companions. He walked about the town with Jessaume at heel, showing him how things worked, and talking, aimlessly, hopelessly, trying to hit on anything to elicit a response of comprehension or intelligence.

"I am a Royal Archmason, Jessaume. You needn't know what that is, but it involves the Mystery School. That is where you are now. There is much lore, but you need only bother yourself with the tools. The gavel or hammer is willpower. The gauge or measuring rule is self-estimation. The chisel is suffering. The level is judgment. And the plumb, which hangs down from Heaven, as it were, is spiritual law. Do you understand? Of course you don't. But all one needs to know is one's three lower natures, the physical, emotional, and mental. Your clothing represents your prejudice. Your shoes symbolize your power to advance yourself via the body. To love is to act in a manner of unity or identity with the object itself. As it is among the highest, so it is also among the lowest. You must not ever let yourself be confined by the triple fences of ignorance, prejudice, and dogma. And avoid the three ruffians, too, which are ignorance, selfishness, and sensuality."

Lewis let that sink in, then said, without slowing or more than glancing at Jess, "Do you understand, even a little, the importance of these things?"

"No, but 'tis interesting," Jess said, head bobbing, Adam's apple glugging. The boy cleared a gob of phlegm and spat and continued tromping along in an ungainly, off-kilter way.

Naturally, Lewis thought. *My apprentice would naturally be a mental defective.*

"Look, Jess," he said. "I can tell you much more. I am an expert on the topic of old bachelors. I can recite to you, chapter and verse, the accidents that assail us in matters of love. I'll teach you the nature of an honest mind, and how to dispatch one's duty, regardless."

"Regardless of what?" Jess said, glancing up as if slightly outraged.

"Regardless of everything, Jess. One's duty is performed regardless of regard. Regardless of breathing."

The boy gave a short, disdainful laugh. "I think you're cracked," he said. "I'm already tired of listening to you. People told me about you. . . ."

Lewis stopped in the street and grappled Jessaume by one bony, truculent shoulder. "Listen, you," he said with a shake, "I have five thousands in land. I have crossed a continent on my hands and knees, dragging thirty-two men after me. And what are you, pray tell me? Name to me one thing that you have or are!"

Jessaume went stiff in the face, and a cold shadow of hatred dulled his features like a cloud blocking a weak, chilly sunlight. With a jerk, he knocked Lewis's hand off and walked away, alone.

Lewis sighed, his whole body shaking. Perhaps it was right, after all, that he had no wife, no sons. Perhaps God knew best. He walked behind Jess for a few paces, then caught up and stopped him.

"Forget all that, Jess," Lewis said. "I know nothing about boys, and am only a musty fusty rusty old bachelor."

Jess gazed disaffectedly at nothing. He seemed to be hung an inch or so above the ground by a cord which bent him at the middle. He was furiously, painfully morose and horrified at being forced to leave home. His big hands were crooked forth as if to shake. He was not cheeky or a dandy, and his collar was too high and too starched for tipping his head any way but forward. He had bright red cheeks and a bulbous nose, and red hair that stuck out all downy pinfeathers.

"And yet, I must repeat, Jess," Lewis said, using the pet name as a way to like that face, "there is duty and there is nothing else. Duty is all we have."

"Well, there's money," Jess said.

"No, there isn't," Lewis said. "And the sooner you get that out of your head, the better. It's nonsense. It's lies."

"And there's girls. Lots of pret-ty girls," Jess said toyingly, mockingly, checking Lewis from the corner of his eye. They again started along feebly to the office.

"No, there are not," Lewis said. "You only imagine there are. And when you try to get one, you'll find that out." He was trying to hold Jess's eye while crossing, and hopping over streams and puddles of urine and horse pats, which the boy splashed straight through.

"I can get them if I please," Jess said. "I've had four already."

"Not that kind," Lewis said. "I mean a true woman to whom you are true! You must find a thing and be true to 't all your miserable days. And many will be miserable, I promise you that."

"My God, you're cracked," Jess said, but softly. "I knew 't soon as I saw you, God help me."

"You've never heard honesty, that's your trouble," Lewis said. "I'm saving you year upon year of fruitless seeking."

"I plan ta get some land, that's all," Jess said, with a shrug.

"I already have land, sir, and 'tis nothing!" Lewis said, causing the boy to move off a yard. More gently, he said, "You must be true, Jess. You must swear an oath. Pick a hard track—medicine or law or, perhaps in your case, a trade. Be unswerving. Put on blinders and never look behind you."

"I'll just take some land, thank you," Jess said lightly, then belched the breakfast Lewis bought for him.

After this day, Lewis continued to call for him every morning, but they spent less time in dialogue. Jess kept himself two steps to the side, kicking a small, hard horse pat.

Clark was away just then at Independence, establishing a fort in Osage territory. For some reason, Lewis felt almost frightened when Clark was out of town, but didn't know what he feared, or what Clark might do were he there.

Then, sickening news: the attempt to return Big White upriver to his people had failed. Worse, Shannon had lost a leg. The very man he'd saved, twice! from wandering the world forevermore. A man he'd carried, nearly, four thousand miles and back without a scratch!

His distress at this had no voice. His muscles seemed frozen to his limbs, his spine a row of brittle coral points. He wrote a requisition to Washington, the War Department, for five hundred muskets, three hundred rifles, a ton of gunpowder. Sending notes here, there, he recruited half a battalion of men to settle the Arikara, to wipe them from the earth once and for all. He needed to hurry, before the only thing he'd ever done was picked down to bones.

The next day, his familiar squatting on his chest, crushing out his air, and gasping after scant mouthfuls of breath, he walked quickly, hoping not to see anyone. Catching his image in a window, hair wild, eyes and mouth screwed into an appalling scowl, he almost turned back. The dark, simple, rectangular white-brick building was daylit, with open doorways at either end. Up a staircase, 'round a corner, he found Shannon in a wheelchair in the hall, bandaged stump oozing into cotton dressings, the smell of bedpans insinuating as perfume. They'd shaved him and oiled his face and hair so he was shiny, skin red as a demon's after stoking a pitch-pot. A funny smile lay crookedly on his lips, over broken teeth wetted by his fat tongue. Embarrassed was how he looked, a man with a secret shame.

"O, Shannon!" Lewis said. "What sort of business is this, now? My God, what have they done to you?"

A nurse, folding sheets nearby, didn't like to hear his tone, apparently. She left with a bang, through a side door.

"'Ey did it to my leg, sir, not me," George said. "I was jus' attached to 't when they shot it from under me."

A stout, formerly robust fellow, his eyes sagged with a mysterious sadness, like he'd seen two hundred years of troubles. God needn't bother with Shannon any longer: the worst had happened.

"O, Shannon. Forever lost," Lewis said, sitting on the marble bench before his dizziness could make him fall. "Forever miles and miles ahead of everyone."

"I tweren't never lost, Cap'n," he said. Then seemed to recollect something, and frowned and looked down. "Hit's jes' like you say. I was jes' way out ahead."

"All right, but what about this gangrene?" Lewis asked. "Will they never stop inventing ways to kill you?"

Shannon grinned faintly and licked his broken teeth. "Who's 'they,' Cap'n? Who d' ya mean?"

"O! *They*, Shannon. *They*. The ones who make designs and plots to crush the innocents who simply find themselves in the way!"

"When I was 'up ahead,' I did suffer, Cap'n," Shannon said. "An' I had long dreams 'bout what's goin' ta happen." His heavy chorus-girl eyelashes fluttered and his hazel eyes winked sadly.

"You'll get better, that's what will happen," Lewis said. "You'll run for the Senate, of course."

"I will?" he asked unhappily, with wider eyes.

"Of course. Or whatever you wish, George," Lewis said. "I simply mean you'll do something useful with your life. You all will."

Shannon glanced at him, darting his eyes like minnows, and nodding with a bare, doubtful movement.

"Yes, sir," he said.

Then Lewis wished he hadn't said it, since a blood clot might kill the man in the next moment.

"You'll get married," Lewis said, as if his tongue had no law. "A woman will set you up nicely. She'll do things for you you can't imagine."

Shannon looked wistful at that. He seemed to be thinking of a woman, one he couldn't have, whom he'd lost and now couldn't find, whose whereabouts were unknown. She was so hidden, only his heart knew she existed on earth. Only his lips remembered her. He was trying to call up her face. Tears started to his eyes and his tongue groped after her name, but could not fashion it.

"Don't," Lewis said. "Don't try to name her. Don't try to remember her. It will only pain you and it pains me to watch you. If not her, you'll have another. Don't suffer over her all your days."

"I was thinkin' on somethin' else, Cap'n," he said, tears wetting his face.

"You've had an awful shock," Lewis said. "Get well. I will visit you. But I must warn you: they are attempting to undo all we did, Shannon. They are trying to feed themselves on what we made, you and I."

"But who are *they*, ek-zakly, Cap'n?" Shannon asked.

"I mean certain types. The pragmatistical men. The pollsters. The statistical men of our insane, numerical new age," Lewis said. "They are founding a new world based on two mathematical systems called profit and loss."

"I had a dream," Shannon said, concealed behind a white handkerchief, which he drew hard down his face, leaving red and pink streaks and paler blotches. With two flat, watery discs, like wounds, where his eyes ought to be. Or was this some awful trick of the light?

"O? Did you dream you lost your way?" Lewis asked.

"Never mind. I can't recall it," he said. He looked down the hall as if for the answer. "What is it these new-age men want, sir? What're they after?"

"Always the same thing," Lewis said, "and they are not new at all. All along, they plot ways to keep the people frightened and servile, like children." Lewis cracked his knuckles for emphasis. As he looked, new drops of blood were born in Shannon's dressing, blooming through the cotton. Lewis recalled his French mistress whose poor head he'd held, as she lay as if dead, and so heavy, the blood seeping from that puckered fissure he'd made in her.

George looked as if he'd had a dark thought.

"What's the matter, son?" Lewis asked.

"All my plans and fond hopes," George said. "Everythin' I was goin' ta be."

Lewis thought on that, blackly, for a moment. Not only would he mount an army against the Arikara, he'd invite other nations, Minnetarries and Mandans, to join in the massacre. How good it was, though, to see an end of things. He did not expect to last much more. Now, anyone who struck at him or one of his would get a terrible surprise.

Dimly there, in the half-light of the empty hallway, surrounded by windows that glow'd and shook, Lewis sensed a change. History held her breath and the sun stopped its motion. He was no longer trying to find ways to stay. Which meant a new freedom stretched out spaciously before him, to the east. No longer bitter because no longer unknown, the future was suddenly all his.

And O, those hallways with planks waxed almost black and all the tightly shut walnut doors and dull transom lights! He had aching kidneys, a sore back, and a whinging pain behind his eyes. This was his body, all right. He kept waking to find himself back inside it and his life.

"No plans means a clean slate, son," he said at last to George. "You'll forge new ones."

Shannon nodded weakly. It was like Lewis had to go about breathing his will into every last one of them. Each was maimed in some way, in need of being made anew. Like God, he hovered in suspense over this man, feeling torn. Should he mash him back into raw clay or attempt a new remedy?

"Ah-about my dream," George said, stammering. "I was some sorta gardener or caretaker on a big, big estate or somethin' . . . with little white flags. . . ."

"Never mind it," Lewis said. "Dreams belong to the dreamer. Keep your dreams."

"Yes, sir," Shannon sighed. He fell back in the chair, sweating, gray, and exhausted from the interview.

When Lewis started away from the hospital, he tried to turn west, toward Clark's, but the lane was darkening toward evening and vanishing into a wooded, blind curve. He couldn't make much headway, like tacking into a gale. His anxiety so increased with each step he took that he trembled. Going along by little bursts, five or six steps at a time, he'd be suddenly overtaken by knots of women out for a stroll. Pretending to notice something rare on the ground, he let them by. Invariably, they were wives of men he owed money. And he could not e'en walk a straight course home, let alone pay his debts or govern this second new nation. Giving up, he turned east, his steps immediately easy. And got home after dark, weak and wet through like he'd pushed a boulder there ahead of him.

What are you up to? he asked *it,* as he panted in a chair.

The following morning, he turned east out the door and wondered if he'd be able to come back west at day's end. He was losing ground, quite literally.

At the office a letter was waiting, from Tom. His eyes blundered into it until a phrase stopped him: "I never had a line from you . . ." He blinked painfully and tried again, but his guts swam like he was falling. Quickly he put it away from him, laying it out dead on a pile he planned never to answer. Yes, and here is for you, sir! Welcome to oblivion.

A letter from a Mr. Dearborn, War Department, arrived. A rebuke for his vast order of guns and men, with war against Britain so imminent. He spent some hours then, 'til the middle of the night, working on a treatise, "True Ambitions of an Honest Mind." Reading it over, he couldn't recognize the person who wrote it.

That night, he covered the mirrors in his rooms. He then sat and wrote his mother, Lucy, his first letter in a year, telling her of the fur company he'd formed with several others, and land he'd bought. He broke news that might well kill her: he was selling Locust Hill, where she and Reuben had long resided. They must try to bravely face this fact, and pack for St. Louis.

Meanwhile, Clark was having trouble with York, who was relentless to be freed, for his wife had been sold far off. Lewis started to laugh. But his laughter was so strange now, a wheezing from a broken pipe organ, he stopped. O, black abomination! To keep any man from any woman who loved him!

Through hot, endless, dust-blown days, nobody came into the office except Bates, his assistant. Bates, whose brother was runner-up for the plummest job ever. Bates of the long upper lip and pale round eyes, the white healed gash in his forehead, a childhood injury, whose large head must've made a seductive target for ev'ry boy with a rock. Then, his long, thin arms and legs, severe, narrow temples, and gray, numeric gaze. Immobile as a crocodile, legs spraddled and feet flat before him, he observed your approach in a pinched collar. With diabolic energy, he kept notes in a crabbed hand in black ledgers.

Lewis had a horror of the office as of the grave, but Bates was much at home there. Recently, Lewis came upon a letter, fallen out of the carrier's pack, in the middle of the hall. In it, Bates told his brother he was unhappy, that it was "a strange world" in St. Louis; he found himself in "acrimonious differences" with everyone he met.

Tired of borrowing from friends, Lewis went in to see Bates. The fellow sat in the arched gloom, so stacked up with official papers they blocked the windows. Bates gave him a curious, prehistoric smile. He thought Lewis had come to begin anew, here and now, and not be his enemy any longer. With grotesque forehead and protruding temples like some saint. And the ticking of a clock. But when Lewis said nothing, an unhappy discovery touched Bates's mouth. The tight jaw grew hard, the black-rimmed eyeballs dried up like peas.

Lewis sat lower, as one did in Bates's company.

"What, Mr. Lewis? What?" he asked. "You visit, then say nothing."

"I have a question for you, sir," Lewis said.

"And I have an answer," he said, with a ferocious lunge, opening a drawer and taking out money. "How much do you need? And forgive me for saying, but you are losing ground! There is growing unrest."

Lewis nodded, with a fever'd grin. "Indeed, you are right about losing ground. My legs no longer travel west. It's just east, east, east now."

Bates smote his hand with ten pounds British, like Lewis's fate was writ on 't. "Lewis, how from love I pity thee," he said. "You are now at such a height that when you fall, you will dash yourself to pieces!"

Then stared at Lewis with a mix of contempt, envy, and a dog-like desire for the rabbit to run. The black peas never moisten'd, stung with eternal, dry, envenomed hurt, like a boy struck by a drunkard father. But terrified, too, wanting a guide thro' this strange world and praying Lewis wouldn't abandon him.

"I need go," Lewis said. "But know this, sir: you are ideal for the age that is coming. It was made for thee, and you may stay! It is I who am misfit and must go!"

Lewis burst out the door. He went on hearing Bates's clock, tho, and had finally come to like the sound. For it was no longer interminable, not horrible, like the infinite stars. It would end.

Getting across town was formidable. An alley was impossible. And any road entering a blind, wooded curve. Or under a stone bridge. Or any rise too tall to see over. He chang'd course a dozen times, until worked up into a full, twisting sweat. The thing in him glowered and warred against him. But where did it live? How did one plot against what lay in the very next breath? The only tack that worked was three or four days of sleepless work and pacing, and drink and opium lozenges, and then collapse.

Meantime, the Great Osage were not in accord with policy, and would need be wip'd from the earth, too, like the Tetons, like the Arikara. He was no longer in any mood for half measures, and anyway, not every human could be suffered to live.

A letter appeared, the War Department again. This one he held, then pretended to lose, then found again at the last instant of the day. Its white edge blazed forth from under its duller cousins. He broke the seal. He threw it toward the open window. It fell short.

With a sigh, a hard-beating heart, he prized it open and looked at his draft for $18.50, refused. Refused. An accompanying note explained that it was refused, though any idiot could see that. Not a vast sum. But the cold, numbing shock was like the time Peter shot him. For if all the drafts were refused, by the dozens, by the hundreds . . . He could not breathe. Shivering with amazement, in delirious tremors, mouth open to suck wind, he went to his knees, then fell, shuddering, forehead pressed to the black, waxed walnut boards.

"There! Enough!" he managed to croak. "This much and no more!"

It gradually let him up to a knee.

"O, one day, I shall settle thee!" he told it. "And where will you go then? Who will feed you then?"

Sitting up in a chair, he thought of the Nations, stealing goods they had no means to pay for, their morality all but ruined. Now he was being finished, too, by another sort of parasite which kept him out of the generous stream, human contact, lest he meet a woman who might save him. O, *if only she'd loved him!*

But the stupid, wretched, jealous thing would kill him first. Hating people and yet needing people. So, in fact, his eternal guest loved people— a dread irony—but was hated by them and hunted, its blood sought.

Lewis fought back. He managed to write a letter, commending a half-Indian boy to West Point. But his friend's counterpunch was twice as strong and staggered him with vertigo and crushed his lungs. Any day now, Janey and her children were expected at the Clarks'. But he could not see her like this, as a craven, muttering, gaunt shadow-self.

That next night, he went to a ball (permitted by his creature because it was his last). He stood at that cotillion in the coolest humour, recalling the day he was sure she loved him. Alert and able to look at each bare shoulder, at each face, frozen yet in motion, and at the black marble columns and pink mica floor, the blood on the nape of a neck from a crushed bedbug. He smelled slivered bitter almonds from the cake, the gassy, tiny stink of champagne, the sweet, dead dried lilacs, and chloroform from the moth-nibbled gowns and gloves.

The beast knew where he was, but could not interfere. Which increas'd its frantic pacing, raging up and down his torchlit marble corridors and stairways, claws clicking and slipping.

Bates was there, at a table for six. With two unhappy ladies who wished he would go or drop dead. The man coloured brightly at the sight of his employer. Lewis dragged up a chair very noisily and almost overturned the table, which set the glasses sloshing.

As he sat, Bates stood. With a thrust of his forehead at the ladies, he walked away. Lewis wished he imagined the rest, when the orchestra wheezed to a stop, or stuttered in a strange way, when all eyes were fixed on the spectacle. When all of St. Louis saw his shame! And the two ladies exploded from wooden chairs in their bright plumage as if catapulted into the air. Using fans like wings, they beat their way downstream away from him to the punch bowl with a flurry and a rustling, like a new bride being ripped from her wedding dress in the dark of a carriage.

He waited for the laughter, the jeering, the gleeful mockery. But ev'ry face had turned and pretended nothing had occurred.

Now real laughter came from deep down below. The thing met him with its careful, gloating smugness. *I told you, did I not? I warned you about people.*

Going home, he was in a frenzy. His legs tried to spasm and lock. Any moment, he'd put down roots like an ash tree after the castration of Uranus. Formed by splashes of bloody semen, he'd take root on a lonely beach for all eternity.

He got there in a helpless sweat, with nothing left. Apparently, he'd used all his footsteps on that long march to the sea.

The next day was his birthday. The world outside was horses, drays, carts, and workmen and widows in their mourning weeds. Women carried cakes iced and studded with candied bloody currants or squashed bedbugs. The cemetery with its willy-nilly, silly tipping headstones. A stone hand pointing straight upward as if offering directions. He felt himself being jerked along the street, body outlined in ragged rays of angry light.

The next day, another letter. The War Department.

He sat outside in the courtyard next to Chouteau's house and worked it open with teeth and fingernails. It hovered, very whitely, on his knee. Refused. Over $500 this time. The beast laughed furiously. Then, calmer, *All right, we knew this was coming; do not pretend surprise.*

Shut up! he told it.

There was still the journal, after all. That might bring something, except the world didn't deserve it.

He wrote his own letter, telling his enemies to expect him. His country might try to bankrupt him, but she could never make a Burr of him. He made plans to go by water, because he could not go by land.

Tom's letter came, but he was past feeling. It said Tom felt fully "bankrupt" in the eyes of his friends, who'd been promised copies of a nonexistent book. Either barking mad now, or very sane, he put it carefully aside on the "dead" pile and decided it had not come. A prince forgot the favors you did him, as Gulliver said, but never the one you refused to do.

Word spread. One by one, one by one, they came. All through the night and the next morning, he was visited by the ghosts of those who'd given him credit, until he'd handed over his last deed to the last gray-faced, blue-jawed gent, red-eyed with hangover, angry at being forced from bed before 2 P.M. In less than a day, it was done.

He looked down at what was left, some clothes, luggage, and papers. A sealskin she'd given her girdle for. A broken pike he'd used to face down a charging ton of claws and teeth.

Having no plan, he'd arrived at wisdom, for without plans, one needed no confidants. He went to the office, but Bates was out. Instead, he'd left a note in which he said he loved Lewis and was full of sorrow for him. Unsigned.

He went to Clark's, who already knew and met him at the garden gate, and shrugged and grinned terribly, as if to keep from weeping, pulling faces in a very queer way. O, how sorry he was, and not just for this cruel turn. He kept rubbing his hand very hard over his features. They sat opposite, on opposing benches. "I say, it will come 'round right in the long run," Clark said. "I know it will."

Then he leaned toward Lewis and shook him by the knee, like some theatrical older brother. "Come now, Lewis! Shake it off, man! It will be all right, won't it?"

"O, will it, then? Very well, then," Lewis said.

"Lewis, you are the most honest man I ever knew," Clark said, freckled and plump and dowdy with domesticity. His hair thinning, his frame sagging toward the earth. "I never knew an honester one."

"Honest ruined men are common as folk," Lewis said. "Swing a cat and hit ten."

"Come, you will be all right!" he insisted. "A few days in Washington. You will return to our shores with colours flying."

They sat for a long moment in a silence that seemed to hum and faintly shriek. The sky trail'd clouds that glowed and shook. Clark felt it, too, Lewis knew, the stillness, the strange violet colour of the light. The trees in the orchard stretched away in straight lines toward a point in infinity. But the lines never met, not even where the world shivered to a stop. Sweet horror, of a judgment coming exactly at sundown, affected every particle of light.

"We have made the infinite finite," Lewis said. "We are the murtherers of mystery."

"Yes. And what of the Arikara now? Where are the Osages now, and the Tetons?" Clark asked, adjusting his tricorner on his skull as he used his stick to mutilate the ground.

"All gone," Lewis said, because he knew the future. "When they trifled with Shannon, they made love with extinction."

The pegs squealed in the wood bench. The air was heavy with dust and beeswax and the scent of dying flowers and pumpkin vines.

"All seems amusing, absurd to me," Lewis added. "Beds, linens, chairs, doors, houses with locks and keys. And yet I fret how I appear to you."

"What will you do, Lewis?" Clark asked.

"Do? I won't do a thing. Let us have no more ambitions," he said. "We have had too much already. Already the dead are clamouring to know: Was their massacre worth this triumph?" And he gestured in a way to include the continent.

Clark shook his head. A pang of conscience caused Clark to think of her, on that far shore, washing. She would be thinking on all she'd done and seen, her heart sore, tender, rueful, and stuffed so full it ripp'd along its seams.

"But what can we do, Lewis?" Clark asked almost impatiently, striking a brick viciously with his stick.

"Nothing," Lewis said. "I was one of the world's living, Clark. Like every human, I lived my true life elsewhere, amid wholly different scenes. God Herself cannot find me. I am thoroughly immured."

Clark ignored the gaffe at God. "But we sought this, Lewis. We did." Clark looked put off and disappointed suddenly in his choices. Lewis wished he hadn't come.

"O, you will be all right," Lewis said. He gazed downward at some sunflower seeds, thrown in the dirt for the scratching hens. "But I—I could never live in Tom's world. I am a creature starv'd by this stuff you people call life."

Clark snapped his branch in two with an involuntary jerk.

"By believing that, you make it true, Lewis," he said.

"Clark, I was only the custodian of this body," he said. "And as you know, adventuring is already done with. Life need not include great feats. Why, a fine sort of life can be led by any farmer 'thout stirring five miles from home!"

"Easy, easy, sir," Clark said. "Rest yourself."

"I will try," he said. But couldn't ignore how the lowering light settled in the branches of the apple trees. The dust was awake and sifting upward in the angled rays. A sweet scent of chicken waste stung his nostrils like the most exotic spiced oils. He was in desperation for how to end. "I cannot relieve distressed humanity, after all," Lewis said.

"Who says you should?" Clark asked.

"Now I go to Washington, in white stone," he said. "Worked with chisels, it sits amid a checkerboard of farms. Clouds steer its skies like ships."

Clark nodded. "Remember New Year's on the Pacific coast, drinking water so cold it hurt the teeth?" he said. "Eating elk meat so green with sour it fizzed going down, like cider? Talking of the all-water route, never found?"

"Sent to prove a folk tale," Lewis muttered. He threw down some seeds in the dirt, and they formed the Big Dipper. He chose to ignore it.

"Sometimes," Clark said, "I think we walked out of a wilderness into a much harder place."

Lewis refused to be kind to Clark anymore, and said nothing.

"Then something happened," Clark said. "What was it, Lewis, that used to erase the distance between us?"

"Need," Lewis said gruffly. "The best glue of all."

Clark whinged, stung. But—for Christ's sake!—how was he supposed to've known Lewis loved her? What sign had he ever shewed?

"As for husbands," Lewis said, "they are a tool for defense, a position in the world, that is all. A woman doesn't need a man to map the labyrinth of her soul."

"Husbands, now? I cannot catch up to you today." Clark laughed, casting his broken branch away.

"By the way, none of the men got the extra wages they deserved," Lewis said. "Yet that creature collected every last cent."

"Lewis, you need rest," Clark said. "Your eyes are otherworldly."

"I know." He smiled. "I would change them but like the effect on visitors to my cell."

"What about our book?" Clark asked.

Lewis sat just the same, making that his answer. "Meanwhile, the men lunge forward with their deathless accounts, this one, that one, until I am ruined buying them all up."

"Why not let them go ahead?" Clark asked. "What's the harm?"

"They miss the underlying story," Lewis said.

Clark fixed him in an interrogative way, with that arrogant cant to his head. "Lewis, forgive me, but what ever went wrong with F.?"

"F. was fine," he said. "Also, she was high-strung, noble, compassionate, and firm, and will die of childbirth. She'd turn to salt if she glimps'd my heart."

"But why? Once for all, just tell me why," Clark said, keeping one bluey eye trained steadily.

"Tell me, Clark. Do you find men remarkable?" Lewis asked.

"No," Clark said. "Nor do I find humanity precious, because most people are very ordinary. Half could be killed without causing a ripple to the rest. The trouble is in determining which half."

"Tom hath said I was the fittest person in the world to send," Lewis said. "Yet, one hand is forever taking the other from my throat. Theseus slew the Minotaur and then escaped back out by winding up his silver cord."

"Lewis, I think you leave something out," Clark said. "I can't follow . . ."

"Don't you?" Lewis laughed, then stopped because it made a sound like wood ripping. "Isn't a river silver, like a cord? My mistake was in bringing an army. Theseus went alone."

"But where is the Minotaur in this fable?" Clark asked, smiling foolishly, for his friend was quite clearly completely mad.

Lewis stared into Clark's face. "Don't jest, for I am looking eye to eye with it. This is an event that *must* take place."

Clark sat with a desperate impatience, grinding big farmer's fists into his knees, and showing his lower teeth, face hot with passion as if about to fall down and shake. It was time to go, Lewis knew, and spare Clark what he plainly couldn't bear.

"Look," Lewis said, pointing at the sunset. "Obscured by a cloudy horizon, shrouded in red-streaked dazzlement, we witness a spectacle of terrible majesty. The dawning of a new race. The Americans."

"So you regret it?" Clark asked, sitting up straighter.

"I no longer know," he said.

"But where will you go?" Clark asked.

"To wrest a victory from those who pronounce over success, and call it, alas, a failure in disguise," he said.

"Is that all, Lewis?" Clark asked. "Will you say nothing more to me?"

"Only this," Lewis said, rising uneasily. "God damn the little men! God damn the little fellows who cannot journey two towns from home for the uncertainties involved!"

He felt safe and sure that his time had passed. Standing with some struggle, swaying, he smelled the illness. Preparing for transformation, he now stank differently.

"Are you all right? Do you need my help?" Clark asked.

"For this tiny hardship? Why, this is some merry lark compared to mapping North America!"

He felt a dangerous joy; it threatened to career out of control into convulsive laughter. He covered his mouth. What he needed was many, many drams, an ocean of whiskey, to pour his whelming dread out into cups and swallow it back down again.

They shook hands. Lewis got up into the saddle on his own.

"Still and all, 'll see you in Washington in six weeks, Lewis," Clark said. "You must last as best you can 'til I arrive."

"I will last out my time," Lewis said, "and not a minute less." And gave a kick to his horse.

At bottom, watching Lewis ride away, Clark knew what it was all about, but had said nothing. Deeds done in the dark belonged there; even Lewis would say the same. But O, why was Lewis the sort of man one could not resist harming? He extended to you a very great temptation, then waited 'til you did what he knew you would all along. And while he hoped you'd be different, better, as good as he was, you never were.

On the other hand, how good was the man who'd consigned the Arikara to extermination? O, yes. Yes, it helped all right, for a moment anyway, to try to judge at Lewis, to blame him. But only a moment.

25.

"...whether my mother is yet living..."

In bed, a pillow packed down tight on his head, Bill groaned and wallowed in the covers and gripped his forehead in agony, because it was Saturday, time to do the grocery shopping. He'd have to tell Emily today, too, about the money. And ought to visit his mom, also, pay his respects. But all he really wondered, staring at the wall in his dilemma, was how to be alone with his cell phone, to see if Rita'd left him a message. Somehow, along the way, his life had started splintering into subplots, making it hard to find the main thread. For now, she was all he had.

The same thing'd happened in Africa, and with Crazy Horse, and the interned Japanese Americans, the village of My Lai. Somebody'd lost the thread.

In getting up and leaving the house, he took the checkbook with him, resolving that issue for a few hours. He smoked four cigarettes behind the garage, growing dizzier with each drag, heart twitching like a scared, blind, cave-dwelling fish in an earthquake. The plot unfolding with Rita already happened, it seemed. He'd come this way before, snapshots of his last major depression flashing in his head. Along the way, control was wrested from his hands. And since he didn't know who'd seized it, every man was his enemy. Every woman, too, but not Rita.

In a little while, he'd gotten to the store and parked, and found a wobbly cart. His head inside the door of a freezer, fumbling after a slippery brick of vanilla, he realized someone was watching him. A woman had stopped her cart a few feet away. Somehow he knew without looking: it was she, his mother.

The ice cream slipped from his grasp and fell where he couldn't reach it.

"Oh, you'll have to eat cake!" she said with a laugh.

He grinned and straightened up, feeling, as he always did with her, chastised and large. He knew he was fatter than when he'd seen her last, and stank of cigarettes.

"Mom, how're you?"

"Oh, fine. I'm just fine." She looked in his cart, then pretended she hadn't.

He'd been stooped too long in that comical fashion, red-faced from effort. Also, his parents made him nervous. And she was not a big jolly mother, but more on the extremely thin side. She wore long, drapey coats that showed how well-off she was, never went without earrings or gold buckles on her black patent-leather shoes. Marie always acted glad to see him, but he wasn't so sure. She seemed to wait for him to say something very serious. He'd never yet said it, but she kept waiting, encouraging. He felt some despair that he'd disappoint her, in the end.

"You see your father lately? How's he?" she asked, with a small, polite cough.

She always asked, and the question seemed too complex to answer. He felt like a double agent, one who'd gone so deep under cover, even he wasn't sure who he worked for. Cut off in enemy territory, now he just waited for orders, or to be brought in from the cold. Fortunately, he was immune to torture because he knew no secret plans. Sometimes he thought he worked for Lloyd, other times Marie. Lately, though, he wondered if there'd ever been a mission. The war was over, and neither side had really won.

"He's okay," he said at last.

After an hour in the store, he didn't have much in his cart. Plus, he was shopping the wrong way, left to right, and sometimes backtracking. He had baker's chocolate, cranberries, a turkey baster, trussing twine—a bizarre survival kit—complete with breadcrumbs for finding his way home.

"I thought *I* was doing the turkey," she said.

"This is for something else," he said. His coat was losing a button, he noted, his threads unraveling.

"Jesus, you're going backward, Bill," she said, teasing him. "It's right to left, silly, like reading Hebrew."

"I know, I know," he said, blinking, nodding, trying to smile. Why so painful, so difficult, just attempting to talk to one's mother? He had to say something fast or lose his toehold on the slippery slope of their history. "Ya know, Ma, I really miss how the holidays used to be," he said. "I mean, with the whole family there and all."

"Bill, open your eyes!" she said. "We *are* the whole family. This is it. We're all that's left."

She made steady, serene eye contact, head slightly tipped, with that troublemaking gleam in her green irises. She'd like him to snap out of it for a change, just for once. Why so miserable? Why'd she have to have such an unhappy, hangdog little boy? But how great it must be for her now, for both his parents! To have his youth behind them, and look back on it from shore, from complete safety, and recall the tight scrapes, the near misses.

"I can't help it," he said. "I keep thinking about the big family Henry could've had."

"Yeah, I know, Bill. Too bad about all that stuff," she said. "So what was Henry for Halloween?"

"Nothing. He wouldn't even go out."

"Now, who was that boy you used to trick-or-treat with?" she asked, gazing across the aisle like she needed to remember to write "capable son" on her grocery list. "What was his name?"

"J. C.," he said. She pretended not to recall the best friend who'd gone nuts in high school, tried suicide, found Jesus, tried suicide again, joined the service, then gone AWOL, and was still out there somewhere, living on a bench or under a bridge.

"Neither of you got much male contact," she said. "I mean, with the crazy way men were then. They just didn't come home."

He almost blurted it out then. That if men hadn't come home, and still didn't want to, it was because of the mission, the one every man was secretly enlisted in, to go far away into enemy territory, to explore, reconnoiter, kill the enemy, win the girl, come back a hero. But, no matter how many years passed, that stayed classified, still triple-super-top-secret. And wasn't discussed, not even among men. Nor could you torture a man into admitting it existed.

Her eyes were on his cart again, disapproving of what they'd resorted to to entice Henry, smoked sardines, canned beef stew, a brick of sharp cheese, a banana-cream pie. That store was so colorful and bright, so odorless and weatherless, it was giving him a dizzy, overinflated feeling. Plus, something strange had intervened to keep people out of the aisle.

"I always felt sorry for you and J. C.," she said. "With all of our fighting and divorcing and trying to kill each other, I think it confused you about what to want from life."

She turned one foot the other way, indicating they needed to part. Her cart drifted away about an inch. "I need to go, baby, but we'll see you all next Thursday," she said. "Love you." She beamed at him. About halfway down the aisle, she looked back and waved. Then she stopped a little farther on and did it again.

He had tears in his eyes. The hardest thing about it, seeing her this way, was that she was gone. She'd died about two years ago. Now when he saw her, the whole thing had to happen this way, in his head.

Out in the parking lot, he simply sat, looking through the smeary windshield, recalling J. C. and the monster that took him. J. C.'d gone crazy that summer before senior year, and fled headlong into the arms of Jesus. Who couldn't save him. Bill was lost, too, the monster pursuing him, too. But it got J. C. first, who kept it occupied while Bill ran away, holding his ears against J. C.'s screams.

But had he really gotten away?

And the answer was . . . the answer was . . . Joaney? No, it was not Joaney with those tight curls of lemony permed hair. Could it be Rita? It wasn't Jesus, obviously, crucified on the cross, because the Jews and Muslims and Buddhists didn't even believe that. It was hard to be calm.

He started driving, weaving in and out of too-slow Saturday traffic, the sunshine-filled lie of clear weather, wanting a cigarette and hating how bad he wanted it. The groceries slowly warmed, the milk no longer cool to the touch. When he squinted, he could almost see the antiheroic, postsacred, antimacho, tolerant New World shouldering its way in. Never mind. It was too late for that, much too late.

And that check. What would Emily make of that, and what would he say, and what was the truth? *Look, Em, it was either that or take her in my arms. Don't you see? I had no choice!*

The crazy things happening almost formed a deranged pattern. So WWPD? What would Pablo do? Meanwhile, the milk was spoiling, the meat was thawing. Like a coward, a gigolo, a liar, a fraud, a clown, a conscienceless con man and opportunist, an enemy of men and a fugitive, he thought of Rita. He neatly divided her from Pablo in his mind like he'd never existed. (*Adios, Pablo, adios! Go with God, you good-hearted fuck!*)

345

Across the railroad tracks, breaking free to the east side, he cruised the little wooded byways. Scowling at where he'd lived as a kid, that first abode of boyhood nightmare. He glided through the empty streets, the three-way and four-way stops, with nobody around to witness his sorrow. A sunny Saturday afternoon, and yet so sickening and unhappy. Meanwhile the mission in this new age lay sunken and wrecked, its back broken on the floor of the male soul.

And grief the lot of every boy because he didn't know how to undertake it, or what to do with the half-killed thing tossed back to him by his own sweet dad.

He went on, past the postwar cracker box Lloyd couldn't afford to own. Jesus. There it went, the commodious American dream. In crummy white, dingy-roofed and dirt-yarded. And yet it stood there, despite nuclear blasts in Hiroshima and Nagasaki.

It wasn't a place to do anything tragic. *Police found him outside his boyhood home.* Jesus.

Still, he had failed, squandered that male dream of interminable going, of unending freedom. Of many loves and no cumbrous ties.

His mind turned to Lewis. His first check, written on the War Department, had bounced that July. Which'd caused him "infinite concern." Not "deep" or "profound" but infinite. No brakes on a mountain road. A toy arrow sunk in your child's eye.

The next one to bounce, the mortal one, was for $500. Word spread fast through St. Louis, which was right at one thousand people, about as big as a rural high school. Within a few days, he handed over everything to panicked creditors, $4,000 worth. All he had left was his clothes, the seal fur she'd bought for him, a broken spear. Unlike Ahab, he would not give up the spear.

He had his patriotism. He said America could do what she wished to him, but she could never make a Burr of him. He briefed Clark about how to do his job. He left with everything and clearly wasn't coming back. You'd think his best friend could figure this out.

Just before going, Lewis wrote a letter to Theo, saying basically, *Dearest Theo, Looks like I'll be dead soon. No time to explain just now, but I'll see you shortly. Love, M.*

He never got there. For three straight years since the expedition, he'd been trying to justify the trip. Now he was lying to everyone, bleeding money and reputation from a dozen wounds. If asked, he'd look you right in the eye and say the book was almost done.

Dead on his feet, he's just looking for a place to fall.

Driving, making a big circle around town, Bill was getting where he'd been going all along, he realized. He was having a bad trip, wandering deeper and deeper into the maze of boulevards. But somewhere along these gracious streets, among the monument-like houses, dwelt the last beautiful woman on earth. And Pablo wouldn't be there today, because it was a football weekend.

How clever it was of him not to follow sports! Because it left him free to go exploring among these houses while the other men were away. Yes, very cunning of him, and low-down.

He turned the engine off. Now the only sounds were of the lettuce wilting and shifting and the meat thawing. Looking up at the huge windows and long Frank Lloyd Wright lines of Casa Pablo Garcia, a patchy sort of bug-eaten yard, lots of big Mexican-bright pots, trees festooned with bird feeders.

The front door hopped open, and his breathing quickened. It was Rita, and he thrilled at the sight. She stepped out on the front step, wearing jeans and flats, an old brown sweater ripped at the elbows, hugging herself against the cold. Waving, she came to him down the steps, one by one.

She was at his window. He put it down with a steady stab of a finger, a curtain of dirty water parting between them. She was smiling and puzzled, pleased and uncertain, like she might kiss him or bolt at the least sign. Oh, that thin nose and those troublemaking eyes of green! That seductively crooked red mouth, nice as pie. Her hand quaked slightly, brushed back a strand of copper. "Hi, Lewis," she said carefully. "My God, what brings you here? I just happened to look out the door and there you were." Her eyes swept the sacks in the backseat, his ruined fenders.

"Nothing. I'm not doing anything," he said, with the sorrow coming through clearly in his voice. His wrist draped casually over the wheel. Smiling shakily upward at her.

"Are you sure? You don't look so good."

"You're not the first to say so," he said. "I saw my muh, um . . . but how are you, Rita? I've been worried about how you're doing with Pablo's friends. Are you okay?"

"Oh." She shrugged. "Is anybody really okay these days? I feel so on-edge for some reason. I'm by myself too much."

"Now you're *not* by yourself," he said.

"I guess I'm not." She grinned. But then took a half step back, as if to let him see her better. Oh, so lovely, so exquisite. The delicate, strong articulation of feet and legs, the good tendony forearms and red, cold hands. Her breath making steam where it came out, mouth trembling. He scared her apparently, tempted her to sin against her vows.

"But why not?" he said. "Clark did it, so why not? If other people are going to lie and cheat, Rita, why shouldn't we be like them?"

"What are you talking about, Bill?" Another half step back. "You're pale. You're worn to a frazzle, Lewis. You're even shaking."

"I shake," he said, nodding. "I'm right on the edge."

She bent down to see better, crossed her arms tighter. "Do you want your book, Bill? Did you come for that? And, by the way, how is your book going?"

"I'm at a very delicate point," he said. "Lewis hired a boat to Natchez. It's hot and very humid. September. I think that's why I'm sweating." He wiped his face. "He's going into his worst despair and I'm trying to break

348

out of mine. It's been hard for me since my mom died. She used to help me through my worst spells."

"You've got a lot in common with Lewis, don't you?" she asked.

"Way too much," he said.

She looked back suddenly at the house, like she'd smelled smoke or heard a loud boom. "Would you want to come in? I really think you should."

"I can't seem to go home," he said, shaking his head. "I try, but I wind up other places. In the river. Two times."

"Who was in the river? You? Or Lewis?"

"Yeah, Lewis. Twice. Just on the way to Natchez," he said. "Got to Fort Pickering straight out of his mind. Completely off the reservation."

Her eyes changed and he glanced up quickly at her. "Am I scaring you, Rita?"

"Well, yes, to be honest!" She laughed, with a lovely blush of fright. "You are kind of scary. Please come in, Bill. Or let me call someone."

"I just need a breather," he said. "It's this goddamned book! Here's some advice for you: never ever write a book about a guy who kills himself!"

He laughed, shrugging and shivering, wet, cold, and fevery all together.

"You aren't him, though," she said, shaking her head. "Right, Bill? You aren't him."

"Are you sure, Rita? Are you completely sure?" he asked.

"Oh. Pablo warned me about this. That you can be a little scary," she said.

"Ha! Pablo said that? I'm scary? *I'm* scary?" he said. "Maybe he was murdered by the innkeeper." He happened to glance again at her beauty. With beauty, you had to keep checking it, because it had this mirage-like quality. You were always doing double-takes, making sure you weren't being fooled.

"You mean Lewis," she said.

"Right. He's supposed to be escorted up the trail, Natchez to Nashville, but this guy—this Neelly—sends Lewis ahead with only his servant for protection," he said. Checking his face with a hand. Still sweating.

"Sounds fishy," she said.

"Right. It does, doesn't it?" he asked gratefully. "Here's this deranged public official, vulnerable, physically weak. You don't send someone off alone like that. Then he turns up later with Lewis's guns."

"Neelly, you mean," she said.

"Right. I thought I said Neelly." He had a sudden notion she was just trying to keep him talking, maybe hoping Pablo would show up.

"So they get to, whatchacallit, Grinder's Inn, right?" she said. "Then what?"

"Pernier takes away his opium, his whiskey," he said. "The caretaker's wife gives up her own bed and sleeps in the adjoining summer kitchen. She's alarmed at Lewis's manner. Here he is, ruler of half of North America, parading around in a dressing gown!"

"Boy, Bill. Writing this book has sort of taken you over, hasn't it?" she asked. "I never realized. You're really eating and sleeping this thing, aren't you?"

"Sleep? What's that?" he asked. "But I'm going to stop scaring you soon, Rita, I promise."

"Are you sure? Look, why don't you let me drive you?" she asked.

"No, no. I'll go in a second. It's just that—"

"It's just what?" She came forward and almost touched the car's rumpled fender. Of course she knew. She knew all about it, chapter and verse, his devotion to her, his need for her and all women. But women suffered, too. Women also dreamed of more passionate loves. He wasn't the only one twisting through long, sore days of bitter doubt.

"I can't go home," he said. "I'm ruining things there. My marriage is over the moment I show my fat face."

Her bluey-green eyes were open wide into his. Now, here was the sort of thing she'd been craving, this intensity. "But maybe it only feels that way," she said.

"What's the difference?" he said. "Who can change how they feel?"

"I don't know," she said. "I mean, you love Emily—"

"Do I?" he said. Then he almost told her about Joaney. But knew he couldn't; it'd be like confessing to cheating on her, on Rita, with Jo. It led in a circle, a snake eating its own tail, and was coming back around to Em.

"Well, yes," she said, warningly, eyes flashing, "don't you?"

"But there's something you don't know," he said, "I mean, about Lewis. These three guys come riding up to the inn after dark. Let's call them the Three Wise Men. For some reason, Lewis goes out and mixes it up with them, gets into a loud argument, and they ride on. Later, when he's mostly gone, Lewis thinks he hears a rider approaching. He thinks it's Clark, coming to his rescue."

"Oh, how heartbreaking," she said. "I suppose he's miles away."

"No, he's *hundreds* of miles away. Anyway, Lewis is dead by morning."

She sighed and backed up. Her face then did a peculiar thing, shape-shifting so that her lovely nose stood apart from her eyes. The eyelids drooped a little. Her mouth had no relation to the rest. Her collarbones were hard knobs. Then the whole thing reversed and Rita was reassembled. Then it all jumped apart. Then coalesced again. His mouth was open. His tongue was drying.

"The question is why," she said.

"That's all anyone wants to know," he agreed, nodding. "It drives me fucking nuts."

"Bill, you'll figure it out," she said. He shook his head. No, no, he wouldn't. Something about it was beyond him.

"Seems like old Pablo's never here when I come by," he said finally, thrusting his jaw forth sadly.

"Yes, it does seem that way," she said.

"Maybe old Pablo doesn't need to know I was here," he said.

"Really? Are you sure?"

He smiled, bravely, he hoped, and backed out before she could reply. *"The last I saw of him, he was smiling," Mrs. Garcia said.* She was halfway up the steps and waving. He put up the window and shot off around the corner and saw himself racing away from her vantage point, with one of his brake lights out.

With the groceries spoiled, he pulled off for a while in a small park to smoke about seven cigarettes, flicking the ash onto the grass. He tossed what couldn't be saved into the trash barrel and drove away.

The one thing that refused to melt, though, was his gutful of ice, because nothing lovely remained between him and home, no pretty girls or women. The great problem of the age—what the real Lewis would've hated—was what Bill hated, too: its plain-spoken self-mockery, its irony, its lack of romance. Its vulgar terms for the sex parts and sex acts. Its lack of mystery.

At home, with the checkbook in his pocket, he carried everything in. Emily quickly rifled the bags in the kitchen, and he waited in the dining room, breath tight in his lungs. Where was a knife? He had to do it fast, before he heard her voice.

"Bill, where's the meat?" she asked. "Where's the milk?"

He was too tired to lie, and anyway it was too late.

"I cannot tell a lie," he called. "I threw it away."

"You did what?" She came out to look at him, but he couldn't quite meet her eyes.

"Right. I was out driving around for a while, and it got too warm, so I had to pitch it."

She stared at the dining table, then slightly nodded, like she'd been expecting this.

"Aren'tcha going to ask me where I was?" he asked. He took out the checkbook and threw it toward her across the heavy antique table.

"Maybe, maybe not," she said vaguely. She pulled out a chair and sat, looking at the little book. "Did you know Henry hasn't been out of his room all day? Not once. The door hasn't budged and he won't let me in."

He shrugged. "Like I know what to do for him, Em," he said. "Like I know what to do for anybody."

She looked down at the little book, like a triggering mechanism she wasn't afraid to push.

"Guess what, Bill?" she said. "I'm fed up with your bullshit. Your son is up there starving himself to death. And you can't even make it home with the groceries I asked you for eight hours ago!"

Her voice was breaking, face darkening. She was breaking, starting to shake, to cry. And he was just starting to open his mouth to tell her about the check for Joaney when there came a crash and tumble from above, and down came Henry's body, thudding and smashing, into the doorway, stopping almost at his mother's feet.

At the hospital, Bill was checking messages on his phone, desperate for something to do, when he found one from his principal, Doug Malard. Doug always used both names when he called you, and it was never to give you some good news. Lewis wanted to laugh. Anytime he found proof of evil in the universe, he laughed, and then he looked forward to telling Emily, hearing her rebuttal.

He'd left Emily behind in the room with Henry, who'd broken his right forearm in the fall, snapped it cleanly, and was now taking food and fluids through a feeding tube and IVs.

She came out in the hall to intercept him. "What's the name of that girl you said he liked?" she asked.

"Oh, God, it started with a D. Why can't I think of it? Was it Debbie? No, wait! *Delilah*."

353

"That's who it is," Emily said, pointing her finger at him. "That's what this was about."

"Didn't I say so?" he asked. But because they were at war over the kid's soul, she didn't answer, going back in.

He stayed out in the hallway, thinking about Lewis and what he'd said at the end, that he was doing it to deny his enemies the pleasure. Yet everyone insisted he had no enemies. Then, a few weeks later, Neelly turned up in possession of his guns, and his servant Pernier showed up wearing his clothes.

Down in the hospital cafeteria, he bought a sandwich, cheese and bread that was hard to choke down. But he did it anyway, for Henry. He felt woozy, big body disobeying him in the hallways and bumping into things, weaving. Back upstairs, Henry was hard asleep from taking so much nutrition at once. Engulfed by the massive, mechanical bed, he seemed to be sliding down into its throat. Emily had left the room. Henry opened his exhausted eyes, then blinked. "Hey, Dad."

"Hey, yeah. Whatsamatter? Are you going to hang on or what?"

He nodded, but shrugged, too, like he scarcely cared, either way.

"Jesus Christ," Bill said. "Jesus, Henry! You're all we have." As if Henry didn't know that. As if that alone could make life attractive.

Henry looked at his feeding tube and gave it a contemptuous flick with a finger.

"Fattening me for the slaughter," he said. For the first time, he sounded no longer like a child.

"What's wrong, Hen? What's so awful?"

"Me. Just me," he said, shifting his eyes away, tears coming. "It's always me."

"What's so wrong with you?" Bill asked.

"I'm not shit!" Henry said, with all the force he had, which was very little. He was left panting and pale. He'd expected to be, was trying desperately to be, something more than just Henry. He seemed to need it, even. Anything less was fucking pathetic, not worth it.

"Hen, this is all my fault," Bill said.

"No, it's not!" Henry snapped. "It's nothing about you. Maybe you guys are getting a divorce, maybe you're not. Maybe you'll die of lung cancer, maybe not. Jesus, do whatever the fuck you want! I can't worry about it anymore!" He grabbed the Kleenex box and hurled it. Then lay in the pillows and moved his eyes one way, then the other. Shrugging. Tears running backward onto the pillowcase from his exhausted face.

"You've gotta stop this," Bill said.

Henry's eyes got cool, cynical, as they regarded this adult, his father.

"You've gotta stop this," he mocked.

Bill shrugged, thinking of at least two things that could refer to.

"Why'd you start, anyway? Your friends dare you?" Henry asked.

"I don't remember now," Bill said.

Henry nodded and scratched the adhesive holding his nose tube in place.

"Hen, your mom is worried sick over you," Bill said. "Most days, she can't decide if she should dial 911 or just drink until she passes out."

Henry scratched the adhesive. Shrugging. Backward-flowing tears.

Lewis looked down on his son. The protein infusion was making his eyelashes flutter. Henry drifted in and out.

"Kid, you're cursed," Lewis said. "You've got my eyes."

"What, Daddy?" he asked, eyes straining, fighting to stay conscious. When Bill thought Henry might die someday, it was like somebody blocking all the exits. Like he was buried alive with only a soda straw to breathe through.

"I'll send Mom in now," he said, and left the room.

Emily sat with Henry until he fell hard asleep, panting, heart racing. When Lewis came back in, she held the checkbook. "So now you're giving her money," she said.

"I have even better news. Doug Malard called me," he said.

"Oh, Jesus! What does he want?"

"He didn't say. They never say over the phone."

"Well, this is perfect," she said.

Lewis went home alone to sleep in their bed, with Emily staying behind, on a fold-out in Henry's room to watch the green numbers of his monitor flicker higher or lower, depending on what he dreamed.

Unable to sleep, Bill lay in bed and thought about Clark, picking up a newspaper in Kentucky and noticing a little item, almost two weeks old, about the governor of Louisiana having cut his own throat.

Clark gave no credence to murder theories. Neither did Jefferson, who said the suicide was no surprise; it ran in the family. Clark worried now about his remaining friends, telling one to "write to me freely" and "let nothing weigh heavy on your mind."

In the morning, he lined up a sub for his class, then called Doug Malard while looking down out of the office's window at a bird perched dejectedly on a murky, reflective disk of ice in the birdbath. "Yeah, hi, Doug, this is Bill," he said. "What's up?"

"Bill. Hey. Hang on a second."

The second turned into a long, long minute. "Still there?" Doug asked. "Hey, are you sure you wouldn't rather come in and talk?"

Lewis pictured him, legs crossed at the knee, dark-haired, dark-eyed, an almost dog-faced sort of guy, very lean and sober. When he spoke, it was either a sudden laugh or bark, or something almost too quiet to hear, with teeth very white, caps. You had the feeling he liked the world as it was.

"I'd rather not. My son's still not doing so great," Bill said.

"I'm sorry." There was a pause. Was Bill supposed to try and fill it, or should he wait? "Listen, Bill, do you know an Annette Pfeffercorn?"

"That'd be Joaney Pfeffercorn's foster mom. She was one of mine last year, until she had her baby. Joaney was, I mean." He said it with a hot, dizzying flush and a cold prickling in his scalp.

"She's made a complaint," Doug said, almost too low to hear. "Can you hear me all right?"

"Not really, but what's she saying?"

"Did you loan her daughter some money?" Doug asked.

Ah-so. Joaney had gotten into it with Annette, telling her she could just cram her monthly check, that she didn't need it now.

"That's not against the law," he said.

When Doug didn't say anything, Lewis knew it was worse than he'd guessed. Annette must've said a lot, made wild innuendoes, accusations. But Doug wouldn't show his whole hand. Those things could just stay submerged for now, until the rope rotted and they popped to the surface. So now, Bill was embroiled in an unfolding foster-care scandal, complete with nubile girl, middle-aged male teacher, and lurking, sexually obsessed foster dad.

"It just doesn't look that great," Doug said at last.

"So are we talking a formal complaint?" he asked as he envisioned a black pall coming down over his entire career.

"I'd rather not get into our whole talk," Doug said. He sounded a little sickened by the whole mess, indignant at the stain seeping across his desk.

"Next time she calls, just give her my number," Bill said. "My home number. I'm happy to talk to her."

"You really ought to get clear of this matter, Bill," Doug said. "Completely clear."

"I plan to take care of it," he said. Then waited to see if that was all.

"Do that. And come in and talk to me after the holiday," Doug said. "No big deal."

"Actually, that sounds like a big deal," he said.

"Not at all. Doesn't have to be. See you later, Bill," Doug said.

Lewis held the dead phone and stared down at the leaf-flecked yard, the birdbath, through water-spotted panes of glass bisected with white wooden crosses. He felt affirmed again in feeling that, like most men in his life, Doug was his enemy.

·　·　·

357

Then it was Thursday, and they were cooking Thanksgiving dinner.

Henry waited at the front window for the company, with the wounds on his arms and forehead still livid, red in the winter light, a cast up past his right elbow. With his hair down over one eye and as thin as Gandhi. In jeans big enough for two Henrys. Emily sent him out to the garage for the orange string-sack of Idaho potatoes.

"Oh, and happy Thanksgiving, Henry!" she called after him.

"Yeah, happy whatever," Henry said.

"Hey, where's your girlfriend?" Bill called.

No answer. In the quietness and emptiness of the house, as they waited for Henry to come back from the garage, Bill felt the fear again, very profoundly, of how painfully spare life would be if they lost him.

"She's a friend," Henry said at last, muscling along with the bag. "And she might come by, but she might blow it off, too. It's not like she promised."

"Whatever," Emily said. "It's all right either way."

A canned ham sat draining on the counter, along with the silver two-slice toaster and a set of kissing Pilgrims boy-and-girl salt and pepper shakers Emily bought for the occasion. She set Bill and Henry up at the sink and made them peel and chop potatoes, carrots, yams, onions, and loaves of stale bread. Bill kept cutting everything too big, and Henry, pinning things down with his cast, diced them finer, onion-tears running down his face. The crying aggravated him and he kept blinking and wincing, slapping away the teardrops.

Emily was still bringing grocery sacks in from the car.

"So what about this girl, hey?" Bill asked, nudging him. "Hey?"

Henry just shoved a pile of onions at him. "God, cut these smaller, Dad. They're still too big."

Then put the knife down and walked out of the room. Emily came back in and looked around for Henry.

"What's the matter?" she asked.

"I don't know exactly."

"Well, what happened?" she asked. "What'd you do to him? Bill?"

"I didn't do anything!" he stage-whispered. "Jesus. Why shouldn't he take a break, if that's what he wants?"

"Because that's not what he wants," she said. And left the kitchen.

He got the ham into the oven, and soon heard the sizzling of fat and the rumble of vegetables boiling in big pots. Emily returned and made up a pie filling out of peeled quartered apples and golden raisins and cream. "He's in his room," she said finally.

Bill tried to concentrate on making the stuffing, but kept thinking about the Nez Percé. When the party was starving, they'd scraped together some trinkets, all they had, to trade for horses. But the chief refused to see any man give his last dime for food, and let them have all the horses they needed.

Emily'd also bought a smoked turkey, so he carved it. After all, he was the patriarch, or what was left of one, anyway. All over the world that old system was faltering, fading, wheezing, teetering, collapsing, and he didn't mind wielding the knife, slicing up what remained. Nor could he give a crap about its passing, since it'd never done him much good. He hacked the turkey up joyfully, whistling while he worked.

As for the true patriarch, Lloyd, he was on a cruise with a lady friend, the Panama Canal, gazing "in wild surmise" on the Pacific.

Henry came down at last, got himself a root beer, and turned on the game. Emily set him up at a TV tray, working with brown paper and stubby scissors, his cast banging about, making pilgrim hats and turkeys to fill with candy corn and caramels for each place. Meanwhile, Bill mashed everything with lots of butter and brown sugar, then salted and peppered it within an inch of its life. Emily ironed the tablecloth for the ironic holiday, a day to eat all you could in honor of those robbed and pillaged, raped and slaughtered.

Bill thought about Jefferson, who, after the fact, had made a $100 claim against Lewis's estate. That's how hard up he was after trying to bail his sister's kids—her sons, Lilburne and Isham—out of a bad money jam. Clark at last found an editor named Biddle for the journals.

Together they waded in, wallowing, hacking, and slashing through the lush undergrowth of Lewis's prose. Like Lewis, Biddle believed in the knife, copious bleeding, and wielded a pen and red ink unsparingly. He asked probing questions, and Clark wrote them down, making cryptic notes to himself: "Qu: as to hands. Blood on."

Emily placed a pitcher of ice water, a cold crock of milk, and a bottle of a nice Syrah on the still-warm tablecloth. The front door opened, Henry letting in the guests. Before Bill could move, Joaney bumped in with Jack on her hip.

She looked carefully around the room, for someone else, not him. Then pushed a hot dish of green beans crisscrossed with strips of sweated prosciutto into his hands. "Don't drop it, Mr. Lewis," she said. "Have you got it? Are you sure?"

Her use of "Mr." made his face hot. Henry just stared. Joaney was Henry's Everest, his Northwest Passage, his deep, dark continent rolled into one. Whatever she felt about seeing Lewis again, and meeting his wife, was submerged under her flushed, pleased expression. "Happy Thanksgiving, everybody!" she said.

That left two empty chairs.

But Emily liked to do that, leave a vacant chair at the table, just in case Jesus dropped by, disguised as a blind man or crackhead, for a surprise inspection of the troops.

When all the food was on, Henry sat down at the table across from Joaney and Jack, and eyed the dish nearest like John the Baptist was looking back at him. The dishes started around. Henry took such tiny amounts onto his plate, it was shocking, like he was flipping off the Statue of Liberty.

Now began the elaborate dance of knife and fork, spearing, sawing, trading, repeating.

"I don't really know a prayer," Emily said, "but what's everybody thankful for?"

Joaney, in her clingy red velour top and hip-rider jeans, tight ringlets of hair like wire coils glowing yellow with heat, ate one-handed and knock-kneed, Jack on her lap. Henry started to say something. Then the doorbell rang. He leapt up first, returning in a moment followed by a hoary angel with a body like a hydrant and the bearing of a thug. His hair was blond and bushy, his quilt-coat bulky and dirty, goatee nearly invisible on sallow skin. And blue eyes that could make a nun cry for mercy.

Tommy trudged forward into the room, head bowed, mouth working, and eyes full, looking straight at Joaney. Who also showed tears. He just stood there, so sure he was unwanted, his forehead touched with light and no hope. His shoulders impulsive, ready for trouble. Joaney knew of his coming, but blushed anyway, hands all atremble.

"Just in time," Emily said. "I think you know us already, Tommy."

Bill shook the hand, fat-fingered, as it reached for him across Joaney's lap, and dodged the kid's searching eyes.

"Henry, what were you going to say, baby?" Emily asked.

"Um, I just think this is a weird holiday," he said. "It's got to look really crazy and sort of nuts to Native Americans. Also, I'm thankful to get the damn tube out of my nose." And began to check under everything on his plate with his fork, as if for trip wires.

"I'm thankful for my ceiling," Joaney said. "And thankful for Bill, because he saved my little ass. And you, too, Emily."

"Yes, thankful for Bill," Tommy said, nodding dutifully. "And for being a Christian."

Bill shrugged at that, because exactly how Christian was it to smack one's girlfriend? Tommy sat gazing eye to eye with his new little son, Jack, in a manly, brutal way, like they'd already disagreed about something.

"When're you getting married?" Henry asked. Tommy smiled and looked at the ceiling.

"Not everybody gets married, Henry," Joaney said quickly.

"Nor should they," Emily said drily.

Everyone laughed, and that gave them a chance to finally settle down to the meal and eat. Henry kept turning around in his chair to see the mute television. They chewed with steadfast resolve, gaze blunted by concentration, determined to eat until much, much too full.

"Hey, how's your book, Dad?" Henry asked, crunching a half bite of celery he'd been working on for a full minute.

"I've gotten all the way to Big White. He's a Sioux chief who comes back with the captains. Then he spends years trying to get home again. And when he finally does, nobody believes a word of his story. Not about visiting the White House or seeing a whole city carved out of white marble. Nothing."

"That's kind of hard to believe," Tommy said, eyes carefully downward. "I bet at least one person believed him."

"Aren't you about done, Bill?" Joaney asked. "I mean, isn't Lewis about dead by now?"

Bill nodded. "Any day."

"But Bill, you keep saying that!" Joaney laughed. "For months now! You've gotta end it."

He could only nod, since it was logical. Yes, that only made sense.

They finished eating, after seconds, after thirds. Soon the dishes were all off the table and the dishwasher was churning. The western light from the sunporch started its change from blue and warm to gray and decolorized, the light of late-winter afternoon. He was aware of a slowing, of little stops in time, and the faces in the room, Joaney's, Emily's, Henry's, holding still. He realized these people weren't always meant to be. This was him living now, but not forever. He was in a two-edged moment, with time stopped and yet also moving. Nobody watched or judged, for this one instant, whether he did it right, caught up as they were in their own rich feeling. The light was phasing forward toward a new mood. He was older now, no longer the Bill who'd gone on that float trip.

As for the famous Lewis, he'd been dead just a few years when his two cousins, Lilburne and Isham, followed. They'd been discovered burning the body of their slave, George, who Lilburne killed in a fit of temper. It seemed George accidentally broke a favorite water pitcher of Lilburne's dead wife. Also, the farm was bankrupt. After being sentenced to hang, Lilburne shot himself. Isham then ran off to the War of 1812. But by 1813, he was dead, too.

Bill took his coffee with brandy out on the sunporch, and stood looking out on the square of cement, the birdbath, its frozen puddle. Henry came out to gaze, too, where his father was looking.

"Dad, how come you don't finish it?" Henry asked. "Have you got writer's block?"

Bill smiled at that innocent question. As Henry's father, he probably needed to hurt the kid, badly, into some later phase of life. He wasn't doing his job.

"Henry, the fact is, nobody gives a crap," Bill said, swirling the black liquid. "It was all too goddamn long ago."

"Oh."

"And I'll tell you something else," he said. "Lewis was just a stooge. He was just an errand boy for some big deal called the Enlightenment. Which never actually happened, because we've clearly been saying one thing and doing another ever since!"

Tommy, who'd been standing behind him in the dining room, left and went back into the living room. Which foiled Bill's plans to corner and threaten the kid, to tell him that if he ever saw Joaney with another bruise, he'd smash his head in.

But just the thought of saying it made his heart leap like a rushing deer, and turned his vision dark and pounding. He followed Tommy, anyway, to where Emily put the pies. They hacked out their slivers, side by side. Bill tried but couldn't calm down, nerves shredded by the strain of these weeks. So Tommy would get away clean with the golden bounty.

"What do you do, Tommy?" he asked, standing there, perceptibly shaking, holding the little plate.

"Dry-fitting," Tommy said. "I'm a stand-piper, basically. I set all the angles and then my chief comes in behind me and sets all my joints, steals all my glory."

He had drifting blue, sort of sky-struck eyes, and was looking a bit above and to the right, like he saw the answer. Bill saw it, too, that the marbled world rolled on and on.

Later, Joaney sat on the couch with Tommy and watched him clean vomit off Jack, a series of dabbing right jabs. Emily leaned in the doorway, wiping her eyes, blowing her nose, having just released Henry's shoulders, coming down from her tiptoes.

Whatever that was about, Bill chose not to know. He sat on one hip on a bar stool, feeling unreliable, like a dog who'd run away from home and now couldn't recall why.

When he looked up, a girl walked in the front door, sober and small, hands in the pocket of her string hoodie, straight black hair combed neatly, resigned shoulders.

"Hey," she said to him, and wandered into the kitchen. He heard Henry introducing her, Emily trying to fix her a plate, and the girl begging off. She wasn't hungry, she'd eaten, and so forth, another whip-thin noneater. She and Henry went out onto the back patio and Bill spied on them, as she leaned within about six feet of his son, drank a Diet Coke, and smoked. Henry didn't even look at her, but they were together; clearly, she was Henry's girlfriend. So there, too, was love.

Now, looking at his life as if from outside it, Bill saw that nothing had really happened in the past year. But real change was often invisible.

After the expedition, it looked like Lewis wasn't doing anything, either. But in fact, he'd been doing two things, (1) furtively searching for the right time and place to kill himself, and (2) desperately trying to find a way not to.

Nobody ever wanted to do it. But since it was going to happen, had to happen, the only choice left was the method, the time and place. Ultimately, Death was going to prove to be Lewis's great love, the dark angel with the full, bare breasts and the hooded face.

At the last, the wall between Lewis's conscious and unconscious minds apparently came tumbling down, maybe because of his chronic insomnia. Which released Pandaemonium, psychosis, the babbling host, into his waking world.

Lewis had everything to live for but a woman. His money troubles were bad but not insoluble. In his final hour, he was heard to cry out, "O, Madam! Give me some water, for I am so strong and it is so hard to die!"

And died. And to Her he flew.

Bill stood inside, thinking, listening to the dishwasher churn, sipping wine, wanting a cigarette. Outside, Delilah offered Henry a drag from hers, and he took it without looking and passed it back, like they'd done this for a million years.

Tomorrow, Bill didn't have to teach, so he'd go up to his office. He wasn't always sure why he went. But then again, why did a monk keep returning to his cell? Because his coffin was there.

And all sorts of crazy shit still needed to go into the book, that Lilburne and Isham only got caught because the New Madrid earthquake—largest ever in middle America—happened to strike that day and knock down the chimney. They built it back up, but an aftershock came and leveled it again, exposing their grisly crime.

And there was more. The Great Comet of 1811 had just visited Earth. Before the quake, tens of thousands of squirrels swam the Ohio River, fled the area. People reported giddiness and an emotion they termed "absence" both before and after. Noxious clouds of sulfur billowed up from the ground, poisoning the air and the wells.

Bill knew he'd have to leave things out. For instance, when you pulled money from your pocket, the coins winking up at you were probably Spanish or British. And you could be fined severely for saying "by God" or "by Jesus" in public.

Sitting, he grew drunker, settling deep into the recliner's embrace and dimly following the battle for turf, the war of inches, on the screen. At that moment, he knew why Lewis did it, but doubted he could find the right words.

By 1812, with Lewis dead for three years, the War Department had ruled in his favor and paid his rejected drafts. In 1813, Theo, her ship, and her whole crew vanished off the Carolinas. Reportedly the prey of pirates, Theo either walked the plank or was kept as a sex toy for some weeks, chained by the throat to the mast.

He'd try to write it. And if the lines didn't scan this time, he'd tear it all up and never try again, so help him. He passed out, writing it, his lips moving, until Emily finally roused him and helped guide him to their bed.

26.

"...I never had a line from you..."

The Pilot's Tale

❀ The next leg of that derang'd gent's tour was mine, from St. Louis, and he came on board there, having swallow'd opium tablets enough to drop an ox, and was a source of alarm to my crew. At one point, early on, I heard the boatman shouting, and turn'd to find him in the river, look-ing up at me from our wake, in cold water to the chin. All water on earth has communication with all other, so, whoever she was, perhaps he'd tried to swim to her. We came about, and haul'd him up. The mate spoke angrily in his face. "What year is it? Who is now the president?" he in-quir'd. "Jefferson," quoth my cargo defiantly, wrongly. We secur'd his drink from easy reach. I order'd him observ'd. To teach manners to the impudent, he drew a pistol from his bags, and from behind we swarm'd over him, which forc'd the discharge, into the air, of the load and bullet.

You see, I'd taken aboard a charter to Natchez, and a ruin, and a scan-dal, and a skeleton just barely cloth'd in flesh. Wet from his adventure in the river, panting from fail'd attempts to die, he was gaz'd upon by my credulous helmsman with his cap shov'd back to better observe the shipment. A look of care, concern, and fear of the insane great person was on the mate's face, too. Mine also, I am sure.

He seem'd desp'rate to talk about some book he was writing. "I wish each word to 'light precisely," he gasp'd, eyes hallow'd into mine. "If you wish, 'll tell it to you but the task is like placing live birds on perches. One must pray the first will remain 'til the last is install'd."

So this pilot (myself) now pull'd up a nail barrel and shouted an order to the helm, then fish'd for a pipe.

"First of all, 'tis no pleasure bark you master," quoth my cargo, "for this is not the Mississippi but the Styx, and that is not your mate but the noble Charon. I was not always as you see me. Once I had hopes, a vocation . . . I was like you. . . ."

With a pipe out, packing it, I stopp'd and waited. Then, the fire struck, the match exploded and lit up my cargo's face like that of a demon's, white-eyed, his teeth and lips leaking light, and smoke, like a stove-grate. Sparks flew in the dark of my boat's open hold. His head was on a coil of rope, with stars behind it, and the curv'd line of the gunwale.

". . . I hath made finite the infinite, sir," he sayeth. "I made the locality of dreams into places on maps."

It was such a sultry, steamy night, I could not tell the sweat about my ribs from the river licking around the hull of the craft. "Come! What ails thee?" I ask'd impatiently, for I was angry at the trouble already with this man. I glimps'd a superstitious fear of madness in the mate's face as he stood watch afore me on the bow.

"I was like you . . . , " he said.

"Now! You've said that. Go on. Say summat else or be silent forevermore!"

"There is no west any longer," he said. "Remove its letter from your compass. That is over and done with."

"What're ya sick from?" I ask'd.

368

"I cannot tell. But it stopp'd my pen four times in three years," he said. "Recently I gave orders to exterminate the Sioux."

"Stick to one course," I said, and shifted to check the channel. "You are much too changeable."

"I cannot remain. For I never wish to see turn'd-down beds or linens, or chairs, or locks with keys thrust cruelly down their throats," he said. "But I was once like you."

"Now back to this again!" I said. He star'd at my boots lac'd to the knee, and my white canvas trousers and tiny blue uniform jacket, which I detested for making me look like an ape in the circus, like a reflective, pipe-chewing simian. Meanwhile, he had a fine, brute face with beautiful eyes and long lashes. And shivering in the wet bottom, he said, "I take you back to the beginning, for it begins long, long ago . . ."

Next, he told it. He stopp'd briefly, now and again, for sunrise or to change out of his clothes (clothes no longer seem'd to suit him) and into the long white shroud-like dressing gown. He kept telling it, while sitting here or there about the open craft like a prophet from Bible days, reviv'd now and then by draughts of whiskey. When he got too sober, his hands turn'd frantic in their play about his garment, wishing to rend it, and about his thin hair, wishing to tear it. So we let him have a little more.

'Twas a strange tale. And if I seem'd fatigu'd by it, he'd make it wilder and more romantic, with more hand-to-hand combats with savages and grizzlies, and cruel beatings to unrepentant husbands, abject apologies from weak and disloyal best friends, punches in the nose for deplorable assistants. Also, the size of fortunes changing hands kept doubling and trebling. He finish'd by insisting the entire epic, penn'd and flawless, lay awaiting print in the very trunks the mate snor'd on.

It may have been true, parts of it. But I doubt that he knew anymore which from which. "One gets so sick of being sick in the world, of starving and choking on that same nutriment that causes others to thrive, marry, and reproduce," he said. "And look at you. A river pilot! Why, you ought to be a sea captain! Our true lives are liv'd elsewhere, by other men."

The illness or madness made his muscles jump. His skin stank faintly of urine, and his farts of onions and eggs, tho' he ate nothing. He trembl'd after a way to stop trembling, squeezing himself tight. "So immur'd am I in this country, and this river, and this debt, God Himself cannot see me," he said. "I'm shaking and tortur'd. I have a malaise. And yet I fret o'er how I appear to you."

"Never mind. Find some peace, sir, if you can. Find some peace," I said, checking my pouch and finding it empty of tobacco.

"The dead wish to know," he said. "Were their deaths worth our triumphs? Meanwhile, she washes clothes on a distant shore and thinks on all she did and saw, her heart sore, tender, and rueful. She is sorry now for what she said."

What could one say to him? He was a miserable, sodden fellow.

"Beware the great man," he said, for we had been speaking of the former president, Mr. Jefferson. "Fear him, I say, for his gratitude is fatal."

"Ay, you know him, so you say," I nodded. He shrugg'd the slight shoulders.

"Do you know," he ask'd, "that life nowadays need not include great feats? Why, a perfectly good life can be liv'd by an old farmer 'thout stirring five miles from home!"

"Is it true what you said before?" I ask'd, checking the channel and tossing a clinker at the mate. One meant one degree port or starboard, depending on where it hit him. "His best friend stole his savage queen? And violated her practically before his eyes?"

"This looks like a river, sir," he answer'd, "but in fact it is my silver cord I am unfurling behind us so we may retrace our way."

"O, I know that old story as well as you," I said. "I went to school, well and all."

"Do not ever die," he said, with a cadaverous smile. "Nor seek to relieve distress'd humanity, for they will only stare and stare with stunn'd despairing eyes, for they expected something rather better."

We didn't always talk. Sometimes he simply look'd, at the water, the mate, the shores, trees, moon, stars, my face. I now think he was seeking desperately after a way not to end.

"Listen, and 'll tell thee of an all-water route, not found," he said. "You see, I was sent to prove a folk tale."

A shar'd sense of sorrow could almost erase the distance between us. For I too had arriv'd at my station in life and could not go farther. I, too, walk'd out of the wilderness of youth into a much harsher place. He was sorry for himself. "I think," I said to him, "that you are almost what could be call'd a self-destructive type."

He smil'd at me exhaustedly. "Works will be the test," he panted. "If even one Indian is alive at the end of it all, remember: I said to leave them be!"

I did not wish to test him, tho'. I only wish'd to deliver him and be quit of that face.

"A husband is merely a tool," he said. "Useful for defense and a stable place in the world. A woman doesn't need a man to stroke the pinfeathers of her soul."

"You sound like a married man!" I replied. And he look'd at me with his softest eyes yet, approaching gratitude.

"Do I, now? Is that how one sounds, then, when married?"

He star'd out at the water, fondly or bitterly, at a love that almost was and would never be. "Since about thirteen," he said, about himself, "he would make you a duel over nothing, over the least slight, or remark."

"But why?" I ask'd, seizing a chance to make him make sense.

"He thought he was a coward," he said. "Not liked by his fellows, he was moon'd over by girls. Until they came close and saw what was truly in his eye!"

Then seiz'd his skull as if struck a blow. "But, O, those curs-ed men! Now they all wade forward, this one, that one, eagerly tendering their accounts. Each thinks he is remarkable, and needs awaken the world to the fact!"

I may have gotten a hard expression at that remark. Above all, he fear'd you'd leave him and start away in disgust.

"Forgive me, kind sir, Captain, sir, but they miss the underlying truths," he said. "Still, I love them to weakness. But they prefer Captain Clark. Er, that is, *General* Clark."

"So, a favourite among women, are ye?" I said.

He took some strain around the eyes.

"There was F. High-strung, thoroughbred, noble, with a firm young . . . mind. On her, I could never visit my beast."

"What beast?" I ask'd.

"It is here," he said. Pointing to his breast and groin.

For a time, he tried to rest. Then he drank. Then more stuporous slumber, tho' not sleep. You saw, by and by, the sort of man he was, one hand forever taking the other from his throat.

Still, when awake, one could not keep oneself from him. "Is there more about the savage girl?" I ask'd.

He rais'd up on one elbow. "Look at the light," he said, pointing. "We shall call this light Unnameable. O, obscure horizon! O, cloudy sky shrouding a red-streaked morning. In this spectacle of terrible majesty, I see a new savage race of people coming, no less savage than the ones before. The Americans."

He was bound for some sort of reckoning in the East, in a white and pillar'd city in greenery, gentle hills, basins, and vales, and pale sunshine on stone work'd with chisels. What had my small life to do with his? But madness in the great never goes unwatch'd. I was his witness.

"O, ironies heavy as anvils!" he cried, holding his head. "Thick fog of days and nights!"

While he was not looking, I secur'd his whiskey, locking it in the possibles box. And his powder.

"Twenty-five boxes, straight to the bottom!" he cried.

His mania was aging him rapidly. It was as if he'd linger'd here too long, and his own time was fast passing while we spoke, and almost gone.

The romance was all out of this journey, for him and for me. A dreaminess was lost from the scene. The nineteenth century began, in my little opinion, at that instant.

When I look'd again, he was all the more faded. "I am being eras'd," he said. "New people are coming."

And, a little after: "God damn the little men who could not travel to the next village for the uncertainties involv'd!"

Of talking to him, I was grown weary, tho' not tired, per se. For, each evening with him, I was growing more grateful for George, the silent mate, and look'd forward to putting this man ashore and being done with Man's Nature.

At dawn of the last day, the whole earth spread itself open for us, and set fire to its own edge, and was playing the mild, unreproving behemoth. But with a shrug of its shoulder, it might unseat us forever.

"Did I tell you of E. B.?" he ask'd. "She had sobriety and gravity and a passion barely restrain'd."

He liked to talk of women, as unmarried men do, like they were all bewitching gypsies, dark-eyed and dazzl'ng. "Tho' I could never dally," he lamented. "Could never flirt or mock. I never understood what we now call 'small talk.'"

Were it not for fame, he would not have caught the world's eye. Yet my days with him have had a signal effect, which I now wear like a cloak against rougher weather. Misfortunes that dash other men's hopes to pieces, I can now barely stoop to notice.

When I met him, I have to admit it: I was a perfect widower in respect to love. I'd thought I would steer my pleasure bark up and down the Mississippi all alone, for all eternity. But lately, I have put to shore. What will be my next adventure, God only knows, but on this I am determin'd: to get a wife.

" . . . to await that which will last forever . . ."

Fort Pickering

⌘ Yes, it was I (call me "Horatio"), who receiv'd him next, from the pilot—and quite out of his mind. The first thing he did was to beg me: I was not to repeat anything he said, especially *regardez* several women he knew back in the East.

"You must not attach my name to a certain L., or a Miss ——, or a Miss ——, or I am undone!" he said.

But later, when we had him bedded down, he summon'd me, and spoke more lucidly about the first lady, L., describing ". . . her impertinent remarks, her nervous hands, her deep unhappy, insomniac eyes. How stunn'd, terrified, we'd've been with each other in love! How lucky for her she escap'd!"

He spoke often of some other fair creature, of "her brutal forthright eyes!"

I did not wish to listen, but could not help it—he said such curious things.

One night, as a boy, he'd dreamt of a beating heart and a mighty river issuing out of it. I'd heard about his struggles, of his doubt and crisis on the Pacific shore. In fact, he was yet in pain from a wounding there, a cureless infected spot that made him limp. "Why must I go on point before all humankind?" he once ask'd me.

"But another went before ye, yes?" I reminded him. "A Canadian?"

He seem'd not to notice, but I regretted saying it. One hated to add pains to those eyes. In his state, his ev'ry doubt caus'd him visible agonies.

"I am a vessel for Man's blasphemous desires," he said. "By and by, you will need to hurt me."

And I saw that I might wish to, if he continu'd this way. But on the third day, without opium or whiskey, he seem'd better. "My dear Horatio," he started calling me, now that we were intimates, "do you see how this nation is being founded? By Spanish and French fortunes, pillag'd during the Crusades."

He fuss'd continually with the wound on his hip, inflam'd as tho' from within. "You see? My old friend Peter mistook me for a stag, and was correct. For I had grown horns!" His laughter was the most terrible ever, and you hop'd he'd not repeat it. Apparently, a woman misled him in love.

"I recall my crib," he told me, "I was calling for Mother. Then I heard my father's voice, forbidding her to go to me. E'en now, I recall the infant hatred, the patricidal rage that well'd in me! O! Even in the nursery, dear Horatio, we are ready to kill for woman-love!"

He meditated a great deal on women and love, like some new-made, modern Ovid.

"You know, Horatio, how we should be asham'd of our—intimacies—with them," he said. "How much better is a distance of respect, regard, and affection. For we only love what remains enigmatic to us, like God."

I told him to be still, to rest, but he rambl'd like a mad thing and shouted like a lawyer. "God Himself, Horatio! God Himself never mov'd so many men so far as I have!" he inform'd me. "But with great boons come great debts!"

Lately, I'd been urging friends and my family to join me out here, on the frontier. But recently, after seeing its effects on certain types, I pause. I believe he might have lasted longer had he come sooner, when we were romantic in our outlook.

Now that he is gone, I scarce know what to do with myself, how to spend my new-earn'd knowledge. What began as a small affair takes on mass with time. His simple visit left me with a strange pain. I think on him as if we were friends.

I plann'd, once, to go upriver myself. Now that abandons me. I think he was a higher-flying Icarus, and 'tis better he is dead. Whether I envy him must remain my secret. At the least, he taught me about great boons and awful catastrophes.

"'Tis an event coming," he told me. "I am barely two moments from 't all the time. The trouble is, I don't know if I race on ahead of it, like poor old George Shannon. Or is it ahead of me, and I need to catch up?"

"Perhaps try to stay still and wait," I suggested.

"But then I seem to fall further and further behind." He laugh'd unhappily.

On the ninth day, I found him almost lucid, resolute, fatigu'd, with eyes starry. "All my life, Horatio, I have hated another man," he confess'd. "I cannot stomach my own sex."

"And yet we seem to get on, you and I," I said.

"Curious, isn't it?" he said. "Nor can I recall, now, what it was all about. The other boys used me badly. I vow'd to get even. I'd set a mark impossible for them to surpass. My whole life, I've been the secret spy among my fellows, finding out their weaknesses, planning and lying in wait."

"Perhaps it is not too late to change," I said.

He chuckl'd, then went to coughing. "You've no idea, Horatio," he gasp'd, "You don't know what's in store for me back East. The places they've prepar'd for me!"

I was helpless to help him, tho' he gave me very much. Before his coming, my life was one continual press of business. And now, at 5, I look up and see I've dream'd the day away.

"I think I am some third sex God plann'd," he told me once. "But I am a botch'd job! Time to sweep away the monstrosity and make a clean slate!"

I grow older, and maudlin, but his ev'ry word now seems full with import, and carries an ache of loss. He did it to make sure that such cares weighing on him would not be mine. And now I try to comfort those likewise afflicted.

Here, on this ledge, out on this frontier, the ones we like best are soonest parted from us. Americans now go up this river to craft a far-flung string of log forts and tiny outposts. Once more, we hear the call for young men to lay down all for the Republic, like their fathers in '75.

His excursion to the ocean only partly cured him, apparently. Forc'd into civiliz'd pursuits, he was soon mad again. Tho' after fifteen days with me, he said he was feeling better.

"What exactly is the affliction?" I ask'd him that day. But he just smil'd at me.

" 'Tis more demon than affliction," he grinn'd, shakily upright. "And sore need. I am like a negro slave betray'd by his own skin. I must restore myself to honour and respect, somehow. The trouble is that how."

"Give it up!" I said to him. " 'Tis no use."

"No, I must keep trying, tho' the liver is eaten out of me," he said. He gaz'd forth out the window as tho' life were a grim, fatal lark, with a sportive grief in pale eyes, watching a buzzard circle.

And now? Well, now that he is gone, I am not so mov'd by death.

He once told me that the passions—love, lust, jealousy, hatred—were why the Enlightenment could never come. Probably he was right.

Little by little, tho', sometimes, I look out at dawn, and believe we are almost awaken'd to what truly is, what we truly are. "You must understand and not regret," he told me. "I was captain of this ship. For the captain, who pledges to stay with his vessel no matter what, every voyage is a suicide."

Some are calling him an absurd artifact of a bygone world, useless relic of an older faith. Tho' they ought to read his journals, for, in them, the truth thunders forth from ev'ry line.

Meanwhile, the men he hated, the Bates-like men, riot o'er the earth. One by one, here and there, the new people begin to appear, and the world treats them with incredible brutality. Ah, well. He made his choice. In the face of such cruelty, he said, he felt his heart growing less and less human. But the only charge that ever truly troubl'd him was the one of treason.

He hasten'd his departure so as to end our torment, watching him die.

The day he left, the river was slow and heavy as milk, rolling with its bounty of whole trees, a pig carcass, with boats all a-tremble on its shiny warm skin. As he headed off, up the Trace, I at last had time to regret the engagement I'd abandon'd to come west. This was what he did to you, forc'd you to examine your life.

The truth was, I'd left her but was already ruin'd by her fineness. Home, which I'd thought could be anywhere, she had vanquish'd. I saw that I was no place and had nothing.

But now—before any who will listen—I make the following declaration: whatever will be my next adventure, God knows, but on this I am determin'd: to leave this place tomorrow and head east, and not cease again 'til that lady is my wife!

28

"...a sweet evening..."

Grinder's Inn

✻ Wishing not to ever forget the distant bright world, sobbing after it already with longing, he went in the cabin, loaded the pistol, and shot himself in the skull. Then, lying on the floor, he shrieked forth, "O, Madam! Give me some water, for I am so strong and it is so hard to die!"

Having passed out, he was now awake again, feeling his head had split nearly in half. Amazed, he loaded a second time, pressed the muzzle to his rollicking, panicked heart, and fired, the exploding gunpowder nicking and pitting his face with a shower of fiery hornet-bites. And somehow, still did not die. He took out his shaving razor, flicked it open, and started on his left arm, making rows of deep parallel cuts, with blood blooming as tho the blade itself were dying, exsanguinating all over him. The thing in him sobbed and ran in helpless circles, trying to stop up the many holes. He sifted each arm and leg with the friendly knife, and at last found the creature's lifelong hiding place.

Pernier came in just then, and looked, and saw. He threw the blade down. "Fetch me some water, my good servant, for I have done the business!" he said.

In the last of his time, he reached forth a trembling hand as if to touch a scene rising up before him, and began to make strange curlicues in his own blood on the floor, like a teacher writing lessons on a blackboard. . . .

" ...no all-water route ..."

✳ So, at long last, Bill came to the place, a hollow by the side of the road, an inn simple as the one that snubbed Mary. Here, finally, was a little log cabin of rough-cut timber. But erected by the Park Service. Now, there was no barn with a trotting-horse weather vane or honeysuckle vines on the postbox. Also, no arbor, no limestone steps, and no dirt lane between house and privy. And no house and no privy!

The smokehouse door was not propped with a stone, flies swirling, and glazed hard rinds of hams. Nor was there a Pernier to stare at the ground and make philosophical discoveries, and hold the horses. No, the poor guy had "followed his master's example" just six months later. Killed himself.

And finally, no keeper's wife to greet them, and livery their horses, and no horses. No weak coffee and lardy-tasting morning cake. No honest kind lady, hard as bricks if tried, to offer them her bed.

But trees still overarched the road. And were so thick in every direction, Bill couldn't tell west from east. He sought a vantage point in order to find the sun. The clouds were spread out across the horizon, filtering the light. The rays tried to break forth in every direction, signaling the Judgment, but couldn't quite get free.

Bill had come far, but was still standing on asphalt. He felt a heaviness which promised a hard sleep at the motel, dreamless and damp. Still, there was no joy in anything. But at least it was evening, and the end of the journey.

He sat, in the lengthening light, in the car. Right over there, that lady had brought her sewing out and sat in her rocker. Lewis had watched her nimble hands, separate from her intent, still form as they labored to restore order to a chaotic void. And it wasn't her chair that rocked, but the world that moved while she'd stayed in place. That night, she'd been the center of the universe, O, Copernicus!

Never content as just himself, Bill was not now. He was the industrious only son and supposed to be the wonder boy, large and in charge. And was indentured, too, like Lewis. But the hardest part of being in charge was keeping watch over oneself. As for what was wrong with the world, he couldn't seem to do much to right it.

Later, he'd guzzle his whiskey from a little flask in the motel bathroom, mind stumbling and staggering while he drank and drank and stayed perfectly sober. 'Twas still up to Mrs. Grinder to hold it all in place, with her chickens scratching in the dirt, her horse kicking in the barn, and her sun plunging into her Pacific Ocean while its waters lapped about her vast, impious soul. Once again, she'd never finish her sewing by dark.

Wishing he could somehow speak to her, Bill's mind was a tangle. Sitting in the car by the cabin as Emily and Henry walked off to use the porta-potties, he was trying to outrace his fate. The truth was, he'd produced no real accounting, and the answer was nowhere. Maybe that lady, rocking and sewing just miles from where she was born, was the whole thing. Maybe Columbus, dying of the syph in the tropics, knew this, too, in the end.

When Lewis was a boy, they'd told him the world revolved at furious speed. Now Bill tested it by leaping into the air. And came down in the same place.

A lady's eye was on him, but whose? Mrs. Grinder's? Joaney's? Rita's? His mom's? Emily's? They knew the distresses of his soul, how to recognize the signs in cows, pigs, and men. He wouldn't speak to them. And had no companion, no Pernier, to attend all from the shade of a flowering crab, and to know and know and say nothing.

And no Clark to never come riding to his rescue. He simply had to last it out, until things were prepared for his own crossing.

Meanwhile, he'd toiled back upstream, back to this place. Overreached by trees, struck by hard lines of radiant light, it had blindly waited. And Locust Hill and snowy mornings and Mother's face. Plus, that sad monster called boyhood.

His throat constricted, and swallowing became impossible. In the end—he just had to face it—everyone outlived their usefulness. O, Ray, O, Joaney, O, Rita! None were truly his. He'd been put on earth to do good through some action, but not 'til the end would he be shown *which* action it was.

By marrying, he was being spared nothing.

Later, night would come crashing and breaking in pieces, shards and motes of black, but no cow would fall quiet, no dog would bark. The corn cribs . . . well, there wouldn't be corn cribs. This was a national park.

"A pleasant evening—" he said.

"Yes, Bill?" Emily brightened, back from the bathroom. For here at last was conversation.

Painful reflections swarmed to goad him away from her, his only comfort and aid. He might beat his head now and cry out and be truly insane. Mosquitoes gnattered demonically in his ears.

But they got back in the car and began to circle the monument, until he was pointed west, where the sun went each day to die. The clouds had weak gold along their bottoms. When that light stopped, so would the world. The world against which he could not stop fighting. It was baffling, why it was ever made. Somebody needed to come end it. Sparing Henry, of course, and Emily, Delilah, Joaney, Tommy, little Jack, Rita, Lloyd, Skyler, Richard, and T. And maybe even old Pablo.

A cardinal said, *Where are you? Hey, where are you? Where? Where?*

O, for a world made the way the captains believed! With one long river top to bottom and side to side. Just one lasting proof that the creation really was for Woman and Man, that all lovers weren't just castaway in it.

Tonight, as he put down the car window and gazed out, the planet was a lonely outpost in a forgotten corner, the garden all but dismantled. They'd found the woolly mammoth all right, on ice, and the Northwest Passage, too, but too far north. Much too far.

Still, what was the mission? What had it been?

Later, the dark would come down heavy as iron on these leaves and branches. And through the crushing weight, stars would very gently press, Venus, too. Bill had only a few moments left. Some natural thing was happening, a death.

Twice he'd tried for her embrace, that angel in black. One time looking like Joaney, and the next like Rita. He'd been trying madly to douse the fire that burned in his every nerve, to silence the growl of his familiar.

The new world was coming on, though, heedless, and the park was closing soon. Light at last broke the clouds open and spread all around. But this time without Pernier to be silent and forbear and foresee it all.

He didn't want it to be over. His visions ended, and then what? The book was almost done. But was any dead hero really worth the anguish of this year?

As for the journals, they'd appear at last in 1814, with a sort of apology by Biddle for the delay, citing the melancholy fate of the author as a factor. Naturally, it made it hard on the editor when the artist shot, stabbed, or hung himself prematurely.

Mary Shelley's book was out in 1818, Irving's in 1824. When Irving returned to America in 1832, he went west to see the Indian burial mounds in Illinois, an earthwork vast and sobering as the Great Pyramids. And to drop in on Clark in St. Louis.

History made for some crazy bedfellows with Lewis, Theo and Aaron Burr, Mary Wollstonecraft, Percy and Mary Shelley, and Washington Irving all mashed up in that one moment. Then Percy drowns while sailing, which frees Mary to moon over Irving at the opera, before he goes to visit Clark to talk about Lewis, and there you are. Or were.

As for York, he did get free of Clark, and set up a cartage business. And when it failed, went back and damned his freedom to Clark's face, saying he hadn't had a happy day since he got it. Then died of yellow fever, in 1812, in Tennessee. Or went west, became a Crow chief, and survived in the territory for dozens of years.

The previous night, Bill had written the last scene, that interview of Clark by Irving, in which they talk of Rip Van Winkle, a man who slept for a whole generation and awoke in an America he could no longer recognize.

The story began and ended with Irving, in a way, a fantasy writer, someone who found Ponce de León's search for the fountain of youth utterly laughable. Who praised Mohammad, but called his doctrine of the sword a great weakness. Who predicted, in 1833, the American Civil War.

Now, with Emily beside Bill and Henry in back, plugged into his music, an abridged copy of the journals in his lap, they sat next to Lewis's grave. She closed his manuscript and held it. "So that's the end, huh?" she mused. She took off her glasses and stuck the arm in a mouth-corner.

"Not at all," he said. "The husband turns up again, when he's over eighty years old. He travels sixteen hundred miles to the Indian Bureau in Sioux Falls, demanding his back pay as a federal interpreter. And you can bet your ass he gets it, too."

"God. I wish I didn't know that." She laughed. "Jesus." She surveyed the greening grass, still mostly brown, though this was early May. Rain droplets streamed up the windshield, against gravity.

"And don't forget the dream of the all-water route," he said. "That one hangs on all the way until Fremont's expedition in the 1840s."

"What about poor old Shannon?" she asked. "Is he still wandering the countryside?"

"He goes on to write some interesting things. About the prophetic nature of dreams," he said. "He dies in 1836, a Missouri senator."

"But here's something I don't get, Bill. How come nobody ever comes forward claiming to be *Lewis's* love child?" she asked.

"Oh. Well. Think about it," he said.

And she did, and nodded. "Yeah. Okay. I see what you mean."

Should he now take her hand, just an inch or two from his? Marriage was for those who could take it, the wear and tear, the supreme tests of patience. He couldn't always feel plainly if he loved her, couldn't always see if she was beautiful. And what a crying shame, because people often said so. But how could you trust what couldn't be empirically proven? So he simply resolved to go on looking, like at an abstract painting, one of Picasso's women.

"Sergeant Gass shows up again in 1854," he said, "applying for veteran's benefits. The only one to make it to the Civil War, to see the slaves freed, and Lincoln killed."

"No more, Bill," Emily said, covering her eyes with a hand. "No more time travel today."

"That's all," he said. "That's all I know about Lewis and Clark. I thought I'd know everything. I can't even tell you why he did it."

"Don't you think he tried very, very hard not to?" she asked. "And who are we to ask for more than that?"

The woodsy road wound in an oval through the monument park, and the earth around it was very red. The place was deserted, as if nobody noticed what was there and nobody cared. It was merely a park in Tennessee, south of Nashville, north of Graceland.

"But what about the golf ball?" Emily asked. "How can Reed find that golf ball?"

"He can't," he said. "I just needed to hold something in my hand that Lewis had held in his. Or vice versa. I hit it into the river, and Reed found it. Worked like a charm."

"So you really think . . . ?" she asked. "Him and Sacagawea?"

"Why not?" He shrugged. "Why should he wind up with nobody? Why should Clark get all the girls?"

"Clark agrees to take Pomp because . . . ?" she said.

"I think he *should* take him, don't you?" Lewis said. "It's the decent thing."

At last he was ready, and exited the car and walked back in the woods a ways, to gaze as far as he could down the Natchez Trace until it was swallowed by a blind curve. O, ancient track and lonely road of boat crews walking home from New Orleans! Which was now carefully mowed and kept. But did anybody in America really know of "the melancholy fate of Captain Lewis"? Would they care?

He walked back toward the monument. Emily joined him with her digital. "What are you thinking?" she asked.

"That I want a cigarette," he said.

"No, I mean before. Back there."

"That I wanted a cigarette," he said. "And that he treated his life so casually, and dueled over it so easily. He risked it all so gladly, the way I do in my dreams. Like America was just some dark, awe-some, fantastic dream to him."

Then he shivered. Life went on, whether you suffered in continual passion or not. And when things were over with, it didn't apologize or look around for something else to give you. In the long run, Henry would get the girl. And Bill himself would get the girl. Even Jesus got the girl, evidence suggested.

They walked around it, circled it, among the leafing trees and into a long, narrow field, big enough for a friendly game of touch. Dusk was just coming on, making the air swim and look murky. Nobody really wanted to go over there. Henry went first, going sort of on his toes across the space. Behind them, a flag hung limp on a pole over a circle of grass. Blinking, rubbing his eyes, Henry waited for them. Emily glanced into the car, at the uneaten half of his sandwich from lunch, anxiety rippling her expression. "Okay, c'mon, Lewis," she said. "This is your mecca."

"Where'd he do it?" Henry called. "Was it over here?"

"More over that way," he said, gesturing.

It was a fairly brief piece of ground. A lonely piece of business, as Clark would say. "Aren't you going to look at it?" Henry asked.

"Coming."

He tiptoed around the other, smaller stones, in his favorite loafers with broken soles, and corduroys, and the Member's Only jacket he'd worn since college. A rock in his shoe, which he was ignoring, made him limp slightly. The monument itself was a dais of limestone, rough-cut and foursquare, with a column, unpolished. And broken off at the height of a basketball rim. An uncompleted life.

Emily took shots of it from all over, every angle, while Henry read all the plaques, calling them out in a clear voice. Finally he shrugged. "So much for the Northwest Passage," he said.

"Actually, it finally shows up," Bill said. "Amundsen found it in 1904, one hundred years too late."

"Poor guys," Emily said. "You poor babies."

"Yeah, poor us," he said.

Personally, he was still looking for something. He wanted more than just this. Some sign, a cold chill, anything. His yearning eyes stopped on several gray, faintly vibrating objects in the trees, just past the road. One by one, they emerged and stood looking right at him. Several does and a fawn.

"There're your ghosts," Emily said. "I'm getting cold."

Later, at the restaurant, at the motel, he'd click through all the pictures, one by one, in the two-by-two-inch viewer. Emily was doing that right then when she stopped on one. "Oh, hey, now. Bill? Look at this," she said, and handed him the camera. He pulled out his glasses, and carried the camera to the car, opened the door, and bent down in the dome light.

He had to get down on a knee. Though there wasn't anything left of Lewis, or Mrs. Grinder, or her beautiful arbor, with the overreaching branches stretching tendriled fingers, and the dead milkweed pods and vines clinging to a limestone, he thought he saw something. He felt cut off from joy. A nameless, bottomless thing kept telling him there was nothing. And at sunset each day, an explosion happened, which threw up doom-filled colors in the west, the sun falling into the sea, making clouds from the steam.

And past and present ground into each other, like lovers, erasing his time on earth. The road came loose and the columns toppled. Lewis would finally stir from there on the day She came to free him. Meanwhile, all about Heaven, Shannon traveled place to place, asking after and looking for the captain, in increasing alarm.

Like Lewis's last night, the sunset now jerked, becoming streaks of light, then shrill rockets screaming in every direction. Each mote of light flowed and sparked and did tricks in the air, like countless swallows of gold whiskey, red wine, green absinthe. Around Bill, the universe vibrated and flickered, and at such velocity that it looked real and felt solid. Sensations happened, but arrived nowhere in him and meant nothing. He'd come so far, but could not take the last step. And felt his enemies trading satisfied looks.

Probably, Lewis hadn't gotten off that Pacific shore. It was over that day on the beach, when she scorned him.

The trail dead-ended here, for both Bill and Lewis. And it seemed he'd always seen it ending here, in his mind's eye. And through it all, heard a whistling sound, a hurtling, of that bullet that missed him on the Maria's.

Bill wiped his eyes and looked again at Emily's silver camera, because it seemed that this particular shot of the tomb was showing a bright crimson flare, right across its foot. "Oh, shit!" he said, tears blocking his sight again.

"What's the matter, Bill?" Emily asked. "What's wrong?"

"It's Lewis!" he said. "Oh, shit, it's him! I mean, it's either a trick of the light, or it's him. Which means he's still with us and death is an illusion! Or it's a trick of the light. Or it's him, Em. He's coming through to tell us to keep holding on here, not to lose hope . . .!"

Author's Note

The material for this novel was derived from many popular and scholarly books about Meriwether Lewis and the Lewis & Clark expedition. No single source was more important to the creation of this book than the daily journals of the expedition kept by the captains and several other members of the Corps of Discovery, including Charles Floyd, Patrick Gass, John Ordway and Joseph Whitehouse. The bulk of the journals—over two million words' worth—was written by Meriwether Lewis and William Clark, though the primary charge to keep a daily accounting of the journey was given to Lewis by Thomas Jefferson. It was William Clark's responsibility to read Lewis's entries regularly, produce a fair copy in his own journal, and add his own notes and remarks. Clark took this one step further, often, by reporting on the same events but in his own words. At several points, the journal contains only entries from Clark, suggesting that part of Lewis's journal was lost or that he kept it up only sporadically.

This remarkable document, containing passages that have an almost dream-like or visionary power, such as one for the day Lewis stands off the charge of a grizzly bear with a spear, was essentially the whole inspiration for this novel, its style, and the order of its events. For the mood and tone of the narrative and dialogue, and for the overall nineteenth-century turn of phrase, letters by various historical figures featured in the book—Lewis, Clark, Jefferson, Theodosia Burr, and others—were also important. A novelist's approach to this material is naturally more fluid than that of a historian's, and where a historian is allowed only to write what happened and stop, a novelist picks up from there, using imagination, and writes why it happened—or one possible reason why. For storytelling purposes, the historical characters in *Melancholy Fate* often say or think a thing they are actually known to have written in the journals, or in a letter or speech, and vice versa. But any statement that is quoted word-for-word, directly from the journals, appears in quotation marks in the novel. The chapter titles, for example, are quoted directly from the journals.

As a final note, reading this novel is in no way a substitute for reading the journals of the expedition, or other documentation of these events. The expedition journals contain what appears to be an almost impenetrably deep mystery about a first encounter between some of the founders of the Enlightenment and Native Americans, and the natural world. If this book encourages readers to seek out and read this remarkable document, it will have served a valuable purpose.